Entrepreneurs

The Boston
Business
Community
1700–1850

Entrepreneurs

The Boston
Business
Community,
1700–1850

Conrad Edick Wright
Katheryn P. Viens

EDITORS

Published by the
Massachusetts
Historical
Society
Boston
1997

Distributed by
Northeastern University Press

Massachusetts Historical Society
Studies in American History and Culture, No. 4
© 1997 Massachusetts Historical Society

Published at the Charge of the Publication Fund

Editing of this book was made possible in part
by the proceeds of an endowment fund
created with the assistance of a Challenge Grant
from the National Endowment for the Humanities,
a federal agency that supports
research, education, and public programming
in the humanities.

Designed by David Ford

ISBN 0-934909-70-9 (cloth)
ISBN 0-934909-71-7 (paper)

Contents

v

Contents

Contents

Preface

POLITICAL COMMENTATORS, particularly conservative analysts, sometimes posit what they call the "iron law of unintended consequences"—the doctrine that well-meant initiatives necessarily produce completely unanticipated outcomes. It goes without saying that most pundits who subscribe to this axiom assume that the fruits of dogoodism are inevitably poisonous. We offer the collection that follows as a small demonstration that good deeds can indeed produce desirable results.

The essays that make up this volume were first offered at the Massachusetts Historical Society on May 20 and 21, 1994, at a conference entitled "Entrepreneurs: The Boston Business Community, 1750–1850." The conference, itself, had grown out of another M.H.S. initiative, its program of short-term scholarly fellowships. In the early 1990s, in the course of considering applications for research grants the Society's fellowship committee began to recognize a burgeoning interest in the business history of colonial Boston, British North America's first important commercial center. Not only were there a great many applications on the subject, the proposals on business topics that the committee received included many of its most promising. Persuaded by the evidence of the applications that there existed a critical mass of capable scholars working on various aspects of the economic history of Boston from the colonial period to as late as the Civil War, the Society set about to bring them together.

The conference organizers had an agenda, albeit a limited one. Great merchants, investors, and industrialists had long dominated the historiography of Boston business, but the fellowship proposals the Society began to receive in the late 1980s directed attention farther down the social and economic scale. Without denying the economic importance of the major traders of colonial Boston, or the merchants in the China trade between the late 1780s and the 1820s, or the Boston Associates, the men who built New England's textile industry beginning in the 1810s, younger scholars were finding signs of vigorous entrepreneurial activity in untraditional places—for instance, among artisans, women, immigrants, and the members of minority communities. The simple objective of the conference organizers was to search out entrepreneurial activity in Boston wherever it was between the early 1750s and 1850—we eventually determined that 1700 was a more appropriate starting date—and to take its full measure.

The essays in this collection provide undoubted evidence of the breadth and diversity of entrepreneurship in Boston in the eighteenth century and the first half of the nineteenth century. While scholars have long recognized a few colonial craftsmen—most notably Paul Revere—who grew from artisanal roots to business prominence, they have rarely looked beyond Boston's countinghouses to trace the city's economic growth in the period before the Civil War. They need to do so. As the pieces that follow show, entrepreneurship flourished in Boston on many different rungs of the social and economic ladder over the century and a half this volume covers.

What is an entrepreneur? By the simplest dictionary definition it is "one who organizes, operates, and assumes the risk for business ventures."[1] In common usage, though, the term normally carries an added connotation. Entrepreneurs have a vision of the future, a plan for developing their initiatives. In organizing this collection of essays, we have assumed that our subjects were builders—men and women who believed that they would have more at the end of the day than at the beginning.

Such expectations do not predominate in all times and all places. In the view of some historians, within a few miles of colonial Boston a different *mentalité* was ascendant. Over the past generation, scholars have argued at length over whether or not most colonial farmers sought to maximize profits. If James A. Henretta and other historians of his persuasion are correct, "lineal values" prevailed in the colonial countryside. Rather than imperil the futures of children and grandchildren by taking unnecessary risks, according to this argument, prerevolutionary yeomen made the preservation of family assets their paramount concern: "farm families usually trained and encouraged their children 'to succeed *them*, rather than to "succeed" by rising in the social system.' "[2]

Whatever the situation was in the countryside, in Boston by the early eighteenth century entrepreneurs—builders, profit-maximizers—were becoming apparent in action and idea not only among the town's great merchants, who could trace their commercial lineage back to the earliest days of settlement, but also among its small shopkeepers and artisans. Retail traders now struggled, not always successfully, to turn marginal endeav-

1. *American Heritage Dictionary of the English Language* (Boston, 1969).
2. James A. Henretta, "Families and Farms: Mentalité in Pre-Industrial America," *William and Mary Quarterly*, 3d ser., 35(1978):30.

ors into thriving enterprises. Craftsmen, at least in some trades, now attempted to grow their businesses either by adding workers to their shops or by retailing goods they had not produced. And an emerging ideology of growth, bound up in a movement to ease credit, now began to provide a blueprint for economic development.

If the articles in this volume unambiguously demonstrate the diversity of burgeoning entrepreneurialism in Boston in the early 1700s, they lead to more mixed conclusions about a second, related issue, the town's place in the development of capitalism in America. The emergence of capitalism is contested historical terrain (one leading participant in this debate has cordially termed her rivals "dear enemies"[3]), and scholars advancing conflicting views on the subject often seem to talk past each other. Advocates of both major approaches to the debate—Allan Kulikoff, focusing on rural economic development, has recently characterized them as "market" historians and "social" historians[4]—will find grist for their mills in the essays that follow.

"Capitalism," no less than "entrepreneur," demands a definition, and none seems capable of satisfying every scholar or theorist. Divided at the outset by their presuppositions, "market" historians influenced by neoclassical economics and "social" historians (many of them sympathetic to Marxist formulations) have found themselves using the same word to describe different phenomena. Functioning, efficient markets are fundamental to neoclassical thought, and historians of this school have pointed to their development in such commodities as land, grain, capital, and labor (seen through the convergence of prices) in the eighteenth century as evidence of the presence of a capitalist economy. Labor relationships, in contrast, are the central concern of Kulikoff's "social" historians, especially of scholars writing in the Marxist tradition. Distinguishing between commerce, which they recognize in early America, and capitalism, which by their definition requires a class of owners of property (including land, machinery, and financial assets) and a second class of wage laborers, they have attempted to identify capitalists who expropriated a share of the value of the goods workers produced. Some scholars in the neoclassical tradition

---

3. Winifred Barr Rothenberg, *From Market-Places to a Market Economy: The Transformation of Rural Massachusetts, 1750–1850* (Chicago, 1992), ix.

4. Allan Kulikoff, *The Agrarian Origins of American Capitalism* (Charlottesville, 1992), 14–16. The first chapter of Kulikoff's book provides a valuable survey of recent work on capitalism in America; for another broad survey, see Paul A. Gilje, "The Rise of Capitalism in the Early Republic," *Journal of the Early Republic* 16(1996):159–181.

maintain that the first European settlers brought a market economy with them to the New World—that is to say, they contend that the American colonies were capitalist from the outset. And some "social" historians insist that the class relationships that they consider to have been at the heart of a transformation to capitalism within the American economy did not take shape until the nineteenth century.

As the following essays show, there is ample room for "market" historians, "social" historians, and what one might call "non-denominational" scholars to contribute to the business history of Boston. Essays by Barbara McLean Ward (on goldsmiths) and Patricia Cleary (on Elizabeth Murray, an eighteenth-century shopkeeper) attest to the early spread of market values into parts of Boston society previously uninvestigated. Ward's contribution outlines the alternative strategies goldsmiths used to grow their businesses; Cleary shows how Elizabeth Murray promoted shopkeeping among women. In conjunction with Margaret E. Newell's essay on the aspirations for economic growth that underlay efforts to establish a land bank in provincial Massachusetts, Ward and Cleary provide unambiguous evidence of entrepreneurialism before the Revolution outside the circles of the great merchants. David Hancock's contribution on the town's Madeira wine traders adds an ironic coda to the theme that Newell, Ward, and Cleary sketch out. As Hancock shows, a failure of nerve and a failure of vision cost some of these merchants their prominent place in the wine trade.

Among the essays in this collection, the concerns of Kulikoff's "social" historians appear most clearly in Lisa B. Lubow's contribution on building construction in postrevolutionary Boston, although several of the other articles provide additional insights. As Lubow shows, Boston's building industry experienced a fundamental transformation during the half century following the American Revolution. Spying an opportunity for substantial gain, by the late eighteenth century investors began to replace carpenters as the principal organizers and financers of major real-estate development projects. Lubow is especially interested in the increasing role that class played in Boston's building industry; three of the volume's other essays point out further aspects of the community's growing stratification. In her study of Massachusetts politics in the 1820s, Harlow W. Sheidley reveals how the Boston-based elite struggled to overcome differences on the issues of the day to form a coherent governing order. Peter Dobkin Hall, in his investigation of uses of wealth, outlines the measures that Boston's richest citizens took to secure the futures of their families and estates. The forces of proletarianization were evident throughout the period, among Lubow's carpenters and those engaged in other crafts; in their essay on the book trades in this volume, Ronald J. and Mary Saracino Zboray outline how developments within that industry enlarged many workplaces and reduced the value of many artisanal skills.

In probing the rise or transformation of capitalism in America, scholars are attempting to question some of the axioms that the present generation has inherited about the development of the American economy. Without challenging basic premises about the nature of the capitalism and economic growth, it is still possible to revise what we think we know about our past. Three of the essays in this volume reconsider specific pieces of received wisdom and find them wanting. Did the Revolutionary War force the colonies' merchant aristocracy to flee, creating a vacuum for a new commercial class to fill? In his contribution, John W. Tyler tests the assumption that the war caused an unusually high rate of merchant attrition and finds it to be an overstatement for Boston. What factors were at the root of debtor unrest in Massachusetts in the mid 1780s? Jonathan M. Chu investigates this question in his essay and concludes that the failure of consumers to limit their borrowing, and not hard-money policies or exploitation by creditors, left debtors vulnerable when inflation rapidly gave way to deflation after the war. How did business corporations replace partnerships during the first half of the nineteenth century? Naomi R. Lamoreaux, in her article, determines that historians who have taken this transformation for granted have misstated the question. She finds that in Boston partnerships were actually an increasingly important business form during the period.

Finally, many of the articles in this volume contribute to the historiography of business in Boston through new research on understudied topics. The Zborays' findings on proletarianization within the Boston book trade, for example, are part of a broader study of the development of a major industrial sector between 1789 and 1850. Their work, which relies on a large computer database, also covers the size, composition, and geography of the sector. In his study of marine insurance, William M. Fowler, Jr., investigates how Boston merchants learned to manage risk in the eighteenth and early nineteenth centuries. Lois E. Horton and James Oliver Horton show how in a climate of racial bias many African-American businessmen recognized an obligation to promote the social and political interests of the black community. And Benjamin W. Labaree, focusing on the relationship between Boston and Essex County, reveals how the metropolis expanded its influence over smaller, neighboring towns between 1750 and 1850.

No collection of essays can hope to offer the systematic coverage of a topic that a monograph provides, and this volume is no exception. As we organized the conference from which this collection emerged, we were disappointed in our efforts to add contributions on such subjects as business and immigration, the development of banking, investors and rural land speculation, and the Boston business community and internal improvements, to name only a few of many possible topics. Nevertheless, this book will serve its purpose if it contributes to the ongoing discussion about American economic growth in the eighteenth and nineteenth centuries and stimulates new consideration of Boston's place in this development.

The publication of this volume marks the culmination of a five-year project. It is a pleasure to acknowledge the many individuals and institutions who made it possible. We received generous support for the conference from the Bank of Boston (now BankBoston), the Fidelity Foundation, and John W. Adams. We owe a word of thanks to the twelve commentators at the conference who provided insightful advice on individual essays: John L. Brooke, Richard D. Brown, Robert F. Dalzell, Jr., Donald M. Jacobs, Gary J. Kornblith, Bruce Laurie, Pauline Maier, Russell R. Menard, Thomas H. O'Connor, Glenn Porter, Richard A. Ryerson, and Tamara Plakins Thornton. We are also grateful to Robert A. Gross, who drew on his vast research on Concord in the age of the Transcendentalists for a paper. It will appear elsewhere. We owe a debt of thanks to Ann Harrer, who prepared the maps. Neither the conference nor the resultant volume would have been possible without the aid of the staff of the Massachusetts Historical Society, especially the following present and former members: Anne E. Bentley, Christopher A. Carberry, Catherine S. Craven, Peter Drummey, Edward W. Hanson, James P. Harrison III, Joice Himawan, Brenda M. Lawson, Barbara A. Mathews, Jennifer Smith, Len Travers, Louis L. Tucker, Seth M. Vose III, and Donald Yacovone.

Conrad Edick Wright
Katheryn P. Viens
Boston, September 1996

Entrepreneurs

The Boston
Business
Community
1700–1850

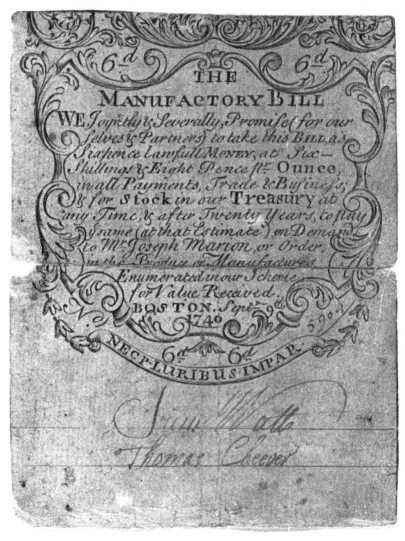

Manufactory bill, Sept. 9, 1740. Collection of the Massachusetts Historical Society.

A Revolution in Economic Thought:
Currency and Development in
Eighteenth-Century Massachusetts

Margaret E. Newell

REVIEWING THE EVENTS of the Revolutionary era, John Adams observed that "the act to destroy the Land Bank scheme raised a greater ferment in this province than the Stamp Act did."[1] Adams's assertion reminds us that economic and constitutional issues were intimately intertwined in the minds of the revolutionary generation. His comment also indicates that the complex debates over banking and currency in Massachusetts, and their ideological contribution to the Revolution, merit further scrutiny. Embracing independence—and repudiating an imperial economic system upon which Boston depended—required a corresponding revolution in the colonists' economic thought, a reconceptualization of their interests and their dependent relationship with the metropolis. When James Otis and other pamphleteers of the 1760s castigated English commercial regulation, they set forth a distinct political economy that advocated both free trade in external commerce and the development of the internal economy. In defining this political economy of revolution, Massachusetts critics of English policy drew upon arguments first articulated during the land bank and paper money controversies of 1712–1751.

Recently, several historians have explored the connection between currency issues and the Revolution, but most focus on the conflict between debtors and creditors, bullionists and critics of intrinsic value, Lockeans and Harringtonians.[2] Yet the Massachusetts currency debates were far

1. Charles Francis Adams, ed., *The Works of John Adams* (Boston, 1851), 4:49.
2. Building upon Andrew Davis's work, Richard Bushman argues that Massachusetts's money policy, so intimately tied to taxation, raised popular fears regarding debt, personal dependency, and political corruption—fears which resurfaced during the Stamp Act crisis. Richard Bushman, *King and People in Provincial Massachusetts* (Chapel Hill, 1985), 198–203. William Pencak, in *War, Politics and Revolution in Provincial Massachusetts* (Boston, 1981), does connect the paper money debates and the Revolution, but he focuses upon

more complex than a creditor versus debtor schema would suggest. Farmers and traders who supported paper money did so not merely because they feared bankruptcy, but because the currency debates touched upon issues of commercial access and the legitimacy of credit, consumption, and internal trade.[3] Advocates of paper money offered more than a market-oriented, individualistic ideology, a defense of debtors' interests, or a critique of government regulation; they offered a distinct vision of the colony's economic future.[4]

---

currency's role in fomenting the assembly's anti-executive political culture. It is my contention in this essay that the ideological *content* of paper money proponents' discourse, not just their political opposition to governor and Council, proved significant during the imperial crisis because it helped unite New Englanders' economic and constitutional concerns on the eve of revolution. Other works on paper money and the Massachusetts currency debates include Leslie V. Brock, *The Currency of the American Colonies, 1700–1764: A Study in Colonial Finance and Imperial Relations* (New York, 1975); Joseph Dorfman, *The Economic Mind in American Civilization, 1606–1933* (New York, 1946–1959); Joseph Ernst, "Massachusetts' 'Great Currency Debate'" (unpub. ms., 1989); Andrew McFarland Davis, ed., comp., *Colonial Currency Reprints, 1682–1751* (1910–1911; reprint, New York, [1971]), hereafter referred to as *CCR*, and his *Currency and Banking in the Province of the Massachusetts-Bay* (New York, 1901); William D. Metz, "Politics and Finance in Massachusetts, 1713–1741" (Ph.D. diss., Univ. of Wisconsin, 1946); Margaret E. Newell, "Economic Ideology, Culture, and Development in New England, 1620–1800" (Ph.D. diss., Univ. of Virginia, 1991); and Edwin J. Perkins, *American Public Finance and Financial Services* (Columbus, 1994). For contemporary accounts, see Thomas Hutchinson, who devoted considerable space in his "History" to the currency debates. Hutchinson, *The History of the Colony and Province of Massachusetts-Bay*, ed. Lawrence Shaw Mayo (Cambridge, Mass., 1936).

3. For example, Bushman notes similarities between paper currency critic Edward Wigglesworth and pro-paper writers on the subject of debt without exploring the banking advocates' distinct understanding of credit's importance for economic expansion. Bushman, *King and People*, 200–201.

4. In his study of Worcester County, John Brooke notes that the 1741 Land Bank battle mobilized backcountry support for the Popular party's attack on the governor, Council, and local representatives of this "court" patronage network and generated a political culture of insurgency which Bay colonists employed during the Revolution. While his account of the bank war's provincial political implications is persuasive, his characterization of the political economy issues at stake is incomplete. Although he notes the presence of some discourse regarding internal development, Brooke concludes that bank supporters articulated an interest-based, Lockean ideology that failed to overcome the Bay colonists' allegiance to their corporate, commonwealth notions. John Brooke, *The Heart of the Commonwealth: Society and Political Culture in Worcester County, Massachusetts, 1713–1861* (Cambridge, 1989), xiii–xv, 41–65, 97–142. William Pencak's *War, Politics, and Revolution* also places the currency debates of 1691–1751 in the context of the political battles between successive royal governors and the "popular party" in the Massachusetts Assembly. Pencak

The key to paper money's appeal was its association with internal development and an optimistic vision of economic diversification and physical expansion. As John Brooke's work reminds us, the pamphleteers and political figures who wrote about currency in the context of these debates were not just engaging in philosophical arguments; they were trying to mobilize voters in Boston and the hinterlands, as well as officials on both sides of the Atlantic, in support of specific currency policies. In order to do so, they had to offer a diagnosis of the colony's economic ills—currency shortages, Boston's loss of trade to rival ports in the northeast—and solutions that would appeal to a varied constituency of farmers, traders, and artisans. Although the pamphleteers whose writings supply the evidence for this essay differed on many particulars—whether a private bank or a public loan represented the best means of augmenting the money supply, for example—they agreed that credit and paper money would unleash the productive, entrepreneurial energy of individual New Englanders upon which public prosperity depended.

The defense of paper money led these writers to reject traditional balance-of-trade theory. They criticized local regulations that interfered with the flow of commerce, instead advocating free trade and the promotion of commerce through broadened access to credit and currency supplies. Without disputing the value of foreign commerce, they shifted the focus of debate away from New England's foreign trade deficits to the issue of stimulating domestic development. More important, they defended these activities as compatible with Puritan notions of industry, morality, and the common good. By linking their policy recommendations to issues of increased productivity, credit, and internal exchange, proponents of banks and public loans offered solutions to collective as well as private concerns. And by viewing the locus of policy and government regulation as Boston, rather than London, they precipitated a crucial shift in the colonists' conceptualization of their economy with important consequences for resistance and revolution.[5]

Beginning in 1690, Massachusetts experimented with a variety of public and private financial institutions. The Bay government initially adopted

offers a compelling account of the political contests that swirled around public loans and military appropriations, but he is less interested in the content of pro- and anti-paper discourse.

5. For a fuller discussion of political economy issues during the imperial crisis, see Margaret E. Newell, *Economic Revolutions: Political Economy, Culture, and Development in New England, 1620–1775* (forthcoming), esp. chap. 13.

paper money as a means of emergency revenue-raising in response to a string of costly imperial wars and planned prompt redemption of the bills through taxes. The bills proved so popular as a form of circulating currency, however, that following the Treaty of Utrecht many Bay colonists championed paper money as a means to avoid economic stagnation and to promote development in peacetime. Unlike Bank of England notes, the Massachusetts notes, issued in small denominations and with the status of legal tender after 1712, functioned "as a medium of commerce in the business and trade of the province, greatly facilitating payments for goods imported from Great Britain and other places."[6] The General Court approved additional emissions in 1714, 1716, 1721, 1728, and 1736; by 1728, A.M. candidates at Harvard could affirm that "the use of paper money contribute[s] to the public good." In addition to these public loans, groups sought charters for private banks in 1714, 1720, and 1739.[7]

These proposals, coupled with concern over the depreciation that accompanied the increased volume of bills in circulation, sparked an ongoing debate over currency in Massachusetts. Aside from influential exceptions like the younger Thomas Hutchinson, few New Englanders anticipated or desired a complete return to specie alone. Defenders and critics of paper money shared certain assumptions in their analyses of the region's economic problems and in the political-economy traditions upon which they drew. Participants in these debates clashed over particulars, such as public versus private control, the backing of bills, and legal tender provisions. But more significantly, the contest over banking and currency reflected a divergence of two visions of commerce and development in provincial New England. Those on each side of the issue voiced spirited and articulate arguments in support of their respective positions.

One group, which largely drew its members from the ranks of Boston's Atlantic merchants, accepted the temporary necessity of bills but wanted controlled, regulated emissions and the eventual return of specie. These writers identified balance-of-trade problems as the source of economic disorder and currency shortages in the Bay Colony and saw international trade as the only means of redress. They argued for retrenchment of imports, advocated manufactures for import substitution (but only those not in competition with English goods), criticized the expansion of retail mid-

6. *Acts and Resolves of the Massachusetts Bay* (Boston, 1869), 1:700–701.
7. See Davis, *Currency and Banking*. The reference to Harvard A.M. presentations appears in Dorfman, *Economic Mind*, 1:148.

dlemen and internal trade, and advocated greater state intervention in the economy in the form of laws restricting credit and consumption. This group viewed development as desirable but wished to achieve it in a more regulated fashion.

Thomas Hutchinson and other members of this faction charged that paper currency would damage New England's international trade. Adherents of a mercantilist, balance-of-trade conceptualization of economic affairs, which they applied to the Massachusetts context, these writers privileged international commerce and saw little value in domestic exchange. They defined wealth in terms of specie in circulation and a positive balance of payments in external trade, and they found the Massachusetts economy lacking on both scores.[8]

Rather than solving the colony's money shortage, charged Thomas Paine, a minister and sometime merchant who left his pulpit in 1730 to pursue commerce full time, the public bills exacerbated the fundamental economic problems that had caused the crisis in the first place. Paper money by its nature functioned as currency only in internal transactions; backed by public faith, it had no value outside the borders of the colony that issued it. Given their conviction that internal transactions offered "no advantage to the Publick," Paine and other importers found the uselessness of provincial bills in foreign exchange a serious drawback.[9] Problems of depreciation in the 1720s and 1730s further increased the reluctance of merchants on both sides of the Atlantic to endorse such a "false Medium." English correspondents generally refused to accept paper bills from the Bay Colony, and British factors in Boston unwillingly received colonial paper only under the duress of legal tender laws. Thus the colony's recourse to paper money impeded Boston merchants' ability to engage in foreign trade. "The generous foreign Adventurer or Merchant, and consequently Trade in its genuine Sense," contended William Douglass, "is hurt; the Gainers are the *Shopkeepers* and *Merchant Hucksters*."[10] Others complained that neigh-

---

8. Quoting John Locke on the intrinsic value of money, Samuel Mather asserted in 1734 that "it is only by *having a greater Quantity of Silver* that Men grow rich." [Samuel Mather,] *The New-England Weekly Journal*, Feb. 4, 1734, *CCR* 3:21–24.

9. *The Present Melancholy Circumstances of the Province Consider'd, and Methods for Redress humbly proposed* (Boston, 1719), *CCR* 1:355.

10. Money substitutes might function well in a primitive, strictly domestic economy, he conceded, but Massachusetts's dependence on foreign trade dictated that the colony adhere to a universal commercial medium–silver–which maintained a steady value. [William Douglass,] *An Essay Concerning Silver and Paper Currencies; More especially with Re-*

boring colonies' emissions of paper had eroded Boston's predominance as the region's center for international exchange.

Indeed, paper money served the needs of local exchange so well that it freed the population from its dependence on scarce specie. Thus irresponsible merchants had seized the opportunity to remit ever larger amounts of specie to England in exchange for imported goods, instead of returning "Fish, Lumber, Horses, Grain, Beaf, Pork," or other labor-intensive remittances.[11] Only increasing productivity and domestic exports while simultaneously decreasing imports would enhance the prosperity of Massachusetts.

According to numerous anti-bank pamphleteers, however, the most pernicious impact of paper money upon the balance of trade was its tendency to democratize credit. Public loan emissions and private banks extended credit indiscriminately beyond the circle of "opulent merchants" who were capable of managing it properly. Writers who favored strictly regulated currency expressed doubt that "middling sorts," laborers, or farmers could be trusted to invest in capital improvements. "If there be but a Bank to run and borrow at," warned Edward Wigglesworth, Hollis Professor of Divinity at Harvard, "the Ill-husbandry, Vanity and Folly of the People is such; that in a short time most of the Estates in the Country would become involved."[12] Given contemporary political culture, such debt risked the inhabitants' personal independence and political virtue. Several pamphleteers cast the issue in terms of a conflict between a corrupt city and a virtuous countryside, in which devious merchants and paper credit combined to tempt the hinterlands with "fine things far fetcht and dear bought."[13] Land bankers, they charged, would eventually hold the mortgages of many Massachusetts farmers, endangering the inhabitants' personal economic and political independence.

An increase in personal indebtedness raised moral and social as well as

gard to the British Colonies in New-England (Boston, [1738]), 11–13; Douglass, *A Discourse Concerning the Currencies of the British Plantations in America* (Boston, 1740), *CCR* 3:309–310.

11. Edward Wigglesworth, *A Letter from One in the Country* (Boston, 1720), *CCR* 1:420, 418; *Present Melancholy Circumstances*, 351–352.

12. Wigglesworth, *Letter from One in the Country*, 439, and *Present Melancholy Circumstances*, 351–352.

13. Wigglesworth, *Letter from One in the Country*, 421–422; Thomas Paine, *A Discourse, Shewing That the real first Cause of the Straits and Difficulties of this Province of the Massachusetts Bay, is it's Extravagancy* (Boston, 1721), *CCR* 2:282.

economic concerns. Attorney General Paul Dudley singled out the colonists' habits of consumption, "excessive retailing," and too-easy access to credit, all of which had led to a chronic trade imbalance with England and precipitated the flight of silver: "if we Import from Abroad, more than we can Pay for, by what we Produce our selves, or Purchase from others with our own Commodities, we shall unavoidably grow Poor, and a Million of *Paper-Money* won't help the matter."[14] Exhibiting a more cautious attitude towards economic growth than their opponents, the faction in favor of regulating paper money bills wondered if commercial expansion in the Bay Colony had proceeded too rapidly. New England's increasingly rich material culture left one anonymous author unimpressed, since he associated this paper prosperity with indebtedness and "Bubbles"—the speculative spirit behind the South Sea Bubble and John Law's failed Mississippi stock company, which now threatened to infect Massachusetts.[15] Boston had long abandoned itself to luxury and extravagance, and now the countryside was beginning to show signs of the new spirit of open acquisitiveness. Like Adam Smith describing the spirit of emulation as a normal human impulse, Thomas Paine noted that "we all scra[m]ble after it as naturally, and with as much Resolution and Shuffling Sedulity as heavy bodies to the Centre of Gravity." But unlike Smith, Paine lacked the concept of a marketplace that would channel such acquisitive impulses into socially useful, productive actions.[16]

To observers like Wigglesworth, credit and internal commerce encouraged "the honest country People" to spend beyond their means. By removing the spur of economic necessity, complained Dudley, paper money and easy credit undermined the inhabitants' commitment to industry and frugality.[17] Running through this commentary was a conviction that too-easy credit and consumption threatened the social order as well as the balance of trade. Inhabitants flocked to purchase imported luxuries inappropriate to their stations; as Thomas Paine mourned, "ordinary Tradesmen's

14. Paul Dudley, *Objections to the Bank of Credit Lately Projected at Boston. Being a Letter upon that Occasion, to John Burril, Esq.; Speaker to the House of Representatives for the Province of the Massachusetts-Bay in New-England* (Boston, 1714), CCR 1:254.

15. *The Second Part of South-Sea Stock* (Boston, 1721), CCR 2:330.

16. Paine, *Discourse*, 283.

17. It was not consumption and the import trade in general that Dudley decried, but specifically a striving beyond one's station, the "Extravagance that People, and especially the Ordinary sort, are fallen into, far beyond their circumstances, in their Purchases, Buildings, Families, Expences, Apparel, and generally in their whole way of Living." Dudley, *Objections to the Bank of Credit*, 254–255.

Wives . . . shall be dressed in Silks and sattens. . . . Inferiour Apprentices
and Servants, having just obtained their Freedom shall be dressed like
Lords of the Mannours." When Gov. Jonathan Belcher issued a broadside
prohibiting the circulation of private land bank bills in 1740, he warned
Bostonians especially to guard against their servants' participation in the
bank, "as such a thing may serve to give 'em an entrance into Credit, which
would prove of dangerous consequence."[18]

Consumption patterns and credit access engendered more than vague
class fears on the part of the top officials, merchants, and council members
who formed the core of the anti-paper circle. Political economy reinforced
private interest in the case of many Atlantic merchants and their spokesmen who argued for tighter regulation of paper emissions and a repeal of
legal tender laws. Their attacks on "over-trading," "selfish, contriving Spirit[s]," "Merchant Hucksters," and "needless Retailers" were aimed at a
new commercial order that drew its energy from the expanding internal
economy. The appearance on the Boston scene of merchants and military
contractors with extensive interior contacts, such as John Colman, William
Paine, and Oliver Noyes, threatened the dominance of the Hutchinsons,
the Sewalls, the Dudleys, and other powerful Boston importers. Paper
money also provided alternative sources of credit for middlemen, retailers,
shopkeepers, and others active in the domestic market. Coupled with the
growing tendency of British factors in the mid-eighteenth century to by-
pass Atlantic merchants and to deal directly with smaller traders and retailers, these new credit arrangements eroded the top international merchants' control of the trade in West Indian goods and British manufactures.
According to critics, country traders infiltrated Boston's hinterlands and
created demand for previously unnecessary goods like spirits, chocolate,
and fine clothing; although they drew new producers into the market, their
competition drove up commodity prices, which made gathering remittances for England even more difficult.

In order to stabilize paper and pave the way for a return to specie, many
writers and government officials argued in favor of a comprehensive program of social and economic reform. They advocated laws limiting the
extension of credit in domestic transactions, restricting imports, and cutting consumption. Proponents of measures "shortening credit" recognized
that such limitations might impede legitimate transactions and make it

18. Broadside, *By His Excellency Jonathan Belcher Esq. . . . Whereas a Scheme for
emitting Bills or Notes by John Colman* [Boston, 1740].

impossible for entrepreneurs to accumulate capital for various enterprises. But they expressed a willingness to sacrifice more dynamic growth in favor of reducing consumption.[19] In addition, they appealed for a return to habits of hard work, industry, and frugality—values for which paper bills could never substitute, according to Gov. Samuel Shute.

In contrast, proponents of paper money stretched the limits of balance-of-trade theory. Although they agreed that the Massachusetts economy faced a crisis, paper money advocates supported a different policy response. Rather than retrenchment of consumption and imports, banking supporters pushed for expansion of trade, farming, and manufacturing to augment exports and contended that enlarging the money supply would tap the productive energies of New England's inhabitants. In presenting their arguments, the pro-bank, pro-paper faction examined the role of interest and the market. They questioned money's intrinsic value and defined wealth as the satisfaction of wants. In their more expansive and dynamic understanding of the economy, proponents of paper money saw credit as the key to rapid development.

Targeting their rhetoric to rising merchants, land speculators, farmers, artisans disgusted with the truck-pay system, and other supporters of Boston's "Popular party," advocates of paper money urged the expansion of both internal and external trade. They rejected the "mean Contracted spirit" of retrenchment and pointed out that trade was necessary to secure the standard of living to which the inhabitants of Massachusetts had rightly become accustomed. While opponents of paper money tended to portray Massachusetts's material prosperity as illusory, supporters of bank schemes constantly referred to the very real improvements in material life that paper money had wrought in Boston and its hinterlands: "Tell the new Towns and Parishes" that paper money and internal trade failed to increase wealth, challenged one anonymous writer; "observe the Buildings, the furniture, the Habit and Diet of the people in general."[20] Rather than in specie, advocates of paper suggested that the colony's wealth inhered in the fine homes, furnishings, farms, and enterprises that filled Boston and dotted the countryside.

19. See Edward Wigglesworth, *A Vindication of the Remarks of One in the Country* (Boston, 1720), *CCR* 2:35–36. Wigglesworth advised that the Court regulate book debt by charging a penalty of 10 percent interest on any accounts that ran over the legal time limit.

20. "A Modest Apology for Paper Money," *Boston Weekly Rehearsal*, Mar. 18, 1734, *CCR* 3:93–94; for similar sentiments see John Wise, *A Word of Comfort to a Melancholy People* (Boston, 1721), *CCR* 1:177.

John Colman chided Wigglesworth and other doomsayers for their unso-
phisticated application of balance-of-trade theory to New England's complex web of international commerce. Critics of consumption exaggerated
the extent of New England's trade deficit, Colman charged, by focusing
solely on direct exchange with England and ignoring the carrying and
plantation trades. "When did we Raise sufficient to Pay for our Import!
Doth not our Import from one place, pay for what we Import from another
place? . . . Do we not Export one Commodity, and Bring in another; and
then Export that, and Bring in another?" Boston served as the hub of the
entire American trade, upon which the southern colonies and the Caribbean depended. Curtailing imports would undermine this delicate mechanism; duties and restrictions merely invited retaliation, diverted trade to
New York, Philadelphia, and other competing ports, and harmed the market for Massachusetts goods abroad. For Colman, this trade justified even
the export of specie, as it had for Thomas Mun a century earlier. "[B]y
encouraging every body to come to us," and "let[ting] Trade go in a manner
free," Bostonians could look forward to a higher volume of shipping, lower
prices, and general prosperity.[21]

Supporters of public bills and private banks also departed from the
traditional balance-of-trade formulation by emphasizing the value of internal commerce. They embraced a more instrumental notion of both currency and public policy, and they utilized naturalistic models to characterize the workings of exchange and to decry laws restricting credit. Their
free-tradism regarding external commerce, however, did not preclude
their support for specific mercantilist forms of government intervention to
promote internal development.[22] Although the American writers lacked
their European counterparts' theoretical sophistication and comprehen-
siveness, their ideas, grounded in a specific political and economic milieu,
combined liberalism with a commitment to other values.[23] Writers like

21. John Colman, *The Distressed State Of the Town of Boston Once more Considered*
(Boston, 1720), *CCR* 2:71–72, 68–69.

22. As Cathy Matson notes, free trade and mercantilism were not rigid, exclusive intellectual categories but points on a spectrum of arguments and positions which the colonists
assumed at different times and in different contexts. Private communication, March 1992;
see also Cathy Diane Matson, "Fair Trade, Free Trade: Economic Ideas and Opportunities
in Eighteenth-Century New York City Commerce," (Ph.D. diss., Columbia Univ., 1985).

23. Janet Riesman contends that American political economy was largely emulative in
the colonial period and that change awaited the postrevolutionary period, but evidence
presented here indicates that the Massachusetts paper money debates anticipated many of

Colman, Ipswich minister John Wise, Huguenot merchant Hugh Vance, and Elisha Cooke, Jr., and Oliver Noyes, the leaders of the Popular Party in the Massachusetts Assembly, all made arguments regarding internal commerce, the benign effects of individuals' pursuit of economic betterment, and the role of government that resembled the works of the Scottish moral philosophers David Hume and Adam Smith as much they did Locke's works.

These advocates of paper money emissions marshalled moral and social as well as economic arguments in favor of their policies. Like their opponents, the pro-banking writers evoked the Puritan qualities of industry and frugality, but they contended that these virtues functioned best in a growing, healthy economy. They blamed economic crimes on a lack of economic opportunity, rather than on "over-trading." Straitened economic conditions led to competition, selfishness, and laziness, they insisted, while policies that permitted wide access to credit, trade, and goods stimulated productivity, thus benefitting the commonweal. "The Law of God and Nature," proclaimed Wise, mandated that "by their Frugality and Painful Improvement," people "ought to make a clear Gain."[24] Instead of portraying a conflict of interest between frugal country inhabitants and Boston's rapacious merchants and retailers, supporters of paper money sought to convince farmers that the market inseparably bound city and rural interests. Without money and trade, rural land and commodity prices would fall. Monetizing exchange made for fairer bargains than did a barter system, which sometimes failed to satisfy both parties' needs.

This benign view of exchange made the pro-bills pamphleteers much more tolerant of consumption and imports than their opponents. Thus a decade before Hume, Massachusetts pamphleteers were distinguishing between "good" and "bad" luxury—between consumption that served to stimulate production and useless extravagance.[25] By 1761, Harvard A.M. candidates could affirm the position that a spendthrift who kept his money in circulation advanced the common good more than a frugal miser, while

---

the Scottish school's and the Physiocrats' later writings. See Janet Riesman, "The Origins of American Political Economy, 1690–1781" (Ph.D. diss., Brown Univ., 1983).

24. [Oliver Noyes,] *A Letter From a Gentleman* (Boston, 1720), *CCR* 2:12; [John Wise,] *A Word of Comfort to a Melancholy Country* (Boston, 1721), *CCR* 2:186, 196–198.

25. This shift in attitude towards luxury was also made possible by a constant redefinition–upwards–of what the colonists considered a reasonable material "competency." See Daniel Vickers, "Competency and Competition: Economic Culture in Early America," *The William and Mary Quarterly*, 3d ser., 47(1990):3–29.

John Wise dismissed sumptuary laws and import restrictions as "Theams more proper for Pulpits then Statesmen to Talk of."[26] These arguments amounted to more than merely a Mandevillean cynicism equating private vices with public virtue, however; banking supporters asserted that participation in trade and credit fostered private virtues as well as the public good. The Boston paper money faction presaged many of Montesquieu's and Hume's arguments in particular: that luxury could replace coercion as a stimulus for development; that commerce brought numerous civilizing benefits in its wake; and that domestic industry served as a key source of national wealth.[27] Assuming that people naturally wished to improve their holdings and to engage in commerce, pro-bank writers asserted the need for currency and economic expansion in order to free individuals to pursue these rational, socially beneficial inclinations.[28] Their appeals to interest did not repudiate notions of commonwealth; the two appeared mutually reinforcing.

Proponents of banking and paper money also sought to strip indebtedness of its negative moral and practical connotations. Rather than signifying bankruptcy and failure, public and private debt played a constructive role in the contemporary commercial world as a source of investment credit. "Most men of thought may see, that Day we are out of Debt, we are out of Credit," asserted one land bank supporter.[29] Numerous authors echoed Locke on the labor theory of value, arguing that paper currency monetized the Bay Colony's most valuable assets—land and the industry of its citizens—and extended the benefits of credit beyond a selfish circle of power-

26. [Wise,] *Word of Comfort*, 201–202; Dorfman, *Economic Mind*, 1:141.

27. For Hume, Montesquieu, and other contemporary writers, see J. E. Crowley, *The Privileges of Independence: Neomercantilism and the American Revolution* (Baltimore, 1993), 6–9; Istvan Hont and Michael Ignatieff, eds., *Wealth and Virtue: The Shaping of Political Economy in the Scottish Enlightenment* (Cambridge, 1983); and Albert O. Hirschman, *The Passions and the Interests: Political Arguments for Capitalism before its Triumph* (Princeton, 1977), 17–19, 25–26, 56–66. James Kloppenberg's "The Virtues of Liberalism: Christianity, Republicanism, and Ethics in Early American Political Discourse," *Journal of American History* 74(1987):9–33, also notes the compatibility of liberal and republican thought in the writings of the Scottish political economists, and their influence upon revolutionary-era American political thought.

28. J. E. Crowley, *This Sheba, Self: The Conceptualization of Economic Life in Eighteenth-Century America* (Baltimore, 1974), 92; [Noyes,] *Letter from a Gentleman*, 11; Wise, *Word of Comfort*, 160–161, 165, 177, 180, 215–218.

29. *A Letter from One in Boston, To his Friend in the Country* (Boston, 1714), 9.

ful merchants.[30] Mortgaging one's land to a public or private bank did not represent a loss of independence, but rather a means of achieving it.[31] Responding to criticism, the Reverend Mr. Wise submitted his own case to the *Boston Gazette* as proof of how an ordinary farmer could benefit from credit to advance "the business of the Family." A £1,000 loan from the public bank of 1716 permitted Wise to pay off debts, make improvements, increase productivity, and enhance the value of the property he planned to pass on to his sons: "We thought it might be very proper both for the Publick good and our own profit so to do . . . and by the Assistance of the Auspicious and Prosperous Bills, we do not fall short of Three Hundred Pounds Annual Income."[32]

This emphasis on productivity, exchange, and the internal economy led a number of writers to endorse more sweeping plans for entrepreneurship and internal diversification. Several authors asserted that public loans and private banks provided more than merely a circulating medium, but also "great sums of Bills for inabling Particular Men to carry on any useful and beneficial Works," such as fishing, hemp cultivation, ironworks, naileries, slitting mills, glass-making, comb-making, and linen and cotton manufactures, all of which would cut the region's dependence on imports and help balance its foreign exchange.[33] One pamphleteer linked the public bank to an almost Hamiltonian program of expansive regional development that focused on the domestic economy as well as international trade. Along with

30. See, for example, Hugh Vance, *An Inquiry into the Nature and Uses of Money*, *CCR* 3:367–379; [John Wise,] *Trade and Commerce Inculcated* (Boston, 1731), 11; "Modest Apology for Paper Money," 92; Dorfman, *Economic Mind*, 1:164, 141.

31. Land bankers refused to abdicate country political rhetoric to their opponents on the subject of debt and mortgages. Indeed, some private bank advocates turned such arguments on their head. Whereas Paul Dudley attacked the power that owning mortgages would confer on bank directors, at least one anonymous bank supporter retorted that **public** control of individuals' estates through official loan emissions represented a much more pernicious threat to liberty. *A Vindication of the Bank of Credit Projected in Boston from the Aspersions of Paul Dudley, Esq.* (Boston, 1714), *CCR* 1:308–309.

32. [John Wise,] *Boston Gazette*, Feb. 20–27, 1721; Thomas Franklin Waters, *Ipswich in the Massachusetts Bay Colony* (Ipswich, Mass., 1905–1917), 2:144–146. Daniel Vickers notes that providing for one's children–the ideal of familial economic security–necessarily required a range of entrepreneurial activities from farmers, from land speculation to production for market. Vickers, "Competency and Competition."

33. *Some Considerations Upon the several sorts of Banks Propos'd as a Medium of Trade: And Some Improvements that might be made in this Province, hinted at* (Boston, 1716), *CCR* 1:336–337.

loans to private enterprises, the bills could be used to fund internal improvements designed to link Boston with the interior—a channel at Cape Cod, a new bridge for the Charles River, a public granary to facilitate the marketing of agricultural goods, and the establishment of new towns and mills in the hinterland to attract settlers. Other writers called on the General Court to use the bills as bounties for entrepreneurs who imported workers from Europe, for those who undertook to develop cloth making or naval stores, and for individuals who improved western lands.[34] Another anonymous writer credited paper money with promoting "Ropewalks, Ship-yards, still-houses, Sugar-houses, and the other Trades Depending upon these, the Number of Ships and Vessels . . . and many other Things not to be numbr'd, increasing daily."[35] This list of enterprises in fact comprised an accurate accounting of the bankers' own assets. Elisha Cooke, Jr., owned three ropewalks in Boston and numerous sawmills on the eastern frontier, Noyes operated a sugar refinery, and both speculated avidly in Maine lands. Other Boston land bank signatories in 1714 and 1740 had interests in shipbuilding and fisheries. Taken together, such industries accounted for an increasingly large portion of New England's credits in foreign trade by mid century.[36]

In their recommendations regarding internal development, paper money advocates generally promoted only those manufactures not in direct competition with English interests, and they remained convinced of the value of foreign trade. But they hinted at an economic nationalism that made Boston, not London, the metropolitan center of a developing hinterland. Many contemporaries watched anxiously in the decades after 1714 as competition from Salem, Portsmouth, Newport, New York, and other minor and

34. *Some Considerations*, 342–345; [Noyes,] *Letter from a Gentleman*, 8.

35. "Modest Apology for Paper Money," 93–94.

36. Noyes was a partner in the Pejepscot Company, and had sawmill and fishery operations near Augusta; Cooke headed the Muscongus Company in Maine, where his sawmills and speculative activities involved him in frequent clashes with His Majesty's Surveyor of the Woods William Bridger. On the enterprising land bankers, Andrew Davis noted that the 1714 signatories included John Oulton, who had interest in fisheries, and shipbuilder Timothy Thornton. *CCR* 1:312–316; Hutchinson, *History of . . . Massachusetts-Bay*, 2:155; John L. Sibley and Clifford K. Shipton et al., *Biographical Sketches of Graduates of Harvard University* (Cambridge, Mass., and Boston, 1873–), 4:260–264, 349–356. John J. McCusker and Russell R. Menard, *The Economy of British America, 1607–1789* (Chapel Hill, 1985), 81–86, 290–294, note the importance of shipbuilding as a component in New England's returns, and the boom in processing and "linkage" industries related to the import/export economy in the region by the mid-eighteenth century.

major ports ate into Boston's share of trade. In response to these fears, Colman and Noyes stressed the connection between expanding internal and external commerce and proposed to enhance Boston's trading connections with the countryside by widening the Boston Neck even as they helped construct the Long Wharf.[37]

The paper money advocates' commercial vision and promise of development proved equally compelling outside the hub. Although the anti-paper faction that dominated the Council had managed to block the land bank in 1714 and 1720, Colman, Cooke, and Noyes used their positions in the House to push for more liberal currency policies. Before 1720, residents of Boston and its immediate environs generated most of the discourse regarding currency and banking. The large public emissions of 1716, 1721, and 1728—concessions to the land bankers' pressure—led to the creation of public land banks administered through the towns, which in turn broadened the constituency for paper money.[38] By the 1730s, town meetings in Dighton, Hadley, Dedham, Ipswich, Billerica, Worcester, and other communities in central and western Massachusetts were holding public discussions on currency, petitioning the Court for new emissions, and occasionally instructing their representatives on specific provincial votes. Echoing the Boston pamphlets, town resolutions demanded easy access to public paper and set maximum limits per individual to ensure widespread participation in the benefits of credit. In addition, town fathers experimented on a small scale with banking's developmental possibilities by using paper profits to fund school and road construction, for example.[39] Thomas Hutchinson and other opponents in the General Court noted uneasily that Massachu-

37. Riesman, "Origins of American Political Economy," 170–171; Sibley and Shipton, *Biographical Sketches of Graduates*, 4:260–264, 349–356; Henry H. Edes, "Note on John Colman," *Publications of the Colonial Society of Massachusetts* 6(1904):86–89.

38. While earlier emissions were administered through appointed directors, after 1716 they were distributed to the towns in proportion to their tax assessments. The towns in turn disbursed paper in exchange for five-, ten-, or twenty-year mortgages on the borrowers' lands. Borrowers promised to pay fixed interest rates, usually 5–6 percent. This interest represented income for the towns, which they could apply to internal improvements or other public expenses. The 1716 emission limited individual loans to £200, but many of the towns thought this excessive; Dedham, for example, set limits of £50, although individuals could apply for additional loans if funds remained.

39. Helen H. Lane, *History of the Town of Dighton Massachusetts* (Dighton, Mass., 1962), 43–45, 52–53; Sylvester Judd, *History of Hadley* (Springfield, Mass., 1905), 301–304; *Early Records of Dedham, Massachusetts* (Boston, 1885–1968), 6:215, 232–233, 7:55–56; Waters, *Ipswich in the Massachusetts Bay Colony*, 1:148–157.

setts's physical expansion after 1714 had created new towns empowered to affect public policy through their representatives, while the accompanying boom in land speculation had increased the number of Bay Colonists eager to transform their holdings into "coined land."[40] As a result of this growing support within and beyond Boston, currency positions formed the core of the Popular Party's electoral success through the early 1740s.[41]

By that time, however, the currency debate had become a transatlantic contest. Under pressure from anti-paper Boston traders and British merchants, after 1730 the Board of Trade began to instruct Governor Belcher to limit paper emissions. While the pro-paper faction's calls for internal development steered clear of openly questioning English regulatory policy regarding trade and manufactures, several town resolutions and pamphlets greeted British interference in colonial currency policy with dismay. Numerous town resolutions attested to the colonists' vigorous opposition to even the mildest of British restrictions; in 1736, the Boston Town Meeting instructed its representatives to demand more paper money and to prevent the "rigorous execution" of the royal instructions, which jeopardized New Englanders' commercial interests, "laws, liberties and properties."[42]

Conflicting positions regarding currency and trade clashed most dramatically over the Land Bank project of 1739–1741.[43] John Colman and his fellow organizers envisioned a credit institution that would facilitate a range of agricultural, commercial, and manufacturing enterprises.[44] Bank supporters had pragmatic political reasons for linking their proposals to internal development. Economic development offered a recipe for social cohe-

40. Hutchinson, *History of . . . Massachusetts-Bay*, 2:298, 300.

41. Brooke, *Heart of the Commonwealth*, 56–65, 97–106; Pencak, *War, Politics and Revolution*, 66–76, chaps. 4–5.

42. *CCR* 3:16–17; Brock, *Currency of the American Colonies*, 179, 182; Hutchinson, *History of . . . Massachusetts-Bay*, 2:289, 306, 288; "Committee Report of April 28, 1736," *Report of the Record Commissioners of the City of Boston* (Boston, 1876–1909).

43. A group headed by John Colman proposed to issue £150,000 in notes against security of land or personal property; borrowers agreed to pay 3 percent interest and to repay the principal in 20 annual payments, either in the bank's notes or in equivalent amounts of specified goods–flax, hemp, bar- and cast-iron, cordage, sail cloth, and tanned leather. The bank's organizers and officers included Peter Chardon, Colman's merchant son-in-law; William Stoddard, a speculator in Connecticut lands; Robert Auchmuty; Samuel Adams, Sr.; inland merchants like the Choate family of Ipswich; ministers John White and Ebenezer Parkman; Peter Thacher of Middleborough, who also had interest in ironworks; and Samuel Ruggles, a Billerica land speculator. *CCR* 3:290–292; George Billias, "The Massachusetts Land Bankers of 1740," *University of Maine Studies*, 2d ser., 74(1959):19–22.

44. Hutchinson, *History of . . . Massachusetts-Bay*, 2:300.

sion; by arguing that public loans or private banks stimulated development, political figures like Colman could appeal to the interests of a varied coalition of investors and supporters including artisans, farmers, and petty traders. Settlement of the interior would increase the number of Bay Colony residents clamoring for ways of converting their landed wealth into capital through land banks and public loans. Thus although the Land Bank was based in Boston, and Bostonians filled most of the institution's offices, the land bankers worked hard to extend their base of support beyond the town, enlisting as many as 1,253 signatories from 64 communities.[45] Through advertisements and newspaper accounts, Colman attempted to recruit merchants, urban artisans, and farmers as subscribers.[46] Shopkeepers, retailers, and Boston merchants interested in expanding their commercial ties to the interior "gave credit to the bills."[47]

Led by Hutchinson and Governor Belcher, the anti-bank faction marshalled its forces to block the Land Bank's charter. One group of "opulent" Boston merchants, including the Hutchinsons, Samuel Sewall, Jr., Joshua Winslow, Andrew Oliver, Peter Faneuil, Thomas Oxnard, and Edmund Quincy, boycotted the Land Bank notes and established a rival specie-backed venture. The governor's complaints and anti-Land Bank petitions from Boston merchants eventually attracted the attention of Parliament. At the New England petitioners' own demand, Parliament applied the provisions of the Bubble Act—a measure passed in the wake of the South Sea debacle, which regulated English corporations—to the Land Bank in 1741, suppressing its operations. Members of the Massachusetts House helped

45. *CCR* 3:302; Billias, "Massachusetts Land Bankers," 11, 14; Pencak, *War, Politics and Revolution*, 101–103. Rosalind Remer has noted a correlation between support for the Land Bank and New Light church affiliations in Boston. See Remer, "Old Lights and New Money: A Note on Religion, Economics, and the Social Order in 1740 Boston," *The William and Mary Quarterly*, 3d ser., 47(1990):566–573. John Brooke finds a similar correlation in Worcester County, despite the differing status and occupation of urban and rural bank supporters. Brooke, *Heart of the Commonwealth*, 70–71.

46. Billias, "Massachusetts Land Bankers," 9. The bank's advertisements attempted to attract artisans, who were leery of paper money because depreciation hurt wage-earners, on the grounds that notes were preferable to truck pay and that the bank would provide a stimulus to manufactures. Although this strategy enjoyed only limited success, a group of Boston caulkers expressed support for the bank in an advertisement that appeared in *The Boston Weekly News-Letter* of Feb. 12–19, 1741. "Artificers and Traders" could obtain credit on collateral other than land. To appeal to farmers, the subscribers noted that the bank would serve as a collective marketing agent; farmers could deposit their produce in exchange for credit, leaving the bank officers to arrange its sale or export.

47. Hutchinson, *History of . . . Massachusetts-Bay*, 2:300.

organize protests, petitions, marches, and other expressions of popular outrage at the closing of the bank, and Hutchinson blamed Belcher's eventual removal on the outcry, but the bank scheme remained moribund.

In the decade following the collapse of the Land Bank, proponents of a hard-money policy in Massachusetts achieved a stunning policy reversal under the aegis of English authorities. Belcher's successor, William Shirley, allowed a public emission of bills, but insisted upon legislation that protected creditors and established official indexes for measuring depreciation. The pressure for regulation abated briefly during the war years, when necessity demanded liberal credit for colonial governments. But after the successful expedition to Louisbourg, British merchants in 1747 petitioned Parliament for the forced retirement of outstanding colonial bills. The fact that Parliament had already considered such a move in 1745 made the Board of Trade receptive to Thomas Hutchinson's plan to use the specie reimbursement granted to the colony by a grateful England to redeem bills and return to a specie standard in 1750. Some paper remained in circulation, but Massachusetts bills lost their legal tender status. Thus the Currency Act of 1751, which prohibited all the New England colonies from issuing any additional bills of credit, passing legal tender laws, or extending the loan periods of existing bills, merely reinforced actions that Massachusetts had already taken in the preceding two years.

Hutchinson and a few hard-money advocates hailed the General Court's actions as a vindication of their political economy. Yet although Bay colonists adjusted to the new conditions of trade, Shirley and the Council had essentially forced the new policy upon an unwilling population. As Hutchinson himself admitted, a majority of Massachusetts voters approved of the paper money; even critics of new emissions like William Douglass desired only a stabilization and reduction of provincial bills, not their elimination.[48] Only complex political jockeying among several competing interests, and the fortuitous specie grant from England, allowed the passage of Hutchinson's proposal after successive defeats.[49] In addition, after 1751 Parliamen-

48. A popular alternative plan would have deposited the specie in the Bank of England and used the interest to redeem outstanding bills gradually, thus avoiding a severe economic contraction. Hutchinson, *History of . . . Massachusetts-Bay*, 2:335.

49. Riesman, "Origins of American Political Economy," 217–218. Joseph Ernst attributes the return to specie to the defection of a critical group of Boston middlemen-merchants. The growing tendency of these traders to import goods directly from England on their own account, rather than through British factors, made them more sensitive to the drawbacks of long credit and depreciating paper; see Ernst, "Massachusetts' 'Great Cur-

tary regulation all but forced the colonists to adopt and maintain hard-money policies.

Certainly, a number of commentators in the 1750s continued to echo the balance-of-payment worries of those who opposed paper money. Observing the rising tide of English imports in 1753, the organizers of the Boston Society for Encouraging Industry and Employing the Poor expressed concern over Massachusetts's imbalance of trade with the mother country and noted a disjunction between Boston's "fair outward shew" and the "poverty" that chronic currency shortages and trade deficits seemed to indicate.[50] But although they assessed their economy according to mercantilist criteria, Bostonians' mercantilism after mid century implicitly rejected a metropolitan focus. The colonists did not question their relationship with Britain; they struggled to improve their fiscal and commercial situation within the framework of the imperial system. But even amidst their economic worries, the Society's members applied mercantilist principles to their situation as if Massachusetts were independent rather than a colonial outpost of empire.

This shift was telling. Although the Currency Act of 1751 retired colonial bills of credit, it failed to retire the land bankers' innovative ideas. Indeed, the ideological outcome of Governor Shirley's contest with bank proponents proved analogous to the aftermath of England's recoinage controversy in 1690.[51] The anti-paper faction's victory was short-lived; the Seven

---

rency Debate.'" John Brooke suggests that the western counties' support of the Louisbourg expedition translated into allegiance to the Shirley administration, which led a few former land bankers to vote in favor of the specie measure. Brooke speculates that most constituents opposed the return to specie, however, and notes that they elected a large number of representatives associated with paper currency and the Land Bank to office in 1749 and 1750; Brooke, *Heart of the Commonwealth*, 112.

50. [Boston] Society for Encouraging Industry and Employing the Poor, *Industry and Frugality Proposed As the Surest Means to Make us a Rich and Flourishing People* (Boston, 1753).

51. As Joyce Appleby notes, although recoinage signaled a victory for the bullionists, the more liberal economic ideas of their opponents proved more influential in the eighteenth century. Joyce Appleby, *Economic Thought and Ideology in Seventeenth-Century England* (Princeton, 1978). This interpretation is at odds with the work of Janet Riesman. Riesman argues that defeat retired the land bankers' radical economic ideas along with the bills of credit. Discredited, their theories concerning wealth, the market, the balance of trade, and internal development failed to influence colonial political economy; true change and liberal economic ideas awaited the postrevolutionary era. But the writings of Colman, Wise, and their fellow pamphleteers suggest that fundamental change preceded the Revolution.

Years' War prompted both a return to paper currency in Massachusetts and a further expansion of internal trade, importation, and the class of traders who serviced both. More crucially, in the debates over currency Bay colonists began to recognize that a lack of specie only masked New England's very real prosperity and developmental potential. Paper money and the discourse that surrounded its adoption helped to create a constituency of farmers and traders who found a political economy that endorsed development, diversification, and internal trade compelling. Finally, Parliament's suppression of the Land Bank and interference with colonial currency forced Americans to examine whether their interests coincided with those of the mother country—a question that New England commentators raised with greater frequency after 1763, when British regulation sparked a new round of debates over the region's economic future.

Thus the Massachusetts currency debates contributed to independence in several ways. During the imperial crisis, Bostonians drew upon ideas first articulated in the contests over banking to devise a political economy that complemented political opposition to Great Britain. In formulating their protests against the new Revenue Acts and enhanced customs enforcement, James Otis, Oxenbridge Thacher, and numerous writers for Boston newspapers adapted the liberal economic discourse of the currency debates and applied its insights to Massachusetts's relationship with England. These authors attacked economic regulation using naturalistic models and a language of interests to defend free-trade principles, and they asserted the colonies' growing economic potential and power. At the same time, the emphasis on internal development and diversification so prominent in the works of Wise and Colman also re-emerged during the 1760s, particularly in the context of the non-importation movement. Many Bay colonists embraced the boycott of English goods as a quasi-mercantilist program that aimed to redress long-standing deficiencies in the colonial economy, rather than as an effort to restore lost virtue or to obtain political leverage in the short term. Those in favor of the boycott asserted the virtues of manufactures, internal trade, and consumption of locally-made goods.

Along with providing ideological reinforcement, then, Massachusetts's paper money policies also helped to create a constituency for political resistance. The audience for this argument was similar to the group that proponents of paper money had courted for decades—an audience that paper money had itself augmented: farmers and traders who recognized the benefits of international trade but whose livelihoods did not depend on tight commercial connections with the mother country. In the end, these groups were far more likely to embrace revolution than the "opulent" merchants who depended upon transatlantic ties and opposed non-importation, just as they had opposed paper money decades earlier. British regulation after 1763 convinced many New Englanders of the political necessity of independence; the paper money advocates' hopeful vision of a rich, diversified, and developed interior linked to international markets offered reassurance that independence was not just economically feasible, but desirable.[52]

52. McCusker and Menard make this same argument from a material standpoint. See *Economy of British America*, 93.

Two-handled covered cup, Boston, 1744. By Jacob Hurd. Mabel Brady
Garvan Collection, Yale University Art Gallery.

Boston Artisan Entrepreneurs
of the Goldsmithing Trade
in the Decades before the Revolution

Barbara McLean Ward

N O   O N E   W H O   H A S   S P E N T time analyzing
eighteenth-century artisan account books or the brief accounts filed as part
of civil suits in the Court of Common Pleas can fail to be impressed by the
broad range of goods in which artisans were forced to trade, especially
during times of inflation when cash was scarce or of dubious value. In 1715,
the anonymous author of a pamphlet attacking the proposal to turn Boston
into a municipal corporation commented that the restrictions that such a
system would impose would be unfair to Bostonians, because few tradesmen could afford to practice only one trade and most had to pursue every
potentially profitable calling in order to earn a living.[1] In such an economic
climate, artisans had to develop a broad knowledge of the trades and establish a wide network of business contacts in order to obtain access to desirable commodities. Unfortunately, the "raw" records of these transactions
are nearly always incomplete and therefore the information about complex
webs of interdependency that they contain is difficult to interpret.

This essay is an attempt to make sense out of some of the records left by
Boston goldsmiths (or silversmiths) who worked during the first three quarters of the eighteenth century. It draws directly on my own research and on
the cumulative efforts of a group of scholars who have collaborated on a
biographical dictionary of goldsmiths, silversmiths, and jewelers working in
Massachusetts before the Revolution. The dictionary, to be published by
the Yale University Art Gallery, includes information on the lives, works,
and business practices of these artisans and contains thousands of bills and
inventories related to the careers of more than 300 men and women.[2]

1. G. B. Warden, *Boston 1689–1776* (Boston, 1970), 74–75.

2. See Barbara McLean Ward, "Boston Goldsmiths, 1690–1730," *The Craftsman in
Early America*, ed. Ian M. G. Quimby (New York, 1984), 126–157; "The Edwards Family

During the last two decades, historians have greatly enhanced our understanding of the crisis that confronted skilled artisans of the late eighteenth century as they faced competition from unskilled workers and changes in the organization of production.[3] As a result, we now have a more sophisticated understanding of the artisan's transformation from skilled mechanic to wage laborer. Recent works have focused less attention on those artisans who became entrepreneurs, partly in reaction to the contentions of earlier scholars that the crafts offered unlimited possibilities for economic advancement and that the typical artisan's life followed the rags-to-riches scenario of a Horatio Alger novel. Nonetheless, with a greater understanding of the substantial differences that existed within the crafts between journeymen or jobbers, who eked only minimal rewards from their labor, and the successful artisan-entrepreneur, we can now attempt more fully to understand the mechanism by which some producing aartisans diversified into general merchant and shopkeeping activities.

Who engaged in merchant ventures in the eighteenth century? How did they obtain the capital to do so? Historians have not fully explored those questions, perhaps in part because of the confusion created by contempo-

---

and the Silversmithing Trade in Boston," *The American Craftsman and the European Tradition*, ed. Francis J. Puig and Michael Conforti (Minneapolis, Minn., 1989), 66–76; and "Hierarchy and Wealth Distribution in the Boston Goldsmithing Trade, 1690–1760," *Essex Institute Historical Collections* 126(1990):129–147. *The Dictionary of Colonial Massachusetts Silversmiths*, under the general editorship of Patricia E. Kane (New Haven, 1997), contains contributions by Jeannine Falino, Deborah A. Federhen, Patricia E. Kane, Gerald W. R. Ward, and myself and draws upon extensive documentary and genealogical research conducted by Francis Hill Bigelow, John Marshall Phillips, and Josephine Setze between 1920 and 1980. In addition to the biographies that have been published as part of the *Dictionary*, the Yale University Art Gallery in New Haven, Conn., maintains an archive of notes and photocopies of documents relating to the careers of Massachusetts silversmiths for future researchers. Significant original documents collected by Bigelow and Phillips as part of the project will be transferred to the Beinecke Rare Book and Manuscript Library at Yale University.

3. See Bruce Laurie, *Artisans into Workers: Labor in Nineteenth-Century America* (New York, 1989); Charles S. Olton, *Artisans for Independence: Philadelphia Mechanics and the American Revolution* (Syracuse, N.Y., 1975); Howard B. Rock, *Artisans of the New Republic: The Tradesmen of New York City in the Age of Jefferson* (New York, 1979); Billy G. Smith, "The Vicissitudes of Fortune: The Careers of Laboring Men in Philadelphia, 1750–1800," *Work and Labor in Early America*, ed. Stephen Innes (Chapel Hill, 1988), 221–251; Richard Walsh, *Charleston's Sons of Liberty: A Study of the Artisans, 1763–1789* (Columbia, 1959); Sean Wilentz, *Chants Democratic: New York City and the Rise of the American Working Class, 1788–1850* (New York, 1984).

rary occupational labels.[4] This is particularly true for Boston, where probate records often offer our best aggregate information on eighteenth-century trading practices. Thus, a merchant who appears in the records is presumed to have been a merchant all of his life, and an artisan listed in the records is presumed to have confined his efforts to his craft. Because many producing artisans who became involved in merchant ventures maintained their craft businesses and identified themselves by their artisanal skills, their contributions as merchants have proved hard to assess. Likewise, the titles "merchant" and "esquire" sometimes mask the fact that individuals trained as artisans often maintained their craft shops as the basis for their merchant ventures, even after they themselves had stopped working side-by-side with their journeymen. The most famous example of such an arrangement is probably the business of Paul Revere II, who, as Deborah Federhen has clearly demonstrated, used the profits from his silversmithing business to branch out into other, more speculative ventures, such as his copper mill operation in Canton, Massachusetts.[5] Billy G. Smith has observed that in Philadelphia, once master artisans achieved prominence in their crafts, they rarely abandoned those positions. Instead, they continued to dominate the market for craft production while diversifying into general merchant ventures, thus preventing lesser artisans from moving up in the socioeconomic hierarchy.[6]

4. For instance, statistics such as those gathered for Boston by Gary Nash count only those individuals who were called merchants in the probate records—that is, who were identified with merchant activities at the time of their deaths; see *The Urban Crucible: Social Change, Political Consciousness, and the Origins of the American Revolution* (Cambridge, Mass., 1979), 387–391. Eric Hobsbawm makes a distinction between "bourgeois" and working-class activism in *Workers: Worlds of Labor* (New York, 1984), 15–32, that acknowledges broad conceptual differences among the persons who referred to themselves by artisan labels. Billy G. Smith, "Vicissitudes of Fortune," discusses the mobility of master artisans, particularly those in high-status trades such as goldsmithing, into the merchant class in Philadelphia, but does not deal with these people in depth. Thomas M. Doerflinger found that merchant-artisans played only a minor role in the Philadelphia business community in the years preceding the Revolution (*A Vigorous Spirit of Enterprise: Merchants and Economic Development in Revolutionary Philadelphia* [Chapel Hill, 1986]), a fact that may account for the attitudes that made it possible for skilled and unskilled labor to unite in the labor reform efforts of the early 19th century. (See Bruce Laurie, *The Working People of Philadelphia, 1800–1850* [Philadelphia, 1980]).

5. Deborah Federhen, "From Artisan to Entrepreneur: Paul Revere's Silver Shop Operation," Paul Revere Memorial Association, *Paul Revere—Artisan, Businessman, and Patriot: The Man Behind the Myth* (Boston, 1988), 84–85.

6. Smith, "Vicissitudes of Fortune."

This trend was evident in the Boston goldsmithing trade even as early as the first decade of the eighteenth century, when the town's economy experienced a brief period of prosperity. Jeremiah Dummer (1645–1718), for instance, trained as a goldsmith in the shop of John Hull (1624–1683) and established a substantial business in the trade by the 1670s. Dummer eventually became an active merchant with investments in at least eleven ships, issued a number of bonds that indicate that he was lending money, was one of the members of the Council of Safety in 1689, and served for many years as a justice for Suffolk County. Nonetheless, he maintained a goldsmithing operation managed by a journeyman even after he was unable to work in the trade himself because of "Such a numness in his hands that he could not wright." By the time of his death in 1718, Dummer styled himself a gentleman.[7] One of his apprentices, Edward Winslow (1669–1754), fol-

7. Hermann Frederick Clarke and Henry Wilder Foote, *Jeremiah Dummer: Colonial Craftsman & Merchant, 1645–1718* (New York, 1970), 28–35; John Coney and Jeremiah Dummer of Boston to John Higginson of Salem, Mar. 11, 1708/9, box 2, folder 1, Curwen Family Manuscripts, American Antiquarian Society, Worcester.

In England many goldsmiths developed significant businesses as bankers, but American goldsmiths do not appear to have been any more actively involved in loaning money, and keeping money on account for others, than many merchants were at the time. (For information on the activities of goldsmith-bankers in 17th-century London, see Stephen Quinn, "Balances and Goldsmith-bankers: The Co-ordination and Control of Inter-banker Debt Clearing in Seventeenth-century London," in *Goldsmiths, Silversmiths and Bankers: Innovation and the Transfer of Skill, 1550–1750*, ed. David Mitchell, [London: Centre for Metropolitan History, University of London, 1995], 53–76.) Jeremiah Dummer had money on account for several individuals at the time of his death in 1718, but evidence is lacking for other Boston goldsmiths (Suffolk County Probate Records, docket no. 4055, Suffolk County Court House, Boston). Several Boston silversmiths assisted merchants involved in a banking scheme in the late 1730s by valuing and weighing the silver left on account and by engraving and printing the bank's notes, but the major investors and organizers of this and other Boston banking schemes were merchants (Memorandum Book of Isaac Winslow, entries involving "Subscribers to the Scheme," Massachusetts Historical Society [hereafter M.H.S.]; Warden, *Boston*; John L. Brooke, *The Heart of the Commonwealth* [New York, 1989]). Jacob Hurd kept silver owned by Gov. Charles Knowles of Louisbourg on display in his shop, presumably for safekeeping, but possibly also to impress the people of Boston (Benjamin Walker Diary, vol. 3, entry for Oct. 7, 1747). Other silversmiths, because they were used to providing for the security and safekeeping of such objects, may have provided similar services for other clients. Because of their knowledge of the exchange rates among various coins and paper currencies, goldsmiths such as Edward Winslow were called upon to provide information on the value of silver at certain times (see, for example, Supreme Judicial Court Record Series, Suffolk County Court Files, docket no. 46659, Suffolk County Court House), and Benjamin Greene appears to have been involved in buying and selling colonial currencies (Benjamin Greene Ledger, M.H.S.). Without the strong guild

lowed a similar course, maintaining a goldsmithing business throughout most of his life even though he began a career as sheriff of Suffolk County in 1716 and probably never again picked up a hammer. He referred to himself as Edward Winslow, Esq., as early as 1720/21, but continued to finance a goldsmithing operation run by a talented journeyman and counted on the business to provide him, and later his widow, with a substantial income.[8]

Some individuals, such as Samuel Edwards (1705–1762) and Benjamin Burt (1729–1805), were able to build upon their fathers' success in the goldsmithing business and to combine large production shops with general merchandising operations that featured imported small metalwares and tools. In addition, Samuel Edwards occasionally invested in shipping ventures with his brother-in-law Isaac Smith and acted as his mother-in-law's agent in investing her substantial wealth. Burt also made speculative investments in real estate and made numerous mortgage loans, mostly to colleagues in his trade. When he died in 1805, he held shares in the Charles River Bridge and the Union Bank. Both men referred to themselves as goldsmiths throughout their lives, taking pride in the source of their wealth.[9]

Unlike the emerging industrialists of England, these producers were managers not of large-scale factories employing legions of workers, but of

---

restrictions that limited artisanal activities in England, however, there was no attempt to limit lending activities to people within a particular craft, and, in fact, many women were actively involved in holding mortgages and in financing businesses.

8. Winslow's earliest recorded use of the title "esquire" appears on a deed dated 1720/21 (Suffolk County Deeds, 35:100, Suffolk County Registry of Deeds, Suffolk County Court House). Benjamin Walker mentions going to "M[r] Sherif Winslow['s] Shop" and conversing there with "Tom Cully his Journyman" on Jan. 16, 1742/43 (Diary of Benjamin Walker, vol. 3, M.H.S.). In his will, dated 1748, Winslow made provisions for housing his journeyman, now referred to as Thomas Maccollo, with the expectation that he would continue to work in the goldsmiths' trade for "M[r] Hurd or any others that may employ him" and that the amount he earned in excess of his wages of 20s. per week would go toward Winslow's wife's and his grandchild's support (Suffolk County Probate Records, docket no. 10609). Edward Winslow's letters to his sons Isaac and Joshua, now in the collection of the Yale University Art Gallery, make it clear that he supported their merchant ventures and suggest that he may have instigated them. See also Francis Hill Bigelow-John Marshall Phillips files, Yale University Art Gallery, and Patricia E. Kane, s.v. "Edward Winslow," *Dictionary of Colonial Massachusetts Silversmiths*.

9. Ward, "Edwards Family," and s.v. "Samuel Edwards," *Dictionary of Colonial Massachusetts Silversmiths*. Samuel Edwards's extensive estate inventory and accounts of his business dealings with Isaac Smith and with Abigail Fowle Smith Edwards are contained in the Smith-Carter Family Papers, M.H.S. Deborah A. Federhen, s.v. "Benjamin Burt," *Dictionary of Colonial Massachusetts Silversmiths*.

small shops that combined work by a handful of journeymen and apprentices with the subcontracting of piecework to independent jobbers. Nonetheless, they shared with their more highly organized and capitalized English counterparts the notion of production as the ultimate basis of wealth. Critics, including artisans, often noted that merchants failed to enrich society because they engaged in the *"meer handling of goods one to another,* [which] no more increases any Wealth in the Province, than Persons *at a Fire* increase the *Water in a Pail,* by passing it thro' *Twenty* or *Forty hands."* Rather than being parasitic like merchants and shopkeepers, artisans enriched the province through their enterprises, based on the "produce of their labour for the Publick Good." Nonetheless, in diversifying their businesses, successful artisans recognized that, as historian Richard Grassby observed in his study of seventeenth-century English business fortunes, "abundant labour and inelastic demand made marketing more vital than production." The survival of Boston's business community depended on the free pursuit of trade by its members.[10]

As master artisans gained experience in the marketplace, some were able gradually to develop the skills and business contacts that allowed them to expand into broader mercantile ventures with the confidence that they had sufficient knowledge of market conditions to succeed in trade. Where goldsmithing, cabinetmaking, or upholstering might be closed to persons not trained in those callings, no such restrictions prevented master artisans from broadening their base of operations into merchant activities. While the economic safety valve for rural artisans was their ability to engage in agricultural pursuits, the safety valve for urban artisans was often diversification into retail and service occupations. The transition to general merchandising was a natural one for many goldsmiths. As producers of luxury goods, they inevitably counted some of the most affluent members of colonial society among their customers. In settling their accounts with these

10. [John Colman], "The Present Melancholy Circumstances of the Province Consider'd . . ." (Boston, 1719), as reprinted in Andrew McFarland Davis, *Colonial Currency Reprints, 1682–1751* (Boston, 1910–1911), 1:356; Richard Grassby, "English Merchant Capitalism in the Late Seventeenth Century: The Composition of Business Fortunes," *Past and Present* 46(1970):98; Winifred Barr Rothenberg identifies this free pursuit of sources and customers as the essence of a modern market economy in *From Market-Places to a Market Economy: The Transformation of Rural Massachusetts, 1750–1850* (Chicago, 1992). For the conflict between mercantilist theory and emerging liberalism, see Joyce Appleby, *Liberalism and Republicanism in the Historical Imagination* (Cambridge, Mass., 1992). For the full development of efforts to expand demand for consumer goods, see Neil McKendrick, John Brewer, and J. H. Plumb, *The Birth of a Consumer Society: The Commercialization of Eighteenth-Century England* (Bloomington, 1982).

individuals, goldsmiths often obtained substantial quantities of merchantable wares. Conversely, goldsmiths frequently found that they were unable to satisfy the demands of tradesmen and yeomen who supplied them with routine necessities. What did a farmer or truckman want with more than one pair of fancy silver buckles or more than one set of gold buttons? The market for luxury items was limited. It thus became commonplace for goldsmiths to accept textiles and other sought-after items in trade with merchants and to import small metalwares and tools such as scissors, pins, knives, awls, hammers, and nails to satisfy the needs of common tradesmen. For some master artisans this trade became significant enough to merit importing these wares to enhance their retail stock.

By expanding their trade, these artisans hoped to forestall the ill effects of fluctuations in the economy and inflationary trends. By becoming successful general shopkeepers, they could actually benefit from inflation. However, the master artisan who concentrated on production had to contend with rising costs of raw materials and found that prices set for finished goods often could not keep up with increasing costs, especially when accounts might remain unpaid for several years. Merchant ventures, shopkeeping, retailing of liquor, and tavern keeping therefore provided important outlets for those artisans who did not choose, or did not have sufficient clientele to support, increased shop production.

During the late seventeenth and early eighteenth centuries, most goldsmiths or silversmiths who achieved a level of prominence strove to utilize their gains to establish themselves as gentlemen and to retire to other pursuits, most notably public service. During this period, there were as many as fifty goldsmiths active in Boston at any one time. Of these, approximately one third seem to have worked as journeymen or as jobbers filling orders on a piecework basis for the larger shops. Another third worked as small-time independent producers and retailers. The final third can be considered to have achieved the rank of artisan entrepreneurs. The wealthiest goldsmiths came from among the ranks of this last group. Using productivity[11] as an indicator, we can establish that in 1700 the craft of gold-

11. See Barbara McLean Ward, "The Craftsman in a Changing Society: Boston Goldsmiths 1690–1730," (Ph.D. diss., Boston Univ., 1983), 25–27, 58n, 71–73; Kane, *Dictionary of Colonial Massachusetts Silversmiths*, will include even more comprehensive figures on surviving objects by individual makers. I determined productivity figures primarily by using marked objects in public collections and supplemented these figures with the limited documentary evidence of objects that I was able to find. Tool ownership provided additional documentation of the types of objects made in a specific shop, but this information could only be used qualitatively.

smithing was dominated by approximately 14 percent of its members, whereas by the 1740s, the craft was dominated by approximately 10 percent of its members. This assessment, however, limits our understanding of the dynamics of the trade. We can only use figures based on surviving objects to measure the activities of individuals who were large-scale producers of silver objects, and these totally exclude the leading jewelers in Boston, as jewelers did not always mark their wares, and jewelry has often been melted down or refashioned. As early as the 1730s, there were actually two different types of artisan entrepreneurs who were beginning to emerge in Boston: 1) large-scale producers and 2) merchant-artisans. These two groups developed different strategies for economic survival during the decades preceding the American Revolution.[12]

The first group, made up of a small number of large-scale producers, routinely employed journeymen and jobbers (sometimes members of their own families) to increase their productive capacity. This strategy worked well for goldsmiths in the early decades of the century—John Coney (1655/56–1722), John Burt (1692/93–1745), and John Edwards (c. 1671–1746) all invested most of their assets in their businesses, and amassed comfortable estates.[13] These producers began to think of themselves more as managers of journeymen making goods for a wider clientele than as working artisans. In the highly inflationary decade before the reissue of Massachusetts currency in 1750 and the uncertain times immediately preceding the Revolution, however, the survival of producing goldsmiths became increasingly precarious.

The most important of the large-scale gold and silver producers in the Boston goldsmithing trade at mid century were Thomas Edwards (1701/2–1755), Samuel Edwards, and Jacob Hurd (1702–1758).[14] Although the records are incomplete, Thomas Edwards and Jacob Hurd appear to have been two craftsmen who confined their operations to the manufacture and sale of gold and silver wares. Hurd's experience during the highly inflationary period between 1742 and 1749 points out the risk involved in pursuing such a course. Hurd was engaged in large-scale production and offered his customers and fellow goldsmiths a full range of services—he made jewelry and did small repairs; made large presentation objects for customers; raised and

12. See Patricia E. Kane, s.v. "John Burt"; Patricia E. Kane, s.v. "John Coney"; Barbara McLean Ward, s.v. "John Edwards," *Dictionary of Colonial Massachusetts Silversmiths*.

13. See Ward, "Craftsman in a Changing Society," esp. 45, 71–72.

14. For a fuller treatment of these three artisans, see Ward, "Edwards Family"; "Hierarchy and Wealth Distribution"; and s.v. "Thomas Edwards," "Samuel Edwards," and "Jacob Hurd," *Dictionary of Colonial Massachusetts Silversmiths*.

cast parts of objects; and finished, engraved, and polished items for other goldsmiths. Hurd made no significant investments in real estate or shipping ventures—nearly all of his capital was tied up in his goldsmithing business. Documents relating to a court case in 1746 may help to explain why Hurd eventually went bankrupt. They may also help to explain why other goldsmiths chose to diversify their operations to allow for maximum flexibility and a more favorable cash flow rather than to expand their production.

In 1745 Hurd borrowed large sums of money at the rate of 30 percent per year from a man named Benjamin Bourn. In the litigation that followed, Hurd testified, and several deponents supported his allegation, that when Bourn had insisted upon having his notes paid "before the Court for tomorrow," the goldsmith had said that he could "pay off the Least Note which was for 476:18:0 old Tenor Dated June 12th 1745 payable in three moneths from the Date theirof but if he did he could not pay for a Large Quantity of Silver which he had bargain'd for," and asked Bourn to "Tarry tell next week." When Bourn asked Hurd how much he could give him, Hurd answered, "if I must offer anything it must be Lawfull Interest, which is six p Cent, for the Last notes were put att 30 p Cent in which you were very hard with me." Hurd agreed to sign new notes for the amount of the old notes plus interest at the rate of 30 percent per year. Even though Bourn was convicted in court of unlawful usury as a result of the civil litigation and suffered from considerable public criticism, Hurd evidently continued to accumulate substantial debts and was forced out of business by his creditors about 1750.[15]

The second group, merchant-artisans, included craftsmen from all levels of the trades. By the middle of the eighteenth century, many individuals in this group began to regard the production of objects as secondary to other enterprises and to use the capital gained from their craft production to finance a whole host of other ventures. This group of merchant-artisans includes some individuals who never established themselves as leaders in their own craft but maintained only small-scale production shops while branching out into general shopkeeping. Successful artisans sometimes also decided to diversify their businesses in this way in an effort to achieve economic security. Some of the ventures these merchant-artisans undertook were successful, and some were not. For those with the capital to become import-export merchants, risks were considerable and it often took

15. Supreme Judicial Court Record Series, Suffolk County Court Files, docket no. 62302; Suffolk County Probate Records, 54:58. Benjamin Walker, Diary, vol. 3, one of the entries for Aug. 29, 1746, M.H.S.

years before an initial investment returned a profit. During this time their craft production provided them with a solid financial basis for their mercantile investments and gave them something to return to if their ventures collapsed. For those with less profitable shops and little money to invest, the revenues from shopkeeping and petty retailing often ended up being essential to their livelihoods; most of them probably only made enough money for their families to live at a subsistence level.

Samuel Edwards is one example of an artisan with a lucrative silversmithing business who decided to invest in shipping and to sell a wide variety of imported goods in his retail shop. He developed a more diversified business than his brother Thomas or his colleague Jacob Hurd, trading in metalwares, small notions, and tools of all descriptions as well as in the usual merchant's stock of imported textiles. The inventory of his estate shows that he had thousands of items of general merchandise—wooden, horn, and ivory combs; penknife cases; toothbrushes; tweezers; sewing and knitting needles; fishhooks and stay hooks; corkscrews; scissors; key rings; buttons of every description; shoemakers' and silversmiths' tools; nails; tacks; brads; brushes; small pictures and "paperback pictures"; trumpets; looking glasses; padlocks and locks with keyhole escutcheons; tin, lead, and wooden toys; whistles; birdcalls; and even one dozen boxes of ninepins—as well as hundreds of yards of ribbon, braid, and cloth (mostly "Oznabriggs," "Striped Holland," "White Fustian," "Coarse Diaper," "Baze," "Crocus," and "Linnen"); handkerchiefs; and mittens. He also had enough tools and workbenches in his goldsmithing shop to allow him to employ at least three journeymen and apprentices. The list of silver goods on hand in his shop is impressive (in uninflated 1762 currency, the value amounted to more than £600, about twice the value of the general merchandise).

Unlike Hurd, Edwards had the advantage of being related by marriage (both his own and his father's—Samuel's father married Samuel's widowed mother-in-law) to the Smiths, a large merchant family, which made it possible for him to obtain general shop merchandise at a favorable price. Unfortunately, no detailed accounts from his business dealings survive. From the personal account of his brother-in-law Isaac Smith, we know that Edwards had a regular account with him, and that Edwards was in the habit of assisting his mother-in-law/stepmother, Abigail Fowle Smith Edwards, in letting out her black slave Caesar and in collecting payments on money she had lent out at interest. With his connection to Isaac Smith and excess capital available from his mother-in-law/stepmother, Edwards had a distinct advantage in business. Nevertheless, he lived in a relatively modest house—brick, three stories high, but only one room deep—conducted at least a portion of his work in and around his own home, and continued to display "1 Goldsmith's Arms" in his best lower room.[16]

Benjamin Greene (1712/13–1776), in contrast, never established himself as one of Boston's leading goldsmiths, but he is an example of one artisan (his brother Rufus [1707–1777] followed a similar path) who plunged into general merchant activities very soon after completing his apprenticeship. Greene's one surviving ledger book, for the period 1734–1756, provides a picture of how merchant-artisans apportioned their investments and made craft production just one element of their merchant ventures.[17]

Greene was born in Boston, the fifth and youngest son of Nathaniel Greene and Anne Gould Greene, shopkeepers of Boston. Nathaniel, who was born in Warwick, Rhode Island, in 1679, died while trading in Surinam when Benjamin was only a year old. His mother, Anne Gould Greene, continued her husband's business and amassed a fortune of her own; she died when Benjamin was fifteen. Benjamin was lucky to have older brothers who were established merchants and artisans as well as numerous other relatives to provide him with significant business contacts.[18]

Benjamin probably served his apprenticeship with William Cowell, Sr., of Boston, a successful goldsmith who also had a significant business as an innkeeper. Under his tutelage, Greene must have practiced more than just simply goldsmithing, possibly learning the simple single-entry bookkeeping system that he would use in his own ledger. Greene may have worked for Cowell as a journeyman after finishing his apprenticeship, and he received day wages from his older brother Rufus Greene in the early 1730s. Benjamin probably started his independent business sometime before 1734, because his own ledger book, which begins in that year, mentions accounts carried over from "the paper book." In 1734 he sold his interest in his parents' estate to his oldest brother, Thomas, a Boston merchant, for £180.[19] In February 1736/37 Benjamin wed Mary Chandler, the daughter of Judge John Chandler (1693–1800) of Worcester and Hannah Gardiner Chandler, originally of New London, in New London, Connecticut. By

16. Inventory of the estate of Samuel Edwards, executor's accounts, June 1762; and executors' accounts for the estate of Abigail Fowle Smith Edwards; both in Smith-Carter Family Papers, M.H.S.

17. Benjamin Greene Ledger, 1734–1756, M.H.S.

18. Barbara McLean Ward, s.v. "Rufus Greene"; Patricia E. Kane, s.v. "Benjamin Greene," *Dictionary of Colonial Massachusetts Silversmiths*.

19. Suffolk County Deeds, 48:206.

marrying, Greene further widened his business contacts; the connection was more logical than seems apparent at first. Thomas, Benjamin's elder by eight years, was married to Mary Chandler's aunt, Elizabeth Gardiner. Benjamin and Mary Greene had six children who lived to adulthood: Benjamin, Hannah, Mary, Lucretia, Sarah, and Gardiner.[20]

When Benjamin Greene's father died, in spite of trading ventures in the West Indies, the family estate was relatively modest. Significantly, his mother carried on the business and over the next fourteen years enhanced the family's fortune. Anne Greene helped to establish her sons in their own businesses and at the time of her death was assembling a set of goldsmithing tools to help her son Rufus (who was still serving his apprenticeship) furnish his own shop. She continued to operate the business begun by her husband, and when she died in 1728, her estate—including an impressive inventory of shop goods—amounted to £6,232.[21]

In establishing her sons in trades, Anne Greene attempted to place them in lucrative professions that would enhance the wealth and trading opportunities of the extended family. And, in fact, the Greene brothers were frequent business partners. Thomas attended Yale College, graduating in 1727, and became a merchant. The second son, Rufus, was apprenticed to a goldsmith. The third son, Nathaniel (d. about 1743), became a merchant like his oldest brother. The fourth son, William, was living in Surinam in 1736, probably working as a merchant, and died before 1743. Benjamin, like Rufus, was apprenticed to a goldsmith.[22]

The first entries in Benjamin Greene's account book demonstrate that early in his career goldsmithing was his primary occupation. Lengthy accounts with other goldsmiths and jewelers are among the earliest transactions and clearly demonstrate that Greene was a working goldsmith who specialized in the production of small wares—teaspoons, tea tongs, strainers, buckles, buttons, rings, and beads.[23] Nonetheless, in 1735, only a year or two after establishing himself in business, Greene mentions the "Ballance of my Acco[tt] with M[r] Samuell Dowse in Surranam" under accounts

20. Kane, s.v. "Benjamin Greene," *Dictionary of Colonial Massachusetts Silversmiths.*
21. Suffolk County Probate Records, docket no. 5574.
22. Ward, s.v. "Rufus Greene." See also, Jules D. Prown, *John Singleton Copley* (Cambridge, Mass., 1966), 1:56, 57, 61, 62, 163–164; Kathryn C. Buhler, *Colonial Silversmiths: Masters and Apprentices* (Boston, 1956), 33–34. According to the ledger, Benjamin Greene consigned goods to his brother William in Surinam in 1736 (Benjamin Greene Ledger, folio 65).
23. Greene's most extensive early accounts are with jewelers James Boyer and Stephen Winter (Benjamin Greene Ledger, folios 1, 4, 64, 68, 93).

with his brother Nathaniel.[24] Apparently from the outset Benjamin planned to use his craft as the basis for a larger business. After 1750, he would largely abandon goldsmithing in favor of merchant activities.

Benjamin made his first investments in shipping in 1736, when he sent an "adventure" to South Carolina. In 1738, his consignment on a vessel bound for Surinam consisted primarily of silver objects worth £41.15, one third of which were shipped back to him unsold. In spite of this poor return on his goods, he sent silver items to Surinam again in 1740, apparently this time with some advice from his contacts there, and everything found a buyer.[25] Many of Greene's most successful ventures were undertaken to North Carolina. In 1738 he sent shop goods—ivory combs, fishhooks, pins, and so on—to John Anderson of "Paquimance" in return for pork and beeswax. Subsequent "adventures" to North Carolina were more extensive in nature, involving purchases of tar, coal, and deer skins, which were then sent to England. By 1740, Greene had several old acquaintances with whom he could trade in North Carolina—former Boston goldsmith Charles Simpson, former Boston brazier James Calf, and merchant Daniel Blinn.[26]

In addition to frequent consignments of goods on vessels owned by others, Greene held major shares in more than a dozen sloops, schooners, brigantines, and ships. In May 1747 he and his brothers Thomas and Rufus, all referring to themselves as merchants, entered into an agreement with Oliver Luckis, Jr., and John Richardson, shipwrights, for the building of the ship *Three Brothers*. The vessel was to measure 70 feet by the keel, and 11 feet 9 inches in the hold and was to be made with "good substantial White Oak Timber." According to Benjamin Greene's ledger, the ship was built to undertake voyages to North Carolina and London, and Benjamin invested approximately £6,597 in its construction and outfitting. The contract called for Benjamin and his brothers to obtain all of the ironwork, pitch, tar, and oakum for the vessel.[27]

Other ships similarly consumed Benjamin Greene's capital resources, and many of his overseas ventures were far from successful. The sloop *Three Sisters*, in which Greene purchased a one-third interest in 1744, did not give him a profit on his investment until 1747 after three voyages to North Carolina and to Louisbourg, Nova Scotia. Other ventures brought

24. Account with Nathaniel Greene, 1735–1736, Benjamin Greene Ledger, folio 7. In addition to this venture in Surinam, the account mentions Nathaniel's payment to Benjamin of "45/ Sterling Received of Mess.rs Storke & Gainsboroug" in goods.

25. Benjamin Greene Ledger, folio 65.

26. Benjamin Greene Ledger, folios 49, 51, 79, 85, 103, 104, 128, 130.

27. Document 347.4, Bostonian Society, Boston. Benjamin Greene Ledger, folio 160.

returns that seem small in comparison to the amount of capital expended, but occasionally a first voyage yielded a significant profit that more than paid for Greene's investment. The ship *Lyon*, for instance, in which Greene owned a one-fifth share, brought him a return of £1,320 on an investment of £1,080 after only one voyage in 1745.[28]

Greene's ventures involved trading in a number of different currencies as well as in goods. One of his most frequent customers in North Carolina, Charles Simpson, usually paid Greene in that colony's currency for silver and gold wares and manufactured goods. Greene used these notes to purchase large quantities of tar and pitch, which were either shipped back to Boston or sent on to London and Bristol. Greene often shipped cash— apparently both North Carolina and Massachusetts bills—to these English cities in exchange for pounds sterling credits with various merchants. Some of Greene's accounts of voyages include the transfer of large amounts of money—both in cash and in silver bullion—shipped in payment for goods purchased in the southern colonies, the West Indies, and England. The silver bullion had to be bargained for, usually at 6 percent interest, in much the same way that Greene bargained for metal to use in his craft. In these transactions Greene's experience as a goldsmith, and his knowledge of the exchange values of different types of silver coins, must have given him a distinct advantage over other artisans seeking to undertake merchant ventures.[29]

Benjamin Greene used his credits on London and Bristol merchants to obtain manufactured goods which he then traded to merchants and shopkeepers in Boston, Milton, Medford, and Worcester, Massachusetts, and Woodstock, Stonington, Hebron, Hartford, Groton, and New London, Connecticut. He also accepted butter, cheese, and other farm products (including firewood for use in his home and shop) in exchange for small silver, gold, and brass items or for mending of various kinds and general shop goods, tools, and "sundrys." Greene's goldsmithing business also made it possible for him to service a wide variety of artisans and tradespeople from surrounding country towns, particularly in the early years of his business. Most country customers paid with cash, often as much as a year after making their purchases, and some eventually became more steady trading partners in other goods and services.[30]

By engaging in commercial ventures, merchant-artisan goldsmiths such as Benjamin Greene and his brother Rufus made a contribution to Boston's

28. Benjamin Greene Ledger, folios 15, 137.
29. Benjamin Greene Ledger.
30. Benjamin Greene Ledger.

economy that went well beyond the exercise of their artisanal trade. Craft production provided a steady income, which the more affluent producing artisans could then invest in other ventures. As craftsmen in a luxury trade, goldsmiths had been challenged to find ways to obtain goods that they could trade for the necessities of life, or to pay in cash. The high level of investment involved in plying their trade—gold and silver were expensive and sometimes difficult to obtain in quantity—also encouraged goldsmiths to diversify into general merchant activities rather than merely to step up their own production. Artisans in other trades faced the same dilemma, and many of them, like James Calf, the Boston brazier turned North Carolina merchant, recognized that merchandising was becoming more profitable than producing. Only after the Revolution, and then haltingly, would artisans such as Paul Revere II find it lucrative to become what we would term manufacturers. Even then, as he launched his copper business and other ventures, Revere was careful to maintain the trade that had brought him his prosperity. He regularly made deductions from the profits of his silversmithing business in order to underwrite his manufacturing ventures.[31]

By understanding the way in which these goldsmiths expanded the definitions of their craft and considered the pursuit of their trade to be only part of a larger scheme for their own personal economic growth, we can gauge the extent to which these artisans developed a "bourgeois" definition of their own identities. Not only did they utilize their craft skills to establish the basis of their businesses; they called upon fellow goldsmiths and silversmiths as trading partners and may well have worked with them to devise strategies for existence in an unstable economy—as the relationship between Benjamin Greene and Charles Simpson suggests. Further investigation into the business practices of men like Greene may also offer us a greater understanding of the extent of Boston's involvement in coastal trading with the southern colonies on the eve of the Revolution and give greater meaning to the commercial ties that bound Americans from different colonies together in the decades before independence.[32]

31. Deborah A. Federhen, s.v. "Paul Revere II," *Dictionary of Colonial Massachusetts Silversmiths*. See also, Paul Revere Memorial Association, *Paul Revere—Artisan*.

32. Thomas Amory was another Boston merchant who traded in North Carolina and South Carolina and also had dealings in the West Indies. Like Greene, Amory seems also to have done some trading in currency. Thomas Amory Account Book 1720–1728, M.H.S.

Imported from *LONDON*,

By *Elizabeth Murray*,

And to be Sold by Wholefale or Retale, at her Shop oppofite to the Brazen Head in Cornhill *Bofton*, Cheap for the Cafh.

Capuchins, flower'd Velvet and Capuchin Silks, black Fringes, Bone Lace, a variety of brocaded ftriped and crofs'd bar'd Stuffs and Poplins for Winter Gowns, Feather Swan and Ermine Muffs and Tippets, brown Padufay and black ditto, ftriped and enam'd Mantuas, Luteftring ditto, Sattins of all Colours, Sattin Perfian & Stuff quilted Petticoats, the neweft fafhiou'd Hoops, Caps, Ruffles, Stomachers, Tipets, and a variety of Gauze and Paris-Nets, Trimmings of all Sorts, black Pink and   k Mitts, Kid Lamb and Sattin Gloves and Mittens, Stone   d Flofs Necklaces and Earings, Silver and Flofs Flowers   s, Shoes and Golofhoes, neat Englifh Stays, Shades and Lorains, Womens Hatts and Heives of all Sorts, Silver Girdles, Twitchers, Spangles and Bugles, Umbrilloes, Millinet, flower'd and plain Lawns, flower'd Border'd Aprons, Ruffies. Canvas, Flofs, fine Shade Silk, Slacks and Crewells, Pound Silks, Silk Lacing, Ferret, Mourning Crapes and Hatbands, Galloom and Worfted Binding, Cotton Leifle, Flanders and Scots Threads, Tape and Bobin, Silver Lace for Shoes, Everlaftings, Ebony, Ivory, Bamboo, Church and Leather mount Fanns, Waddin for Caupachins, Silver and Gold Thread, Cord, Flat and Plate for Embroidery, Macklin, Bruffels, Flanders, Millenet, Dott, Trally and Englifh Cap Lace, Lappets and Lappet Heads, a variety of fafhionable Ribands, fmelling Bottles, Hungary and Honey Water, Bagg Hollands, Long Lawns, Cambrick and Muflin, Silk and Guaze Handkerchiefs, Fans Mounts &c. &c. &c.

Trade bill of Elizabeth Murray, ca. 1749. Collection of the Massachusetts Historical Society.

'Who shall say we have not equal abilitys with the Men when Girls of 18 years of age discover such great capacitys?': Women of Commerce in Boston, 1750–1776

Patricia Cleary

IN 1749, ELIZABETH MURRAY sailed from England, intending to return to North Carolina, where she had lived with an older brother some years earlier. When the ship put in at Boston, however, she disembarked, contrary to expectations that she would accompany her family to the southern colony. Deciding instead to set up shop in Boston, Murray went on to become one of the town's prominent shopkeepers, engaging in a variety of commercial enterprises that tested her abilities and strained gender conventions. In an advertising leaflet printed after her arrival, Murray announced a vast array of goods available "Cheap for the Cash" at her shop in Cornhill. Proclaiming the metropolitan source of her merchandise by heading the flyer "Imported from *LONDON*," she described silks and satins as well as the necessary accompaniments to such fine fabrics: petticoats, hoops, and trimmings. To complete the fashionable woman's outfit were "neat English Stays," necklaces, and earrings.[1]

In establishing herself as a purveyor of imported goods and in publicizing her stock, Murray seized the opportunity to participate in commercial developments that were transforming consumption in the eighteenth cen-

1. The list, which mentions over one hundred individual items and categories of goods, ends with the additional lure of "&c. &c. &c," as if to suggest that the stock was simply too extensive to enumerate fully. Elizabeth Murray, trade bill, [Cornhill, Boston, 1749?], Massachusetts Historical Society (hereafter M.H.S.). Murray's last name changed with her marriages to Thomas Campbell, James Smith, and Ralph Inman. I include her maiden name in all references.

tury.[2] Her experiences point to the influence of gender upon women's entrance into this commercial world. Her choice of occupation, trials and successes, and later efforts to establish other women in retailing suggest that women in the colonies found keeping shop a relatively accessible and rewarding trade.

The absence of Murray and many women like her from the historical record is the result of oversight, not of their lack of importance.[3] An examination of the working lives of Murray and other women retailers offers important insights. The economic processes that they engaged in reveal the existence of women's commercial networks. In addition, in keeping shop these women encountered situations that enlarged their opportunities for independent thought and action. Shopkeepers like Murray linked colonial consumers to British manufacturers and merchants on both sides of the Atlantic.[4] Selling imported merchandise did more than provide such women with a livelihood; their economic activities had political ramifications and

2. See Neil McKendrick, John Brewer, and J. H. Plumb, *The Birth of a Consumer Society: The Commercialization of Eighteenth-Century England* (Bloomington, Ind., 1982); T. H. Breen, " 'Baubles of Britain': The American and Consumer Revolutions of the Eighteenth Century," *Past and Present* 119(1988):73–104, and "An Empire of Goods: The Anglicization of Colonial America, 1690–1776," *Journal of British Studies* 25(1986):467–499; Carole Shammas, *The Preindustrial Consumer in England and America* (Oxford, 1990); and the collection of essays edited by John Brewer and Roy Porter, *Consumption and the World of Goods* (New York, 1993). Lorna Weatherill connected an expansion of women's role as purchasers to an increase in shops in "A Possession of One's Own: Women and Consumer Behavior in England, 1660–1740," *Journal of British Studies* 25(1986):131–156.

3. For a discussion of historians' treatments of women shopkeepers, see Patricia Cleary, " 'She Merchants' of Colonial America: Women and Commerce on the Eve of the Revolution," (Ph.D. diss., Northwestern Univ., 1989). Earlier examinations of women's commercial activities appear in Julia Cherry Spruill, *Women's Life and Work in the Southern Colonies* (1938; reprint, New York, 1972), and Elisabeth Anthony Dexter, *Colonial Women of Affairs: A Study of Women in Business and the Professions in America before 1776* (Boston and New York, 1924). In the only article written about Elizabeth Murray, Mary Beth Norton describes how Murray's spirit of independence influenced the way she raised or assisted several women and how she acted as a role model for younger women. In tracing the biographical details of Murray's life–particularly her three marriages and the unusual pre-nuptial agreements she had with her second and third husbands–Norton offers her portrait of "an extraordinary woman" and "her beliefs and experiences" as a venue for 20th-century individuals to learn about self-reliant women of an earlier era; Norton, "A Cherished Spirit of Independence: The Life of an Eighteenth-Century Boston Businesswoman," *Women of America: A History*, Mary Beth Norton and Carol Ruth Berkin, eds. (Boston, 1979), 60, 49.

4. Thomas Doerflinger's study of Philadelphia's economy details the evolution of and mobility within the mercantile community; *A Vigorous Spirit of Enterprise: Merchants and Economic Development in Revolutionary Philadelphia* (Chapel Hill, 1986).

personal implications that shaped their sense of identity and gender consciousness. Through keeping shop, women became more aware of the choices, constraints, and expectations that governed their social, economic, and political roles.

Born in Scotland in 1726, Elizabeth Murray settled in Boston and pursued retailing only after years of geographic mobility and dependence. With both of her parents dead by 1737, she became the charge of her older brother James, who had already established himself in North Carolina. After settling the family estate, James brought Elizabeth to the colony, where he assigned her housekeeping responsibilities. By late 1740, she had assumed the "station" of her brother's "only Housekeeper."[5] That position evaporated when James returned to Scotland, taking his sister with him, and married in 1744. The Murrays' sojourn abroad stretched to five years, and during a part of this time they lived in London. There, Elizabeth Murray may have considered taking up trade back in North Carolina. When the ship put in at Boston during the Murrays' return voyage, however, Elizabeth disembarked with her shopkeeping ambitions and without her brother's wholehearted approval.

Presumably Murray determined to stay in Boston only after considering her prospects and options as well as the range of economic choices open to a young, single woman and immigrant in eighteenth-century colonial America. If she were not a dependent in a household—that is, if her lot in life involved self-support outside her immediate family circle—she had to settle where there were available economic opportunities. Even using the phrase "economic opportunities," however, immediately raises the specter of the "golden age" interpretation of colonial women's lives and demands qualification.[6] To argue that Murray found shopkeeping accessible is not to suggest that the period witnessed unrestricted opportunities and autonomy for women. Rather, some women worked to seize opportunities, drawing upon female networks to do so and creating a niche for themselves in the expanding commercial economy. Certain occupations were simply not

5. James Murray to Mrs. Bennet of Chesters, September 1740, reprinted in Nina Moore Tiffany, ed., *Letters of James Murray, Loyalist* (Boston, 1901), 47.

6. Historians who have supported this interpretation have drawn upon Dexter's study for its presentation of women "carrying on work, apparently in a legal and social atmosphere of almost entire freedom" and posited the corollary of deteriorating status in the 19th century. See Dexter, *Colonial Women of Affairs*, 185; Gerda Lerner, "The Lady and the Mill Girl: Changes in the Status of Women in the Age of Jackson," *Midcontinent American Studies Journal* 19(1969):5–15; and for a critical overview of women's status, Mary Beth Norton, "The Evolution of White Women's Experience in Early America," *American Historical Review* 89(1984):593–619.

open to women; others were accessible only to those with income or the ability to obtain credit. Clearly, women's options for employment varied according to their assets, as well as their class, training, and place of residence.

Ports, in effect the urban centers, provided a range of employments for women, especially for those with skills or capital. In these settings, women acted not only as servants, but as midwives, teachers, and tavernkeepers.[7] Where women appeared among the ranks of shoemakers, gunsmiths, printers, shipwrights, and in other trades less typically feminine, they were usually operating businesses established by deceased spouses. Eighteenth-century Boston in particular attracted large numbers of women, especially widows, in the aftermath of wars. The poverty of many of these women inspired the unsuccessful plan at mid century to put them to work manufacturing cloth in a central facility; too few women proved willing to leave the household setting for this employment.[8] For women, the ability to tend shop and children at the same time must have added to the appeal of retailing as an occupation.

Many women in Boston pursued trade in the quarter century preceding the Revolution. Women retailers were neither unprecedented nor rare phenomena.[9] They ran specialty shops and general stores, advertised regularly, and were respected members of their communities. Although shopkeepers primarily retailed goods, some sold merchandise wholesale and engaged in small-scale importing; trading activities somewhat blurred the distinctions between shopkeepers and merchants. However, while the business practices may have overlapped, merchants were typically, and almost exclusively, male. Furthermore, the buying patterns of female shopkeepers were often identifiable. Most women traders, including those who both imported and sold British products as well as those who dealt pri-

7. For treatments of women's participation in a variety of trades, see Claudia Goldin, "The Economic Status of Women in the Early Republic: Quantitative Evidence," *Journal of Interdisciplinary History* 16(1986):375–404; Spruill, *Women's Life and Work*; and Laurel Thatcher Ulrich, *A Midwife's Tale: The Life of Martha Ballard, Based on Her Diary, 1785–1812* (New York, 1990). Also see Jean R. Soderlund, "Women in Eighteenth-Century Pennsylvania: Toward a Model of Diversity," *Pennsylvania Magazine of History and Biography* 115(1991):163–183.

8. Gary B. Nash, *The Urban Crucible: Social Change, Political Consciousness, and the Origins of the American Revolution* (Cambridge, Mass., 1979), 189–197.

9. Women engaged in a variety of trading activities in Europe. See, for example, Merry Weisner Wood, "Paltry Peddlers or Essential Merchants? Women in the Distributive Trades in Early Modern Europe," *Sixteenth Century Journal* 12(1981):3–13; Alice Clark, *Working Life of Women in the Seventeenth Century* (1919; reprint, Boston, 1982), 198–209.

marily in retail, tended to concentrate upon dry goods such as cloth, lace, and millinery wares.

As wives, mothers, widows, and spinsters, these female shopkeepers carved a niche for themselves and their businesses. They supported other women shopkeepers, forming personal and professional networks. Estimates of the percentage of eighteenth-century colonial shopkeepers who were women vary widely.[10] New York and Philadelphia had fair numbers. The presence of women selling goods at mid century suggests that the expanding import trade and rising consumer demand facilitated their participation in commerce.[11] With each passing decade, more women traders advertised goods for sale in Boston newspapers. In addition, despite economic instability, Boston's women retailers conducted business for extended periods. Twenty-five women, or nearly half of the fifty-five women whose business careers in the three decades preceding the Revolution can be traced, kept shop for more than ten years; eight were in business for over twenty years.[12]

10. Figures based largely on advertisements in 18th-century colonial newspapers have ranged between 2 and 10 percent. Dexter estimated that women accounted for a little less than 10 percent of colonial retailers; *Colonial Women of Affairs*, 38. Jean P. Jordan concluded that Dexter's figure was too high and that at most, women comprised 2 percent of New York's commercial community. Mercantile and other sources reveal more women involved in trade in New York in the 1760s alone than Jordan did for the period 1660–1775. Jordan, "Women Merchants in Colonial New York," *New York History* 58(1977):436. Another low estimate counted only ten women of business in New York between 1768 and 1775; Robert Michael Dructor, "The New York Commercial Community: The Revolutionary Experience" (Ph.D. diss., Univ. of Pittsburgh, 1975), 15–16. Goldin found that women accounted for 28 percent of Philadelphia's shopkeepers in 1791. "Economic Status of Women in the Early Republic," 402. Colonial shopkeepers may have accounted for closer to half of all retailers; according to a Philadelphia tax list from 1756, 38 women kept shop, comprising 42 percent of the town's assessed shopkeepers and almost two thirds of the women listed with occupations. Hannah Benner Roach, "Taxables in the City of Philadelphia, 1756," *Pennsylvania Genealogical Magazine* 22(1961):3–41. The tax assessors noted occupations for 59 out of 184 women on the list; no woman was described as a merchant. The tax lists, which offer a rough sense of the proportion of shopkeepers of each sex, also show that in the 1750s and 1760s, male shopkeepers, in general, were more prosperous than their female counterparts. For a discussion of the difficulties involved in using tax lists, see Doerflinger, *Vigorous Spirit of Enterprise*, 63–67, 384–386.

11. From 1745 to 1754, 33 women kept shop in Boston. That figure rose to 43 in the ten years from 1755 to 1764 and to 46 between 1765 and 1774. Overall, 41 women ran shops between 1745 and 1759 and 64 from 1760 until the Revolution. Cleary, "'She Merchants' of Colonial America," 78, 91–95.

12. Nine other women engaged in commerce for six to ten years (16 percent), and 21 for

Because she was still single, Murray was unlike the majority of women shopkeepers. Roughly two thirds of them were widows, most of whom continued businesses established by their spouses, while just under one third were spinsters. Murray began to trade without family networks in place,[13] a situation that may even have prompted the implicit criticism of her brother John, who did not fully support her decision to reside in Boston. He expressed concern about her future and, in 1752, invited her to join him in England "if she found that Boston did not ans[we]r her Expectations." His generous but qualified offer, described in a letter to their brother James, underlines the precarious position of the unmarried woman. As John relayed his message, "If I continue Bachelor she will be my Housekeeper, if I marry she may do something in this growing Place to acquire a handsome livelihood." If she did not support herself in the eventuality of his marriage, she would, he said, "be ever Welcome in my Family."[14] In other words, she could accept the status of dependent.

Although records that detail Murray's early years in Boston are scarce, leaving only an incomplete sense of her life during that period, her few existing letters present a picture of struggle and inexperience that could inspire her brothers' doubts. To James, she related the story of how some people called her "the broken shop keeper," apparently for running out of stock. After finding herself with a bare looking display, she decided to protect herself from such future charges by ordering a gross of boxes which she planned to label with "letters & numbers on them & set them on the shelves." While she could have gone into debt to keep her shop fully stocked instead of just maintaining that appearance, she admitted that previous mistakes with her finances made her wary of that solution. She

---

at least two to five years (38 percent). It should be noted, however, that the longer a woman kept shop, the more likely it is that her work left some evidence. Thus, women who engaged in trade for very short periods are more difficult to discern. A variety of evidence from newspapers, mercantile records, correspondence, and probate documents forms the basis for calculations of business tenure.

13. Widows clearly predominated. Out of 63 shopkeepers whose marital status could be determined, almost two thirds were widows; less than one-third were single women. Two others began to keep shop while single and continued to do so after their marriages. Two others, Jane Eustis and Henrietta Maria East, were either divorced or separated during most of their business careers. East discovered the risks of wedlock after her husband's debts made it difficult for her to carry on business. Henrietta Maria East, Suffolk Files #129736, "Divorces 1760–1784," Suffolk County Court House, Boston.

14. John Murray to James Murray, Feb. 28, 1753, box 1, J. M. Robbins Papers.

reminded James of what she had "suffer'd allready," adding that although she could obtain goods on credit, she chose "to keep clear."[15]

Murray acknowledged that staying out of debt was difficult in Boston. She described to her brother the predicament of another woman retailer, Mrs. Ken, who found herself "obliged to sell all her goods" and was "a great many hundreds worse than nothing." This example troubled Murray: "such things makes me double my dellegence & endevour to keep my self as clear as is possible in this place." Her dependence upon her brother for credit added to her worries; she wrote, "your being so much ingaged for me gives me great uneasyness." To avoid his ruin if her finances failed, she proposed switching her business to two merchants who would supply her without a letter of credit from James.[16] This arrangement points to two important aspects of colonial trade. First, it suggests that British merchants were willing to give credit directly to shopkeepers, small traders who lacked the backing of the sort that merchants enjoyed. Second, it emphasizes the precariousness of commercial endeavors, and how the financial ruin of one individual could destroy a family's well-being in an age when business ties frequently followed family lines.

In their efforts to avoid economic difficulties and drum up business, Murray and other shopkeepers publicized their wares repeatedly. Advertisements in colonial newspapers reveal an increasing variety of consumer goods available after mid century.[17] As importation and consumer demand grew, merchants and retailers began to promote their stock in new ways. Rather than simply announcing the arrival of new merchandise, they employed fancy type, illustrations, and borders to attract attention to their notices, which they filled with superlatives. Shopkeepers described in detail "Superfine Dutch Hollands, and choice Irish Linens" and "All sorts of the Newest Fashion Millinary" imported from London.[18] In the 1750s, Murray participated in this development, placing large notices in the *Boston Evening-Post*, which announced her location in Cornhill as well as the variety of her wares. She notified the newspaper's readers that her goods were "just imported" and included varied fashionable items such as cloth ruffles, hoop petticoats, women's shoes, stockings, gloves, and threads. In

15. Elizabeth Murray to James Murray, May 27, 1753, box 1, J. M. Robbins Papers.

16. Elizabeth Murray to James Murray, Sept. 27, 1754, box 1, J. M. Robbins Papers.

17. For a discussion of advertising changes during this period, see Breen, " 'Baubles of Britain.' "

18. Advertisements in *Boston Evening-Post*, Jan. 21, 1754, and Sept. 5, 1757.

1759, she announced a change of location, from next door to Doctor Boutineau to a shop lately occupied by Mr. Gilbert Deblois at the corner of Queen Street, where she would continue to sell imported wares which came in the last ships.[19] After a decade in business, Murray still advertised similar goods: cloth, bonnets, lace, and stockings.

Throughout her career, Murray offered the latest fashions, which she had first selected carefully for the Boston market. In 1753, she decided to travel to London to order goods in person, intending to undertake the voyage once she had disposed of her out-of-season merchandise. Sounding like an experienced observer of consumer desires and purchasing behavior, she explained, "I had a gr[e]at many articals come this fall that was fitt for summer[;] therefore I advertised my going away & by that means I have sold a good many of thim." For her siblings' benefit, she relayed that "every body thinks my going home will be a very great advantage to me as I can chuse such goods as I know will suit this place."[20] Her knowledge of the Boston market, combined with the financial wherewithal and willingness to travel, would give her an advantage over her competitors.

Murray's decision to return to London to lay in a stock of goods represents a turning point in her maturation as a trader and in her independence from familial guidance. Without including in her correspondence her usual request for approval of her plans, she guessed that her siblings would "be very much surprised" by her scheme; she did not have the time to enlist their support. She needed to travel soon "in order to return early in the spring with the newest fashions." Clearly no longer a "broken" shopkeeper, Murray arranged to have a widowed woman handle the shop goods in her absence. For her pains with Murray's remaining goods, which were "all Mark'd" with prices, Widow Boyen would earn one shilling on the pound for what she sold.[21]

Murray planned to do business in England with merchant Edward Bridgen, from whom she previously had received goods. When she arrived in London in February 1754, after a passage of six weeks, she went directly to Bridgen's home. The merchant, whom she described as "a most generous friend," insisted upon her staying with his family. During her short visit, Bridgen accompanied her on her rounds while she chose "a very net assortment of goods" that would "suit [the] Boston market very well." She acquired these wares through Bridgen on the presumption that her brother

19. *Boston Evening-Post*, May 14, 1759.
20. Elizabeth Murray to James Murray, Dec. 4, 1753, box 1, J. M. Robbins Papers.
21. Elizabeth Murray to James Murray, Dec. 4, 1753.

would give her a larger letter of credit. Although she wrote that she was "very much ashamed" for not having discussed the matter with him beforehand, she hoped James could oblige her request. Therefore, she wrote, "please let me know by the first opportunity to Boston without reflecting the least on Mr Bridgens conduct."[22] Perhaps she thought James would interpret Bridgen's assistance as a self-interested design to drive her into greater involvement with his firm.

Murray's relationship with Bridgen and his partner, James Waller, proved mutually satisfying. After her return to Boston, Murray remitted large sums to the pair well within the allotted nine or twelve months of credit. She told her brother James that she planned to remain "as Clear as is possible" in her finances and reported that Bridgen would continue to oversee personally the selection of her stock.[23] Her correspondent's personal attention could only work to her advantage, she believed.

Murray continued to keep shop during her marriage to Thomas Campbell, whom she wed in 1755; letters subsequently addressed to her described her as a "Milliner in Boston."[24] However, her husband appears to have assumed responsibility for handling her commercial correspondence, writing about trade to brother-in-law James Murray and responding to Bridgen and Waller's letters. Although Murray gave up retailing after the death of her first husband and her remarriage in 1760 to James Smith, a wealthy distiller much older than she, she continued to arrange business dealings with Bridgen and Waller on behalf of other women shopkeepers, including two nieces whom she established in trade. Her goal in so doing was to enable women to achieve economic independence; there is little indication that she benefitted financially from her role as facilitator.

Murray's efforts to assist others in becoming shopkeepers point to the existence of female networks that enabled women to take advantage of opportunities available in the world of colonial commerce. Two sisters, Anne and Elizabeth Cuming, who became shopkeepers under her tutelage, expressed gratitude for the selfless assistance Murray showed them after their mother's death. Anne Cuming claimed that their mentor had directed them "in the way that would most contribut to [their] Mutual Happiness." In helping the sisters, Anne wrote, Murray did not consider how much her interest and property might suffer "in the hands of two young unexperinced Girls no way qualifyed for Business." They were not, she admitted, bred "to

22. Elizabeth Murray to James Murray, Apr. 3, 1754, box 1, J. M. Robbins Papers.
23. Elizabeth Murray to [James Murray], Nov. 1, 1754, box 1, J. M. Robbins Papers.
24. See the J. M. Robbins Papers for correspondence from 1756–1757.

hard labour," and were therefore "unfite" to get their "bread in that way."
Thus the two found themselves unprepared to meet the challenge of supporting themselves. Reflecting upon that time, Anne asserted that Murray's
help made it possible for them to stay together and made them independent of everyone but her.[25] In 1756, Murray proposed a similar plan for
another young woman, Jeany McNeal. Murray thought her a likely candidate for a career in shopkeeping and was surprised when McNeal decided
to leave Boston for North Carolina. According to Murray, the young woman
was very industrious. "I flater'd my self," she told her brother James, "that
she might doe something for her self here much better than in Cape
Fear . . . every one that knew her was of the same oppinion."[26]

When the goal of economic independence and self-sufficiency similarly
prompted Murray to set up her brother John's daughter Polly as a shopkeeper in the early 1770s, she found her actions criticized in some quarters.
Although John Murray had initially supported his sister's plans, he later
changed his mind. In a 1783 letter to John, Elizabeth Murray offered a
defense of her actions with regard to her niece. Responding to a comment
he apparently made that she knew that Polly "gave up all her consequence
& most favourite hopes to comply with her [aunt's] request," Elizabeth
answered, "If this means business, I am sorry the desadvantages arising
from young Ladys going into business did not occur to you [in] time enough
to prevent it." She demanded of her older sibling, "Did not you occation
me to form this plan by saying what wou[l]d you do with so large a family?"
She further reminded him of her own experiences: "Could I be blamed for
pointing out that mode of life from which I had recieved the greatest
advantage & satisfaction?"[27]

The idea of installing Polly Murray as a shopkeeper in Boston first occurred to Elizabeth Murray when she visited her brother's family in England in 1770. When she broached the subject of Polly's future with her
brother James, who had relocated to Boston, Murray outlined the reasons
for her choice of career for her niece. As she explained to James, "Polly has
been at Boarding school since she was ten years old, she has now finished
her education & is a very capable girl [who] understands writing & areth-
mitc very well." With these skills in mind, Murray resolved that her teen-

25. A[nne] Cuming to [Elizabeth Murray Smith], November 1769, J. M. Robbins Papers, oversize.
26. Elizabeth [Murray] Campbell to James Murray, Mar. 20, 1756, box 1, J. M. Robbins
Papers.
27. [Elizabeth Murray] Inman to John Murray, Sept. 18, 1783, box 3, J. M. Robbins
Papers.

aged niece should sail to Boston with a stock of goods, as she had done twenty years earlier. Once in Boston, Polly Murray would be connected to Murray's commercial network. Anne and Elizabeth Cuming could help to train her. If she boarded with them, suggested Murray, "she might gain experience by attending to thier selling things." With James's supervision, Polly "might keep thier books." So the shopkeeping sisters would guide her in the skills of retailing, while James would offer his hand in her accounting. In other necessary skills, Elizabeth Murray informed her brother, Polly was prepared: "as to making up things she can do that very well."[28] Polly, then, resembled many other women, who, while predominantly retailers, possessed some basic millinery abilities. With her niece's training in mind, Elizabeth Murray launched Polly, then sixteen, upon a transatlantic voyage destined to end with retailing in Boston.

In the process of setting Polly upon the path she had taken in the 1750s, Elizabeth Murray undertook negotiations that point to differences between the consumer worlds of the colonies and the mother country. Murray began by enlisting the advice and assistance of her business associates in London, Bridgen and Waller, in plotting Polly's career in retailing. In response to Murray's queries about where Polly should go to acquire the necessary skills, Bridgen suggested that the young woman train "with some prudent Milliner and there learn the Genteel way of Making up things" and at the same time "also learn the Nature of Shopkeeping." While Bridgen thought that an initial stint in a London shop—which Murray considered—could help the young woman, he doubted it would fully or accurately prepare her for the different endeavor of colonial retailing, distinctive in the lesser degree of specialization involved. "As to her Learning the Generall Method of Shopkeeping used at Boston," he wrote, "it is Impossible here as you Sell at Boston all sorts of Shopkeepers goods in one Shop, and here are 20 Shops for that purpose."[29] Indeed, he believed that "shopkeeping in London & Boston [were] so diffrent that [Polly] wou'd have it all to learn over again." The merchant asserted that the most Polly needed was "an exactness in arethmitic [and] an acquain[t]ance with the people & the money," which he thought could not be learned in London.[30]

Bridgen's assessment of differences in the trade points to an intriguing possibility: that the less specialized stock and lesser skills required for

28. Elizabeth [Murray] Smith to James Murray, Feb. 26, 1770, box 1, J. M. Robbins Papers.

29. Edward Bridgen to [Elizabeth Murray Smith], Jan. 26, 1770, box 1, J. M. Robbins Papers.

30. Elizabeth [Murray] Smith to James Murray, Feb. 26, 1770.

selling it in the colonies rendered shopkeeping more accessible to women in New England than in Old. Advertisements for imported goods placed in colonial newspapers by single female immigrant shopkeepers support the perception that the trade was accessible to women. While there is little indication that merchandise correlated precisely with gender—with both men and women selling dry goods—women retailers were less likely to sell hardware. Contemporaries believed that a woman could earn a living in the colonies by selling British fashions. In the early 1770s, Elizabeth Murray's friend Christian Barnes argued that a young woman, Jackie Day, and her mother, Jannette Barclay, former residents of Boston who were then living in London, could easily earn livelihoods if they returned to Massachusetts. Jackie, Barnes averred, could "soon be made capible of giting a Genteel living on this Side the water." Her mother's "Character [was] so well established in Boston that She might enter into any way of Bussiness with almost an assureance of Success."[31] Barnes added that she hoped to be "the first Person that imploys Miss Day upon her arrival in New England."[32] These comments convey the perception that women could make a "Genteel living" as well as the importance of name and a cultivated clientele.

The expense attending London training, the different characteristics of shopkeeping in that city, and the presence of numerous "friends" in Boston ultimately deterred Elizabeth Murray from pursuing a metropolitan apprenticeship for her niece. Upon inquiring in local shops, Bridgen and Waller discovered that the principal ones refused to negotiate reasonable terms of apprenticeship for a short period; thus, her contacts advised Elizabeth Murray accordingly: "We are of [the] Opinion as she is not to set up in London that it would be so much Money lost." By spending a year in Boston, she would become "Acquainted with the People before she Enters largly into Business."[33] Concurring with their assessment, Murray sent her niece to Boston in early 1770.[34]

31. Christian Barnes to Elizabeth [Murray] Smith, Apr. 28, [1770], Christian Barnes letterbook, Papers of Mrs. Christian Barnes, Library of Congress, Mss. div.

32. Christian Barnes to Elizabeth [Murray] Smith, [undated], Christian Barnes letterbook.

33. Bridgen and Waller to [Elizabeth Murray Smith], Mar. 15, 1770, box 1, J. M. Robbins Papers.

34. As further reason for quick action in sending Polly, Elizabeth Murray added: "I should not be anxious about her going into business so early if she was not so forward in her education." If something were not done quickly, Polly could be ruined. According to her aunt, "if she stays here any longer she must enter the gay scenes of life & become a fine Lady, in my opinion that will enervet her so much that business will ever be irksome to her." Murray believed not only that commercial endeavors were appropriate for young

Throughout the process of making a decision about her niece's liveli-hood, Elizabeth Murray took into consideration a number of factors. She weighed her niece's skills and lack of particular kinds of experience against her own shopkeeping past and the importance of a network of family members and female retailers who would assist the young woman. The business options Murray considered for her niece illuminate the fluidity of trading relationships and the partnerships of women retailers. In addition to considering the Cuming sisters, Murray suggested that a Mr. Pearce might assist Polly, "as he used to do Mrs. Eustes," a Boston retailer and friend of hers. If neither the Cumings nor Pearce seemed feasible, Eliz-abeth Murray recommended to James Murray that perhaps he "could make an agreement with Miss Rand to go into business with her."[35]

Many women shopkeepers knew each other and were friends, sharing commercial concerns as well as ties of affection. In a variety of legal docu-ments, particularly wills, they acknowledged their relationships. When shopkeeper Jane Gillam deeded property to her sister Elizabeth, the Cum-ings were on hand to witness the transaction.[36] For some, these friendships may have provided the social and emotional support that marriage might otherwise have given them. Several women shopkeepers expressed their regard by giving partial or entire estates to other women retailers. Sarah McNeal, a widowed Boston trader, left all of her substantial property, including a house and land, to her "faithfull Maid Servant & Friend Ann Dearden."[37] At the time of McNeal's death in 1761, Dearden was already keeping shop.[38]

---

women, but that engaging in selling goods could prove a corrective to the dissipating influences of a genteel education. Elizabeth [Murray] Smith to James Murray, Feb. 26, 1770. A detailed discussion of Murray's views of education and commercial endeavor appears in Cleary, "'Nothing but Parties of Pleasure': Educating Women as Cultural Consumers in Eighteenth-Century Britain and America," chap. 4 in *Elizabeth Murray and the "Spirit of Independence": Public Roles and Private Lives in Eighteenth-Century Amer-ica* (manuscript).

35. Elizabeth [Murray] Smith to [James Murray], Apr. 14, 1770, box 1, J. M. Robbins Papers. Abigail Rand had been in business in Cornhill as early as 1765, when she adver-tised in the *Boston Evening-Post*. Rand sold millinery wares, fans, stays, hair powder, and similar fashionable goods.

36. Jane Gillam, Suffolk County Deeds, 117:153, Suffolk County Registry of Deeds, Suffolk County Court House, Boston.

37. Sarah McNeal, Will, Suffolk County Probate Records, 58:282–284, Suffolk County Court House.

38. Both women reported losing property after a 1760 fire that began in the house of Mary Jackson, another Boston retailer. McNeal and Dearden presumably sold their re-

Boston retailers who bequeathed property to other women shopkeepers did so on the basis of years of personal affiliation and business association. When Sarah Todd, a retailer since the mid-1750s, wrote her will in 1776, she left her entire estate, "Real, personal and mixt," to her "dearly beloved friend Mary Purcell."[39] Purcell first tried to support herself teaching needlework with her sister Elinor in 1751. By 1755 she had become the partner of divorced shopkeeper Jane Eustis. Although she dissolved her partnership with Eustis after only a few years, she continued to keep shop. By 1759, Purcell had joined spinster Todd in selling millinery wares. Their business relationship and friendship lasted almost twenty years, until Todd's death in 1777. Purcell's switch from teaching to shopkeeping suggests confidence in the potential financial reward of retailing as well as an awareness of the commercial enterprises of other women.

Advertisements offer further evidence, both of women's business relationships and of the prominence of some women retailers. While some shopkeepers described their location as near the post office or a tavern, for example, others alluded to neighboring shops. In reporting a change of address or the opening of a business, they listed the name of their shop's previous inhabitant or located themselves by referring to their proximity to an established retailer. For example, in the summer of 1759, a few months after Elizabeth Murray had announced her relocation, Todd and Purcell described their new venue as the shop lately inhabited by Elizabeth (Murray) Campbell.[40]

Some retailers strengthened female bonds by training their daughters in trade, taking them as partners, and bequeathing substantial legacies to them. Abigail Whitney, Sr., willed the family business and most of her estate to her daughter Abigail Whitney, Jr., rather than to her son Samuel, an upholsterer.[41] Hannah Newman, who operated a Boston shop with her

---

spective wares from McNeal's house; while the fire damage assessors described losses in personal estate for both women, they recorded a loss of real estate for McNeal alone. Dearden lost £137 in personal estate and was identified as a person of "middling" wealth. The assessors described McNeal as a "rich" person with losses of £400 in real estate and personal estate losses valued at £2,005 "Lawfull money." Boston Fire Records, Ms. Am. 1809 (2), Boston Public Library; and *Report of the Record Commissioners of the City of Boston* (Boston, 1876–1909), 29:37.

39. Sarah Todd, Will, Suffolk County Probate Records, 76:593.

40. *Boston Evening-Post*, Aug. 20, 27, 1759.

41. Whitney willed 400 pounds lawful money each to her son Samuel and daughter Anna and the rest of the estate to Abigail. It cannot be determined whether Samuel had already

daughter Susannah, bequeathed only paltry sums to her two sons.[42] In her will, Newman elaborated on the attributes her daughter possessed that earned her esteem and estate. Susannah, Newman wrote, "has been a great Comfort, & Support to me, in my advanced age, & has taken Care of my Business; & by her Diligence & Industry," contributed immensely.[43] By giving their daughters substantial legacies in excess of an equal division of their estates, these women formally and legally recognized the role their female children had played in their businesses.[44] Their actions further confirm a sense of retailing as an appropriate occupation for women in colonial America; women who earned their livelihoods keeping shop could bring daughters into the trade hopeful of their ability to maintain themselves in the future.[45]

As a beneficiary of her aunt's assistance and largesse, Polly Murray appeared poised to earn her livelihood as a shopkeeper. Bridgen and Waller expressed confidence that Polly would make "good all the Prophesies . . .

<hr/>

received parental assistance in the form of training and education. Abigail Whitney, Will, Suffolk County Probate Records, 66:89–90. When Abigail Whitney, Jr., married, she had a marriage settlement that included the provision that she would be entitled to half of the profits she and her husband made "if by their Care Industry & Skill in Commerce & Trade" they increased their estate. Suffolk County Probate Records, 91:583.

42. Hannah Newman, Will, Suffolk County Probate Records, 51:657–660.

43. Newman, Will, 659.

44. Male testators in colonial America discriminated more against daughters than female testators did, increasing equality in their sons' portions to their daughters' detriment. Although women showed more favoritism toward their daughters than men did, their testamentary behavior did not make up for the overall difference in children's portions. Carole Shammas, Marylynn Salmon, and Michel Dahlin, *Inheritance in America From Colonial Times to the Present* (New Brunswick, N.J., 1987), 45, 55. Suzanne Lebsock explored the personalism of women's bequests in *The Free Women of Petersburg: Status and Culture in a Southern Town, 1784–1860* (New York, 1984), 135, 142.

45. Men may have recognized the financial stability shopkeeping promised women as well. For example, New York shopkeeper Samuel Pell's two daughters earned their living as shopkeepers; Hester Pell kept shop as a single woman, while her sister Elizabeth Pell Sleght took up shopkeeping after her merchant husband died. In his will, Pell left all of his real and personal estate to his wife during her lifetime, and only after her death ordered that the estate be divided between their two offspring; he believed their commercial activities could support them. Samuel Pell, Will, file 2818, 1776, Historical Documents Collection, Queens College, New York. In Philadelphia, shopkeeper Mary Coates clearly trained her daughters to follow her shopkeeping path while pushing her son toward becoming a merchant. See Cleary, " 'She Will Be in the Shop': Women's Sphere of Trade in Eighteenth-Century Philadelphia and New York," *Pennsylvania Magazine of History and Biography* 119(1995):181–202.

viz.: That She would turn out the Notable dilligent & Cleaver Shop-keeper."[46] Although the political unrest of 1770 delayed her entrance into trade, by early 1772 she was well on her way to a thriving business career. By that time, her younger sister Anne and Jackie Day had arrived from England to join her in the enterprise. Together, the young women sold and made stylish merchandise. An invoice dated April 1771, for the first order of goods selected for Polly Murray, captures the scale and range of their stock. It lists a variety of cloth, millinery wares, and trimmings, as well as specific clothing items, all of which came from Bridgen and Waller. The order included articles of apparel for both sexes, such as six dozen men's hose and three dozen women's cotton double heels, for a bill totaling several hundred pounds.[47] Over the next several months, the stock was augmented by more merchandise from Bridgen and Waller ordered by Elizabeth Murray, who was still overseas. Murray had the merchants send quantities of cloth, nine dozen men's gloves, five dozen women's gloves, six dozen fans, as well as catgut and lace.[48] Waller described the attributes of several items: the "strip'd Mantua's are all the Taste here and . . . must sell well in Boston."[49] Expressing a confidence in both the wares and the young Murrays that was tempered only by an awareness of their competition, he wrote, "We are certain nothing can prevent the Sale of the Goods sent but the large Quantities that have been sent to Boston from other Houses."[50]

Waller's confidence was well placed. Customers attracted to their stock and assured by their reputation kept the young women busy. According to Elizabeth Murray, the three behaved "charmingly" and were very in-dustrious.[51] Their bookkeeping was simple, with the extension of credit strictly limited, thereby eliminating the necessity of complicated, long-running accounts. Elizabeth Murray had insisted that Polly not sell goods on credit. She declared, "It is much better to say as Mr. Deblois does that he keeps no Books, only to people that he is well acquainted

46. Bridgen and Waller to [Elizabeth Murray] Inman, June 25, 1773, box 2, J. M. Robbins Papers.

47. Invoice no. 1, Apr. 26, 1771, Invoice Book, Mary Murray & Co., 1771–1775, Account Book of James Murray, 1766–1779, M.H.S.

48. Invoice no. 7, July 13, 1771, Invoice Book, Mary Murray & Co., 1771–1775, Account Book of James Murray, 1766–1779. This order alone was valued at over five hundred pounds.

49. J[ames] W[aller] to Elizabeth [Murray] Smith, July 18, 1771, box 2, J. M. Robbins Papers.

50. J[ames] W[aller] to Elizabeth [Murray] Smith, Aug. 10, 1771, box 2, J. M. Robbins Papers.

51. Elizabeth [Murray] Inman to Lady Phillipaugh, [1772], box 2, J. M. Robbins Papers.

with."[52] Although the young women's shop location is not clear, apparently Murray found them a propitious venue. Prior to their opening, Bridgen and Waller opined, "The corner Shop which you mention in a former Letter is the very thing the Situation &c must do, and the sooner they get into the Shop the better."[53] Once at work, Polly Murray found admirers. One woman wrote approvingly of "the amiable Polly Murray so content with her situation[;] she is a pattern to every Girl in my opinion."[54] In letters to her cousin Betsy Murray, Polly wrote that customers kept the retailers occupied and working long hours, noting in one report: "We have made 4 more of the Persian Hatts this week—they are getting very much into fashion."[55]

Christian Barnes, Murray's close friend, expressed great satisfaction with the young women's progress and held high hopes for their future achievements. She told Elizabeth Murray that she sincerely wished that the young women's undertakings would "be crowned with success for their own sakes, as well as for the Honour of the Sex." As she declared with remarkable gender consciousness, "Who shall say we have not equal abilitys with the Men when Girls of 18 years of age discover such great capacitys?"[56] Barnes's assertion that their youth, rapid acquisition of shopkeeping skills, and early promise of financial success attested to feminine ability prefigured the claims and demands of reformers who began to reconsider the content and purpose of women's education in the last quarter of the century and urge its redesign for more practical and civic ends.[57]

The successes that Polly and her partners enjoyed encouraged the Murrays to consider shopkeeping for Polly and Anne's younger sister Charlotte. In 1773, John Murray wrote to his sister Elizabeth that "agreeable to [her] desire [he had] pushed Charlotte forward in her Arithmetic" and that as soon as she was "fit for book-keeping," she would be instructed in it as well.[58] Before Charlotte Murray could join her sisters, however, political and personal developments derailed their business.

52. Elizabeth [Murray] Smith to [James Murray], Apr. 14, 1770, box 1, J. M. Robbins Papers.

53. Bridgen and Waller to Elizabeth [Murray] Smith, Sept. 21, 1771, box 2, J. M. Robbins Papers.

54. M. Spence to Mother Spence, Oct. 16, 1774, box 2, J. M. Robbins Papers.

55. Polly Murray to Betsy Murray, May 8, 1772, typescript, box 5, J. M. Robbins Papers.

56. Christian Barnes to Elizabeth [Murray] Smith, Mar. 6, 1774, Christian Barnes letterbook, Papers of Mrs. Christian Barnes.

57. Linda Kerber, *Women of the Republic: Intellect and Ideology in Revolutionary America* (Chapel Hill, 1980).

58. John Murray to [Elizabeth Murray Inman], July 12, 1773, typescript, box 5, J. M. Robbins Papers.

In 1774, Elizabeth Murray had decided that Polly deserved a visit home. Elizabeth assessed Polly's skills proudly: "Pollys capac[i]ty for business is so great & that I thought going home woud be a great advantage to her & she ought to be indulged with a sight of her Friends." Polly Murray's return to England initially followed the same pattern as had her aunt's commercial voyage of the 1750s. From London, she wrote to her aunt at length about her business affairs. Immediately upon her arrival, she was visited by Edward Bridgen. "I delivered him the bills," she reported, "the amount of which you know was small and at the same time offered him the account I had by your desire prepared for his inspection." Polly went on to tell him "exactly how [their] affairs stood." For his part, Bridgen seemed "quite satisfied and returned . . . the book without once looking into it." Polly's business associates planned to usher her around while she conducted her affairs: "to-morrow Mr. Bridgen and Mr. Hayley's Clerk are to attend me in search of goods."[59]

While abroad, Polly Murray continued to oversee her Boston business. It had been difficult for Elizabeth to convince Anne Murray to guard the shop in her sister's absence. On the eve of Polly's departure, Anne had to face the prospect of assuming sole responsibility for the operation. Given that Polly had dominated the business, Anne dreaded replacing her. Her aunt wrote that "it was with great dificulty" and only after many tears that she "perswaded her she was capable to take care of the shop & accounts."[60] Despite her fears, Anne Murray proved her mettle. In a letter to their uncle James in 1775, Polly wrote that her sister "Annie has made me better remittances than I expected at this time, so I am less anxious than I was about her success."[61]

Political upheavals ultimately cut short Polly Murray's shopkeeping career. By July 1775, she had decided to postpone her expected fall return to the colonies. Although the outbreak of war prevented her from following her aunt's shopkeeping path for long, Polly never rued the experience. She declared in 1783 that the "spirit of independance" that her aunt had cherished in her was "not yet extinct."[62]

Other women retailers found their economic activities similarly plagued by political developments. In the midst of the unrest that had initially

59. Mary [Polly] Murray to Elizabeth [Murray] Inman, July 12, 1774, typescript, box 5, J. M. Robbins Papers.

60. [Elizabeth Murray Inman], Feb. 11, 1774, box 2, J. M. Robbins Papers.

61. Mary [Polly] Murray to James Murray, Jan. 8, 1775, typescript, box 5, J. M. Robbins Papers.

62. Mary [Polly] Murray to [Elizabeth Murray] Inman, Nov. 30, 1783, typescript, box 5, J. M. Robbins Papers.

forestalled Polly's entrance into trade, the Cuming sisters came under attack for dealing in imported wares. In 1770, they were publicly chastised in the *Boston-Gazette* for audaciously "importing British Goods contrary to the Agreement."[63] Relaying the news to Elizabeth Murray, then overseas, that the Cumings and her own husband Henry Barnes had been so described, Christian Barnes wrote that she longed to have "one political Laugh" with her friend. Barnes thought Murray would be diverted "to see Squire Barnes and the Two little Miss Cuminges Posted together in a News Paper as Enimys to their Country."[64]

While the Cumings may not have construed their economic activities in a larger political context, other Bostonians did. The Cumings discovered that their small shop was visible within the mercantile community and that their individual business decisions carried political implications. When a merchants committee first accused the sisters of violating the non-importation agreement, Elizabeth Cuming answered that they had never entered into any sort of a pact. Moreover, she was amazed that the merchants would "try to inger two industrious Gerls who ware Striving in an honest way to Git there Bread."[65] After their names were published as enemies, Anne Cuming reported that their friends were inspired to buy goods from them and that they had "mor[e] custom then before."[66] By purchasing imported English wares from the Cumings rather than boycotting them, those "friends" who frequented the sisters' shop expressed both their personal loyalties and political leanings. Other shopkeepers and traders who continued to deal in imported wares attracted violent reprisals from angry colonists in 1770.[67] Apparently loyal to the crown and apprehensive of such actions, the Cuming sisters were among those Bostonians who fled the town when the British evacuated.[68] Removing to Halifax in 1776, however, did not signal the

63. "Boston Gazette of March 12, 1770," printed in *Proceedings of the Massachusetts Historical Society* 59(1926):255.

64. Christian Barnes to Elizabeth [Murray] Smith, Dec. 23, 1769, Christian Barnes letterbook, Papers of Mrs. Christian Barnes.

65. Elizabeth Cuming to Elizabeth [Murray] Smith, Nov. 20, 1769, box 1, J. M. Robbins Papers.

66. Anne Cuming to Elizabeth [Murray] Smith, Dec. 27, 1769, box 1, J. M. Robbins Papers.

67. In Boston in 1770, intimidating mobs deterred customers from entering proscribed shops, defaced importers' signs, and broke store windows. Pauline Maier, *From Resistance to Revolution: Colonial Radicals and the Development of American Opposition to Britain, 1765–1776* (New York, 1972), 128–129.

68. Samuel A. Green, "List of Refugees from Boston in 1776," *Proceedings of the Massachusetts Historical Society* 18(1880–1881):266.

end of their commercial ventures; in 1780, Betsy Murray, James Murray's younger daughter, reported with pleasure "that the Miss Cummings [were] so successful in busines" in their new home.[69]

Shop work caused some women retailers to contemplate their personal abilities and gender as well as their political loyalties. In the midst of the "great disturbances" of 1770, Christian Barnes was hard at work in her husband's shop. In November, she apologized to Elizabeth Murray for not writing; "ploding behind a counter from Sun to Sun" left her no time for correspondence. Apparently, she did not relish the shopkeeping life as much as Murray had, asserting that it could "Stagnate the Blood and Stupifie the Senses."[70] As Barnes kept shop over the course of the next year, she expressed ambivalent feelings about her employment, mixing protestations of ignorance and inability with evaluations of her skill and accomplishments as she undertook mercantile activities. "It would divert you to see what a parade I make with my business," she told Murray; "to one Gentleman I write for insurence, to another to secure freight, to a third to purchase Bills." In summing up her negotiations, she wrote, "all this is done in such a Mercantile Strain that I believe many of them think me a Woman of great capacity."[71]

Barnes's assertions of feminine "capacity" in matters of business highlight the intersection between familial enterprises and female entrepreneurship. Clearly, she undertook commercial endeavor in a family context. Like many other women who kept shop, Barnes did so as an adjunct to a trading spouse. In her spouse's absence, she filled the role of "deputy husband."[72] Yet her shopkeeping transcended family duty. She saw her work as a challenge and opportunity on the grounds of gender; in its pursuit, she found that she possessed skills that reflected well upon women's abilities, as did the success of Polly Murray. Moreover, Barnes's sense of the relative ease with which she took up trade to assist her husband added to her view of shopkeeping as accessible to women. The world of men and business lost some of its mystery once she entered it.

69. E[lizabeth Betsy] M[urray] to James Murray, May 14, 1780, typescript, box 5, J. M. Robbins Papers.
70. Christian Barnes to Elizabeth [Murray] Smith, Nov. 24, 1770, Christian Barnes letterbook, Papers of Mrs. Christian Barnes.
71. Christian Barnes to Elizabeth [Murray] Smith, Feb. 20, 1771, Christian Barnes letterbook, Papers of Mrs. Christian Barnes.
72. Laurel Thatcher Ulrich, *Good Wives: Image and Reality in the Lives of Women in Northern New England, 1650–1750* (New York, 1982), 35–50.

Barnes's understanding of commerce and its significance in the civil disturbances afflicting Boston, her friends, and family led her to offer political commentary. After both her husband and the Cumings had been published as enemies, she decided she would try to sway her husband's behavior. She preferred that he not incite the rabble by publicizing his goods; "what the consequence of that would be," she worried, "I know not." She determined to use her "influence with him not to be the first" to advertise.[73] When some goods arrived for him, a committee from "those dareing Sons of Libberty" waited upon him to demand the wares be stored. Their behavior was tyrannical and their rule shaky, asserted Christian: "People will not be much longer imposed upon with a Cry of Libberty when they see Private property is only Sought after." Expressing to her friend Elizabeth Murray a hope that "the deluded multitude" would turn upon their radical oppressors, Barnes added that this was her "Private opinion."[74]

Almost apologetically, Barnes declared that she was mystified by her own forthrightness, because she "never chose to dabble in" politics. She excused her exercise of political voice as the result of the intimacy of her relationship with Murray: "I can account for it no other way, then as I am writing to you. I have a pecular pleasure in gieveing vent to every sentiment that rises in my Heart."[75] The following month, she moved from rationalizing her commentary to asking for the latest political news. Writing to Murray, Barnes neatly connected politics and commerce in a simple request. "Send us a Little Dash of Politics from t'other side the Water," she urged, "that we may see something that has the appearance of truth, for our well disposed import such a vast quantity of lies with their other articles that they begin to find a Difficulty in vending them."[76]

Some of Boston's women traders were treated as men when they expressed their political sentiments. In early 1768, seven women were included on "A List of the Subscription of Those Gentlemen . . . immediately concerned in importing Goods from great Britain" who would "not import any for a year."[77] Jane Eustis, the only one of these women closely associ-

73. Christian Barnes to Elizabeth [Murray] Smith, Nov. 20, 1769, Christian Barnes letterbook, Papers of Mrs. Christian Barnes.

74. Christian Barnes to Elizabeth [Murray] Smith, Nov. 29, 1769.

75. Christian Barnes to Elizabeth [Murray] Smith, Nov. 29, 1769.

76. Christian Barnes to Elizabeth [Murray] Smith, Dec. 26, 1769, Christian Barnes letterbook, Papers of Mrs. Christian Barnes.

77. Non-importation agreement, Boston, 1768, S. P. Savage Papers, M.H.S.

ated with Murray, was again ordering goods from Bridgen and Waller in 1769.[78] Although Eustis signed the 1768 agreement, she did not subscribe to a 1769 non-consumption pact supported by ninety-five men and eight women, two of whom had endorsed the earlier action.[79] Like Barnes and the Cuming sisters, these women became participants in political activity through their involvements in commerce.

For her part, Elizabeth Murray's opinions about the civil struggle changed over the course of the Revolutionary years. In 1770, while visiting Great Britain, Murray had expressed hopes for peace in her chosen home.[80] She also urged her brother James not to involve himself in politics and to conciliate with those patriots from whom they had received so much friendship rather "than try to reform them." She argued that such people saw it as their "duty to stand up for so valuable a country & not be tax'd to feed the worst set of men that ever lived." Indeed, she told him, "if I was in Boston I wou'd drink no tea and advise all my friends to sign" the petitions then circulating.[81] Reflecting upon her decision to send her brother's children into the turmoil of colonial society, she claimed, "I may be allowd a partiality for a Country & people where & from whom I have received unmarited friendship & civilitys that I shall ever Glory to Boast off."[82] Although she heard of incidents of young women being tarred and feathered for saying they would drink tea "in spight of the Liberty folks," she retained her positive view of life in the colonies.[83] Her attitudes underwent a dramatic shift during the next decade, however, as she witnessed her family and friends suffer and her own reputation come under attack in the press.[84]

78. Correspondence from Bridgen and Waller to Elizabeth Murray from early 1770 describes the orders Eustis placed. The merchants sought Murray's advice on the disposal of the goods after Eustis died while visiting London and suggested that Polly Murray could sell them (see J. M. Robbins Papers). Ultimately, Polly received a parcel of goods originally ordered by Eustis. This lot included lace, cloth, hats, women's mitts, and silk gloves. Invoice no. 5, July 24, 1771, Invoice Book, Mary Murray & Co., 1771–1775, Account Book of James Murray, 1766–1779.

79. "Non-Consumption Agreement Signed by 113 Inhabitants of Boston," July 31, 1769, Boston, Mss. L., M.H.S.

80. [Elizabeth Murray] Smith to [Ezekiel] Goldthwait, May 17, 1770, box 1, J. M. Robbins Papers.

81. Elizabeth [Murray] Smith to James Murray, May 19, 1770, box 1, J. M. Robbins Papers.

82. Elizabeth [Murray] Smith to [Christian Barnes], November [1770], box 1, J. M. Robbins Papers.

83. Elizabeth [Murray] Inman to Lady Don, [fall] 1773, box 2, J. M. Robbins Papers.

84. A detailed discussion of Murray's experiences in the 1770s and 1780s appears in

While Murray's political opinions changed, her positive assessment of shopkeeping never wavered. In the 1780s, more than thirty years after she first advertised her business, she reflected upon both the material and intangible benefits she had gained in her pursuit of commerce. Explaining her attitudes to her older brother John, she wrote: "I rejoice that the spirit of Independence caused such exertions as to place me in a setuation that I am content to pass the remainder of my days in."[85] She acknowledged that she was "untaught" when she began; given that inexperience, she remarked, "I am surprised & my heart overflowes with gratetude at the success I have met with." Murray's economic achievements suggested to her the accessibility of shopkeeping for women who possessed energy but limited training and led her to assist several young women in similar endeavors during the 1760s and 1770s.

In looking at Murray's life, we see how shopkeeping could shape women's identities, as well as their political and economic experiences. Shopkeepers' roles as arbiters or handlers of fashion made them important sources of information; in displaying their stock of British styles, they revealed their skill as consumers themselves. Shops may have been the female counterpart to the largely male establishments of the coffeehouse and the tavern, with women's gossip and conversation about fashions in dress or chinaware the analogue to men's inquiring about the latest news over a drink and meeting business associates. Perhaps female consumers felt more comfortable in public going to a woman's shop. As a center for consumer activities, the shop provided a stage for women to interact with each other. Similarly, the relationships that developed among women shopkeepers expressed professional and personal camaraderie, sometimes in the form of partnerships and financial assistance. Women retailers constructed and took part in alliances that grew out of common commercial experiences. Engaging in commerce brought these women into the distinctively masculine realm of politics, as shopkeeping revealed its obvious political connotations. Their experiences force us to rethink the precise nature of gender roles and the distinctions between public and private spheres.

Cleary, "'I have acted many parts in life but never imagen'd . . . being a Generall': the Revolution in Women's Roles," chap. 5, *Elizabeth Murray and the "Spirit of Independence."*

85. Elizabeth [Murray] Inman to John Murray, Sept. 18, 1783, box 3, J. M. Robbins Papers.

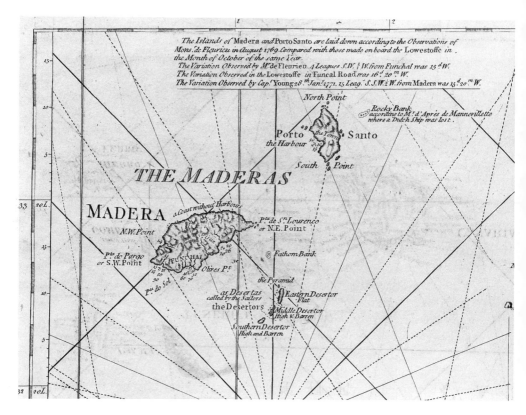

The Islands of Madera and Porto Santo are laid down according to the Observations of
Mons. de Fleurieu in August 1769. Compared with those made on board the Lowestoffe in
the Month of October of the same Year.
The Variation Observed by M. de Fleurieu 4 Leagues S.W. ¼ W. from Funchal was 15 ¼ W.
The Variation Observed in the Lowestoffe in Funcal Road was 16.ᵈ 20.ᵐ W.
The Variation Observed by Cap. Young 28.ᵗʰ Jan. 1771. 13 Leag. S.S.W. ½ W. from Madera was 15.ᵈ 20.ᵐ W.

North Point

Rocky Bank
according to M. d'Aprés de Mannevillette
where a Dutch Ship was lost.

Porto
the Harbour
the Town

Santo

South Point

THE MADERAS

MADERA
a Coast without Harbours

N.W. Point

P.ᵗᵃ de S.t Lourenço
or N.E. Point

P.ᵗˢ do Pargo
or S.W. Point

FUNCHAL

Olives P.t

Fathom Bank

P.ᵗᵗ do Sol

the Pyramid

as Desertas
called by the Sailors

Eastern Desertor
Flat

the Desertors

Middle Desertor
High & Barren

Southern Desertor
High and Barren

"Chart of the Maderas," *The Oriental Pilot: Or, East India Directory*
(London, 1801), pl. 9. The chart bears the date 1794. Collection of the
Massachusetts Historical Society.

Markets, Merchants, and the
Wider World of Boston Wine,
1700–1775

David Hancock

AT THE BEGINNING of the eighteenth century, Boston merchants involved with the shipping and trading of wine dominated the importation of the commodity from southern Europe's Wine Islands to North America. By the outbreak of the American Revolution, their dominance had been eroded, much of their share of overseas trade having passed to merchants in Philadelphia, New York, Charleston, and Salem. How and why did Boston merchants lose control of a profitable wine commerce?

An answer does not readily emerge from the existing historical literature. When historians have addressed the subject of the state of Boston commerce during the eighteenth century, they have either adopted an optimistic perspective based on the ultimately regenerative effects of the Revolution and concluded that trade was "in a fairly flourishing condition," or argued that, limited by its geography and population, Boston experienced "unrelieved economic depression," "a bewildering conglomeration of very slow overall increases, sudden losses, slow decreases, see-saw ups and downs, and only limited signs of variable growth after 1750."[1] A more realistic answer probably lies somewhere between these extremes, but even that is uncharted territory. In surveying the field, what seems most surprising is that, to date, the studies of the prerevolutionary Boston economy are remarkably devoid of comment on Boston merchants' commercial activities and how they relate to the growth of Boston business. This study of Boston's wine traders attempts to begin providing such a perspective.

---

1. Samuel Eliot Morison, "The Commerce of Boston on the Eve of the Revolution," *Proceedings of the American Antiquarian Society*, 2d ser., 32(1922):49; G. B. Warden, "Inequality and Instability in Eighteenth-Century Boston: A Reappraisal," *Journal of Interdisciplinary History* 6(1976):589–590.

Much the same situation prevails in the larger field of research on trans-atlantic commerce. While comprehensive overviews of British foreign commerce in the seventeenth and eighteenth centuries, detailed studies of British shipping, and numerous analyses of trades in specific goods like slaves, sugar, and tobacco have been conducted, wine and Britain's trade with the Wine Islands (Madeira, the Azores, and the Canary Islands) have been neglected in the extensive scholarship on the overseas business of British America.[2] A few historians—E. D. Beechert, D. J. Mishkin, T. B. Duncan, and R. C. Nash—have looked at the subject but have focused on narrow aspects of the trade, such as the literary record of wine's role in the development of mercantilism or the statistical share that wine held in Great Britain's export and import portfolio. No scholar has yet examined the role that wine played in strengthening colonial America's economic connections to southern Europe.[3] The present essay also makes a first attempt at analyzing this role.

This essay is part of an ongoing project that seeks to understand the trade

2. Ralph Davis, *The Rise of the English Shipping Industry in the Seventeenth and Eighteenth Centuries* (London, 1962); Philip D. Curtin, *The Atlantic Slave Trade: A Census* (Madison, 1969); Jacob M. Price, *Capital and Credit in British Overseas Trade* (Cambridge, Mass., 1980); John J. McCusker, *Rum and the American Revolution* (New York, 1989). The oversight and neglect are surprising. As the character and volume of coastwise and oceanic trade developed and expanded, wine grew in importance as a commodity throughout the colonial period. As early as the 1580s, wine was shipped to the New World and, at the same time, considered a crop that could be cultivated there and brought back to the Old. Throughout successive waves of discovery and settlement, wine continued to capture investors' and settlers' imaginations. Among Europeans, the British were particularly intrigued by the possibilities of the vine, and, although nothing substantial came of their efforts to cultivate native or imported vines in the New World, their desire for wine persisted. As a result, through the first decade of the 19th century, European wine, as an import to America, figured prominently among transatlantic commodities.

3. E. D. Beechert, Jr., "The Wine Trade of the Thirteen Colonies" (M.A. thesis, Univ. of California, Berkeley, 1949); David Mishkin, "The American Colonial Wine Industry" (Ph.D. diss., Univ. of Illinois, Urbana, 1966); T. Bentley Duncan, *Atlantic Islands: Madeira, the Azores and the Cape Verdes in Seventeenth-Century Commerce and Navigation* (Chicago, 1972), 61; R. C. Nash, "English Transatlantic Trade, 1660–1730: A Quantitative Study" (Ph.D. diss., Cambridge Univ., 1982). In particular, they have failed to examine the provocative hypothesis put forth by more general economic and social historians of early America that, as the demand for food in southern Europe (the Iberian Peninsula and the Mediterranean) increased in the second third of the 18th century, southern Europe exported large quantities of wine, fruit, and salt from the Wine Islands under its control, for which it received large quantities of colonial rice, wheat flour, and codfish directly from the British colonies.

in one transatlantic bulk commodity, Madeira wine—from the cultivation of the vine and manufacture of the drink in Madeira to its consumption in British America—by examining the links between its production, distribution, and consumption in the first three quarters of the eighteenth century. It focuses primarily on colonial Massachusetts and on imports from the Portuguese islands of Madeira and the Azores, for they were always the principal source of British America's wine. The story, therefore, is somewhat incomplete, for it omits a full discussion of wines from the Spanish Canary Islands, from the Iberian peninsula (wines like port, malaga, and sherry), and from France (claret).[4] However, from preliminary investigations into the eighteenth-century Atlantic wine trade in general, it appears that Madeira's and the Azores' connections with Massachusetts were similar to those between other wine regions and Massachusetts, as well as other British American colonies.

This paper suggests that three, and perhaps four sets of factors combined in the middle decades of the eighteenth century to alter patterns of commerce and cause Boston merchants to lose their share of the American wine trade. First, in the Atlantic, the desire of Madeira's municipal chamber, customs house, and resident exporters to control the price and distribution of their wine caused them aggressively to seek out new customers and correspondents in other colonies. Second, in America, the growth of the colonial economy led to the formation of merchant communities and networks in New York, Philadelphia, and Charleston, among those who wanted actively to establish and develop their own commercial ties to Madeira. Third, with respect to New England, Boston became relatively uneconomic compared to Salem as a wine entrepôt. Finally, there is some suggestion of a "sclerosis" of the Boston commercial community's entrepreneurial spirit, at least as measured against its competitors' in other colonies and in its home market.

The importation and consumption of wine, as well as an attempt at domestic production, began with the founding of the colonies. The Puritans stowed 10,000 gallons of wine in the hold of the *Arbella*, and wine was "very plentiful, and cheap, in the country" surrounding Winthrop's Boston. In 1651, one commentator observed that leniency in collecting imposts on

4. On the Canary trade in the 1750s, especially the ways Canary merchants packaged wines as Madeira products, see A. G. Ravina, " 'Las Islas del Vino' y La America Inglesa durante el siglo XVIII: Una Aproximacion a su estudio," in *Actas Do Colóquio Internacional de História da Madeira 1986* (Funchal, 1990), 900–932.

wine opened "a door of encouragement" to wine shippers and traders, who in previous years had "filled the country with that commodity, to the over-flowing of luxury and other evils." A ship laden with Madeira or Fayal—what John Josselyn called "a walking tavern"—was widely considered a legitimate and profitable "means for the Merchant to increase his gains."[5] Additional encouragement came from the Act for the Encouragement of Trade in 1663, the second of the Navigation Acts. Under its terms, England was to be the staple for European commodities imported into America, and European goods were to pass through England before being exported to America. Wines from the Continent were subject to the law, but exceptions were made; among these were wines from Madeira and the Azores.[6]

5. Thomas Pinney, *A History of Wine in America* (Berkeley, 1989), 29–31. James Savage, ed., *The History of New England from 1630 to 1649, by John Winthrop, Esq.* (Boston, 1826), 95; William Hubbard, *A General History of New England, from the Discovery to 1680, Collections of the Massachusetts Historical Society,* 2d ser., 6(1815):520. For 17th-century shipments, see Savage, *History,* 95; *A Volume Relating to the Early History of Boston containing the Aspinwall Notarial Records from 1644 to 1651* (Boston, 1903), 296 (1650); John Josselyn, *An Account of Two Voyages to New-England,* 2d ed. (London, 1675), *Collections of the Massachusetts Historical Society,* 3d ser., 3(1833):213–353. One 1680 partnership agreement between Samuel Shrimpton and Stephen Wesendonck estab-lished a firm "in the trade and secret of making & managing" Rhenish, Canary, French, and Pesado wines. Shrimpton was to buy the wines, and Wesendonck to blend and package them. Miscellaneous Bound Manuscripts Additional, Massachusetts Historical Society (hereafter M.H.S.). Contrary to popular belief, 17th-century Massachusetts inhabitants did not turn from the glass or bottle when proffered it. Most seem to have agreed with Increase Mather that "the wine is from God, but the Drunkard is from the Devil." Wine, cider, and beer flowed freely at church-related functions; drinking was closely tied to family and community events. Mather, *Wo to Drunkards* (Boston, 1673). Mark E. Lender and James K. Martin, *Drinking in America: A History* (New York, 1987), 4–37, discuss the prevalence of drinking wine and spirits in New England. On drinking legislation in Mas-sachusetts, see David W. Conroy, "The Culture and Politics of Drink in Colonial and Revolutionary Massachusetts, 1681–1790" (Ph.D. thesis, Univ. of Connecticut, 1987).

6. For the 1663 statute, see 15 Car. II, c. 7, v. A detailed discussion of the exceptions appears in Charles M. Andrews, *The Colonial Period of American History,* vol. 4, *England's Commercial and Colonial Policy* (New Haven, 1938), 109; Lawrence A. Harper, *The English Navigation Laws: A Seventeenth-Century Experiment in Social Engineering* (New York, 1939), 401, 406. Why the exception was granted is unclear. It is possible that wine was recognized because, unlike cloth, it was an article that could not "be supplied by Great Britain to Advantage." Moreover, the importance for the northern colonial economies of the direct exchange of New England fish, timber products, and wheat for southern Euro-pean salt and wine seems to have weighed heavily on the bill's principal supporters. Finally, the increasingly close link between Portugal and England, solemnized in the 1662 mar-riage of Charles II to Catherine of Braganza, daughter of the king of Portugal, plus the

Because of Madeira's strategic location in the Atlantic trade winds and Britain's long-standing alliance with Portugal, nearly all west-bound British vessels not traveling north of Ireland stopped at Madeira for fresh water and southern European food provisions. As a result, Madeira became a mid-Atlantic entrepôt. Its wine was an easy and useful cargo for trans-oceanic shippers to procure, and these transactions complemented the traders' dealings with other regions and commodities. Through the first third of the eighteenth century, Boston enterprisers dominated North American wine importation. Initially, in the seventeenth century, they "supplied themselves with wines advantageously," exchanging their fish, timber, butter, beeswax, and candles in the Wine Islands for European wine and salt, which they then peddled in Boston and its environs. At the end of the seventeenth and beginning of the eighteenth centuries, their trade was significant and they began to re-export such commodities.[7] By 1709, Capt. Nathaniel Uring noted, Boston enjoyed both "a very good trade to the islands of Azores and Madeira, whom they furnish with pipe staves, dried Fish, salted Mackerel, and Bees Wax, for which they purchase wines," and a superior re-export trade to less-well-supplied towns in other colonies.[8] According to naval office shipping lists compiled by the Boston naval office's clerk (an appointee of the governor), Boston directly imported at least 350 pipes of wine each year from southern Europe and the Wine Islands in the second decade of the eighteenth century. Charleston imported 100

long-standing personal enmity between the kings of England and France (heightened by the ascendant economic theory, which encouraged keeping English wealth out of French coffers), made such a commercial arrangement sensible. In Britain, Madeira's competitive advantage was enhanced by the favorable terms of the 1703 Methuen Treaty, which allowed Portuguese wine to enter Britain at a third less the rate imposed on French wine. Lewis Hertslet, ed., *A Complete Collection of the Treaties and Conventions . . .* , (London, 1840), 2:24–25.

7. Account of the Consul and Factory of Madeira, in Lords of Trade to Earl of Shelburne, Sept. 3, 1766, Joseph Redington, ed., *Calendar of Home Office Papers of the Reign of George III, 1766–1769* (London, 1879), 75. At the turn of the century, Boston's presence appears to have been constant. The presence of Boston ships in Funchal (Madeira) harbor is documented in the William Bolton letterbooks. In the period 1695–1700, 4 ships originated in Boston; 5 left for Boston. In the succeeding period, 1701–1714, 29 vessels arrived from Boston and 5 departed for Boston. João Adriano Ribeiro, "A Casquinha na Rota das Navegações do Atlântico Norte nos Séculos XVI–XVIII," *Actas III Colóquio Internacional de História da Madeira* (Funchal, 1993), 363–364, 372; and Graham Blandy, ed., *The Bolton Letters* (Funchal, 1960).

8. Capt. Nathaniel Uring, *A History of the Voyages and Travels* (London, 1726), 79.

pipes, New York, 99 pipes, and Philadelphia even less—some directly from the Wine Islands but many more via Boston and her re-export merchants.[9]

Boston's taste for and trade in wines continued to grow during the eighteenth century, at least in absolute terms. The number of merchants involved in shipping and trading wine rose between 1700 and 1775. Moreover, the number of ships carrying wine increased, and the amount of wine they brought into the port grew substantially. The records left by the naval office clerks—the only available records for the years 1714–1719 and 1752–1765—provide irrefutable evidence of the growth in this sector of the economy. As Table 1 notes, a total of 17 ships arrived from the Wine Islands, dropped anchor in Boston, and unloaded wine cargoes containing a total of 772 pipes in the three years 1716–1719. In periods of equal duration in the 1750s and 1760s, entrances and imports were greater. Some 44 ships holding 911 pipes arrived in 1753–1756, the merely moderate rise in the quantity of wine probably due to a decline in production on the island of Madeira caused by bad weather and the interruptions of war. By 1762–1765, the increase was more apparent: 53 ships unloaded 1,718

9. CO 5/848–851, CO 5/1222–1229, CO 5/508–511, Public Record Office, London. The clerk was, among other things, responsible for obtaining detailed information regarding every vessel that arrived at and cleared the port: the date of arrival or departure, the name of the ship, its shape, the place where and date when the ship was built and registered, the name of the captain and sometimes the owner, the number of tons, guns, and crewmen aboard, the cargo it held, and the name of its previous or next port. W. E. Minchinton, *The Naval Office Shipping Lists for Massachusetts, 1686–1765, in the Public Record Office, London* (Wakefield, England, [1968]). On the small scale of the Philadelphia trade with the Wine Islands in the early decades of the 18th century, see Beechert, "Wine Trade," 40–42. In the present essay, the unit of measurement will be the English "pipe," the 18th-century commercial equivalent of 110 gallons, one gallon equaling 231 cubic inches. A pipe would have filled roughly 440 quart bottles. Much confusion, however, still surrounds the measure. Contemporary chroniclers, like Henry Crouch and Malachy Postlethwayt, and modern historians, like E. Beechert and R. Zupko, measure a pipe at 126 gallons, relying on the outdated statutory definition of a pipe as the equivalent of 126 gallons. R. Zupko, *A Dictionary of English Weights and Measures* (Madison, 1968), 128–129. Further complicating matters, the Madeira custom house (but not Madeira's merchants) considered the pipe equal to 136 gallons, and the Lisbon customs house, to 126 gallons. Then, too, other gauges, like the Gunter gauge sometimes used in New York, produced casks of greater size. British and British American merchants working in Madeira did not adhere to statutory or foreign standards; rather, they measured and valued their pipe by the commercial standard of 110 gallons. See Johnston & Jolly to Newton & Gordon, Mar. 5, 1765, Cossart & Gordon Papers, Liverpool University Archives, Liverpool. John McCusker has done much to clarify the problem. *Rum and the American Revolution*, vol. 2, Appendix C, 768–878.

Table 1. Wine Arriving in Massachusetts, 1714–1719 & 1752–1765

	Boston Ships			Salem Ships			Other Ships			All Ships		
	Number	Registered Tons	Pipes of 110 Gallons	Number	Registered Tons	Pipes of 110 Gallons	Number	Registered Tons	Pipes of 110 Gallons	Number	Registered Tons	Pipes of 110 Gallons
'14												
'15												
'16				1	80	35				1	80	35
'17				2	81	108				2	81	108
'18	9	390	423							9	390	423
'19	8	280	349							8	280	349
total	17	670	772	3	161	143				20	831	915
'52	2	120	71							2	120	71
'53	16	156	331	1	40	4				17	196	335
'54	13	763	485	2	85	44				15	848	529
'55	5	225	37	2	125	98				7	350	135
'56	10	530	157	2	140	147				12	670	304
'57	3	95	39	2	110	72				5	205	111
'58	3	100	49	3	165	113				6	265	162
'59	8	345	515	3	110	110				11	455	625
'60	3	90	8	2	150	119				5	240	127
'61	10	440	477	4	215	108				14	655	585
'62	9	415	182	4	295	333				13	710	515
'63	14	737	235	6	303	296	1	40	1	21	1080	532
'64	22	1350	632	1	75	12				23	1425	644
'65	8	460	669	4	270	62				12	730	731
total	126	5826	3887	36	2083	1518	1	40	1	163	7949	5406

Source: CO 5/848-851, Public Record Office, London.

pipes. Over the course of five decades, shipping had trebled and cargoes more than doubled.[10]

Yet, by the late 1760s and early 1770s, Boston's relationship with other ports had changed. According to customs ledgers, Boston imported 415 pipes of wine each year from Europe and the Wine Islands between 1768

10. CO 5/848–851, Public Record Office, London. Only one ship returned from the Wine Islands without wine in her hold. James Lydon's approximations are slightly different. For the ports of Boston and Salem in the years 1752–1773, Lydon adds hypothetical averages to quarters for which no data survive, basing his averages on comparable quarters in adjacent years. After doing so, he finds that Boston imported an average 171 pipes in 4

and 1772, but Philadelphia was importing 681 pipes, New York, 656 pipes, and Charleston, 528 pipes, and Boston's re-exports had fallen to 61 pipes per year on average.[11] Similarly, Philadelphia, New York, and Charleston outranked Boston in coastwise imports of wine, and in coastwise re-exports of wine.[12]

Why did this happen?

Part of the answer lies in the island of Madeira. The trade of that island was always uppermost in the minds of Boston's prerevolutionary wine merchants. Many had visited the place and most had corresponded with British merchants resident there. The island they knew was a "circumscribed spot," about seventy miles long and twenty-five miles wide. Extremely mountainous, it enjoyed "an exceedingly rich soil" of light red tufa and a highly diversified set of micro-climates that were perfectly suited "to grow fruits and plants of the southern and northern growth" equally well.[13] The 120,000 inhabitants were mainly involved in the production and distribution of wine and, for most years in the century, were unable to feed themselves on their own produce; they depended heavily on British and, after 1740, North American foodstuffs. The bulk of the population was Portuguese, but the presence of a substantial number of other European exporters and their coterie created for the island the reputation of an international port. The French, the Dutch, and the Swedes all had consuls and merchants at work in the port capital Funchal, situated on the south side of the island. But the dominant foreigners, in terms of wealth, population, and trade, were the British and British Americans.

Madeira's wine production rose during the early years of the century, according to export figures occasionally noted by informed observers and participants or intermittently recorded in customs books. Nearly constant average production occurred from the 1730s through the 1770s. Exports

ships each year between 1752 and 1773. James G. Lydon, "Fish for Gold: The Massachusetts Fish Trade with Iberia, 1700–1773," *The New England Quarterly* 54(1981): 575, Table 8.

11. CUST 16/1, Public Record Office, London. Quebec led in imports into North America with 788 pipes.

12. Average annual coastwise imports: Charleston (110 pipes), Philadelphia (106 pipes), Quebec (66 pipes), New York (61 pipes), and Boston (49 pipes). Average annual coastwise re-exports: New York (319 pipes), Philadelphia (241 pipes), Charleston (111 pipes), and Boston (61 pipes). CUST 16/1, Public Record Office, London.

13. Account of the Consul and Factory of Madeira, 74–76.

rose 71 percent over the first few decades, from approximately 7,000 pipes in 1700 to 12,000 pipes in 1728, and then remained constant on average through 1775.[14] Much of this significant early growth was the result of Madeirans' putting to use unemployed land; any later, smaller gains accrued from their using existing production resources more efficiently.

These macro-trends were true, on average, but during certain decades the outward flow of Madeira's wine fluctuated frequently and wildly, rising as high, for example, as 20,000 pipes in 1764, falling to 1,700 pipes in 1771, and then rising back to 13,000 the following year.[15] The unpredictable gyrations bedeviled enterprisers on both sides of the Atlantic. That "the markets are constantly fluctuating" became a commonplace in their transatlantic correspondence, as scarcity and glut determined the dynamics of the global wine trade.[16]

Various events caused these fluctuations. The easiest to identify are those that sprang from international war and diplomacy. War cut normal lines of distribution. The War of Jenkins' Ear (1739–1742), the War of Austrian Succession (1740–1748), and the French and Indian Wars (1755–

14. Production figures have not survived. One present ongoing study assumes that exports engrossed roughly three-quarters of the vintage in most years. For consignments to residents and exports to foreigners, from which export figures can be derived, see *Livros dos Direitos dos Entradas dos Navios, nos. 146–174 (1727–1808), Alfândega do Funchal, Provedoria & Junta da Real Fazenda do Funchal, Arquivo Nacional da Torre do Tombo,* Lisbon, Portugal, and *Livros dos Direitos dos Saidas dos Navios, nos. 272–360 (1727–1833),* and *Livros das Visitas de Bordo, nos. 215–228 (1740–1778).* There are significant gaps in the *Saidas* wine export series, but the fuller complementary shipping series of the *Entradas* allows for some comparisons. This series, recorded in Table 2, gives a picture of long-term decline between the late 1720s and early 1760s. After a flurry of activity in the first quarter of the century, shipping soared to an all-time high in 1728, when 420 vessels, including 325 British and British-American vessels, entered the port of Funchal. Yet, from there, shipping by foreigners or Portuguese in foreign ships dropped to a low in 1762, when roughly 87 ships, including 50 British and British-American ships, were counted. Unfortunately, neither entrances nor clearances fully document the activities of Portuguese merchants aboard Portuguese ships arriving in or leaving the port. There is, however, no reason to believe that they do not present an accurate state of the trade of foreigners or of Portuguese using foreign vessels.

15. Newton & Gordon to Thomas Newton, May 15, 1765, Francis Newton to Newton & Gordon, Oct. 11, 1771, Cossart & Gordon Papers. The year 1764 was "the greatest vintage we have had" since 1745, wrote one resident. The year 1763 also witnessed an abundant harvest. Newton & Gordon to Thomas Newton, Nov. 15, 1764, Cossart & Gordon Papers.

16. Charles Chambers, Jr., to Richard Derby, July 8, 1770, Felt Family Collection, James Duncan Phillips Library, Peabody Essex Museum, Salem.

Table 2. Ship Entrances and Clearances in Funchal (Madeira), 1727–1775

Year	All Ships	British & British- American Ships	Year	All Ships	British & British- American Ships
1727	150	122	1752	190	155
1728	420	342	1753	183	149
1729	335	273	1754	190	155
1730	320	260	1755	233	190
1731	307	250	1756	265	216
1732	303	247	1757	153	123
1733	312	254	1758	185	149
1734	299	243	1759		
1735	375	305	1760	140	113
1736	317	258	1761	160	129
1737	315	237	1762	87	70
1738	317	238	1763	301	243
1739	340	256	1764	335	270
1740	230	173	1765	360	290
1741	230	173	1766	302	243
1742	300	226	1767	298	240
1743	278	209	1768	384	309
1744	240	181	1769	402	330
1745	225	169	1770	352	278
1746	215	162	1771	329	275
1747	210	171	1772	357	299
1748	269	219	1773	410	343
1749	323	263	1774	407	340
1750	337	274	1775	331	277
1751	255	208			

Source: *Livros dos Direitos dos Entradas dos Navios, nos. 146–174 (1727–1808), Alfândega do Funchal, Provedoria & Junta da Real Fazenda do Funchal, Arquivo Nacional da Torre do Tombo,* Lisbon, Portugal, and *Livros dos Direitos dos Saidas dos Navios, nos. 272–360 (1727–1833),* and *Livros das Visitas de Bordo, nos. 215–228 (1740–1778).*

1763), as well as the depredation of privateers during these periods, all seriously hindered the movement of ships between Boston and the Wine Islands. During the last conflict, several Massachusetts wine-trading vessels were captured or warned off by the threat of capture or by the high price of insurance premiums. Surplus wine sat in lodges in Funchal and eventually joined the next year's vintage as cargo. On other occasions, international conflict could favor consumption of Madeira. The prosecution of the conflict with Spain in 1762 and the Order in Council that was issued the following year prohibited the import of Spanish Canary wines into British North America; importers of beverages from Madeira and the Azores found themselves advantaged with the only low-duty wines on the market.[17]

The vagaries of harvest and weather further contributed to the instability. In the year 1764, for instance, the island experienced unusually plentiful rain and warm weather as well as an absence of ice or wind storms, leaf or root blight, and pestilent insects; in the end, 1764 produced the greatest crop ("the longest vintage") Madeira had seen in twenty years, much more than island firms could sell. A succession of large vintages throughout the mid 1760s (1763–1767) drove exports upwards. Yet, on account of an excessive amount of fog, hail during flowering, leaf fungus, and rain during the pressing, the crop "failed greatly" from 1768 through 1771, after which large vintages were again the norm for at least a half decade.[18]

17. Chambers, Hiccox & Chambers to Richard Derby, Jan. 13, 1757, and Lane & Booth to Richard Derby, Oct. 3, 1757, Richard Derby Papers, Peabody Essex Museum; and letters of June 22, 1762, Sept. 21, 1763, and Feb. 1, 1764, Newton & Gordon Letterbook, Cossart Archives, London. On privateers, see letters for Aug. 16, Oct. 20, and Nov. 12, 1761, in Newton & Gordon Letterbook. Conversely, peace saw the return of previous levels of movement and, usually, an increase in the flow of wines to America and Britain. The post-Seven Years' War period was especially good for the island's export trade, for in several years, shipping rose six-fold, nearly returning to its 1728 level, and exports climbed to a phenomenal 15,000 pipes.

18. The growers, occasionally wealthy landlords but more often peasant tenants, harvested grapes between mid August and early November and subjected them to two or three pressings. The sugar of the juice was fermented out, and often some of the juices were exposed to the heat of the sun and/or blended. The blended or unblended must was then sold to Funchal's export shippers, whom the growers and pressers often agreed in advance to supply over the long term; occasionally, it was sold to Portuguese middlemen (often landlords) who held the must in store until they sold it to the exporters at a considerable markup. The shippers or middlemen selected the must, often with the help of a full-time taster in their employ; directly or indirectly exposed it to the air and the heat of the sun for a time; perhaps blended it with different colors, tastes, or years; or perhaps let it sit

Throughout the glut of the 1760s, Madeira exporters and Massachusetts shippers brought the drink to America in greater and greater quantities. Wine traders in major American towns like Boston complained of Madeira wines as "a drug upon the market." In Halifax, Francis White could not get rid of the five pipes and eleven hogsheads that Richard Derby had first unloaded in Boston Harbor and then re-exported to Nova Scotia, hoping for a sale there. White's town was "full of wines," he complained to Derby in the summer of 1761, and "no demand." Public vendues and private auctions there killed the prospects of profitable private sales. The situation was no better later in the decade, when one finds Derby sending five pipes to Portsmouth, where they sat for twelve months, and then moving them to Philadelphia, where for two years he tried to sell them at public or private auction, but in vain. In the end, he sent them back to Madeira with five more equally unmarketable pipes he had stored in a rented Boston warehouse. In the midst of the surplus, one Madeira firm, Newton & Gordon, acutely perceived that, "as the London Market and all our Colonies are so glutted with our Wines," Madeira exporters had "no reason to expect a great demand."[19]

Notwithstanding the precariousness of the supply from year to year, the number of wine exporters continually grew over the course of the century, and this dramatically influenced their relationships with the Bostonian wine traders. Early in the century, as many as nine British merchants were resident in Madeira; by 1775, four times that number shipped wine across the sea, and at least six of these exporters had come from North America.[20] The "Factory," a trade association that served as the representa-

---

as common beverage wine; fortified the remainder with *aguardente* (brandy) if that was desired (fortification was not common practice until at least the 1760s and 1770s); placed the wines in casks; and housed them in stores in the vicinity of the capital city Funchal and scattered around the island. In fortifying wine, it was common to add 2 to 3 gallons of brandy to 110 gallons of wine at the time of the fermentation, and 2 to 3 more at the time of shipment.

19. Francis White to Richard Derby, Sept. 17, Nov. 19, 1761, Feb. 27, 1762, May 7, 1766, Richard Derby to Chambers, Hiccox & Denyer, Sept. 4, 1769, Richard Derby Papers; Newton & Gordon to Thomas Newton, Nov. 15, 1764, Thomas Newton to Newton & Gordon, Feb. 15, 1765, Newton & Gordon to Thomas Newton, May 15, 1765, Cossart & Gordon Papers.

20. Only two Americans, Richard Hill of Philadelphia and John Searle of New York, are known to have established mercantile houses in Madeira before 1763; they employed at least ten other Americans. From their arrival in 1739 and 1754, respectively, since their "interest . . . was naturally in America," they made use of their connections in appointing

tive of the British and British-American shippers resident on the island, supervised the activities and managed the complaints of the larger and more successful wine exporters against the governments of Madeira and Portugal.[21] Over the century, it grew from six to twelve firms. But even it could not control the explosion in the number of wine traders. New entrants into the merchant group—not all of whom became members of the Factory—received their first mention from other exporters during the 1750s. But by 1763 the presence of so many newly-established firms in the island began to "unavoidably hurt . . . Business."[22] New and old houses alike fought over the uncertain supply, competed over old customers, and vied for new ones; in general, they undertook "large adventures in wines" of both high and low quality and procured "business on any terms."[23]

New entries into the Madeira export group were, to a considerable degree, an unintended consequence of collusively maintained prices, a final conditioning factor that affected the behavior of Boston shippers, importers, and retailers. Indeed, the system of pricing wines—a cartel-like operation in which aldermen set the prices paid to the growers, and the customs house and the Factory set the prices charged by the exporters— worked against the interests of the Bostonians, insofar as it allowed "the

---

agents and finding customers overseas, and in becoming part-owners of American vessels and cargoes, by which means they engrossed the trade of the regions from which they had come. Thomas Lamar to Henry Hill, Feb. 8, 1766, Sarah Smith Papers, Historical Society of Pennsylvania, Philadelphia. In the 1750s and 1760s, the British residents who were principals of firms and also Factory members included: Robert Bissett, John Catanach, Charles Chambers, Thomas Cheap, James Denyer, James Gordon, William Haddock, Matthew Hiccox, Thomas Lamar, John Leacock, James Mowat, William Murdoch, Francis Newton, Michael Nowlan, John Pringle, John Scott, George Spence, and John Russell Spence. But there were many more British resident and working on the island than this list suggests. In 1728, there were 160 firms or exporters in Madeira, of which 15 were British. The bulk were Portuguese. In 1768, by contrast, the total number of exporters had only grown to 216, but the number of British and British Americans had climbed to 34, and there were many more actual exporters, since non-Portuguese merchants tended to cluster in firms.

21. There was a Factory in Madeira as early as 1722 (Graham Blandy, ed., *Copy of the Record of the Establishment on the Chaplaincy and Notes on the Old Factory at Madeira* [Funchal, 1959]). It was headed by the vice-consul, an official appointed by the British consul resident in Lisbon, whose office dated to 1583. Madeira did not gain its own consul until the British Crown appointed William Naish in 1754.

22. Johnston & Co. to Newton & Gordon, Oct. 25, 1763, Cossart & Gordon Papers.

23. Francis Newton to Newton & Gordon, Dec. 7, 1769, Cossart & Gordon Papers; and Feb. 18, 1767, Newton & Gordon Letterbook, Cossart Archives.

natives not only . . . an opportunity of making their own prices which have been and are still extravagantly high but also [a chance] of altering the mode of payment, by insisting on having bills of exchange on Lisbon or London for their best wines."[24] The prices the export shippers and middle-men paid the growers and pressers were set by the *vereadores* (aldermen) of Funchal's *camara municipal* (municipal chamber) in the middle of October after the first harvest and pressing.[25] In late December or early January, the officers of the *alfandega* (customs house) met and, after consulting the exporters, established a valuation price, which served as the basis of the duty that was levied on exports of the vintage. Soon thereafter, usually in January, the British Factory, taking into consideration the valuation price, met as a body and set shipping prices for the several qualities of export wines; no merchant who was a member of the Factory was to sell below the set prices.

As far as the extant records show, the price floors held among Factory members and non-members alike, at least throughout the eighteenth century. Moreover, in Madeira, the official Factory price of nearly all qualities of export wine at least doubled between 1725 and 1775, a period when the composite price index went up by only 34 percent.[26] The cost of London "Particular" (sometimes known as just "Particular"), the choicest wine, rose from £8 per pipe to £30. The increases on lower grades were less dramatic. From 1721 until 1759, prices rose sharply (by 325 percent); they stabilized between 1759 and 1769, jumped 15 percent in 1770, and finally leveled until the outbreak of the Revolution. On the other side of the Atlantic, in Massachusetts, the retail prices of Madeira also tripled, from roughly £9 per pipe in the second decade of the century to £29 in the 1750s.

How did this affect the wine trade of Boston's merchants and retailers? First of all, it led to increasingly high prices for them and their consumers. Soon, public patterns of consumption and attitudes toward the drink

24. Account of the Consul and Factory of Madeira, 74–76.

25. On the work of the *camara municipal* in the 17th century, see Duncan, *Atlantic Islands*, 61. In addition, the governor and his officers, as well as the Crown, introduced a host of laws and orders regulating the wine industry. See, for instance, letters of Mar. 28, 1763, July 7, 1768, May 13, 1770, Feb. 10, 1773, and Nov. 15, 1775, Newton & Gordon Letterbook, Cossart Archives. Export shippers bought in one of two ways: by exchanging their own imported dry goods or provisions for the growers' wines, or by paying for wines with currency (usually Spanish pistareens) or Lisbon bills of exchange. Often the merchants paid the growers in advance of the vintage.

26. Figures for the general price level over 50 years are given in John J. McCusker, *How Much Is That in Real Money? A Historical Price Index for Use as a Deflator of Money Values in the Economy of the United States* (Worcester, 1992), 341–342.

shifted. In 1767, when he temporarily declined doing any more business with his Madeira correspondent, Richard Derby uttered what many in Massachusetts had already concluded: "The price of your wines being so very high hath occasioned the consumption thereof to become very small in these parts." Derby's complaint came at the end of the four long vintages of the 1760s, when he may have sought some advantage in being recalcitrant. Four years later, even after a series of bad harvests, John Rowe wrote much the same to his own correspondents, Newton & Gordon: "The price of Madeira wines are so high that I cannot at present venture to speculate in them."[27] The fixing of high prices encouraged a "spirit of oeconomy" and forced many of Madeira's traditional consumers to forego the pleasure.

Moreover, these prices and the resulting public "oeconomy" contributed to the image of Madeira wine as a luxury good. Elite families like the Hancocks annually ordered two and sometimes four pipes from Madeira in the 1750s and 1760s, regardless of price, which they used at their own table. Similarly, they procured a pipe or two of "the very best Madeira wine" for friends and colleagues: Thomas Hancock did this in 1759 for the colony's governor; his nephew John Hancock did the same in 1767 for its treasurer. Then, in the same letter by which he placed the treasurer's order, John Hancock requested two pipes for his friends John and Jonathan Amory, two wealthy Boston merchants who were at that time strangers to Madeira's exporters, and six more pipes, which he planned to resell to several Boston "Public Houses, where the Best Company resorts."[28]

Secondly, as an eventual result of escalating prices overseas, Boston's merchants and retailers were forced to compete with new importers, retailers, and agents in the colonies. As the trade lost consumers, island exporters looked farther afield than they had previously in order to maintain their business. Some wine export firms took up a complementary trade in dry goods, although this was considered a risky move. Other firms began

27. Richard Derby to Scott, Pringle & Cheap, June 1, 1767, Richard Derby Letterbook 1760–1772, Acc. # 15,442, Peabody Essex Museum; and John Rowe to Newton & Gordon, Sept. 16, 1771, box 1/bundle 5, Cossart & Gordon Papers. On the price of wines in Madeira and America, see David Hancock, "Prices of Madeira Wine, 1703–1807" (unpublished paper, 1995). Massachusetts's wine prices were usually higher than those in New York, Pennsylvania, or South Carolina.

28. John Hancock to Lamar, Hill & Bisset, Jan. 20, Nov. 12, 1767, Hancock Papers, Special Collections, Harvard Business School, Boston. After the Revolution, Lamar, Hill & Bisset resumed shipping two pipes per year to Hancock. The luxury image of the wine was further burnished by the appearance at mid century of fine crystal drinking paraphernalia, such as decanters with "Madeira" etched in their sides, specially-sized tasting glasses, and silver bottle tags.

dealing in cheaper, lower-grade wines, newer Madeira varietals and blends, and traditional Canarian and Azorean wines. Still more firms extended their customer and correspondent network. The increasingly varied and heavily stocked stores of Madeira growers, middlemen, and exporters caused the exporters to seek out new markets for their wines: in America, where they believed the taste for their wines still raged but where consumers had never bought at lower prices or tasted finer grades; in England and Ireland, where the wines had not been popular before 1750; and in India, after the 1757 Battle of Plassey and the East India Company's subsequent push for territorial and military control.[29] In short, Madeira exporters began marketing their wine extensively by pushing their goods in new markets in Britain and India, and intensively by establishing new contacts in America and encouraging their old correspondents there to expand their customer bases.

Madeira's merchants sent more wine to America on their own account, in particular, and pressured their correspondents to accept the consignments. In 1764, after the Sugar Act slapped a £7 per ton duty on wine, but before it was levied, Newton & Gordon took the bold step of loading a ship with the beverage and sending it to New York. Most firms did the same. Once taken, this measure became a commonplace, even after the duty was well entrenched. The inducement for such a risky venture, Newton & Gordon informed their correspondent Thomas Newton, was that it appeared "obvious & clear to us that the prices of wine must rise considerably with you on account of the high Duty laid on Wines imported into America." Such a move on their own account, of course, could be doubly hazardous, for dumping overseas forced the firms to grant lenient terms of repayment and left them "in very great advance" to those they supplied.[30]

As a consequence, island exporters pushed their correspondents to peddle their wines and seek new orders more aggressively in the areas the colonists had long managed.[31] And they forcefully introduced themselves into new, largely untapped markets like Charleston and Philadelphia in

29. Account of the Consul and Factory of Madeira, 75. For an example of one firm's efforts in Britain, sending a partner expressly to London "to be of service to the House" and, in particular, to capture the metropolitan tavern trade, see Newton & Gordon to Thomas Newton, May 15, 1765, and Francis Newton to Newton & Gordon, May 6, 1759, and Oct. 11, 1771, Cossart & Gordon Papers.

30. Newton & Gordon to Thomas Newton, May 26, 1764, Jan. 24, 1765, Cossart & Gordon Papers.

31. Newton & Gordon to Thomas Newton, Nov. 15, 1764, Cossart & Gordon Papers. A similar push is noticeable in the dealings of Burgess & Nowlan, Spence & Leacock, Searle Brothers, and Lamar, Hill & Bisset.

search of more customers. Newton & Gordon, for instance, first made an attempt on Boston in the early 1760s, begging Thomas Newton, a partner in the business along with his brother Francis, to visit the town and solicit the merchants there. After numerous delays, Newton traveled north in July 1762, only to find that Lott Hall had engrossed the retail wine business of "most the whole of the people in the place."

Nevertheless, Newton was undaunted. He befriended John Rowe, whom he found to be "a person of much Worth & good Fortune" with "very great Interest" in the town; in Rowe, he saw the best possible "means of procuring an Opening to a larger Correspondence" despite Hall's dominance. For his part, Rowe offered "at any time" to ship Newton & Gordon any fish they desired and proposed that if the Funchal market proved encouraging a joint concern between Rowe, Jacob Oliver (a Marblehead sea captain and fish exporter), and Newton & Gordon might be launched. "Whenever you think convenient to consign anything to me," Rowe suggested, "you may depend on attention to your interests." In response, there ensued several transactions, which involved relatively large shipments—20 or 21 pipes of wine on Rowe's account and risk, as return for 1,000 quintals of cod; another consignment of 20 pipes of best London Particular the following year for 400 quintals of cod, 13,490 feet of pine boards, and 1,500 white oak barrel staves; and finally in 1764, 15 pipes—until the relationship collapsed in a squabble over the weight of a cargo of Newfoundland fish, Rowe claiming that the fish he had sent weighed more than the poundage Newton & Gordon acknowledged receiving.

On the same trip to New England, Thomas Newton struck up similar correspondences with Jeremiah Lee of Salem, Thomas Gerry, Sr. and Jr., of Marblehead, Jacob Fowler of Marblehead, and Col. Jonathan Bagley near Newburyport. Two years after Newton's Boston journey, in 1764, when Newton & Gordon realized that no Madeira merchant had captured the Philadelphia market for "particular wines," they again requested their representative to use his "best endeavours to introduce us" in that town, and there ensued a long and profitable correspondence with the house of Baynton & Wharton.[32]

32. John Rowe to Newton & Gordon, Nov. 9, 1762, Thomas Newton to Newton & Gordon, July 10, 1762, Newton & Gordon to Thomas Newton, Nov. 15, 1764, Cossart & Gordon Papers. Rowe's debt of 714$765 (approximately £195 sterling), the balance of his Account Current, was still unpaid in 1788, several years after his death. Before Thomas Newton made his journey to Boston in 1762, Newton & Gordon had only infrequently and somewhat unsuccessfully corresponded with Alexander Gordon, Robert Sloane, and Richard Wiltshire, all of Boston.

Ultimately, this growth in the number of wine importers, retailers, and agents in Britain's colonies led to a rise in the number of Madeira consumers. More people were buying the drink and storing it in their homes. This was dramatically so in Britain and India, where by all accounts imports were inconsequential before 1750. But it was also true in Boston. From a preliminary comparative investigation of the inventories of those individuals who lived or worked in the vicinity of Boston and whose estates were probated during the 1710s, it appears that only one out of every thirty-eight estateholders kept Madeira or Azorean wines in his cellar in the early years of the century. Fifty years later, at a time when the wine's luxury status was emerging, one out of every eighteen held them. But personal stores are only the tip of the iceberg. Surely, far more people consumed wine at the numerous taverns and inns of Suffolk County and more taverns offered the drink on a regular basis with each passing decade. So much so that by mid century one Englishman visiting Boston commented that, while "no good beer" was to be found anywhere in New England, Madeira wines and rum punches made from Caribbean sugars distilled in New England were "the liquors they drink in common."[33]

The emerging merchants and entrepreneurs of New York, Philadelphia, and Charleston responded to the overtures from the Madeira traders, while merchants from other cities broke into the trade with greater frequency and effectiveness. Before 1739, for example, only one or two of Philadelphia's firms had conducted a direct correspondence with a Madeira exporter. Rather, a merchant like John Reynell preferred to avail himself of the intermediating services of New Englanders. Soon, however, the establishment of a firm by the erstwhile Philadelphia doctor Richard Hill and the remarkable growth of Philadelphia's wheat and flour trade alongside the rising need of southern Europe for these foodstuffs motivated the city's largest firms, including Baynton & Wharton, Kearny & Gilbert, Francis & Tilghman, and Willing & Morris, to establish direct relations. Thereafter, as importers in other colonial cities began to establish dominance over their own hinterlands, Philadelphia's suppliers served as the conduit by which gentlemen and tavernkeepers in Baltimore and Lancaster, as well as customers in a host of much smaller towns, procured Madeira wines.

33. Probate Records, Massachusetts State Archives, Boston. For Joseph Bennett's "The History of New England, 1740," see Mss. Sparks 2, Houghton Library, Harvard University, Cambridge. Cider was what "the generality of the people drink with their meals."

Yet other factors were also at work. In Boston as in competing markets, importers began to promote their wines more aggressively. With the increase in shipments came a proliferation of varieties. An exhaustive survey of Boston newspapers covering the years for which naval office shipping lists have survived reveals not only the expansion of consumer choice in Atlantic wines in the town, but also the desire to exploit such expansion. During 1717 and 1718, for instance, seven named Boston merchants and two unnamed traders selling at "public vendue" advertised on fifteen occasions. Through tersely written ads, they hawked four different kinds of imported wines—Madeira, Fayal, Canary, and "Strong Spirits of Wine." Their adjectives were plain, the most descriptive being either "choice" or "good." In three of the ads, wine was one of a number of goods listed, along with brandy, aniseed water, and cinnamon water; new cables from four to ten inches; Holland, German, and Lubeck duck; Spanish iron; best Dutch twine; and the like.[34] By the 1750s and 1760s, a marketing explosion had occurred. Some twenty merchants advertised in the newspapers in these decades; seventeen notices appeared in 1758, and sixty-four in 1765.[35] In addition to Madeira, Fayal, and Canary wines, these offered white and red French, Malaga, Mountain Malaga, Lisbon, Caccovillo, Perferdor, and St. Michael's. Now importers and retailers pronounced their wines "rich," "old," and "excellent," and they "warranted [them to be] good and stored from the kiln." Their descriptions had become more elaborate, and they paid greater attention to color and quality.[36]

In part a function of similar aggressive entrepreneurial activities by merchants elsewhere, Boston's loss of market share in Madeira wine accords strongly with what historians have discovered about Boston's general decline before the outbreak of the Revolution. Unlike other towns at mid century, Boston's economy was not growing or, at least, not growing much. Although there was recognizable expansion before 1720, the butchering, distilling, and shipbuilding industries fell into decline in the decades that

34. The known advertisers were: John Colman, Thomas Grosse, Thomas Steel, George Bethune, Ambrose Vincent, Abiel Walley, and Jacob Wendell.

35. Among them were: Nathaniel Bethune, William Buttar, Chase & Speakman, Nathaniel Cossin, Andrew Craigie, Samuel Fletcher, James Griffin, Samuel Hughes, William Hunt, Ralph Inman, Daniel Malcom, John Moore, John Marston, Poole & Clarke, Edmund Quincy, Dr. Bezaleel Tappan, and Jonathan Williams.

36. Nearly every advertisement for wine is concluded with an extensive list of "sundry other goods." Surprisingly, these wines, which were increasingly varied, were more frequently coupled with a greater assortment of other goods than they had been in 1717 and 1718.

followed as similar enterprises sprang up elsewhere; at the same time, Boston's tax base dwindled, and the value of Massachusetts's provincial currency fell. After 1740, even the town's fishing industry, long a bulwark of the economy, stagnated.[37] Most dramatic was the stagnation of shipping in and out of Boston's port. The naval office shipping lists provide a rough comparative picture. On average, some 457 ships cleared the port each year, from 1714 to 1717. Forty to fifty years later, in the period 1753 to 1764, that number had fallen to 400.[38] The comparison with other ports is striking: Charleston clearances more than doubled over the decades, from 198 in 1731 to 429 in 1768; New York clearances rose in a similar fashion, from an annual average of 215 in 1715–1718 to 480 in 1768; and Philadelphia clearances more than tripled—from 185 in 1733 to 641 in 1768.[39] Whereas Boston had dominated mainland American shipping in the early part of the century, it had dropped to fourth place in clearances by the 1760s.

Various reasons account for the general relative decline.[40] First of all, in an age without communications technology, so that individuals were unable to influence events when they were absent the scene, geography frustrated business activity. The rocky, swampy land surrounding the port town checked Boston's commerce, as did the lack of easy, natural access to the interior via a deep and extensive navigable river system such as Newburyport enjoyed with the Merrimack; the Charles and the Mystic were relatively useless for that purpose. Moreover, New England contained no vast tracts of easily improved farmland; the region's mediocre soil discouraged agricultural production. Cities like New York, Philadelphia, and Charleston were better endowed with rich hinterlands and easier routes to them.

War and the opportunities it provided to other colonies also frustrated the growth of Boston's imports and exports. Conflict with Spain between

37. Warden, "Inequality," 589; Lydon, "Fish for Gold," 556, 561–563, Table 2. See also James Birket, *Some Cursory Remarks . . . 1750–1751* (New Haven, 1916), 23.

38. However, average total registered vessel tonnage clearing the port rose nearly 20 percent, from 21,000 to 25,000 tons, because shippers employed larger, heavier vessels as the century wore on.

39. U.S. Department of Commerce–Bureau of the Census, *Historical Statistics of the United States, Colonial Times to 1979*, part 2 (Washington, D.C., 1976), Ser. Z 266–285, 1180–1181.

40. The most powerful analysis of Boston's development as a port town appears in Jacob M. Price, "Economic Function and the Growth of American Port Towns in the Eighteenth Century," *Perspectives in American History* 8(1974):123–186. The paragraphs that follow draw heavily on this account.

1739 and 1748 temporarily cut Boston's commercial ties to southern Europe. During the War of Austrian Succession, provisions merchants from the middle colonies prospered in contrast to those in New England. They developed a business of delivering to Europe foods grown in their interiors; at the end of the war, the same enterprisers rushed in to fill the orders of the Spaniards and Portuguese who, because of bad harvests and population growth in Iberia, needed wheat and corn in particular. The middle colonies excelled in growing these crops, which Britain could not provide on account of its own disastrous harvests; the crops fared poorly in New England in any event. Thus war opened a channel that was not easily closed.[41]

Population figures offer some evidence about commercial growth. After 1740, the population of Boston stopped growing. From some 6,700 inhabitants in 1700, Boston's population rose to 17,000 in 1740, when it peaked. It did not reach that height again until the 1780s, even though the population of Massachusetts more than doubled and that of the thirteen colonies quadrupled in the fifty years between 1740 and 1790. In 1750, Boston was still the most populous town in the colonies, but by 1775, it had fallen to third place, behind Philadelphia and New York.[42] The static customer base was as much a frustration to the further expansion of trade in Boston as it was a by-product of that expansion elsewhere, especially in the 1750s and 1760s when Boston was rocked by frequent short-term economic dislocations.

In short, Boston lost its dominance in the North American wine trade for the same reason that it lost in most other trades—other towns in other colonies grew faster and larger, at a time when Madeira exporters were aggressively seeking new customers and correspondents overseas. The subsequent burst of transatlantic commercial activity is not really surprising; merchants in growing communities, with rapidly developing economies, frequently establish their own mercantile links to the source of bulk commodities. The demographic and economic rise of all America made Boston's loss almost inevitable.

One question arising out of Boston's relative decline in the wine trade is, why did the town lose so much of its home market to other coastal commu-

41. The want of institutional endowments also kept Boston from competing effectively with much younger port towns. Unlike Philadelphia, for instance, Boston possessed no banks and few insurance houses. It enjoyed few regulations or organizations that controlled the conduct of trade. And its currency, fluctuating wildly, moved generally downwards.

42. Carl Bridenbaugh, *Cities in Revolt: Urban Life in America, 1743–1776* (New York, 1971), 5, 216–217; Rossiter, *Century of Population Growth*, 11, 78; Price, "Port Towns," 176.

nities, Salem in particular? The growth of the North Shore town especially bedeviled the Boston merchant groups. While Boston's population stabilized or declined, Salem's rose from 2,200 in 1692 to 3,300 in 1759 and 7,921 in 1790, and with the increase, there emerged a bigger, more aggressive importing and retailing community. In the seventeenth century, Boston merchants had satisfied the bulk of this population's needs, and Salem merchants acted as their agents. But as the eighteenth century progressed, Salem merchants began to assert their independence. By moving into branches of overseas trade long dominated by the Bostonians, they started to satisfy as principals the growing demand in Salem for foreign manufactures and comestibles.

Part of the explanation for this is that Salem was an easier and cheaper place to carry on a trading business at mid century. Facilities and services were as available there as in Boston: in 1760, Salem had thirty wharves, forty warehouses, and registered ninety-seven ships. A preliminary investigation seems to suggest that wharfage, truckage, and storage fees were half what they were in Boston, and commission fees for selling another's goods were two-thirds the Boston rate. Wharf hands were as plentiful as in Boston, but their wages less. Wharves were not so crowded, a circumstance that reduced the time that ships sat idle at anchor. Shippers favoring Salem with their custom thus enjoyed lower operating costs. Then too, in a smaller, more closely-knit community like Salem, it may also have been less likely that cargo would be pilfered or handled by unknown persons.[43]

In effect, Salem had what Boston had to offer, only cheaper. Shipping regulations did not differ markedly between the two towns. No guild-like rules of who could and could not trade or how the trade should be conducted were ever enacted in either place. Wine exports to both communities were subject to the same colonial impost. Yet it does seem that, in the decade after 1764, Salem may have been more relaxed with respect to the enforcement of imperial laws. In Boston, where officials made strong attempts to enforce the Sugar Act with high-profile raids on the cargoes of wine traders like Daniel Malcom and John Hancock, the illegal or questionable importation of certain kinds and amounts of wine was scrutinized by officer and merchant alike. In Salem, where no such *cause célèbre* arose, the mood was such that minor infractions were overlooked. The custom prevalent in Massachusetts of allowing wine merchants to import several

43. Richard J. Morris, "Urban Population Migration in Revolutionary America: The Case of Salem, Massachusetts," *Journal of Urban History* 9(1982):3–30; and Richard Derby Letterbook, passim.

hogsheads of wine for their own or their friends' private consumption or "to pass them off as ships' stores" was certainly questioned and to some extent curtailed in Boston, for instance, whereas in Salem it flourished much as it had before.[44]

In addition, with respect to the wine trade, Salem enjoyed a closer proximity to shipping-related industries. With easier and quicker access to the Atlantic fisheries and the rivers and bays suitable for harvesting timber, Salem replaced Boston as a center for fishing and shipbuilding. Consider just the fisheries. At its height, Massachusetts shipping satisfied a quarter of the Iberian demand for this commodity. Boston traders' share of that quarter fell precipitously after the outbreak of the French and Indian Wars, from roughly 40,000 quintals in 1755 to 5,000 in 1774; in contrast, Salem's exports only fell from 123,000 quintals in 1756 to 117,000 in 1774. Proximity to the fishing banks and the fishermen (who had always chiefly resided at Marblehead and Gloucester) gave Salem shippers a few days' or weeks' edge over their Boston competitors in supplying the Wine Islands with cod, the one commodity, after bills on London, that served as a medium of exchange in the Madeira trade. Since fish still operated as a form of alternative currency in the wine trade and Salem fish were fresher and cheaper than Boston fish, which were generally purchased through Salem suppliers, Boston suffered.[45] The daily presence of Salem's wine-trading merchants on the docks and ships wrangling with men who were often their relatives allowed the merchants of the North Shore to engross the better catches of fish.[46]

Three economic reasons why Boston traders lost their commanding share of the North American market for Madeira wine over the second and third quarters of the eighteenth century have emerged: the new Madeira exporters' response to high prices and their solicitation of new customers; the decision of shippers, importers, and retailers in other American ports to disintermediate the Bostonians; and the higher costs of doing business in Boston compared to local competitors. Still, one should ask who the Boston

44. The custom is described in Francis Bernard, *Select Letters on the Trade and Government of America* (London, 1774), 2, 4.

45. Bartered goods were often preferred to London bills of exchange. Henry Leddel to Robert Treat Paine, May 15, 1753, Stephen T. Riley and Edward W. Hanson, eds., *The Papers of Robert Treat Paine, Collections of the Massachusetts Historical Society* 87(1992): 195.

46. Newton & Gordon to Thomas Newton, Feb. 28, 1765, Cossart & Gordon Papers.

traders were, and whether there was something about this group that helps to explain the town's loss.

Initially, Boston's "community" of wine traders was small. At least nine men sold wine in Boston in the first two decades of the eighteenth century: wealthy merchant and rum distiller Thomas Amory, George Bethune, John Colman, Thomas Grosse, tavernkeeper Thomas Selby, Thomas Steel, Ambrose Vincent, Abiel Walley, and Jacob Wendell. At least ten others were involved in shipping it to the town.[47] One in this group, Thomas Selby, had emigrated from England in the first decade of the century and with the assistance of wealthy merchant Jonathan Belcher had managed the Crown Coffee House on Long Wharf from 1714; at his death in 1725, he possessed a cache of drink valued at £1,538. Three different qualities of Madeira wine comprised 49 percent of the supply; the rest was spread among Fayal and Vidonia from the Azores, Port, Tent, and Canary. Selby's tavern offered a relatively elite wine drinker's fare: seven times as much wine as spirits was available for consumption.[48] Nevertheless, Selby's operation was typical, in the sense that it was from tavernkeepers like him that the bulk of the population bought wine and spirits; the remainder, usually the well-to-do, arranged for individual consignments directly from island exporters.

Wine merchants and, in particular, tavern proprietors and dram-shop retailers multiplied in each succeeding decade of the first half-century. Their growth, David Conroy convincingly reports, was the result of "persistent popular resistance to the repression of customary drinking habits," the increase in the number of unemployed workers in Boston for whom tavernkeeping was regarded as useful employment, and the spread of more relaxed attitudes among London-appointed and -oriented royal officials

47. The number of early shippers and importers is difficult to determine with precision. The records of the port kept by the clerk of the naval office ("the naval office shipping lists") name only the captains of the ships. Nevertheless, the names of retailers and importers can be gleaned from contemporary probate inventories, account books, and newspapers. As an example of the latter, see *Boston News-Letter*, May 6, July 8, 10, 15, Aug. 12, 19, 26, Sept. 9, 16, Oct. 14, 21, Nov. 25, 1717, June 30, Aug. 11, 25, 1718. Vol. 2 of William Bolton's Madeira letters for the years 1701–1714 lists 15 ships (naming 11 captains: Armitage, Joseph Barry, Bedford, Cravatt, Stephen Eastwick, Thomas Gwyn, John, John Osborn, Richard Pilcher, Samuel Sanders, Thomas Steel) that carried wine from Madeira to Boston. Blandy, *Bolton Letters*.

48. Inventory of Thomas Selby, Oct. 23, 1727, vol. 25, ff. 534–535, Suffolk County Probate Records, Massachusetts State Archives, Boston. Conroy, in "Culture and Politics" 181–182, presents incomplete data on Selby's cellar. The holdings of a less-well-endowed innholder, James Pitson of Boston, are listed on ff. 360–364 of vol. 34 of the Suffolk County Probate Records. Pitson dealt mainly in cider.

and their local political allies.[49] But it was equally the result of the aggressive overtures made by Madeira's exporters, especially during the 1740s and 1750s. Indeed, by mid century, the local merchant group had grown startlingly: between 1752 and 1765, some 383 men shipped, imported, retailed, or exported wine in Massachusetts; of these, 198 lived and worked in Boston.[50] The structure of the business had not changed to this degree; in these years wine trading was still dominated by a small number of principals, although now it embraced a large number of secondary and tertiary participants. One might have recognized only seventeen merchants, men like John Rowe, as carrying on a trade in the commodity, inasmuch as each imported it on six or more occasions.[51] (Significantly, none of the seventeen imported wine at a rate of as much as one shipment per year.) Some 114 merchants imported only once. Most of Boston's traders appear to have been importing for their personal or their friends' use, acquiring one or two pipes from time to time. Over the fourteen-year period, the seventeen large-scale traders each averaged eight incoming shipments; each of these shipments contained on average seventeen pipes; thus, over the whole period, each large trader brought in the equivalent of 1,870 gallons of wine, which would have filled roughly 468 bottles. The remaining 181 traders averaged three shipments, each of which contained, on average, fourteen pipes.[52]

Throughout the century, Boston's wine traders typically were "general merchants." They did not specialize in the sense that they imported and sold wine exclusively. In the 1752–1765 period, more than half of the 198 Boston traders—shippers and importers of wine—were described simply as "merchants," a term that, earlier in the century, meant any trader in goods.

49. Conroy, "Culture and Politics," 179.

50. A database of the vital statistics and social activities of the 383 has been constructed, drawing on the Thwing Index at the M.H.S., and the various reference works and manuscript collections cited in the notes that follow. To the 383, culled from owner entries in the naval office shipping lists, should also be added 9 firms–Chase & Speakman, Nathaniel Cossin, Andrew Craigie, Samuel Fletcher, William Hunt, John Moore, Poole & Clarke, Edmund Quincy, and Jonathan Williams–who advertised in newspapers or left manuscript papers but did not concern themselves with shipping. See *Boston News-Letter*, and *Boston Weekly Advertiser*, 1758, 1765; Amory Letter Books, Amory Papers, Library of Congress, Washington, D.C.; and Edmund Quincy (1703–1788) Papers, M.H.S.

51. These 17 imported wine on at least 6 different occasions between 1752 and 1765: John Winniett (15 vessels), John Rowe (13), Robert Gould (10), John Homer (10), William Wimble (10), Sylvester Drew (9), Samuel Sturgis (8), Solomon Davis (7), William Mackay (7), Murtaugh McCarroll (7), Edward Payne (7), Noah Doggett (6), Timothy Fitch (6), James Griffin (6), William Powell (6), Samuel Welles (6), and Samuel Wentworth (6).

52. Amounts of wine imports are given in Table 1.

But by 1750, its original meaning had been considerably narrowed, to indicate an importer or exporter who had dealings with foreign countries.[53] Yet even this refinement was broad enough to encompass, in addition to wine importing and re-exporting, the work of tavernkeepers and shop-keepers who sold for consumption on or off their premises and dealt indi-rectly with Madeira's exporters. John Rowe, himself a prominent fish ex-porter and the second most frequent wine importer of the period, was in the common sense of the day no more notable a wine merchant than John Marston, the proprietor of the Golden Ball in Merchants Row, or Enoch Brown, a substantial dry goods merchant, who died with 2,100 gallons of the wine and brandy that he sold to his customers along with his silks, linens, hose, and waistcoats.[54] Yet, whatever their specific focus, most of the wine traders in this group operated as sole enterprisers. Firms were infre-quent: only sixteen men worked in partnership, none of whom worked in a firm with more than two principals.[55] One-sixth of the traders, including sea captains, were known as "mariners." The other third worked as apothe-caries, bakers, boat builders, braziers, bricklayers, brokers, cabinetmakers, chandlers, distillers, innholders, ministers, or schoolmasters.[56] Not a single

53. Samuel Johnson, *A Dictionary* (London, 1755); Thomas Sheridan, *A General Dic-tionary of the English Language*, vol. 2 (London, 1780); and Timothy Cunningham, *The Laws of Bills of Exchange, Promissory Notes, Bank-Notes, and Insurances* (London, 1761), 4, n. 1. Other contemporary descriptions appear in R. Campbell, *The London Tradesman* (London, 1747), 284–285; Wyndham Beawes, *Lex Mercatoria Rediviva: Or, The Mer-chant's Directory* (London, 1761), 29–40; and Thomas Mortimer, *The Universal Director* (London, 1763), 3:3–4. According to Campbell, one who mixed and blended wines was a "wine-cooper"; one who bought "neat Wines" and then sold them was a "vintner." *London Tradesman*, 268–270. An examination of the newspaper advertisements and business pa-pers of the 198 merchants in the sample reveals that a merchant's portfolio was often filled with items running the gamut from clothing, books, and candles to sugar, tobacco, and spices; it underscores the general nature of the trade of many entrepreneurs.

54. Inventory of Enoch Brown, vol. 86, ff. 473–475, Suffolk County Probate Records. John Marston, the proprietor of the Golden Ball in Merchants Row from at least 1757 until 1775 and of the Bunch of Grapes on King Street (now State Street) from 1775 to 1785, appears to have sold wines for consumption on or off the premises. For the stock of his tavern at the time of his death in 1786, see vol. 86, ff. 12–15, Suffolk County Probate Records. On Marston and his taverns, see Samuel A. Drake, *Old Boston Taverns and Tavern Clubs* (Boston, 1917), 83.

55. Partnerships included: Nathaniel & George Bethune, Peter Boyer & William Thompson, Bossenger & Foster, Chase & Speakman, Benjamin & Edward Davis, Henry Lloyd & Shrimpton Hutchinson, Poole & Clarke, and John & Thomas Stevenson.

56. See, for example, the non-wine orientation of wine importers in the D. S. Greenough Papers, box 1751–1758, folder January–March 1757, and Account Book 1770–1771, bound vol. 1, Amory Family Papers, M.H.S.

trader in Boston was ever called a "wine-merchant," "vintner," or "wine-cooper," to wit, a specialist, between 1752 and 1765.

Wine merchants' primary and secondary business concerns were varied. Four of the larger traders, for instance, were widely recognized as leading American suppliers to North America's coastal communities; another four had significant dealings in southern Europe, and nine in the British West Indies. The business of Bostonian John Rowe serves as an important example. Regarded by many as primarily a fish merchant, in a typical year during the 1760s he would leave Boston with his New England or Newfoundland cod and return with cloth, clothing, stationery, or wine that he had picked up in Madeira.[57] A similar custom grew up among Joseph Green, who shipped New England-distilled rum, Samuel Welles, who exported New England-grown foodstuffs to the West Indies, his brother Arnold, who shipped them to Quebec, and the Bethune brothers, who provided them to the Newfoundland fisheries; for these merchants, Madeira products were frequently the only return cargo. Yet others, like Rowe, found their own valuable trading commodities and exchange mediums to complement their import portfolios: Thomas Cushing, who imported British woolens, John Phillips, who imported West Indian produce, and Benjamin Brandon, who imported English dry goods and stationery.[58] Overall, bilateral traders were perhaps the most common, yet some dealt with several regions at the same time, as did Samuel Sturgis, who imported raisins, rum, dry goods, and marine supplies from at least four different parts of the British Atlantic community. Not one wine trader dealt exclusively with the Wine Islands.[59]

In contrast to the variety of their primary or complementary businesses, the Boston wine traders were characterized by a pervasive cultural homogeneity. Boston's wine-trading community at mid century was not as diverse as that of Philadelphia. Many traders appear to have been born in the vicinity of Boston but not necessarily in the town itself, although a general lack of hard evidence about places of birth makes it difficult to be precise.[60]

57. Anne Rowe Cunningham, ed., *Letters and Diary of John Rowe, Boston Merchant, 1759–1762 & 1764–1779* (Boston, 1903), passim. For similar behavior earlier in the century, see Thomas Amory Account Book, 1720–1728, ff. 2–8, M.H.S.

58. The receipts of the grocer Caleb Davis provide excellent examples of the complementarity of wine to the trades of most Boston businessmen. Caleb Davis Papers, vols. 1–61 (1752–1765), M.H.S.

59. Since the necessary account books do not exist, it is not possible to determine for Boston merchants what share of their businesses they devoted to wine at various times in their careers.

60. Further evidence of this provinciality is found in a study of career paths. No mer-

Seven of Boston's 198 wine shippers and traders definitely were born in Britain—one in Ireland, two in Scotland, and four in England—and, given the state of our knowledge about colonists' places of birth and the extent of migration in the eighteenth century, this is certainly a minimum.[61] While they followed a variety of career paths, most traders appear to have been born into families of middling rank with some previous connection to overseas commerce, like the noted humorist Joseph Green, the son of a sea captain, or Joseph Lee, the son of a Boston shipbuilder. Many were the sons or nephews of merchants, like Nathaniel Bethune, the son of wine trader George Bethune, or Samuel and Arnold Welles, the sons of the merchant and councillor Samuel Welles. Only three were members of commercial dynasties spanning three or more generations in the colony.[62] Very few were born or married into families possessing significant wealth or power. John Erving, Sr., the son of a merchant reputed to be the richest man in colonial Boston and the son-in-law of Gov. William Shirley; Samuel Wentworth, the son of Lt. Gov. John Wentworth; Arnold Welles, son of a provincial councillor; and John Brandon, who married the sister of Josiah Willard, the province secretary—these are exceptions.

Few wine traders were extensively educated. Although it would have been surprising if these merchants had not received some form of primary and secondary education before they went into the counting house, as Joseph Green, Jr., did at the South Grammar School, most did not attend college. Only 17 of the 198 attended Harvard; none went to Yale. Nor is there a record of any merchant taking the Grand Tour or attending an Inn of Court or a university in Britain.

Birth and education notwithstanding, the men in this group were firmly fixed in Boston's establishment. Nearly all adhered to traditional creeds: of the forty-seven merchants whose religious affiliation can be determined with certainty from church and testamentary records, 60 percent were Congregationalist and 38 percent were Anglican. Only 2 percent were Presbyterian. As a further testament to their orthodoxy, nearly all seem to have participated in government at some level. Over a third held a signifi-

---

chant, for instance, appears to have acquired his start in trade through foreign contacts or experiences.

61. In Ireland: Hugh Tarbutt; in Scotland: John Erving, Sr., and Archibald McNeil; and in England: John Rowe, Richard Smith, Nathaniel Taylor, and James Thompson.

62. These were Thomas Cushing, Shrimpton Hutchinson, and Thomas Cushing III. Indeed, a majority did not marry, or at least their marriages were not recorded by Boston churches or in probate records. Only 41 percent are known to have wed at least once.

cant town or county political office, such as treasurer, warden, register and clerk of probate, justice of the peace, or selectman—an unusually high percentage in an age when it was wholly acceptable and common to pay a fine rather than hold an office. Several wine traders held judgeships, as did Samuel Wentworth, a J.P. of Suffolk County; one, Thomas Cushing, rose to become lieutenant governor.[63]

Although this was not a trade dominated by "merchant princes," most of the wine shippers and importers enjoyed a significant degree of comfort, somewhere near the top of the scale. In 1771, the Boston wine traders for whom records have survived owned, on average, £544 sterling in assessed taxable wealth (the sum of the value of their merchandise, factorage and commissions, money lent at interest, and the annual value of their real estate), roughly twice the amount owned by the average 1771 taxpayer. At the same time, each Boston wine trader owned on average 172 tons of shipping, the approximate equivalent of three ships' cargo.[64] None later went bankrupt, although many fell on hard times, especially as the Revolution advanced. Furthermore, probate inventories indicate that at the time of their deaths, these wine traders owned estates valued on average at £2,068 sterling, four times the average wealth of the probated Boston inhabitant in 1774.[65]

The estate of Capt. Daniel Malcom was typical. In 1769, he left a house

63. Offices held are listed in Robert F. Seybolt, *The Town Officials of Colonial Boston, 1634–1775* (Cambridge, Mass., 1939).

64. Unless otherwise stated, monetary amounts will be expressed as pounds sterling; conversions are calculated with the assistance of John J. McCusker, *Money and Exchange* (Chapel Hill, 1978). Some 67 merchants of the 198 were rated in the 1771 assessment, and their assessed wealth ranged from £9 to £11,290. Another 25 of the 198 had already died, and 2 had moved from Boston. About the rest, nothing is known. The tax list is published as Bettye Hobbs Pruitt, ed., *Massachusetts Tax Valuation List of 1771* (Boston, 1978), 2–46. For averages, see James A. Henretta, "Economic Development and Social Structure in Colonial Boston," *The William and Mary Quarterly*, 3d ser., 22(1965):75–92, esp. Tables II and III. For a discussion of the interpretative problems raised by this list, see Warden, "Inequality," 604–608.

65. Some 46 probate inventories were recorded or have survived for this group. In addition, four merchants left wills without inventories, and one inventory listed no value at the end. For contemporary levels of wealth, see Gary B. Nash, "Urban Wealth and Poverty in Pre-Revolutionary America," *Journal of Interdisciplinary History* 6(1976):569; Alice H. Jones, *Wealth of a Nation to Be: The American Colonies on the Eve of the Revolution* (New York, 1980), 357, 377 (per capita total physical wealth without slaves and servants averaged £318); Gloria Main, "Inequality in Early America," *Journal of Interdisciplinary History* 7(1977):565, Table 2 (the average probated estate = £163).

and land on Fleet Street, a house and land in Boylston Street, a warehouse and land in King Street, shares in the *Rose*, the *Fanny & Jenny*, and the *Rainbow*, a gold watch, and 112 pounds of candied raisins. The appointments of his house in Boylston Street bespeak a life of comfort and ease: furniture made of mahogany or walnut filled the rooms, an eight-day clock stood in the hall, four looking glasses and twenty-five framed and glass-covered prints (including one "glass picture of Mr. Wilks") graced the walls, Scotch carpets covered the floors, and two pipes of Fayal wine, one hogshead of Jamaica rum, and six gallons of raspberry rum lay in the cellar. But nowhere does one find gold service or silk fabrics, or even much silver tableware or china.[66]

Unlike Malcom, who became one of the most belligerent opponents of the government in the 1760s, most of the traders left no indication of their political beliefs; they were seldom given to public or even written expressions of non-commercial opinions.[67] As for the quarter who did make their views known, the revolutionary agitation that slowly drove a wedge in Boston's commercial society found them on both sides of the issue. The majority (thirty merchants) opposed the general trend of imperial legislation in the 1760s (which among other things doubled the duty on Madeira wine) and supported the war effort as "Patriots." Nearly all of them were charter members of the 1763 Society for Encouraging Trade and Commerce; a third were later accused of smuggling; and a similar number owned or invested in privateering voyages against the British during the Revolution. Another thirteen merchants were "Friends of the Government" and eventually adopted Loyalist positions. Only four—Samuel Grant, Shrimpton Hutchinson, Joseph Lee, and John Welch—are known to have stayed neutral, although, in light of the silence of so many others, the actual number may have been much greater.[68]

66. Probate Inventory of Daniel Malcom, Nov. 24, 1769, vol. 68, f. 388, Suffolk County Probate Records.

67. Some 14 percent of the group had died prior to this period, 2 percent left the country before they could give vent to their beliefs, and another 60 percent kept quiet or left no record.

68. I have consulted E. Alfred Jones, *The Loyalists of Massachusetts* (Baltimore, 1969), and James H. Stark, *Loyalists of Massachusetts* (Boston, 1910), and have adopted John W. Tyler's evidence for smuggling and tests of loyalty or patriotism. *Smugglers & Patriots: Boston Merchants and the Advent of the American Revolution* (Boston, 1986), 13–22, 253–277. Such tests include evidence of signing the 1755 petition to abate Boston's taxes, the 1756 agreement to inform on smugglers, a petition that warships be used only to guard the coast, the 1760 *Gray* petition, the 1761 petition against the writs of assistance, and the 1761 petition for the restoration of Barons, membership in Boston's Society for Encouraging

Thus, when compared to the society at large, a Boston wine trader was a member of a group that was middling in origins, relatively well-to-do, Protestant, mainly politically reticent, and commercially involved in several services (export, re-export, import, or retailing), geographical regions, and commodities. Although the necessary socio-economic dimensions of the lives of Boston's non-wine-trade merchants have not been studied in any detail to allow close comparisons between the two groups, preliminary consideration suggests that Boston's wine traders stood as a cross-section of the town's trading class. On the surface, at least, there appears to have been nothing that specifically encouraged or facilitated the loss of markets that Bostonians experienced. The answer must lie deeper.

Does it lie in their "spirit of enterprise"? To ask a question posed by Thomas Doerflinger of Philadelphia's merchants, how "vigorous" were Boston's enterprisers? Some economic historians may regard this as a gratuitous, unnecessary question, believing that the growth of Philadelphia and New York alone explains the decline of Boston's markets; other scholars might point to Salem's advantage in shipping and trading operating costs as sufficient cause. However, whether causal or not, the commercial spirit in Boston does seem to have flagged in the third quarter of the eighteenth century, at least among its wine traders. The Boston mercantile community's entrepreneurial spirit hardened. This "sclerosis" blocked it from taking the aggressive action needed to meet rising competition from other colonial port towns and provincial coastal settlements. This dimension is extremely difficult even to adumbrate; it is only suggested by the silence of one group and the activities of traders elsewhere, activities witnessed and commented upon by the former.

Boston's fall was not a case of decline through inadvertence. It is true that for most of the traders wine imports were not their principal concern. But that is not to say that wine was an afterthought; it was critical to the economics of a voyage. Often, as in the case of fish export, it was the only return commodity. Wine figured as both a medium of currency in barter exchanges and as necessary ballast. Accordingly, wine required a great deal of time and attention. Still it seems that the Bostonians did not match the efforts of others. The wine trading of Boston merchants was generally stiff and inflexible. They waited for orders to come to them before they contacted their customers or their correspondents; they acted more as agents

---

Trade and Commerce, and the like. Members of the society are listed in the Ezekiel Price Manuscripts, ff. 78–81, M.H.S. The subject of privateering, especially as a business, remains largely unstudied.

than as principals. When they did act, they moved sluggishly.[69] Richard Derby of Salem, for example, kept five ships constantly plying the waters between Madeira and Salem from 1757 to 1765; John Hancock, by contrast, relied on one or two carriers who only occasionally stopped at Funchal.[70] Boston traders did not speculate with large orders in this period, as did Derby and some of his neighbors; most Boston traders' requests were for small amounts. They were unwilling to grant the longer terms of credit that had become commonplace in Salem and towns to the south, such as Philadelphia. No one in Boston appears to have attempted to make a killing in advance of the implementation of the Sugar Act by buying wine in bulk and holding it in store in advance of a rise in price, as their compatriots did in Philadelphia.[71] And despite much grumbling and protest, Boston's wine traders generally complied with the imperial regulations that interfered with the conduct of the direct trade with Madeira, unlike wine traders in other towns. As opposed to many Salem traders, whose shipping remained direct with Madeira and the Azores despite the high price of the duty (for they "creatively" got around the law), Boston traders either paid the high price or rerouted their purchases through London, in compliance with the 1764 Act as a way of reducing their duty.[72]

When high prices persisted or when Madeira wines glutted their market,

69. John Rowe to Newton & Gordon, July 10, 17, Nov. 9, 1762, Jan. 20, 1763, Dec. 26, 29, 1764, Feb. 28, 1765, Cossart & Gordon Papers.

70. A brief overview of the career of Richard Derby appears in James Duncan Phillips, *The Life and Times of Richard Derby, Merchant of Salem, 1712 to 1783* (Cambridge, Mass., 1929). Derby's family firm–Richard Derby, Sr., Richard Derby, Jr., John Derby, Elias Hasket Derby, George Crowninshield, and John Gardner–had more partners than any Boston firm that traded wine. Its large size, which seems to have been characteristic of Salem firms in general, may explain its more vigorous approach to the trade.

71. Alexander Barclay to Newton & Gordon, June 16, 1764, Cossart & Gordon Papers.

72. Consider one typical plan for disguising imports. The inhabitants of Philadelphia had "for a long time been accustomed to the Lisbon wine," but such wine was more highly taxed. Accordingly, a proposal was made to systematize a method "of introducing them into" Madeira and "afterwards shipping them *as Madeira* in English Bottoms," and thereby reap "very great profits." To "avoid giving cause of Suspicion," it was considered necessary to order "the Lisbon wine to be put in pipes of the exact dimensions and make of the Madeira." Baynton & Wharton to Newton & Gordon, Oct. 2, 1763, Cossart & Gordon Papers. See John Crosse to Board of Trade, Jan. 8, 1719, in Historical Manuscripts Commission, *Report on the Manuscripts of Lord Polwarth* (London, 1911–1961), 2:14. Richard Derby frequently took French wines from Guadeloupe, carried them to Madeira, and passed them off as Madeira wines, thereby avoiding the duty on foreign wines. Richard Derby to Ancrum, Lance & Loocock, Dec. 4, 1764, Richard Derby Letterbook.

Boston wine traders sat back. Not one dumped his goods at private auction or public vendue in the 1750s and 1760s in an attempt to decrease his stock and undercut his competitors. Richard Derby, in contrast, frequently shipped cargoes of both choice and unsalable wine to Canada and Carolina with orders to dump whatever could not be privately sold.[73] Moreover, no Boston wine merchant moved quickly and decisively to capture a different or larger share of consumers. Again Derby's trade provides a contrast. In the troublesome 1760s, the Salem merchant dispatched agents and factors to Halifax, Montreal, and Quebec and established relations with merchants and agents in Kittery, Portsmouth, Philadelphia, Georgetown, and Charleston.[74] Derby's behavior reflects what other, larger traders in New York, Philadelphia, and Charleston were doing.

Why, then, did Boston's share in the Madeira wine trade decrease between 1700 and 1775? There were large economic factors at work. Market relations in Madeira shifted, prices rose, and wine exporters sought out new correspondents and markets. At home, population and geography worked against Boston's wine traders, as new, more advantageously poised communities prospered in other colonies and other parts of Massachusetts. Moreover, the port of Boston may have priced itself out of much of the New England market. In addition to these market forces, there seems to have been a dearth of spirited individuals at work in the town's wine trade, which assured its decline. It is difficult to say whether the difference in spirit is a story of two competing towns or two markedly different men, one lame— say, John Rowe or Lott Hall—and the other manic—Richard Derby or James Kearny, for example. Enough instances of Boston passivity and Salem or Philadelphia enterprise have survived, however, to suggest that the difference was more widespread and took on an almost pathological form in Boston, a form that was markedly reshaped by the wholly transforming effect of the Revolution on American commerce.

73. Ancrum, Lance & Loocock to Richard Derby, May 23, 1764, May 9, Oct. 17, 1767, Richard Derby Papers.
74. In Halifax, Derby dealt with Francis White; in Quebec, the biggest port for wine imports in North America, Joseph Choate, Calvin Gay, Jeffrey & Faneuil, Jonas Clarke Minot, and Gamaliel Smethurst; in Kittery, Nathaniel and John Sparhawk; in Portsmouth, John and Samuel Sparhawk; in Philadelphia, Richard Smith; in South Carolina, Shackleford & Lupton, of Georgetown, and Ancrum, Lance & Loocock of Charleston.

Joseph Barrell (1740–1804), 1767–1769. Pastel by John Singleton
Copley. Collection of the Worcester Art Museum, Worcester, Mass.

Persistence and Change within the
Boston Business Community,
1775–1790

John W. Tyler

When you come you will scarcely see any other than new faces. . . .
The change which in that respect has happened within the few years
since the revolution is as remarkable as the revolution itself.
—James Bowdoin, 1783[1]

AS BEFITS AN ADMIRAL, Samuel Eliot
Morison was good at telling other people what to do. One of the tasks he
was always urging on younger or less well-informed scholars was to write a
social and economic history of Massachusetts during the American Revolution, a far-reaching project, for which he saw great need. Others have noted
a gap in the historiography as well. John McCusker and Russell Menard,
writing in *The Economy of British America, 1607–1789: Needs and Opportunities for Study*, point out that "the period from 1776 to 1789 is among
the least studied in American history." But unlike Morison, McCusker and
Menard candidly admit that the appalling condition of the evidence is one
reason why more scholars have not undertaken the task.[2]

Lacking carefully researched monographs on the war years, narrative
historians attempting to describe Revolutionary society have relied instead
on the pithy quotation to paper over the gaps. Robert Treat Paine's words to
Elbridge Gerry in 1777 might be an example: the war "has thrown property

1. James Bowdoin to Thomas Pownall, Nov. 20, 1783, *Collections of the Massachusetts Historical Society*, 7th ser., 6(1907):22. Cited in Robert A. East, *Business Enterprise in the American Revolutionary Era* (New York, 1938), 214.

2. Samuel Eliot Morison, "Remarks on Economic Conditions in Massachusetts, 1775–1783," *Publications of the Colonial Society of Massachusetts* 20(1920):191; John J. Mc-Cusker and Russell R. Menard, *The Economy of British America, 1607–1789* (Chapel Hill, 1985), 358–359.

into channels, where before it never was, and has increased little streams to overflowing rivers: and what is worse, in some respects by a method that has drained the sources of some as it has replenished others."[3] Those who find Paine's metaphor too extended may prefer James Warren's more succinct style: "Fellows who would have cleaned my shoes five years ago, have amassed fortunes, and are riding in chariots."[4] No one except Allan Kulikoff in a highly regarded article (now almost a quarter century old) has sought to test the truth of Paine's and Warren's observations.[5]

The myth of a Loyalist elite has further compounded the difficulties of unraveling the truth about social change during the Revolutionary era. It is a perception that seemingly will not die despite all the scholarly debunking of the last two decades. The view that Loyalists somehow constituted a displaced American aristocracy probably owes its origin to contemporary observations, which have been repeated over and over (just like those of Paine and Warren) without a systematic investigation of their validity. The first nineteenth-century pioneers of Loyalist studies piously repeated the Loyalists' own claims to social distinction, and once enshrined in the convenient form of J. Franklin Jameson's *The American Revolution Considered as a Social Movement*, the belief has metastasized, spreading through textbooks and novels until it has become something every schoolboy knows (or thinks he does) about the impact of the American Revolution.[6]

The relevance of the Loyalist myth to a study of mobility among Boston merchants rests on the expectation that if Loyalists were indeed an elite,

3. Robert Treat Paine to Elbridge Gerry, Apr. 12, 1777, New York Public Library. Cited in Ralph V. Harlow, "Economic Conditions in Massachusetts during the American Revolution," *Publications of the Colonial Society of Massachusetts* 20(1920):171–172 .

4. James Warren to John Adams, June 13, 1779, *Collections of the Massachusetts Historical Society* 73(1925):105. Cited in East, *Business Enterprise*, 227.

5. Allan Kulikoff, "The Progress of Inequality in Revolutionary Boston," *The William and Mary Quarterly*, 3d ser., 28(1971):375–412.

6. The list of books that view Loyalists as a political and economic elite is extensive, but a distinguished sampling might include: J. Franklin Jameson, *The American Revolution Considered as a Social Movement* (Princeton, 1926); Carl Becker, *Political Parties in the Province of New York, 1760–1776* (Madison, 1909); and Merrill Jensen, *The Articles of Confederation: An Interpretation of the Social-Constitutional History of the American Revolution, 1774–1781* (Madison, 1948). That Loyalists should more properly be regarded as a cross-section of Revolutionary America has been one of the principal themes of Loyalist studies since the Bicentennial. Specific analysis of Boston Loyalists can be found in Richard D. Brown, "The Confiscation and Disposition of Loyalists' Estates in Suffolk County, Massachusetts," *The William and Mary Quarterly*, 3d ser., 21(1964):534–550, and in John W. Tyler, *Smugglers and Patriots: Boston Merchants and the Advent of the American Revolution* (Boston, 1986), 242–246.

and particularly a mercantile elite, then the departure of this group for Halifax at the end of the Siege of Boston must have created an upper-class vacuum into which rushed interlopers from the North Shore, men with strange new names like Cabot and Lowell.

Gone were the Hutchinsons, Olivers, Belchers, and Apthorps, leading merchant clans for much of the eighteenth century, and in came emigrants from the outports, like Stephen Higginson, Joseph Lee, and Thomas Russell, penetrating the uppermost ranks of the Boston society. Such evidence gives credibility to the notion that Boston's merchant aristocracy was somehow transformed by revolutionary struggle, and once again, contemporary observers can be quoted to support this view. One dyspeptic Loyalist grumbled in 1780, "The Cabots of Beverly who, you know, had but five years ago a very moderate share of property, are now said to be by far the most wealthy in New England. Hasket Derby claims the second place on the list."[7] The presence of newcomers within the Boston merchant community of the 1780s is undeniable, but how much the phenomenon is the result of the special circumstances of the war and how much it is attributable to normal rates of attrition and death remains to be seen.

The goals of this essay are modest. It is not Morison's long-hoped-for history of the society and economy of Revolutionary Massachusetts. Nor will it resolve to any significant degree how much social change we should associate with the American Revolution. It merely attempts to trace for a sample of Boston merchants (derived from the only complete tax records that remain for the 1780s)[8] who stayed and who departed, whose fortunes rose and

---

7. East, *Business Enterprise*, 228.

8. It is necessary to make clear the limitations of the evidence. Anyone using Boston tax records from this period should not expect to find anything so marvelously complete as the 1771 tax list, which in addition to the annual value of real estate includes such items as the amount of stock in trade, money lent at interest, tonnage of vessels, superficial feet of wharf, and the number of shops, distilleries, or warehouses a merchant might own. Such complete information exists for some years for some wards, but it is not again available for the entire town until 1790, some 29 years after the 1771 list. Instead, one is forced to rely on Taking Books, which list only the annual value of real estate but do offer the advantage of naming the taxpayer's occupation (merchant, trader, retailer, shopkeeper, and so forth.) Taking Books still exist for all twelve wards for the years 1780, 1784, and 1790, thus enabling one to examine the Boston merchant community at more frequent intervals than reliance on just the 1771 and 1790 tax lists allows. The Taking Book for 1780 was published by the Bostonian Society as its Publication #9 in 1912. The other Taking Books can be found in the Town of Boston Records Collection in the Rare Book Room of the Boston Public Library.

Some may object to the idea of making judgments about a merchant's wealth based only on the annual rental value of his real estate holdings. Unfortunately, this is the only option

whose fell. To a certain extent the question of how much opportunity the departure of the Loyalists created is an integral part of the story, as is the fate of those few Loyalists who attempted to return. This essay will also take note of how many newcomers there were during this era and what levels of the Boston commercial community they entered. Finally, it will make a few provisional observations about the sources of wealth for those merchants, both new and established, who were most successful during the period.

In *The Emergence of a National Economy, 1775–1815*, Curtis P. Nettels sketches a general outline of what one might expect to find for business conditions during the war years. Their initial phase lasted from June 1, 1774 (the effective date of the Boston Port Act), through April 1776, when restraining legislation issuing from both Parliament and Congress resulted in few imports and great shortages of goods. Imports and exports revived, especially through trade with the foreign West Indies, in the second phase, once Congress opened American ports to unrestricted foreign trade in April. The height of United States commerce during the war years occurred from mid 1778 to early 1782, when France joined the war and the British Navy was forced to divert its attention from North American shipping to the protection of its home ports. The American merchant marine suffered heavy losses during the last phase, from early 1782 to the final signing of peace on September 3, 1783, as the Royal Navy returned to the American theater of war with renewed vigor. Other, more recent studies appear to confirm Nettels's periodization.[9]

The depressed conditions that existed at the end of the war seem to have persisted through 1786, according to most observers, and were followed by

one has. It may be reassuring to note that a list of the top 10 percent of Boston merchants in 1790 according to their real estate holdings is not notably different from a list of those with the greatest personal wealth. See Table 7 and John D. Forbes, "The Port of Boston, 1783–1815," (Ph.D. diss., Harvard Univ., 1936), 249–255.

9. Curtis P. Nettels, *The Emergence of a National Economy, 1775–1815* (New York, 1962), 13–14; McCusker and Menard, *Economy of British America*, 361; and James A. Henretta, "The War for Independence and American Economic Development," Ronald Hoffman et al., eds., *The Economy of Early America: The Revolutionary Period, 1763–1790* (Charlottesville, 1988), 75–76. Although local military circumstances and fluctuations in the demand for tobacco and flour account for some minor variations, two recent studies of merchant communities elsewhere confirm this general pattern. Thomas M. Doerflinger, *A Vigorous Spirit of Enterprise: Merchants and Economic Development in Revolutionary Philadelphia* (Chapel Hill, 1986), and Edward C. Papenfuse, *In Pursuit of Profit: The Annapolis Merchants in the Era of the American Revolution, 1763–1805* (Baltimore, 1975).

a weak recovery in the closing years of the decade. Particularly afflicted by the depredations of the Royal Navy and British privateers, the loss of the New England fishing fleet, and the closure of the British West Indies to American vessels, Boston was slower to recover economically than were some other parts of North America. Nor should the extent of the late-1780s recovery be overstated: American exports per capita were 25 percent lower in 1791–1792 than they had been in 1768–1772. Per capita gross national product had dropped perhaps as much as 46 percent from 1775 to 1790, a figure McCusker and Menard provocatively compare to the 48 percent drop of the Great Depression.[10]

In its actual size, the merchant community in Boston appears to have responded to the larger economic trends outlined above. Although the 1771 tax list does not include the taxpayer's occupation, it cites 399 persons whose assets (stock in trade, vessels, shops, and warehouses) suggest an involvement in overseas or retail trade. (One should also remember that the 1771 list does not include the eleventh ward in the South End, which, as Kulikoff notes, was a popular residence for merchants. Other tax lists suggest that, as a consequence, the 1771 list understates the total number of merchants by 20 to 30, bringing the total to perhaps 429.)[11]

Many merchants, most notably John Hancock, believed that by the late '60s and early '70s the Boston merchant community had already expanded beyond a number that trade could reasonably support. Composed of perhaps as few as 300 or 330 persons early in the 1760s, its numbers had risen considerably from two sources. Late in the decade, the number of factors (agents of merchants who were situated elsewhere, most notably in Scotland) had grown to about 30. An additional 68 traders were what one observer disdainfully called "mushroom merchants," former retailers who, encouraged by liberal terms of credit from British suppliers, had begun to make limited importations of their own. Indeed, some commentators have seen the non-importation controversy as an effort by well-established

10. Benjamin W. Labaree, *Patriots and Partisans: The Merchants of Newburyport, 1764–1815* (Cambridge, Mass., 1962), 57–58; William M. Fowler, Jr., "'Trye All Ports': The Port of Boston, 1783–1793," Conrad Edick Wright, ed., *Massachusetts and the New Nation* (Boston, 1992), 44; and McCusker and Menard, *Economy of British America*, 367, 369, 373–375. Morison, writing in 1921, called conditions following the war "the worst economic depression Massachusetts has ever known." Samuel Eliot Morison, *The Maritime History of Massachusetts, 1783–1860* (Boston, 1921), 30. Philadelphia rebounded more swiftly, while Annapolis never recovered from the depression of the mid 1780s and was soon eclipsed by nearby Baltimore. Doerflinger, *Vigorous Spirit of Enterprise*, chaps. 5 and 6. Papenfuse, *In Pursuit of Profit*, chap. 4.

11. Kulikoff, "Progress of Inequality," 398.

merchants, heavily stocked with goods, to drive out these presumptuous newcomers.[12]

By 1780, the size of the Boston merchant community had ballooned to 480; presumably, many persons had been drawn into commerce by the boom conditions that the presence of the French fleet and the heightened wartime trade had created. The abrupt reversal of conditions after mid 1782, however, trimmed the number of merchants and traders appearing on the 1784 Taking Books to 350, fewer than three-quarters of the number that had been counted four years earlier. By 1790, the merchants' numbers had recovered to 393, a 12 percent increase in six years, bringing the size of the business community back to within less than 10 percent of what it had been in 1771. Philadelphia followed an even more pronounced pattern of depression and recovery, with 320 merchants in 1774, 200 late in the war, and 500 in 1785.[13]

The entry of new traders into the Boston merchant community was heaviest from 1771 to 1780, a nine-year interval in which their numbers increased to 167 and newcomers came to represent 63 percent of the total. In contrast, the proportion of newcomers in 1784 was only 46 percent and in 1790 just over 50 percent. Only a quarter of the merchants doing business in Boston in 1790 had traded there in 1771. One wishes that a complete set of tax records existed for Boston for a year midway between 1771 and 1780, because normal attrition from aging and death undoubtedly plays a part in these figures. (My research for the prerevolutionary period of 1760–1775 notes the disappearance through death and bankruptcy of 17 percent of a sample of 439 persons.[14] The ratio seems to hold throughout the 1780s as well: 18 percent of those who disappeared from the sample

12. John Hancock to William Reeve, Boston, Sept. 3, 1767, Hancock Papers, New England Historic Genealogical Society, Boston. The Loyalist printer John Mein was the first to indict the self-interested behavior of the "well-disposed dons" at the head of trade in his *Boston Chronicle* on Sept. 21–25 and Sept. 28–Oct. 2, 1769. That there is some truth to Mein's charges is a principal theme of chapters three and four in Tyler, *Smugglers and Patriots*.

13. Doerflinger, *Vigorous Spirit of Enterprise*, 215. It is only fair to note a considerable discrepancy between my 1790 total and the figures supplied by Kulikoff, who puts the number of "merchants," "traders," and "retailers" alone at 352. It made more sense to me to include the allied occupations of "auctioneer," "brazier," "chandler," "broker," and "distiller" in my calculations, for an additional 98 people according to Kulikoff. Thus, a total that relied on his figures for all of these occupations would be 450 (about 16 percent of the 2,754 taxpayers on the list in 1790) instead of my 393. I am at a loss to explain the discrepancy except to speculate that Kulikoff's use of city directories perhaps enlarged his count. Kulikoff, "Progress of Inequality," Appendix, 411–412.

14. Tyler, *Smugglers and Patriots*, 241–242.

between 1780 and 1784 had died; 19 percent of those who left the sample between 1784 and 1790 had also died.)[15]

The war years and the period immediately following were tumultuous times for everyone. Even higher rates of turnover prevailed in Philadelphia, where, as Thomas Doerflinger notes, there were 50 percent more merchants after the war than before. Only 50 percent of those present in 1785 had been in business three years earlier, and about 30 percent of those left by 1791. Considering non-merchants in Boston, Alan Kulikoff observes that 45 percent of the taxpayers of 1780 had disappeared from the tax list by 1790.[16]

The most obvious special circumstance causing such turnover was the exodus of Loyalist merchants in March 1776. My earlier research has determined revolutionary tendencies for 392 Boston merchants. According to my own rather narrow definitions, 118 were Loyalists (30 percent) and 163 active patriots (41 percent). Even though 30 percent of the Boston commercial community departed with the British troops for Halifax, there is no reason to assume this group somehow constituted a mercantile elite. The average assessed annual value of property in 1771 for both Loyalist and patriot merchants was remarkably similar: £38.5 for patriots and £36.7 for Loyalists. A comparison of the different levels of wealth between the two groups (Table 1) reveals frequency values that are admittedly small, but a disproportionately high number of those who ranked among Boston's wealthiest citizens with assessments of over £70 annual value were patriots.[17] The departure of the Loyalists created opportunity but not necessarily at the highest levels of the Boston merchant world.

The fierce inflation of the war years and the 1780s renders it difficult to track any gains in real wealth made by either groups or individuals during this era. The composite consumer price index for the period shows that by 1780 prices had advanced to 170 percent of their 1771 levels. Between 1780 and 1784, they had dropped back 25 percent, and a further 9 percent deflation took place between 1784 and 1790. Thus, the net increase in

15. Boston Athenaeum, *Index of Obituaries in Boston Newspapers, 1704–1800* (Boston, 1968).

16. Doerflinger, *Vigorous Spirit of Enterprise*, 249; Kulikoff, "Progress of Inequality," 401–402.

17. Only someone who actually emigrated or was listed by state or town authorities as an "inimical person" was regarded as a Loyalist. Active patriots included those for whom there was evidence of military service, government office, or the sponsorship of privateers. Tyler, *Smugglers and Patriots*, 241–243.

Table 1. Frequency Distribution: Assessed Annual Values of Merchants'
Property in 1771

Wealth in Annual Rental Value	Observed Values				Expected Values		
	Patriots	Loyalists	Neutrals	Total	Patriots	Loyalists	Neutrals
£10–19	8	7	1	16	9.4	4.8	1.8
£20–29	32	8	7	47	27.7	13.9	5.3
£30–39	11	7	3	21	12.4	6.3	2.4
£40–49	24	21	4	49	28.9	14.6	5.5
£50–59	10	2	3	15	8.8	4.5	1.7
£60–69	8	5	1	14	8.2	4.2	1.6
£70–79	2			2	1.2	0.6	0.2
£80–89	3			3	1.8	0.9	0.3
£90–99	1			1	0.6	0.3	0.1
Totals	99	50	19	168	99	50	19

Source: Tyler, *Smugglers and Patriots*, 243.

prices from 1771 to 1790 was about 15 percent.[18] To survivors of the 1970s, such inflation may not seem as grim as one might have guessed, but real estate assessments in Boston advanced at much more terrifying rates. The mean assessments of a random sample from 1780 were 328 percent of their 1771 figure, 38 percent higher in 1784 than in 1780, and 61 percent higher by 1790. Thus, an average assessment was nine and a half times greater by 1790 than it had been in 1771.[19]

It is interesting to set the mean assessments for merchants who appear on the same tax lists against the figures for the overall Boston population. Merchants' assessments increased 346 percent from 1771 to 1790, reflecting a 72 percent rise from 1780 to 1784 and 58 percent growth from 1784 to 1790. Thus average real estate assessments for merchants closely paralleled the figures for the general population, except for the period of 1780–1784, when merchant-owned real estate appears to have advanced in value at a much faster rate.

18. John J. McCusker, *How Much Is That in Real Money?: A Historical Price Index for Use as a Deflator of Money Values in the Economy of the United States* (Worcester, 1992), Table A-2.

19. These figures are derived from a random sample of the 1771, 1780, 1784, and 1790 tax lists as described in footnote 8.

It will come as no surprise to anyone familiar with the social structure of America's seaport towns to learn that merchants dominated the upper ranks of society. The mean real estate assessment for all of Boston in 1771 was £14.5; for merchants it was £32.5. In 1780, an average estate of £62.1 belonged to hucksters, wheelwrights, constables, and the like. For a merchant the average assessment was £145.8. The gap widened even further in 1784 to £85.6 versus £250.9 for the general population and merchants alone, respectively. In 1790, the gap remained just about the same or was a little less: £138 to £396. Already more than twice as rich as their neighbors in 1771, merchants had accumulated wealth at an even faster rate than the overall population during the war years and their immediate aftermath. Samuel Hazard was shocked; he remarked, "The rich . . . are more luxurious and extravagant than formerly. Boston exceeds even Tyre." Meanwhile, landlessness in Boston ran at rates of between 30 and 40 percent.[20]

In order to circumvent the troubling issue of price inflation, the best route for examining prospects for persistence and economic mobility within the merchant community itself lies in dividing the sample into deciles and then observing a merchant's movement up and down this arbitrary ranking system in each of the four years for which we have complete records: 1771, 1780, 1784, and 1790. Examining change in the merchant community by deciles yields some predictable observations and some surprises (see Tables 2–4). One might have guessed that in the lower deciles (those reflecting lower assessments) the numbers of newcomers would be highest, often two to three times greater than those occurring in the highest deciles. Such a pattern would reflect the entry into the community of young merchants with scant capital resources at the outset of their careers. But would one necessarily have anticipated that their penetration of the commercial community would be so thorough at all levels, with even the highest decile replenished by merchants new to the sample at rates of between 45 and 17 percent? Here is an indication of how tumultuous conditions were and just how tenuous a merchant's grasp on prosperity might be.

The numbers of those leaving the sample reveal the other face of the same process. Once again, it is logical to expect that persistence rates would be higher in the upper deciles and that those merchants who had been in business the longest would have had the best chances of survival. The numbers appear to bear this out. But would one have surmised that

20. Samuel Hazard to Jeremy Belknap, Apr. 1, 1780, *Collections of the Massachusetts Historical Society*, 5th ser., 2(1877):47. Cited in East, *Business Enterprise*, 35. Concerning landlessness, see Jackson Turner Main, *The Social Structure of Revolutionary America* (Princeton, 1965), 191–192.

Table 2. Merchants in the 1780 Tax Taking Books (Divided by Deciles)

Deciles	Average Assessment (in £, s)	Increase since 1771 (in £, s)	Percent Persisting since 1771	Percent New to Sample	Percent Out by 1784	Percent Still Present in 1784, Out by 1790	Percent Out by 1790
First	382	5.5	55	45	24	13	37
Second	241.9	4.8	50	50	25	8	33
Third	193.8	4.6	50	50	23	30	53
Fourth	173.6	4.8	56	44	29	19	48
Fifth	139.9	4.5	24	76	39	19	58
Sixth	107.6	3.9	24	76	50	17	67
Seventh	83.5	3.4	25	75	55	13	68
Eighth	54	2.8	10	90	52	8	60
Ninth	34.5	2.5	14	86	64	14	78
Tenth	20.1	2.3	20	80	70	10	80

Source: 1771 Tax List; Boston Tax Taking Books, 1780, 1784, 1790.

rates of attrition would be so high? The exodus is greatest (at 66 percent) in the nine-year period from 1771 to 1780 (which, of course, includes the Loyalists' departure). But attrition continues at a very high level in the 1780s as well, with 43 percent of merchants leaving the sample between 1780 and 1784 and 47 percent leaving between 1784 and 1790.[21]

One should not assume that everyone who left the sample did so because of faltering business prospects; as Edward Papenfuse notes, bankruptcy did not always mean departure from town.[22] Death accounts for near 20 percent of the attrition. Then there were others, like Isaac Sears, John R. Livingston, and Pascal N. Smith, who, drawn to Boston by the lure of privateering and the fact that it was the United States's most active port during the war years, left soon after making a killing. Papenfuse in his study

21. Doerflinger notes that 61 percent of elite Philadelphia merchants in 1791 had not been there in 1774. Doerflinger, *Vigorous Spirit of Enterprise*, 248–249. Examining a similarly elite list, Labaree finds that only 9 out of the top 25 families on the 1782 Newburyport tax list were still at the top in 1790, and of that group only 5 had persisted since 1767. Fifteen of the leading 25 families had left the list by the end of the war, and another 5 had disappeared by 1790. Labaree, *Patriots and Partisans*, 84.

22. In Annapolis, 4 out of 13 shopkeepers went bankrupt during the 1780s, but only one left town. Papenfuse, *Pursuit of Profit*, 157.

Table 3. Merchants in the 1784 Tax Taking Books Divided by Deciles

Deciles	Average Assessment (in £, s)	Increase since 1780 (in £, s)	Increase since 1771 (in £, s)	Percent Persisting since 1771	Percent Persisting since 1780	Percent New to Sample	Percent Out by 1790
First	521.4	1.3	7.4	43	29	28	54
Second	400.7	2.1	8.0	37	34	29	43
Third	327.9	1.7	7.8	33	37	30	41
Fourth	275	1.6	7.6	12	50	38	47
Fifth	230.2	1.6	7.3	24	40	36	51
Sixth	197.7	1.8	7.3	20	30	50	60
Seventh	159.5	1.9	6.6	23	37	40	53
Eighth	131.6	2.4	6.8	5	20	75	65
Ninth	89.7	2.6	6.6	7	7	86	71
Tenth	54.4	2.7	6.3	12	3	85	62

Source: 1771 Tax List; Boston Tax Taking Books, 1780, 1784, 1790.

of Annapolis merchants sums up the situation neatly when he says that in the midst of an atmosphere of declining opportunity like the depression of the mid 1780s, "those who had the most to lose or the most to gain found it easiest to leave."[23]

Table 2 shows faster rates of property accumulation in the upper deciles from 1771 to 1780. The rate of increase in the average assessments of the upper deciles is nearly twice that which occurs in the lower ranks. The overall rate of increase in average assessments slows considerably by 1784 (see Table 3), but it is curious to note that the momentum has shifted since 1780, with the lower deciles now making faster rates of gain than the upper, thus tending to even out the comparative increases since 1771. The period from 1784 to 1790 (see Table 4) shows once again only modest gains when measured against inflation, but the upper levels have reasserted their lead, albeit at a slower rate.[24]

Storekeeping had traditionally been regarded as a stage on the way to wealth. Indeed, the experience of the prewar years, Papenfuse notes,

23. Papenfuse, *Pursuit of Profit*, 156.
24. Once again the comparison with Kulikoff is instructive. Kulikoff speculates that among those who remained for the entire 10-year period of 1780–1790, opportunity may have been closing slightly at the top and opening at the bottom. Kulikoff, "Progress of Inequality," 405.

Table 4. Merchants in the 1790 Tax Taking Books Divided by Deciles

Deciles	Average Assessment (in £, s)	Increase since 1784 (in £, s)	Increase since 1780 (in £, s)	Increase since 1771	Percent Persisting since 1771	Percent Persisting since 1780	Percent Persisting since 1784	Percen New 1790
First	1198.1	2.3	3.1	17.1	46	29	7	17
Second	735.6	1.8	3.0	14.7	37	20	6	37
Third	553.8	1.7	2.9	13.2	24	30	19	28
Fourth	442	1.6	2.5	12.3	23	26	12	38
Fifth	385.9	1.7	2.8	12.3	21	27	15	36
Sixth	322.4	1.6	3.0	11.9	23	30	11	36
Seventh	272.4	1.7	3.3	11.2	16	24	12	48
Eighth	204.5	1.5	3.8	10.6	18	20	24	38
Ninth	148.1	1.6	4.3	10.9	7	13	16	64
Tenth	70	1.3	3.5	8.0	21	13	8	59

Source: 1771 Tax List; Boston Tax Taking Books, 1780, 1784, and 1790.

would have encouraged such expectations, but the economic fortunes of the 1780s dealt such aspirants a cruel blow. The gap between the richest merchant and the poorest shopkeeper widened considerably from 1771 to 1790. In 1771 the average assessment for the top decile was eight times that of the lowest, whereas in 1790 the top decile's average assessment was 17 times greater. As the above figures for different rates of property accumulation suggest, this gap was widest in 1780 (with the top decile's assessment 19 times greater) before it narrowed somewhat in the following decade. Although the record is mixed, inequality among merchants, the richest segment of Boston society, seems to have grown in much the same way that Kulikoff describes it for the entire population. In discussing a similar situation among Philadelphia merchants, Doerflinger writes, "While the base of the merchant community was broadened by the entrance of many newcomers, the peak thrust higher," and "an enhanced spirit of emulation and material display" was one of the most visible consequences of such increasing concentration of wealth.[25]

Despite growing inequality and a precarious business climate, the prospect of moderate success still acted as a magnet drawing large numbers of newcomers to Boston. How realistic were their expectations? Kulikoff pro-

25. Papenfuse, *Pursuit of Profit*, 143, 147–148; Kulikoff, "Progress of Inequality," 409; Doerflinger, *Vigorous Spirit of Enterprise*, 250.

nounces occupational mobility "very moderate" and possibly declining from 1780 to 1790: only 28 percent of taxpayers changed jobs, and 14 percent made minor changes in status (presumably measured for Kulikoff's purposes by the step up from "trader" or "shopkeeper" to "merchant," for example). While these distinctions were undoubtedly meaningful in the eighteenth century, today such changes in title offer only a very slippery way of measuring social mobility. Clearly, the scavengers of the various wards each had a different understanding of how to apply such distinctions. Although "merchants" (the term generally implied some involvement in overseas trade) occur more frequently in the upper deciles and "retailers" and "shopkeepers" in the lower, such humble titles were no bar to the accumulation of wealth, as the presence of shopkeepers Samuel Elliot and Arnold Welles, Jr., in the top decile of 1790 testifies. Nor should one discount as major figures in the commercial scene distillers, whose enterprises required a high capital investment in facilities. In the end, Kulikoff concludes that about the same number of Bostonians rose in status as declined.[26]

The division of the merchant sample into deciles affords one an opportunity to record mobility with a little more precision, even if it does tend to support Kulikoff's insight. Among those who appear in both the 1771 and 1780 tax lists, roughly a third dropped more than two deciles from one list to the next, a third remained more or less where they were (with about a quarter of that group being rich men holding onto their position at the top), and a third rose in rank by more than two deciles. One person rose a spectacular eight deciles, but in general upward mobility was more moderate.

From 1780 to 1784, despite the shrinking size of the merchant community, those who did not leave Boston appeared to have better chances than formerly of holding onto what status they had and perhaps improving their wealth. Only 18 percent dropped more than two deciles, 41 percent remained where they were, and an additional 41 percent advanced more than two deciles. An interesting distinction also emerged between those senior merchants who had been in Boston since 1771 and the newcomers of 1780. Only a third of those who had arrived in 1780 had advanced in rank by 1784 (with no one rising more than five deciles), while 53 percent of the pre-revolutionary group rose more than two deciles (and a third of that group advanced *more* than five deciles.) There were clear advantages to an established reputation and access to greater credit.

26. Kulikoff, "Progress of Inequality," 404. Kulikoff also notices a certain "inflation of honors" toward the end of the period; for instance, the once exalted title of "gentleman" seemed by 1790 to indicate nothing more than a retired tradesman. Kulikoff, "Progress of Inequality," 409–410.

Table 5. Members of the First Decile in 1780

Assessment (in £)	Name	Decile in 1771	Loyalty, Occupation
500	Joseph Jackson	1	PATRIOT, general merchant
500	Timothy Fitch	1	PATRIOT, general merchant
480	Thomas Amory	1	LOYALIST, distiller
480	Jonathan Amory, Sr.	2	NEUTRAL, general merchant
480	John Rowe		PATRIOT, general merchant
450	Mungo Mackay	10	PATRIOT, privateer
450	Daniel Parker	6	distiller
450	Adam Babcock		PATRIOT, privateer
400	James Perkins	4	LOYALIST, general merchant
400	John Cunningham	5	dry goods merchant
400	John Hancock	1	PATRIOT, general merchant
400	Isaac Smith	1	merchant, West Indies & southern Europe
400	James Bowdoin		PATRIOT, investor
400	Thomas Hill		PATRIOT, distiller
400	William Porter		trader
400	Thomas Russell		from Charlestown, general merchant
400	Pascal N. Smith		PATRIOT, from N.Y., privateer
400	Josh. Witherly		brazier
380	Joseph Hall	9	distiller
360	Jonathan Mason	1	PATRIOT, brazier
360	Oliver Wendell	4	PATRIOT, whale oil merchant
360	John Gray		NEUTRAL, ropemaker
350	William Phillips	1	PATRIOT, general merchant
350	William Greenleaf		dry goods merchant become auctioneer
350	Daniel Austin		shopkeeper
325	John Bryant		trader
320	John Scollay		general merchant
300	Samuel Breck	10	PATRIOT, general merchant
300	John Barrett	1	PATRIOT, general merchant
300	Henry Hill	8	PATRIOT, distiller
300	John Andrews	7	brazier
300	Joseph Russell	4	
300	Samuel Hewes	4	general merchant
300	John Herskins	2	
300	Timothy Newell	2	brazier

Table 5. *Continued*

Assessment (in £)	Name	Decile in 1771	Loyalty, Occupation
300	Isaac Peirce	1	PATRIOT, distiller
300	Ralph Inman		LOYALIST, dry goods merchant
300	John Kennaday		distiller
300	William Molineux, Jr.		
300	Nathan Pierce		trader
300	Nathaniel Barrett		PATRIOT, lawyer become army contractor
300	Samuel Barrett		

Source: 1771 Tax List; Boston Tax Taking Books, 1780.

What of the end result by 1790? Twenty-three percent of those persisting from earlier years had dropped in rank, 47 percent had remained where they were (with 18 percent of that group holding on to top rankings), and 30 percent had risen by more than two deciles. This time those new to the sample in 1784 were more likely to be gainers (35 percent versus 25 percent of the 1780 newcomers and 27 percent of those resident since 1771). The most dramatic advances (of nine deciles) among the 1771 group were made by Samuel Breck, supply contractor to the French navy, Joseph Coolidge, Jr., an early entrepreneur in trade with the Far East, and Mungo Mackay, a former distiller now turned ship owner thanks to a fortune made in privateering. Among those present since 1780, similar gains were made by Joseph Barrell, another contractor to the French, Ebenezer Parsons, and the Codmans (John, Jr. and Sr.), out-of-towners who had made heavy investments in privateers (see Tables 5, 6, and 7).

The list of those merchants who had tenaciously hung on to their positions in the top decile ever since 1771 reads like a list of leading patriots: John Hancock, James Bowdoin, William Phillips, Sr., Moses Gill, Jonathan Mason, Arnold Welles, Sr., Timothy Newell, and Thomas Walley (nearly all had served either as selectmen or as members of the General Court in the tumultuous prewar years). Among those who joined the sample in 1780, some men like Thomas Russell and Stephen Higginson had accumulated capital elsewhere and entered directly into the highest circles of the merchant community. Both had been heavy investors in privateers, and Russell now usurped Hancock's traditional status as the richest man in Boston.

Among the wealthiest merchants in Boston, the loyalty of only a handful

Table 6. Members of the First Decile in 1784

Assessment (in £)	Name	Decile in 1771	Decile in 1780	Loyalty, Occupation
1600	Thomas Russell		1	general merchant from Charlestown
1600	William Foster		2	merchant, southern Europe
1600	John Rowe		1	PATRIOT, general merchant
900	Joseph Barrell	8	2	PATRIOT, privateer
900	Samuel Breck	10	1	PATRIOT, agent for French navy
800	Jonathan Amory, Sr.	2	1	NEUTRAL, dry goods merchant
750	Ebenezer Parsons		8	PATRIOT, from Newbury, privateer
750	John R. Livingston		4	PATRIOT, privateer from N.Y., returned there by 1784
700	William Molineux, Jr.		1	
700	William Breck		3	brazier
700	John Dean	4		PATRIOT, privateer
700	Joseph Russell, Jr.			
700	John Coffin Jones			PATRIOT, from Newbury, privateer
650	John Boies			
600	Ebenezer Storer	1	3	PATRIOT, prize agent
600	Leonard Jarvis		3	PATRIOT, privateer, partner of J. Russell
600	Samuel Pitts		3	
550	Stephen Greenleaf			"old gentleman"
550	Jonathan Williams	1	2	general merchant
500	Samuel Barrett		1	lawyer become army contractor
500	Nathaniel Frazier		5	
500	Capt. Isaac Phillips	6		PATRIOT, privateer
500	John Barrett	1	1	PATRIOT, general merchant
500	Timothy Fitch	1		PATRIOT, West Indies slave merchant
500	John Reed, Jr.			
500	Daniel Sargent			PATRIOT, from Salem, privateer

Table 6. *Continued*

Assessment (in £)	Name	Decile in 1771	Decile in 1780	Loyalty, Occupation
500	Robert Harris			
500	Elisha Doan			
450	Nathaniel Ingraham			gone to N.Y. by 1784
450	Samuel Welles, Jr.			West Indies merchant
450	Joseph Hall		1	distiller
450	William Greenleaf	2	1	dry goods merchant become auctioneer
450	Henry Hill	8	1	PATRIOT, distiller
450	John Herskins	2	1	

Source: 1771 Tax List; Boston Tax Taking Books, 1780, 1784.

was politically suspect. John Rowe had been one of the most adroit trimmers of the prewar years, but his widow still managed to rank seventh on the list in 1790. Jonathan Amory, Sr., appeared twelfth on the list. Some might call him a Loyalist, but his politics were more complex than that. He remained in Boston during the siege and negotiated the entry of Washington's troops into the city at its conclusion. His brother Thomas was even exiled to Waltham for a time by the town's loyalty committee. No one who has observed the Amorys' skillful maneuvering to bring about the end of the non-importation agreement in Boston[27] can be very surprised that they survived, and even flourished, in the postwar period. John Gray, who also remained in Boston during the siege, is much further down the list of rich merchants. The owner of a ropewalk, he supplied the Royal Navy with cordage during 1775–1776.

Most Loyalists did not fare so well. Seventeen of them (representing 14 percent of the total group of Boston Loyalists who have been identified in my previous study) appear on the town's tax rolls for 1780–1790. Of the seventeen, only two rose more than two deciles in these years, eight remained where they were, and seven dropped in rank, a very unsuccessful showing compared to that of other merchants during the period. The most spectacular collapse of all was John Erving, Jr.'s. An in-law of the Bowdoin-Pitts clan, his wily father, John Erving, Sr., had managed to be both a smuggler and a member of the governor's council at the same time.[28] John, Jr.,

27. Tyler, *Smugglers and Patriots*, chap. 4.
28. Tyler, *Smugglers and Patriots*, 30–32.

Table 7. Members of the First Decile in 1790

Assessment	Name	Decile in 1771	Decile in 1780	Decile in 1784	Loyalty, Occupation
3000	Thomas Russell		1	1	PATRIOT, general merchant, from Cambridge, privateer
1800	John Hancock	1	1		PATRIOT, general merchant
1600	Joseph Barrell	8	2	1	PATRIOT, contractor to the French fleet
1525	Mungo Mackay	10	1		PATRIOT, distiller become ship owner, privateer
1525	Joseph Russell	4	1		PATRIOT, auctioneer become general merchant, privateer
1500	Joseph Coolidge	10	3		early China trader
1400	widow of John Rowe			1	NEUTRAL, general merchant, smuggler
1400	William Phillips, Jr.	6	3		PATRIOT, distiller
1400	Samuel Elliot	5	4	2	shopkeeper
1300	William Phillips, Sr.	1	1		PATRIOT, dry goods dealer, "A Rich man, *very rich*"
1300	James Bowdoin		1		PATRIOT, gentleman, "A rich man"
1275	Jonathan Amory, Sr.	2	1	1	NEUTRAL, dry goods merchant
1275	David Sears			5	PATRIOT, West Indies & China merchant
1250	Daniel Sargent			1	PATRIOT, merchant from Salem, privateer
1200	Abial Smith				"gentleman of fortune"
1200	Isaiah Doan			4	merchant "going" in 1790
1200	Arnold Welles, Sr.	1	2		PATRIOT, "merchant of respect & note"
1200	Charles Miller	5			merchant
1200	Moses Gill	1			PATRIOT, brazier
1200	Theodore Lyman				merchant
1200	William Forster				merchant
1100	Samuel Breck	10	1	1	PATRIOT, agent for French fleet
1100	James Tisdale			3	merchant
1050	Samuel Salisbury			2	merchant from Worcester
1000	widow of John Gray		1		LOYALIST, ropewalk owner, died 1782

Table 7. *Continued*

Assessment	Name	Decile in 1771	Decile in 1780	Decile in 1784	Loyalty, Occupation
1000	Martin Brimmer		2		PATRIOT, merchant
1000	William Powell		2		PATRIOT, southern European merchant become underwriter
1000	Ebenezer Parsons		8	1	PATRIOT, merchant from Newbury, privateer
1000	John Codman, Jr.		9	2	PATRIOT, merchant from Charlestown, privateer
950	Joseph Hussey		9	5	merchant
925	Caleb Davis		5	3	PATRIOT, agent for prizes and confiscated Loyalist estates
925	Thomas Inglish				merchant
900	John Andrews	7	1		merchant, remained in Boston during siege
900	Samuel Parkman	5	5		early China trader
900	Stephen Higginson		2		PATRIOT, merchant from Salem, privateer
900	William Burgis				merchant
850	Jonathan Mason	1	1		PATRIOT, brazier become broker
850	John Carnes		4	2	shopkeeper
850	Jonathan Freeman				merchant
850	Arnold Welles, Jr.				shopkeeper
850	Henry Hill	8	1	1	PATRIOT, distiller
850	Timothy Newell	2	1	3	brazier

Source: 1771 Tax List; Boston Tax Taking Books, 1780, 1784, 1790.

had emigrated to Halifax in 1776 and his property had been confiscated in 1779, yet he still appeared in the second highest decile of the 1780 tax list. Despite rich and well-placed connections, his business failed late in the 1780s, and he died in Bath, England. A certain stigma appears to have attached to the Loyalists, which hindered the postwar prospects of most of them.[29]

29. Both Jonathan Amory, Sr., and Thomas Boylston (someone who tried to remain neutral but was eventually forced to emigrate) were targets of food riots during the war. Wise merchants may have considered a full warehouse to be the best hedge against

Conspicuous among those who were most successful during and after the war were those who invested in privateering. Such activity was probably widely diffused throughout the merchant community, with most participants taking only small fractional shares in privateering voyages in order to limit their risk. There is little way of tracing such small investments. Historians have generally depended on Gardner Allen's "Massachusetts Privateers of the Revolution,"[30] which contains information from a variety of bonds and certificates of ownership but unfortunately usually lists only a few principal owners before concluding an entry with a vague but tantalizing reference: "and others." Thus, we can only examine those most heavily involved in the practice.

Thirty-two merchants from the Boston tax rolls of 1771 to 1790 appear in Allen's compilation as the principal owners of three or more privateering voyages. Of that group only one dropped more than two deciles during the period, while seven made little or no change, and eleven were significant gainers. Among the big winners were Mungo Mackay, who advanced by nine deciles; John Codman, Jr., and Stephen Bruce, who advanced by eight; and Ebenezer Parsons, formerly of Newburyport, who advanced by seven. Thirteen of the thirty-two heavy investors appear on only one of the tax lists for 1780–1790, which perhaps can mean one of two things: either they made a killing and left the town, or they were ruined and disappeared from the sample as a result.

Fortune was sometimes fickle for privateers. William Shattuck, who invested in twenty-four ventures, disappeared after 1780. Mungo Mackay, second on Allen's list with fifteen ventures, rose spectacularly, as has already been noted. Isaac Sears, who made twelve ventures, does not appear on the tax rolls after 1780, probably an indication that he returned to New York. Stephen Higginson and Daniel Sargent, with eleven and nine ventures, respectively, were both Salemites who stayed on in Boston to become major figures in the political and commercial worlds of the capital.

Although historians have frequently taken notice of the role privateering played in elevating some newcomers to the upper ranks of the Boston merchant community, less attention has been focused on the effects of military contracts and positions of profit dispensed by Congress and the

inflation, but their fellow townsmen viewed it as selfish "engrossing." Given who their targets were, these food riots had a distinct anti-Loyalist tinge. Barbara Clark Smith, "Food Rioters and the American Revolution," *The William and Mary Quarterly*, 3d ser., 51 (1994):17, 26.

30. Gardner Allen, "Massachusetts Privateers of the Revolution," *Collections of the Massachusetts Historical Society* 77(1927).

state government. Thomas Russell, grandest of the new merchants, was the confidential agent of Robert Morris, the superintendent of finance. Joseph Barrell and Samuel Breck, as noted earlier, received a 5 percent commission on supplies they provided to the French fleet while it was based in Boston.[31] Caleb Davis, who rose from the fifth to the first decile, was the state agent for the sale of prize vessels after 1781 and the Boston agent for the Continental Board of War. John Bradford handled over half a million dollars in prize money for the Continental Navy in four years. Samuel Allyne Otis and John Andrews were appointed collectors of clothing for the Continental forces in November 1777, from which position, Otis himself admitted, the "emoluments were considerable." Government contracts offered perhaps an even surer way to wealth than privateering's wheel of fortune.[32]

Several members of the top decile in 1790 were intimately involved in the closely related businesses of financing the war and speculating on the war debt. Nathaniel Appleton owed much of his rise to his role as the continental loan officer for Massachusetts. The list of the largest subscribers to the national debt in 1790 could serve as a roster of top Boston merchants: Samuel Breck ($104,300), William Phillips, Sr., ($94,000), Jonathan Mason ($89,000), David Sears ($72,000), and William Phillips, Jr., ($49,000). Only small parts of these totals were "original holdings," (bonds purchased by the merchants themselves from the government, as opposed to those purchased from other bondholders as a form of speculation). Thus such speculators would receive a considerable windfall when Alexander Hamilton's financial plan took effect.[33]

Robert East has remarked that Boston merchants were not very innovative in the decade following the American Revolution and that they tended to

31. McCusker and Menard reference an estimate of French military expenditures in America totaling $6,000,000, an amount that helped offset declining exports during the war years. McCusker and Menard, *Economy of British America*, 363. French demand for flour in the first five months beginning May 1779 was 45,000 barrels, triple the amount of bread and flour exported from New England to the West Indies from 1768–1772. Henretta, "War for Independence," 75.

32. East, *Business Enterprise*, 54–57; William M. Fowler, Jr., *Rebels Under Sail: The American Navy during the Revolution* (New York, 1976), 70. Doerflinger downplays commissary work as the road to wealth among Philadelphia merchants, preferring to say that staff officers, because of the contacts they made during the war, were well positioned to make money once the war had ended and credit began to flow again from Europe. Doerflinger, *Vigorous Spirit of Enterprise*, 233, 235.

33. East, *Business Enterprise*, 56; E. James Ferguson, *The Power of the Purse: A History of American Public Finance, 1776–1790* (Chapel Hill, 1961), 274–275.

return to prewar patterns of trade rather than explore the new commercial possibilities opened to them by their release from British mercantilist restrictions.[34] The list of the richest merchants of 1790 (Table 7) tends to confirm this observation. In 1787, fourteen men invested in the famous first voyage of *Columbia* to Canton via the Pacific Northwest. Only four were Bostonians, and of the four only Joseph Barrell appears in the top decile of Boston merchants in 1790. In the early years of trade with the Far East, there was not so much a direct trade with Canton or Calcutta, but instead a tentative exploration of a variety of ports in the "Orient."[35] Only three early entrepreneurs of this trade appear in the first decile: Thomas Russell, Joseph Coolidge, Jr., and Samuel Parkman. Commerce with the Far East belongs more properly to the next phase of Boston's history, but as a kind of precursor of things to come, there appears in the obscure ranks of the tenth decile the name of Thomas Handasyd Perkins, "just returned from the Eastward," the man who would eventually succeed to Thomas Russell's role as the grand arbiter of Boston society.[36]

Trade with southern Europe and the West Indies had been among the most successful of prewar activities, earning valuable credits that made possible the purchase of British manufactures. Special circumstances closed these regions to Boston merchants during much of the 1780s. British Orders in Council prohibited American vessels from entering the British West Indies after 1783, and the French eventually imposed some discriminatory duties and limits on tonnage in their own islands as well. Massachusetts retaliated against the British in June 1785 by forbidding the export of Massachusetts produce in foreign vessels, as well as slapping those that entered with an additional 5s. per ton port duty. The restoration of free trade with the British West Indies would be a major goal of United States foreign policy for the next fifty years.[37]

Expelled from British islands in the Caribbean, American vessels also faced new hazards posed by Barbary pirates off the shores of southern Europe. Soon after the end of the Revolution, a new British consul in Algiers made it clear that American ships no longer enjoyed his government's protection. At first, war between Spain and Algiers kept most of the

34. East, *Business Enterprise*, 250. Kenneth Wiggins Porter concurs with this observation in *The Jacksons and the Lees: Two Generations of Massachusetts Merchants, 1765–1844* (Cambridge, Mass., 1937), 1:24.

35. Porter, *Jacksons and the Lees*, 1:31.

36. Morison, *Maritime History*, 129.

37. Fowler, "'Trye All Ports,'" 39–41; McCusker and Menard, *Economy of British America*, 286.

corsairs bottled up within the Mediterranean, but soon after the warring parties concluded a treaty in 1785 they captured the Boston schooner *Maria* off Cape St. Vincent. Thus did the *Maria* become one of the first American victims of the pirates who had now begun to roam the Atlantic as well. The effect of the news was dramatic: fifteen vessels either arrived in Boston from the Mediterranean or left the town for those parts in 1784–1785; in 1786 none did. Some of the vessels diverted from this once lucrative area of trade found their way into the Baltic, but Bostonians (except for Thomas Russell and his Codman in-laws) were slow to identify new opportunities even there before 1790.[38]

Boston recovered only gradually from the commercial disruption caused by the American Revolution. Many formerly profitable trade routes were now closed to its merchants, and some commercial contacts, who had once been so liberal in supplying credit, now turned their backs on the community. The departure of Loyalist merchants in 1776 did create some degree of opportunity for aspiring entrepreneurs, but the change was not as dramatic an event as some theorists of revolutionary social turnover have implied. As many as one-sixth of the Loyalists eventually returned to take up business in Boston once again, though few were very successful in the effort. Some North Shore merchants who, during the Siege of Boston, had gained an early lead in the business of privateering did find their way into the upper echelons of Boston's merchant establishment, but supplying the American and French armies could be an equally effective road to wealth.

Pressure from newcomers who sought entry into the Boston commercial world, although greatest between 1771 and 1780, was relentless throughout the '80s as well, as between 20 and 60 percent of the names in each decile were regularly replaced. Predictably, the well-established merchants of the top deciles proved most tenacious in holding onto their wealth and social position, but by the end of the decade those who had done business before 1771 comprised no more than 19 percent of the highest decile and 3 to 8 percent of the lower ones. The presence of new faces in the Boston merchant community had come about more slowly than the shocked comments of many contemporaries like Sam Adams and James Bowdoin might imply, but death and attrition had taken their inevitable toll, and the commercial possibilities of the 1790s really belonged to a new generation.

38. Fowler, " 'Trye All Ports,' " 41–43; Forbes, "Port of Boston," 64–66.

Commonwealth  of Maſſachuſetts.

By His EXCELLENCY

JAMES BOWDOIN, Eſquire,

Governour of the Commonwealth of Maſſachuſetts.

A Proclamation.

WHEREAS information has been given to the Supreme Executive of this Commonwealth, that on Tueſday laſt, the 29th of Auguſt, being the day appointed by law for the ſitting of the Court of Common Pleas and Court of General Seſſions of the Peace, at *Northampton*, in the county of *Hampſhire*, within this Commonwealth, a large concourſe of people, from ſeveral parts of that county, aſſembled at the Court-Houſe in *Northampton*, many of whom were armed with guns, ſwords and other deadly weapons, and with drums beating and fifes playing, in contempt and open defiance of the authority of this Government, did, by their threats of violence and keeping poſſeſſion of the Court-Houſe until twelve o'clock on the night of the ſame day, prevent the ſitting of the Court, and the orderly adminiſtration of juſtice in that county :

AND WHEREAS this high-handed offence is fraught with the moſt fatal and pernicious conſequences, muſt tend to ſubvert all law and government ; to diſſolve our excellent Conſtitution, and introduce univerſal riot, anarchy and confuſion, which would probably terminate in abſolute deſpotiſm, and conſequently deſtroy the faireſt proſpects of political happineſs, that any people was ever favoured with :

I HAVE therefore thought fit, by and with the advice of the Council, to iſſue this Proclamation, calling upon all Judges, Juſtices, Sheriffs, Conſtables, and other officers, civil and military, within this Commonwealth, to prevent and ſuppreſs all ſuch violent and riotous proceedings, if they ſhould be attempted in their ſeveral counties.

AND I DO hereby, purſuant to the indiſpenſible duty I owe to the good people of this Commonwealth, moſt ſolemnly call upon them, as they value the bleſſings of freedom and independence, which at the expence of ſo much blood and treaſure they have purchaſed—as they regard their faith, which in the ſight of GOD and the world, they pledged to one another, and to the people of the United States, when they adopted the preſent Conſtitution of Government—as they would not diſappoint the hopes, and thereby become contemptible in the eyes of other nations, in the view of whom they have riſen to glory and empire—as they would not deprive themſelves of the ſecurity derived from well-regulated Society, to their lives, liberties and property ; and as they would not devolve upon their children, inſtead of peace, freedom and ſafety, a ſtate of anarchy, confuſion and ſlavery,—I do moſt earneſtly and moſt ſolemnly call upon them to aid and aſſiſt with their utmoſt efforts the aforeſaid officers, and to unite in preventing and ſuppreſſing all ſuch treaſonable proceedings, and every meaſure that has a tendency to encourage them.

GIVEN at the COUNCIL-CHAMBER, in BOSTON, this ſecond day of September, in the year of our LORD, one thouſand ſeven hundred and eighty-ſix, and in the eleventh year of the Independence of the United States of AMERICA.

JAMES BOWDOIN.

By his Excellency's command.

JOHN AVERY, jun. Secretary.

BOSTON : Printed by ADAMS and NOURSE, Printers to the GENERAL COURT.

Broadside, Sept. 2, 1786. Proclamation following the Aug. 29 riot in Northampton. Collection of the Massachusetts Historical Society.

Debt and Taxes: Public Finance
and Private Economic Behavior
in Postrevolutionary Massachusetts

Jonathan M. Chu

PITY THE POOR TAX COLLECTOR and the bankrupt. Like stepparents at a wedding, their presence is too frequently reminiscent of unpleasant times. Some historians of postrevolutionary Massachusetts have seen in the debtor and tax collector the causes of the upheavals that marked Shays's Rebellion and, by extension, the demise of the Confederation government. An extraordinary tax burden levied upon an exhausted, indebted population broke the state's economy and led to an armed rebellion that intimated the need to restructure the existing national government—or so the story goes. Yet for others, debt and taxes were not at the bottom of riot and rebellion; rather, they were the catalyst that precipitated divisions between class and cultural interests conveniently exemplified by Boston's and Eastern Massachusetts's hegemony over western and rural parts of the state.[1] These scenarios, however, do not take into account the fact that debts and taxes are variables that shape and are shaped by greater forces that define, limit, and encourage different economic behaviors. Moreover, in the aftermath of the American Revolution, the insolvent and the tax collector, like the stepparents at the wed-

---

1. Forrest and Ellen Shapiro MacDonald are the most explicit of those who see the rebellion's roots in "a level of taxation that was not only unbearably heavy but also grossly unjust." *Requiem: Variations on Eighteenth-Century Themes* (Lawrence, 1988), 68. For a more detailed defense of this position, see E. James Ferguson, *The Power of the Purse* (Chapel Hill, 1961), 245–248, and Roger H. Brown, *Redeeming the Republic: Federalists, Taxation, and the Origins of the Constitution* (Baltimore, 1993), 108–117. For the alternative view of taxation as cultural catalyst, see Van Beck Hall, *Politics without Parties: Massachusetts, 1780–1791* (Pittsburgh, 1972), 96–100; Robert A. Becker, *Revolution, Reform and the Politics of American Taxation, 1763–1783* (Baton Rouge, 1980), esp. 115–121; and David P. Szatmary, *Shays' Rebellion: The Making of an Agrarian Insurrection* (Amherst, 1980), 32–33.

ding, represented disconcerting links to the past and dark portents for the future.

The Revolution altered the economic world in which all Americans lived. The mere fact of declared independence compelled the restructuring of the commercial spheres in which both the Empire and America operated. While the acts of trade and navigation were central to the debate between Britain and America over the larger issue of sovereignty, they also served as boundaries that defined incentives and shaped individual economic behavior. Whatever the nature of its long-term economic impact, independence immediately denied the colonies their position within the Empire and compelled them to search for new trade relationships.[2] Ironically, Congress's reliance upon economic boycotts as a means of forcing British concessions demonstrated that it still operated within the conceptual limitations of mercantilism: it fervently believed it should not disregard imperial commercial practice even as it tried to amass the matériel for waging war against Britain. At the same time, those who saw the negative consequences of maintaining colonies within a mercantile system challenged Congress's desire to sustain the colonies' privileged economic position.[3] Nonetheless, as the war made reconciliation increasingly difficult, it compelled the establishment of commercial relationships with France and the Dutch Republic whose implications would ripple through the postrevolutionary domestic economy. Dutch merchants recognized that the Revolution offered them the chance to recapture a lost market, reestablish Amsterdam as a major Atlantic commercial power, and resurrect the Netherlands's golden age. Weighing Holland's traditional alliance with Britain

2. Curtis P. Nettles, "British Mercantilism and the Economic Development of the Thirteen Colonies," *Journal of Economic History* 12(1952):106–107, 112–113, notes the negative effects upon northern colonial development, in particular. See also Thomas M. Doerflinger, *A Vigorous Spirit of Enterprise: Merchants and Economic Development in Revolutionary Philadelphia* (Chapel Hill, 1986), 199–201.

3. See, for example, Josiah Tucker's argument that the British taxpayer and consumer paid higher prices on tobacco and hemp because of imperial restrictions and subsidies. Calling for the liberalization of domestic and foreign trade, Tucker criticized commercial regulation as an extension of privileges to the few at the expense of the many and concluded that no economic advantage followed from the political possession of colonies. *Josiah Tucker: A Selection from His Economic and Political Writings*, ed. Robert Livingston Schuyler (New York, 1931), 315. George III made a similar observation. John L. Bullion, "George III on Empire, 1783," *The William and Mary Quarterly*, 3d ser., 51 (1994):307. John E. Crowley, *The Privileges of Independence: Neomercantilism and the American Revolution* (Baltimore, 1993), 8–11, 52–54, 55–57.

against the new economic opportunities of America, Dutch merchants stepped up smuggling gunpowder and other goods through St. Eustatius and extending credit to private individuals and subsequently to Congress as well.[4]

In addition to a triumph on the battlefield, independence required a demonstrated confidence in America's economic viability. Without that confidence the new nation could not sustain the trade both at home and abroad that it needed to finance the war. A willingness to invest in American ventures in the absence of hard currency reserves or a proven system of tax collection came to depend upon the availability of credit and a money supply that sustained its specie-equivalent value. Congress hoped that its promises to redeem its paper dollars and debt instruments in specie at a future date would provide the basis of trade until a system of revenue collection could be established.[5] In actuality, the plummeting value of the congressional and state paper issues, combined with wartime shortages, produced runaway inflation and rapid and real fluctuations in prices which, taken with public fiscal policies, altered incentives and behavior for everyone. Nowhere was this more apparent than in the processes of economic exchange. Interest fluctuations or adjustments to price variations suggest a subtle, but significant and sophisticated, comprehension of the distinctions between the future and present values of goods and services, as the Revolution called into question how Americans ascertained value in their economic transactions.

The exchange of goods in abstract, monetary terms indicates a presumption that value can be transferred over space and time. As such, the expression of the worth of exchanges in abstract, fungible monetary designations renders any debate over the existence of subsistence or market economies in North America during this period largely irrelevant for the purposes of this essay. Once goods and services are assigned an abstract unit of exchange, that is, a price, they become fungible equivalents of commodities, one of which is money itself. Because it, too, varies in quantity and quality, money may have fluctuating value relative to other goods and services in the economic culture. In any economy, the use of non-metallic media of exchange including goods and labor means simply that the supply of metal, or its more obvious functional equivalents such as bills of exchange, is

4. Jan Willem Schulte Nordholt, *The Dutch Republic and American Independence*, trans. Herbert H. Rowen (Chapel Hill, 1982), 34–37, and Simon Schama, *Patriots and Liberators: Revolution in the Netherlands, 1780–1813* (London, 1977), 59–60.

5. Ferguson, *Power of the Purse*, 26–29.

insufficient to meet the demands of trade or subsistence because the economy, whether local, regional, or self-sufficient, suffers from a chronic balance of payments deficit. Such a monetarist approach does not deny the
existence of small-scale, marginal producers and markets limited by technologies, or moral, communitarian pressures that moderate individual, acquisitive behavior. However, the presence of these factors, which restrain
unbridled greed in a culture, does not preclude either fluctuations in value
or an individual assessment of the consequences of those fluctuations,
which compels a response or an appropriate change in behavior.[6]

In a relatively stable economy, money and the relationship of value between credit and debt remain in rough equilibrium. Inflation, however
virulent, would have had little impact upon producers of goods or services
in revolutionary America had it moved uniformly through the economy. On
the contrary, price inflation varied substantially among services and commodities and taught real, and not very difficult, lessons on how to reorient
one's economic behavior. Abigail Adams's farm hand Prince learned in
1777 that he did not have to be satisfied with his previous year's wage of
eight dollars a month. He quit, and Adams had to offer twelve to fill the
position, noting that she was "put to great difficulty to hire a Hand even at
that price."[7] Prince was not alone in adjusting his demands to the realities
of inflation in revolutionary Massachusetts. Charles Chauncy reported to

6. What follows in this essay will illustrate my agreement with those who recognize the
presence of capitalism or commercialism in America before the Industrial Revolution.
Allan Kulikoff has an excellent summary of the debate in *The Agrarian Origins of American Capitalism* (Charlottesville, 1992), 5–6, 21–23, as does Michael Merrill in "Putting
'Capitalism' in Its Place," *The William and Mary Quarterly*, 3d ser., 52(1995):315–326.
Winifred Barr Rothenberg, *From Market-Places to a Market Economy: The Transformation of Rural Massachusetts, 1750–1850* (Chicago, 1992), 52, 124–125, and Bruce Mann,
Neighbors and Strangers: Law and Community in Early Connecticut (Chapel Hill, 1987),
37–46, demonstrate unequivocally that value can and does transcend time and space in
18th-century America. Ironically, I find the most eloquent expression of the cultural subsistence perspective, Merrill, "Cash is Good to Eat: Self-sufficiency and Exchange in the
Rural Economy of the United States," *Radical History Review* 4(1977):42–71, the most
compelling argument for a monetarist approach to the problems of the revolutionary
economy. See also Barbara Clark Smith, "The Politics of Price Control in Revolutionary
America, 1778–1780" (Ph.D. diss., Yale Univ., 1983), 49–53. The bases for my theoretical
perceptions may be found in Ludwig von Mises, *The Theory of Money and Credit*, trans.
H. E. Batson (1934; reprint, Indianapolis, 1981), 47–48, and Ronald I. McKinnon, *Money
and Capital in Economic Development* (Washington, D.C., 1973), 38–41.

7. On Prince, see Abigail Adams to John Adams, June 1, 1777, L. H. Butterfield et al.,
eds., *Adams Family Correspondence,* (Cambridge, Mass., 1963–), 2:251.

Richard Price in 1779 that merchants, farmers, manufacturers, tradesmen, and day laborers had raised their rates "in proportion to the depreciation of the currency and the rise of the necessaries of life."[8]

Inflation, the overarching characteristic of the Revolutionary economic universe, disrupted conventional assessments of value. Unfortunately for some but fortunately for others, inflation moves through economies unevenly shifting relative values of goods and services according to the propensity of each to make adjustments. The result of currency depreciation and a demand that varied in response to local conditions, inflation altered relative prices, caught most creditors unprepared, and drove home to debtors shifts in the real value of their assets. As Eumenes observed in the *Boston Gazette*, many widows and orphans who had loaned money had to accept payment at nominal values when the discount was "two, four, six, eight or fifteen for one."[9] Creditors might have offset the losses by exacting higher rates of interest on the debts, but it is doubtful that one raised in a colonial society whose tendencies were to deflate the economy through hard money policies or, for that matter, in any economic environment other than hyperinflation, could have accurately foreseen the general collapse of currency values after 1776.[10]

Creditors, in particular, were caught in a bind. Credit and debt are the warp and woof of commerce; neither exists without the other. If debtors longed for the depreciation of their debts, merchants and shippers could not conduct a profitable trade without offering credit. In 1778, Elias Hasket Derby of Salem issued a bill of lading instructing the—presumably English—purchaser of his Virginia tobacco to pay ship captain Stephen Higginson on his account. The bill represented a chain of credit beginning with the delivery of tobacco to Higginson, at which time he became indebted to Derby. Higginson could then satisfy his obligation to Derby either by payment to a third party on his account or delivery of the bill.[11] Credit also facilitated third-party transactions and thereby increased eco-

8. Charles Chauncy to Richard Price, May 20, 1779, Bernard Peach, ed., *Richard Price and the Ethical Foundations of the American Revolution: Selections from His Pamphlets, with Appendices* (Durham, 1979), 315.

9. *Boston Gazette*, Jan. 3, 1780.

10. Joseph Ernst, "Shays's Rebellion in Long Perspective: The Merchants and the 'Money Question,'" Robert A. Gross, ed., *In Debt to Shays*, in *Publications of the Colonial Society of Massachusetts* 65(1993):57–58.

11. E[lias] H[asket] Derby, Sept. 8, 1778, box 2, Higginson Family Papers, Massachusetts Historical Society.

nomic activity. S. Phillips, Jr., provided a letter of introduction for William Abbot in which he asked Caleb Davis to advance Abbot articles on credit "as he is a stranger to you." At the same time, Phillips offered to stand as surety for the debt.[12] Like Abbott, farmers in need of cloth, rum, and other goods and storekeepers dependent upon their custom could not have engaged in trade if they had had to wait upon the cyclical reckonings of agricultural production and the sale of farm products.

Furthermore, in an inflationary economy those holding assets had to keep them constantly at work. Even one with productive enterprises, like Derby, could ill afford to leave them idle in the face of rampant inflation, which eroded the value of assets. Credit properly adjusted for inflation and risk through interest and discounts could be a means of keeping assets at work and compensating for inflation's ill effects. Thus, in his September bill to John Higginson, Derby offered to discount the note. If Higginson could repay the debt at least four months prior to the completion of the transaction, he could calculate his payment at the state's scale of depreciation and make "a saving of 50 prct—& so likewise shall [Derby] loose [it]."[13] Upon borrowing money from Caleb Davis before and during the war, James Noble Shannon turned around and loaned it to his neighbors who were cutting timber and building sawmills in Maine.[14]

Adjusting the values on loans to account for the risk of currency depreciation and inflation during the war, however, was extremely problematic, and few creditors could have guessed correctly on their timing. Prices had to reflect a variety of factors in addition to the forces of supply and demand, among them investor confidence and seasonal and regional fluctuations in the value, supply, and velocity of money.

Through mid 1776, paper issues sustained their sterling equivalent values and increased the amount of money in circulation, either because the promise of redemption appeared sound in the first blush of revolutionary enthusiasm or because currency issues enhanced economic activity.[15] In-

12. S. Phillips, Jr., to Caleb Davis, July 23, 1784, vol. 11, Davis Papers, Massachusetts Historical Society.

13. Bill of exchange, Sept. 8, 1778, box 2, Higginson Family Papers.

14. James Noble Shannon to Caleb Davis, May 13, 1784, vol. 10a, Davis Papers.

15. Charles W. Calomiris, "Institutional Failure, Monetary Scarcity, and the Depreciation of the Continental," *Journal of Economic History* 48(1988):55–57. See his Table 2 and Figure 1. In 1775 Continental notes exchanged at par; in November 1779, at 50:1; and in April 1781, at 146.67:1. Ferguson, *Power of the Purse,* 56–67. See also, Charles Bullock, "The Finances of the United States from 1775–1789," *Bulletin of the University of Wis-*

creasing the money supply facilitated small exchanges and lowered transaction and credit costs, thereby raising demand and contributing to real
rises in prices. Paper issues reduced the costs of payment, especially when
they came in what were considered more stable smaller units of currency.
These either eliminated the shipping costs for specie or increased the
reliability of third-party exchanges and endorsements to create more flexibility in the size and nature of transactions. Furthermore, substituting
paper for specie alleviated the problems caused by the chronic adverse
balance of payments, general illiquidity, and shortage of specie endemic to
British North America in general and Massachusetts in particular.[16]

During this period, moderate levels of inflation minimized the risk of
investment while encouraging creditors to put their liquid assets to work
and introduce more money into circulation. Lower transaction costs, coupled with upward pressure on commodity prices, encouraged risk-taking
by offering seemingly assured rates of return. In the first stages of revolutionary finance, investor confidence that nominal paper issues represented
real value further explains the ability of continental and state paper to
retain its worth through the summer of 1776, as does another significant
fact: the early rise of the demand for imported goods and agricultural
commodities was matched by the need for additional labor. The call to
expand production came at a time when the supply of labor was disrupted,
and the uncertainty of the moment fueled a brief scramble for cash.[17] Thus,
while commodity producers and importers benefited from wartime conditions, they were not immune to the impact of changes in the money supply.

Paper's ability to retain its sterling equivalents, however, depended upon
the government's promise of redemption. Once that pledge soured, confidence in the value of money ebbed, and the process of currency depreciation and inflation accelerated. Commodity producers could adjust for depreciation in the form of higher prices and on occasion could sell to the
British or, after 1778, the French; but the rapidity with which paper issues

consin: Economic, Political Science and History Series 1(1895):125, and Anne Bezanson,
Prices and Inflation during the American Revolution: Pennsylvania, 1770–1790 (Philadelphia, 1951), 65.

16. Calomiris, "Institutional Failure," 53. Larry Neal, *The Rise of Financial Capitalism:
International Capital Markets in the Age of Reason* (Cambridge, 1990), 67.

17. Calomiris, "Institutional Failure," 52–53, 61. See also Roger Weiss, "The Issue of
Paper Money," *Journal of Economic History* 30(1972):776–777. Neal argues that war and
economic crises produce demands for liquidity that lead to short-term appreciation of
domestic currencies. Neal, *Rise of Financial Capitalism*, 67–69.

declined in value imposed considerable hardships, especially on those who loaned money or were dependent upon fixed incomes.[18] When inflation exceeded the nominal rate of interest, the real value of assets shifted from creditor to debtor and, ironically, further impelled the former to continue to lend. Money, particularly that which was eroding in value because of inflation, had to be recirculated quickly on terms that would minimize its loss. In theory, the freeholders and farmers Chauncy described could have satisfied their debts without damaging their creditors' finances by adjusting the value of their notes. For their part, investors could have anticipated the problem of inflation and compensated for it by demanding repayment in commodities or services that kept pace with or exceeded the rate of economic change. Prudent creditors indexed their loans to the rate of inflation or established a sufficiently high rate of interest to compensate for the risk of depreciation in the notes' value.[19]

Wide swings in the rates of inflation marked the period 1777–1780, however, and in these conditions creditors naturally found it difficult to do business. Some relief was attempted in 1780, when Massachusetts established an official schedule of equivalents for specie in credit instruments of the United States that was to be used to discharge all private and public debts. The schedule illustrates the extreme difficulty of coping with the ramifications of a volatile economy. Assuming that the official rate of currency depreciation approximates the rate of inflation in Massachusetts, the annualized inflation rate for the first eight months of 1777 was 64.3 percent, but for the last third of the year, it was 386 percent. The next year's

18. Ferguson, *Power of the Purse*, 57–69. Richard Buel, Jr., "The Committee Movement of 1779 and the Formation of Public Authority in Revolutionary America," *The Transformation of Early American History: Society, Authority, and Ideology*, ed. James A. Henretta et al. (New York, 1991), 155. See also Michael D. Bordo's comment on Charles Kindleberger, "The Panic of 1873," *Crashes and Panics, the Lessons from History*, ed. Eugene N. White (Homewood, Ill., 1990), 70–73.

19. Rothenberg suggests that it is during the Revolution that interest becomes conceptualized as the money value of time. *From Market-Places to a Market Economy*, 122–123. While it may not have been as pronounced before the Revolution, the perception that interest represented the replacement of lost profits has a long history. Peter Spufford has uncovered evidence of this dating from as early as 1271. *Money and Its Use in Medieval Europe* (Cambridge, 1988), 260. Mann's description of the shifting nature of book debt and notes of hand in 18th-century Connecticut suggests a clear understanding of the trade-offs among custom, liquidity, risk, and rates of return. *Neighbors and Strangers*, 36–41. Rothenberg's observation of revolutionary concern about interest can be explained by creditors' anxiety over what would constitute the real rate of return in a highly inflationary environment.

inflation rate of 95 percent escalated to 249 percent in 1779 and then slowed over the first four months of 1780 to an annualized rate of 110 percent.[20]

When Congress and the state attempted to cope with such rates of inflation, their successes paradoxically further compromised public confidence in the money supply and, accordingly, redirected the incentives shaping economic behavior. In 1780 Congress attempted to stabilize the value of its notes through a new emission, which it guaranteed. The bills were to be issued at par by the states, which would then provide a sinking fund to redeem them in specie. In theory the differences between the new currency and specie would wither away, and prices would stabilize. Most importantly, buyers and sellers would become indifferent to the medium of exchange, and, as more money entered the marketplace, tax revenues and the extension of government loans would further diminish the fiscal burden of the war.[21] Massachusetts complied with Congress's plan, producing the aforementioned schedule of depreciation, and emitted £400,000 in new bills, its share of the continental obligations.[22]

Over the short term, these efforts seemed to arrest the cycles of monetary inflation in the Commonwealth. Cotton Tufts reported to John Adams in November 1780 that over several months the exchange for old currency had stabilized at between 65 and 75, but the public perceived this to be falling, as prices generally were.[23] As late as the following April, Abigail Adams related to her husband that the exchange had in fact held stable at 75 for five months.[24] But starting in May, the value of old currency plunged precipitously, falling by the end of June to "200, 250 and even 300 —in one Week it fell from 75 to 150." Paper money was "Breathing its last gasp . . .

20. *The Acts and Resolves . . . of the Province of the Massachusetts Bay, 1769–1780* (Boston, 1886), chap. 12 (1780), 1413–1414. If anything, this assumption underestimates the real inflation rate. Abigail Adams informed John Adams on June 23, 1777, that "I was offered an article the other day for two dollors in silver for which they asked me six in paper." Butterfield, *Adams Family Correspondence*, 2:270. In June, the official rate was 1:1.2.

21. See, for example, the explanations for the legislation in Cotton Tufts to John Adams, Nov. 27, 1780, and Richard Cranch to Adams, Jan. 18, 1781, Butterfield, *Adams Family Correspondence*, 4:23, 66.

22. E. Whitney Bates, "The State Finances of Massachusetts, 1780–1789" (M.A. thesis, Univ. of Wisconsin, 1948), 81–82.

23. Cotton Tufts to John Adams, Nov. 27, 1780, Butterfield, *Adams Family Correspondence*, 4:23.

24. Abigail Adams to John Adams, Apr. 23, 1781, Butterfield, *Adams Family Correspondence*, 4:104–105.

and being much debauched in its manners communicated the contagion all of a sudden and is universally rejected."[25]

The rapidity of such changes placed the costs of inflation upon those unable to respond by selling goods at higher prices or renegotiating the rate of interest.[26] Those most wronged were "salary men [and] those who depended on the value and interest of their money for a subsistence."[27] Creditors soon found that nominal interest rates, generally set at 6 percent, could not begin to protect the real value of obligations in a rapidly inflating economy. Based on the official scale of depreciation any debt entered prior to January 1777 could be satisfied three and a half years later at 2.6 cents on the dollar. A loan made in April 1781 was one-fourth its value two months later. Under these circumstances, the wisest course of action was to assume debt, circulate depreciated dollars, go long on commodities, and hoard specie, tactics well known and widely employed. As early as 1779 Rufus King, hardly the model of a struggling, indebted yeoman, asked Robert Southgate of Newburyport to "send me three or four hundred of those good for nothing paper dollars, you would enable me to pay some honest debts I owe."[28]

25. Cotton Tufts to John Adams, June 20, 1781, and Abigail Adams to John, May 25, 1781, Butterfield, *Adams Family Correspondence*, 4:156, 130.

26. See the examples of Weimar Germany and the Confederacy in Philip Cagen, "The Monetary Dynamics of Hyperinflation," and Eugene M. Lerner, "Inflation in the Confederacy," *Studies in the Quantity Theory of Money*, ed. Milton Friedman (Chicago, 1956), 88–89, 174–175. Ernst, "Shays's Rebellion in Long Perspective," 58–59. Ernst sees the Money Question as an issue that defines and sifts long-term economic and cultural interests. Great merchants, argues Ernst, would favor hard money policies that enhanced the value of their assets. So too would the poor. What is at issue at the most elemental level for anyone who holds cash in any amount is the preservation of a money supply that can be relied upon to retain its value. See Janet Riesman's argument that during the mid 1700s paper was only a temporary substitute for specie and only insofar as it stimulated the kinds of enterprise that led to the greater accumulation of specie. "Republican Revisions: Political Economy in New York after the Panic of 1819," in William Pencak and Conrad Edick Wright, eds., *New York and the Rise of American Capitalism: Economic Development and the Social and Political History of an American State, 1780–1870* (New York, 1989), 2–3.

27. Charles Chauncy to Richard Price, May 20, 1779, Peach, *Richard Price and the Ethical Foundations of the American Revolution*, 315. See also James Lovell's complaint that he was being squeezed by an obligation of £80 lawful money that could not be satisfied by a farm mortgaged to him and by a state per diem for his services to the Congress. To Abigail Adams, June 16, 1781, and editors' note to letter of July 13, 1781, Butterfield, *Adams Family Correspondence*, 4:149, 176.

28. This, after all, is the classic example of Gresham's Law: bad money driving good out of the marketplace. Charles R. King, ed., *The Life and Correspondence of Rufus King*, (New York, 1894–1900), 1:30. As Rufus King indicates, Doerflinger is mistaken in his

For creditors, the strategy of debtors left few alternatives. One might follow Derby's lead and adjust the discounts on loans to counter—however imperfectly—anticipated depreciation. Or one might play upon debtors' inclination to avoid payment and bet on the reversal of depreciation at some time in the future. William Bant, shortly before his death in 1781, deferred Benjamin Shepherd's offer of payment. As Shepherd recounted the episode, "the money was Depreciated altho many then took it for Debts[,] he told me he had much Rather Not take the money[,] I did Not insist he Should."[29]

Shepherd's ambivalence at clearing his debt illustrates how easily inflation created opportunities for debtors to expand their productive capacity with little risk. As long as Bant declined satisfaction, the costs of carrying the loan—the interest—and even the real value of it would essentially be rendered worthless by inflation. Moses Whitcomb of Hardwicke advised Davis that in the first few years of his indebtedness he intended to pay only the interest and not the principal on the loan that had enabled him to buy his farm.[30] When investments were funded by loans that were declining in value and the capital liability that had spawned them amortized, the costs of producing new income were reduced.

Investors, had they been able to foresee the future, could have exploited price differentials and inflation to excellent advantage. In Philadelphia, prices of West Indies goods rose rapidly during the first two years of hostilities, because the Empire was closed to American trade. Thereafter, the prices of agricultural commodities increased. Pennsylvania farmers experienced difficulties sowing their crops and insect damage in the year following a poor harvest in 1778; in 1778–1779, the arrival of the French expeditionary forces exacerbated the resultant shortages, and the prices of agricultural goods surged. The 1779 Pennsylvania harvest, while bountiful, brought three times the price of the previous year.[31] Richard Cranch, Abigail Adams's brother-in-law, estimated that in Massachusetts pieces of linen could fetch two to three times their European wholesale prices.[32] Charles

comment that inflation necessarily transfers wealth from debtors to creditors. Much depends upon the terms of repayment of the debt. King recognized that he was satisfying an obligation with assets whose real worth was far less than his "honest debt." Doerflinger, *Vigorous Spirit of Enterprise*, 201.

29. Benoni Shepherd to Mary Anna Bant, Aug. 6, 1783, vol. 10b, Davis Papers.

30. Moses Whitcomb to Caleb Davis, June 23, 1784, vol. 11, Davis Papers.

31. Bezanson, *Prices and Inflation during the American Revolution*, 14–15.

32. Richard Cranch to John Adams, June 22 , 1781. See also Abigail Adams's use of her husband's connections to the Dutch firm of Jean De Neufville & Sons to obtain goods like

Chauncy, in his letter to Richard Price, described how Massachusetts free-holders and farmers could also benefit from price fluctuations. After they cleared themselves of their debt, they "got their farms enlarged and stocked beyond what they could otherwise have done."[33] Chauncy was only partly correct in relating how one might profit from currency depreciation. King had the far better suggestion: borrow to the hilt, expand capacity, then pay off debt in worthless dollars.

Although inflation was an obvious and omnipresent characteristic of revolutionary society, coping with it also meant responding to spasmodic and unpredictable fluctuations in real prices. They posed a snare that was difficult to avoid or escape. Engrossing commodities alone would have been a simplistic and potentially disastrous tactic. Consolidating one's gains ultimately required finding a stable repository of value. In the absence of efficient markets,[34] using agricultural commodities or imports to guard against price and currency inflation falters on the problems of liquidity and the preservation of value. As armies moved away or as the sale of agricultural goods became more difficult, profits on them and many other goods declined because of lower demand and higher freight charges. Mercy Otis Warren confided to Abigail Adams in December 1780 that she had not sold a single article consigned to her and that the town had a surfeit of handkerchiefs which could not be sold at their asking price.[35] Upon the establishment of

---

"a large Quantity of ordinary black ribbon, which may possibly sell for double what it cost." Abigail Adams to John Adams, Nov. 24, 1780, Butterfield, *Adams Family Correspondence*, 3:xxxii; 4:16, 159.

33. Charles Chauncy to Richard Price, May 20, 1779, Peach, *Richard Price and the Ethical Foundations of the American Revolution*, 315. See also Richard Buel, Jr., "Time, Friend or Foe of the Revolution?" Don Higginbotham, ed., *Reconsiderations on the Revolutionary War* (Westport, Conn., 1978), 133, and "Samson Shorn: The Impact of the Revolutionary War on Estimates of the Republic's Strength," Ronald Hoffman and Peter J. Albert, eds., *Arms and Independence: The Military Character of the American Revolution* (Charlottesville, 1984), 156–160. The response was not unique to America. Inflation in Weimar Germany proved to be an initial boon to agriculture because it lowered the cost of credit while stimulating yields. Frank Graham, *Exchange, Prices and Production in Hyperinflation: Germany, 1920–1923* (Princeton, 1930), 286–287.

34. On this point, Rothenberg and her critics find common ground, the latter by their argument that moral restraints restricted the rise of efficient markets, the former by asserting the process of their development in this period. *From Market-places to a Market Economy*, esp. 239–243, and "Markets, Values and Capitalism," *Journal of Economic History* 44(1984):174–178. Michael Bernstein and Sean Wilentz, "Marketing, Commerce and Capitalism in Rural Massachusetts," *Journal of Economic History* 44(1984):171–172.

35. Mercy Otis Warren to Abigail Adams, Dec. 21, 1780, Butterfield, *Adams Family*

the French alliance, merchants who otherwise engrossed commodities envisioned the resurrection of international trade and new opportunities requiring more liquidity. Finally, currency's instability made extending credit, a normal lubricant of commercial exchange, a much riskier proposition.

But in moving to cash, one needed to avoid holding a risky, depreciating currency. "The whole value of paper," wrote Hugh Williamson, "is imaginary, and men do not believe by compulsion." Sound money, hard currencies that gave a reliable indication of value over the long-term, provided a better solution. Bringing the balance of goods and money into equilibrium by deflating the amount of money in circulation would restore prices to their proper levels. "Gold dear Gold," wrote Abigail Adams, would lessen the evil of rising prices and define fair values.[36]

French subsidies and Dutch loans buoyed confidence in American debt issues by providing specie in support of the new government. For the Dutch, American independence reconciled domestic political factions with the promise of a significant new market. Patriots, those opponents of the Orangists, could champion American trade as the vehicle to restore Dutch commercial supremacy in the Atlantic without overtly antagonizing those sympathetic to England. As the war wound down in 1781, the French prevailed upon private Dutch investors to subscribe to a loan of five million guilders. The next year, John Adams negotiated a similar loan with three Amsterdam banking firms. So eager were the Dutch firms of Willem and Jan Willink, Nicholas and Jacob van Staphorst, and de la Lande and Fynje to secure the privilege of underwriting the loan for the new nation that they offered extremely favorable rates and made few inquiries into the state of American finances.[37]

Intermittent though the Dutch loans were, when combined with French

Correspondence, 4:42. John J. McCusker and Russell R. Menard, *The Economy of British America, 1607–1789* (Chapel Hill, 1985), 362.

36. Janet A. Riesman, "Money, Credit, and Federalist Political Economy," Richard Beeman et al., eds., *Beyond Confederation: Origins of the Constitution and American National Identity* (Chapel Hill, 1987), 132–137. Buel, "Time: Friend or Foe," 133. [Hugh Williamson], *Letters from Sylvious to the Freemen Inhabitants of North Carolina Containing Some Remarks on the Scarcity of Money, Paper Currency, Foreign Luxuries, the Federal Debt, and Public Taxes* (New York, 1787), 3. Abigail Adams to John Adams, June 23, 1777, Butterfield, *Adams Family Correspondence*, 2:270.

37. Pieter J. van Winter, *American Finance and Dutch Investment, 1780–1805, with an Epilogue to 1840* (New York, 1977), 1:83–94, and James C. Riley, "Foreign Credit and Fiscal Stability: Dutch Investment in the United States, 1781–1794," *Journal of American History* 65(1978–1979):654–657.

and Spanish subsidies, they ensured confidence in the American economy and, by implication, its credit instruments. For example, the proceeds from the Dutch loans went to satisfy foreign obligations that could not otherwise have been met after 1784 because of the breakdown in the Confederation's requisition system. Furthermore, the subsidies and loans permitted Americans to conserve domestic specie at a time when French and English expenditures in North America were beginning to peak. Therefore, despite the loss of the compensating balances provided by the Empire before the war, Americans still seemed to be able to meet the demand for specie through 1784.[38]

Indeed, just as the value of paper issues was eroding, the money supply was being supplemented by infusions of specie. In markets like Philadelphia, southeastern Massachusetts, and the Connecticut Valley, the British and French armies provided livre and sterling as stable sources of value.[39] Henry van Schaack, writing from New York in the summer of 1783, advised Massachusetts Commissary Theodore Sedgwick to use his spare money "to good advantage": buy goods to ship to New York and resell them to the British occupying forces, thereby achieving a variation of the alchemist's dream, changing paper into sterling. Since rumors persisted that the British were considering an evacuation, this would probably be the last opportunity to take advantage of their presence.[40]

Sedgwick was not the only American to prosper from the infusion of specie. Between 1780 and 1783, approximately $6 million in hard currency entered North America, promoting further liquidity by its very presence. Meanwhile, with the demand for agricultural goods, in particular, still high because of the presence of three armies in the field, real prices rose and precipitated a boom that drew even more hoarded specie into circulation.[41]

38. Riley, "Foreign Credit and Fiscal Stability," 660–661. Murray Wildman, *Money Inflation in the United States: A Study in Social Pathology* (New York, 1905), 62–63. McCusker and Menard, *Economy of British America*, 362–363.

39. Doerflinger, *Vigorous Spirit of Enterprise*, 201; Richard Buel, Jr., *Dear Liberty: Connecticut's Mobilization for the Revolutionary War* (Middletown, Conn., 1980), 243–244, 263. Calomiris, "Institutional Failure," 52–53. Wildman, *Money Inflation in the United States*, 62–63. For a specific report of the demise of paper currency, see Abigail Adams to John Adams, May 25, 1781, Butterfield, *Adams Family Correspondence*, 4:130.

40. Henry van Schaack to Theodore Sedgwick, Aug. 13, 1783. Van Schaack, a Tory, also asked Sedgwick's advice on whether it might be possible for him to immigrate to Massachusetts. Sedgwick I Papers, box 1, vol. A, folder 1.5, Massachusetts Historical Society.

41. James Swan estimated that the amount of specie in America was three times its prewar totals. *National Arithmetick: Or, Observations on the Finances of the Common-*

Park Holland, a Petersham farmer, Revolutionary War veteran, and government loyalist during Shays's Rebellion, observed in 1785 that money was plentiful in New England because of a sudden flow of specie attributable in part to the presence of the French fleet, which came needing "all kinds of provisions, thus raising prices to an unusual height."[42]

The rise in the quantity of specie confirmed the revolutionary model of investment as it pertained to credit and debt. Creditors had no incentive to pursue debtors if the obligation could be met with depreciated currency at the official scale of depreciation. Rather, they would await payment in the specie that was now increasingly available. In light of their experience over the previous five years, debtors also were not inclined to satisfy their obligations with specie. However, the nature of the economy was soon to change, as investments that once offered sure returns had to be approached more cautiously. Toward the end of the war, high prices for agricultural commodities did not promise rewards for increased production. In the South, tobacco planters let fields remain fallow despite high prices; in Massachusetts, the demand for agricultural products became more sporadic as the centers of military activity shifted south.[43] Furthermore, investors had discovered more desirable uses for specie. The sudden flow of hard money enabled them once again to stock for resale imported goods, the consumption of which had been curtailed by the war.

The imminence of the British withdrawal did not imperil the flow of capital and specie to America because it promised to open the young nation to new patterns of international trade. The Dutch and the French, eager to gain access to American markets and to build up their exports, expected that wartime hostility would manifest itself in an American dislike for English goods. Unfortunately, Dutch and French merchants misjudged the influence of habit and taste and the long-term structural integration of British goods into the American economy. Dutch goods of comparable or superior quality sometimes could not be sold because Dutch ships would only release them for cash or short-term credit; goods sent on order occasionally fell into the hands of unscrupulous traders or remained unsold, and

---

wealth of Massachusetts (Boston, 1786), 82. Donald F. Swanson, "The Origins of Hamilton's Fiscal Policies," *University of Florida Monographs: Social Sciences* 17(1963):39.

42. Park Holland, "Reminiscences" (unpub. typescript of the original, n.d.), 37–38. A copy is located in the Petersham Historical Society.

43. Jacob Price, *France and the Chesapeake: A History of the French Tobacco Monopoly 1674–1791, and of Its Relationship to the British and American Tobacco Trades* (Ann Arbor, 1973), 2:715.

specialty items like Haarlam braid could not compete after the British began to produce the same articles. Americans simply preferred English dry goods; when Boston merchants could not sell their French cloth, they put English trademarks on it. Even when issues concerning the credit and quality of non-English imports were settled, some goods were simply unsuited to the American market; for example, Bohemian glass was sized improperly for American windows. American rum distillers preferred English copper boilers because they had customary shapes and used traditional English weights and measures.[44]

Despite Britain's commercial advantages, all was not well within the Empire. The loss of the colonies compelled its merchants and manufacturers to make some readjustments. Diplomatic isolation and the ravages of privateering had led to a recession at home, and British firms eager to sustain their sales in America extended credit to spur consumption and hold their share of the market. In 1784 exports to America jumped to 256 percent of their 1783 sales, and the influx appears to have been far in excess of any prewar boom, with dry goods imports at twice their previous high, recorded in 1771–1772.[45]

Little of the postwar foreign trade brought with it infusions of specie; rather, the capital invested in America took the form of goods and credit. As the supply of specie available for the continued purchase of imported goods became depleted, both foreign and American merchants extended credit to sustain consumption. Habituated to the processes of inflation and debt accumulation as an investment strategy, Americans with the encouragement of English and Dutch merchants continued to count on cheap credit and easy money through 1784. Unfortunately, the import boom only masked the states' adverse balance of payments and the vulnerability of their money supply to narrow shifts in the quantity of their specie. Unlike the prewar years, there were no imperial institutions to provide compensating balances over the long term.[46] Congress and the states hoped that their promise to redeem debt instruments in specie would prevent the further depreciation of other forms of currency. However, since American

44. Only Dutch gin sustained its command of the American market. See van Winter, *American Finance and Dutch Investment*, 130–137, 153–194.

45. Gordon C. Bjork, *Stagnation and Growth in the American Economy, 1784–1792* (New York, 1985), 97, 14–17, 107. Doerflinger, *Vigorous Spirit of Enterprise*, 243–244.

46. James F. Shepherd, Jr., and Gary M. Walton, "Estimates of Invisible Earnings in the Balance of Payments of the British North American Colonies, 1768–1772," *Journal of Economic History* 29(1969):230–253.

paper continued to lack government support in the form of adequate tax revenues, foreign merchants declared it unreliable and would not allow it to function as an alternative to hard money. Having reached its credit limits by the end of the war, after 1784 the United States could not continue to depend upon the French and the Dutch for loans of specie. Like Britain, France had been drained by the demands of the American Revolution; unlike its former enemy, its system of public finance was in grave difficulty.[47] The Dutch had particular reason to doubt American promises: their previous loans had been paid with new ones, and for the 1784 loan it was difficult to find subscribers.[48]

Thus, just as public sources of reliable money were drying up, private citizens were spending their reserves. British exports of the 1780s peaked in 1784 while American exports approached their lowest levels in the decade and stood at only two-thirds of their 1775 level. In addition, farm prices fell approximately 30 percent in Massachusetts between 1783 and 1784. They rebounded the next year, only to fall below 1784 levels in 1786.[49] When British exports flooded the American market and their quantity exceeded their demand, merchants who were unwilling to accept paper currency coped with the shortage of specie by offering credit to stimulate sales. But British merchants became overextended, and rather than helping sales, credit became a liability that added to the cost of doing business and led to demands for payment. John Lathrop complained to Richard Price in early 1786 that while English merchants had filled America with goods through the extension of large amounts of credit, many of the loans remained outstanding because creditors were reluctant to allow remittances in the prewar fashion and had instead demanded cash payments.[50]

47. John Brewer, *The Sinews of Power: War, Money, and the English State, 1688–1783* (Cambridge, Mass., 1990), 130–131. Peter Mathias and Patrick O'Brien argue that per capita levels of taxation in France were significantly lower than they were in England, but that the rates and forms of taxes were bitterly attacked for their regressive characteristics and geographical and social differentials. "Taxation in Britain and France, 1715–1810: A Comparison of the Social and Economic Incidence of Taxes Collected for the Central Governments," *Journal of European Economic History* 5(1976):605–608, 631–635.

48. Riley, "Foreign Credit and Fiscal Stability," 661.

49. Bjork, *Stagnation and Growth*, 107. Winifred Rothenberg, "A Price Index to Rural Massachusetts, 1750–1855," *Journal of Economic History* 39(1979):983, and Ruth Crandall, "Wholesale Commodity Prices in Boston during the Eighteenth Century," *Review of Economic Statistics* 16(1934):127.

50. March 1786, Bernard Peach et al., eds, *The Correspondence of Richard Price* (Durham, 1983–1994), 3:13. See also Holland, "Reminiscences," 38.

These developments reversed the incentives to investment with stunning effect and with consequences for the money supply. The export of specie had repercussions of a magnitude beyond its face value, for behind the relative worthlessness of continental and state paper stood the Banquo's ghost of the tax collector. As early as 1780, Massachusetts floated two loans that promised to pay both principal and interest in specie. The first loan was intended to support Congress's efforts to refinance paper money through a new emission that both paid interest and would be redeemed in specie. The General Court issued £72,000 worth of notes to be exchanged over the next seven years. The second loan, in the form of a £400,000 emission authorized in February 1781, paid an interest rate of 6 percent and promised a 4 percent premium upon the purchase of a bill of credit within the first year. A tax collected over the next four years would allow the state to repay the principal in silver, gold, or bills of credit, while an additional tax of £90,000 would cover the interest, the first installment of which would be due in September 1781 with succeeding payments due in May for the next six years.[51] A third issue of state treasury notes due in 1785 also allowed redemption in the form of consolidated notes, the 6 percent interest and principal of which were payable in specie. Like the previous two issues, this was designed to take extensive amounts of paper currency and army depreciation notes out of circulation, reduce the money supply, and engender confidence in the replacement currency by committing the state to its redemption in sound credit instruments supported by ample tax revenues.[52]

Given the economic circumstances of 1781–1783, the General Court's plans to begin the redemption of its notes in 1785 probably seemed reasonable and were certainly consistent with colonial and state policies. By timely redemption, the state would avoid further interest payments and return taxes to their prewar levels more quickly, while presumably stabilizing the value of its issues.[53] The General Court was intent on dispelling the public attitude recounted by Cotton Tufts, who thought that currency's precipitous fall in the spring of 1781 had largely convinced people of the

51. *Acts and Resolves, 1769–1780*, chap. 40 (1779–1780), 1178–1181; *Acts and Laws of the Commonwealth of Massachusetts, 1780–1781* (Boston, 1890), chap. 12 (1780), 20–23.

52. Bates, "State Finances of Massachusetts," 83–90.

53. Edwin J. Perkins argues persuasively that in retrospect the desire for quick redemption of the state debt was foolish and precipitated Shays's Rebellion. *American Public Finance and Financial Services, 1700–1815* (Columbus, Ohio, 1994), 174, 180–181, 184–186, 358–359, and Ernst, "Shays's Rebellion in Long Perspective," 57, 63–65.

folly of depending upon paper.[54] The state's tax policy also would encourage a shift in the public's investment strategy from imports and commodities to specie. Abigail Adams noted the need to reorient her financial plan as early as August 1781. Commenting to her absent husband that she had sold her commodities and collected a large sum of paper in anticipation of paying her taxes, she declared, "It now will avail me not a groat." Adams began to barter goods and demanded only hard money while looking for the kinds of commodities, like Bohea tea, that could be converted quickly into cash. Despite the deflationary impact of currency devaluation, Adams was able to change her plan because specie remained sufficiently liquid, and "difficult as the times are," she reported, and "dull as Buisness [*sic*] is, we are in a better situation than we were before."[55] Two years later, while the strategy remained sound, the ability to follow it had profoundly diminished. When Massachusetts attempted to fulfill its congressional and state responsibilities in 1784, the combination of economic stagnation, the demands of tax collectors, and the end of the boom led citizens to a search for cash that in turn produced a classic money panic.

In that year, Massachusetts decided to reassess the value of its tax base and thus redistribute the burden of taxes to reflect changes that had taken place since 1781. The plan was, not surprisingly, politically controversial. Routine questions involved, for example, calculating the share of taxes to be collected in towns like Gardner that had formed during the period of the appraisal after their property had been allocated to other communities. Simple errors in assigning individuals to the right town also vexed the legislators. In perhaps their most acrimonious exchange, members of the House spent the morning of February 22, 1786, debating an additional three-pound levy on residents of Suffolk County. Referred to committee for drafting in May 1784, the final reassessment bill was not passed until 1786. In the interim, of course, the state had to defer its 1785 tax collection.[56]

The hiatus only hinted at the underlying collapse of the tax collection system in Massachusetts and the pent-up demand for hard currency. Provisions for the collection of specie had been structured into the system as early as 1780, and the volume of delayed payments only aggravated the

54. Cotton Tufts to John Adams, June 20, 1781, Butterfield, *Adams Family Correspondence*, 4:156.

55. Abigail Adams to John Adams, Aug. 1 and Sept. 29, 1781, Butterfield, *Adams Family Correspondence*, 4:191, 221.

56. Massachusetts House Journal, May 1784–1785, 23, 77; House Journal, 1785–1786, 404, 408–409, 422, 432, 434, 439, Massachusetts State Archives, Boston.

money shortage. In Worcester County, tax delinquencies rose dramatically from 1783. As of November 11, 1785, 70 percent of Worcester's taxes for 1781–1782 were in arrears. Overall, however, defaults were weighted toward the taxes assessed after 1783, indicating a lag on the part of many people consistent with the tendency to defer payments on debts while accumulating assets.[57] As late as 1786 Brookfield residents, for example, paid 95 percent of their New Emission tax and 87 percent of their Specie Tax (October 1781), but only 35 percent of their Continental #1 (1782) tax before their delinquencies were put out for execution.[58]

The distribution of towns in Worcester County with a high proportion of tax delinquencies does not seem to reflect any cultural division between cosmopolitan-capitalist towns and their rural-subsistence counterparts. There appears to be no correlation between the amount of personal, as opposed to real, property held by a town's population and their promptness in paying their taxes. Indeed, towns whose citizens possessed the greatest amount of liquid assets in the form of money loaned at interest proved to be among the most problem-plagued collectors in Worcester County. Lancaster, with the second highest total valuation, paid only half of its taxes on money (1780) and specie (1781) and none of its Continental #1 tax, while Upton, which ranked fifth from the bottom in Van Beck Hall's index of commercial cosmopolitanism, collected all of its money and Continental #1 taxes and 96 percent of its specie taxes. The town also produced 84 percent of its Continental #2 and all of its state taxes in 1783, 1784, and 1786.[59]

57. Brown, *Redeeming the Republic*, 101–102.

58. Brookfield had the highest valuation in Worcester County in 1781, and it had the highest amount of money loaned out at interest. I am grateful to Ms. Susan Storch for the collection of this data. Treasurer's Records, 1464X: Temporary Ledger for New Emission Tax, and Temporary Ledger for Money Tax of May 1781, 224–269; Treasurer's Records, 1465X: Abstracts #1 and 2, 1783, 61–75; Continental Tax Book #1, 95–117, all at the Massachusetts State Archives. *Acts and Laws, 1780–1781*, chap. 43 (1780), 84–104, chap. 16 (1781), 503–524, chap. 28 (1781), 555–557. Tax Valuation 1781, 162:38, Massachusetts Collection, Massachusetts State Archives. Note that the MacDonalds misread the tax valuation records as money at interest owed, rather than money at interest due. There is no way to assess the total amount Massachusetts citizens owed from the tax valuation records. The entries for monies due could very well represent obligations from outside the state. *Requiem*, 62.

59. Treasurer's Records, 1464X: Temporary Ledger for New Emission Tax, and Temporary Ledger for Money Tax of May 1781, 224–269; Commonwealth Tax Book #3 (1783–1787), 101–123; Commonwealth Tax Book #4, (1784–1785), 100–121; Commonwealth Tax Book #5 (1786), 104–126. Treasurer's Records, 1465X: Abstracts #1, 62–75, and 2,

The obvious solution to delinquencies, efficient tax collection, only increased the need for specie, placing further pressure on the money supply. The General Court tried to make tax collection more effective after 1785, when it charged a committee to ascertain the obstacles several towns faced before delivering their taxes and "to report suitable measures to be taken for the more speedy collection of them." Among other measures, legislators ultimately proposed to call constables before the House and to levy writs of execution upon them for uncollected revenues.[60] Holding the constable liable for the delinquencies of his neighbors, however, exacerbated the problems of illiquidity by expanding the pool of insolvency and frozen, unproductive assets—tying up the assets of collectors or, even worse, compelling their forced sale at depreciated prices.

Nor could redeeming private debt produce specie that did not exist. While Massachusetts citizens were doubtlessly deeply indebted, they also were creditors. Holding notes, however, did not indicate the ability to fulfill one's tax obligations. Between 1781 and 1784, the amount of money loaned at interest in Worcester rose dramatically, from £4 4s. 8d. to £19 1s. per capita. The change indicated Worcester's rapid growth in the immediate aftermath of the war. Before long it would replace Lancaster and Brookfield as the economic center for the county. Yet the town forwarded no payments toward Continental Tax #1 and its people had their Continental Tax #2 abated.[61] Desperately short of cash, the town's residents could not change their notes into specie.[62] Writing from his post in Springfield to State Treasurer Thomas Ivers in 1782, Elisha Porter despaired of his ability to collect any of the 1781 taxes: "The scarcity of money . . . I fear will prevent the wish[d] for success."[63]

At the same time, the rise in debt litigation, the greater occupancy of the

1783, 61–75; Continental Tax Book #1, 95–117; Continental Tax Book #2, 98–117, all at the Massachusetts State Archives. *Acts and Laws, 1780–1781*, chap. 43 (1780), 84–104, chap. 16 (1781), 503–524, chap. 28 (1781), 555–557; *Acts and Laws of the Commonwealth of Massachusetts, 1784–1785* (Boston, [1889?]), chap. 25 (1784), 62–84, chap. 74 (1785), 580–605. Tax Valuation 1781, 162:36, 58, Massachusetts Archives.

60. Massachusetts House Journal, 1785–1786, 282, Massachusetts State Archives.

61. The total amounts owed rose from £1,563 to £6,812 13s. while its polls declined from 389 to 342. Continental Tax Book #1, 95–117; Continental Tax Book #2, 98–117, Massachusetts State Archives; Tax Valuation 1781, 162:36, 58, Massachusetts Archives.

62. The large sum of notes is the criteria Hall uses to justify Worcester's top rank among commercial cosmopolitan towns in the county. *Politics without Parties*, Appendix 3.

63. May 19, 1782, Miscellaneous Letters, 1781–1794, Treasurer's Records, Massachusetts State Archives.

debtors' prison, and the increased time it took to execute debt judgments in cases brought before the Supreme Judicial Court in Worcester indicated renewed efforts to raise cash. "In every quarter of the Commonwealth," wrote James Swan, "we hear men complaining of the times and of the scarcity of cash. Ask the collector of taxes why the list committed to him to collect is not discharged. . . . Ask a man to pay his just debt and still the same answer is heard—no money."[64]

The patterns of tax delinquencies reflected the supply of specie in the colony and the general rise in litigation. The years 1784–1785 were crucial: as the economy stagnated, the wise businessman sought a safe, secure haven for his assets. In the face of declining farm prices and an accumulation of imported goods on merchants' shelves, he would be foolish to invest in new stock and trade or expand agricultural production. Yet, even those who wished to divest themselves of farm lands found it difficult to do so. As early as 1782, declining prices coupled with currency depreciation and a tax system based upon real property made such sales increasingly problematic. According to Abigail Adams, Thomas Alleyne possessed a farm in Braintree valued at £3,000 sterling, for which he could find no buyers.[65]

Two alternative strategies, the purchase of state or continental notes redeemable in specie and the liquidation of assets into specie or specie equivalents, seemed more sensible. Continental and state securities were, however, long-term investments whose worth ultimately depended upon the ability to prevent the passage of laws authorizing paper tender, something Rhode Islanders had proven politically incapable of doing. It was far less risky to move immediately to cash and specie, in anticipation that the funds derived would help preserve the values of assets, provide flexibility for future investment, and, not so incidentally, stave off the tax collector, who had been largely ignored in the recent past. Indeed, the liquidation of private debt was already long overdue because of the wartime suspension of the courts. Now, the deflationary economy's high rate of indebtedness, the state's early decision to begin redeeming its notes in 1785, and Congress's need to pay its international debts in specie dictated this course of action. Unfortunately, the liquidation of private debt simply could not generate the sums of specie needed to satisfy tax collectors and avert panic. Prescient investors began trying to liquidate their private assets beginning

64. Robert A. Feer, *Shays's Rebellion* (New York, 1988), 60. Swan, *National Arithmetick*, 82.

65. Abigail Adams to John Adams, Apr. 25, 1782, Butterfield, *Adams Family Correspondence*, 4:315–316.

in 1783 through the fall of 1785 before the General Court had begun to tighten its collection processes and in the midst of its deferral of the 1785 state tax.[66]

In 1784 the Bay State's economy once again followed Charles Kindleberger's model for monetary panics.[67] In an inflationary economy people took on substantial obligations, expecting them to reap benefits from a depreciated currency, long-term debt instruments, or the continued price increases of their goods and services. But once the cycle reversed, deflation ratcheted up debt burdens by increasing the values of loans and raising the real rates of interest while lowering the incomes and assets that supported those debt burdens.[68] Some of the creditors' bets paid off: John Trumbull reported to Nathaniel Paine that he had obtained a judgment against a debtor on a note drafted in 1778. Although the defendant's counsel had argued that the balance should reflect the state's scale of depreciation, "the Court, after long argument, gave judgment in full."[69]

Conditioned to assume debt, people like Trumbull's defendant continued to do so until changed circumstances drove home the fact that their actions had passed the point of maximum utility and they were being made insolvent by the very forces that had enabled them to prosper only months earlier. The export of specie, coupled with the increased demand for hard currency to satisfy state and continental requisitions, reversed the situation that had characterized the closing years of the war. Specie now became dear as people scurried to raise the cash they needed to remain solvent.

66. See, for example, the rise in the number of cases for debt in the Worcester sessions of the Supreme Judicial Court, Supreme Judicial Court Archives Project, Massachusetts State Archives. Feer, *Shays's Rebellion*, 60.

67. Wildman, "Monetary Inflation in the United States," 62–63. See, especially, Charles P. Kindleberger's model for describing financial panics. According to Kindleberger, short-term expectations tend to control investment decisions. Because there are no absolute, fixed wrong prices in financial or commodity markets, changes in those prices occur as investors seek to place their assets in safer repositories of value. When those markets are volatile, their very movements create a new opportunity for investment; more assets follow, but the tendency among investors is to overshoot the equilibrium between risk and return and thus create the very conditions that require changing expectations. *Manias, Panics and Crashes: The History of Financial Panics* (New York, 1978), and *Laws and Economic History* (Cambridge, 1989), 60–63, offer his most recent iteration of the model.

68. Perkins argues that had Massachusetts done nothing but maintain the debt service during the second half of the decade, the state's creditor position vis-à-vis the national government would have provided sufficient funds to redeem the principal and tax rates would have been 75 percent lower. *American Public Finance*, 184–186.

69. John Trumbull to Nathaniel Paine, Dec. 1, 1784, vol. 11, Davis Papers.

Inflation became deflation, and the specter of illiquidity, insolvency, and forced sales loomed. When the General Court began to demand that taxes be satisfied in specie, it accelerated the dumping of assets and the pursuit of debtors in search of hard currency to pay the tax collector.

Recession added to the demands that already plagued strapped debtors. In a climate of deflation and falling prices, the profitability of capital investments depended upon a cash flow that the economy could not sustain in the aftermath of the war. Revolutionary veteran Long Bill Scott used a continental promissory note as a down payment on a farm in Groton. Unfortunately, he could not come up with the balance of the purchase price, was rendered insolvent, and forfeited the property.[70] Although not everyone lost his land, farmers were particularly vulnerable, especially in comparison to people in commercial centers like Boston, because they were less able to respond to changes in economic incentives. Long Bill Scott and others whose livelihoods rested upon agriculture were at a decided disadvantage in a world of short money, commodity surpluses, and falling prices. Because deflation shifted asset values from debtor to creditor, delay raised the costs of debt even as incomes fell. Thus, delay for the cash-short farmer or debtor was inescapable and unforgivable. Trying circumstances complicated James Noble Shannon's use of lumber to satisfy his obligation to Caleb Davis. First, Shannon's stock was not ready for immediate delivery. The best price for the lumber not only depended upon the nature of the trees cut but upon the job's timing. In the absence of adequate storage facilities, exposure to the elements lowered the wood's prices, so it had to be readied just prior to its date of delivery. When Davis's ship arrived in July six months after the deal had been closed, it had insufficient room to take on all the lumber. Finally, because of price decreases, the value of the stock was lower than expected, and the product's deterioration added to the real value of Shannon's debt.[71]

To avoid Shannon's situation, others tried to move more quickly to cash in order to rescue a few assets from the collapse, but they only aggravated

70. Jonathan Smith, *Peterborough, New Hampshire in the American Revolution* (Peterborough, 1913), 316–324.

71. Note the decline in the agreed price of lumber from 48 shillings per merchantable foot and 72 shillings, clean, to 36 and 55 shillings, respectively. Further complicating the process, Shannon and Davis needed to negotiate who should bear the burden of the loss. Peter Cunningham to Caleb Davis, Jan. 26, 1785; J[ames] Noble Shannon to Davis, Jan. 26, 1785; Ja[me]s Avery to Davis, May 17, 1785; Shannon to Davis, July 5, 1785, vols. 12a, 12b, Davis Papers.

the problem of plunging values. As market values of assets and real incomes fell, the burdens of debt increased, and it became more difficult to extricate oneself from one's obligations. Debtors had to put more crops, commodities, livestock, and property on the market and collect more notes to salvage their solvency. But as these assets entered the stream of commerce, they created surpluses for which there were no outlets, further depressing prices. Worcester Sheriff William Greenleaf reported to Treasurer Ivers that he had taken personal property and put it up for sale, but there was "not one bidder: I have levied on twenty farms, have advertized for sale [and] am afraid I can't sell them."[72]

The values of agricultural assets were particularly sensitive to the cycles of the season, further limiting farmers' ability to respond to demands for repayment. The January sale of his Leicester farm, argued Thomas Andrews, would not satisfy his obligations to Worcester merchant and storekeeper Samuel Salisbury, but he continued, "I am in hopes and expect to sell my farm in the Spring which I trust will enable me to do justice to all." In June schoolmaster Peter Rowell asked Salisbury to wait until fall for his payment; then he could get some pigs to sell and pay double the agreed rate of interest.[73]

Opposite Rowell and Andrews in their situation were, of course, Salisbury and Davis, who with their stores and shipping enterprises enjoyed a more reliable flow of income. Although they frequently offered credit, merchants could choose to demand cash for goods if they needed it.[74] Indeed, the integration of promissory notes and bills of exchange into the money supply provided them with alternatives to currency that paid interest. Further, merchants could more easily dump the smaller, elastically priced goods they carried and, though taking a loss, raise some of the cash they needed to avoid insolvency. Like the merchants, lawyers and judges whose incomes were spread out over the course of the year and were guaranteed by legal process also experienced financial security. Because their fees were either prepaid or given priority in the execution of judg-

72. Oct. 24, 1785, Miscellaneous Letters, Treasurer's Records, Massachusetts State Archives. See also Robert J. Taylor, *Western Massachusetts in the Revolution* (Providence, 1954), 134.

73. Thomas Andrews to Samuel Salisbury, Jan. 5, 1786, and Peter Rowell to Salisbury, June 6, 1785, Salisbury Family Papers, American Antiquarian Society, Worcester.

74. See, for example, the Stephen Salisbury Account Books in the American Antiquarian Society. For a description of the evolution of this process well before the Revolution, see Mann, *Neighbors and Strangers* (Chapel Hill, 1987), 12–17, 34–41.

ments, particularly in cases of debt, growing insolvency in the larger society was inconsequential to them.[75] Indeed, the incomes of lawyers and judges were protected, continuous, and growing.

Among these privileged individuals, some would have had fewer difficulties in meeting the demand for liquidity than others. Their profits—if not their survival—depended upon ready access to hard currency or fortuitous timing and circumstances. Davis's business, for example, was extensively diversified. By 1784, he had begun to call in loans and had invested widely. Shipping expeditions to Port-au-Prince, the West Indies, and Glasgow meant access to ports where merchants were more liquid. In January 1786, at the very moment that money was most hard to come by, Charles Fleischer, a St. Croix merchant, offered to buy a third or fourth share in the brig *Juno*. In behalf of his partners, Davis instructed Lemuell Weeks, the *Juno*'s captain, to try to get £1,000 sterling in either cash or produce from Fleischer, acknowledging that £900 sterling would also be acceptable.[76] Other infusions of cash from abroad provided marginal reserves of liquid assets to support a wider expanse of extended families. Abigail Adams sent by way of Charles Storer £17 sterling to be credited to her family's accounts. In turn, these allowed her to instruct Cotton Tufts to settle an annual income of $20 upon her mother and to promise aid to other family members whose lives were less than comfortable.[77]

Davis's and Adams's liquidity illustrates the central advantage of their transatlantic connections. Yet all commercial centers, including Boston, had greater liquidity, if only because of the velocity at which money moved through their economies.[78] Sending him £63, James Avery instructed Caleb Davis to pay Mr. Benjamin and Norman Balch £12 and £20, respectively, and to hold the remainder on account. In this particular transaction Davis's net assets did not increase but his liquidity did, as did that of other Boston citizens.[79]

But urban residents' access to freely-flowing cash did not guarantee

75. *Acts and Resolves of the Commonwealth of Massachusetts, 1786–1787* (Boston, 1893), chap. 73 (1786), 226–238.

76. Caleb Davis to Lemuell Weeks, Jan. 26, 1786, vol. 13, Davis Papers.

77. See, for example, Abigail Adams's letters to Mary Smith Cranch, Sept. 11, 1785, and to William Stephens Smith, Sept. 18, 1785, Butterfield, *Adams Family Correspondence*, 6:359, 364.

78. Hall, *Politics without Parties*, 194–195; Joseph A. Ernst, *Money and Politics in America, 1755–1775* (Chapel Hill, N.C., 1973), 356–358.

79. James Avery to Caleb Davis, Nov. 12, 1785, vol. 12b, Davis Papers.

them refuge from monetary panics. Like other investors, they could succumb to misjudgment or overspeculation. Some, like the Lancaster husband of Hannah North, simply guessed wrong. Mr. North had loaned a Revolutionary war veteran $97 and been talked into accepting notes at par in repayment when they only purchased a bushel and a half of Indian corn. Having dissipated his assets in this fashion, he was unable to satisfy his own obligations to Caleb Davis. North's acceptance of the notes may have been merely a sympathetic response to the "manly tear" shed by the soldier, but it also typified a transaction fraught with opportunity and risk. By moving to notes, North could have been better off. After all, he had eliminated a debt that might otherwise have gone unpaid and had obtained more liquid assets capable of future appreciation.[80] Unfortunately, Davis was unprepared to wait until North's holdings increased in value.

On a larger scale, Worcester residents' quadrupling of their holding of debt between 1781 and 1784[81] suggests a similar transition to more liquid assets and reflects an astute anticipation of deflation's impact. While interest rates may have remained unchanged, deflation ratcheted up their burdens and increased the real value of the notes themselves. On the other hand, events in Worcester also indicated a greater vulnerability to changes in the commodity value of money and the solvency of others. One individual's getting stuck with the wrong currency at the wrong time or holding notes drawn on insolvents could precipitate the fall of a complex fiscal pyramid. North and his fellow debtors in Worcester reflected different facets of economic behavior whose success ultimately depended upon liquidity and timing, and all found it difficult to cope with the highly volatile circumstances released by independence.

While shifting economic circumstances may have minimized the hardships of some people and commercial centers, most were unprepared for the way in which public policy exacerbated the problems of liquidity. As the General Court encountered difficulties in securing tax revenues, it began to enforce collections through executions against delinquent taxpayers' property, only adding to the urgency to liquidate debt. Panics, argues Michael Bordo, are avoided either when confidence restores value to assets or when there is an active lender of last resort to act as a barrier against mass

---

80. Hannah North to Caleb Davis, Sept. 19, 1785, vol. 12a, Davis Papers. Indeed, had North been able to hold the notes until 1791 he would obviously have benefited from Alexander Hamilton's assumption of the public debt at par.

81. See above, p. 141.

insolvency.[82] In Massachusetts, the state government reversed modern practice, refused the role of lender in any form, and positioned itself at the head of the collection line. Taxes added to the forces raising the real value of debt since they were the demand of a creditor with low marginal costs and claims that took priority over private indebtedness. Unlike private lenders, the state had difficulty lowering its citizens' tax obligations. While a private creditor in need of cash might be prevailed upon to settle for less than his expected return, a constable could not negotiate taxes downward for fear of being held personally liable for the outstanding amount. To make a claim for hardship, one would have to get an abatement from the General Court, at best a cumbersome process that only created more ripples of illiquidity through the private and public sectors.

Still, taxes were only one manifestation of the changed economic conditions wrought by independence and peace. The losers in this particular game were not the poorest, the dispossessed. Indeed, one reason for their becoming losers was that they owned the resources to enter the game.[83] To be indebted was not necessarily to be poor or an exploited victim of another socio-economic cultural group. Giving money to the destitute is called charity; conversely, expecting repayment rather than mere gratitude assumes the recipient has assets and will be able to satisfy the obligations assumed, including the interest.[84] Similarly, liability for taxes in postrevolutionary Massachusetts presumed the existence of private assets—either real or personal property or, in the case of polls, a faculty to earn an income. The inability to pay taxes, like private debt, was but one consequence of illiquidity; declining incomes and asset values, higher costs of debt, and the drying up of European investment capital were others. Insolvents, for the most part, had not anticipated the switch in the economy in 1783 and 1784 and lacked sufficient liquidity to meet their immediate obligations. They had borrowed while spending on foreign gee-gaws, or they had been struck by the return of the pendulum that shifted real wealth back to creditors. As

82. Michael D. Bordo, Comment, in White, *Crashes and Panics,* 73.

83. As Daniel Vickers pointed out, competition can be the flip side of the coin of a modest economic competency. "Competency and Competition: Economic Culture in Early America," *The William and Mary Quarterly*, 3d ser., 47(1990):17, 28.

84. Theresa A. Sullivan et al., *As We Forgive Our Debtors: Bankruptcy and Consumer Credit in America* (Oxford, 1989), points out the truism that money given to the poor is called charity. No one willingly loans money to someone he or she presumes cannot pay it back. Bankruptcy, the authors argue, occurs not because someone is poor, but because something interrupts income. Insolvency, even more than bankruptcy, only denotes the short-term inability to satisfy demands on one's liquid assets.

such, the seeds of discontent in postwar Massachusetts did not come from a sudden transition to hard money policies by a capitalist or commercial culture exploiting subsistence farmers, widows, and orphans. Rather, taxes were the highly visible representation of governments and people struggling to respond to the consequences of wartime finance and investment when they had not fully reckoned with the economic impact of the fall of the first British Empire.

Ship *Ulysses* of Salem ("Cap Cook Cast a Way on Cape Cod 1802").
Gouache attributed to Cornè. Courtesy, Peabody Essex Museum,
Salem, Mass.

Marine Insurance in Boston: The Early Years of the Boston Marine Insurance Company, 1799–1807

William M. Fowler, Jr.

HAD WILLIAM SHAKESPEARE known more about marine insurance he might have altered the script of *The Merchant of Venice*. For in this drama the unfortunate Antonio loses all as a result of a disaster at sea in which his vessel and cargo go down in a raging storm. This is the point around which the plot swings. It is an unlikely scenario, for no reputable merchant of Venice would have risked such an enterprise without insurance. Antonio might have been distraught at the news of the sinking, but he would have quickly recovered as he scurried off to find his even more unfortunate underwriters.

Yet if Shakespeare knew little about marine insurance he certainly knew enough history to place his tale of seaborne commerce gone awry in Venice. This city more than any other represented the birth of modern commerce and the reemergence of Mediterranean shores as the great mart of the western world. In the heyday of the Italian city-states the Mediterranean sea routes were alive with vessels carrying goods and people among dozens of ports and nations.

But the perils of nature, compounded by the sinister activities of man, made sea voyaging an uncertain enterprise. Reducing this uncertainty and assigning risk to others became of paramount interest to shippers in Mediterranean cities. Here, among the company of merchants, shippers with risk sought men with capital who were willing to insure against the perils of voyaging and, for a fee (premium) underwrite their names to an agreement (policy) promising compensation should disaster strike. Precisely where this business began is not certain. However, by the twelfth century it had achieved a recognized orderliness and form generally associated with the northern or Lombard region of Italy and was referred to as marine insurance.

As a device both to protect commerce and to concentrate capital marine insurance worked wondrously well. At the very moment that Europeans set sail across dangerous waters seeking new lands and trade, marine insurance stood by as a steady friend helping to guard against financial disaster. Seafarers, however, were not the only ones to benefit, for as underwriters—first in Europe, and later in Boston—pooled their money they created new sources of capital to finance other ventures.[1]

The English were bystanders in the early development of maritime commerce, but as their nation ventured onto the sea during the reign of the Tudors its merchants, too, sought protection through insurance. Marine insurance was certainly not unknown in England, but those shippers who embarked overseas before the Tudors usually obtained their policies in foreign ports. The first policy known to have been issued in England is dated 1547 and is written entirely in Italian. Embedded in the text is the rule that any dispute is to be settled according to the customs of "Questa Lombarda di Loudra." Within a few years policies would no longer be written in Italian, but the reference to Lombard Street would remain, amended slightly by including the Royal Exchange.[2]

In London the business was informal. No one specialized in insurance. It was simply an activity undertaken by various brokers who also engaged in a variety of other enterprises. In his widely regarded *Dictionary* (1670), Thomas Blount described marine insurance as

> a course taken by those who adventure wares or merchandise by Sea; whereby those unwilling to hazard their whole adventure do give some other person a certain rate or proportion as 6, 8 or 10 in the hundred, or such like, to secure the safe arrival of the ship and so such Wares at the place agreed on. So that if the Ship and Wares miscarry the Assures or Insurers make good to the Venture so much as they undertook to secure[;] if the Ship arrive safely, he gains that clear which the venturer agrees to pay him. And for the more certain dealing between them in this case there is a clerk or Officer ordained to set down in writing the effect of their agreement called Policy, to prevent any differences that might afterwards happen between them.[3]

A shipowner seeking insurance engaged a broker who then opened a policy and invited interested parties, as they came by, to sign their names

1. Florence E. de Roover, "Early Examples of Marine Insurance," *Journal of Economic History* 5(1945):198.

2. Charles Wright and C. Ernest Fayle, *A History of Lloyd's* (London, 1928), 40.

3. Thomas Blount, *Law Dictionary* (London, 1670).

and indicate the amount they wished to subscribe to the agreement. The system was fraught with problems, particularly fraud. How, for example, would brokers and underwriters know whether or not a shipowner had floated more than one policy on a single voyage? Nor was it always easy for underwriters to know much about the voyage, vessel, or men undertaking the adventure. For information upon which to calculate the risk the subscribing gentlemen depended upon a combination of personal knowledge, information from the broker, and rumors on the street. Not surprisingly, the wisest among the underwriters were cautious in signing policies.

Although the merchants who underwrote the risks were scattered throughout London and even beyond, those who acted as brokers tended to congregate within a particular section of the city. In his colorful travelogue *A New View of London* (1708), E. Hatton described the neighborhood where brokers gathered as a place of "Fountains, Bridges, Conduits, Ferries . . . Insurances of All Kinds, Bagnios, Baths Hot and Cold." To Hatton, at least, there seemed to be a plethora of these gentlemen:

> Offices that Insure Ships or their Cargo are many about the Royal Exchange, as Mr. Hall's. Mr. Bevis's. etc. who for a Premium paid down procure those that will subscribe Policies for Insuring Ships (with their Cargo) bound to or from any part of the World, the Premium being proportioned to the Distance, Danger of Seas, Enemies, etc. But in these Offices 'tis customary upon paying the Money on a Loss to discount 16 per Cent.[4]

While the precincts of the Royal Exchange provided a convenient and convivial financial center for the business of an island nation with relatively modest trade, the arrangement was totally inadequate to suit the needs of a burgeoning empire with worldwide interests. The physical premises of the Exchange were hard pressed to accommodate the comings and goings of legions of merchants transacting the business of empire. Cramped in one location, they cast about for other places wherein they might do their business. Some found their way to a new kind of shop in the city—the coffee house.

Unlike raucous taverns, coffee houses were sober places where respectable gentlemen might come, sit, visit, refresh themselves, and conduct business in an atmosphere far more genteel than that of the boisterous alehouse. Coffee houses had the added virtue of being cheap. For a penny or so a customer could purchase a dish of coffee and linger for as long as he desired, talking with friends, hearing and reading the latest news. The

---

4. Quoted in Wright and Fayle, *History of Lloyd's*, 40.

houses were, in brief, a wonderful place to do business. Among the best known was a shop run by Mr. Edward Lloyd opened sometime during the early 1680s in the neighborhood of Tower Street. Lloyd prospered, and in 1691 he moved his coffee house to Lombard Street not far from the General Post Office. He was now at the very center of London's information and financial network.

Although only one of many coffee houses in the vicinity, Lloyd's soon emerged as the preeminent center for maritime business. In October 1692, an advertisement appeared in the *Gazette* confirming Lloyd's role in maritime affairs:

> On Tuesday the 8th of November next, at Bennet's Coffee-House in Plimouth, will be exposed to sale by Inch of Candle, 3 Ships with all their Furniture; the Names whereof are the Teresa, the St. Thomas, and the Palme, two of 400 Tuns and the other 100. The Inventories thereof to be seen at Lloyds Coffee-House in Lombard-street, London. The said Ships are enter'd out for Barbados or Virginia.[5]

The rooms at Lloyd's were heavy with the elegant aroma of coffee, thick smoke, and the chatter of men sharing the latest intelligence concerning shipping. In 1696 Lloyd took an important step towards marking his coffee house as the center for information. He inaugurated *Lloyds News*, a thrice-weekly newspaper carrying the latest foreign and domestic intelligence as well as shipping advice.

By the turn of the eighteenth century, Lloyd's Coffee House had become an institution, raising Edward Lloyd to an exalted station far above that of a simple coffee-house proprietor. His shop was one of the most important maritime marts of the empire. His bustling waiters carried more than food and beverages on their trays. Deftly navigating the crowd, they placed before their customers offers to buy and sell vessels. They circulated insurance policies that still awaited the requisite number of names to be undersigned. But by far the most important commodity in circulation at Lloyd's was information. News of ships, captains, weather, war, and politics filled the room. Every scrap of intelligence and rumor was grabbed up, the better to inform decisions being made about risks and rates.

Edward Lloyd died in February 1713. Following his death questions arose about the conduct of marine insurance in London. A sizable number of merchants complained that the current method of doing business, that

5. *Gazette*, Oct. 20–24, 1692, and in Wright and Fayle, *History of Lloyd's*, 19.

is, of individual underwriters operating independently, was inadequate to service growing trade. They claimed that as the value of cargoes increased it was necessary to collect together many underwriters in order to secure a policy. One or just a few underwriters could not raise enough capital. They also suggested that in the current unregulated and seemingly chaotic market, numerous frauds were taking place, and that in some instances underwriters pledged to a policy could not deliver when called upon. The answer, according to these merchants, was a single corporation granted exclusive rights to issue insurance.

Over the loud objections of the subscribers at Lloyd's and other private underwriters, but with the aid of generous bribes well placed, Parliament passed a bill calling for the establishment of two corporations. Key to the bill was the twelfth clause, which prohibited

> All other Corporations or Bodies Politick, before this Time erected or established, or hereafter shall or maybe entered into by any Person or Persons, for assuring Ships or Merchandizes at Sea, or for lending Money upon Bottomry.[6]

The law then went on to state that private underwriting might still continue, but no "Persons acting in a Society or Partnership" could engage in the activity. The presumption was that insurers would abandon individual underwriters and seek the greater security and capital of the corporation.

The timing of those who supported incorporation was abominable. Unfortunately, the charter was granted at a time when reckless stock jobbing was at its apogee and about to plunge to its nadir. As the market collapsed in a rotten stench of corruption and fraud, few investors were willing to put their money into yet another new and suspect corporation. In a perverse twist the law of 1720 actually strengthened the hand of those doing business at Lloyd's, for the patrons in the coffee house were certainly not incorporated nor were they in formal partnership. They were simply private individuals who drank and ate together but did business independently, following the precept "each for himself and not one for another." All this was completely within the law. Furthermore, despite the slanderous propaganda spread by those favoring incorporation, the underwriters gathered at Lloyd's and other such places had performed well and had always been able to summon sufficient capital for the underwriting at hand. In the decades to come, Lloyd's Coffee House would become synonymous with

6. Wright and Fayle, *History of Lloyd's,* 61.

marine insurance, despite the fact that in truth it was only a meeting place where individuals congregated to do business.[7]

Whatever might be said of the idiosyncrasies of Lloyd's "organization," merchants who wished to share risk knew that on Lombard Street one could find underwriters with capital who shared a wit and a willingness to do business. While not unique to London, the fundamental elements that formed the marine insurance business—information, capital, and men willing to act as underwriters—were not easily assembled elsewhere in the empire.

In the American colonies, for example, Boston and Philadelphia merchants found themselves heavily reliant on London underwriters, a situation they deemed to be a particular inconvenience. Already obligated to their London correspondents for a variety of services rendered to them—shipping, banking, marketing—insurance simply represented an additional burden requiring payment. Shipowners of these towns recognized the benefits of local underwriting for the simple ease of doing business while at the same time keeping profits at home. However, until capital, risk, and underwriting fell into an American alignment, the choice was either to do without or do with London.

The first sign of American underwriting appeared in 1721 at Philadelphia. On May 25, John Copson placed an advertisement announcing

> Assurances from Losses happening at Sea ect. being found to be very much for the Ease and benefit of the Merchants and Traders in general, and whereas the merchants of this City of Philadelphia and other Parts, have been obliged to send to London for such Assurance, which has not only been tedious and troublesome, but even very precarious. For remedying of which, An Office of Publick Insurance on Vessels, Goods and Merchandizes, will, on Monday next, be Opened, and Books kept by John Copson of this City, at his House in the High Street, where all Persons willing to be Insured may apply: And Care shall be taken by the said J. Copson That the Assurors or Underwriters be Persons of undoubted Worth and reputation, and of considerable Interest in this City and Province.[8]

Although Philadelphia took the lead, Boston soon followed. In 1724 Joseph Marion, a notary of the town, announced the opening of his insurance office on "the North side of the Court House, near the head of King Street." Marion's style of business was in keeping with the tradition of

---

7. James Allan Park, *A System of the Law of Marine Insurances* (Boston, 1799).

8. C. Mitchell Bradford, *A Premium on Progress* (New York, 1970), 9.

Lloyd's. He drew up policies noting vessel, master, intended voyage, and the premium rate. He then left the document on a table, inviting those who would to sign the policy and note the amount they wished to subscribe. When the full amount was underwritten, the policy was sealed. While Marion's notarial office was not as busy as Lloyd's Coffee House, nor did it offer refreshment, it was nonetheless a public rendezvous where men of business were accustomed to visit. For these gentlemen, Marion was simply expanding his line of services.[9]

Boston merchants welcomed Marion's new venture. For generations, the town's most important trade had been along the coast and to the islands. It was a thriving traffic dominated by small vessels, sloops, and schooners owned by merchants of modest means. These were men who often lacked the capital and contacts to insure at Lloyd's, even if that august institution would deign to gamble on such a small and distant trade. Marion offered a chance to insure and, for those with capital to risk, an opportunity to underwrite. Bostonians were eager to engage.

These were good years for the port of Boston, and the town's rising tide of trade buoyed Marion's business and made his office a busy place. More policies were placed on the table and more underwriters sought. It was much like Lloyd's—informal, unregulated, and open to all who had a spirit of adventure and money to risk. In another respect, however, Marion's was unlike the London operation.

At Lloyd's, traffic was heavy enough through the house that when a policy was laid on the table it was fully subscribed only a short time later. At Marion's it was otherwise. Boston was not London; substantial amounts of time elapsed before enough men with sufficient capital came by to undertake risk. The best solution to this problem was the creation of a permanent pool of capital that could be tapped for risks. This of course was precisely what a corporation was intended to do, but since Boston was governed by the same laws as London, that could not happen. Other ways of accumulating capital had to be found. In December 1739 Benjamin Pollard, another notary of the town, announced that his office on "the South Side of the Town House" was open for those who sought marine insurance. Pollard promised "that a certain Number of Ge[n]tlemen of this Town[,] of good Estates, are Agreed and Ready, to make Insurance upon any Vessels or Cargoes, or both, in a lawful Trade."[10]

9. E. R. Hardy, *An Account of the Early Insurance Offices in Massachusetts from 1724 to 1801* (Boston, 1901), 29.
10. *New England Weekly Journal,* Dec. 18 and 25, 1739.

Pollard's innovation was lining up underwriters in advance. While no formal papers were signed (it would have been illegal in any case), Pollard nevertheless created and managed a pool of capital that could be quickly assigned to risks. While members of this pool might float in and out, the fact remained that capital was being organized on a dependable, albeit informal, basis. This was a rare occurrence in the colonies. Only in ports like Boston and Philadelphia, with a sufficient critical mass of commerce, could this take place.

Pollard stayed in the business a half dozen years. In 1745 he was succeeded by Joseph Dowse, who announced his office "at the lower end of King Street near the sign of the Elephant." Dowse remained at that location until 1763, when he moved up the coast to Salem.[11]

In the decades leading to the Revolution several other gentlemen, both merchants and notaries, sought business in marine insurance. The entry of new faces often coincided with war, a time of high rates and equally high profits. As business expanded, so too did the interests of the brokers and underwriters. Some ventured into fire insurance, although Boston's tightly packed wooden buildings presented a particularly hazardous risk for subscribers. Indeed, tradition suggests that Joseph Dowse's relocation to Salem was hastened by the great fire of 1760, in which he took a heavy loss.

Boston's regional dominance meant that shipowners in outports such as Salem and Newburyport looked to offices in the provincial capital for insurance. Boston underwriters also took shares in vessels from other New England colonies and, occasionally, even on vessels out of New York and Philadelphia. For the most part, however, underwriting in Boston focused on coastwise trade north to Nova Scotia and Newfoundland and south along the coast and to the islands.

It was not only the availability of capital that enabled Boston's marine insurance business to flourish. Central to the success of the enterprise were timely intelligence and a coordinated effort. Shipowners, underwriters, and brokers constantly prowled for news. Sure knowledge was the best basis for assigning risk and establishing premium rates, while to disregard risks was to court disaster. Insurance offices in Boston were thus clearinghouses of information. In some instances this ravenous appetite for intelligence extended to fixing the location of His Majesty's ships and customs officials. Boston underwriters were known on occasion to write policies for vessels involved in illegal trade under the rubric of "private adventures." Here, of

11. *Marine and Fire Insurance in Boston* (Boston, 1873), 37.

course, the best insurance was to know the location of His Majesty's ships and the disposition, geographic and political, of the local crown officers.[12]

At the outbreak of the Revolution, Boston had more than a half century of experience in marine insurance, and no one was more prominent in the business than Ezekiel Price. Born in Boston in 1728, Price was well connected. Like most of his fellow brokers he was a notary, but in addition he served as secretary to three royal governors—William Shirley, Thomas Pownall, and Francis Bernard. He was also at various times clerk of the Court of Common Pleas and Sessions, registrar of deeds, and a Boston selectman. He kept his insurance office on King Street opposite Kilby. In some ways, Price was the archetypal insurance man—he knew everyone and everything.[13]

Price opened his office in 1759, at the height of the French and Indian War and continued in business almost to the close of the Revolution. He issued his first policy, on March 19, 1759, on the brigantine *John Roger* bound for Gibraltar. She was insured by four underwriters, each taking an equal part of the £200 policy. Price wrote the policy in the form of Lloyd's, promising that it "shall be of as much Force and Effect as the surest writing or Policy of Assurance heretofore made in Lombard Street or in the Royal Exchange or elsewhere in London."[14]

Although Price launched his business by insuring a trip to Gibraltar, for the most part his normal range of activities, like that of his fellow Boston brokers, involved commerce closer to home—voyages along the coast in both directions and ventures to the islands. Since this sort of trade generally involved relatively small vessels carrying modest cargo, Price's policies were never large, rarely exceeding £200 and generally written with a premium of not more than 10 percent.

For marine insurers, war often meant prosperity, for it permitted underwriters to raise premiums beyond the level of actual risk. Indeed, just the anticipation of losses was enough to drive up rates. The Revolution was no exception. In Boston, once the British evacuated on March 17, 1776, trade in the port resumed. Since risks were rated high, insurance rates rose to unheard of levels of 40, 50, and 60 percent. The promise of rich profits

---

12. John Tyler, *Smugglers and Patriots: Boston Merchants and the Advent of the American Revolution* (Boston, 1986), 13.

13. The Ezekiel Price Papers are located at the Boston Athenaeum. A smaller collection may also be found at the Massachusetts Historical Society.

14. Price Papers, vol. 8, policy no. 1, Boston Athenaeum.

drew new men into the insurers' ranks, including Edward Payne, who set up an office on King Street, and James Jeffries, who opened his office on School Street.[15]

Boston's waterfront was now alive with activity. With near giddy abandon merchants rushed to fit out privateers lest all the good prizes be taken before they could set out. Extravagant prices on commodities drew investors into risky trade with distant ports hitherto closed to them. These were gambles, of course. Men were betting that the Royal Navy was either too impotent or too incompetent to put a stop to their business. Heeding the risks, however, they took out insurance. Owners engaged insurers on the odds that they would lose their ships. Underwriters wagered that they would not.

Like a rising storm at sea, it took the Royal Navy a while to make up a force, but when it did it was able to unleash its fury on the Americans. As more and more losses were tallied the blush of war paled. British cruisers became a common sight along the coast. They overtook American merchantmen and privateers and cast their crews into grim rotting hulks at New York or hauled them off to Dartmoor and Mill prisons. Trade and profits evaporated. In 1780 Price wrote forty-six policies, about half the number of the prior year. In 1781 he wrote just seven.[16]

Seventeen eighty-one was a bleak year for Boston's commerce. Yet the tide was turning. As the war drew to a close a new nation was taking shape. Even before the treaty of peace, in testimony of their separation from England, Boston's underwriters changed the form of their policies. Although it still smacked of the Lloyd's style, the insurers altered its key wording. No longer, for example, did policies make reference to settling disputes in accordance with the customs of Lombard Street and the Royal Exchange. Henceforth, policies issued in Boston would be adjudicated "agreeable to Rules and Customs in Boston."

Good sense and tradition dictated that the "Customs in Boston" ought not to vary widely from the course set by Lloyd's. Maritime trade and commerce were by their very nature international and thus had to abide by certain accepted rules that were beyond the exclusive control of the American merchant community. At the same time, however, Boston brokers came to appreciate that the traditional way of doing business, that is, of

15. Hardy, *Account of the Early Insurance Offices*, 93.
16. Price Papers, Boston Athenaeum.

keeping policies open while waiting for underwriters, was inefficient and slow. Two men in particular, both experienced brokers, saw the ill effects of such informality and took steps to organize capital resources in a more modern fashion.

In 1781 John Hurd, son of Boston's well known gold and silversmith Jacob Hurd, announced the opening of an insurance office at the Bunch of Grapes Tavern. While apparently new to the business, Hurd was well aware that the success of an insurance office depended upon its ability to attract and keep underwriters. The long and tedious process of finding them was an ordeal most new insurers feared. To avoid that obstacle, Hurd worked out a deal with Ezekiel Price, who seems to have been ready to retire. Hurd took over Price's business.

For the first two years, at least, he handled affairs in the old-fashioned way. He kept his office in the front room of the Bunch of Grapes Tavern, laid policies on the table, and waited for men to come by and underwrite their names. It was a time-honored and convivial way of doing business. Nonetheless, it was awkward, slow, and uncertain. Perhaps it was the end of the war and the release from British restrictions that convinced Hurd that he ought to try a different manner of writing insurance. Whatever the reason, in December 1783 John Hurd created a standing "company" of underwriters. Each man who agreed to list his name stood ready to underwrite a fixed amount of money without reference to any particular venture. When an insurance proposal was made, any three of the names on the list or the office keeper and any two could sign and pledge all to the policy. Twenty men signed on: sixteen from Boston, two from Salem, and one each from Cambridge and Medford. Hurd's "company" was not an incorporated body, to whom the General Court had granted a charter; nonetheless, in everything but law Hurd had formed a company.[17]

Edward Payne saw the virtues of Hurd's innovation and followed suit. He and his son William also gathered a group of regular underwriters. Twenty-two men agreed to join them. Apparently all Bostonians, they did business in the manner of Hurd and his associates.

As part of the membership agreement, each group required the underwriters to place a certain portion of their liability in the hands of the organization. As a result, the Hurd and Payne associations very quickly came to command considerable sums of money. These sums could not

17. Agreement, Dec. 10, 1783. Private collection.

remain idle waiting for a disaster, so their custodians sought safe and profitable havens into which they could funnel their capital. In 1784 the General Court created just such an investment opportunity when it incorporated the Massachusetts Bank.[18]

Although neither Hurd nor Payne was among the original petitioners for the bank, they and many of their associates invested heavily in its stock. Indeed, both Payne's and Hurd's offices were listed in the advertisement announcing the bank as a place where subscriptions were being taken. In addition, three of Hurd's regular underwriters served as bank directors, and eight of Payne's held the same post. Those who organized this bank were part of a complex social and commercial Boston network, held together in part by a shared interest in marine insurance. Perhaps it was the profitable experiences with insurance underwriting that prompted them to risk a more formal relationship. Certainly, profits from insurance helped to finance the bank, which in turn generated its own profits to be invested elsewhere.

For the next decade and a half the Paynes and Hurd satisfied the bulk of Boston's marine insurance market through their unincorporated companies. Other individuals also acted as brokers. Moses Michael Hays kept an office, as did William Cleland and Joseph Taylor, but the key figures remained the Paynes, Hurd, and their associates. Hurd seems to have been particularly successful. In great measure this was due to a young man, Peter Chardon Brooks, whom he took into his office in 1789.

Born in 1767 in North Yarmouth, Maine, Brooks was the son of the town's minister, Edward Brooks. Barely two years after the birth of his son the Reverend Mr. Brooks ran afoul of his congregation over a theological matter. He lost the dispute and returned to his small family farm in Medford, Massachusetts, near the Mystic River. During the Revolution the elder Brooks enlisted in the Continental Navy and served aboard the frigate *Hancock*. He was serving in her when she was captured and taken into Halifax. The rigors of confinement in the Halifax jail so weakened him that by the time he returned to Medford he was ill and unfit for continued naval service. He died at home on May 6, 1781, leaving behind a family that, while not poor was, nonetheless, in need. Under the circumstances Peter Brooks, age fourteen, was dispatched to Boston to be apprenticed in a

18. N. S. B. Gras, *The Massachusetts First National Bank of Boston, 1784–1934* (Cambridge, Mass., 1937), 17–30.

counting house. Brooks did well enough to catch the eye of John Hurd, who brought him into his business.[19]

In the years following the Revolution, Boston's trade suffered. The general travail of postwar adjustment, coupled with exclusion from traditional British markets, caused a considerable falling off of arrivals and clearances. In the first year of peace, they totaled only 408, most of them small vessels plying the coast and to the islands. That figure and pattern remained fairly constant throughout the decade.

Boston's somber trade prospects brightened a bit in the late 1780s. In 1787 *Columbia* and *Lady Washington* departed the town bound for the northwest coast and thence to Canton. Of the four Bostonians who were shareholders in the voyage, three—Crowell Hatch, Joseph Barrell, and Samuel Brown—were part of Hurd's underwriting group. After a long and arduous voyage, *Columbia* and *Lady Washington* reached Nootka Sound on Vancouver Island. *Columbia* then sailed for Canton, while *Lady Washington* remained on the coast. From Canton, *Columbia* struck a course for Boston, where she warped alongside the wharf on August 9, 1790. *Columbia*'s triumphal return buoyed the town and announced Boston's entry into the China trade.

Columbia's success was a harbinger of good tidings for the port. Equally welcome was the news from Philadelphia. In 1787 *Columbia* had cast off from Long Wharf leaving behind a nation governed under a weak confederation. By the time of her return, Americans had crafted a republic under the Federal Constitution.

First on the agenda of the new government was the issue of revenue and trade regulation, which neatly combined into the first tariff legislation enacted on July 4, 1789. This law set in place a discriminatory schedule that gave a 10 percent discount to goods imported in American vessels. The law also required the domestic construction of ships seeking American enrollment or registry. Within a few weeks the First Congress enacted additional legislation aimed even more directly at protecting and encouraging the American merchant marine and shipyards. This set standard tonnage duties for vessels entering American ports: those entering with United States registry paid six cents per ton, those built in the United States but regis-

19. Freeman Hunt, *Lives of American Merchants* (New York, 1856–1858), 1:133–183.

tered under a foreign flag paid thirty cents per ton, and those foreign built and foreign owned paid fifty cents per ton.[20]

All this was good news for Boston commerce. Entrances and clearances climbed. Not only did the number of vessels trafficking the port increase, but so too did the value of cargoes and their insurance. Between 1789 and 1795, 1,152 vessels were either enrolled or registered at the Boston custom house. Of that number 860 gave Boston as their home port.[21] No greater testimony to the rising profits in trade and insurance could be offered than the fact that this burgeoning business drew the attention of the tax collector. In 1788 the General Court levied a 12s. fee on all marine insurance policies.[22]

Boston's experience in the postwar world was mirrored in other American ports, particularly Philadelphia. Philadelphians had underwritten their commerce in much the same way as Bostonians, that is, at first as individuals and then, through an evolution, in more formal associations. These associations paved the way for a meeting held in the city on November 3, 1792, at which a group of underwriters and investors decided to organize a company for the purpose of writing marine and other insurance. The state granted a charter, the company sold shares, and on December 10 the stockholders met to elect directors and officers. The company had a capital fund of $600,000.

The example of Philadelphia was not lost on Boston. Incorporation offered numerous advantages for merchants and underwriters alike, including access to greater capital as well as a fair degree of permanence and stability. On the other hand, the old ways of doing business were hard to shake off and, in fact, seemed for the moment quite capable of handling what was required.

By the mid nineties, marine insurance in Boston was dominated by Hurd's protégé, Peter Chardon Brooks. Having succeeded Hurd, in a few short years Brooks had managed to amass a considerable following of underwriters to accompany a large fortune. In his later years of retirement,

20. William A. Baker, *A Maritime History of Bath, Maine, and the Kennebec River Region* (Bath, Me., 1973), 149–170.

21. Ship registers and enrollments of Boston and Charlestown compiled by the Survey of Federal Archives, Division of Professional and Service Projects, Works Progress Administration (Boston, 1942). Typescripts at the Massachusetts Historical Society, Mystic Seaport, and the Peabody Essex Museum.

22. *Massachusetts Laws and Resolves* (Boston, 1788), chap. 15 (June 18, 1788), 203.

Brooks mused that the 1790s were a time when he "made money enough to turn any man's head."[23]

Given the remarkable growth in Boston's commerce, it is somewhat unusual that marine insurers did not follow the example of the Massachusetts Bank and legally incorporate in order to amass greater capital resources. That they did not seems to indicate that private underwriters, particularly Brooks, could supply local demand. It may also be that Brooks and his associates used whatever political influence they could muster to block any attempt at incorporation. Since corporations were often viewed as greedy abusers of the public trust, opposition to them was politically popular and easily undertaken. Massachusetts did not have a general incorporation law until 1818, so every request for a charter required special legislation, which could bring unwanted attention to its proponents.[24]

Despite public skepticism, the number of corporations in Massachusetts grew. In the first decade of the commonwealth's existence (1780–1790) the General Court created approximately one hundred corporations. Almost all of the special acts of incorporation created either a public entity, such as a town, or brought into existence a charitable, educational, or medical institution. On only a few occasions (e.g. in the case of the Massachusetts Bank) did the law create a for-profit company.

In June 1795 the General Court chartered the first insurance company in the commonwealth, the Massachusetts Fire Insurance Company. It was capitalized at $300,000, with 3,000 shares. Three years passed before the next insurance company appeared. The General Court chartered the Massachusetts Mutual Fire Insurance Company with a capital of $2,000,000 in 1798.

Philadelphia's example, coupled with the apparent success of local fire insurance companies, led the way to Boston's first incorporated marine in-

23. Hunt, *American Merchants*, 1:152.

24. Julius Clarke, *History of the Massachusetts Insurance Department: Including a Sketch of the Origin and Progress of Insurance, and of the Insurance Legislation of the State, from 1780 to 1876* (Boston, 1876). For additional discussion of the issue of incorporation see Pauline Maier, "The Debate over Incorporations: Massachusetts in the Early Republic," Conrad Edick Wright, ed., *Massachusetts and the New Nation* (Boston, 1992), 73–117; Oscar and Mary Handlin, *Commonwealth: A Study of the Role of Government in the American Economy: Massachusetts, 1774–1861* (New York and London, 1947); and Edwin M. Dodd, *American Business Corporations Until 1860, With Special Reference to Massachusetts* (Cambridge, Mass., 1954).

surer. On January 16, 1799, the Boston Marine Insurance Company (BMI) received its charter "to make insurance upon vessels, freight, and goods or for the ransom of persons in captivity and in cases of money lent upon bottomry and respondentia." The capital fund was set at a minimum of $500,000, not to exceed $820,000. Shares sold at $100 each, with investors required to pay $30 per share by March 27 and the remainder in five installments within one year.[25]

Nearly 150 men stepped forward and quickly bought up the offering. While the majority, 92, hailed from Boston, two other Massachusetts seaports were represented as well. Thirty-one men from Salem purchased shares, and 19 from Newburyport adventured their money. No one person took more than fifty shares, and many took far less. Ownership of the company was widely distributed. On March 14, 1799, the stockholders held their first meeting at the Concert Hall in Boston to elect a president, secretary, and a board of directors. Thomas Davis became president, at a salary of $2,000 per year, Col. Joseph May took office as secretary at $1,500 per year, and twelve directors (including Davis and May) were chosen. The act of incorporation called for an annual meeting of stockholders, monthly meetings of the directors, and a committee of three to meet even more often, on a daily basis if necessary, to assess risks and set rates. Company records indicate that in practice, the annual meeting did take place to elect officers and directors. It is much less certain whether or not regular monthly meetings took place, nor is the evidence clear about the role of the three-man committee. What does emerge from the records is the clear impression that from their rented office in the Union Bank on State Street Davis and May ran the company.

It was not surprising that the directors elected Thomas Davis to be their president. A native of Plymouth, Davis had served the town in the General Court and represented it at the Massachusetts ratifying convention in 1788. Like many of his contemporaries, Davis saw in the creation of a new republic great opportunity for himself, and so he left provincial Plymouth and set off for Boston. The move worked. A firm Federalist, he became a successful merchant, was elected to the State Senate, and became treasurer of the commonwealth. With his strong links to the both the business and political worlds, he was a natural choice to lead the new company.

Davis's good right hand was Col. Joseph May. A member of an old and

---

25. *Massachusetts Laws and Resolves* (Boston, 1796), chap. 22 (June 25, 1795), 362–365; *Laws and Resolves* (Boston, 1798), chap. 67 (Mar. 1, 1798), 456–459.

noted Boston family, May was married to a descendant of Judge Samuel Sewall and was, like his wife's distinguished ancestor, a prominent member of the Old South Church. Born in 1760, May had done a brief apprenticeship with Stephen Salisbury, a prosperous Worcester merchant, and then returned to Boston after the British evacuation to set up his own mercantile business. He was also prominent in the Independent Corps of Cadets, of which he was colonel. In 1798, May's business went bankrupt. It was then, according to his grandson, that "After some days of deep depression, he formed the resolution never to be a rich man; but to withstand all temptations to engage again in the pursuit of wealth." The next year he became secretary of the insurance company. According to his grandson, he accepted the post because it gave him a small income while allowing him afternoons free to participate in charitable works. May remained secretary from the company's formation until its demise in 1838.[26]

By the conditions of its charter, the BMI was required to place most of its capital in bank stock. It did, making its largest investment in notes of the Bank of the United States and putting smaller amounts in Boston banks, including the Massachusetts and Union banks. Its only non-bank investment was $20,000 allocated to real estate. Thus the company launched its important role as a key provider of bank capital.

Critical to the success of the BMI was the skill with which the company calculated and assigned risks. Although the company records are not specific in this matter, it seems likely that the president, in consultation with May and selected directors, played the role of principal actuary. The company wrote insurance to all parts of the world including a variety of American ports. Key to its success was its creation of a network of correspondents who channeled business and information to the office on State Street.

The company made its entree to the profitable Newport market through the firm of Gibbs and Channing. The Browns in Providence were important BMI clients as well; in fact, they were among the first to query Davis about insurance. They wanted to insure the *Ann and Hope* to Batavia and Canton. She would carry specie out and merchandise back. According to the Browns, insurers Willing and Francis of Philadelphia quoted a premium rate of 12 percent, 10 percent to Batavia and then an additional 2 percent to Canton. Was Davis interested in insuring the voyage? He was, he replied, and indeed, the company had several vessels with policies

26. Samuel May, "Col. Joseph May, 1760–1841," *New-England Historical and Genealogical Register* 27(1873):116.

to Canton but at 10 percent. The Providence men were persistent and shrewd. They replied that since *Ann and Hope* was a new and well armed vessel, they expected 7 or 8 percent. Davis compromised at 9 percent. The policy was issued.[27]

Davis was aggressive in soliciting new business. He wrote policies for owners as far south as New York and Philadelphia and as far north as Portland. Boston, however, was his principal arena, and the vessels and merchants of this port proved to be the mainstay of his business. In its first five months of operation the company wrote 233 policies at an average premium of 10 percent with a total face value of $1.4 million. In the same period, it had four losses for $13,700. Premium income was $191,806.

Whether it insured a voyage to Canton or to Philadelphia, the company understood the complexities of coping with the sea. It looked for a good ship, an able commander, and an experienced owner. If all seemed well and the voyage was on a known route, coastwise or deep sea, then the company was likely to take on the risk of storms, wrecks, and strandings. Ironically, what the company feared most was not the vicissitudes of nature, but the perversity of man.

Two wars were underway at the time of the company's launching. In the West Indies, the United States's undeclared war with France was winding down, while in Europe Great Britain and France showed no sign of letting up in their incessant struggle. For Boston merchants the troubles in the West Indies were most annoying, but thanks to aggressive patrolling by the infant American navy, and the gradual weakening of the French at sea, the threat to commerce from that quarter was much reduced. As far as Europe was concerned the situation was far less threatening than might be imagined. First, since the United States was a neutral power a certain amount of trading could be carried on under that guise. Both England and France, while prone to dismiss the rights of neutrals whenever convenient, were equally likely to respect those rights when it served their purpose. Boston had a full complement of clever neutral traders who could do well in such confused times.

Being clever meant avoiding capture. Despite romantic tales of chases at sea and rollicking fights, merchant vessels on the high seas were in very little danger of being captured. In fact, once off soundings the chance of encountering an enemy on the open sea was fairly remote. Traders faced

27. Thomas Davis to Brown & Ives, May 29, 1799, letterbook, Boston Marine Insurance Company Papers (hereafter BMI), Massachusetts Historical Society; Brown & Ives to Thomas Davis, June 1, 1799, box 1a, BMI.

their greatest danger entering and leaving port where traffic was concentrated and the enemy could lie in wait. Moreover, since the British navy controlled European waters it could, for the most part, blockade the enemy in port. Those few warring rascals who did elude blockaders might make the men on State Street a bit nervous, but in reality they posed nothing more than a minor nuisance. Rates charged by the BMI indicate that Davis and his associates had faith in the Royal Navy and disdain for the French. From 1801 to 1807 the rate to England and Ireland never rose above 3½ percent, and in general the rates to open ports north of Gibraltar remained relatively low and stable.

Europe was not the only place where war threatened the company's insured. Even after the end of hostilities with France in 1800, war, revolutions, and general lawlessness were frequent visitors to the West Indies and spawned a variety of predators. In 1800 for a voyage from Jamaica to Honduras and thence to Liverpool the company quoted a rate of 15 percent. This, at a time when the rate on a voyage to Canton hovered at 10 percent. Such a high rate was the sum of navigational hazards and the risks of predators.

Another area that drew particular attention, and thus compelled high rates, was the Mediterranean. The culprits here were the notorious Barbary corsairs. Their method was direct—nations wishing to transit their waters had to pay tribute or risk attack. Over the years most European nations had opted to pay. It was cheaper than maintaining naval patrols in the region. Great Britain was no exception, and as long as Boston vessels flew the Union Jack they enjoyed protection. Independence brought the unhappy realization that American vessels had to fend for themselves.

Whatever the hazards, for Bostonians the Mediterranean trade was too important to be abandoned. The exchange of fish for salt and wine was key to the town's prosperity. Small wonder that in the early 1790s Bostonians were strong advocates for the creation of an American navy. Congress's authorization of six frigates in March 1794 was a direct answer to the Barbary threat.

Uneasiness over conditions in the Mediterranean was reflected in the offices of the BMI. Early in 1801 at the height of American troubles Israel Thorndike, owner of the ship *Sally*, asked for insurance to the region. Davis quoted him 15 percent out and back, but only on condition that Thorndike agree to arm *Sally* with eight cannon. This was more than double any of the company's rates for voyages to northern Europe. Furthermore, to limit its exposure the company noted "in the present state of things in the Mediterranean they do not incline to take more than twenty thousand dollars on our risk."[28]

Of course, the perils of sea voyaging did not threaten only vessels and cargo. Crewmen sailing in the Mediterranean feared being captured and held for ransom. Who would pay for their return? Daniel Sargent and Eleazer Johnson, both of the brig *Traveller* bound for those waters, were worried about their prospects, so after insuring their vessel and cargo for $10,300 they turned to the BMI to insure their "personal liberty." On September 16, 1801, the company wrote a policy in the amount of $3,000 on the personal liberty of Johnson at a premium of 2½ percent. Two weeks later it did the same for Sargent at a slightly lower premium of 2 percent. The difference may well have been the result of the good news from the Mediterranean that Commodore Richard Dale's squadron had arrived safely and was enjoying success rounding up some of the corsairs.[29]

Lives were also at risk in other trades. In February 1800 Eliphalet Butter took out a $600 policy on the life of his brother John bound for the north-west coast aboard the schooner *Rover*, commanded by George Davidson. The rate was 5 percent, a clear indication that the risks to life on the coast were judged greater than those in the Mediterranean—and indeed they were. *Rover* was never heard from again. She may have been lost at sea, or she may have been the American vessel reported in June 1801 to have been cut off by the natives. In any case, in April 1802 Eliphalet Butter collected $594.[30]

Almost as soon as the company opened its doors, inquiries arrived concerning insurance on voyages to the east. Shipowners in Salem, Providence, and New Haven, who hitherto had enjoyed only a limited number of options for insurance, welcomed the appearance of a new company. These gentlemen were anxious to shop for the best rates. Between 1799 and 1807, premiums for voyages to eastern ports (Isle de France, Calcutta, Sumatra, and Canton) ranged between 8 and 10 percent. A slight additional charge was levied when the cargo was specie, usually 1 or 2 percent.

Although these eastern voyages were long, they actually posed fewer risks than did many shorter runs. The vessels themselves, for example, tended to be larger, newer, and under the command of better officers than

28. Tho[mas] Davis to Israel Thorndike, June 17, 1801, letterbook, BMI.

29. Policies 1491 and 1504, Policy Records G, BMI.

30. Policy 446, BMI; Proposals of February 1800, Proposals No. 2, BMI; F. W. Hovey, "A List of Trading Vessels in Maritime Fur Trade, 1785–1794," *Royal Society of Canada Transactions*, sec. II (1930), 134.

those involved in other trades. Although many Boston vessels sailed round the Horn to the northwest coast for sea otter and thence to Canton, the company seems not to have been interested in insuring on those routes. For the most part its clients traveled east via the Cape of Good Hope and the Isle de France.

For such long voyages the company was apt to add conditions. For example, the rate was lower if the insured agreed not to make any stops en route to the final destination. Intermediate port calls added risk to the venture. There was, of course, the natural risk of navigating in and out of port. There was also the threat of complications with local authorities or natives. This concern may explain why the company avoided insuring vessels trading on the northwest coast.

The company also tried to stay away from illegal trade, not always an easy task, for the question of legality was complex. One of the company's most interesting cases involved the *Aurora*. In the fall of 1805 while allegedly bound from Leghorn to the Isle de France, she was taken by an English privateer. *Aurora* carried a handsome cargo of wine, oil, perfumes, soap, capers, olives, and marble tiles. She also had on board $45,000 in specie. *Aurora*'s value merited the cost of an appeal to the British government, in hopes of recovering the loss. Samuel Williams, the company's representative in London, undertook the case, asking the British Court of Vice Admiralty for full restitution. The court decided that the cargo was a private adventure belonging to the captain and mate. It ordered the return of the cargo and vessel to the owners, but seized the specie as, in the words of the court, part of "an illicit voyage to the Isle de France . . . intended for the purpose of carrying on the Trade and Commerce of the Colonies of the Enemies of the Crown."

In the matter of the *Aurora* the company had wisely only taken part of the risk. It had written $15,000 at 11 percent. Suffolk Marine Insurance Company, New England Marine Insurance Company, Newburyport Insurance Company, and at least three individuals—William Payne, Aaron Dexter, and Jonathan Amory—had also taken a risk.

Although unhappy with the Vice Admiralty Court's decision the company recognized the legitimacy of the royal claim. But before it would settle with the owner certain adjustments had to be made. First, because the premium on the specie had not yet been paid (owners often did not pay until the end of the voyage, since it was only then that cash would be available), the claim was reduced to $13,350. The company took a second deduction for "prompt payment." This simply meant that once the company agreed to pay it would make good within sixty days. In the end BMI paid the *Aurora*'s owners $13,067 as its share on the loss.[31]

Dividing up the risk, as was done in the case of the *Aurora*, was a common practice. A company might be willing to undertake fully the modest risk of a few thousand dollars on a coastwise or island voyage, but the situation was quite otherwise where large vessels and rich cargoes bound halfway around the world were concerned. In seeking partners, BMI had no lack of candidates. Within a half decade of the company's incorporation Massachusetts chartered at least seventeen additional corporations to do business in marine insurance. BMI shared risks with other underwriters in Boston as well as with firms and individuals in New York and Philadelphia, where many more companies had been established.[32]

By sharing risks at sea marine insurance companies were among the first businesses in the new republic to engage in interstate commerce. Cooperating with various out-of-state companies and individuals worked to create pools of capital sufficient to underwrite large ventures. In June 1800, for example, the company shared in underwriting $100,000 in coverage on *Northern Liberties*, a New York vessel bound on a voyage from that port to Tenerife and thence to Vera Cruz. Three other companies also participated: New York Insurance Company, Columbian Insurance Company, and North American Insurance Company. Also venturing were a group represented by Joseph Taylor's office in Boston and several individuals. Each participant underwrote on its own in a range between 17½ and 22½ percent.

31. Box 4, BMI, contains the papers relating to this case. The Suffolk Marine Insurance Company seems not to have been a legally incorporated entity. The Newburyport Marine Insurance Company was incorporated in 1799, and the New England Marine Insurance Company was incorporated in 1803. *Acts and Resolves* (Boston, 1803), 315, 224.

32. The seventeen companies included: Newburyport Marine Insurance Company (1799); Maine Fire and Marine Insurance Company (1799); Salem Marine Insurance Company (1800); Merrimac Marine and Fire Insurance Company (1802); Lincoln and Kennebec Marine Insurance Company (1803); New England Marine Insurance Company (1803); Essex Fire and Marine Insurance Company (1803); Marblehead Marine Insurance Company (1803); Gloucester Marine Insurance Company (1803); Cumberland Marine and Fire Insurance Company (1803); Portland Marine and Fire Insurance Company (1803); Bedford Marine Insurance Company (1804); Union Marine Insurance Company (1804); Nantucket Marine Insurance Company (1804); Kennebec Marine Insurance Company (1804); Plymouth Marine Insurance Company (1804); and Nantucket Union Marine Insurance Company (1804).

Unfortunately, *Northern Liberties* was lost at sea. Her settlement un-veiled differences among the underwriters. While all understood the gen-eral arrangements of the voyage, certain details of the ship's ownership, which if a loss had not occurred might well have never been discovered, emerged to cloud the claim. The men in Boston refused to pay over their share to an individual not specifically mentioned in the policy. This, appar-ently, was not the position of the underwriters in New York and Phila-delphia. The case eventually found its way to the Supreme Court, where the Boston company's position was upheld.[33] In years to come, as com-panies grew more accustomed to cooperating, such disputes diminished as both custom and law became standardized.

In settling on losses, company and shipper alike generally followed the traditional practices of marine insurance. If an insured vessel or cargo suffered damage during a voyage, as soon as he came to port the captain filed a "protest." In this document, which served as the first step in the claim process, the captain described the extent of the loss. If possible, he might seek to have an independent party (perhaps another captain from Boston) verify the damage. If not, it was simply his own testimony, perhaps notarized by an American consul if one were present. Once received at the company offices in Boston, the protest was vetted by the officers and direc-tors. If the directors felt they needed more information, or independent judgment concerning the veracity of the claim, they might engage an agent (surveyor) to assess personally the alleged damage to ship and cargo. If everything were found to be in order, then within sixty days the claim would be paid. If a dispute arose, then by mutual agreement the matter would be resolved by "Referees chosen by each Party." Ultimately, of course, as in the case of *Northern Liberties,* the dispute could go to court.

Edmund Bartlett of Newburyport was the first policyholder to deliver a protest to the BMI. His schooner *Dolphin,* laden with flaxseed and staves, departed the Merrimac River in February 1799. Once to sea she suffered heavy damage in a winter storm. Bartlett claimed damages of £250. The company demurred and offered less. He agreed. Bartlett's quick acquies-cence to the company's determination of loss was fairly common. With only a few exceptions, between 1799 and 1807 the BMI speedily and without difficulty paid its claims. The amounts forthcoming were nearly always less

33. *Graves and Barnwell* v. *Boston Marine Insurance Company,* in B. R. Curtis, *Reports of Decisions of the Supreme Court of the United States* . . . (Boston, 1855), 1:514–520.

than what the insured sought, but were close enough so as to make legal action cumbersome and unprofitable.[34]

If a vessel were "abandoned," that is, if the owners surrendered all rights to the underwriters, the company paid the adjusted claim. The vessel and her cargo now belonged to the company. In many instances salvage then became a possibility, particularly if the vessel had been wrecked or had gone aground close to home. In February 1805, for example, the company paid off on two strandings, both abandoned, one at Provincetown and the other on the Marshfield beach. In both instances, they turned to an experienced salvager, Thomas Smalley of Provincetown, to manage the recovery operation. On the scene, Smalley determined that although the vessels could not be refloated, much of their equipment, sails, rigging, and the like could be saved. These were placed in storage to be auctioned at a later time.[35]

When matters to the north needed attention, the company often turned to Capt. Henry Jackson. Jackson occasionally handled salvage projects, but he also acted as a surveyor. Vessels putting into Portland with claims against the company could expect a visit from the captain. Jackson was a thorough man and served the company well. In most instances a vessel's cargo was of greater value than its hull, so Jackson was careful to inspect below to determine if the hogsheads, bales, or boxes had been stowed properly. Should he find any negligence, the company might refuse full payment. Nearly every cargo carried a certain deductible for normal damage at sea, and Jackson's task was to determine just what a reasonable owner's loss might be. The company had a regular relationship with Jackson and Smalley.[36]

Losses reported in distant parts of the world presented the firm with special problems. For example, when a vessel insured by the company put in at Lisbon for repairs her master, John Hamilton, forwarded to the BMI a lengthy bill of costs for labor and food in that port:

> I thought a fair charge upon the underwriters arising from the great quantity of hired Labourers which were fed all on board. Add to this the number of Custom house officers that a ship in Lisbon is crowded with expecially in distress that must be all victualled at the ship's expence that it seems to be the principle business for everyone to get as much out of the distressed as possible. I have conversed with Cap. Salter & he says & the Mate likewise that $500 would be no compensation for what was swallowed by these

34. Thomas Davis to Edmund Bartlett, Sept. 16, 1799, letterbook, BMI.
35. Jos[eph] May to Thomas Smalley, Feb. 4, 1805, letterbook, BMI.
36. Henry Jackson to [Thomas Davis], Feb. 15, 1804, box 3, BMI.

Louzy devils & that they left Lisbon with but little more than half the quantity of provisions that they had when she sailed.[37]

The company responded with its own list of queries, and the matter went back and forth until finally the parties reached a settlement.

The case at Lisbon was not particularly unusual. Boston's considerable trade with the Baltic region, for example, often resulted in plaintiff letters from captains who had come to grief in those shallow and confusing waters. Settling disputes at such distances required considerable diplomacy, tact, and expertise. Only under the most extraordinary circumstances would the company go to the extreme of dispatching its own agent to a distant place to investigate a claim. The costs intending upon that inclined the BMI to negotiate a settlement even when it suspected misconduct. In at least one instance, however, the company elected to send a representative to investigate a claim, namely, that of the owners of the brig *Traveller*.

Traveller, apparently the same brig that had previously been insured in Mediterranean service, was now sailing round the Cape of Good Hope into the Indian Ocean. She was lost somewhere near the Isle de France. The vessel was insured for a handsome sum, and when the owners delivered their protest the amount involved warranted sending Charles G. Cabot as a company representative to determine the facts. Cabot's mission cost the company $500. His report is unrecorded, but the absence of correspondence and legal action would seem to indicate that the owners must have received all, or nearly all, of what they expected.[38]

Of all the trades to the various parts of the world there were only two kinds of business in which the company refused to participate. It would not insure vessels in the slave trade, nor would it insure voyages to the La Plata region. Whether the company's antipathy to the slave trade was a result of moral revulsion or simple actuarial calculation is not certain. The trade was legal under the Constitution and would remain so until 1808, when Article I, section 9, of the document permitted Congress to ban the business. However, whatever the legal status of slaving it did pose a high risk. There was always the danger of an attack by angry natives along the African coast, to say nothing of the perils of the voyage during which disease might decimate the crew and cargo. Boston merchants had little financial interest in the business, anyway. Most of the New England slave trading originated in Narragansett Bay, particularly at Newport and Bristol, so that even if the

37. Jona[than] Hamilton to Thomas Davis, May 10, 1802, box 2, BMI.
38. Receipts, Apr. 8, 1801, BMI.

company had offered to underwrite the business there would not have been much demand for its services in Boston. The case of La Plata was different.[39]

Spain's American empire was falling apart. The demise had been underway for several generations, and the tumult of the wars of the French Revolution hastened the process. The political and economic situation throughout Spanish America was confused and vexsome. Nowhere was this more apparent than in the vice royalty of Rio de la Plata. The heart of the vice royalty was the port of Buenos Aires, a vibrant commercial center located on the river about 135 miles west of Montevideo.

In 1796, when war broke out between England and Spain, the merchants of Buenos Aires found themselves isolated and cut off from Spain by the wooden walls of the Royal Navy. Having festered for decades under inept Spanish rule, local leaders had little compunction about seeking alternative, albeit illegal, routes of trade. Too feeble to stop them, but desperately trying to maintain the pretense of authority, in 1797 the king allowed trade in neutral vessels, but only if they pledged to "return to the ports of Spain." The United States was the principal neutral carrier left in the Atlantic world, and American ships, including vessels from Boston, flocked to take up the business. Precious few of these neutral bottoms, however, ever dropped anchor in a Spanish port, preferring instead to carry goods where they might fetch a handsome price.[40]

The sham of this neutral trade was so glaring that in 1799 the king revoked his permission. American ships were once again subject to seizure for taking on Spanish cargo. At the same time, of course, they were also subject to British capture. Reports of seizures alarmed the company. This game of double jeopardy was not to its liking, and so in the year following the king's act it informed its clients, "The risks to River la Plata are not among those to which our Directors are partial."[41]

In the eight years studied (1799–1807) the Boston Marine Insurance Company prospered. Under the guidance of Thomas Davis and Joseph May, the company returned annual dividends of between 10 and 14 percent. During the same period returns from the Massachusetts Bank averaged 8.5 percent; the Insurance Company of North America in Phila-

39. Tho[ma]s Davis to Eben Stocker, Mar. 19, 1802, letterbook, BMI.
40. H. S. Ferns, *Britain and Argentina in the Nineteenth Century* (Oxford, 1960), 1–15.
41. Joseph May to John Clark, Nov. 24, 1800, letterbook, BMI.

delphia was pleased to return 9 percent; and obligations of the Bank of the United States were at 6 percent.[42]

That the BMI was able to return such a healthy dividend is not surprising. As the European nations warred on one another, neutral American shippers rushed to carry trade formerly prohibited to them. The port of Boston flourished. When the company was formed in 1799, Boston had more than 1,000 vessels entering and clearing in foreign trade each year and nearly twice that number sailing in the coastwise business. Those numbers grew steadily each year, so that by 1807 foreign trade had risen by nearly 50 percent and coastwise trade by a like amount.

In great measure the good fortune of the company was a tribute to the sound management of Thomas Davis. While technically answerable to his directors, Davis was a power unto himself. He may well have consulted with other directors, but if he did it was in quite an informal manner. The company's act of incorporation required the directors to meet monthly; however, surviving records give no indication whether such meetings actually took place. The only reference to meetings in the company's papers is a notation that the president could convene the directors when "he thought proper."

On January 21, 1805, the company suffered a great loss, one for which it was not insured. At age forty-nine Thomas Davis died. The directors remembered their friend and president at a special meeting called the day after his death by voting to erect a marble tablet and column on which they would inscribe a tribute to the "undeviating rectitude, . . . great ability, and . . . universal acceptance" by which he conducted the affairs of the company from its founding until the very day of his death.[43]

With the founder gone the company moved quickly to reorganize lest its reputation suffer by rumor or innuendo. Two days after the funeral the board met and by unanimous vote elected James Lloyd president. Four days later he resigned claiming ill health. Having lost two presidents in the space of two weeks the directors took a bold and curious step. They offered the post to Peter Chardon Brooks.[44]

42. Lester W. Zartman, *Fire Insurance* (New Haven, 1909), 311.

43. BMI Committee Report, Jan. 22, 1805, box 4, BMI; *Columbian Centinel*, Jan. 23, 1805. Davis is buried in the Central Burying Ground. *Gravestone Inscriptions and Records of Tomb Burials in the Central Burying Ground* (Salem, 1917), 51.

44. Minutes, Jan. 25, 1805, box 4, BMI; Ja[me]s Lloyd to Company, Jan. 29, 1805, box 4, BMI.

Brooks had only a slight association with the company. He owned a few shares of stock, but he had never shown more than a passing interest in company affairs. Indeed, since 1803 he had entered semiretirement to enjoy the bucolic surroundings of his Medford estate. At 11:00 in the morning on January 31 the directors elected Brooks president of the BMI. Immediately they dispatched a committee to wait upon him. Brooks received them well enough, listened to their invitation, queried them about the conditions of employment, and then responded that he would have an answer that afternoon. Accustomed to independence, Brooks was undoubtedly leery about working in a corporate environment. His concerns deepened as he learned that the directors intended to rein in the powers of the president. By the time the gentlemen returned at 3:00 he had made his decision. He would not serve.[45]

Brooks's suspicions were on the mark; the directors were planning to reduce the powers of the presidency. Six years of benevolent despotism under Davis had brought profits, but now events abroad conspired to make continued growth uncertain. In Europe war raged, while the British continued to harass American trade. In such worrisome times the directors needed insurance that the BMI's next president would fall under their scrutiny and control.

On February 11, the directors met for the first time since the unhappy news from Brooks. They had two main items on their agenda, the election of yet another president and the approval of a list of resolutions that defined certain policies within the company. It is not clear which item came up for discussion first, although it seems likely that the resolutions preceded the election. The directors voted

> That it shall be the duty of the President to cause to be made out, and laid before the Directors on the first Monday of each month, an accurate, detailed and perspicuous exhibit of the concerns of the office—which account shall be recorded in a Book, to be kept exclusively for that purpose, and each account copied therein shall be verified by the signatures of the President & Secretary.
>
> That a Book also be kept for the purpose of registering the losses that may befal[l] the Company, and, that the adjustment of each loss shall be entered in detail therein and be authenticated as above mentioned.
>
> That from the interest the Boston Marine Insurance Company possess[es] In the Boston Bank, it is the duty of the Directors of this Institution

45. Minutes, Jan. 31, 1805, box 4, BMI; P. C. Brooks to T. C. Amory, Jan. 31, 1805, box 4, BMI.

to support the said Bank—In order to effect this object, as well, that the utmost regularity should pervade the affairs of the Company, and that a distinct record should be kept of the most trivial disbursements for accounts thereof—Be it resolved.—that the evidences of all the funds and property belonging to the Boston Marine Insurance Company, and all notes taken, and all monies received for accounts of said Company shall, immediately on the receipt be deposited in the Boston Bank, and that no payments however small be made except by check on the said Bank.[46]

The directors also resolved that the books of the company must always be available for examination by any director and that the current books must be closed and a new set opened by the first of July. With these stringent rules in place the directors chose a president—Samuel Cabot. He accepted and settled down to work at the same salary Davis had received.

The degree to which this corporate reorganization and rationalization affected the fortunes of the company is difficult to assess. At the end of 1806 the company's capital stock stood at a record $593,000, with about 45 percent in Boston Bank stock, 24 percent in obligations of the Bank of the United States and the remainder scattered among other local banks. There had been no untoward losses, and the company declared a year-end dividend of 10 percent. Unfortunately, this was the BMI's last normal year of operation, for beginning with a French decree in November 1806 the two warring powers escalated their bedevilment of neutral trade. This diplomatic maelstrom would soon draw the American republic into embargo, non-intercourse, and finally war.

Although only one of several marine insurance companies in New England by 1807, the Boston Marine Insurance Company was clearly among the most important. By the manner in which it conducted its business, it provided a safe and profitable haven for profits gained from trade. It offered a measure of financial security for those owners and captains venturing overseas and provided banks with a source of capital. The services offered by the BMI and other companies were essential to the development of America's maritime enterprise, which in turn fueled the growth of the nation's economy and set Boston on a course to becoming one of the nation's most important financial centers.

46. Vote of the Board, Feb. 11, 1805, box 4, BMI.

Plan of two tenement houses under one roof, 1773. Caleb Davis Papers, Massachusetts Historical Society.

From Carpenter to Capitalist:
The Business of Building
in Postrevolutionary Boston

Lisa B. Lubow

IN THE FIFTY YEARS following the American Revolution, the character of entrepreneurship fundamentally altered in Boston's building industry. In eighteenth-century Boston, a "builder" or "building contractor" was, by definition, an artisan: a skilled craftsman laboring in a business he also owned. House carpenters—like artisans in all areas of manufacturing—actively engaged in production while maintaining financial and administrative control of their enterprise. In the nineteenth century, however, nonlaboring speculators—largely drawn from the merchant elite—intervened in the business of building, assuming the role of "builder" or "building contractor." Intent upon securing new avenues for lucrative returns, honing the economic and productive efficiency of real estate development, and channeling a greater part of the profits into their own pockets, these men altered the terms of investment and risk. While some carpenters continued to function as laboring proprietors, most found general contracting prohibitively expensive. As a result, the artisanal linkage between labor and property broke down. Rising numbers of house carpenters were forced into a lifetime of dependent labor, while nonlaboring financiers retained entrepreneurial control of a growing proportion of Boston's building projects. Entrepreneurship—with all of the proprietary rights and responsibilities once intrinsic to artisan life—shifted, from artisan to investor, from laboring carpenter to nonlaboring capitalist.

Boston's Artisanal "Builder" in 1790

The entrepreneur of Boston's eighteenth-century building industry was an ordinary artisan: a master house carpenter (or housewright) working in a business he also owned. In 1790, this intersection of labor and property characterized Boston's majority. Of 3,000 adult males, 60 percent were members of the "middling sort": laboring proprietors, holding 36 percent of the town's taxable wealth. Most were craftsmen (also known as mechanics or tradesmen), skilled in one of nearly one hundred specialized trades.[1] Jonathan Lambert, for instance, was a cooper, living in a small house and sharing a shop in Boston's North End. Joseph Lovering, Jr., carried on his family's tallow business, working out of their candle works in the southern part of town.[2] Of the 150 craftsmen trained in carpentry, 77 percent owned property, worth an average of $400.[3] While such holdings might impart to these men a certain economic, political, and social independence, however, the era was not a "golden age." The need for hard labor, along with ownership, frames the burdens and privileges confronting the eighteenth-century building entrepreneur.

This intersection of labor and property not only characterized artisanal carpenters, but also distinguished them from, and defined their relationship to, others in society. Like all Americans, the 18,000 who lived in Boston in 1790 arranged themselves hierarchically. At society's apex were the town's "better sort": merchants, gentlemen, and professionals who often invested in various forms of commercial endeavor and who controlled the bulk of society's assets. The top 1 percent of Boston's taxpayers held 27 percent of the town's taxable wealth; the top 10 percent held as much as 65 percent.[4] John Codman, Jr., a merchant, possessed real estate worth over

1. Allan Kulikoff, "The Progress of Inequality in Revolutionary Boston," *William and Mary Quarterly*, 3d ser., 28(1971):376–385, 411–412. There were 7,912 males to 9,642 females. Lemuel Shattuck, *Report to the Committee of the City Council Appointed to Obtain the Census of Boston for the Year 1845* (1846; reprint, New York, 1976), 2–6, 26, 43, 45, 53; Gary Nash, *The Urban Crucible: Social Change, Political Consciousness, and the Origins of the American Revolution* (Cambridge, Mass., 1979), 16–17; Myron F. Wehtje, "A Town in the Confederation: Boston, 1783–1787" (Ph.D. diss., Univ. of Virginia, 1978), 21–23, 44.

2. Boston tax taking lists, 1791, Rare Book Room, Boston Public Library (hereafter BPL).

3. For a full analysis of property holding in the trade, see chapter 6 in Lisa B. Lubow, "Artisans in Transition: Early Capitalist Development and the Carpenters of Boston, 1787–1837," (Ph.D. diss., Univ. of California, Los Angeles, 1987). Statistics and examples profiling Boston carpenters used in this paper are derived from the Boston tax taking (or transfer) lists and the tax valuation lists for 1790, 1796, 1800, 1805, 1810, 1815, 1820, 1825, 1830, 1831, and 1834, Rare Book Room, BPL. All carpenters listed in each were used, except for those named in 1830, since the population proved prohibitively large for that year; a random sampling was based on every fifth name listed on each page of the 1830 tax lists. Some anecdotal material was also taken from the 1791 tax taking lists.

4. Men whose interests were associated with mercantile activities lived in lavish style, dominated institutions of power, hired others to do their productive labor, and had money

$9,000 in 1791. He owned several shops, stores, and wharves, as well as a number of carriages (a real luxury in a "walking city" barely a few miles wide).[5] Thomas Russell, Esq., a merchant, storekeeper, and director of the Massachusetts Bank, lived in Boston's South End with his two black servants, Richard and Belfast. According to the tax collector, Russell owned a personal coach, chariot, and chaise, as well as a wharf, store, house, and pasture worth more than $11,000.[6] As property owners, facilitators of commercial exchange, and organizers of business, these members of Boston's elite—like their artisanal neighbors—fit the profile of the American entrepreneur. Unlike the artisans, however, they did not engage in productive labor.

Also distinguishing themselves from the mechanics were society's "lesser sort": the laboring poor or near-poor who lacked the means to support themselves independently. As of 1790, 30 percent of the taxable population were propertyless.[7] Among them were the aged, sick, widows, and unemployed who often relied on charity to survive. In 1791, tax collectors noted that Joseph Crane and Charles Woodman had been living in one room and were so "very poor" that, by tax day, they had moved "in the almshouse." Joshua Davis was "sick, poor, and old"; tailor James Dodge was "crazy and poor"; Widow Martin was simply "poor"; while "black men" John Polley and Peter Williston were "as poor as possible."[8] Also among the "lesser sort" were the unskilled laborers, servants, seamen, and journeymen who

---

to reinvest in commerce, land, and financial speculation. Kulikoff, "Progress of Inequality," 380–381; Wehtje, "Town in the Confederation," 37–42.

5. Boston tax taking lists, 1791. Some estates were assessed as high as $17,000 in 1790.

6. Boston tax taking lists, 1791.

7. The number of poor and near poor in Boston swelled over the course of the 18th century, due to chronic postwar depression, a growing dependence on a mercurial commercial economy, as well as the influx of rural migrants suffering the long-term effects of partible inheritance, land shortages, and soil exhaustion. As Allan Kulikoff has commented, "more men lost than gained wealth" in this era. Kulikoff, "Progress of Inequality," 380–383, 409–410. Wehtje, "Town in the Confederation," 9, 37–43. See also James A. Henretta, "Economic Development and Social Structure in Colonial Boston," *William and Mary Quarterly*, 3d ser., 22(1965):75–92; Billy G. Smith, *The "Lower Sort": Philadelphia's Laboring People, 1750–1800* (Ithaca, 1990); Douglas L. Jones, "The Strolling Poor: Transiency in Eighteenth-Century Massachusetts," *Journal of Social History* 8(1975):28–54; Raymond Mohl, *Poverty in New York, 1783–1825* (New York, 1971); Gary B. Nash, "Poverty and Poor Relief in Pre-Revolutionary Philadelphia," *William and Mary Quarterly*, 3d ser., 33(1976):3–30.

8. Boston tax taking lists, 1791.

worked for others for a daily wage. Nathaniel Kidder, a "poor" sailor with three children, had "gone to sea" at tax time. John Baker, who "tends at market," was "poor" and living in one room with Edward Hawes, who was "lame in one arm" and "very poor." George Hardy, a laborer, also crowded into a single room with his wife and four children.[9] On building projects, laborers such as Hardy might saw wood, haul stuff, or dig holes. Carpenter Braddock Loring, working on a house on Franklin Street in 1796, paid his laborers $4.33 to cart 14 loads of dirt.[10] Although these workmen engaged in practical labor, as did the artisan, in other ways they were set apart from those above them in Boston's social hierarchy: their lack of property—and the dependency that conveyed—denied them the opportunities of entrepreneurial endeavor.

In this context, Boston's "middling sort"—representing the bulk of the town's productive labor and the majority of its property holders—stood as a critical interface between the laboring poor and the proprietary elite. Although wage earners were increasing in number, both in Boston and in the nation as a whole, they remained a minority throughout the eighteenth century. They therefore were not representative of America's "working class." Rather, it was the independent producer—the urban artisan and his rural cousin, the freehold farmer—who was the mainstay of the northern workforce and the majority of the population. Moreover, while artisans were fundamentally committed to maintaining the autonomy they derived from ownership, they rarely expected, respected, or obtained the unfettered mobility and freedom from productive labor that someday would be associated with the nineteenth-century entrepreneur. On the contrary, most of Boston's eighteenth-century artisans accepted persistent notions of "natural hierarchy," while also taking pride in labor's virtue and utility.

9. Boston tax taking lists, 1791. Journeymen were distinguished by the more or less temporary nature of their poverty. In 1790, the aggregate wealth of journeymen carpenters was 3 percent of that held by their trade; 68 percent were propertyless. Yet these men at least had a decent chance of rising to independent master. Lubow, "Artisans In Transition," chap. 6 and, on mobility patterns, chap. 4.

10. Bill, Braddock Loring for house at 18–20 Franklin Place, January 1796, Jonathan Amory Papers, Massachusetts Historical Society (hereafter M.H.S.). In another example, Thomas Briggs and his partner Wilkinson, presumably truckmen or laborers, billed "for 10 hours work Shoveling mud under wharfe," and "½ days work loading gravel," "15 loads of mud—twice thrown and Carted," "½ day work throwing dirt back of House," "Carting 20 loads of Wood to Distillary House," "Extra Diging Cellar by Agreement," and "2 Hours Work making Drain in Cellar." Account, Wilkinson and Briggs with Ralph Haskins, 1810, Society for the Preservation of New England Antiquities (hereafter SPNEA), Boston.

These views, together with the constraints of circumstance and opportunity, confined them to a "decent competency," that is, a laboring and modest independence.[11] It was, in fact, the unique combination of work and property that distinguished the "middling sort" from the elite who owned but did not engage in productive labor, and from wage earners who labored but did not own.

Labor, for the preindustrial artisan, meant working from sunrise to sunset, custom-crafting a product with a few hand tools. In 1788, a farmer "just outside Boston" commented on the importance of work to both urban and rural producers. "The tradesmen of Boston, and the farmers in the country, I have always considered as brethren," he wrote, for they "get their living, as we do, by the labour of their hands."[12] That year, when nearly 1,500 workmen marched in procession following state ratification of the Constitution, local carpenters proudly carried the tools of their trade, a testimony to their support for the new federal government and their hopes that it would revive the economy and stimulate production.[13] And, as late as 1825, master carpenters reminded their journeymen of "that wise and salutory maxim of Mechanics 'MIND YOUR BUSINESS,'" for which they "consider idleness to be the most deadly bane to the usefulness and honourable living." A pride in labor was central to Boston's independent producers.[14]

That labor, moreover, was a skilled labor: unlike ordinary workmen, the mechanic possessed the expertise needed to design, fabricate, and merchandize a product from start to finish. In 1818, housewright Joseph Jenkins informed members of the Massachusetts Charitable Mechanic Association, "You still have much, for which to be grateful; for that skill you possess, which is a capital in business." Look, he said, at how the earth is cultivated and its products made salutary for food. Look at how man is clothed comfortably, how he is furnished with convenient, elegant dwellings. Look also at the vehicles of communication, commerce, and travel, at all the comforts and luxuries brought to his storehouse and table. "And what," he asked, "short of Heaven . . . are the means, by which he enjoys

11. On the issue of labor's value in the producer tradition, see for example, Ronald Schultz, *The Republic of Labor: Philadelphia Artisans and the Politics of Class, 1720–1830* (New York, 1993), chap. 1. For a fine discussion of notions of producer "competency," see Daniel Vickers, "Competency and Competition: Economic Culture in Early America," *William and Mary Quarterly*, 3d ser., 47(1990):3–29.

12. *Massachusetts Centinel*, Jan. 9, 1788.

13. *Boston Gazette and the Country Journal*, Feb. 11, 1788.

14. "Meeting of Master Carpenters," *Boston Daily Advertiser*, Apr. 19, 1825.

these benefits? Methinks I hear you answer, 'Tis the operation of the *Mechanic Arts*."[15] The arts—or skill—that Jenkins celebrated remained essential to manufacturing well into the nineteenth century. Moreover, it was
that skill, the artisans insisted, that created the basis by which society both
survived and flourished.

For house carpenters—a subdivision of general carpentry—skilled labor
was more extensively defined than it had been for the early country carpenter (who made everything from carts to coffins), but was not yet as specialized as it would become in the nineteenth century.[16] In Boston, it meant
expertise in designing, building, altering, repairing, and selling any of a
number of structures made of wood, including homes, stores, offices, man-
ufactories, public edifices, bridges, canals, and wharves.[17] As in most trades,
skill began in the form of product design. There was no profession of
trained architects in America before 1790. It was the housewright who
created the building plans, often working with the future owner, aided by
manuals and pattern books.[18] Boston's many building guides included *The*

15. Joseph Jenkins, *An Address Delivered Before the Massachusetts Charitable Mechanic Association, December 17, 1818* (Boston, 1819).

16. For a few general discussions of the changing division of labor, see Adam Smith, *An
Inquiry into the Nature and Causes of the Wealth of Nations*, 4th ed. (London, 1786), 1:1–
32; Karl Marx, *Capital: A Critical Analysis of Capitalist Production* (First German edition,
1867; New York, 1967), 1:322–368; Carl Bridenbaugh, *The Colonial Craftsman* (New
York, 1950), 65, 75–78; Robert A. Christie, *Empire in Wood: A History of the Carpenters'
Union* (Ithaca, 1956), 19–20; "Trades and Occupations in Eighteenth-Century New England: Gleaning from Boston Newspapers," *Old Time New England* 18(1972); Edward
Hazen, *The Panorama of Professions and Trades; or Every Man's Book* (Philadelphia,
1836).

17. While house carpenters specialized in buildings, some craftsmen specialized in other
woodworking trades: cabinetmakers, chairmakers, shipwrights, ship carpenters, mast makers, ship joiners, headbuilders, wheel makers, chaise makers, harness makers, coopers,
carvers, joiners, and turners. Boston tax taking lists, 1791. Others continued in general
carpentry, making closets, shelves, shutters, blinds, locks and keys, sinks, sewers, theater
props, stepladders, boiler covers, butter boxes, tools, coffins, fences, racks to hold fire
hoses, etc. Account, Thomas Hearsey, Jan. 12, 1796, Boston Theatre Papers, BPL; Bill,
Simeon Wade to Harrison Gray Otis, May 10, 1799, Harrison Gray Otis Papers, SPNEA;
Account, James Bird, September 1804, Boston Theatre Papers; Braddock Loring Survey
of Work by Richard Hills, Atkinson Street, 1809, Jonathan Amory Papers, M.H.S.; Bill,
James Armstrong to Fife and Brown, Aug. 22, 1825, Boston City Records, BPL; Bill, Seth
Copeland for Work on Engine House Number 5 in School Street, January, 1826, Rare
Book Room, BPL.

18. The same has been said of English construction, although some suggest that "architects" designed some of that nation's grand buildings. Nineteenth-century scholars tended

American Builder's Companion by Asher Benjamin and Daniel Raynerd and *The Architect, or Practical House Carpenter, for the Use of Carpenters and Builders*, which Benjamin also wrote.[19]

The housewrights' skill, however, went beyond simply following established customs and published pattern books. Mechanics often generated building plans by integrating new designs and techniques observed elsewhere, in accordance with developing technologies, consumer fashions, and customer preferences. When housewright Samuel Beals agreed in 1817 to erect a house on Purchase Street for Daniel Sigourney, he indicated it would be built "similar to Mr. Briggs' situated on said street." In 1813, housewright Ephraim Marsh agreed to build "four tenements" for Ralph Haskins on his wharf near South Street, "to be exactly like the building next to the cooper shop on said wharf and to be as good as that building outside and in every respect."[20] Moreover, of fundamental importance— and distinguishing building construction from many areas of manufacturing—housewrights needed to be sufficiently skilled to select, adapt, compose, and combine plans appropriate to the varied complexities of a given worksite. A significant architectural expertise, therefore, was an intrinsic characteristic of the preindustrial building entrepreneur.

Also basic to such builders was a mastery of the complete range of hands-on activities construction required. The 1795 *Carpenters' Rules of Work, in the Town of Boston*, published in order to standardize prices, listed a pan-

---

to view the production supervisor as an "architect," so as to inflate estimates of their number. See Bridenbaugh, *Colonial Craftsman*, 11, 14, 77; Roger W. Moss, Jr., "The Origins of the Carpenters' Company of Philadelphia," *Building Early America: Contributions toward the History of a Great Industry*, ed. Charles E. Peterson (Radnor, Penn., 1976), 41.

19. Asher Benjamin and Daniel Raynerd, *The American Builder's Companion; or, a New System of Architecture* (Boston, 1806), and Asher Benjamin, *The Architect or Practical House Carpenter, for the Use of Carpenters and Builders* (Boston, 1845). See also William Pain, *The Practical House Carpenter* (1796). On the use of pattern books, see Harold and James Kirker, who argue, "Boston building before Bulfinch was the uncultivated domain of carpenters whose knowledge stemmed from pattern books. Their field was only rarely contested." *Bulfinch's Boston: 1787–1817* (New York, 1964), 31. The published Constitution of The Social Architectural Library of Boston (chartered Nov. 15, 1809), contained a catalogue of holdings. The list consisted mainly of books of buildings and designs, published in 18th-century London, among which were pattern books with specific plans, elevations, and designs.

20. Contract, Samuel Beals and Daniel Sigourney, Nov. 19, 1817, Bostonian Society (hereafter BS). Contract, Ephraim Marsh with Ralph Haskins, Mar. 18, 1813, SPNEA.

oply of woodworking jobs. These included the construction of cellar floors, rough floors, brick house floors, water tables, and "sundry sorts of floors"; rough partitions, planed partitions, lining rooms and closets, brick house sides, brick house ends, and wooden house frames; rough ceilings, brick house roofs, turrets, and shingling; brick house fronts, wooden house fronts, "Pent Houses" and frontpieces; various casings (timber, chimneys, etc.); capped windows, sashes, window seats, frames, casings, shutters, shop windows, and windows "broak in"; outside cellar doors, double doors, quarter round doors, inside door cases, outside door cases; rough boarding, clapboarding, fascia, mop, saddle, weather, and corner boards; cornicing in rooms, quarter round wainscot and dado, with bases and capping; stone mouldings and pediments over windows; sundry sorts of stairs, fences, and gates; shelves in closets; and trunks and gutters.[21] In addition, building contracts mentioned many other tasks. To be an eighteenth-century "builder," one had to know how to build.

If labor helped to define Boston's preindustrial entrepreneurs, the fact that they owned property—both real and personal estate—was equally essential.[22] In 1790, William Andrews was a master housewright, with a house and a lot on North Essex Street assessed at $671. Over the next decade, Andrews bought more land on Pleasant Street, building a house and shop in the yard. By 1805, there were 388 carpenters living in Boston, 95 percent of whom owned property worth an average of $1,141. Andrews was doing quite well by then, his holdings assessed at $3,300.[23] Similarly, William Ellison, Sr., and Moses Eayers, Sr., both master housewrights, owned a house and shop on the east side of South Street in 1790. By 1796, they had been joined in their business by their sons, William Ellison, Jr., and Moses

21. *The Carpenters' Rules of Work, in the Town of Boston* (Boston, 1795).

22. Adam Smith argues that an independent manufacturer "who has stock enough to both purchase materials and maintain himself until he can carry his work to market" was paid a price representing both wages and profit. Smith, *Wealth of Nations*, 1:80–81. Karl Marx added, "in order that a man be able to sell commodities other than labour-power, he must, of course, have the means of production, as raw materials, implements, etc. . . . he also requires the means of subsistence." Marx, *Capital*, 1:167–171. J. R. Commons and associates state, "in the case of prices, the labourer's compensation was his net income dependent upon the margin between the price received from the consumer and the price paid for the raw materials. The artisan was merchant as a seller of personal services, and labourer as the producer of those services." J. R. Commons et al., *History of Labour in the United States* (New York, 1921–1935), 1:32–33.

23. Boston tax taking and tax valuation lists, 1790, 1796, 1800, 1805; Lubow, "Artisans in Transition," chap. 6.

Eayers, Jr., both carpenters. By 1805, the combined worth of the property owned by the four men was $5,400, enhanced, perhaps, by Ellison's work as a building surveyor. The fact that these men, like other artisans, owned property—invested, in part, in their own businesses—meant that they had secured an economic independence, as well as control of their enterprise.[24]

Control in building construction—as in any trade—rested on the relative ability of a business owner to arrange a price bargain and monopolize the resulting profits. Control of prices and profits, in turn, was reinforced by the extent to which he was able to negotiate directly with his client. In the eighteenth century, a future occupant would make arrangements with the carpenter to build his product. The customer would provide land and indicate his proclivities with respect to design. The housewright supplied the materials, tools, skills, and plans and erected the building in a "workmanlike manner." He then was paid a price for his finished product, from which he realized his "wages" and profits above expenses. In this way, client and carpenter met in the marketplace as producer and consumer. Until the building was transferred to the new owner, it was the artisan who retained control of production, product, price, and profits.[25]

The business controlled by the housewright was modest in size, but it also was large in risk. In this "era of small things," most artisan production was restricted by the limits of markets and technology, as well as by the fact that the mechanics' skill was all-encompassing, with a single craftsman performing all of the time-consuming tasks needed to complete a product. Shops were tiny, worked only by a master, family members, and, perhaps, an assistant or two.[26] Boston's artisan shops in 1790 had, on the average,

24. Boston tax taking and tax valuation lists, 1790, 1796, 1800, 1805; Lubow, "Artisans in Transition," chap. 6.

25. Betsy Blackmar comments, "Colonial builders produced houses primarily for simple commodity exchange, that is, for their purchase by known customers who put up the capital and consumed the 'use value' of a shelter for both production and reproduction." Betsy Blackmar, "Rewalking the 'Walking City': Housing and Property Relations in New York City, 1780–1840," *Radical History Review* 21(1979):134; see also W. S. Hilton, *Foes to Tyranny: A History of the Amalgamated Union of Building Trades Workers* (London, 1963), chap. 1 and p. 20.

26. On shop size, see I. J. Prothero, *Artisans and Politics in Early Nineteenth-Century London, John Gast and His Times* (Kent, 1979), 24; Eric Foner, *Tom Paine and Revolutionary America* (New York, 1976), 29; Bridenbaugh, *Colonial Craftsman*, 129; Howard B. Rock, *Artisans of the New Republic: The Tradesmen of New York City in the Age of Jefferson* (New York, 1979), 155; Susan E. Hirsch, *Roots of the American Working Class: The Industrialization of Crafts in Newark, 1800–1860* (Philadelphia, 1978), 8. Richard B.

three workers.[27] Fabricating a product as elaborate as a building, however, required major financial investments. Although the clients supplied the land, the size and complexity of most construction meant high expenditures over a lengthy building season. If the work proved more extensive, costly, or time-consuming than originally estimated, the carpenter needed the resources to absorb the difference until he was paid. In 1794, merchant Henry Jackson wrote his friend Henry Knox that the costs for one building under construction would be double the sum "originally mentioned." And the Boston Theatre, estimated to cost $20,000, already had consumed $35,000, although all the materials, Jackson insisted, had been bought with cash, at the cheaper rates, and work performed on the most reasonable terms. "It goes to show you," he said, "the uncertainty of the best calculation." In the case of the ordinary carpenter with a limited income, unexpected expenses could prove devastating.[28]

Such risks were compounded when large projects were involved, requiring extensive investments and cooperative labor among various building tradesmen (masons, glaziers, bricklayers, painters, stonecutters, plasterers, etc.). While construction was once performed by carpenters working alone (as, presumably, was still the case in some rural areas and on smaller urban projects), eighteenth-century developments had deepened Boston's division of labor. The resulting craft interdependence on some construction projects impinged on each trade's autonomy. When housewrights agreed to "do all the carpenters work wanted" for a building project on India Wharf in 1805, they agreed to "go on and finish said work as fast as the stone and brickwork for the said stores will admit." An 1806 account by James Tillebrown for repairing a Cambridge church requested an additional payment of $10.52 "for the damage he supposes he sustained by the whole quantity of Shingles not having been delivered him reasonably." In 1809, John Bates promised housewright Samuel Waldron that "masons shall be so far completed that said Waldron may without inconvenience finish his work before the first of October Next." The cooperative nature of the building process demanded that each tradesman schedule his work and pace his labor in a

---

Morris says some shops may have been larger, but most had one or two apprentices and a like number of journeymen. Morris, *Government and Labor in Early America* (New York, 1946), 42.

27. Kulikoff, "Progress of Inequality," 376, 378.

28. Henry Jackson to Henry Knox, Apr. 13, 1794, Henry Knox Papers, Morgan Library, New York.

manner facilitating harmony among tradesmen and the synchronization of their respective duties.[29]

Housewrights nonetheless retained significant autonomy, enhanced by a system in which members of their trade often emerged as general contractors. This occurred because clients preferred to hire one artisan (who engaged others) and because wood dominated construction into the nineteenth century. When carpenter Jonathan Bell built a "Necessary" for Dr. Nathaniel Saltonstall in 1788, it was Bell who arranged for the labor of "Two Men and Boy" to erect the building and plank the new vault.[30] When Braddock Loring built a house on Franklin Place in 1796, he not only billed Harrison Gray Otis for carpentry, but also for Mr. Edwards for "28 yards priming," for Mr. Brewer for "glasing and pipes," and for laborers for "carting dirt."[31] When Ephraim Marsh contracted in 1813 to build tenements on Ralph Haskins's wharf (modeled on a nearby building), he agreed to do everything to make "every part of said house to be as complete in every respect." That included "finding all materials which are to be as good as in said house & free of expense . . . two coats of paint, outside and in, the shingles to be of the very best quality, & the iron work, glaziers work, stock etc. equally good . . . windows blinds, properly painted i.e. slate colour and secured to each window . . . a sash in each kitchen outside door & to lay the drain and find all the materials therefor." Haskins would pay him $200 cash and $1,550 in goods ($700 in lumber and $650 in cordials). Marsh would arrange for the digging of the cellar and drain at his own expense, while billing Haskins for the "labour and stock" of plasterers, glaziers, and other mechanics.[32]

When the housewright was the general contractor, he functioned as a facilitator, not employer, of the various independent tradesmen. The tradesmen worked at his side, selling to the customer their products, rather than beneath the housewright, selling to him their labor. Billing practices varied, although general contractors often included in their bills itemized references to jobs done by members of other trades. In certain cases, carpenters

29. Schedule of Carpenter's Work for 34 stores, to be built on India Wharf, 1805, Baker Library of the Harvard Business School (hereafter BL); James Tillebrown, Account for repairs of the Episcopal Church, Apr. 25, 1806, SPNEA; Agreement, Waldron and Bates, July 21,1809, SPNEA.

30. Account, Jonathan Bell with Dr. Nathaniel Saltonstall, 1788, Nathaniel Saltonstall Papers, M.H.S.

31. Bill, Braddock Loring, January 1796, Jonathan Amory Papers, M.H.S.

32. Contract, Ephraim Marsh with Ralph Haskins, Mar. 18, 1813, SPNEA.

requested payment for those mechanics, presumably passing the monies they received on to those who had performed the work. In 1830, house-wright Hosea Bartlett charged for thirty-four days carpentry, Allen Litch-field's "Bill for Mason's work," John Bates's "Bill for Painting," and David Tillson's "bill for slating." In other cases, carpenters requested reimbursement for their own "cash paid" to the other tradesmen prior to their billing the client. Bell's account with Saltonstall includes a charge for "cash paid Mr. White for Emptying vault." Because each trade charged for its part of the effort, the product's price became the combined prices of the parts, yet each part remained a commodity controlled by each trade. There is no evidence that housewrights charged fees for coordinating the enterprise, nor that contracting brought them special economic gain. Nonetheless, as general contractors, housewrights did enjoy certain advantages: negotiating with the client, coordinating operations with the various tradesmen, and managing the accounts.[33]

Contracting housewrights also insisted on accounting methods suited to meet the costs of a lengthy building season, thus reducing some of the risk. Melzar Dunbar, like most contemporaries, used "job pricing" when building the Suffolk County Courthouse. In his bill, he separately charged for the costs of building a riser and rail in front of a judge's platform, stepladders, bookcases, and thirty-six spit boxes (for which he asked twenty-five cents apiece).[34] *The Rules of Work* were published, in part, to establish price standards for housewrights negotiating with customers in their community.[35] When Beals agreed to build a house for Sigourney in 1817, he requested he be paid "for such a sum as the labour and materials shall

33. Accounts, Hosea Bartlett, 1830, Boston Theatre Papers, BPL; Account, Jonathan Bell with Dr. Nathaniel Saltonstall, Nathaniel Saltonstall Papers, M.H.S. Their role as general contractor apparently elevated carpenters to positions of leadership among the building tradesmen in England and America. See Hilton, *Foes to Tyranny*, 22; William T. Ham, "Associations of Employers in the Construction Industry of Boston," *Journal of Economic and Business History* 3(1930):55–80.

34. Accounts, Melzar Dunbar, 1821–1822, Judge Elijah Adlow Papers, Rare Book Room, BPL.

35. Housewrights could ask whatever price they wanted, but many adhered to guidelines "suited to the means of an honest livelihood, and equitable reward for faithful industry" set by the trade as a whole. The *Rules* of 1800 were reviewed by a "Committee of 21," approved by "the whole body of tradesmen," and printed on the basis that "work will be measured by them and executed in the best possible manner." *The Rules of Work, of the Carpenters in the Town of Boston formed and most accurately corrected, by a large number of the workmen of the TOWN* (Boston, 1800).

amount to," with bills made out "according to the rules of work."[36] Carpenters also requested payments throughout the construction process. Amos Lincoln, at work on the Massachusetts State House between 1795 and 1799, was paid $200 on October 3, 1795, $200 on November 20, 1795, $100 on December 31, 1795, $200 on March 12, 1796, and $1,000 at "sundry times since."[37] Most artisans, moreover, requested regular reimbursements for materials. In 1796, Loring's bills for work on Franklin Place included $16.16 for "661 feet of clear board and carting," forty-four cents for a pound of glue, ninety cents for four pounds of two-penny nails, and six cents for six copper drains.[38] These practices—itemizing tasks, payment in installments, and billing for materials—helped carpenters retain financial and administrative control throughout the eighteenth century.

The perpetuation of the artisan-dominated business also required a system by which generations of carpenters could secure both skill and property.[39] A demand for skilled carpenters allowed the British system of craft training to flourish in Boston.[40] Until the age of twenty-one, an apprentice

36. Contract, Beals and Sigourney, 1817, BS. References to the *Rules* in sundry contracts and accounts indicate that they were respected and consulted by tradesmen and clients. Even the occasional willingness or request to work below the standards of the *Rules* testifies to their perceived legitimacy in the community. See Bid, Theodore Phiney, Mar. 3, 1798, and Bid, Ebenezer Dunton, 1798, Boston Theatre Papers, BPL; Request for Proposals, Work on the new Suffolk County Courthouse, Aug. 20, 1810, Judge Elijah Adlow Papers.

37. Receipt Book for the Building of the State House, Boston, 1795–1800, Edward H. R. Robbins Papers, BL.

38. Bill, Braddock Loring, January 1796, Jonathan Amory Papers, M.H.S.

39. Hirsch writes, "The artisan class was part of a pre-industrial class structure and was not comparative to any class in our later industrial sector. The different statuses within this class were no barriers to advancement but clearly defined stages of transition for the individual, and the unity of the artisan class originated in the expectations of its lowest members that with age, experience, and hard work they could rise to the highest level as self-employed master craftsmen." Hirsch, *Roots of the American Working Class*, 7.

40. In Europe, unlike America, occupational distinctions and mobility between the three tiers were maintained by craft guilds in this era. On guilds in the building trades, see R. W. Postgate, *The Builders History* (London, 1923), 2–3; Hilton, *Foes to Tyranny*, 12–13; Moss, "Origins of the Carpenters' Company," 36, 41. In America, the scarcity of skilled labor rendered guilds superfluous, and early efforts to regulate the trades failed. Morris, *Government and Labor*, 3; Victor S. Clark, *The History of Manufactures in the United States* (Washington, 1929), 1:5; Alan Dawley, *Class and Community: The Industrial Revolution in Lynn*, (Cambridge, Mass., 1976), 18; Sean Wilentz, *Chants Democratic: New York City and the Rise of the American Working Class, 1788–1850* (New York, 1984), 4–5; Hirsch, *Roots of the American Working Class*, 8.

learned the "mysteries" of the trade from a given master.[41] Upon completing his indenture, he became a journeyman, often remaining with that
master until he acquired the capital to set up his own enterprise. While
"journeyman" would someday mean only a skilled worker, in the eighteenth century it meant one on his way to becoming a master.[42] And while
assumptions of intra-craft mobility did not suggest unrestrained movement
across the classes, the hope of owning a business lay at the heart of individual persistence in a trade.[43] Theophilus Burr, for example, born in Hing-
ham in 1795, was apprenticed to Boston housewright Jesse Shaw. By age

41. W. J. Rorabaugh, *The Craft Apprentice: From Franklin to the Machine Age in
America* (New York, 1986); Bridenbaugh, *Colonial Craftsman*; Bruce Laurie, *Artisans into
Workers: Labor in Nineteenth Century America* (New York, 1989), 35–36; Nash, *Urban
Crucible*, 15–16, 116; Foner, *Tom Paine*, 29, 43–44; Rock, *Artisans of the New Republic*,
152–157; Commons, *History of Labour*, chap. 2; Hirsch, *Roots of the American Working
Class*, 8–9.

42. Although European guilds maintained distinctions between masters and journeymen, no official mechanism for assigning status appears to have existed in America. Such
distinctions were apparently made on an informal basis by the community or trade. Tax
collectors in Boston understood the criteria for such distinctions, as demonstrated by their
consistent use of the terms "journeyman" and "master" in the tax rolls. The pattern in the
rolls suggests that the distinction was tied to economic independence or "ownership" of a
business, rather than simply the acquisition of skill. This view is reinforced by evidence of
reversion to journeyman status when a master experienced a major loss of ownership
(surely one cannot experience a loss of skill). Of course, in any society with an elaborate
system of credit, mortgages, loans, and rents, notions of "independence" remain relative.
The difficulty is compounded by the fragmentary evidence available to reconstruct that
network of financial interdependency. Nonetheless, the acceptable degree of indepen-
dency required to achieve and maintain master status—with whatever levels of loans,
mortgages, etc. might be buried within it—was apparently understood by tax collectors and
community members. Lubow, "Artisans in Transition," chap. 4.

43. Most historians assume that easy mobility from journeyman to master existed
throughout the colonial era. See Foner, *Tom Paine*, 39; Morris, *Government and Labor*, 49;
Bridenbaugh, *Colonial Craftsman*, 128, 134–138. The extent to which notions of posses-
sive individualism, ideals of political equality, and personal ambitions for unfettered mobility permeated American society is part of several large historiographic debates. For a few
of the differing views and applications, see Vickers, "Competency and Competition";
James A. Henretta, "Families and Farms: Mentalité in Pre-Industrial America," *William
and Mary Quarterly*, 3d ser., 35(1978):3–32; Joyce Appleby, "The Social Origins of American Revolutionary Ideology," *Journal of American History* 64(1978):935–958; Nash, *Urban Crucible*, 7–9, 12–13, chap. 13; Foner, *Tom Paine*, 39–42; Dawley, *Class and Community*, chap. 2; Bridenbaugh, *Colonial Craftsman*, 165; Rock, *Artisans of the New Republic*,
chap. 6. On the liberal arguments, see C. B. MacPherson, *The Political Theory of Posses-
sive Individualism: Hobbes to Locke* (Oxford, 1962), and Albert O. Hirschman, *The Passions and the Interests: Political Arguments for Capitalism Before Its Triumph* (Princeton,
1977).

twenty-five, Burr had become a master carpenter. He later took his own apprentice, William Leavitt, who, in turn, became a journeyman by 1836.[44] As of 1790, most carpenters (87 percent) were masters, suggesting something of the ease of craft mobility. Nearly half the journeymen present that year rose to master status while living in Boston.[45] If only the men would persevere, insisted master carpenters as late as 1825, "all journeymen of good character and skill, may expect very soon to become masters, and like us the employers of others."[46] Craft mobility—by facilitating the transfer of skill and property—provided the mechanism by which the artisan system reproduced itself in Boston.

Intervention by Building Speculators

In the postrevolutionary era, the entry of the "better sort" into construction profoundly challenged Boston's business of building. What had been a gradual process of change, largely characterized by increasingly specialized skills and a deepening interdependence among building tradesmen, was qualitatively transformed by a fundamental shift in proprietary control of the industry. For more than a century, members of the local elite had depended largely on mercantile activity to accumulate their fortunes. And, although the economy flourished after 1790, Boston industry trailed mercantile pursuits. The seaport lacked the waterpower and large numbers of unskilled laborers needed to supply cheap labor for mass production. Moreover, Boston investors seemed reluctant to jump quickly into unexplored and capital-intensive industrial projects. Preferring those ventures in which their primary role was that of merchant and facilitator, they per-

44. Shaw appeared on the tax lists as a journeyman in 1805. By 1810 he was a master, and would continue in his business through 1825. He died in 1861. Over the years, Shaw took on several apprentices, including Burr. There is no record of Burr as a journeyman, since he first appeared in the rolls of Boston carpenters in 1820, continuing as such in 1825, 1830, and 1836, and possibly thereafter. His wife died in 1870, and his son, Theophilus Burr, Jr., continued as a carpenter and was admitted to the Massachusetts Charitable Mechanic Association in 1856. Burr's apprentice, Leavitt, completed his indenture, was listed as a journeyman in 1836, and later set up the partnership of Leavitt and Bourne. Ultimately he retired to Cambridgeport, Massachusetts. Another of Shaw's apprentices, Isaiah Rodgers, became a prominent architect, studying with Solomon Willard. He was chief architect of construction in Washington, D.C., and designed the Boston Custom House. His son, Willard Rodgers, was also an architect. Boston tax taking lists, 1805, 1810, 1820, 1825, 1830, 1836; Records of the Massachusetts Charitable Mechanic Association (hereafter MCMA), M.H.S.

45. Lubow, "Artisans in Transition," chap. 4.

46. "Meeting of Master Carpenters," *Boston Daily Advertiser*, Apr. 19, 1825.

sistently invested in mercantile over industrial enterprises by a five- or six-to-one ratio. Such investments continued to generate substantial capital. Nonetheless, their many avenues of investment—including ships, trade, luxuries, banking, land schemes, insurance, currency, lotteries, mortgages, stocks, and money-lending—diffused that capital and inhibited any urge to sink high concentrations into industry.[47]

In this context, real estate must have appeared as familiar territory—both literally and financially—to Boston's mercantile investors. They were used to buying and selling for a profit and, in addition, were intimately acquainted with the "highways and byways" of the region. Real estate also promised high rates of return, given rising property values and the potential for additional income to be derived from rents, mortgages, and loans. Some investors, moreover, already had dabbled in speculation, investing in large tracts of the distant hinterland with the hope of quick financial gain. In 1791, for instance, Henry Jackson and Henry Knox joined the Duer group of New York in buying two million acres of land in Maine at ten cents an acre. They planned to resell the land in smaller parcels for a much higher rate of return. Although their project collapsed in the financial crash of 1792, other similar efforts to speculate in rural land sales were more successful.[48]

In the early republic, however, a cadre of wealthy Bostonians went further than mere land speculation, investing in the actual "improvement" of urban land in the form of building speculation. They bought up and reparcelled various plots of land throughout the New England seaport, demolishing whatever structures might already have been situated there. They also hired other individuals to design, supervise, and erect new buildings. The fact that they then secured clients and resold the finished product for a profit—rather than retaining it for their own personal use—transformed construction into a speculative enterprise. The collective result was the virtual take-off of the real estate industry, the full commodification of land and housing markets, the physical transformation of the urban topography,

47. As time passed, investors would also divert funds into transportation systems facilitating commercial exchange, including turnpike, canal, and railroad development. Alan Pred, "Manufacturing in the American Mercantile City, 1800–1840," *Annals of the American Association of Geographers* 56(1966):307–325, reprinted in *Cities in American History*, ed. Kenneth Jackson and Stanley K. Schultz (New York, 1972), 117–118.

48. James T. Adams, *New England in the Republic, 1776–1850* (Boston, 1926), 194–195; Henry P. Kidder and Francis H. Peabody, "Finance in Boston," in Justin Winsor, ed., *The Memorial History of Boston, including Suffolk County, Massachusetts, 1630–1880* (Boston, 1881), 4:164.

and—of particular relevance to this essay—the reorganization of the business of building.

The men who moved into construction tended to be merchants and lawyers associated with some of Boston's foremost institutions: directors of newly created banks; subscribers in the building of ships; investors in land schemes, lotteries, and insurance companies; candidates for local, state, and federal offices; and sponsors of numerous civic activities. Some would come to be known as the Boston Associates, whose fortunes would fuel the incipient textile industries of New England's river valleys. Such developers did not devote themselves exclusively to real estate, but several—Uriah Cotting, Harrison Gray Otis, Jonathan Mason, and Francis Cabot Lowell, for example—made it a major concern.[49] The ubiquitous Otis, for one, appears prominently among the real estate developers. Born in 1765 into a wealthy Boston family of both Patriots and Loyalists, he graduated from Harvard, studied law, and gained a substantial fortune working for some of Boston's leading merchants. Beginning in the 1780s, he became active in Federalist politics, as a U.S. congressional representative, U.S. senator, federal district attorney for Massachusetts, speaker of the state House of Representatives, president of the Massachusetts Senate, judge to the Boston Court of Common Pleas, and mayor of Boston.[50] He also achieved enormous financial success in numerous endeavors, including real estate speculation. Between 1790 and 1830, Otis engaged in nearly 1,100 Boston property transactions as either buyer or seller.[51]

Developers like Otis often made real estate a joint venture, forming associations, frequently incorporated, to pool their resources and limit their

49. On the Boston Associates, see Robert F. Dalzell, Jr., *Enterprising Elite: The Boston Associates and the World They Made* (Cambridge, Mass., 1987). On elite activity in building construction, see Lubow, "Artisans in Transition," chap. 2.

50. Samuel Eliot Morison, *The Life and Letters of Harrison Gray Otis, Federalist, 1765–1848* (Boston, 1913); Samuel Eliot Morison, *Harrison Gray Otis, 1765–1848: The Urbane Federalist* (Boston, 1969); Kirker and Kirker, *Bulfinch's Boston*, 152; State Street Trust Company, Boston, *Mayors of Boston: An Illustrated Epitome of Who the Mayors Have Been and What They Have Done* (Boston, 1914), 9–10.

51. Harrison Gray Otis listings, Suffolk County Registry of Deeds, Boston. The indices of grantors and grantees list for Otis large numbers of property transfers and other transactions. In addition to purchases and sales, mortgages, depositions, and instances in which Otis was awarded power of attorney are all recorded. The indices are an important gauge of the sheer volume of real estate transactions in which Otis engaged, especially when his activity is compared with that of other individuals. William Clouston was a relatively successful housewright, yet he appeared only five times as grantor and seven times as grantee in the same period as Otis's 1,100 entries. Many housewrights were involved in far fewer transactions. William Clouston listings, Suffolk County Registry of Deeds.

personal financial liability. In 1795, Otis, Cotting, and Mason joined Benjamin Joy in buying eighteen acres of pasture on the southern slope of Mt. Whoredom (the western peak of Trimountain). Incorporated as the Mt. Vernon Proprietors, the investors paid $1,000 an acre and, for thirty years, oversaw the leveling of hills, the laying of streets, the construction of mansions and row houses, and the sale of finished estates.[52] A desire to spread the risks generated many similar associations in the first half of the nineteenth century. Otis, for example, was active in the Broad Street Association, Liberty Square Warehouse Company, Central Wharf and Wet Dock Association, the New Cornhill Association, the Boston and Roxbury Mill Corporation, the South Boston Association, and the Proprietors of India Wharf, among many others. He also developed property on Fort Hill, Brattle Street, lower Federal Street, Barton's Point, and elsewhere.[53] By 1828, Otis's tax assessments indicated that he owned twenty-two lots of land and seven houses in Ward 6; two lots in Ward 1; five shops, forty lots, two yards, and one wharf in Ward 3; two stores and five lots in Ward 4; and one house and six stores in Ward 9. His total real estate holdings were valued at $147,000. In such cases, men like Otis—by virtue of their investments—assumed the role of "owner," or entrepreneur, of Boston's construction business.[54]

On various projects, nonlaboring investors intervened between artisan and future occupant, rendering construction a speculative endeavor. Their function was to buy land only to sell land—improved—at a profit. In 1804, Otis, Cotting, Lowell, James Lloyd, and others formed the Broad Street Association to erect a new commercial district on the eastern waterfront,

52. Walter M. Whitehill, *Boston: A Topographical History*, 2d ed., (Cambridge, Mass., 1968), 60–63, 161; Edward Stanwood, "Topography and Landmarks of the Last Hundred Years," in Winsor, *Memorial History of Boston*, 4:29, 32; Shubael Bell, "An Account of the Town of Boston, Written in 1817," Bostonian Society *Publications*, 2d ser., 3(1919):21–22; James Kirker, *The Architecture of Charles Bulfinch* (Cambridge, Mass., 1969), 147–148, 156–159, 173–174, 186, 205–209, 226–227; Kirker and Kirker, *Bulfinch's Boston*, 147–158; Harrison Gray Otis Papers, SPNEA; State Street Trust Company, Boston, *Forty of Boston's Historic Houses* (Boston, 1912).

53. Harrison Gray Otis listings, Suffolk County Registry of Deeds. The projects in which Otis participated ranged from the grand mansions on Beacon Hill to the commercial development of wharfs and bridges, to large public buildings, to tracts of ordinary residential homes in South Boston. There is also evidence that Otis and his associates financed smaller projects—e.g., an individual home or office—especially when such projects promised future income, possibly in the form of rents or mortgage payments. Lubow, "Artisans in Transition," chap. 2.

54. These do not include those many properties in which Otis invested and then sold. Harrison Gray Otis Taxed in 1832, Harrison Gray Otis Papers, SPNEA.

between Battery March and India streets. They purchased various properties, leveled many tiny and deteriorating structures, arranged for construction on the cleared site, and oversaw the final sale of the finished properties. The new street was eighty to one hundred feet wide, lined with some sixty brick stores and warehouses, all of uniform construction. In 1807, Otis reported that gross income from the project was $323,460, "Leaving a net profit of $117,295." Twelve years later, Cotting indicated that the association netted a profit of $200,000, suggesting that future mortgages and rents were part of the investment strategy.[55] Because such projects were speculative, they required significant capital outlay without the guarantee of a customer waiting, purchase price in hand. Included in this outlay, moreover, was the cost of land and building materials, expenses once absorbed by the consumer during the building process. Lowell, for instance, as agent for the "Proprietors of India Wharf," agreed to furnish all of the materials needed to build the stores.[56] Arrangements of this kind thus demanded greater resources from those who functioned as building contractors, and promised higher risks.

By raising whole blocks and neighborhoods at a time, investors also introduced the "slop" or mass production of what had long been a custom craft. In 1810, a plan was developed to build nineteen brick buildings along the eastern side of Tremont Street, from West to Mason streets. Five more were erected later in the same style, extending Colonnade Row to the corner of Boylston Street. By the summer of 1811, each completed structure was worth between six and nine thousand dollars. Additional construction followed, and prices rose as the years passed. One estimate found that two-thirds of the houses along the row were built on speculation.[57] Similarly, in 1825, Lewis Tappan announced plans to take down several houses on Federal Street, all of the houses on northwest High Street, and two houses on Summer Street. His intention was "to sell lots for erecting 24

55. Abbott Lowell Cummings, "The Beginnings of India Wharf," Bostonian Society *Proceedings* 15(1962):17–24; Judith McDonough, "Uriah Cotting, Planner and Developer: An Analysis of His Early Career in Federalist Boston," (unpublished paper, Boston Univ., 1975 [courtesy SPNEA]), 5; Whitehill, *Boston*, 84–86; Kirker, *Architecture of Bulfinch*, 32; Bell, "Account of the Town," 30; Uriah Cotting, *The Boston and Roxbury Mill Corporation* (Boston, 1818); Lists of Notes, 1805–1807, Broad Street Association, Mar. 9, 1807, Harrison Gray Otis Papers, M.H.S.; Conveyance of Land, Benjamin Hollowell to the Broad Street Association, Harrison Gray Otis Papers, M.H.S.; Broad Street Association, Suffolk County Registry of Deeds.
56. Schedule, India Wharf, 1805, BL.
57. Kirker, *Architecture of Bulfinch*, 258–260; Bell, "Account of the Town," 23–24; Whitehill, *Boston*, 64–65.

new houses of a Uniform Construction." In this manner, two hundred years of individualized building projects, spontaneously generated in response to human need, were transformed into the consciously planned neighborhoods associated with Sam Bass Warner's studies of the late nineteenth-century city. The enlarged scale of production, moreover—from single homes to whole tracts of buildings—brought a parallel rise in costs to be met by the building contractor.[58]

In addition, speculators altered labor relations in the building industry. On those jobs where nonlaboring entrepreneurs contracted for construction and marketed the final product, they only brought in housewrights as subcontractors or as wage earners. Moreover, rather than hire one mechanic to complete all of the tasks needed, the new contractors—especially on large projects—preferred to employ several artisans, each completing one part of the job. When the Proprietors of the Boston Theatre invited bids in the 1790s, they made different contracts for framing, for the doors and windows, for the interior, for the roof, and for masonry.[59] Similarly, Rolun Hartshorne was paid $380 in 1822 for putting a roof on the new Leverett Street jail.[60] Where possible, employers encouraged the abandonment of contracts altogether in favor of hiring by the day. In 1793, when housewrights Oliver Wiswall and Thomas Hearsey were hired to complete the interior of the theater, they agreed to do so at the rate of 5 shillings, 6 pence (90 cents) per day, "for ourselves and such men as we employ under our direction." Their bill of 1793 and 1794 indicates that they and their men accumulated 6,216 days working at the stipulated rate.[61] In 1821, the agents to build a new jail indicated that they preferred the "moderate rate of day wages" and to have the work done in "the most thorough and perfect manner." This could not be achieved under contract, they insisted. Rather, they hired by the day so they might employ "more or fewer as the work required."[62]

58. Lewis Tappan to the Mayor and Aldermen, Feb. 28, 1825, Boston City Records, Microprint Room, BPL; *Report of a Joint Committee on a Prospective Plan and Elevation of all the Streets in the City* (Boston, 1824); *Boston Daily Advertiser*, Mar. 25, 1825. On later urban development, see Sam Bass Warner, *Streetcar Suburbs: The Process of Growth in Boston, 1870–1900* (Cambridge, Mass., 1962).

59. Request for Proposals, Theatre, 1798, Boston Theatre Papers, BPL.

60. Accounts, Rolun Hartshorne, January 1822, Judge Elijah Adlow Papers, BPL.

61. Bid, Oliver Wiswall and Thomas Hearsey, Feb. 27, 1798, Boston Theatre Papers, BPL.

62. Report of the Appointed Agents to erect a new City Jail to the Justices of the Court in the County of Suffolk, 1821, Judge Elijah Adlow Papers. Hiring by the day has, since this time, coexisted with contracts and subcontracts. While the practice appears to have been

Speculators also introduced new financial terms into the industry, working to make their own construction endeavors financially more efficient. For instance, many new contracts required artisans to bid a price for an entire project before a job began. When Thomas Whitmarsh, Seth Nason, and Joseph Eaton agreed in 1805 to erect several blocks of buildings on India Wharf, they agreed to do so for $350 per store.[63] In such cases, the workmen—whether contractors or subcontractors—were forced to absorb any unforeseen costs exceeding the original bid. However, those outside of production—whether future occupants or nonlaboring contractors—were freed of extra financial obligations. Moreover, a rising number of contracts required that this "whole price" be paid only upon completion of the job. In 1826, Calvin Thompson agreed to build an addition onto the theater for $3,500, to be received when the work was done.[64] Once again, while such terms limited the cash outlay required from nonlaboring participants during construction, house carpenters—as contractors or subcontractors—needed sufficient funds to maintain themselves and the job until the building was completed. In this manner, such arrangements privileged the profits and financial security of nonlaboring contractors over those of working tradesmen.

The financiers also took over many of the administrative duties once reserved for laboring housewrights. In many cases, they did so by introducing new forms of nonlaboring middlemen, including architects, supervisors, and clerks-of-the-works. Charles Bulfinch, Boston's first "architect," was a Harvard-trained gentleman who had studied design but had little background in actual construction. Bulfinch developed the plans for numerous buildings between 1790 and 1844, including the Massachusetts State House, the Old Suffolk County Courthouse, the New North Church, and the Massachusetts General Hospital. When Bulfinch was hired by the Proprietors of the Boston Theatre in the 1790s, trustee Henry Jackson wrote to Henry Knox, "Mr. Bulfinch is a professional man, he calculated the cost of our theatre to a Brick, a foot of Boards, and every other material to complete the workmanship." Bulfinch also worked up the designs and made sure they were properly executed. When Wiswall and Hearsey bid to raise the roof in 1798, they agreed to work "according to Charles Bulfinch's

increasing in this period (especially on large projects utilizing many workmen), fragmentary records prohibit a comprehensive calculation as to the exact proportion of projects employing day labor.

63. Schedule, India Wharf, 1805, BL.
64. Contract, Calvin Thompson, June 20, 1826, Boston Theatre Papers, BPL.

plan." By the 1830s, some thirteen architects had emerged in the tax rolls. Where such architects were employed, housewrights not only had to relinquish the privilege of product design, but also found their role and authority in production subsumed to someone else's requirements.[65]

On some of the new projects, moreover, architects doubled as supervisors. Asher Benjamin first became known in the 1790s when he introduced a series of architectural manuals to Boston's working housewrights. He identified himself as "housewright" in the 1805 and 1812 membership rolls of the Massachusetts Charitable Mechanic Association and as a "carpenter" in the 1810 tax list. He also gained a reputation as an architect, designing, for instance, the West Church and the Exchange Coffee House. By the 1820s, however, Benjamin spent the bulk of his time as a contractor, supervisor, and paymaster for Boston's real estate developers. In 1821, he notarized an account between Otis and mason Caleb Storrell, indicating "This bill is right." In 1829, he signed an Otis account from housewrights Joseph Stoddard and Hezekiah Lincoln to "C. Brooks and Co." for sundry materials, noting that "$16.77 of this hardware was used at your house in Broad Street. Asher Benjamin." His accounts with Otis in March 1830, requesting refunds for a cash outlay to Stoddard and Lincoln (for carpentry), Hadley and Stanwick (for bricks), and John Oakes (for boards), contained a $100 charge, "for my services superintending the finishing of your buildings." Architect-supervisors such as Benjamin, in this manner, further circumscribed the housewrights' role.[66]

A third type of middleman was the "clerk-of-the-works," who represented a commissioning organization. Elisha Sigourney, for instance, as

65. Kirker and Kirker, *Bulfinch's Boston*, passim; Henry Jackson to Henry Knox, Apr. 13, 1794, Henry Knox Papers; Request for Proposals, Theatre, 1798, Boston Theatre Papers; Charles Bulfinch to Elisha Sigourney, 1797, Boston Theatre Papers. Architects were found in the Boston tax taking lists, 1790–1836, BPL Rare Book Room, and in Records of the MCMA. Edward Hazen (writing in Philadelphia in 1836), distinguished carpenters from architects in many cases: "Carpentery and joinery, as well as the other trades connected with building, are subservient to the architect, when an individual of this particular profession has been employed." *Panorama of Professions and Trades*, 205; also Charles A. Cummings, "Architecture in Boston," in Winsor, *Memorial History of Boston*, 4:472–479.

66. *Dictionary of American Biography*, 1:180; Kirker and Kirker, *Bulfinch's Boston*, 201, 280n.; Boston tax taking lists, 1810; Records of the MCMA, 1805, 1812; Account, Caleb Storrell with Harrison Gray Otis, July 11, 1821, and Account, Joseph Stoddard and Hezekiah Lincoln with Harrison Gray Otis, 1829, Harrison Gray Otis Papers, SPNEA; Account, Asher Benjamin with Harrison Gray Otis, Oct. 20, 1830, Harrison Gray Otis Papers, M.H.S.

agent for the new theater, advertised for men, made a few contracts, managed finances, obeyed Bulfinch's instructions, oversaw work, and reported to the trustees. The 1790 proposals were to be submitted to Sigourney. In 1798, he received word from Bulfinch as to what doors were needed, where they should be placed, and what kind of frames must be built to accommodate them. In 1811, Sigourney wrote to the trustees, "Agreeable to your instructions, I have made such repairs and alterations on the Theatre as in my opinion would be for the benefit of the proprietors and convenient to the manager."[67] As these examples indicate, Sigourney obeyed the instructions of his employers but retained significant initiative regarding the actual work. It is true that he lacked the expertise to acquire materials, hire workmen, supervise labor, or participate in the work process. In fact, while he said that he "made repairs and alterations," he did not really participate in production, leaving this to the laboring employees. Despite such limitations, clerks-of-the-works, like Sigourney, nonetheless took over the artisans' role of paymaster, contractor, and general supervisor.

The Impact on Artisanal Builders

These changes in financial and productive relations, as precipitated by elite speculators in postrevolutionary Boston, effectively transformed the business of building, while at the same time shifting control of the industry. Some housewrights, of course, persisted in the customary fashion, contracting directly with future owners. Some found that, while they lacked sufficient capital to obtain general contracts, they nonetheless were able to obtain lucrative subcontracts from the new developers. A few even found it possible to advance to the position of nonlaboring speculator, hiring workmen to produce the goods they later sold on the open market. All together, these three groups of housewrights comprised a small but relatively prosperous sector within the trade. By 1825, the top 20 percent of the housewrights controlled nearly 92 percent of the craft's taxable assets. More than half of the trade's wealth was held by the top 5 percent of its carpenters. Individual holdings ranged as high as $17,000, as compared to the $377 industry mean.[68]

Housewright Joseph Jenkins offers one example of a tradesman who

67. See Boston Theatre Papers, including Request for Proposals, Theatre, 1798; Bid, Oliver Wiswall and Thomas Hearsey, Feb. 27, 1798; Charles Bulfinch to Elisha Sigourney, April 1798; Elisha Sigourney to the Trustees of the Boston Theatre, Sept. 26, 1811.

68. Lubow, "Artisans in Transition," chap. 6.

achieved some semblance of success in these years. He first appeared as a housewright in Boston's South End in 1805, claiming property assessed at $6,000. He was active in city politics and in various civic groups in the 1820s. In 1822, he was chosen as alderman in the first city election and also made a lieutenant colonel in the militia. In 1833, he was appointed Suffolk County justice of the peace. Although the War of 1812 temporarily depleted his assets, by the 1830s he owned several houses, was worth $12,000 on the tax rolls, served as president of the Boston Lyceum, and called himself an "architect." By the 1840s, he considered himself a "builder," speculating on projects where he employed many men but did not engage in physical labor.[69]

Most masters, however, lacked the funds to buy land and erect whole blocks of buildings for unknown clients. Even for Jenkins, the limits of his resources ultimately relegated him to the periphery of capitalist success. In an 1839 building dispute, his ambitions were thwarted by the very entrepreneurs he chose to emulate. He had decided to purchase a valuable tract, erect a costly building (with a museum, warehouses, halls, and shops), and become its proprietor. He estimated a net gain of more than $50,000. After hiring one hundred men and investing $10,000, however, he ran out of funds. Efforts to obtain additional loans found creditors unsympathetic. "The debts already contracted began to press me, some of the persons who loaned me money began to complain, not only to me, but to others." Jenkins believed his inability to obtain funds was due to the competitive nature of his creditors. "I had rivals in the purchase of the estate, who were greatly disappointed in not obtaining it and, I have abundant reason to believe, improved any opportunity to excite prejudice against me, with the designs of frustrating my plans, that they might after all obtain the property." Lack of funds, moreover, only fueled their opposition. "I could make no arrangements with Capitalists," he said, and found it impossible to proceed. He was persuaded by Charles Eldredge, a relative by marriage, to transfer the property on a temporary basis, so as to clear its title and secure a loan. But Eldredge then tried to seize the property himself, and Jenkins was forced to take the matter to court.[70]

During the testimony, Jenkins's hostility toward Boston's entrepreneurial

69. Lisa B. Lubow, "When Labor and Capital Divide: Housewright Joseph Jenkins and the Quandary of the Middling Sort in Boston's Early Republic" (unpublished paper, 1993).
70. *The Case of Joseph Jenkins Versus Charles H. Eldredge, et. Al., in Equity* (Boston, 1843).

elite was apparent, as was the degree to which he was marginalized by their society. "I have no doubt," he insisted, "that most of my difficulties in obtaining a loan arose from the hostility of these people." When discussing Eldredge, Jenkins said that although his in-law was to have nothing to do with the building, he soon began to interfere. Eldredge came to the site, talked to the workmen, told them he was the owner, asked if they had been paid promptly, and gratuitously assured them that he would see to it. In this manner, Jenkins explained, Eldredge was

> thus creating a fear on the part of the workmen as to me, degrading me in their estimation, taking from me if he could the dignity of my position as the builder and owner, and in various instances, rendering it impossible for me to make contracts or to obtain the fulfillment of those already made, on advantageous terms.

Moreover, countless witnesses testified to how bad was Jenkins's credit. "I think," said Jeremiah Bumstead, a dealer in paper hangings, "his reputation was worse than any man's would be, who was not known at all."[71] Compared to rising numbers of wage earners, Jenkins was privileged in ways they would never experience. Yet in the eyes of the new industrial elite, the inadequacies of his investment capital rendered him a virtual non-person. Cursing the "Capitalists" whom he believed conspired against him, Jenkins drew his career to a close. He died seven years later, one of the few examples of a carpenter turned nonlaboring speculator.[72]

Those carpenters with more finite resources avoided the pitfalls of speculative contracting, choosing instead to subcontract to the new "builders." When Hearsey and Wiswall bid for one subcontract on the Boston Theatre, they then proposed to subcontract further or hire others to work under them for a daily wage. Once on the job, they labored beside the employees, submitting accounts to agent Sigourney. As many as twenty men worked under Wiswall at once.[73] Subcontracts, however, further eroded the position of master craftsmen. The new real estate developers, after all, had no need for artisans equipped in every facet of the business. They handled the

71. *Joseph Jenkins Versus Charles H. Eldredge.*
72. *Joseph Jenkins Versus Charles H. Eldredge.*
73. Contract, Oliver Wiswall and Thomas Hearsey, Apr. 29, 1793, and Accounts, Oliver Wiswall, 1798, Boston Theatre Papers. Many accounts show housewrights contracted by a middleman and then further subcontracting to others. For example, Accounts, Joseph Stoddard and Hezekiah Lincoln with Harrison Gray Otis, Nov. 18, Dec. 16, 1829, Harrison Gray Otis Papers, SPNEA. See also Wilentz, *Chants Democratic*, 132–134.

financial and mercantile dimensions themselves, while hiring middlemen for those administrative functions once reserved for the independent mechanic. The one artisan quality that remained in demand was that of skill, but skill was not unique to master artisans: journeymen also were skilled. In this context—in an industry increasingly dominated by a small group of nonlaboring contractors and rising numbers of workmen—competition among skilled housewrights deepened. Subcontracts wrested from that competition, moreover, were won by underbidding, leaving artisans a smaller profit margin and greater vulnerability to debts, delays, and bankruptcy. As a result, the growing subcontracting system, and the intensifying market competition that followed, ate away at the very resources housewrights needed to compete in a changing business.

With general contracts beyond most, and competition forcing down compensation, artisan ownership began to crumble, despite a burgeoning real estate industry. While nearly 1,000 men worked in carpentry in 1825, 62 percent of all carpenters and 93 percent of all journeymen—over 600 men—were propertyless. Although the trade now claimed 9 percent of Boston's 11,673 adult males, they held only 1.4 percent of the town's taxable wealth. Their average property holding was only $377, nearly the same as it had been in 1790.[74] Ebenezer Dyer, for example, was a master in 1810. He owned a house on North Allen Street in West Boston, a second house on Poplar Street, and was worth $2,500. The War of 1812 was hard on Dyer, as it was on most Bostonians. Forced to sell both houses, he moved to Allen Street as a tenant to the new owner, Richard Caswell. Although, in time, society's economic health improved, Dyer's situation did not. He remained Caswell's tenant for fifteen years; by 1825, his estate was valued at only $100.[75]

As property-holding steadily eroded, the nature of the carpenters' trade changed, from one largely characterized by independent masters, to one dominated by wage-earning journeymen. Lacking property, rising numbers of master housewrights were transformed from businessmen into dependent labor, returned—as verified by the yearly tax rolls—to the status of journeyman carpenter. Between 1810 and 1825, 19 percent of Boston's master carpenters reverted. Between 1825 and 1831, 13 percent (in an even larger industry) experienced the downward shift.[76] Darius Holbrook, a

74. Lubow, "Artisans in Transition," chap. 6.
75. Boston tax taking and tax valuation lists, 1810, 1815, 1820, and 1825.
76. Lubow, "Artisans in Transition," chap. 4.

master assessed in 1796 at $700, lived in one end of a house and occupied a shop nearby. By 1805, he occupied a house on Elm Street, rented a shop in a neighboring ward, and held $1,400 in wealth. Whether hard times or opportunity drew him away is unknown, but he disappeared from the rolls of Boston carpenters in 1810. When he reappeared in 1815, he was again a journeyman, renting from another carpenter in the South End, assessed for only $100. By 1820, he was a penniless boarder. Although Holbrook recovered some by 1825—claiming $200 and master status—he never regained the standing he enjoyed fifteen years earlier.[77] Given such insecurities, fewer masters joined the trade or rose from journeyman status. Of the 509 journeymen who appeared in 1825, fifty-four (less than 11 percent) rose to master. Mobility within the trade had collapsed. By 1825, two thirds of all carpenters were journeymen. Most housewrights, lacking the property needed to own their own enterprise, were forced to hire out for a daily wage.[78]

As wage earners, or as subcontractors, carpenters became the employees of others, losing significant entrepreneurial initiative. First, they relinquished control over much of the labor process. They no longer bargained with clients over work regulations or schedules. They were not responsible for product design. They had a limited say in choosing workers, dividing labor, and overseeing the work process. Their influence over the woodwork was diminished. And they lost control of their workday: the hours, pace, and pattern of work discipline. Second, they lost financial control. The product of their labor was no longer theirs to buy and sell, as it was now owned by the financier who paid for its construction. They had little say about prices, the distribution of profits, pay schedules, and amounts. They also lost the

77. Boston tax taking and tax valuation lists, 1796, 1800, 1805, 1810, 1815, 1820, 1825.

78. Lubow, "Artisans in Transition," chap. 4. Mobility figures for those carpenters first appearing after 1810 contain an unknown, since a small but growing proportion remained journeymen as of 1834, the last year checked. Yet the great majority of journeymen appearing in 1810, 1815, 1820, and 1825 either became masters or disappeared from the trade prior to 1834; their number, moreover, does conform to mobility trends set in earlier years. For instance, from among those carpenters who first appeared on the 1825 tax rolls, 54 individuals, or 10.6 percent, became master carpenters in Boston between 1825 and 1834; 384 individuals, or 75.4 percent, disappeared during those years; only 71 individuals, or 14 percent, remained journeymen carpenters as of 1834. Even if the full proportion of carpenters who appeared in 1825 and remained journeymen in 1834 had eventually become masters, those who disappeared without having risen to master status would have remained dominant.

bulk of the benefits realized from a profitable endeavor. While Whitmarsh, Nason, and Eaton were paid $350 for each store they erected on India Wharf, the Proprietors pocketed the $200,000 surplus realized from the job. Profits buried in the price were now appropriated by those men who paid for constructing the product, not by those who actually made it.[79]

In this context, entrepreneurial control of Boston's building industry gradually shifted in the postrevolutionary decades. Although some house-wrights persisted as independent contractors, coexisting with the new non-laboring speculators even to the present day, they found their role increasingly circumscribed.[80] Nonlaboring contractors, assuming proprietary initiative and employing new methods, grew unprecedentedly active, particularly on large-scale, capital-intensive projects. In the years to follow, a growing share of society's commercial buildings, public structures, residential housing tracts, and industrial construction would become the province of the new real estate developers. Moreover, patterns of wealth-holding and occupational mobility reveal that a rising proportion of housewrights— a majority by 1825—lacked the resources to operate as independent contractors, let alone compete on the scale and terms initiated by elite speculators. Consequently, growing numbers of craftsmen—especially on major construction projects—found themselves employed by those speculators, where once they had operated as the owners and entrepreneurs of their trade. In an echo of the industrializing process transforming other sectors

79. Estimate of Stores on India Wharf, 1806, Harrison Gray Otis Papers, M.H.S.; Abbott Lowell Cummings, "Beginnings of India Wharf," 17–24.

80. Fragmentary records make it difficult to quantify the pace of industrial change: the proportion of construction run by nonlaboring proprietors, the degree to which any given housewright worked as wage earner or subcontractor, or the extent to which the new methods of payment and hiring were used. Certainly laboring contractors operate today, on individual housing, renovation, custom crafting, etc. Yet the assumption that carpentry has remained a "traditional" craft is inaccurate. Most commercial buildings, public structures, housing tracts, shopping malls, industrial complexes, etc. are corporately funded and managed by nonlaboring contractors employing wage labor. Also, the trade has experienced a major breakdown of skill. By the 1830s, workmen were producing prefabricated, standardized doors, blinds, stairs, and window sashes. By the 1870s, semi-skilled workers built stairs, laid floors, and hung doors; women, children, and others sublet for piecework, making ready-to-install factory parts. In 1928, the Department of Labor listed 21 different types of carpenters, while subsequent decades brought widespread production of buildings made of structural steel and prefabricated parts, lifted into place by powered machines. U.S. Bureau of Labor Statistics, *Description of Occupations: Metal Working, Building and General Construction, Railroad Transportation, Shipbuilding* (Washington, D.C., 1918); Christie, *Empire in Wood*, chap. 2; Ham, "Associations of Employers," 57.

throughout America, the manufacture of Boston buildings was increasingly the product of elite financiers and dependent employees. The business of building, once the province of the laboring carpenter, now belonged to the nonlaboring capitalist.[81]

81. Although most studies of early industrialization stress technology and labor culture, not proprietary control, the literature is rich and also contains data suggestive of the historical trend regarding property ownership. Included, in part, is Mary H. Blewett, *Men, Women, and Work: Class, Gender, and Protest in the New England Shoe Industry, 1780–1910* (Urbana, Ill., 1988); Dawley, *Class and Community*; Thomas Dublin, *Transforming Women's Work: New England Lives in the Industrial Revolution* (Ithaca, 1994); Paul G. Faler, *Mechanics and Manufacturers in the Early Industrial Revolution: Lynn, Massachusetts, 1760–1860* (Albany, N.Y., 1981); Herbert G. Gutman, *Work, Culture, and Society in Industrializing America: Essays in American Working-Class and Social History* (New York, 1976); Hirsch, *Roots of the American Working Class*; Graham Russell Hodges, *New York City Cartmen, 1667–1850* (New York, 1986); Paul E. Johnson, *A Shopkeeper's Millennium: Society and Revivals in Rochester, New York, 1815–1837* (New York, 1978); Laurie, *Artisans into Workers*; David Montgomery, "The Shuttle and the Cross: Weavers and Artisans in the Kensington Riots of 1844," *Journal of Social History* 5(1972):411–446; Theresa Anne Murphy, *Ten Hours' Labor: Religion, Reform, and Gender in Early New England* (Ithaca, 1992); Jonathan Prude, *The Coming of Industrial Order: Town and Factory Life in Rural Massachusetts, 1810–1860* (Cambridge, 1983); Howard B. Rock, Paul A. Gilje, and Robert Asher, eds., *American Artisans: Crafting Social Identity, 1750–1850* (Baltimore, 1995); Rock, *Artisans of the New Republic*; Steven J. Ross, *Workers on the Edge: Work, Leisure, and Politics in Industrializing Cincinnati, 1788–1890* (New York, 1985); Sharon V. Salinger, *"To Serve Well and Faithfully": Labor and Indentured Servants in Pennsylvania, 1682–1800* (Cambridge, Mass., 1987); Philip Scranton, *Proprietary Capitalism: The Textile Manufacture of Philadelphia, 1800–1885* (Cambridge, Mass., 1983); Schultz, *Republic of Labor*; Cynthia Shelton, *The Mills of Manayunk: Early Industrialization and Social Conflict in the Philadelphia Region, 1787–1837* (Baltimore, 1986); Smith, *"Lower Sort"*; Christine Stansell, *City of Women: Sex and Class in New York, 1789–1860* (New York, 1986); Charles G. Steffen, *The Mechanics of Baltimore: Workers and Politics in the Age of Revolution, 1763–1812* (Urbana, Ill., 1984); Richard B. Stott, *Workers in the Metropolis: Class, Ethnicity, and Youth in Antebellum New York City* (Ithaca, 1990); Daniel Vickers, *Farmers and Fishermen: Two Centuries of Work in Essex County, Massachusetts, 1630–1850* (Chapel Hill, 1994); Anthony F. C. Wallace, *Rockdale: The Growth of an American Village in the Early Industrial Revolution* (New York, 1978); Shane White, *Somewhat More Independent: The End of Slavery in New York City, 1770–1810* (Athens, Georgia, 1991); Wilentz, *Chants Democratic*; Alfred F. Young, "George Robert Twelves Hewes (1742–1840): A Boston Shoemaker and the Memory of the American Revolution," *William and Mary Quarterly*, 3d ser. 38(1981):561–623.

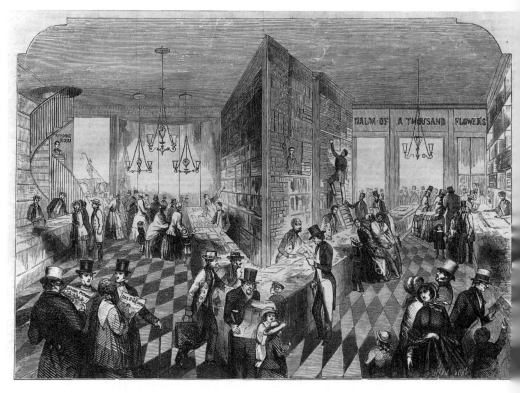

Fetridge & Co. Periodical Arcade, Washington and State streets.
Gleason's Pictorial 3(July 31, 1852):80.

The Boston Book Trades, 1789–1850:

A Statistical and Geographical Analysis

Ronald J. Zboray and Mary Saracino Zboray

RECENT SCHOLARLY WORK in the history of the book in the United States has benefited from a long tradition of research into bibliographical highways and byways. Beginning in the middle of the nineteenth century, librarians, rare book dealers, and other specialists painstakingly compiled information about American imprints and the people who produced them. Some of this work was "antiquarian," though no less valuable than academic studies; it produced reliable lists of early imprints for each of the fifty states, for example.[1]

Many people and institutions have contributed labor, advice, and encouragement to this project. Work began in 1992 under a National Endowment for the Humanities-American Antiquarian Society six-month fellowship. The Society's staff, then and during several subsequent visits, was particularly helpful, as were many other scholars passing through the library who encouraged this study. Of these, Victor A. Berch, Jane Pomeroy, and Willman Spawn deserve special thanks. Our gratitude goes also to John Bidwell, Richard D. Brown, Robert F. Dalzell, Robert Gross, Sidney F. Huttner, Bruce Laurie, Glenn Porter, and Paul Wright for their interest and helpful observations on diverse occasions. During a 1993 visit to the Massachusetts Historical Society, Conrad E. Wright and other staff members expressed enthusiasm for this project, especially in light of the M.H.S.'s similar data base for all trades. Marjorie D. Patterson and other librarians in the Interlibrary Loan Office at Georgia State University (GSU) as well as their counterparts at the University of Georgia took special care to assure us an even flow of city directories in 1994. GSU provided funds for purchasing the directories in 1995 and, through a Research Initiation Grant, for three graduate student assistants to whom we owe thanks for their painstaking efforts: R. Michael Brubaker, Christopher Hawkins-Long, and William Simson. GSU also generously supplied a Research Enhancement Grant for the project's computerization. Finally, the GSU Department of History has provided funds for purchasing reproductions of maps, and it has offered us much steadfast encouragement and support.

1. G. Thomas Tanselle, *Guide to the Study of United States Imprints* (Cambridge, Mass., 1971), xiv–xx. Perhaps the best and most scholarly of these lists is Marcus A. McCorison, comp., *Vermont Imprints, 1778–1820* (Worcester, 1963). Many compilations remain unpublished, such as the Printer's File at the American Antiquarian Society (hereafter AAS) in Worcester, which provides details on printers' lives, their association with firms, and their imprints. It is most complete for Boston up to 1820. Recent scholarship in early-

Book-trades directories, especially, have provided researchers with historical details about specific printers, publishers, booksellers, and other individuals and firms.[2] Beyond their use as reference works, directory compilations can also serve as the basis for a collective biography of the book trades. Fluctuations in the number and relative proportions of types of firms, their changing geographic distribution, even the emergence of new occupational titles within the trades can be traced using directory information. Modern computerized data bases permit analyses of these kinds of patterns, which earlier compilers possibly discerned but could not quantify. Such impressions might be more valid for the smaller book trades of the colonial and early national periods—indeed most compilations focus on those times—but falter before the extensive and complex state of the industry in the mid nineteenth century.

---

national and antebellum book history that calls upon this older tradition includes, Richard D. Brown, *Knowledge Is Power: The Diffusion of Information in Early America, 1700–1865* (New York, 1989); several of the essays in Cathy N. Davidson, ed., *Reading in America: Literature and Social History* (Baltimore, 1989); idem, *Revolution and the Word: The Rise of the Novel in America* (New York, 1986); William J. Gilmore, *Reading Becomes a Necessity of Life: Material and Cultural Life in Rural New England, 1780–1835* (Knoxville, 1989); Robert A. Gross, "Much Instruction from Little Reading: Books and Libraries in Thoreau's Concord," *Proceedings of the American Antiquarian Society* 97(1987):129–188; Mary Kelley, *Private Woman, Public Stage: Literary Domesticity in Nineteenth-Century America* (New York, 1984); and Ronald J. Zboray, *A Fictive People: Antebellum Economic Development and the American Reading Public* (New York, 1993).

2. For a listing to 1971, see Tanselle, *Guide to the Study of United States Imprints*, 398–403. Sidney F. Huttner and Elizabeth S. Huttner, *A Register of Artists, Engravers, Booksellers, Bookbinders, Printers and Publishers in New York City, 1821–1842* (New York, 1993) appeared too late to influence the design of the present study. See also C. Deirdre Phelps, "Printing, Publishing, and Bookselling in Salem, Massachusetts, 1825–1900," *Essex Institute Historical Collections* 124(1988):227–295, which includes a directory of the trade. On an earlier period, see G. Thomas Tanselle, "Some Statistics on American Printing, 1764–1783" in *The Press and the American Revolution*, ed. Bernard Bailyn and John B. Hench (Worcester, Mass., 1980). For a model of geographical analysis based on directories and other sources, see Ian Maxted, *The London Book Trades, 1775–1800: A Preliminary Checklist of Members* (Folkestone, Eng., 1977). Business historians have long made analyses of city directories. See, for example, George H. Evans, Jr., "A Sketch of American Business Organization, 1832–1900," *Journal of Political Economy* 60(1952):475–486; George H. Evans, Jr., and Walter C. Kanwisher, "Business Organization in Baltimore," *Journal of Political Economy* 62(1954):63–67; and Ruth G. Hutchinson, Arthur R. Hutchinson, and Mabel Newcomer, "A Study in Business Mortality: The Length of Life of Business Enterprises in Poughkeepsie, New York: 1843–1936," *American Economic Review* 28(1938):497–514.

Figure 1. U.S. Printing and Publishing in 1850: Value of Product

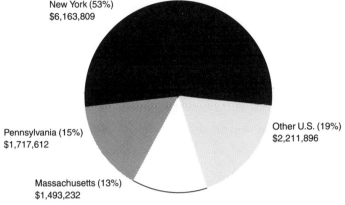

New York (53%)
$6,163,809

Pennsylvania (15%)
$1,717,612

Other U.S. (19%)
$2,211,896

Massachusetts (13%)
$1,493,232

Source: 1850 census. Total $11,586,549.

The difficulties of mastering the mid-century book trades are especially acute for the three leading publishing centers: New York, Philadelphia, and Boston.[3] Nearly all production took place there; for example, in 1850 their states accounted for 81 percent of the value of the nation's printing and publishing output (Fig. 1), almost all of it from the cities. Driven by population increase, transportation access, and general economic development, the industry boomed in these centers. Little wonder that the published directory compilations for the three cities covered only the period up to the 1820s.[4] Yet it is precisely for the ensuing years that an analysis of the

3. William Charvat, *Literary Publishing in America, 1790–1850* (1959; reprint, Amherst, 1993), 17–37. The fourth largest antebellum publishing center was Cincinnati. Walter Sutton, *The Western Book Trade: Cincinnati as a Nineteenth-Century Publishing and Book Trade Center* (Columbus, 1961). One of the best overviews of the trade can be found in Samuel G. Goodrich, *Recollections of a Lifetime; or, Men and Things I Have Seen* (New York, 1856).

4. On Boston, see the source note to Table 2 and the Appendix. On New York, Huttner and Huttner, *Register of Artists*; George L. McKay, "A Register of Artists, Booksellers, Printers and Publishers in New York City, 1781–1820," *Bulletin of the New York Public Library* 43(1939):711–724, 849–858; 44(1940):351–357, 415–428, 475–487; 45(1941): 387–395, 483–499, issued in 1942 as an offprint with additions under the same title; Elizabeth Waterman, "A Register of Publishers, Printers and Booksellers of the City of New York, 1850–55," typescript at the Grolier Club; H. Glenn Brown and Maude O. Brown, "A Directory of the Book-Arts and Book Trade in Philadelphia to 1820 Including Painters and Engravers," *Bulletin of the New York Public Library* 53(1949):211–226, 290–

American book trades becomes critical for historians, since it provides a material foundation for understanding the American Renaissance and other important mid-century cultural developments.[5]

Boston, as the smallest of the three centers, is the most easily studied for the years beyond 1820. Its relatively limited scale has traditionally led book historians to portray the trades there as backward and "parochial."[6] Nonetheless, the city's flourishing literary culture in the early nineteenth century, however small, left abundant materials documenting the local book trades. And modern social historians who have analyzed the city intensively have given a firm descriptive and statistical basis for contextualizing its publishing industry.[7]

The importance of the Boston book trades, however, extends beyond sociocultural history. They also played a significant role in the economic growth and development of the city (Table 1). We can thus trace through them the rapid expansion of a single, large sector of local business. The book trades represented just under a tenth of the firms engaged in manufacturing in 1832; they were the fourth largest occupational group, after dry goods, nautical supplies, and metalworking. The book trades had the

298, 339–347, 387–401, 447–458, 492–503, 564–573, 615–622; 54(1950):25–37, 89–92, 123–145, issued in 1951 as a separate imprint by the New York Public Library.

5. Of the many books and articles that address the linkages between history and literature in the region, one of the most insightful is Lawrence Buell, *New England Literary Culture: From Revolution through Renaissance* (Cambridge, 1986). For considerations of the economic motivations of Boston publishers, see Ronald J. Zboray, "Literary Enterprise in Antebellum Boston," Seminar in American Bibliography and Book Trade History, AAS, Nov. 9, 1992; idem, "The Romance of Trout Fishing: Angles on the Market for Antebellum Novels," Work in Progress in the History of the Book in American Culture, Colloquia Series at the AAS, Aug. 18, 1992. Copies of both papers are on deposit at the AAS.

6. Charvat, *Literary Publishing*, 27–29; John Tebbel, *A History of Book Publishing in the United States* (New York, 1972–1981), 1:386.

7. A selective list includes: Henry C. Binford, *The First Suburbs: Residential Communities on the Boston Periphery, 1815–1860* (Chicago, 1985); Matthew Edel, Elliott D. Sclar, Daniel Luria, *Shaky Palaces: Home Ownership and Social Mobility in Boston's Suburbanization* (New York, 1984); Peter R. Knights, *The Plain People of Boston, 1830–1860: A Study in City Growth* (New York, 1971); idem, *Yankee Destinies: The Lives of Ordinary Nineteenth-Century Bostonians* (Chapel Hill, 1991); William H. Pease and Jane H. Pease, *The Web of Progress: Private Values and Public Styles in Boston and Charleston, 1828–1843* (New York, 1985); David Ward, "Nineteenth-Century Boston: A Study in the Role of Antecedent and Adjacent Conditions in the Spatial Aspects of Urban Growth" (Ph.D. diss., Univ. of Wisconsin, 1963). For the later 19th century, see Stephan Thernstrom, *The Other Bostonians: Poverty and Progress in the American Metropolis, 1880–1970* (Cambridge, Mass., 1973); Sam B. Warner, Jr., *Streetcar Suburbs: The Process of Growth in Boston, 1870–1900* (Cambridge, Mass., 1962).

third highest level of overall capitalization and led all other industries in the amount invested in machinery and other capital goods (accounting for 42.41 percent of all the investment in the city, with the second ranked group, the metal trades, trailing at 21.70 percent).[8] Apart from dry goods, the book trades were the most dynamic producer of mass-market-oriented consumer items, even, in the value of their output for 1832, slightly leading the distillers for which Boston had long been famous.[9] Thus, in their use of capital goods (steam presses, type, and, especially, electrotype and stereotype plates) and their production of consumer goods for a mass market the book trades stood on the cutting edge of economic change.[10]

8. Absolute values of capitalization, however, are probably underestimated due to the lack of depreciation accounting; Judith A. McGaw, "Accounting for Innovation: Technological Change and Business Practice in the Berkshire Paper Industry," *Technology and Culture* 26(1985):703–725. The figures from the table are based on McLane, which though published in 1833 described conditions as reported in the late spring and early summer of 1832. The high capitalization of publishing shows that the various parts of the book trades did not industrialize simultaneously. To some extent, this was due to differentials in technological innovation and adaptation. Stereotype plates (1813) and, later, electrotype plates (1841) became a form of capital accumulation, for they stored text in a convenient, ready-to-use form that eliminated the substantial costs of repeated typesetting and permitted type to be redistributed for use on other jobs—little wonder that the 1820s saw the emergence of "publisher" as a separate occupational designation. Printing would await the later 1830s to be revolutionized by steam presses; during the same decade papermaking machinery came into widespread use. Several machines affected bookbinding from the 1820s through the 1850s. For a summary and analysis of these innovations— and an argument that they alone do not explain the antebellum publishing boom—see Ronald J. Zboray, "Antebellum Reading and the Ironies of Technological Innovation," *American Quarterly* 40(1988):65–82. Judith A. McGaw, *Most Wonderful Machine: Mechanization and Social Change in Berkshire Paper Making, 1801–1885* (Princeton, 1987).

9. On the meaning of the book trades for consumers, see Ronald J. Zboray and Mary Saracino Zboray, "Books, Reading, and the World of Goods in Antebellum New England," *American Quarterly* 48 (1996):587–622.

10. For arguments in favor of the innovative nature of publishing within American economic development, see Ronald J. Zboray, "Literary Enterprise and the Mass Market: Publishers and Business Innovation in Antebellum America," *Essays in Economic and Business History* 10(1992):168–181, 2 leaves. Compare the development of publishing with the pace of change described in Alfred D. Chandler, Jr., *The Visible Hand: The Managerial Revolution in American Business* (Cambridge, Mass., 1977), and Glenn Porter and Harold C. Livesay, *Merchants and Manufacturers: Studies in the Changing Structure of Nineteenth-Century Marketing* (Baltimore, 1971). That publishing stood at the forefront of change is not surprising in light of the argument made by JoAnne Yates, *Control through Communication: The Rise of System and American Management* (Baltimore, 1989). The best general source on the state of manufacturing remains Victor S. Clark, *History of Manufactures in the United States*, 2d ed. (1929; New York, 1949), 1:233–582.

Table 1. Boston Trades in 1832: Capitalization and Work Force

Business Type	% of All Trades	% of Capital				% of Input			% of Output
		Machinery	Real Property	Inventory	Total	U.S.	Foreign	Total	
Book Trades	9.49	42.41	12.37	10.80	15.68	17.60	1.54	8.50	8.67
Building Trades	6.77	4.26	6.86	4.36	5.67	5.48	2.10	3.57	3.61
Carriages	4.55	1.36	5.54	4.58	4.67	3.63	0.70	1.97	1.80
Chemicals	0.51	0.30	0.91	1.42	1.01	0.93	1.20	1.08	0.77
Dry Goods	42.53	3.86	22.66	30.13	22.83	17.15	44.66	32.73	22.97
Food	5.25	1.52	6.15	2.49	4.29	0.91	2.99	2.09	1.53
Furnishings	1.92	2.27	3.38	2.86	3.06	3.70	0.97	2.15	1.28
Instruments	1.11	1.12	1.66	0.49	1.19	0.53	0.40	0.46	1.04
Liquor	2.22	3.00	5.68	0.82	3.66	6.93	22.43	15.71	8.63
Metal Trades	11.11	21.70	18.13	22.71	20.17	25.24	7.19	15.02	12.68
Nautical Supplies	13.74	16.37	14.74	14.18	14.75	12.24	15.30	13.97	35.30
Other Consumables	0.81	1.83	1.93	5.16	3.03	5.66	0.51	2.75	1.72
All°	100.00	100.00	100.00	100.00	100.00	100.00	100.00	100.00	100.00
Actual totals	990	$857,200	$3,522,219	$2,309,572	$6,668,991	$3,412,162	$4,457,665	$7,869,827	$16,484,995

Business Type	Annual Wages (in dollars)				Number (estimated)				Average Daily Wages (in dollars)		
	Men	Boys	Women	Total	Men	Boys	Women	Total	Men	Boys	Women
Book Trades	310,153	34,187	56,054	400,394	709	225	403	1,337	1.41	0.49	0.45
Building Trades	200,745	10,771	155	211,671	444	68	1	513	1.46	0.51	0.50
Carriages	99,882	15,348	340	115,570	264	83	2	349	1.22	0.60	0.55
Chemicals	6,392	155	495	7,042	15	1	5	21	1.37	0.50	0.32
Dry Goods	393,241	33,244	392,487	818,972	870	200	2,328	3,398	1.46	0.54	0.54
Food	44,598	7,155	2,100	53,853	138	39	14	191	1.04	0.59	0.48
Furnishings	29,852	3,797	7,750	41,399	77	22	50	149	1.25	0.56	0.50
Instruments	45,101	852	0	45,953	91	5	0	96	1.60	0.55	0.00
Liquor	24,600	3,100	0	27,700	80	20	0	100	0.99	0.50	0.00
Metal Trades	393,337	20,441	9,590	423,368	938	115	59	1,112	1.35	0.57	0.52
Nautical Supplies	322,767	37,873	0	360,640	697	216	0	913	1.49	0.57	0.00
Other Consumables	16,541	1,550	7,373	25,464	44	10	49	103	1.21	0.50	0.49
All	1,887,209	168,473	476,344	2,532,026	4,367	1,004	2,911	8,282	1.39	0.54	0.53

Source: Based on John S. Tyler, "Document 3, Nos. 198–216, Boston, Schedule of Manufactures, Buildings, &c. Materials Used, Manufactures, Markets, Workmen, Wages," Louis McLane, comp., *Documents Relative to the Manufactures in the United States Collected and Transmitted to the House of Representatives in Compliance With a Resolution of Jan. 19, 1832, By the Secretary of the Treasury* (1833; reprint, New York, 1969) 1:432–468. "Machinery" represents "Values of tools, machinery & apparatus, other than the fixtures."

a May not equal 100 percent due to rounding.

They did so in another regard, too, for the book trades provide a glimpse into the way that certain crafts industrialized. Specifically, in the antebellum years the trades witnessed a great deal of proletarianization. In many areas of print production, artisan shops gave way to industrialized factories, and journeymen who once hoped to become master artisans in later life became instead permanent wage laborers. As early as 1832, the average shop in the trades contained almost nine men, slightly more than the typical Boston industrial firm of the mid forties.[11] The book trades were the only industry in the city that employed an almost equal number of men (709 in 1832) and boys and women (628)—one more indication of the deskilling that accompanied the move to machine-assisted production, often in factories (Table 1).[12]

The industrial development of this one sector of production and distribution had its geographical consequences, as well. Within Boston, places of production and retailing for the book trades increasingly clustered on

11. The average industrial firm in Boston employed eight workers in 1845 according to Ward, "Nineteenth-Century Boston," 42. Jeremy Atack, "Firm Size and Industrial Structure in the United States during the Nineteenth Century," *Journal of Economic History* 46(1986):463–475; Ross Thomson, "Invention, Markets, and the Scope of the Firm: The Nineteenth Century U.S. Shoe Machinery Industry," *Business and Economic History* 18(1989):140–149. Compare these with Lisa Beth Lubow, "Artisans in Transition: Early Capitalist Development and the Carpenters of Boston, 1787–1837" (Ph.D. diss., Univ. of California, Los Angeles, 1987).

12. In dry goods production, women had long predominated. For a survey of the overall transformation of labor, see Bruce Laurie, *Artisans into Workers: Labor in Nineteenth-Century America* (New York, 1989), 15–46, with special notice of printers, 38–39. By 1850, in Philadelphia, only about 3.6 percent of printing firms operated in the artisan mode–see idem, *The Working People of Philadelphia, 1800–1850* (Philadelphia, 1980), 17, Table 3; Alan Dawley, *Class and Community: The Industrial Revolution in Lynn* (Cambridge, Mass., 1976). Some of the larger issues surrounding women's participation in the industrial workforce are treated in Claudia Goldin, "The Economic Status of Women in the Early Republic: Quantitative Evidence," *Journal of Interdisciplinary History* 16 (1986):375–404. The diminishing importance of adolescents in the industrial workforce is underscored by Susan E. Hirsch, *The Roots of the American Working Class: The Industrialization of Crafts in Newark, 1800–1860* (Philadelphia, 1978), 40–47, though she is mostly concerned with industries that demanded higher levels of skills than many of the book trades. In this sense, labor in the Boston book trades more closely resembled that of a textile town like Lowell than it reflected the workforce of a heavy industrial center like Newark. The book trades foreshadowed the erosion of gender-segregated employment; Nancy E. Bertaux, "The Roots of Today's 'Women's Jobs' and 'Men's Jobs': Using the Index of Dissimilarity to Measure Occupational Segregation by Gender," *Explorations in Economic History* 28(1991):433–459.

a few downtown streets. At the same time, the homes of tradespeople emerged from workplaces early in the century and then moved ever outward, scattered mostly in a few residential areas away from the principal business district. In short, the book trades provide a microcosm of the urban spatial development and business specialization that came to characterize American cities from the middle of the century well into the next.[13]

In pursuit of these themes of rapid sectoral development, the impact of industrialization upon work, and geographical specialization, the present study examines the Boston book trades for the years 1789 through 1850. We created a data base of the names, work and home addresses, and occupations of book tradespeople found in any city directories published during the period. We then standardized and coded the information for statistical analysis (see Appendix). The resulting wealth of data, 18,506 records (see Table 2), allows us to delineate to an unprecedented degree the growth and development of these important trades. We present our findings in three broad sections: 1) an overview of the industry, 2) an examination of the numbers, including an analysis of the duration of individual and corporate entities, along with an occupational breakdown, and 3) a geography of the trades.

The number of book-trades entries in the directories expanded dramatically over six decades.[14] This was not simply due to the growth of Boston's

13. Compare the development with that described in Edward K. Spann, *The New Metropolis: New York City, 1840–1857* (New York, 1981), chap. 5; Joan H. Geismar and Bert Salwen (commentary), "Patterns of Development in the Late-Eighteenth and Nineteenth-Century American Seaport: A Suggested Model for Recognizing Increasing Commercialization and Urbanization," *American Archeology* 5(1985):175–184; and Edward K. Muller, "Spatial Order before Industrialization: Baltimore's Central District, 1833–1869," in *Historical and Geographical Aspects of 19th-Century Baltimore: Working Papers from the Regional Economic History Research Center* 4(1981):100–140. The manufacturing portion of the trade, like that in other cities, would remain close to the city center as part of the dichotomization of production in which some primary industries leave a city while other secondary ones, like printing, remain downtown to take advantage of "information" and "external" economies. These secondary industries remain flexible enough to ride the ups and downs of seasonality and fashionable demand. See Richard Stott, "Hinterland Development and Differences in Work Setting: The New York City Region, 1820–1870," in *New York and the Rise of American Capitalism: Economic Development and the Social and Political History of an American State, 1780–1870*, ed. William Pencak and Conrad Edick Wright (New York, 1989), 45–71.

14. Because the directories were published in July and were presumably compiled in the late spring, seasonality probably had little effect on annual fluctuations. Obviously, how-

population, which increased about six-and-a-half times; book-trades entries mushroomed to forty-two times the number represented in the 1789 directory (Table 3).[15] In three of the decades, the 1790s, 1820s, and 1840s, the increase in the number of book-trades entries surpassed the population increase by more than 70 percent; in only one decade, the 1830s, were they about the same.[16]

Rather than population growth, the overall economic development of the city explains much of the increase in book-trades entries. In this light, entries in city directories for all trades provide a better backdrop for comparison than do population figures (Table 4). Not surprisingly, impressive average annual growth rates characterize directory entries as a whole (for the period, these averaged 7.94 percent). Yet the book trades outperformed the norm (averaging 10.98 percent), though the growth was uneven: their seven years of downturn may be measured against only four for all trades combined. At the same time, for every one year in which book-trades entries decreased there were at least two years of double-digit growth.

One should not assume that too much of a parallel exists between the book trades and other businesses, for the trades behaved somewhat independently of all directory entries combined, in terms of their growth patterns (Table 4). In only seventeen of forty-four years was the deviation between the growth of the book trades and the growth of all businesses

---

ever, the figures represent a snapshot of the state of the trades during a single season over these decades, meaning that at other times of the year the numbers might be lower or higher. Two factors helped to compensate for possible distortions: the standard directory practice of including people who were more or less established in business (and hence less likely to migrate due to seasonal flux), and the fact that names were compiled at a midpoint in the yearly life cycle of the trade, after the traditional spring peak and before the one that occurred in the early fall, yet not far enough into the summer to represent the trough. For the most systematic consideration of seasonality, see Richard B. Stott, *Workers in the Metropolis: Class, Ethnicity, and Youth in Antebellum New York City* (Ithaca, N.Y., 1990), 110–119.

15. The increase in numbers of entries also outpaced the overall national decadal growth rate of 39 percent in value-added manufactures. Barry Warren Poulson, *Value Added Manufacturing, Mining, and Agriculture from 1809–1839* (1965; reprint, New York, 1975), 144.

16. John L. Sibley of Boston characterized that state of the trade after the Panic of 1837: "The American Stationers Company has failed. The booksellers to a man say they have never saw the like times–the people buy not a dollar's worth of books if they can help it." John L. Sibley to John E. Wood, Mar. 3, 1838, Book Trades Collection, AAS, courtesy of the American Antiquarian Society.

Table 2. Boston Book-Trades Data Base, 1789–1850: Source of Entries

	Not Included		*Included*	
From prior compilations:				
Driscoll, 1789–1840			5,061	
Silver, 1789–1799				
Undated	12			
Not from directories	121			
Defective	30			
From directories			28	
Total not included		163		
Silver, 1800–1825				
Undated	81			
Not from directories	205			
Defective	235			
From directories			448	
Total not included		521		
French, 1789–1820				
Not from directories	54			
From directories			87	
Total not included		54		
Flint, 1835–1840		499		
Subtotal not included		1,237		
Subtotal included				5,624
Additions and replacements				
from directories 1789–1840			4,459	4,459
From directories, 1841–1850				
From name listings			9,513	
From other listings			1,080	
Total				10,593
Less related occupations from all sources°			−2,170	−2,170
Total Used				18,506

Sources: J. Francis Driscoll, "List of Publishers, Booksellers and Printers Taken from the Boston Directories of 1789–1840," typescript, AAS, c. 1922; Rollo G. Silver, "The Boston Book Trade, 1790–1799," *Essays Honoring Lawrence C. Wroth*, ed. Frederick R. Goff (Portland, Me., 1951), 279–303; idem, *The Boston Book Trade, 1800–1825* (New York, 1949); Hannah Dustin French, "Early American Bookbinding By Hand, 1636–1820," *Bookbinding in America: Three Essays*, ed. Hellmut Lehmann-Haupt (New York, 1967), 1–27; Robert W. Flint, "The Boston Book Trade, 1836–1845" (M.A. Thesis, Simmons College, 1956 [rejected because he duplicated, with unresolvable variations, corresponding names in Driscoll]) and the following items taken from *American Directories Through 1860: A Collection on Microfilm* (New Haven, 1969): *The Boston Directory* (Boston, 1789, 1796, 1798, 1800, 1803, 1805–1807, 1809, 1810, 1813, 1816, 1818, 1820–1823, 1825–1846); *Adams's New Directory of the City of Boston, 1846–47* (Boston, 1846); *Adams's Boston Directory, 1847–1848* (Boston, 1847); George Adams, *The Boston Directory, 1848–1849* (Boston, 1848); *The Boston Directory, 1849–50* (Boston, 1849); *The Directory of the City of Boston, 1850–51* (Boston, 1850).

° This category included "Daguerreotype," "Intelligence Office," "Library," "Paperhangings," "Printed Goods" (usually fabrics and carpets), and "Sign Painter."

Table 3. Boston's Population and the Book Trades, 1790–1850

Year	Population	% Change	Book Trades Entries	% Change	Difference between % Changes
1790	18,038		30		
1790–1800	24,937	+38.25	63	+110.00	+71.75
1800–1810	33,250	+33.34	122	+ 93.65	+15.02
1810–1820	43,298	+30.22	170	+ 39.34	+ 9.12
1820–1830	61,392	+41.78	380	+123.52	+81.74
1830–1840	93,383	+52.10	567	+ 49.21	+ 0.36
1840–1850	136,881	+46.58	1,299	+129.10	+82.52
1790–1850		+658.84		+4,230.00	3,571.16

Sources: United States Bureau of Census, *Return of the Whole Number of Persons Within the Several Districts of the United States* (1790, 1800; reprint, New York, 1990); *City Document No. 9, Municipal Register . . . of the City of Boston for 1845* (Boston, 1845), 58; J. D. B. DeBow, *Statistical View of the United States . . . Being a Compendium of the Seventh Census* (Washington, D.C., 1854), 342. For the sources of book trades figures, see Table 2.

less than 5 percent, and in the same number of years the deviation was more than 10 percent. On an annual basis, the number of book-trades entries fluctuated wildly compared with the total for all entries: in selected book trades, there were sixteen years of change exceeding 10 percent, compared with seven years of 10 percent change (or greater) for all occupations. These fluctuations belie the apparent constancy of net growth.

The instability played differently among major occupations like bookbinder, bookseller, editorial services, engraver, stationery, and printer (as they are named in the directories—see Fig. 2). The number of entries for each seldom remained the same from one year to the next—this despite the natural bias in directory publishing toward preserving as many names as possible with each edition in order to save on typesetting costs.[17] And despite the overall upward trend, few trades moved in synchrony for any length of time. Two trades, printing and editorial services (for

17. Directory publishers apparently left a good deal of composed matter standing from year to year in order to recycle as much as possible cost effectively. The flat lines between 1789 and 1796 and for several other periods in the first two decades of the new century reflect years for which no directory was published, and hence, for the sake of clarity, the numbers from the last published directory have been used as estimates.

Table 4. A Comparison of Total Entries against Book-Trades Entries in Boston City Directories, 1789–1850

Year	No. of Entries[1] All Trades	No. of Entries[1] Book Trades	Change in[2] All Trades	Change in[2] Book Trades	% Change[3] All Trades	% Change[3] Book Trades	Difference[4] between % Changes
1789	1,950	30					
1789–96	3,700	69	1,750	39	89.74	130.00	40.26
1796–98	4,524	74	824	5	22.27	7.25	−15.02
1798–00	4,574	63	50	−11	1.11	−14.86	−15.97
1800–03	4,914	84	340	21	7.43	33.33	25.90
1803–05	4,515	87	−399	3	−8.12	3.57	11.69
1805–06	4,736	104	221	17	4.89	19.54	14.65
1806–07	5,130	98	394	−6	8.32	−5.77	−14.09
1807–09	5,382	114	252	16	4.91	16.33	11.42
1809–10	6,936	122	1,554	8	28.87	7.02	−21.85
1810–13	6,554	148	−382	26	−5.51	21.31	26.82
1813–16	6,734	145	180	−3	2.75	−2.03	−4.78
1816–18	7,280	156	546	11	8.11	7.59	−0.52
1818–20	7,752	170	472	14	6.48	8.97	2.49
1820–21	9,922	185	2,170	15	27.99	8.82	−19.17
1821–22	10,038	208	116	23	1.17	12.43	11.26
1822–23	9,786	203	−252	−5	−2.51	−2.40	0.11
1823–25	10,608	273	822	70	8.40	34.48	26.08
1825–26	10,868	283	260	10	2.45	3.66	1.21
1826–27	11,760	288	892	5	8.21	1.77	−6.44
1827–28	11,808	348	48	60	0.41	20.83	20.42
1828–29	11,719	368	−89	20	−0.75	5.75	6.50
1829–30	12,129	380	410	12	3.50	3.26	−0.24
1830–31	12,384	387	255	7	2.10	1.84	−0.26
1831–32	12,697	432	313	45	2.53	11.63	9.10
1832–33	13,773	430	1,076	−2	8.47	−0.46	−8.93
1833–34	14,613	490	840	60	6.10	13.95	7.85
1834–35	14,870	540	257	50	1.76	10.20	8.44
1835–36	15,636	503	766	−37	5.15	−6.85	−12.00
1836–37	15,881	504	245	1	1.57	0.20	−1.37
1837–38	16,737	540	856	36	5.39	7.14	1.75
1838–39	17,807	560	1,070	20	6.39	3.70	−2.69
1839–40	18,850	567	1,043	7	5.86	1.25	−4.61
1840–41	19,730	608	880	41	4.67	7.23	2.56
1841–42	20,063	673	333	65	1.69	10.69	9.00
1842–43	20,930	764	867	91	4.32	13.52	9.20
1843–44	22,575	790	1,645	26	7.86	3.40	−4.46
1844–45	23,932	801	1,357	11	6.01	1.39	−4.62

Table 4. *Continued*

Year	No. of Entries[1] All Trades	No. of Entries[1] Book Trades	Change in[2] All Trades	Change in[2] Book Trades	% Change[3] All Trades	% Change[3] Book Trades	Difference between % Changes
1845–46	26,543	1,228	2,611	427	10.91	53.31	42.40
1846–47	27,170	1,028	627	−200	2.36	−16.29	−18.65
1847–48	29,907	1,126	2,737	98	10.07	9.53	−0.54
1848–49	34,149	1,236	4,242	110	14.18	9.77	−4.41
1849–50	36,122	1,299	1,973	63	5.78	5.10	−0.68
Tot/Av	587,688	18,506	814	30	7.94	10.98	3.04

Sources: See Table 2.
1. The years for the directories are given, followed by the total number of directory entries for the latest year. If a directory did not contain a count of names, the number was estimated by counting the number of entries on the first full page of the listings and then multiplying that by the number of pages over which the listings ran. The figure for 1846 is the average from the 1846 and 1846–1847 directories. Thereafter, biennial directories stand for the earliest year (i.e., "1847–48" for 1847 and so forth). The number of all book-trades-related entries next appears.
2. The net gain or loss in numbers of all entries and book-trades-related ones.
3. The corresponding changes in percentages for all entries and book-trades-related ones.
4. The deviation between percentages for all entries and those of book-trades-related entries.
Note: The Tot/Av row at the bottom gives the totals where applicable ("No. of Entries") and averages elsewhere ("Change in," "% Change," and "Difference between % Changes").

occupations included in these, see Appendix), deviated the most from the rest (Fig. 2). Printers experienced the most ups and downs in numbers of entries: they began a twenty-year surge in 1810 from just under 50 to over 100 and then plunged in the 1830s back down to just over 50. As this study will show, the decline represents a structural change in the trades in which smaller artisan firms consolidated into larger industrial units that employed ever increasing numbers of workers. Editorial services also vastly expanded, but at a different time, from the late 1830s with under 23 entries to over 200 in 1849. While some of this increase was due to changes in the definition of occupations, particularly the emergence of "publisher" as a distinct category, much of the growth stemmed from alterations in directory practice toward the end of the period, particularly the inclusion of periodical offices. Other occupations fluctuated within a narrower range, usually with fewer than 25 entries before

1830, yet topping 50 in the last two decades of the period (Fig. 2).[18] Engraver and stationer were the most stable, and bookseller and bookbinder less so, reflecting perhaps their greater entrepreneurialism and market sensitivity.[19]

These interoccupational differences resonate in the relationship between entries for workplaces and those for homes (Tables 5–8).[20] In light of the demise of traditional artisan shops in which work, living, and leisure intertwined, the proportion of home to work addresses suggests the degree to which a trade had industrialized (i.e., more home and fewer work addresses usually indicate numerous wage laborers in larger units of production). While generally entries for work addresses only slightly outnumbered those for homes, this was neither the rule over time nor for every occupation. In the 1790s, when most artisans still lived above shops, work addresses overwhelmed by three-and-a-half times those for homes, a proportion that dipped only slightly in the ensuing three decades. In the 1830s, however, the ratio of home to work addresses narrowed, and by the 1840s, it reversed. The home/work relationship bears a class dimension, for during the last three decades traditionally higher-echelon occupations (i.e., bookseller, editorial services, music dealer, and stationer) showed more workplace entries, while, conversely, for bookbinders, printers, and suppliers—the occupations undergoing the most industrialization—home entries dominated.[21] This disparity suggests an increasing proletarianization within these three trades, further evidenced by wide-scale boarding

18. Because 1846 is a "composite" year for which entries from two directories have been combined, its inflated numbers push bookseller and stationery to just over 50.

19. On colonial engraving and copperplate printing, see Arthur Dexter, "The Fine Arts in Boston," in Justin Winsor, ed., *The Memorial History of Boston, including Suffolk County, Massachusetts, 1630–1880* (Boston, 1881), 4:385–386. For a glimpse at the interior of a bookbindery that suggests this market sensitivity, see Mary-Parke Johnson, "An Inventory of the Joseph T. Altemus Book Bindery, Philadelphia, 1854," *Papers of the Bibliographical Society of America* 80(1986):179–191; on a contemporary bookstore, see Zboray, *A Fictive People*, chap. 10.

20. For a discussion of the larger meaning of the home/work relationship within the context of 19th-century development, see R. J. Johnston, *The American Urban System: A Geographical Perspective* (New York, 1982), 157–168.

21. Diana diZerega Wall and Arnold Pickman, "The Beginnings of the Family Consumer Economy," *American Archeology* 5(1985):190–194; Diana diZerega Wall, "The Separation of the Home and Workplace in Early Nineteenth-Century New York City," *American Archeology* 5(1985):185–189.

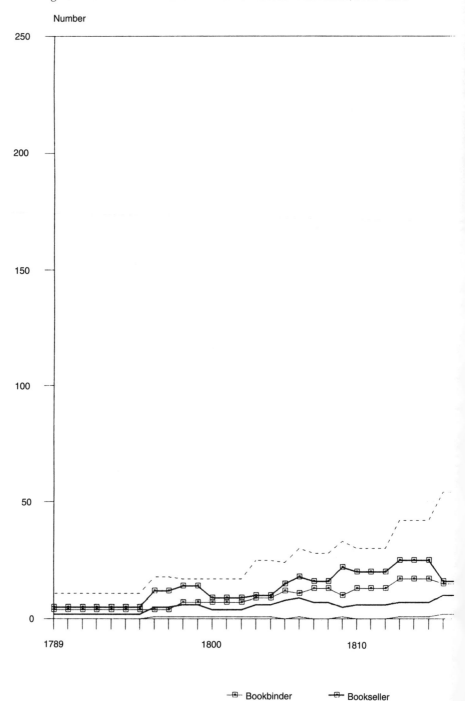

Figure 2. Selected Book-Trades Entries from Boston Directories, 1789–1850

Number

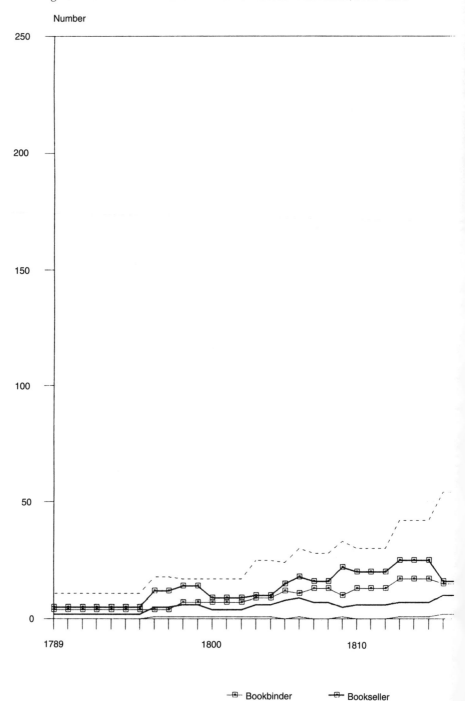

Source: See Table 1. Only entries for workplaces are represented.

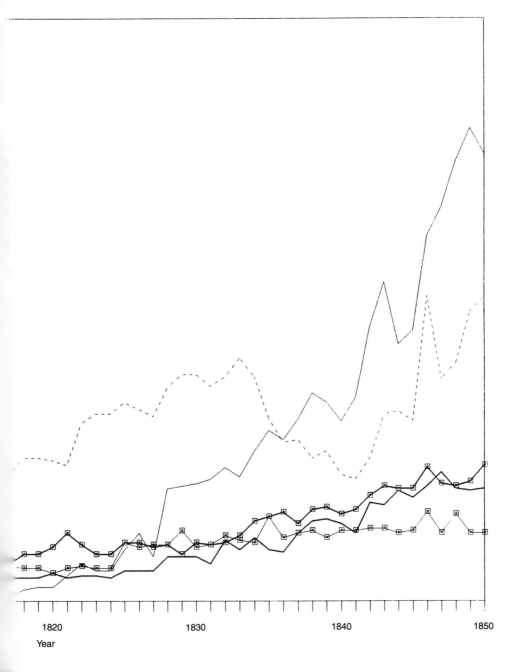

1820   1830   1840   1850

Year

Editorial   Engraver   - - Printer

Table 5. Book-Trades-Related Workplace Entries Appearing in Boston City
Directories, 1789–1850

Occupation	1789–1800	1801–10	1811–20	1821–30	1831–40	1841–50	Total
Bookbinder	22	68	58	192	282	313	93
Bookseller	40	101	84	215	334	494	1,26
Editorial	3	3	14	257	697	1,478	2,45
Electro/Stereotype	0	0	0	3	8	3	1
Engraver	17	41	39	125	265	450	93
Miscellaneous	0	0	0	24	39	71	13
Music	1	1	8	33	22	61	12
Paper and Stationery	32	34	32	165	235	374	87
Printer	63	170	217	745	782	934	2,91
Supplies	5	7	9	137	137	123	41
All	183	425	461	1,896	2,801	4,301	10,06

among workers (involving more than a third of all printers in 1850, up from
one-fifth in 1830), primarily factory hands.[22]

These generalizations about stratification find support in census and
tax documents. For example, already by 1832 proletarianization had proceeded far enough in publishing (whose entries are listed as "booksellers")
that the average firm employed twenty men, four boys, and ten women; the

22. John Townsend Trowbridge's novel *Martin Merrivale: His "X" Mark* (Boston, 1854)
depicts the boardinghouse lives of an author, a printer, and "Miss Tomes," a book folder, in
antebellum Boston. An example of this expanding scale of production: the 1847 directory
reported twelve printers, two bookbinders, a proofreader, and a type founder who worked
at 52 Washington Street with Samuel N. Dickinson, a job printer, publisher of the *Typo-
graphic Advertiser*, and typefoundry owner. He employed around 100 workers in the early
1840s, so these entries represent a portion of his work force. Rollo Silver, " 'The Flash of
the Comet': The Typographical Career of Samuel N. Dickinson," *Studies in Bibliography*
31(1978):68–89; and idem, *Typefounding in America, 1787–1825* (Charlottesville, Va.,
1965). The nature of the life of printers in the period can be glimpsed in idem, *The
American Printer, 1787–1825* (Charlottesville, Va., 1967); W. J. Rorabaugh, *The Craft
Apprentice from Franklin to the Machine Age in America* (New York, 1986), passim.; and,
especially for antebellum Boston, Joseph T. Buckingham, *Personal Memoirs and Recollections of Editorial Life*, (1852; reprint, New York, 1970). On both Dickinson and Buckingham, see Bruce Laurie, "The Political Economy of Antebellum Mechanics," a paper
delivered at the Atlanta Seminar in Comparative History of Labor, Industry, Technology,
and Society, Georgia Institute of Technology, Dec. 5, 1993.

Table 6. Book-Trades-Related Home Addresses Appearing in Boston City Directories, 1789–1850

Occupation	1789–1800	1801–10	1811–20	1821–30	1831–40	1841–50	Total
Bookbinder	3	17	24	86	319	631	1,080
Bookseller	10	43	33	111	199	386	782
Editorial	1	1	6	94	171	515	788
Electro/Stereotype	0	0	0	0	8	4	12
Engraver	1	3	15	49	205	445	718
Miscellaneous	0	0	0	16	30	116	162
Music	0	0	4	10	14	55	83
Paper and Stationery	6	10	11	70	163	299	559
Printer	32	110	65	184	938	2,526	3,855
Supplies	0	0	0	20	105	275	400
	53	184	158	640	2,152	5,252	8,439

three typefoundries averaged a workforce of over fifty-five (Table 9).[23] In the same year, publishers and typefounders together held about 58 percent of the entire capital investment in the book trades and accounted for 61 percent of their total output. The profits resulting from industrialization had their clearest impact upon typefounders. In 1821, while their trade was still in transition from an artisan's craft, their average assessed wealth ($633.34) ranked them alongside printers; by 1844, two owners of industrialized typefoundries could report assessments of over $7,000 (Tables 10 and 11). At that later date nineteen printers reported over $4,000 worth of property and ten publishers, seventeen booksellers, and twelve stationers and paper manufacturers were counted among the wealthiest individuals in the trade.

23. Joshua L. Rosenbloom, "Economics and the Emergence of Modern Publishing in the United States," *Publishing History* 29(1991):47–68. Printers' memoirs and diaries attest to the work specialization that attended proto-industrialization. "It is very common to find journeymen compositors who know nothing about working at the press, and sometimes journeymen pressmen cannot work at the [composing] case," the young apprentice David Clapp observed in the early 1820s. David Clapp, *The Journal of David Clapp Kept While Learning His Trade in the Printing Office of John Cotton, Corner of Washington and Franklin Streets, Boston, 1822–1824* (Boston, 1919), 2. He also poignantly reports his state of mind upon coming to board at the house of his employer, where he is stiffly ushered into the kitchen to eat the genteel family's leavings: "I must confess I felt for a moment no small degree of indignation, and a consciousness that I was degraded" (12).

Table 7. Percentage of Book-Trades-Related Workplace Entries With Corresponding Home Addresses in Boston City Directories, 1789–1850

Occupation	1789–1800	1801–10	1811–20	1821–30	1831–40	1841–50	Overall
Bookbinder	13.64	16.18	25.86	34.90	62.77	70.93	52.9
Bookseller	20	29.70	34.52	47.91	49.40	73.68	55.1
Editorial	0	33.33	42.86	25.29	17.22	27.00	24.1
Electro/Stereotype	0	0	0	0	50	100	50
Engraver	0	4.88	41.03	37.60	50.57	65.11	52.5
Miscellaneous	0	0	0	58.33	61.54	57.75	58.9
Music	0	0	50	30.30	63.64	81.97	61.9
Paper and Stationery	12.50	20.59	31.25	40	62.13	66.04	55.0
Printer	19.05	16.47	13.82	13.83	39.00	72.70	39.7
Supplies	0	0	0	6.57	21.17	53.66	24.8
All	14.75	18.58	23.86	25.52	39.91	54.96	41.5

Note: These are percentages of the sums given in Table 5.

The social stratification of the book trades had only some influence upon persistence at the same home or business address. (Tables 12 and 13). The more genteel occupations—booksellers, editorial services, music, and paper and stationery dealers—tended more than industrialized trades to remain put. Higher status accounts for this to a lesser degree than the amount of walk-in business these firms engaged in; for them, it paid to have a fixed location. In fact, some sites, like that of the famous Old Corner Bookstore, could change hands several times yet continue in the same retail line. But this point does not completely explain the persistence of this genteel group of occupations, for similar patterns of stability (suggesting a greater level of property ownership) emerge through a count of residence changes in each year.[24]

In sum, the book trades in early-national and antebellum Boston experienced both numerical growth and structural development, according to the information contained in the city directories. As they moved from an artisan mode of production toward the types of specialization and social stratification that characterized industrialization, however, they encountered

24. This trend away from persistence contradicts that described in Andrew A. Beveridge and others, "Organizing Running Records to Analyze Historical Social Mobility," in *Data Bases in the Humanities and Social Sciences*, ed. Joseph Raben and Gregory Marks (Amsterdam, 1980), 157–163.

Table 8. Decimalized Ratio of Workplace Entries to Home Addresses for Book-Trades Occupations in Boston City Directories, 1789–1850

Occupation	1789–1800	1801–10	1811–20	1821–30	1831–40	1841–50	Overall
Bookbinder	7.33	4	2.42	2.23	0.88	0.50	0.87
Bookseller	4	2.35	2.55	1.94	1.68	1.28	1.62
Editorial	3	3	2.33	2.73	4.08	2.87	3.11
Electro/Stereotype	0	0	0	0	1	0.75	1.17
Engraver	17	13.67	2.60	2.55	1.29	1.01	1.31
Miscellaneous	0	0	0	1.50	1.30	0.61	0.83
Music	0	0	2	3.30	1.57	1.11	1.52
Paper and Stationery	5.33	3.40	2.91	2.36	1.44	1.25	1.56
Printer	1.97	1.55	3.34	4.05	0.83	0.37	0.76
Supplies	0	0	0	6.85	1.30	0.45	1.05
	3.45	2.31	2.92	2.96	1.30	0.80	1.19

Note: These figures are the result of dividing the number of work entries in Table 5 by the home entries in Table 6 for each occupational group. Thus "4" means that there are four times as many workplace entries as there are home ones, and ".25" means four times as many home addresses as there are workplace entries. An equal number of workplace and home entries equals "1."

much instability, the meaning of which becomes plainer upon a closer examination of the data.

Raw numbers of directory entries indicate growth but can only suggest the development of the book trades. An analysis of entities that appear year after year—persons, partnerships, corporate firms, or even institutions— presents a finer picture, one that portrays the nature of the industry's expansion.[25] The analysis allows for tracing firms over time and offers an-

25. See the Appendix for a discussion of the methods used to construct entities from directory entries. The percentage of businesses that were structured as partnerships differed dramatically among occupations: bookbinder (23.79), bookseller (35.33), editorial (30.68), electro/stereotype (40.00), engraver (15.13), miscellaneous (3.57), music (28.26), paper and stationery (34.28), printer (16.62), and supplies (21.42). The overall percentage of 23.79 is very close to what Naomi Lamoreaux finds in these pages to have been the average for mercantile firms in the 1840s ("The Partnership Form of Organization"). Four groups with among the highest level of partnerships–booksellers, editorial, music, and paper and stationery–were among the most entrepreneurial of the trades and the most demanding of ever increasing amounts of capital. This confirms Lamoreaux's conclusion that the pooling of capital resources inspired partnerships.

Table 9. Boston Book Trades, 1832: Capitalization and Work Force

Establishment	No.	Capital (in dollars)				Input (in dollars)			Output (in dollars)	Wages (in dollars)			
		Real Machinery	Property	Inventory	Total	U.S.	Foreign	Total		Men	Boys	Women	Total
Blank Books	10	6,000	40,000	50,000	96,000	60,000	18,000	78,000	100,000	15,480	3,100	3,100	21,680
Bookbinders	15	15,000	45,000	9,000	69,000	20,100	8,000	28,100	60,000	23,220	4,650	13,950	41,820
Booksellers	20	200,000	160,000	100,000	460,000	403,600	8,000	411,600	800,000	186,000	12,100	24,800	222,900
Colored Paper	1	1,200	1,600	3,500	6,300	2,675	400	3,075	6,850	1,488	372	465	2,325
Copperplate	10	10,000	20,000	10,000	40,000	35,000	500	35,500	80,000	15,500°	1,500	0	17,000
Engravers	17	6,000	40,000	6,000	52,000	4,100	6,600	10,700	50,000	0	1,500°	5,580°	7,080
Inkmakers	4	8,000	3,200	16,000	27,200	3,600	20,000	23,600	75,000	3,100	620	0	3,720
Newsprinters	12	60,000	72,000	6,000	138,000	60,500	0	60,500	168,000	22,120	5,580	0	27,700
Pocket Books	2	800	9,000	5,000	14,800	4,000	3,000	7,000	18,000	4,650	620	775	6,045
Typefoundries	3	56,500	45,000	44,000	145,500	6,800	4,000	10,800	71,500	38,595	4,045°°	7,384°°	50,024
All	94	363,500	435,800	249,500	1,048,800	600,375	68,500	668,875	1,429,350	310,153	34,087	56,054	400,294

Establishment	Average No.			Total Number (estimated)			Daily Wages (in dollars)		
	Men	Boys	Women	Men	Boys	Women	Men	Boys	Women
Blank Books	4	2	2	40	20	20	1.25	.50	.50
Bookbinders	4	2	6	60	30	90	1.25	.50	.50
Booksellers	20	4	10	400	80	200	1.50	.49	.40
Colored Paper	4	2	3	4	2	3	1.20	.60	.50
Copperplate	4	1	0	40	10	0	1.25	.50	.00
Engravers	1.06	.59	1.76	16	10	30	0	.50	.60
Inkmakers	2	1	0	8	4	0	1.25	.50	.00
Newsprinters	4	3	0	48	36	0	1.49	.50	.00
Pocket Books	5	2	2.5	10	4	5	1.50	.50	.50
Typefoundries	27.6	9.7	18.3	83	29	55	1.50	.45	.43
All (Av. or Tot.)	7.6	2.7	4.4	709	225	403	1.41	.49	.45

Source: See Table 1. The booksellers category includes publishers. Among engravers are "2 Lithographic Establishments"—"These branches of trade, viz. engraving and copperplate printing, are said to require some further protection, owing to the introduction of foreign plates at the present book duty." Of the engraver workforce: "16 men, most of them pupils who receive little compensation except the art." Tyler, "Document 3," 458–459.

* Total wages were not given; they were estimated using a 310-day working year.

** Rounded.

Table 10. Average Property Valuation and Taxes Paid by Boston Book Tradespeople, 1821

| Occupation | No. | Valuation (in dollars) | | | Taxes Paid (in dollars) |
		Real Property	Personal Property	Total	
Bookbinder	13	530.77	238.46	769.23	8.49
Bookseller	51	1,435.88	1,188.24	2,624.12	24.11
Editorial	20	1,940	525	2,465	16.37
Engraver	10	410	210	620	6.25
Miscellaneous	2	1,450	200	1,650	14.64
Music	5	1,500	1,060	2,560	23.41
Paper and Stationery	17	1,141.18	482.35	1,623.53	14.85
Printer	57	450.88	200	650.88	6.23
Publisher	1	0	0	0	1.46
Supplies	3	466.67	166.67	633.34	8.70
All (Total/Average)	179	1,005.20	570.39	1,575.59	14.03

Source: Lewis Bunker Rohrbach, ed., *Boston Taxpayers in 1821* (1822; reprint, Camden, Me., 1988). Because in this assessment renters paid according to the worth of the property they rented, the real property column in some cases does not reflect ownership.

swers to the following: Were a few firms doing business over long periods, with the progressive entry of additional firms, or did a welter of firms come to life and then vanish?

During the six decades prior to 1850, 3,814 book-trades entities operated in Boston. For most trades the rate of business entry escalated toward the end of the period (Table 14). Printers led the way with a 160 percent increase in newcomers in the 1820s, and in the 1840s the trades as a whole more than doubled their business entrants. However, the gains in newcomers ran only slightly ahead of losses (Tables 15 and 16), due to death, retirement, changes in occupation to outside the book trades, moves out of Boston, bankruptcy or other types of business failure, and consolidations or break ups, which removed entities from a directory.[26] As might be expected, the panic decade of the 1830s shows a sluggish net compared to the doubling rebound of the 1840s. Despite overall gains in entities, their lifespans averaged fewer years with each new decade (Table 17). For exam-

26. To prevent generating a high number of dropouts for the terminus of the study, the year 1850, which only inflates the figures for the 1840s, that year was not used in the analysis that produced Tables 15 and 16.

Table 11. Book Tradespeople or Firms among Published Boston Taxpayers, 1844: Assessed Taxable Wealth

$100,000 and over

Blank books	1
Editor	1
Total	2

$50,000–100,000

Bookseller	1
Copperplate	1
Paper	1
Printer	1
Publisher	1
Stationery	1
Total	6

$25,000–50,000

Bookbinder	1
Bookseller	2
Paper	2
Publisher	1
Stationery	1
Total	7

$12,000–25,000

Binder Supp.	1
Bookseller	2
Editor	2
Periodical	2
Printer	6
Publisher	2
Stationery	1
Typefoundry	1
Total	17

$10,000–12,000

Bookseller	4
Editor	1
Periodicals°	1
Printer	3
Total	9

$7,000–10,000

Bookbinder	2
Bookseller	2
Engraver	2
Lithographer	1
Music	1
Paper	1
Periodical	2
Printer	2
Stationery	2
Typefoundry	1
Total	16

$5,000–7,000

Bookbinder	1
Bookseller	5
Music	1
Paper	1
Printer	5
Publisher	5
Stationery	2
Total	20

$4,000–5,000

Bookseller	1
Lithographer	1
Printer	2
Publisher	1
Total	5

All

Binder Supp.	1
Blank Books	1
Bookbinder	4
Bookseller	17
Copperplate	1
Editor	4
Engraver	2
Lithographer	2
Music	2
Paper	5
Periodical	4
Periodicals	1
Printer	19
Publisher	10
Stationery	7
Typefoundry	2
Total	82

° i.e., dealer or "depot."

Note: Right hand columns represent the number of each listed trade appearing within the range.

Source: City of Boston, "City Document No. 9," *Municipal Register . . . of the City of Boston for 1845* (Boston, 1845). The document lists only those who paid fifty dollars or more in taxes.

Table 12. Workplace Entries for Book-Trades Occupations in Boston City Directories, 1789–1850: Address Changes from a Previous Year

			% Changed				
Occupation	*1789–1800*	*1801–10*	*1811–20*	*1821–30*	*1831–40*	*1841–50*	*Over*
Bookbinder	22.73	29.41	31.03	26.56	31.56	22.36	27.0
Bookseller	7.50	9.90	15.48	26.05	14.07	12.75	15.1
Editorial	0	0	14.29	28.79	21.23	19.69	21.0
Electro/Stereotype	0	0	0	0	50	33.33	35.7
Engraver	29.41	26.83	28.21	36.80	31.32	27.33	29.7
Miscellaneous	0	0	0	25	23.08	14.08	18.6
Music	0	0	25	27.27	13.64	13.11	17.4
Paper and Stationery	18.75	11.76	15.63	27.27	15.32	19.52	19.3
Printer	14.29	32.35	35.94	36.78	26.21	16.60	26.6
Supplies	20	14.29	11.11	0.73	42.34	21.14	29.4
All	15.85	23.76	27.98	32.59	23.49	18.95	23.3

Note: These are percentages of the totals given in Table 5.

Table 13. Home Entries for Book-Trades Occupations in Boston City Directories, 1789–1850: Address Changes from a Previous Year

			% Changed				
Occupation	*1789–1800*	*1801–10*	*1811–20*	*1821–30*	*1831–40*	*1841–50*	*Ove*
Bookbinder	33.33	35.29	25	34.88	42.01	33.12	35.
Bookseller	20	18.60	27.27	34.23	28.14	31.09	29.
Editorial	0	0	66.67	19.15	27.49	27.18	26
Electro/Stereotype	0	0	0	0	50	25	41.
Engraver	0	33.3	40	44.90	34.63	35.51	35
Miscellaneous	0	0	0	31.25	20	27.59	26
Music	0	0	50	30	7.14	34.55	30
Paper and Stationery	16.67	20	18.18	34.29	23.93	24.41	25
Printer	15.63	33.64	47.69	27.72	36.03	37.09	36
Supplies	0	0	0	0	4.76	32.73	36
All	16.98	29.35	37.97	30.47	34.76	33.83	33

Note: These are percentages of the totals in Table 6.

Table 14. Book-Trades Entities by Decade of First Appearance in Boston City Directories, 1789–1850

Occupation	1789–1800	1801–10	1811–20	1821–30	1831–40	1841–50	Total
Bookbinder	11	23	31	50	92	191	398
Bookseller	19	28	23	39	70	116	295
Editorial	4	2	5	95	184	429	719
Electro/Stereotype	0	0	0	3	3	1	7
Engraver	11	9	14	31	96	129	290
Miscellaneous	0	0	0	11	17	72	100
Music	1	1	3	9	7	24	45
Paper and Stationery	24	7	16	38	49	107	241
Printer	46	65	82	213	326	795	1,527
Supplies	3	3	5	61	40	80	192
	119	138	179	550	884	1,944	3,814

Table 15. Number of Book-Trades Entities by Decade of Last Appearance in Boston City Directories, 1789–1849°

Occupation	1789–1800	1801–10	1811–20	1821–30	1831–40	1841–49	Total
Bookbinder	3	17	20	28	75	169	312
Bookseller	5	27	16	34	60	104	246
Editorial	3	2	2	49	133	332	521
Electro/Stereotype	0	0	0	3	2	1	6
Engraver	4	8	11	21	65	101	210
Miscellaneous	0	0	0	6	14	46	66
Music	1	1	0	8	9	18	37
Paper and Stationery	16	12	11	27	37	88	191
Printer	21	36	64	135	250	607	1,113
Supplies	1	5	3	37	35	67	148
	54	108	127	348	680	1,533	2,850

°, does not include any entity appearing in 1850.

Table 16. Net Gain or Loss in Number of Book-Trades Entities in Boston City Directories, by Decade, 1789–1850

Occupation	1789–1800	1801–10	1811–20	1821–30	1831–40	1841–49°	To...
Bookbinder	8	6	11	22	17	−3	
Bookseller	14	1	7	5	10	−4	
Editorial	1	0	3	46	51	39	1...
Electro/Stereotype	0	0	0	0	1	0	
Engraver	7	1	3	10	31	6	
Miscellaneous	0	0	0	5	3	0	
Music	0	0	3	1	−2	2	
Paper and Stationery	8	−5	5	11	12	8	
Printer	25	29	18	78	76	29	2...
Supplies	2	−2	2	24	5	−5	
All	65	30	52	202	204	72	

° For consistency, in the final decade, first appearances in 1850 were not counted in this table. This yields th... following adjusted figures for 1841–49: Bookbinder (166), Bookseller (100), Editorial (371), Electro/Stereotype (1), Engraver (107), Miscellaneous (46), Music (20), Paper and Stationery (96), Printer (636), and Supplies (62).

Table 17. Average Number of Years Between the First and Last Appearance of Entities in Boston City Directories, 1789–1850, by Decade of First Appearance

Occupation	1789–1800	1801–10	1811–20	1820–31	1831–40	1841–50	Ove...
Bookbinder	14.55	10.09	11.26	10.10	5.25	1.58	5.
Bookseller	11	7.93	10.83	5.05	4.37	1.34	4.
Editorial	5	2	12	7.98	4.30	1.48	3.
Electro/Stereotype	0	0	0	0	4	3	2.
Engraver	12	8.11	13.64	6.61	5.45	1.72	4.
Miscellaneous	0	0	0	3.36	3.76	0.46	1.
Music	0	0	11.67	5.78	2.29	0.79	2
Paper and Stationery	6.13	5.86	4.63	5.87	5.65	1.50	3.
Printer	15.37	11.15	9.34	8.36	5.21	1.32	4
Supplies	4	0	6.80	6.07	5.38	1.15	3
Average	11.66	9.40	9.82	7.51	4.96	1.37	4

Note: Entries appearing only once are averaged in as zeroes.

Table 18. Book-Trades-Related Entities in Boston City Directories by Decade, 1789–1850

Occupation	1789–1800	1801–10	1811–21	1820–31	1831–40	1841–50
Bookbinder	11	31	43	65	140	300
Bookseller	19	41	43	71	106	204
Editorial	4	3	7	113	261	665
Electro/Stereotype	0	0	0	3	3	1
Engraver	11	14	20	39	128	232
Miscellaneous	0	0	0	11	24	95
Music	1	1	3	13	11	38
Paper and Stationery	24	15	20	57	80	175
Printer	46	90	132	281	512	1,225
Supplies	3	4	7	67	75	133
	119	199	275	720	1,340	3,068

Note: Because people or firms appeared in more than one decade, and thus can be counted more than once in this table, for each decade after 1800 the numbers exceed those given in Table 14.

ple, entities first appearing in the 1790s survived about 11.66 years, but by the 1840s they averaged a mere 1.37 years.

The composition of the book trades within each decade emerges from this analysis of entities (Table 18). For example, while only 119 book-trades entities were active in the city during the 1790s, by the 1840s, their number climbed to 3,068. Put another way, 80 percent of all entities founded between 1789 and 1850 did business at some time in the 1840s—the longevity of people and firms from earlier years who survived into the decade explains much of this concentration. The 1840s did not witness the only boom in the industry, however, for the 1820s saw a 162 percent increase in entities over the previous decade. Some of this gain was due to a rebound after the derangement of trade during the War of 1812 and the Panic of 1819, but it was also due to Boston's transformation during the 1820s into the information center of the quickly commercializing and industrializing regional economy.[27] By 1833 city firms controlled about 90 percent of the total volume of printing and publishing in eastern Massachusetts.[28]

27. On larger changes inspired by the recovery, see Andrew R. L. Cayton, "The Fragmentation of a 'Great Family': The Panic of 1819 and the Rise of the Middling Interest in Boston, 1818–1822," *Journal of the Early Republic* 2(1982):143–167.

28. Francis X. Blouin, Jr., *The Boston Region, 1810–1850: A Study of Urbanization* (Ann Arbor, Mich., 1980), especially Appendix 8, 166. He includes Rockingham County, New Hampshire, among his figures for eight eastern counties of Massachusetts (23).

Table 19. Occupations of Entities Appearing in Each Decade As a Percentage of All Book Trades in Boston City Directories, 1789–1850

Occupation	1789–1800	1801–10	1811–20	1820–31	1831–40	1841–50	Overa
Bookbinder	9.24	16.67	17.32	9.09	10.41	9.83	10.4
Bookseller	15.97	20.29	12.85	7.09	7.92	5.97	7.7
Editorial	3.36	1.45	2.79	17.27	20.81	22.07	18.8
Electro/Stereotype	0.00	0.00	0.00	0.55	0.34	0.05	0.1
Engraver	9.24	6.52	7.82	5.64	10.86	6.64	7.0
Miscellaneous	0.00	0.00	0.00	2.00	1.92	3.70	2.0
Music	0.84	0.72	1.68	1.64	0.79	1.23	1.
Paper and Stationery	20.17	5.07	8.94	6.91	5.54	5.50	6.
Printer	38.66	47.10	45.81	38.73	36.88	40.90	40.
Supplies	2.52	2.17	2.79	11.09	4.52	4.12	5.
All (rounded)	100.00	100.00	100.00	100.00	100.00	100.00	100.

° This column corresponds to the Total column in Table 14.

In the face of the decadal ups and downs of the trades, the relative proportions of the various occupational groups of entities remained surprisingly stable (Table 19). Printers always predominated, within a range of nine percentage points (to make up from 38.66 to 47.10 percent of the trades). Except during the first twenty years of the new century, about a tenth of the entities comprised bookbinders. The proportion of booksellers dropped off over time (decreasing from 15.96 to 5.97 percent) as the number of publishers increased, representing a move toward increasing entrepreneurial specialization, rather than a net loss for the trades (i.e., many booksellers sloughed off their retail business and focused exclusively on publishing). Paper and stationery dealers remained for the most part just over 5 percent of the trades. Obviously, some rule governed the distribution of entities into specific occupational groupings. No doubt, to a degree this developed naturally, according to a conventional understanding of the opportunities within the trade matched against the optimal workforce and output levels of each shop, yet at least some of it may be due to purposeful organization.[29]

29. Some of the book trades' efforts to organize are treated in Laurie, "The Political Economy of Antebellum Mechanics." The Boston Booksellers' Papers, 1640–1860, at the AAS contain the records of the Association of Boston Booksellers (vols. 1 and 2), which testify to these measures toward industrial organization.

Table 20. Occupational Changes Reported for Book-Trades Entities in Boston City Directories, 1789–1850

Occupation	1789–1800	1801–10	1811–20	1821–30	1831–40	1841–50	Total
Bookbinder	3	2	9	7	7	8	36
Bookseller	6	4	6	7	6	9	38
Editorial	1	1	3	13	17	29	64
Electro/Stereotype	0	0	0	0	1	0	1
Engraver	2	1	3	4	13	13	36
Miscellaneous	0	0	0	2	3	2	7
Music	0	0	0	1	0	0	1
Paper and Stationery	1	0	1	6	7	7	22
Printer	8	10	7	16	30	15	86
Supplies	1	0	0	4	5	2	12
All	22	18	29	60	89	85	303

Whatever the case, certain forces influenced the entities' occupational identifications (Table 20). The directories reported relatively few occupational changes (only 7.94 percent of all entities reflect a change); the most were within the emerging category of editorial services and among paper and stationery dealers, who often engaged in other types of retail. Among printers the relative permanence of occupational identification challenges the common assumption that the path of occupational mobility within the book trades went from printer to bookseller (or editor) to publisher.[30] For example, by the 1840s, only 1.8 percent of printers changed occupations, down from 17 percent in the 1790s and 9.2 percent in the 1830s.

The constancy of trade identification did not prevent about 12 percent of the entities from having a significant additional occupation (Table 21). After all, according to the 1833 McLane Report:

> The several branches of business . . . are so intimately connected with each other, that the result of the whole should be taken into one view, as constituting one trade. Some of the large dealers in books and stationery, carry on printing, binding, and blank book making. Some of the newspaper establishments print books and pamphlets. Some of each kind of the establishments keep places for vending their manufactures on their own accounts; and others are wholly employed in manufacturing for other establishments.[31]

30. Gary John Kornblith, "From Artisans to Businessmen: Master Mechanics in New England, 1789–1850" (Ph.D. diss., Princeton Univ., 1983), especially 291–349, for a consideration of the printer and publisher Joseph T. Buckingham.

31. See the source note to Table 1 (1:436–437).

Table 21. Significant Secondary Occupations Reported for Book-Trades Entities in Boston City Directories, 1789–1850

Occupation	1789–1800	1801–10	1811–20	1821–30	1831–40	1841–50	Tota
Bookbinder	2	2	5	3	3	2	17
Bookseller	14	6	4	13	10	31	78
Editorial	0	0	0	2	11	34	47
Electro/Stereotype	0	0	0	0	0	0	0
Engraver	1	0	6	6	29	25	67
Miscellaneous	0	0	0	0	2	5	7
Music	0	0	0	1	0	9	10
Paper and Stationery	1	1	0	6	8	27	43
Printer	12	15	15	35	52	37	166
Supplies	0	0	0	2	3	5	10
All	30	24	30	68	118	175	44

Retailers, like booksellers and stationers, tended toward these secondary lines, very often verging upon one another's turf. But there were other, sometimes intriguing variations, as well: booksellers who purveyed navigational books were occasionally listed with ship chandlers; books and toys were another natural combination for a children's market (one bookseller had a sideline in "baby jumpers"); books could also be sold alongside medicines or fancy goods.[32] At least some printers reported a secondary occupation for each decade and their numbers generally rose, but their proportion to all printers declined. For example, in the 1790s 26 percent had secondary occupations, compared with about 5 percent in the 1840s. Throughout the period, the most common secondary occupation of printers was bookseller, reflecting the traditional path of occupational mobility. That this

32. John P. Jewett, who later published *Uncle Tom's Cabin*, started out specializing in nautical literature (including a "Sea Library" of 1,000 volumes aimed at sailors) in Salem before he moved to Boston. Philip M. Fragasso, "John P. Jewett: The Unsung Hero of *Uncle Tom's Cabin*," *New England Galaxy* 20(1978):22–29. See also, Deborah Jean Warner, "At the Sign of the Quadrant: The Navigational Instrument Business in America to the Civil War," *American Neptune* 46(1986):258–263. Genevieve Miller, "The Nineteenth Century Medical Press," in *Centenary of Index Medicus, 1879–1979*, ed. John B. Blake (Bethesda, Md., 1980), 19–30; on the types of medicines sold, see Christopher R. DeCorse, "Elixirs, Nerve Tonics and Panaceas: The Medicine Trade in Nineteenth-Century New Hampshire," *Historical New Hampshire* 39(1984):1–23.

path became less and less traveled over time further indicates the proletarianization of the trade.[33]

So far, we have sketched the expansion of the book trades over time, but how was this growth and development expressed spatially? Where were the main centers of publishing, bookselling, and printing located? Where did people who worked in the book trades live, and did their home locations change over time? Did they generally live and work in the same areas?[34] In pursuit of answers to these questions, we plotted home and work sites upon maps for selected years (1796, 1805, 1838, and 1845), primarily for printers, the largest and most diverse group.[35]

Hints of the eventual centralization of the trades on a few down-

33. On class and occupational categories, see Michael B. Katz, "Social Class in North American Urban History," *Journal of Interdisciplinary History* 11(1981):579–605.

34. Similar questions have been raised within the work of the new urban historical geographers. Among the seminal texts in this area, see James E. Vance, Jr., *The Continuing City: Urban Morphology in Western Civilization* (Baltimore, 1990); idem, *Capturing the Horizon: The Historical Geography of Transportation Since the Sixteenth Century* (1986; reprint, Baltimore, 1990); David Ward, *Cities and Immigrants* (New York, 1971); several works by Allan Pred over the years, for example, *City Systems in Advanced Economies: Past Growth, Present Processes, and Future Development Options* (New York, 1977); Michael P. Conzen, "The Maturing Urban System in the United States, 1840–1910," *Annals of the Association of American Geographers* 67(1977):88–108.

35. Helpful in understanding Boston's ever changing geography throughout the period are: Annie Haven Thwing, *The Crooked & Narrow Streets of the Town of Boston, 1630–1822* (Boston, 1920); Perry Walton, *Devonshire Street: A Collection of Facts and Incidents together with Reproductions of Illustrations Pertaining to An Old Boston Street* (Boston, 1912); Harold Kirker and James Kirker, *Bulfinch's Boston, 1787–1817* (New York, 1964); Lawrence W. Kennedy, *Planning the City upon a Hill: Boston Since 1630* (Amherst, Mass., 1992); Nathaniel B. Shurtleff, *A Topographical and Historical Description of Boston*, 3d ed. (1870; Boston, 1890); Robert Shackleton, *The Book of Boston* (1916; reprint, Philadelphia, 1920); Walter Muir Whitehill, *Boston: A Topographical History*, 2d ed. (1959; Cambridge, Mass., 1968); Ward, "Nineteenth-Century Boston." For other relevant sources on streets see, for Washington St., the Old Corner, or Ticknor and Fields, Houghton Mifflin Company, *Park Street, New and Old, 1828–1923* (Boston, c. 1923); Macullar Parker Company, *Some Old Sites on an Old Thoroughfare* (Boston, 1918); idem, *Washington Street, Old and New* (Boston, 1913); Henry F. Jenks, "Old School Street," *The New England Magazine*, new ser. 13(1895):259–272; John T. Hassam, *No. 47 Court Street, Boston* (Boston, 1903); *Views of Tremont Street Boston* (Boston, c. 1895); Thomas W. Tucker, *Bannisters Lane, 1708–1899* (Boston, 1899). Informative contemporary guides include: Abel Bowen, *Bowen's Picture of Boston*, 3d ed. (Boston, 1838) and Nathaniel Dearborn, *Boston Notions; Being an Authentic and Concise Account of "That Village," from 1630–1847* (Boston, 1847).

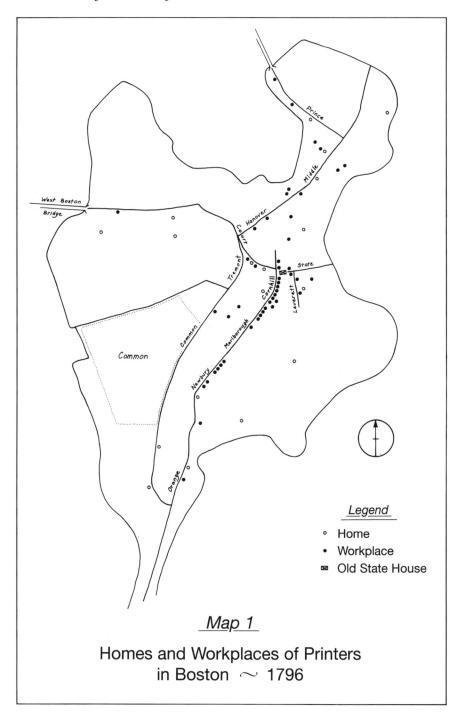

West Boston
Bridge

Prince

Middle

Hanover

Court

Tremont

State

Cornhill

Leverett

Marlborough

Common

Newbury

Common

Orange

Legend

∘ Home
• Workplace
▩ Old State House

Map 1

Homes and Workplaces of Printers
in Boston ∼ 1796

town streets appeared as early as 1796, when the industry was still small (Map 1).[36] Already the clear outline of Washington Street—then actually a string of streets including Cornhill, Marlborough, Newbury, and Orange—emerges with the greatest concentration of workplaces (i.e., bookstores, card and print shops, bookbinderies, an engraver's shop) and a printer's home or two. This north-southwest route would remain throughout the period a common site for workplaces (in the north) and homes (in the south). Workplaces also clustered around the Old State House, on Court, State, and Leverett streets (at the time it was also known as Quaker Lane, and, later, Congress Street). Other centrally located streets with workplaces included Spring Lane, Kilby Street, Dock Square, and Water Street. Indeed, from 1789 to 1800, 38 percent of book-trades directory entries had work addresses downtown on either Congress, Cornhill (already called "Publishers' Row" for its array of booksellers), Court, School, State, or Water streets (Table 22).[37] Some book tradespeople, however, worked outside the downtown area: mainly in the North End, on Back Street, Bridges Lane, and Prince Street; and in the South End, on Essex and Newbury

36. Some information about specific addresses for this map was derived from Benjamin Franklin V, ed., *Boston Printers, Publishers, and Booksellers: 1640–1800* (Boston, 1980). Concerning this map and the ones below, we should emphasize that the names of many streets in Boston changed throughout time, as in any major city, but here names often disappeared and shortly thereafter reappeared in a different location. As one writer put it, "names [are] not thrown away but frugally saved to be used in a new district" (Shackleton, *Book of Boston*, 122). For example, Cornhill, once a street with a north-south direction, was swallowed up by Washington Street but "reappeared" with an east-west orientation. Thus, the maps probably give a more accurate account of streets than the tables do, but the elusiveness of street names and locations, the fact that a lane and a street of the same name could be very far apart, and the twisting, turning quality of Boston streets made locating work and home places–especially those of later periods–difficult. Nonetheless, discernable patterns emerge when the addresses are plotted. For a discussion of the "new" Cornhill laid out in 1816, see Thwing, *Crooked & Narrow Streets of the Town of Boston*, 93. According to Harold Carter, *An Introduction to Urban Historical Geography* (Baltimore, 1983), 54–55: "Perhaps the most extreme example of natural growth in the whole United States is Boston. This is the city where most Americans get confused because it is not set out on the ubiquitous grid, and where the meandering streets were supposedly the result of straying cows."

37. Tebbel, *History of Publishing in the United States*, 1:422–423. Washington Street, of course, technically contained no workplaces, because it was not yet called that; however, Cornhill's numbers reflect business activity on at least a section of what would later be called Washington.

Table 22. Principal Workplace Streets for Book-Trades Occupations in Boston City Directories, 1789–1800

Occupation	Congress	Cornhill	Court	Devonshire	School	State	Washington	Water	Total
Bookbinder	1	2	1	0	0	1	0	1	6
Bookseller	0	21	3	0	0	1	0	0	25
Editorial	0	1	0	0	0	0	0	0	1
Electro/Stereotype	0	0	0	0	0	0	0	0	0
Engraver	0	1	0	0	0	1	0	0	2
Miscellaneous	0	0	0	0	0	0	0	0	0
Music	0	1	0	0	0	0	0	0	1
Paper and Stationery	0	2	1	0	0	4	0	0	7
Printer	1	8	6	0	1	9	0	2	27
Supplies	0	0	0	0	0	0	0	0	0
All	2	36	11	0	1	16	0	3	69

streets, or near Mill Pond on Hanover Street and Link Alley.[38] Although most printers worked on Cornhill, Court, and State streets (Table 22), while their homes were scattered throughout the peninsula, already a few of these tradesmen preferred to live in proximity to one another near the West Boston Bridge on Centre and Temple streets (Map 1). Tradesmen other than printers lived in various neighborhoods on Middle, Essex, and Orange streets. The outlying location of many dwellings necessitated a considerable walk to downtown workplaces, a pattern common from the late eighteenth through the early nineteenth centuries.[39]

The first decade of the nineteenth century saw the beginnings of the book trades' geographical specialization. Most printers still worked in the city center along State, Court, Cornhill, and Congress streets, but more

38. We define the North End here as being north and east of Mill Creek, which dissects the peninsula from Mill Pond down to the harbor.

39. Allan Pred, *Making Histories and Constructing Human Geographies: The Local Transformation of Practice, Power Relations, and Consciousness* (Boulder, Co., 1990). Pred attempts to reconstruct the daily walking path of a late 18th-century Boston merchant capitalist and emphasizes the importance of that daily path in acquiring knowledge from social interactions and printed matter (41–63). He also develops in this book a theory of "time-geography" as a way of understanding the interactions of geography, commutation paths, and social and gender formations (76–111). Binford, in *First Suburbs* (85–87) notes that walking was often favored over other forms of commutation, and that even into the mid-19th century it was not unusual for people to commute long distances on foot.

were employed in marginal areas than previously (Map 2).[40] The homes of printers clustered somewhat in the West End, for three lived on Pinckney Street.[41] Few resided even near the city center. During this period, some trades began to develop spatial patterns that differed from those of printers, and the geographic concentration of the book trades broke down even further. For example, booksellers plied their trade much less on Congress than on Cornhill and adjacent Court Street (but still managed to live downtown), while most engravers worked on Devonshire, all paper and stationery dealers were on State (Table 23), and bookbinders were found on all major thoroughfares, but most commonly on State and Court streets.[42] Many of the engravers, printers, and bookbinders who amassed in this central area performed work for the government and commercial or financial interests (producing certificates and other forms, for example), which offered steady business.

During the 1810s this trend continued, but at a slower pace, owing to economic troubles brought about by the War of 1812 and the Panic of 1819 (Table 24). Engravers concentrated still further on Devonshire, while State Street gave way to Congress as the most common business location for printers, commencing a long-term pattern by which relatively few printers

40. The growth of smaller shops in these marginal areas may be an expression of the apparent paradox that as factory production was adopted, smaller firms proliferated in outlying areas rather than giving way before the superior form of production. Jeremy Atack attempts to resolve the paradox in "The Rise of the Factory: Economies of Scale and Efficiency Gains in the Rise of the Factory in America, 1820–1900," in *Quantity and Quiddity: Essays in U.S. Economic History*, ed. Peter Kilby (Middletown, Conn., 1987), 286–327. He at once points out that the gains in productivity achieved in the move from the artisan shop to the factory were not as great as historians once supposed, but he also adds that the economic growth generated by the new forms of production encouraged this more traditional sort of economic activity.

41. Ward, "Nineteenth-Century Boston," 30–31. Pinckney Street seems to have been marginally exclusive in the late 18th and early 19th centuries. See Kirker and Kirker, *Bulfinch's Boston*, 149, 157.

42. The concentration of booksellers probably reflected a retail strategy in which customers were encouraged to visit but a single location in search of a specific good or service. Boston's emphasis on denominational publishing and retailing also probably allowed for a certain degree of specialization among booksellers on Publishers' Row, which undercut possibly ruinous competitions. Tebbel, *History of Book Publishing in the United States*, 1:387, 1:422–423. Other reasons for the concentration include the fact that such clustering fostered an information community; also, in a city's transition from a mercantile to an industrial economy, districts devoted to a particular business activity naturally occurred, especially for trades engaged in wholesaling. See Pred, *Making Histories and Constructing Human Geographies*, 41–63.

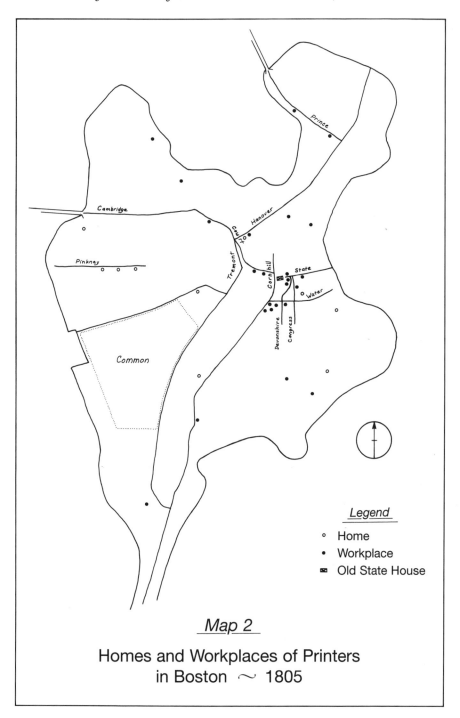

Legend

∘   Home
•   Workplace
▨   Old State House

Map 2

Homes and Workplaces of Printers
in Boston ∼ 1805

Table 23. Principal Workplace Streets for Book-Trades Occupations in Boston City Directories, 1801–1810

Occupation	Congress	Cornhill	Court	Devonshire	School	State	Washington	Water	Total
Bookbinder	4	2	10	3	3	12	0	1	35
Bookseller	2	46	18	0	0	1	0	0	67
Editorial	0	0	0	0	0	2	0	0	2
Electro/Stereotype	0	0	0	0	0	0	0	0	0
Engraver	5	0	0	8	0	1	0	0	14
Miscellaneous	0	0	0	0	0	0	0	0	0
Music	0	0	0	0	0	0	0	0	0
Paper and Stationery	0	0	0	0	0	10	0	0	10
Printer	10	17	18	5	1	25	0	5	81
Supplies	0	0	0	0	0	0	0	0	0
All	21	65	46	16	4	51	0	6	209

would work on State, as banks encroached the street. Some printers' workplaces may have relocated to Congress Street, or elsewhere in the downtown, but they appeared in greater numbers in the North and West Ends, areas outside of the city center.

The surge of book-trades activity during the 1820s had its greatest geographical expression in Washington Street, which came to anchor the city's central business district (Table 25). With the exception of stereotypists, all the book trades found work on Washington, which had "co-opted" Cornhill and three other streets. Still, thirty booksellers remained on a reoriented Cornhill, and another twenty-eight were on Court Street. During the decade directory entries for periodical offices abounded for the first time. The offices could be found on most principal thoroughfares, but especially on Congress Street. Their proliferation did not so much signal an increase in the actual number of periodicals; instead, it indicated a greater recognition of them as businesses rather than mere organs of various groups.[43]

43. For example, none of Boston's 17 newspapers appeared as entries in the 1820 directory. Clarence Saunders Brigham, *History and Bibliography of American Newspapers, 1690–1820* (Worcester, Mass., 1947), 1:271–421. To complicate matters, many nonprofit organizations, ranging from religious denominations to charitable organizations, pursued vigorous publishing programs that produced a wide variety of tracts, reports, sermons, magazines, newspapers, and other imprints. Technically, any of these groups might be considered "publishers" in their own right; since the directories do not usually list

Table 24. Principal Workplace Streets for Book-Trades Occupations in Boston City Directories, 1811–1820

Occupation	Congress	Cornhill	Court	Devonshire	School	State	Washington	Water	Tota
Bookbinder	7	5	2	2	0	8	0	1	2⁵
Bookseller	0	31	15	0	0	8	0	0	5⁴
Editorial	6	0	0	1	0	3	0	0	1(
Electro/Stereotype	0	0	0	0	0	0	0	0	(
Engraver	1	0	6	13	0	2	0	1	2⁵
Miscellaneous	0	0	0	0	0	0	0	0	(
Music	0	0	0	0	0	0	0	0	(
Paper and Stationery	0	0	2	0	0	9	0	0	1]
Printer	26	14	11	5	0	15	2	1	7⁴
Supplies	0	2	0	0	0	0	0	0	⁵
All	40	52	36	21	0	45	2	3	19⁵

The slowdown of the 1830s only slightly affected the downtown concentration of the trades (Table 26). The number of entries for book-trades establishments there increased about 150 percent over the previous decade, while total workplace entries experienced only a 48 percent gain. This suggests that businesses outside the central district were more vulnerable to economic downturns and, perhaps in relation, that a move to the central area was a survival strategy in a time of retrenchment.

The late 1830s witnessed important developments in the residence patterns of printers (Map 3).[44] In 1838 printers lived mainly in the North End,

them that way, though, they have not been counted here in the totals. About 60 charitable organizations operated from 1789 to 1817; see Conrad Edick Wright, *The Transformation of Charity in Postrevolutionary New England* (Boston, 1992), 246–247. It would be wrong, however, to contrast this flood of print with the activity of the marketplace, for many of these items, though they were perhaps partly subsidized, nevertheless were produced by the commercial firms considered here and often sold for profit. Publishers' business papers provide ample evidence of these varying practices. For example, William D. Ticknor published *The Lectures before the American Institute of Instruction* in April 1841. "Deduct cash of American Institute pr agreement" appears in his accounts, but these also list trade and retail prices–thus suggesting a market distribution. *The Cost Books of Ticknor and Fields and Their Predecessors, 1832–1858*, ed. Warren S. Tryon and William Charvat (New York, 1949), 44.

44. While it is difficult to tell exactly where on a street someone lived, we were able to make close approximations in many cases. With the aid of the city directory's appended

Table 25. Principal Workplace Streets for Book-Trades Occupations in Boston City
Directories, 1821–1830

Occupation	Congress	Cornhill	Court	Devonshire	School	State	Washington	Water	Total
Bookbinder	0	12	3	0	2	11	43	14	85
Bookseller	0	30	28	0	3	3	73	0	137
Editorial	90	5	21	0	8	14	33	0	171
Electro/Stereotype	0	0	0	0	0	0	0	0	0
Engraver	19	1	11	1	0	26	18	0	76
Miscellaneous	3	3	3	1	0	0	1	0	11
Music	3	3	6	0	0	0	3	0	15
Paper and Stationery	2	4	4	0	0	58	14	0	82
Printer	79	16	14	4	1	8	55	2	179
Supplies	11	2	3	2	0	0	8	4	30
All	207	76	93	8	14	120	248	20	786

to the west, especially above Cambridge Street, and to the south, above the
Boston and Worcester Rail Road tracks. That they resided in the North
End at this time is not surprising, for Yankee tradesmen and mechanics
occupied this area until the 1840s, after which Irish immigrants succeeded
them.[45] Proximity to bridges affected the residential patterns of some
printers (Map 3). They made their homes near the approaches to the
Charles River Bridge, on Prince Street (4 in total), as well as on Endicott
(2), Snowhill (2), Hull (1), Salem (2), and Cooper (1) streets. This facilitated travel between Boston and Charlestown, where some may have also
worked or had clients.[46] Other Boston printers may have had business

listing of names of streets, courts, places, etc. (for 1800, 1805–1810, 1838, and 1845), wharf
locations, various advertisements, and other miscellaneous information, we could pinpoint
particular numbers on streets, especially at crossroads. For approximating addresses on
long streets, like Washington, Ann, or Hanover, for example, or on short but densely
populated streets, like Court and Cornhill, this data was invaluable. It was less important
for plotting addresses on short streets, where specific points would render themselves
visually meaningless on such small-scale maps.

45. Oscar Handlin, *Boston's Immigrants, 1790–1880: A Study in Acculturation*, rev. ed.
(1959; New York, 1971), 94.

46. Some simply may have wanted to go to a family residence on the weekends, as did
David Clapp, Jr., a printer, who in the summer of 1823 boasted of the regularity of his visits
home: "I have not been obliged to stay in Boston one Saturday night on account of weather
or sickness since I moved in, in May 1822 and have not been detained but two or three

Table 26. Principal Workplace Streets for Book-Trades Occupations in Boston City Directories, 1831–1840

Occupation	Congress	Cornhill	Court	Devonshire	School	State	Washington	Water	Total
Bookbinder	1	32	4	7	19	6	112	21	20!
Bookseller	0	79	32	0	5	0	159	12	28"
Editorial	125	86	36	6	30	32	205	58	57!
Electro/Stereotype	3	0	0	0	0	1	0	1	!
Engraver	1	10	31	2	30	48	109	10	24
Miscellaneous	7	6	0	1	0	0	11	1	2!
Music	0	7	1	0	1	0	11	0	2!
Paper and Stationery	0	1	7	0	1	87	45	11	15!
Printer	71	46	37	27	27	16	124	51	39!
Supplies	16	4	0	1	2	0	17	11	5!
All	224	271	148	44	115	190	793	176	1,96

in Cambridge, for a substantial number congregated near the Canal and Cambridge bridges, on Leverett Street (4), Brighton (1), Spring (1), and Allen (3); and on Cambridge (1), Southack (1), Myrtle (4), Pinckney (1), North Russell (3), Lindall Place (1), and Vine (1).[47] The three railroad lines that served urban commuters attracted as yet only a few printers to their environs, though a few lived near the Boston and Providence Railroad on streets like Warren (1), Fayette (3), Bay (1), and Carver (1).[48]

As printers' homes receded from the central business district in the 1830s, their workplaces remained there, on Congress, Court, Cornhill, Washington, Water, and Devonshire streets. Only one printer listed in the

times Sunday nights." Clapp worked in the office of John Cotton, Jr., who published the Boston city directory from 1829 to 1846. David Clapp, Jr., Aug. 10, 1823, "Journal, 1820–1824," AAS, courtesy of the American Antiquarian Society. See William B. Trask, *Memoir of David Clapp* (Boston, 1894), 14.

47. Since some streets south of Southack and north of the Common in the West End were exclusive at this time, the wealthy printers who lived there (no doubt master craftsmen or the owners of large firms) made a conscious decision to adopt an elite address. For a depiction of exclusive neighborhoods in 1840, see Figure 8 in Ward, "Nineteenth-Century Boston," 365.

48. More research will reveal the locations of boardinghouses and their role as the dwelling place of many printers. Of course, other factors, such as larger patterns of development and relative rent and land values, may be at work in the residential distribution of printers.

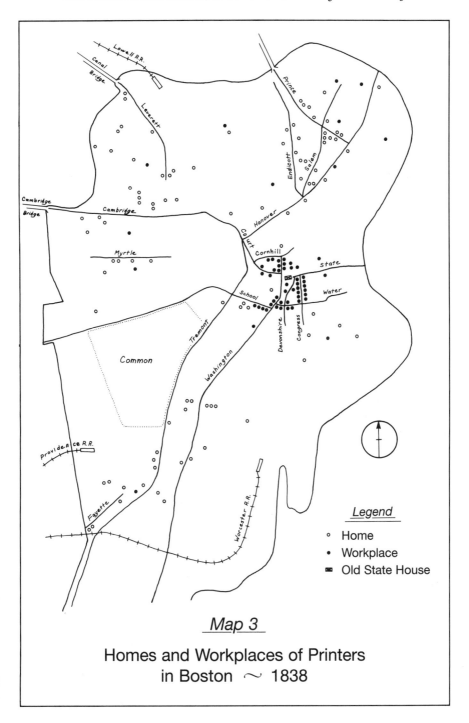

Legend

○ Home
● Workplace
▨ Old State House

Map 3

Homes and Workplaces of Printers in Boston ∿ 1838

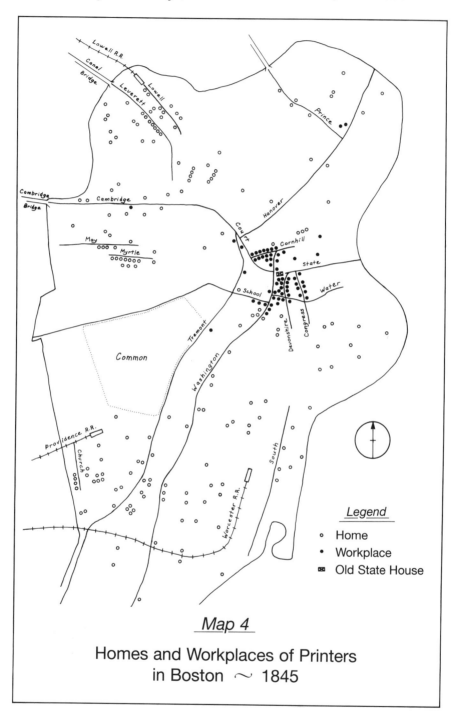

Lowell R.R.

Canal
Bridge

Leverett

Lowell

Prince

Cambridge
Bridge

Cambridge

Hanover

Court

May

Myrtle

Cornhill

State

School

Water

Devonshire

Congress

Tremont

Common

Washington

Providence R.R.

Church

South

Worcester R.R.

Legend

∘   Home

•   Workplace

✇   Old State House

Map 4

Homes and Workplaces of Printers
in Boston ∼ 1845

directory worked on State Street in 1838, reflecting the previous year's panic and the ongoing concentration of banks there (twenty-two in 1837).[49] Printers' shops proliferated in the North End, and a few appeared in the residential area south of Cambridge Street; thus, the centrifugal pattern seen in 1805 continued, suggesting a clientele beyond Publishers' Row and downtown commerce and government.

By 1845 more than half of all printers lived near a few railroad depots and bridges (Map 4). Near the Back Bay, printers clustered around the Providence depot (the number of residences, if more than one, is shown in parentheses): on Carver, Cedar Street Place (3), Church (3), Eliot, Fayette (3), Hamlin, Head Place, Piedmont (2), Pleasant (2), Seaver Place (2), South Cedar (2), Shawmut, lower Tremont (2), and Warren (3). In the South End, their dwellings appeared scattered on streets surrounding the Boston and Worcester terminal: on Bedford, Cove, Essex, Harvard, Kingston (3), Kneeland, Oliver, South (3), South Street Court, South Hudson (2), Oak (2), Oxford, and Tyler. The northwest housed numerous printers, especially near the Cambridge Bridge on Bridge, Cambridge (3), Fruit, Garden, James Place, North and South Russell, West Cedar, and West Center (2) streets. A few blocks south of the Cambridge Street approach to the bridge was a heavy concentration of printers' homes, on May (5), Myrtle (7), and Pinckney (3). Even more printers' homes appeared near the Boston and Lowell Railroad depot and Canal Bridge on Allen, Auburn, Billerica (3), Brighton (2), Leverett (7), Lowell (5), Minot (2), Poplar, Second, Spring Street Place (2) and Court, and Wall. Printers virtually abandoned the North End by 1845 (especially compared with 1838); there, printers now resided only on Ann, Bartlett, Battery, Foster Place, Hanover, Prince (3), Salem (3), and Snowhill.

As printers removed their homes in the 1840s to the south and west of the business district, workplaces for all the trades amassed downtown. The arrival of several more printers on Devonshire and Cornhill was the only major change (apart from greater density) from the 1838 configuration of firms on Congress and Water streets. The parallel line of establishments on Washington to the west (Map 4) continued, and only about three or four printers operated beyond the downtown.[50] On Washington Street, of

49. Ward, "Nineteenth-Century Boston," 41.

50. Only two printers' home addresses could not be pinpointed, both of them on Wesley Street in East Boston. In determining locations on Washington and a few other streets with erratic numbering, we consulted "Re-Numbering of Streets," *The Directory of the City of*

Table 27. Principal Workplace Streets for Book-Trades Occupations in Boston City Directories, 1841–1850

Occupation	Congress	Cornhill	Court	Devonshire	School	State	Washington	Water	Total
Bookbinder	5	36	3	26	28	9	116	37	260
Bookseller	0	112	29	0	15	19	195	7	377
Editorial	83	322	37	39	112	162	369	100	1,224
Electro/Stereotype	0	0	0	0	0	. 0	3	0	:
Engraver	1	8	32	2	24	45	212	13	33?
Miscellaneous	0	21	0	0	3	6	11	0	4?
Music	0	1	20	0	0	0	25	0	4?
Paper and Stationery	2	28	4	36	0	77	48	68	26?
Printer	106	132	39	75	85	49	194	101	78?
Supplies	11	6	3	10	2	0	20	24	7?
All	208	666	167	188	269	367	1,193	350	3,408

course, anything but some types of manufacturing and wholesaling (of blank books, cards, paper, presses, printed goods, and printers' supplies) could be found (Table 27). Otherwise, if shoppers were to walk through the center in search of sheet music on a business day in the 1840s, they would likely find it in Cornhill. For paper (wholesale, probably), or for fancy paper goods sold in stationery stores for personal use, one would head for State Street. There, one could also order some cards for invitations or calling. Bookbinders who worked mainly on Cornhill or upper Washington Street, or on Devonshire, School, or Water could buy their supplies in the immediate vicinity on Cornhill and Water. Thus, within a limited area just about any book-trades-related need could be met.

By 1850 the geographical separation of homes and workplaces that had begun sixty years earlier was nearly complete.[51] In that year, no book tradesperson lived on Cornhill, School, Devonshire, Congress, State, or Water streets; these and neighboring thoroughfares formed a district exclusively devoted to business activities, even without effective zoning laws. Only Hanover (which proceeded from the downtown), Court, and lower Washington contained homes along with work establishments. However,

---

Boston . . . from July 1850, to July 1851 (Boston, 1850), 67–70, which compared old and new numbers and listed cross streets.

51. Ward, in "Nineteenth-Century Boston" (40), notices that this pattern was increasingly evident throughout the century.

there may have been "hidden" residents on these central streets: the apprentices who resided in rooms at printing establishments.

A pamphlet novel by Joseph Holt Ingraham, who was one of the most prolific contributors to Boston cheap fiction in the 1840s, illustrates the life of a printer's apprentice who lives in the room of a print shop on Court Street. "Bruising Bill," as he is dubbed for his fighting skills and anti-Whig sentiments, is resentful of the Harvard students who cross the Cambridge Bridge on the weekends to go to the Tremont Theatre in the city. He despises their display of wealth, when he himself "had been out of work, his employers . . . having failed, and the difficulty of getting work was then very great." At one point in the narrative, Bill fashions a three-foot-square Oxfordian style trencher cap out of paper—apparently the large printers' sheets he works with every day. When he dons the paper hat publicly, in mockery of the "Harvies" who wear their tasseled trenchers to Boston, he provokes his colleagues' laughter and the rage of the students. As one might guess, the students and apprentices settle their differences with brutal fistfights, one of which ends in near death for a student.[52]

This story, published in 1845, not only reveals the precarious proletarian future of printers; it also highlights the importance of bridges in connecting family and foes: Bill's mother lives in Cambridge near the Charles, where he goes on weekends to give her his insubstantial earnings. The climax of the story takes place at the foot of the bridge in Cambridge as the students are returning to campus after a night in Boston. Ingraham's novel with its apparently "mechanic accent" would seem at first to be pointed exclusively

52. Joseph Holt Ingraham, *Alice May, and Bruising Bill* (Boston, 1845), 34. The Tremont Theatre had been out of existence for two years when the novel was published, suggesting that Ingraham wrote about an earlier time, perhaps May 1842 when the first of the "cap" wars apparently occurred. William W. Clapp, "The Drama in Boston," in Winsor, *Memorial History of Boston*, 4:368–369; for background on Ingraham, see Robert W. Weathersby II, *J. H. Ingraham* (Boston, 1980). Leverett Saltonstall discussed the war in a May 29, 1842, letter to his son, Leverett Saltonstall, Jr. See *The Papers of Leverett Saltonstall, 1816–1845*, ed. Robert E. Moody, *Collections of the Massachusetts Historical Society* 85(1991):138–139. The elder Saltonstall, away in Washington, D.C., had foreseen trouble on learning that the Harvard class had decided to affect the Oxford style and found his forebodings confirmed when he read about the war in the Boston papers. "I did not expect that riots, wars & rumors of wars would grow out of it. What a strange time we live in, that 3 or 400 full grown men could be formed to march out of Boston, armed with bludgeons &c. to attack the College buildings and the Scholars. The age of authority has indeed gone." But the father hastens to add, "as a general rule, I must say, that it is not in exact good taste to assume a dress, which from its peculiarity is likely to attract observation." Thanks go to Conrad E. Wright for pointing out this citation.

at the apprentices whom he addresses in his conclusion; he urges them to "combat a prejudice as pernicious as it is absurd." But Ingraham was also a Whig, determined to alleviate class tensions through didactic fiction, and so warned his middle-class readers not to "despise one that is meanly clad." The novel was produced by the country's most notable publisher of fiction in the antebellum period, Frederick Gleason of Boston's Tremont Street, and sold by hawkers in railroad depots, on trains, and, especially, in periodical depots.[53]

In 1845 these depots were mainly situated downtown with only two others: on Hanover Street in the North End and at the U.S. Hotel near the Worcester Rail Road depot. The locations suggest the readership for these publications, insofar as the depots catered to people passing through the business, financial, and shopping districts, and to railroad commuters. The only depots among working-class residences were the two in outlying areas, one of which served travelers on the Worcester line. This strongly suggests that cheap novels like Ingraham's were intended for a wider audience than workers, one that included genteel shoppers and commuters.[54]

Beyond the hints it provides about readership, a geographical analysis of the Boston book trades may contribute to the political history of the factious antebellum years. For example, though the political affiliations of people and firms are often difficult to ascertain, there is some evidence that newspapers of certain denominations or political persuasions clustered

53. Michael Denning, *Mechanic Accents: Dime Novels and Working Class Culture in America* (New York, 1987); for a discussion of the complex reading patterns of mechanics and a consideration of Denning's thesis, see Robert A. Gross, "The History of the Book: Research Trends and Source Materials," *The Book: Newsletter of the Program in the History of the Book in American Culture*, 31(1993):3–7; Ingraham, *Alice May, and Bruising Bill*, 50. For a discussion of Whig rhetoric, see Daniel Walker Howe, *The Political Culture of American Whigs* (Chicago, 1979). On Gleason, see Ralph F. Adimare, "The Dime Novel: Its Place in American Literature," *Dime Novel Round-Up* 2–3 (January 1932– December 1933) 13:2–3; 14:3–4; 15:2–4; 16:2–4; 17:2–4; 18:4–6; 19:2–3; 21:4–5; 22:3–4; 25:3–5; Peter Benson, "Gleason's Publishing Hall" in *Publishers for Mass Entertainment in Nineteenth Century America*, ed. Madeleine Stern (Boston, 1980), 137–145; George Waldo Browne, "Pioneers of Popular Literature: New Hampshire Authors Among Them," *Granite State Magazine* 3(1907):51–55, 111–113; Joseph J. Hinchcliffe and Philip B. Dematteis, "F. Gleason's Publishing Hall, M. M. Ballou" in *American Literary Publishing Houses, 1638–1899*, ed. Peter Dzwonkoski (Detroit, 1986), 1:176–178; "Frederick Gleason," *Frank Leslie's Illustrated Newspaper*, Sept. 21, 1867, 6. Periodical depots demand further treatment, but for an introduction to them, see Zboray, *A Fictive People*, 29–34.

54. Binford, *First Suburbs*, 95–101, discusses the relatively high expense of commutation by train and omnibus.

together. For example, in 1847 various Whig papers, including the *Courier*, the *Daily Advertiser*, and the *Daily Whig* were located at 6, 8, and 10 Congress Street, respectively. Down the road at 27 Congress was the staid, if venerably Whiggish *Transcript,* and in between the former editor of the *Courier*, Joseph T. Buckingham, and the Congregational reform publisher T. R. Marvin had their offices. One wonders whether other nearby book-trades establishments also tended to be Whig throughout the 1840s.[55] And what can be construed from the coexistence on tiny Spring Lane of the *Catholic Observer* and the temperance periodical the *New England Washingtonian*?[56]

Geographical analyses of this sort also help to resolve historical enigmas, like that concerning Frederick Gleason, who published more American fiction titles in the 1840s than any other firm anywhere.[57] Employing an integrated factory system with its own paper mill, he also published a story paper, *The Flag of Our Union*, which featured the work of prominent writers, including Edgar Allan Poe. In 1850 Gleason inaugurated the first pictorial weekly in America (modeled on the London *Illustrated News*), but no evidence has survived to flesh out his biography and, especially, the context out of which his pictorial journalism emerged. Our geographical analysis provides a glimpse of that context, for his office differed from those of all other periodical publishers in that it was located on Tremont Street mainly amid daguerreotypists and engravers.

The Boston city directories show that from 1789 to 1850 the local book trades experienced both developmental expansion and chronic instability. Their growth was dramatic: book-trades entries on average far outpaced

55. The importance of the economic subsidy that partisan newspapers received should not be overestimated, for their owners often understood the papers as a paying enterprise. See, for example, Allen Shepard to Samuel Breck, Apr. 18, 1848, Book Trades Collection, AAS: "The establishment of the Boston Whig is for sale for the sum of $3000. Press–type–subscription and everything connected with the concern. The Press is one of Adams best power presses and is of itself worth $1500[;] the office is well stocked with type and the paper itself was never in better condition. . . . The present patronage [i.e., subscriptions] of the concern amounts to $4,500 (or over that) per year. The cash receipts per week average over $60." Courtesy of the American Antiquarian Society.

56. For a consideration of the literary, the religious, and the political in publishing, see Leon Jackson, "The Two Worlds of William Wells: Ideology and Economy in the Early American Republic of Letters" (D.Phil. thesis, Magdalen College, Oxford Univ., 1993).

57. See Ronald J. Zboray and Mary Saracino Zboray, "American Fiction Publishing, 1837–1857," a paper delivered at the annual convention of the Society for the History of Authorship, Reading, and Publishing, Washington, D.C., July 15, 1994.

overall increases in entries. But just as dramatic were the great fluctuations the trades endured year-to-year, which decennial federal censuses cannot register. However, raw numbers of entries from city directories themselves can be deceptive: the rates of increase differed among occupations, with few inverse relationships (i.e., one occupation gaining at the expense of another). The numbers of entries and entities within each occupation generally rose and fell independently of the others, probably because of the very different types of activities within the trades (i.e., production, wholesaling, distribution, and retailing). Also, since many businesses, such as typefoundries, performed services for a regional rather than a strictly local economy, they responded to largely exogenous influences.[58]

In a reflection of the overall instability, the longevity of entities decreased over time due to failures or mergers, the relative proportions of which remain an open question. Certainly, mergers occurred at a startling rate; for example, in his manuscript on Boston booksellers, the publisher Melvin Lord attempted to trace the complex lineage of Cummings and Hilliard, beginning in 1813:

> About 1821 Timothy H. Carter ^a young man^ who had been an active clerk in the store several years ^in his youthful^ days became a partner in the business ~~concern for a limited period~~ [and?] its chief manager. Cummings ~~decease occurred~~ stet. about 1823, after which ^several^ other parties, ~~at diff' periods~~, in the course of a few years following, were admitted into the concern ^and continued for different periods,^ ~~embracing~~ as Harrison Gray, Charles C. Little, John H. Wilkins, Charles and James Brown, the firm consequently, being several times changed in style: ^in 1825 it was C. H. & Co[.]^ in 1827–1832 ~~it was~~ stet. ^[illegible] Hilliard Gray & Co.^ ^consisting of^ Hill^d, Gray, Little & Wilkins; in 1833–39, ~~1839~~ some of the parties ~~having~~ had retired, but the firm ~~became was~~ was still *Hill^d, Gray & Co.* ~~at the same time~~ notwithstanding, it is believed, Hilliard was one of the retired.[59]

Even with their many mergers, the Boston book trades represent a transitional stage between the more personal forms of business organization

58. On the instability in Boston, see Pease and Pease, *Web of Progress*, 23–39, and Edel, Sclar, and Luria, *Shaky Palaces*, 36–46. The regional orientation of the Boston economy is addressed in Blouin, *Boston Region*, especially Appendix 8, 166.

59. Melvin Lord, "Boston Booksellers, 1650–1860," Boston Booksellers' Papers, 3:91. Courtesy of the American Antiquarian Society. For a similar complex genealogy of mergers, see Jack O'Bar, "The Old Merrill Bookstore: Its Indianapolis Background and History and Its Relationship to the Bobbs-Merrill Company," *Journal of Library History* 20(1985): 408–426.

characteristic of the early nineteenth century and the corporate forms that would predominate later in the century. In many ways the publishing industry stood at the forefront of the development of business practices that included diversification, mass marketing, new forms of advertising and distribution, and increased managerial control.[60] Entrepreneurs like Frederick Gleason could combine under one roof the full gamut of activities related to publishing, from paper milling to bookbinding, including the wholesale and retail distribution of their wares.

As factory organization came to several areas of publishing, the lives of printers, especially, underwent a profound change, for the displacement of artisan production exposed them to the insecurities of a rapidly fluctuating labor market. The ever-increasing number of home addresses reported for printers and the corresponding decline in directory listings for work addresses further indicate their proletarianization, as does their absence, for the most part, from well-to-do neighborhoods. The residential clustering of printers around avenues of transport out of Boston points to the role of the regional labor market in the rapid turnover of local printers. A shortage of local work could drive unemployed printers to seek temporary jobs elsewhere, and this process was perhaps facilitated by the workers' proximity to transportation routes.[61]

Throughout the time period, the book trades' downtown center acted as an anchor for an industry that knew frequent instability, even as the levels of concentration and the distribution of the various trades changed on its principal streets. For printers the downtown provided the majority of workplace establishments. From 1789 on, Cornhill remained an important

---

60. For the presentation of this evidence and a supporting argument, see Zboray, "Literary Enterprise and the Mass Market," 168–181.

61. The expense of daily commutation was prohibitive for most printers, however. Only about 5 percent of the entries for printers' home addresses during the 1840s are for towns outside of Boston, compared with 22.71 percent for editors, a more genteel occupational group. On migration as a response to a fluctuating labor market, see Michael J. Piore, *Birds of Passage: Migrant Labor and Industrial Societies* (Cambridge, 1979). An unfortunate haze of romance surrounds most considerations of itinerant printers; see, for example, John Gordon, *A Memorial to the Tramp Printer, the Intelligent and Intellectual Disciple of the Art Preservative Who Roamed . . . All Over the American Continent, until the Linotype Said–Begone!* (South Brewer, Me., 1927). On the emergence of suburbs, see John Archer, "Ideology and Aspiration: Individualism, the Middle Class, and the Genesis of the Anglo-American Suburb," *Journal of Urban History* 14(1988):214–253; and, on the Boston region in particular, Tamara Plakins Thornton, *Cultivating Gentlemen: The Meaning of Country Life among the Boston Elite, 1785–1860* (New Haven, 1989).

venue for booksellers in particular. Yet in this enclave stability was elusive. Cornhill itself even changed orientation from north-south to east-west. With the rise of some streets for printers' workplaces and the diminution of others, patterns of concentration within the central district mutated throughout time. Increasingly, a few downtown streets in close proximity, especially Washington, became virtually the only major workplace sites within the industry. Concurrently, a distinct home/work division occurred for the trade as a whole.[62]

The irregular growth patterns of the book trades may have had some important political ramifications. For example, Whig socio-economic rhetoric seems less self-serving in light of the instabilities within publishing, itself an area of Whig interest, and these disruptions reflected the uneasy nature of Boston's larger growth patterns. Since the Whig program aimed to achieve a modicum of economic stability (and this seems to have helped the Massachusetts economy during and after the Panic of 1837), perhaps some of that party's success in the state throughout the 1840s can be understood as a favorable response to its practice of directly addressing the concerns of an electorate buffeted by the uneven and unpredictable effects of rapid economic development. Insofar as the Whig press played an important role in rousing citizens during the campaigns of the 1840s, it benefited directly through patronage from the party's surge in popularity. Then, too, perhaps some of the Whig failure around 1850 can be attributed to the party's inability or unwillingness to deliver on its promises of ever greater economic security for common folk.[63]

62. It would be wrong to attribute this concentration to the operations of central place theory, for the local book trades were highly regionalized and engaged in significant wholesaling activity. That Boston book-trades personnel, especially printers, participated in a regional labor market (and hence to some extent accounted for the year-to-year fluctuations of their numbers) suggests the inapplicability of central place theory. If the theory held true, Boston would account for nearly all production, so there would be little work elsewhere. The theory is set out in Walter Christaller, *Central Places in Southern Germany*, trans. Carlisle W. Baskin (1933; reprint, Englewood Cliffs, N.J., 1966); modified by August Lösch, *The Economics of Location*, trans. W. H. Woglom and W. F. Stolper (1939; reprint, New Haven, 1954). For arguments against the theory, see Allan R. Pred, "Behavior and Location: Foundations for a Geographic and Dynamic Location Theory," Part 2, *Lund Series in Geography* [Sweden], B. Ser. 28(1969):17–19; and James Vance, Jr., *The Merchant's World: The Geography of Wholesaling* (Englewood Cliffs, N.J., 1970). On the geographical ramifications of the rise of the rental market for housing, see Elizabeth Blackmar, *Manhattan For Rent, 1785–1850* (Ithaca, N.Y., 1989), especially chaps. 4, 6, and 7.

63. For an explication of the innovations made within the Waltham-Lowell system and

In its dynamism, driven by the mighty currents of socio-economic and political change, the Boston publishing industry thus differed considerably from its standard depiction as a group of small, quaint, traditional, and stable trades. This older image largely results from scholars' over-concentration on a few well-known firms, like Ticknor and Fields and their Old Corner Bookstore.[64] Such an emphasis obscures the contributions of lesser, long-term participants in the book trades, like Moses Jaquith who started as a bookbinder in 1818, became a paper ruler in 1840, and continued in business to the end of the decade. Also overlooked are the many people who came and went within a year or two but who, collectively, constituted a considerable part of the trades, like the pressman William L. Hurd who appeared in the 1834 directory, engraver Gilbert Fox in 1806, or printer Aaron Cutter in 1810.

It is here where the antiquarian tradition and modern social history meet. The antiquarians were motivated by their concern for individual craftsmen and firms, while social historians analyze the behavior of groups and classes to enable themselves to make generalizations about social change. In order to understand the history of the book trades, scholars must pursue both approaches, one particularistic and the other collectivistic. The combination, in the end, allows us to recover and contextualize the lives of the people who created the publishing industry in antebellum Boston.

----

the ways these reflected Whig economic and social thought, see Robert F. Dalzell, Jr., *Enterprising Elite: The Boston Associates and the World They Made* (Cambridge, Mass., 1987), passim, and on the Panic of 1837, 187. For a broader view, see Howe, *Political Culture of the American Whigs*, especially chap. 5; Steven P. McGiffen, "Ideology and the Failure of the Whig Party in New Hampshire, 1834–1841," *New England Quarterly* 59(1986):387–401. The larger political context in Massachusetts during the period is analyzed by Ronald P. Formisano, *The Transformation of Political Culture: Massachusetts Parties, 1790s–1840s* (New York, 1983). Whig economic goals may have been naturally undermined by the economic uncertainty of the workers at the bottom of the labor hierarchy in the book trades; see Michael J. Piore, "Dualism as a Response to Flux and Uncertainty," in *Dualism and Discontinuity in Industrial Societies*, ed. Suzanne Berger and Michael J. Piore (Cambridge, 1980), 23–54. On the patronage of political newspapers, see Gerald J. Baldasty and Jeffrey B. Rutenbeck, "Money, Politics, and Newspapers: The Business Environment of Press Partisanship in the Late 19th Century," *Journalism History* 15(1988):60–69; Gerald J. Baldasty, "The Nineteenth-Century Origins of Modern American Journalism," *Proceedings of the American Antiquarian Society* 100(1990):407–419; Barbara Cloud, "The Press and Profit: Newspaper Survival in Washington Territory," *Pacific Northwest Quarterly* 79(1988):147–156.

64. For example, Henry Walcott Boynton, *Annals of American Bookselling, 1638–1850* (1932; reprint, New Castle, Del., 1991), 189–194.

Appendix: Sources and Methods

Directory studies, as historians have long known, have their limitations. Until the early years of the nineteenth century city directories appeared irregularly and they excluded many residences and businesses. They are biased toward white men with higher incomes. Information can mislead by its omission; the absence of a home address, for example, may or may not mean that a person resided in the suburbs. Conversely, the lack of a work address might suggest that a person worked and lived at the same site, but it could as likely indicate wage labor in a large firm, unemployment, retirement, or transience. And, of course, faced with such a herculean undertaking, directory compilers were bound to make mistakes or be inconsistent.[65]

These limitations affect research on the book trades perhaps less than they hamper studies of other occupational groups. Certain titles, like "publisher," "bookseller," and even "printer" (for those who headed their own industrial firms) were genteel enough to insure their appearance in the directory. Moreover, the directory compilers, publishers themselves, had an intimate knowledge of the local book trade and were therefore more likely to catch the errors and omissions of those who collected the information in the field.

Several sources initially contributed information to this study (Table 2). Three of the sources are prior compilations of the trades made primarily from city directories. The most chronologically comprehensive source remains unpublished: J. Francis Driscoll's c. 1922 "List of Publishers, Booksellers, and Printers . . ." covers the period from 1789 through 1840. Driscoll limited himself to selected occupational titles (i.e., publisher, copperplate printer, bookseller, editor, and printer, and, in a separate list, engraver) and presented his information in a sometimes ambiguous typewritten format, using inconsistently placed ditto marks.[66] The data base, once assembled, revealed that Driscoll dropped "editor" from 1830 through 1840, and he was inconsistent in tracking other occupations as well.

Rollo Silver's two published compilations cover the first part of Driscoll's range (to 1825) but with a greater variety of occupations. Silver augmented

65. Knights, *Plain People of Boston*, Appendix, 127–139; and Thernstrom, *Other Bostonians*, 280–288, address the limitations of the directories.

66. J. Francis Driscoll, "List of Publishers, Booksellers and Printers Taken from the Boston Directories of 1789–1840," typescript, c. 1922, AAS. Copperplate printers worked the specialized presses required for copperplates that were created by the intaglio method of engraving. See Lawrence C. Wroth, *The Colonial Printer* (1931; reprint, Portland, Me., 1938), 286.

his directory research with announcements and advertisements from a few local newspapers. Though this information provided the only glimpse of the book trades for non-directory years, it produced isolated duplications and inconsistencies, which had to be filtered out during data analysis. He also excluded most bookbinders; he left the task of documenting their contributions to the third compilation, Hannah French's "Early American Bookbinding by Hand." She assembled her list (to 1820 only) from a variety of sources, only one of which comprised city directories. Since including this information would have distorted the statistical series for bookbinders, we retained only those entries appearing in directory years.[67]

Since variations in all these sources obviously affected the uniformity of the resulting statistical series, we subsequently proofread the data against the directories on microfiche—and rescanned the fiche for missed entries— to obtain the greatest possible consistency and comprehension. We also added entries from the 1840s, which themselves were subsequently re-scanned and proofread.[68] Thus, we virtually started from scratch, with the advantage that earlier compilations provided another set of eyes, so to speak. In the process of proofreading and scanning, we added for the years before 1841, 4,459 records to our base of 5,624 corrected and verified entries from prior compilations. From our earlier perusal of the 1840s

67. Rollo G. Silver, "The Boston Book Trade, 1790–1799," in *Essays Honoring Lawrence C. Wroth* (Portland, Me., 1951), 279–303; idem, *The Boston Book Trade, 1800–1825* (New York, 1949); Hannah Dustin French, "Early American Bookbinding By Hand, 1636–1820," in *Bookbinding in America: Three Essays*, ed. Hellmut Lehmann-Haupt (New York, 1967), 1–127; Robert W. Flint, "The Boston Book Trade, 1836–1845" (M.L.S. thesis, Simmons College, 1956). This fifth source was rejected in favor of a scan of the original city directories for the years 1841 through 1850.

68. *American Directories through 1860: A Collection on Microfilm* (New Haven, Conn., 1969), based on Dorothea N. Spear, *Bibliography of American Directories through 1860* (Worcester, Mass., 1961), contains the following directories that were used for this study: *The Boston Directory* (Boston, 1789, 1796, 1798, 1800, 1803, 1805, 1806, 1807, 1809, 1810, 1813, 1816, 1818, 1820–1823, 1825–1846); *Adams's New Directory of the City of Boston, 1846–47* (Boston, 1846); *Adams's Boston Directory, 1847–1848* (Boston, 1847); George Adams, *The Boston Directory, 1848–1849* (Boston, 1848); *The Boston Directory, 1849–50* (Boston, 1849); *The Directory of the City of Boston, 1850–51* (Boston, 1850). Beginning in 1846, a new publisher, George Adams, produced the directories under a biennial title range (i.e., 1846–1847) without changing the schedule of their issuance; therefore, information was entered under the earlier of the two years. Entries from the 1846 and 1846–1847 directories were combined and any duplications deleted. The new publisher included suburban home addresses and appended separate lists of newspapers, which somewhat inflated the numbers for the composite year.

directories (which yielded an additional 10,593 entries), we devised an expanded list of relevant job titles: blank books, bookbinder supplies, paper, paper ruler, pens, music, and pocket books were among occupations that previously were not systematically compiled. At first, we included closely allied occupations, like paperhangings, library, sign painter, printed goods, intelligence office, and daguerreotype (2,170 entries in all), but decided at a later stage to delete them from the data presented here in order to keep a tight focus on the book trades.[69] These various levels of sifting and scanning resulted in a data base consisting of 18,506 records (entries with both home and work addresses received records for each).[70]

Once computerized, the information required a good deal of authority work in order to catch ever-present variations in spelling, capitalization, abbreviation, punctuation, and the form of occupational titles, streets, and individual and corporate names.[71] We categorized occupational titles under thirty-nine rubrics and then into ten book trades, those of: 1) bookbinder, 2) bookseller (and periodical depot), 3) editorial (editor, periodical office, proofreader, publisher, reporter), 4) electro/stereotype, 5) engraver (along with copperplate printer and lithographer), 6) miscellaneous (agent, auctioneer, author, paper carrier, secretary, trade association), 7) music, 8) paper and stationery (also blank books, cards, paper ruler, pens, and pocket books), 9) printer (and compositor), and 10) supplies (bookbinder's and

69. A case could be made for the inclusion of daguerreotypists. During a visit to the AAS in 1992, Willman Spawn, Curator of Bindings at the Canaday Library, Bryn Mawr College, explained to us that both bookbinding and the daguerreotype arts use the same types of cases. Daguerreotype prints also began to appear as frontispieces of books very shortly after the techniques of this kind of photography were developed. Yet within this time period, daguerreotypists were seldom considered part of the book trade, so they have not been accounted for in this study.

70. Directory information (consisting of names, addresses, occupation, and dates) was entered into a dBase IV data base. The use of an earlier version of dBase for historical research is discussed in Ronald J. Zboray, "dBase III Plus and the MARC AMC Format: Problems and Possibilities," *American Archivist* 50(1987):210–225; idem, "Computerized Document Control and Indexing at the Emma Goldman Papers," *Documentary Editing* 11(1989):72–75.

71. For the problems commonly encountered with authority work, see Ronald J. Zboray, "Archival Standards in Documentary Editing," *Studies in Bibliography* 43(1990):34–49; Robert H. Burger, *Authority Work* (Littleton, Co., 1985); Lorene E. Ludy and Sally A. Rogers, "Authority Control in the On-Line Environment," *Information Technology in Libraries* 3(1984):262–266; Mary W. Ghikas, ed., *Authority Control: The Key to Tomorrow's Catalog: Proceedings of the 1979 Library and Information Technology Association Institutes* (Phoenix, Ariz., 1982).

printer's, along with ink and typefoundry).[72] The categories reflect the manner in which the various parts of the trade fit together functionally. While the pattern of categorization may have been figured in several alternative ways, one should remember that due to the overlap of occupations, the categories reflect an emphasis upon a certain type of trade activity, not always an exclusive allegiance to any particular specialization.

Upon completing authority work we were able to assign codes to link the various records to unique people or firms ("entities"). The use of the concept of entities discourages errors of judgment about what names are corporate or individual. During this time period, for example, a seemingly individual name could stand for a firm with silent partners or even one owned by a person with an entirely different name. To make matters worse, single home addresses sometimes were given for firms with several partners. The directories presented other problems, like variant spellings and the absence or presence of initials and designations (e.g., "Jr." or "Rev."). During the coding process, all 18,506 records were examined closely to make sure that every variant would be associated with the proper entity and that entities with similar names were separated. If the name of a company remained the same, even though the partners changed, it was designated as a single entity. However, if "Co." was added to a name or partnership, it became a distinct new entity.

72. Of course, such functional classification does not easily distinguish between manufacturers and retailers, or master artisans and wage laborers, yet these cannot be discerned from directory information, but perhaps only through an analysis of manuscript census data. See Michael B. Katz, "Occupational Classification in History," *Journal of Interdisciplinary History* 3(1972):63–88; Carl F. Kaestle, *The Evolution of an Urban School System: New York City, 1750–1850* (Cambridge, Mass., 1973), 31–32, n. 9.

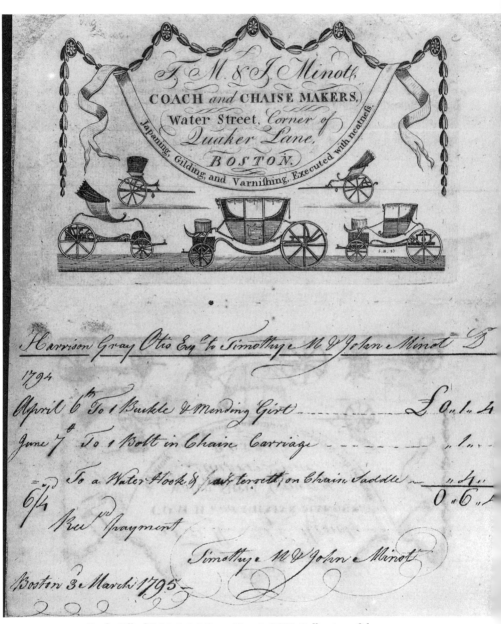

Trade Bill of T. M. & J. Minot, Mar. 3, 1795. Collection of the
Massachusetts Historical Society.

The Partnership Form of Organization:
Its Popularity in Early-Nineteenth-Century Boston

Naomi R. Lamoreaux

H I S T O R I A N S   W H O   W R I T E about industry
during the nineteenth century tend to take for granted the organizational
forms that businesses employed. For example, they are apt to view the shift
from single proprietorships to partnerships to corporations that occurred
during this period as a natural consequence of the growth of the market
and technological change. But firms, like all human institutions, are constructed entities. Their sizes, boundaries, internal structures, and organizational forms are products of social and cultural as well as economic processes and, indeed, vary quite strikingly from one nation to the next.[1] The
purpose of this essay is to take a new look at business forms in the United
States during the nineteenth century in order to explore the processes that
shaped them and determined their use. My focus is the partnership form of
organization, a subject that has received scant attention from a scholarly
community preoccupied with the rise of the corporation. I first review the
weaknesses of the partnership form and present evidence showing that,
despite obvious limitations, partnerships were an increasingly important
form of enterprise during the first half of the nineteenth century. I then
analyze two samples of firms from Boston in the 1840s and 1850s with the
aim of understanding why so many businesspeople formed partnerships
during this period. The answer, I argue, must be sought in the value system
of the Early Republic, in particular in the horror of dependence that made

1. Alfred D. Chandler, Jr., of course, has devoted considerable energy to explaining the
structure of very large firms of the late 19th and early 20th centuries, but the model he
offers is largely technologically determined. Social and cultural factors either account for
only minor differences in the structure of large firms or, conversely, operate to prevent
large firms from emerging (and the economy from prospering). See *Strategy and Structure: Chapters in the History of the Industrial Enterprise* (Cambridge, Mass., 1962); *The
Visible Hand: The Managerial Revolution in American Business* (Cambridge, Mass., 1977);
and *Scale and Scope: The Dynamics of Industrial Capitalism* (Cambridge, Mass., 1990).

independent proprietorship seem so much more appealing to men of that time than salaried employment.

The limitations of the partnership form of organization are (and were) well known. The most obvious—unlimited liability—was important because it constrained firms' ability to raise capital. The only way to invest in a firm was to become a partner, and because all partners were fully liable for the firm's debts, in general only investors who planned to play an active role in management could afford to take the risk.[2] A second obvious and important limitation of the partnership form of organization was its short time horizon. Many partnership agreements expired after fixed periods of time, and most included procedures for terminating the arrangement should one of the partners wish to withdraw.[3] The death of a partner also typically forced the dissolution of a firm, an eventuality that could have potentially disastrous consequences if assets had to be liquidated to pay off the deceased partner's heirs. Firms that were temporarily overextended could end up insolvent, and even a strong firm could suffer serious losses if the timing of the dissolution meant that assets had to be sold at fire-sale prices. Although some contracts contained provisions specifically aimed at avoiding this eventuality, most did not.[4] Apparently, most partners did not wish their heirs' assets to be tied up in the firm after their death.

2. Massachusetts enacted a law permitting limited liability partnerships in 1835, but this form of organization was not much used before the Civil War, perhaps because lenders at this time strongly preferred granting credit on the basis of personal rather than collateral security and typically demanded that a firm's debt be endorsed individually by its partners, thus negating much of the advantage of limited liability. See below.

3. For example, the partnership between Horace Abbott and John S. Gilman of Baltimore was scheduled to last five years. Either partner, however, could terminate the agreement earlier by giving six months notice. See copartnership agreement, Mar. 30, 1857, Horace Abbott Papers, Massachusetts Historical Society (hereafter M.H.S.). Similarly, Nathan Appleton's partnership contracts typically contained a clause allowing any partner to give six months notice if he wished to withdraw from the agreement. Copartnership agreement, May 24, 1810, box 2, folder 19, Appleton Family Papers, M.H.S. See also copartnership agreement, June 1, 1815, box 3, folder 1; copartnership agreement, Jan. 1, 1829, box 4, folder 10; and copartnership agreement, May 7, 1838, box 5, folder 14.

4. One famous example of such a contract was Carnegie Steel's so-called "iron-clad agreement." The minor partners in the firm were so afraid of what would happen if Carnegie died that, in exchange for a clause permitting Carnegie's estate to be paid off gradually, they submitted to a provision that greatly reduced the value of their holdings should they choose to withdraw from the firm. See John Landry, "Corporate Incentives for Managers in American Industry, 1900–1940," (Ph.D. diss., Brown Univ., 1994), 67.

In addition to these obvious limitations, the partnership form of organization was fraught with the kinds of risks that economists call "moral hazard." Problems of joint production meant that partners could not always verify that associates were working as hard for the firm as they claimed.[5] A more important source of difficulty, however, was the ease with which partners could withdraw from their firms. Membership in a partnership gave a potential rival access to such firm-specific assets as business connections and carefully fostered relations with customers, access that a partner could exploit on his own after the firm dissolved. Francis Coffin reported one such incident from France in 1807. An ambitious merchant, who had been taken into a partnership by a more established colleague, used his position to play "so artfull a role towards the Captains & Supercargoes as to instill into their minds the idea that he was the sole acting partner of the house in order to secure to himself their future consignments whenever a seperation took place." He then moved to dissolve the firm.[6] A letter that Boston merchant Jonathan Jackson wrote to reassure a relative about his partnership with John Bromfield suggests that fears of such exploitation were widespread. "As to my Partner's going off with the Business hereafter there wou'd be no fear of that while I chose to give him the advantages I now do M^r B—d confesses an entire Ignorance of Mchts Acct^s. I have undertaken the care of the Books intirely myself."[7]

An even more important hazard was unscrupulous partners who involved the firm in their own debts or exploited the assets of the firm for personal advantage. The disastrous consequences that might result from such complications can be seen in the experience of Philadelphia merchant Thomas P. Cope. Victimized by the "imprudent conduct" of his New York partners, Cope not only lost the capital he had invested in the business but was forced to advance "large sums to pay [his partners'] debts."[8] Investors sometimes attempted to guard against such dangers by writing special clauses into their partnership agreements. For example, Boston merchant Nathan Appleton's 1815 contract with Benjamin C. and William Ward

5. See Armen Alchian and Harold Demsetz, "Production, Information Costs, and Economic Organization," *American Economic Review* 62(1972):777–795; and Bengt Holmstrom, "Moral Hazard in Teams," *Bell Journal of Economics* 13(1982):324–340.

6. Francis Coffin to John Derby, Apr. 20, 1807, box 2, folder 16, Appleton Family Papers.

7. Kenneth Wiggins Porter, *The Jacksons and the Lees: Two Generations of Massachusetts Merchants, 1765–1844* (Cambridge, Mass., 1937), 1:161–162.

8. Eliza Cope Harrison, *The Diary of Thomas P. Cope, 1800–1850* (South Bend, Ind., 1978), 62, 94, 128–129.

specified that "no endorsements shall be made or surety given in the name of the firm for any person whatever out of favour or affection, but if made shall be at the risk of the person making the same." Although the partners might endorse notes for "persons who shall reciprocally endorse notes or become surety to bonds for the benefit of said concern," "such reciprocal endorsements shall not be made without the consent of the said Appleton and one at least of the other parties."[9] Over time Appleton insisted on even more restrictive clauses. In an 1838 agreement revising the terms for the partnership James W. Paige & Co., he required his associates to relinquish their freedom of contract, insisting that "neither the said James W. Paige nor Samuel A. Appleton shall become guarantee or endorser for any person or persons whatever on their own account, excepting as surety on Custom House Bonds."[10]

Few businessmen had the financial clout to impose such restrictions on their partners. Moreover, this kind of agreement was typically not enforceable under the common law.[11] As a consequence, businessmen either had to pay close attention to the details of their business or trust completely the judgment of their associates. Either way, the decision to enter a partnership was not something to be undertaken lightly. Thomas Cope, for one, had not thought through the implications of his agreement seriously enough and, as a result, later came to regret the move. The lessons he learned from hard experience he passed on to his sons: "Be very guarded in forming partnerships. They are sometimes attended with advantages, but often with great vexation & difficulty." "I speak from experience," he added. "I formed several & wish I never had formed any."[12]

9. Copartnership agreement, June 1, 1815, Appleton Family Papers. See also copartnership agreement, May 24, 1810, and copartnership agreement, Jan. 1, 1829.

10. Copartnership agreement, May 7, 1838, Appleton Family Papers.

11. See, for example, U.S. Supreme Court Chief Justice John Marshall's decision in John Winship and Others, Plaintiffs in Error, v. The Bank of the United States, Defendant in Error, 5 Peter's Supreme Court Reports 529. Marshall ruled that the partners of a firm were liable for debts incurred by one of their number in violation of the copartnership agreement, because creditors could not be expected to know the terms of such agreements. See also Joseph Story, *Commentaries on the Law of Partnership, as a Branch of Commercial and Maritime Jurisprudence with Occasional Illustrations from the Civil and Foreign Law*, 5th ed. (Boston, 1859), 163, 351–381. Partners could attempt to use the equity courts to enforce copartnership agreements, but such action was tantamount to dissolution and in any event did not absolve partners from liability to third parties for debts incurred in violation of such agreements.

12. Harrison, *Diary of Thomas P. Cope*, 128–129.

Because of all these problems with partnerships, but especially their short life expectancies and the constraints unlimited liability placed on their ability to raise capital, this form of organization has been conventionally viewed as unsuitable for industrial ventures. Originating in commerce, it is argued, partnerships were replaced in the nineteenth century by the corporate form once industrialization raised the capital requirements and lengthened the time horizons of business. Certainly, by the 1820s most corporations had limited liability and so did not face the same constraints on capital accumulation that partnerships did. Because they also typically had perpetual life, they solved as well the problem of impermanency that made partnerships such an uncertain investment.[13]

The corporate form also had its drawbacks, however. During the early part of the century, charters were available only by special legislative act, and as a result, securing a charter entailed costs that were not easily estimated in advance. Moreover, even after the passage of general incorporation laws, public mistrust of corporations meant that firms that adopted this form of organization were exposed to a greater degree of public intervention than that borne by partnerships. Governments sought to ensure that corporations did not enjoy unfair advantages over other firms and that their managements behaved responsibly. Thus state legislatures inserted regulatory provisions into corporate charters and, after the Supreme Court's decision (in the Dartmouth College Case in 1819) that a corporate charter was an inviolable contract, also routinely added clauses that allowed the state to alter unilaterally a charter's terms. Regulatory provisions ranged from restrictions on the amount of capital that firms could raise and the lines of business in which they could engage to requirements that specific types of corporations, for example banks, submit semi-annual financial reports. Legislatures also imposed particular structures of governance on corporate enterprises, specifying, for example, the size and composition of the boards of directors, the frequency of elections for corporate officers, and the number of votes that large shareholders could exercise. Adoption of the corporate form of organization thus involved a considerable loss of flexibility and contractual freedom compared to partnerships.[14]

13. The charters of banking corporations in Massachusetts all expired at 20-year intervals, but most other corporations were not subject to similar time limits. For a discussion of the early law on limited liability, see Edwin J. Perkins, *American Public Finance and Financial Services, 1700–1815* (Columbus, Ohio, 1994), 373–376.

14. See, for example, Louis Hartz, *Economic Policy and Democratic Thought: Pennsylvania, 1776–1860* (Cambridge, Mass., 1948); James Willard Hurst, *The Legitimacy of the*

It is also important to realize that the advantages of the corporate form for securing capital were not as clear-cut as they might seem at first glance for firms in the first half of the century. As Sidney Pollard and others have demonstrated, the amount of fixed capital required for manufacturing ventures in the early nineteenth century was not large, and entrepreneurs could raise the necessary sums by tapping family savings and plowing back the firms' earnings. Although these scholars recognized that obtaining working capital was a more serious problem for early manufacturers, they argued that much of the necessary credit was provided by merchants who sold the firms supplies.[15] Not surprisingly, Paul Paskoff has found that corporations in the Pennsylvania iron industry did not outperform partnerships before mid century. Although corporate operations tended to be somewhat larger as a result of the firms' superior ability to raise capital, their bigness brought no technological advantage, and productivity growth rates for partnerships were comparable. Not until the second half of the century, when the creation of a national market presented new opportunities for growth, would size give some firms in this industry a competitive advantage.[16]

There were also real limits to the sources of investment capital that corporations could tap in the early nineteenth century, and most companies were in practice restricted to the same familial reservoirs of funds on which partnerships depended. In the first place, the shallow markets and high risks associated with manufacturing during the early industrial period caused people to shy away from investing in industrial securities. In the second, corporations were widely viewed with suspicion. Expressing sentiments that would be familiar to modern-day proponents of principal-agent theory, contemporaries worried that hired managers would not devote the same amount of energy to the firm that they would if they owned it

Business Corporation in the Law of the United States, 1780–1970 (Charlottesville, Va., 1970); and Herbert Hovenkamp, *Enterprise and American Law, 1836–1937* (Cambridge, Mass., 1991).

15. For an excellent survey of this literature, see François Crouzet, Editor's Introduction, in *Capital Formation in the Industrial Revolution*, ed. Crouzet (London, 1972), 1–69. See also Sidney Pollard, "Fixed Capital in the Industrial Revolution in Britain," *Journal of Economic History* 24(1964):299–314; Glenn Porter and Harold C. Livesay, *Merchants and Manufacturers: Studies in the Changing Structure of Nineteenth-Century Marketing* (Baltimore, 1971), 62–78.

16. Paul Paskoff, *Industrial Evolution: Organization, Structure, and Growth of the Pennsylvania Iron Industry, 1750–1860* (Baltimore, 1983), 91–105.

themselves and that profits would be frittered away in excessive salaries and perquisites.[17] Unless a stockholder participated actively in the direction of the firm, he could not be certain that the funds he had invested would be used productively and that he would get the full benefit of the firm's earnings. Although limited liability protected stockholders from losing in excess of their investments, government securities and other financial instruments available at the time did not pose the same level of risk. As a result, only well-established companies or those promoted by the region's most prominent business leaders could attract investment capital from non-familial sources, and even these firms were limited to regional financial markets until the end of the century.[18]

Finally, the limited liability that the corporate form made possible could actually hinder access to the credit markets. Banks and other providers of credit in this period typically lent their funds on the basis of personal rather than collateral security. They preferred to have the debt backed by the full resources of the maker of the loan, as well as of one or more endorsers, rather than limit their security to a particular piece of property. As a consequence, lenders were wary of providing credit to a corporation unless the officers of the concern were willing personally to endorse the firm's notes. This procedure, however, effectively eliminated the advantage of limited liability for these men, and thus removed one of the reasons for adopting the corporate form.[19]

With the advantages of the corporate form so marginal in this period, it is perhaps not surprising that, as Jeremy Atack and Fred Bateman have found, even within the manufacturing sector the number of partnerships

17. For some examples, see Paul F. McGouldrick, *New England Textiles in the Nineteenth Century: Profits and Investment* (Cambridge, Mass., 1968), 23–25.

18. For a list of industrials sold on the Boston exchange in the 19th century, see Joseph G. Martin, *A Century of Finance: Martin's History of the Boston Stock and Money Markets* (Boston, 1898). On the institutional problems associated with trading equities, see Jonathan Barron Baskin, "The Development of Corporate Financial Markets in Britain and the United States, 1600–1914: Overcoming Asymmetric Information," *Business History Review* 62(1988):199–237.

19. For this reason some corporations formed after the passage of general incorporation laws specifically rejected the provision of limited liability. See, for example, Peter J. Coleman, *The Transformation of Rhode Island, 1790–1860* (Providence, 1969), 113–114. On early banks' lending practices, see Naomi R. Lamoreaux, *Insider Lending: Banks, Personal Connections, and Economic Development in Industrial New England* (New York, 1994), 1–2.

grew relative to the number of corporations until the 1870s.[20] The more difficult and interesting question is why businessmen so frequently chose the partnership form of organization over the many other (non-corporate) contractual forms that were available at the time.[21] In order to explore this issue, it is helpful first to think about the economic reasons that might bring businessmen together in partnerships. One possibility is that entrepreneurs sought partners in order to secure some badly needed input for the firm. Their businesses, for example, might require more labor than they themselves were willing or able to provide. Thus Boston merchant Jonathan Jackson formed Jackson and Bromfield when the poor state of his health prevented him from keeping up with the business alone. Similarly, Nathan Appleton formed partnerships with Benjamin C. Ward and James W. Paige in order to free his own time for other pursuits.[22] Partners might also be valued for the capital they brought to a firm. Thus the Jones and Laughlin Steel Company of Pittsburgh got its start when two immigrant German ironworkers sought an infusion of capital for their rolling mill. They first formed a partnership with members of the mercantile firm of Jones and Kier; when they needed still additional funds, another Pittsburgh merchant (James Laughlin) joined the concern.[23] Finally, it is possible that businessmen sought partners who would bring some complementary capability to the concern. Judith McGaw has argued, for example, that firms in the Berkshire paper industry were more likely to survive if their partners were tied to different information networks—for example, if one partner had experience and connections in commerce and another in papermaking.[24]

All of these economic goals, however, could be achieved by means of other contractual forms. Obviously, firms could secure investment capital by borrowing on a variety of short-term and long-term debt instruments,

20. Jeremy Atack and Fred Bateman, "Preliminary Data on the Spread of Organizational Forms Among American Manufacturing Firms in the Nineteenth Century," unpub. paper, National Bureau of Economic Research, 1995.

21. I use the term business*men* deliberately. Although city directories reveal a few instances of partnerships involving women, the overwhelming majority of firms during this period were exclusively male. As I will argue later in this essay, the appeal of the partnership form of organization was closely bound up with early-19th-century notions of masculinity.

22. Porter, *Jacksons and the Lees*, 1:161; Frances W. Gregory, *Nathan Appleton: Merchant and Entrepreneur, 1779–1861* (Charlottesville, Va., 1975), 106, 214–215, 229–230.

23. Porter and Livesay, *Merchants and Manufacturers*, 65–68.

24. Judith A. McGaw, *Most Wonderful Machine: Mechanization and Social Change in Berkshire Paper Making, 1801–1885* (Princeton, 1987), 127–147.

and they could secure labor inputs by hiring wage-earning employees. But there were additional alternatives. For example, in 1817 Hugh Lindsay contracted to provide the United States Navy with a supply of live oak timber. Not having the financial resources to fulfill the obligation on his own, he contracted with John P. Rice to advance him the necessary funds in exchange for one half of the profits.[25] To give another example, in 1851 the East Boston Manufacturing Company (a partnership of William T. Hawes and the firm of Robinson, Wiggin & Company) financed its inventory of manufactured goods (candles) by contracting with the firm of Mixer & Pitman to own the output jointly.[26] Labor contracts could also take a variety of forms. B. W. Dodge of Malden, Massachusetts, negotiated an agreement with Nathaniel L. White in 1842, according to which White assumed responsibility for managing Dodge's store in return for a share of the profits of the business. The two men were not partners; rather, Dodge conceived of White's share as a payment for labor services.[27] In another instance, a man was hired to manage a foundry in exchange for a fixed salary and a share of the profits.[28]

Businessmen also used a variety of non-partnership contracts to combine their complementary talents and skills in joint ventures. For example, the merchant firm of Cabot, Appleton & Co. of Boston signed a contract in 1841 with Hiram Cooper, a manufacturer who had leased a mill in Medford, Massachusetts. The merchants agreed to furnish Cooper with materials, and Cooper in turn agreed "to cause to be manufactured the stock furnished, into satinets, . . . to be thoroughly made in a workmanlike manner in every respect." The merchants were to handle the sales, and Cooper was to receive a fixed rate for each yard of cloth produced as well as a share of the profits.[29] Similarly, the firm of Judson & Company together with one Williams agreed "to furnish such materials as are required for the purpose of manufacturing and making glass bottles" to a man named Foster, who was skilled in the manufacture of glass. Foster agreed "to manufacture said materials, furnished by said Judson & Co. & Williams, into such glass ware as they shall direct, and to do the same in a faithful and workmanlike

25. John P. Rice v. Nathaniel Austin, 17 Tyng (17 Mass.) 197 at 198.

26. William T. Hawes & others v. Pardon Tillinghast & another, 1 Gray (67 Mass.) 289 at 289–290.

27. Edwin Bradley & another v. Nathaniel L. White & another, 10 Metcalf (51 Mass.) 303.

28. Edward Denny & another v. Richard C. Cabot & others, 6 Metcalf (47 Mass.) 82 at 91.

29. Denny v. Cabot, 82 at 83–84.

manner, and to give his whole time and attention to said business." Judson & Company and Williams would handle the sales, and Foster would receive a share of the profits as his remuneration.[30]

We know that such alternative contractual forms existed. Unfortunately, there is no way of knowing how often they were employed in comparison to partnerships or how their relative frequency changed over time. We do, however, have indications that the number of partnerships was increasing relative to single proprietorships during the first half of the nineteenth century.[31] The change can be seen by comparing random samples from the 1800, 1820, 1840, and 1860 Boston directories (see Table 1). In 1800, there were 89 overseas merchants operating as sole proprietors in the sample, but only 16 mercantile partnerships—for a ratio of partnerships to merchants of 18 percent. By 1820 the ratio had increased to 31 percent, and by 1860 to 112 percent.[32] The proportion of partnerships that were engaged in overseas mercantile pursuits increased from 31 percent in 1800 to 38 percent in 1820, but then dropped dramatically to 23 percent in 1840 and 9 percent in 1860. In other words, not only were merchants turning increasingly to the partnership form of organization, but after 1820 a growing proportion of the partnerships in the city were being formed in other types of businesses. Indeed, by 1840 nearly a quarter involved craftsmen and manufacturers.[33] The number of partnerships was also increasing relative to the total population. In 1800 the ratio of partnerships to entries in the city directory was 5.5 percent. By 1820 the ratio had grown to 6.8 percent, and in 1840 it still exceeded 7 percent, despite rapid population growth and

30. Chester Judson & another v. Thomas Adams, 8 Cushing (62 Mass.) 556 at 558.

31. In addition, Atack and Bateman found that between 1850 and 1870 there was a rise in the number of partnerships relative to single proprietorships in the manufacturing sector. See their "Preliminary Data."

32. Over time, the designation "merchant" was increasingly replaced by more specialized occupational labels. Hence the decline in numbers reported in the table. Nonetheless, the trend in the percentages is important. By 1860 it was comparatively rare for anyone listed as a commission merchant to be in business as a sole proprietor. In all years, some men who were merchants were listed in the directory without any occupational designation, but there is no reason to believe that the proportion so listed increased over time.

33. This figure is only an estimate, because it was not always possible to distinguish craftsmen and manufacturers from retailers by using the occupational labels given in the directories. For example, I excluded from the manufacturing category men whose business was listed simply as "shoes" or "drugs," though these occupations undoubtedly included some manufacturers.

Table 1. The Number and Composition of Partnerships, 1800–1840

	1800	1820	1840	1860
1. No. of Mercantile Partnerships	16	45	63	29
2. No. of Independent Merchants	89	146	167	26
3. Ratio of Merchant Partnerships to Independent Merchants	0.18	0.31	0.38	1.12
4. No. of Partnerships	51	118	270	308
5. % of Partnerships That Were Mercantile	31%	38%	23%	9%
6. Total No. of Entries in Sample	914	1,735	3,740	5,434
7. % of Entries That Were Partnerships	5.5%	6.8%	7.2%	5.7%
8. Population of Boston (in 000s)	24.9	43.3	93.4	177.8
9. Sample Entries as % of Population	1.6%	1.7%	1.7%	3.1%
10. Sample Partnerships as % of Population	0.092%	0.12%	0.13%	0.17%

Notes: For 1800, 1820, and 1840 the sample consisted of every tenth directory page. The layout of the 1860 directory was more condensed, so I chose the right-hand column of every fifth directory page. I defined as mercantile all names or partnerships with the occupational label "merchant" (unless the party was clearly engaged in domestic trade), as well as those listed as handling West Indian or other foreign goods. Merchants involved in partnerships were not included in the total for merchants operating independently, so line 3 should be interpreted as the ratio of the two types of firms. In order to insure uniform coverage across directories, I only counted principal entries for partnerships— that is, the entry located by the name of the partner who was listed first in each firm's title.

Sources: Boston City Directory, 1800, 1820, 1840, and 1860; Massachusetts, Secretary of the Commonwealth, *Abstract of the Census of Massachusetts, 1860* (Boston, 1863), 208.

the severe depression that began in 1839. The 1860 percentage was only 5.7, but this drop was an artifact of the dramatically improved coverage of the 1860 directory compared to 1840 and earlier years.[34] The ratio of the number of entries in my samples to the total population of Boston hovered

34. Examination of the directories makes it clear that coverage improved over time and that the improvement was especially great between 1840 and 1860. In the former year, for example, undercoverage of clerks and laborers was severe, but there were extensive listings for these occupational categories in 1860. There were also many more women in the 1860 city directory.

around 1.6 to 1.7 percent from 1800 through 1840 but leapt to 3.1 percent in 1860. At the same time, the ratio of the number of partnerships in my sample to Boston's population nearly doubled, from 0.092 percent in 1800 to 0.17 percent in 1860.

Given the risks associated with the partnership form of organization and the presumption that partnerships would have appeared less attractive over time as a result of industrialization, these figures pose an interesting puzzle. In the remainder of this essay I explore the reasons for the popularity of the partnership form by analyzing two samples of firms from Boston. The first was drawn from the 1845 Boston city directory; the second from the R. G. Dun credit ledgers for the late 1840s and early 1850s. Because the first sample is the more comprehensive, I rely on it to focus my discussion, employing the second mainly to explore issues that cannot be studied using the city directories alone.[35]

The most striking characteristic of the sample from the 1845 Boston city directory was the small size of the firms (see Table 2). The average number of partners per firm was only 2.2, and fully 84 percent of the firms had only two partners. There were a mere ten firms with more than three partners, and none had more than five. The size of firms in the R. G. Dun sample was slightly larger, with the average partnership consisting of 2.4 members. But the R. G. Dun Company only collected information about firms that sought to borrow on the credit markets. As a result, the latter sample was probably biased toward larger firms, a supposition that the different occupational composition of the two samples tends to confirm. Slightly less than two-thirds of the firms in the city directory sample were involved in some commercial pursuit, as opposed to 80 percent of those in the R. G. Dun sample. Because virtually all of the firms in both samples with more than three partners were engaged in commerce, this difference explains much of the discrepancy in average size. Moreover, the R. G. Dun sample in-

35. The first sample, which consists of 443 firms, was selected by picking the first partnership listed on every other page of the 1845 directory. I chose the year 1845 because it occurred at the height of the partnership boom but long enough after the 1839 depression to enable me to trace the firms and their members backwards in time. The second sample (164 firms plus their subsequent avatars) consists of all the partnerships for which entries before 1853 were recorded on the right-hand pages of Massachusetts vol. 67 of the R. G. Dun Co. records. The latter are located at the Baker Library, Harvard Graduate School of Business Administration. There is very little overlap between the two samples.

Table 2. Distribution of Firms by Number of Partners and Occupation, 1845

	No. with 2 Partners	% of Total	No. with 3 Partners	% of Total	No. with 4 or More Partners	% of Total	Total No.
Merchants and Shopkeepers	213	77%	53	19%	9	3%	275
Craftsmen and Manufacturers	107	99%	1	1%	0	0%	108
Professionals and Proprietors	17	81%	4	19%	0	0%	21
Other	11	100%	0	0%	0	0%	11
No Occupation Listed	25	89%	2	7%	1	4%	28
All Occupations	373	84%	60	14%	10	2%	443

Note: Percentage totals may not equal 100%.

Source: Boston City Directory, 1845.

cluded no small partnerships involving shipwrights, housewrights, and other similar craftsmen, such as were listed in the city directory.[36]

Firms in the city directory sample also had very short life expectancies. Indeed, only 33 percent survived to be recorded in the 1850 Boston direc-

36. It is possible that the city directory listings neglected to include silent partners and thus understated the size of firms. Examination of the R. G. Dun credit reports indicates, however, that silent (or special) partners were relatively rare during this period. Only two of the firms in that sample had special partners, though eight others acquired them for brief periods as a result of subsequent reorganizations.

Table 3. Survival Rates for Various Categories of Partnerships, 1845–1850

	Survived	*Dissolved*	*Disappeared*	*Total No.*
All Firms	33% (144)	59% (260)	9% (39)	443
Firms with 2 Partners	29% (106)	60% (219)	10% (38)	363
Firms with More than 2 Partners	48% (38)	51% (41)	1% (1)	80
Merchants and Shopkeepers	32% (87)	62% (170)	7% (18)	275
Craftsmen	34% (33)	53% (51)	13% (13)	97
Manufacturers	45% (5)	45% (5)	9% (1)	11
All with Different Last Names	29% (103)	62% (220)	10% (34)	357
All with Same Last Name	44% (26)	49% (29)	7% (4)	59
Some with Same Last Name	56% (15)	41% (11)	4% (1)	27
All Partners Experienced	53% (62)	44% (52)	3% (4)	118
Some Partners Experienced	33% (55)	62% (104)	6% (10)	169
All Partners Inexperienced	17% (27)	67% (104)	16% (25)	156
Paid Less than $25 in Taxes in 1845	23% (56)	64% (157)	13% (32)	245
Paid $25 or More in Taxes in 1845	44% (88)	52% (103)	4% (7)	198

Notes: Firms were considered to have survived if most or all of their 1845 partners were listed as members of the same firm in the 1850 or 1851 directory. Firms were considered to have dissolved if they were not listed in the 1850 or 1851 directory but at least one of their 1845 members was. If none of the 1845 partners could be located in the 1850 or 1851 directory, the firm was considered to have disappeared. Percentage totals may not equal 100%. Number of cases is indicated within parentheses.

Sources: Boston City Directory, 1840, 1845, 1850, and 1851; Boston, Tax Assessors, "List of Persons, Copartnerships, and Corporations Who Were Taxed Twenty-Five Dollars and Upwards in the City of Boston in the Year 1845," City Doc. 14, 1846.

tory (see Table 3).[37] Large firms were more likely to persist than small ones. Of the firms with more than two partners, 48 percent survived until 1850, whereas only 29 percent of the firms with just two partners did. On average, however, survival rates did not vary much from one type of business to the next. Firms engaged in commerce persisted the five years 32 percent of the time; for partnerships of craftsmen the survival rate was 34 percent. Manufacturing firms fared somewhat better, though their numbers were too small to justify generalization. Of the eleven firms in the sample that were clearly engaged in manufacturing, 5 (45 percent) survived the five-year period.[38]

In 59 percent of the cases it is clear that the firm dissolved between 1845 and 1850, because at least one of the original partners was listed in the 1850 directory as a member of another partnership, as a sole proprietor, or without an occupation.[39] Although it is impossible to tell from the city directories whether the dissolution was caused by failure, the death of a partner, or voluntary agreement, the R. G. Dun records do provide such information. A somewhat larger proportion of the firms in this sample survived over five years, a result that is consistent with the observation that firms listed in the R. G. Dun records were larger on average than those in the city directory. For the Dun sample, 44 percent of the firms for which such a calculation could be made survived from 1850 to 1855.[40] Of those that did not survive, twenty-seven (35 percent) failed, one disappeared from the record, two dissolved as a result of the death of one of the partners, and forty-eight (62 percent) dissolved voluntarily, most likely because the partners no longer wanted to continue in business with one another. In some cases the dissolution was precipitated by losses or other kinds of

37. I am counting as survivors both firms that persisted unchanged from 1845 to 1850 and those that persisted but experienced some minor change in their membership. In order to minimize the effect of errors in coverage by the city directories, I checked the 1851 volume as well as 1850, only counting as missing those firms and partners that were not listed in either 1850 or 1851.

38. Because most of the larger firms (in terms of numbers of partners) were engaged in commerce and survival rates for large firms were higher than for small ones, the survival rate for commercial firms with only two partners was actually below the sample average and below that of craftsmen.

39. In the remaining 9 percent of the cases none of the firms' partners could be found in the 1850 directory. It is likely that these firms had dissolved as well.

40. The calculation included only 139 firms, as 25 had either already left the sample by 1850 or had not yet been organized. Forty-one percent of the firms that survived to 1855 survived to 1860 as well.

Table 4. Distribution of Firms by Number of Partners and the Relationship of Partners, 1845

	No. with 2 Partners	% of Total	No. with 3 Partners	% of Total	No. with 4+ Partners	% of Total	Total No.
All with Different Last Names	311	87%	41	11%	5	1%	357
All with Same Last Name	52	88%	7	12%	0	0%	59
Some with Same Last Name	0	0%	22	81%	5	19%	27
All Partnerships	363	82%	70	16%	10	2%	443

Note: Percentage totals may not equal 100%.

Source: Boston City Directory, 1845.

financial difficulties, but in most cases the R. G. Dun credit reports provide no evidence to support a conclusion that the breakup was precipitated by financial distress. In a few cases, moreover, it is clear that partners removed substantial assets from the firm and used the proceeds to go into business on their own or to join another partnership.

Another striking characteristic of the partnerships in the samples was their composition (see Table 4). Although one might expect, given the risks associated with this form of organization, that partners would tend to be chosen primarily from among kin, the number of firms whose members had the same surname was surprisingly low.[41] For example, in only 13 percent of the cases in the city directory sample did all partners in a firm have the same last name, and in only another 6 percent did at least some partners have the same last name (these, of course, were in firms with more than two partners). All of the partners had different last names in the vast majority (81 percent) of cases. For the R. G. Dun sample, the distribution

41. For a theoretical discussion of the advantages of kinship ties in such situations, see Robert A. Pollak, "A Transaction Cost Approach to Families and Households," *Journal of Economic Literature* 23(1985):581–608.

was similar. In 75 percent of the cases, all of the partners had different last names. In only 17 percent of the cases did all of the partners have the same last name.

Of course, having different last names did not necessarily mean that the partners were unrelated; the individuals involved might have been cousins, or they could have been connected by marriage. In Providence, to give a well-known example, the pioneering textile manufacturing firm of Almy and Brown consisted of merchant Moses Brown and his son-in-law William Almy, as well as cousin Smith Brown. Similarly, the firm Brown and Ives joined two brothers-in-law, Nicholas Brown and Thomas P. Ives.[42] However, in other cases firms brought together individuals not connected by ties of marriage or consanguinity. Brown and Benson, the firm organized by Nicholas Brown to provide apprenticeships for his sons, is a good example, for senior partner George Benson was not a member of the family.[43]

Close examination of the R. G. Dun records suggests that most of the partnerships involving persons with different last names did not involve cousins, in-laws, or any similarly close relationship. Because family members could be called upon to provide badly needed funds for the repayment of debts, the credit reports often included information about partners' relatives. Fifty-six of the 164 cases in the sample included such mentions, but only seven involved links between partners. Of course, lack of mention does not necessarily mean that the other partners were not related to each other. Moreover, even in the case of firms composed of non-relatives it is likely that some kind of personal tie brought the partners together in the first place. It is very unlikely that perfect strangers would have formed partnerships. Nonetheless, the survival rates reported in Table 3 suggest that firms whose partners shared the same last name were in some fundamental way different from those whose partners did not. Only 29 percent of the firms in the latter category persisted to 1850, as opposed to 44 percent of firms in the former. Of the twenty-seven firms in which some, but not all, partners had the same last name, 56 percent survived to 1850. Although the superior record of this last group was in part a consequence of the firms' larger size (in terms of the number of partners), the fact that the survival rate for this category was greater than that for all firms with more

42. Barbara M. Tucker, *Samuel Slater and the Origins of the American Textile Industry, 1790–1860* (Ithaca, 1984), 50; James B. Hedges, *The Browns of Providence Plantations: The Nineteenth Century* (Providence, 1968), 64.

43. James B. Hedges, *The Browns of Providence Plantations: The Colonial Years* (Providence, 1968), 20.

than two partners is further evidence that kinship ties enhanced a firm's chances of survival—and that such ties were not as strong in firms where partners had different last names.[44] In other words, in the vast majority of cases family ties could not be expected to alleviate substantially the risks associated with the partnership form of organization.

The small size of the partnerships in the city directory sample, especially in conjunction with their short time horizons, suggests that any advantage the bulk of these firms had over single proprietorships was modest at best. The subsequent activities of members of firms that did not survive confirm this view. Although some individuals joined new partnerships, others simply continued in business on their own. Only about a quarter of the partners of non-surviving firms who could be traced to the 1850 directory had joined new partnerships by that year. A small number (about 5 or 6 percent) had taken positions as clerks, bookkeepers, officers of corporations, or government officials. But by far the greatest number—about 45 percent of the group—were operating their businesses as single proprietorships.[45]

Why then did so many merchants and craftsmen form partnerships during this period, when the advantages of doing so seemed marginal at best? And why did they join forces in such great numbers with people to whom they appear not to have been closely related? In order to explore these issues, I traced the 979 partners in the 1845 city directory sample back to 1840 to see what resources or capabilities they might have brought to their firms. The hypothesis that firms joined together partners with complementary capabilities is fairly easy to dismiss, because so few of these individuals had experience in other lines of business. Indeed, only about 5 percent of the partners had business interests in 1840 that were clearly different from those they pursued in their 1845 partnerships. Some of the individuals in this small group probably did bring complementary capabilities to their firms. For example, it is likely that a stove firm benefited from the skills of a machinist, a lumber partnership from the knowledge of a former house-

44. The differences between firms whose partners shared the same last name and those in which they did not was also apparent in the R. G. Dun sample. Fifty-five percent of the firms in the former category survived from 1850 to 1855 as opposed to 40 percent of the firms in the latter.

45. The city directory listed no business occupations for the remaining 22 percent Although the absence of information about occupation does not necessarily mean that the men were retired from business (indeed many young men listed without any occupation were functioning as clerks), they certainly were no longer actively involved in partnerships.

wright, and a ship brokerage from that of a former sea captain. In many cases, however, there was no relationship between the occupation in which a partner had previously engaged and the business of his 1845 firm. It is difficult to imagine, for example, what a customs inspector contributed to a music publishing firm, a cook to a partnership of druggists, and a house-wright to a provisions business. More important, 492 of the partners—fully 50 percent—could not be located in the 1840 directory.[46] Although it is possible that some of these individuals were migrants who had obtained considerable business experience in other locales, it is more likely that the vast majority were young men just beginning their careers. In any event, it seems unlikely that any great number of partnerships brought together individuals with significantly different—and complementary—kinds of business experience.[47]

Additional perspective can be gained by looking at the same data from the standpoint of firms, rather than partners. In the case of about a quarter of the firms in the 1845 sample all the partners had been involved in business (of one type or another, alone or in partnership) in 1840. A larger group (38 percent of the cases) consisted of firms in which one or more partners with business experience in 1840 combined with one or more partners not listed in the directory in that year (or listed without any occupation). In yet another large group of cases (35 percent of the total) none of the partners was in business in the city in 1840.

What might these numbers indicate about the reasons for forming partnerships? It seems that many young men (or perhaps simply men who were new to the community) saw the partnership form of organization as a way of entering business. The advantages of such an arrangement from the standpoint of the newcomer were obvious: joining together with one or more individuals who had already acquired local experience, connections, and capital was a good way of making a start. But what might have induced a more established businessman to take on such an inexperienced partner?

46. Three hundred eighty-one of the partners (39 percent) were engaged in the same type of business in 1840 as in 1845. As for the remaining approximately 6 percent, either there was no occupation listed in one of the two years or it was impossible to tell whether the business was the same or not.

47. About 10 percent of the partners who were not listed in the 1840 directory had brief experiences in other businesses in the city between 1840 and 1845. Once again, there was often no relationship between these other businesses and those in which their 1845 partnerships were engaged.

Table 5. Tax Assessments of Partners in 1845, by Occupation

	Avg. Assessment of All Partners (in $)	Avg. Assessment of Partners Paying $25 or More (in $)	% of Partners Paying Less than $25
Listed with an Occupation in the 1840 Directory	7,309	26,819	73%
Listed but with No Occupation in the 1840 Directory	4,084	18,086	78%
Not Listed in the 1840 Directory	730	15,626	95%

Note: The average assessment of all partners is based on the assumption that individuals not paying at least $25 in taxes had no assessed property. The purpose of the calculation is purely heuristic.

Sources: Boston City Directory, 1840 and 1845; Boston, Tax Assessors, "List of Persons."

Although it was possible that newcomers might bring to the firm inherited wealth or the financial backing of family members, it is unlikely that securing capital was the primary motive for taking on junior partners in the majority of cases. Indeed, as Table 5 shows, fully 95 percent of the partners not listed in the 1840 Boston directory paid less than $25 in taxes in 1845 (that is, they owned less than $4,000 worth of real and personal property combined). It is much more likely that junior partners were desired for their labor input—that is, that established partners expected to have too much work to handle by themselves and wanted additional help.[48]

This explanation, however, only raises an additional question: Given the risks associated with partnerships, why did not businessman simply hire

48. Although systematic study is difficult, examination of the R. G. Dun records shows that most junior partners did not bring much if any capital to the firm. Assessments such as "adds little to the responsibility of the firm" were common.

clerks to take up the burden? The answer is that they probably did, though because of problems of undercoverage, one cannot judge the extent of such hiring from the city directories. Only 16 of the 492 partners (3 percent) not found in the 1840 directory were listed as clerks for any enterprise in the city between 1840 and 1845. But this is clearly an underestimate. In order to gauge the magnitude of the problem of undercoverage, I recorded the names of clerks listed in the tax assessors' street-by-street record for one ward in the city (the fourth) in 1844 and then tried to locate these names in the Boston directory for that year. Only 31 out of 176 individuals labeled as clerks in the assessors' records (18 percent) were actually listed as clerks in the Boston directory. Eighty-eight (50 percent) did not appear in the directory at all, and 43 (24 percent) were listed without any occupational designation.[49] Thus it is quite possible that many of the partners who were not listed in the 1840 city directory, or who were included without any occupational designation, were actually working as clerks. The R. G. Dun records confirm this supposition. Credit reports often included background information for men who were admitted to their first partnership. Of the 86 partners for whom such information is available, 45 percent had been employees of the business in which they became partners, and another 22 percent had been employees of other businesses. Only 33 percent were relatives of (or had the same last name as) existing partners, and many of these had also been clerks.

But the willingness of businessmen to take the risk of elevating clerks who were not relatives to the position of partner still requires explanation. It is possible that employers wanted to promote key employees—after a suitable probationary period—because they thought that profit sharing would prevent shirking and induce employees to keep the interests of the firm in the forefront of their minds. As we have already seen, however, other types of profit-sharing contracts were available that could have achieved the same result. Recall B. W. Dodge's agreement with Nathaniel L. White whereby the latter managed the former's store in return for a share of the profits.[50]

49. Most of the rest were listed as having other occupations. In a couple of cases the existence of more than one individual with the same last name precluded identification. The tax assessors' ledgers have recently been removed from the Boston Public Library and are now stored at the Boston City Archives.

50. Bradley v. White, 303. According to Alchian and Demsetz, moreover, the partnership form of organization did not solve the shirking problem. See "Production, Information Costs, and Economic Organization," 777–795.

Another possibility is that employers could only effectively delegate certain types of tasks to a partner, perhaps because customers had a strong preference for dealing with owners rather than with hired hands. Although this hypothesis requires further investigation, it seems an unlikely explanation for the phenomenon. It was precisely their greater status in dealing with customers that made partners such a potential threat to the firm-specific capital of the enterprise—it was a much more serious matter to face competition from a former partner than from a former employee. Moreover, it is difficult to understand why customers would have been reluctant to do business with employees, as a well established body of law gave deals negotiated with agents the same protection that those negotiated with partners enjoyed.[51]

Given the risks associated with granting employees equal standing in a firm, it makes more sense to conceive of the choice as a matter of employee preference in an environment where skilled clerical labor was relatively scarce (or where businesses made substantial investments in their employees to build up firm-specific knowledge and skills). But why might employees prefer partnership contracts to other agreements that enabled them to share in profits without bearing as much risk? One can imagine both economic and non-economic reasons for the choice. With respect to the former, it is possible that employees wanted a say in the direction of the firm so that they could influence the level of profits in which they would share. It is also possible that, for some types of businesses, achieving partnership status was the only way to lay claim to accumulated firm-specific assets such as carefully built up relations with customers.[52]

As for non-economic motives, there is a large literature about the positive value that Americans in this period placed on the independence associated with small proprietorship—and conversely on the negative ways in which they viewed positions of dependence. There is also a growing literature that connects this preference for independence with emerging concepts of masculinity. It may be, therefore, that the popularity of the partnership form of organization during the early nineteenth century resulted more than anything else from young men's abhorrence of relations of de-

51. Indeed, the law of partnerships was articulated in terms of the law of agents. Thus Justice Joseph Story quoted another learned judge: "One partner by virtue of that relation (of partnership) is constituted a general agent for another as to all matters within the scope of the partnership dealings. . . ." Story, *Law of Partnership*, 163–164.

52. I am suggesting, in other words, that it was more difficult for an employee to leave a firm and take customers with him than it was for a partner.

pendence.[53] We know, for example, that men who applied for civil service jobs later in the century were acutely sensitive to the status implications of becoming permanent employees. E. Lac Haskins justified his application for a job in the Census Office in 1890 by claiming, "I have not been lucky in late years in my transactions. . . . I want to go forward again—to go honestly—and it is asked *not* from preference but because at 49 years old I have nearly lost my capital and *must* work as employee instead of doing business for self."[54] According to Cindy Aron, who has studied civil-service employees, such defensiveness was pervasive: "Would-be federal office workers repeatedly apologized for seeking government clerkships, implying that to do so was somehow less than admirable."[55] As one writer put it at the time, a clerk for the federal government had "no independence while in office, no true manhood."[56]

As a result of employees' pressuring for promotion, firms could not meet

53. On clerkships as routes to upward mobility, see Stuart Blumin, *The Emergence of the Middle Class: Social Experience in the American City, 1760–1900* (New York, 1989), 66–137. For a general view of the importance of independence, see Gordon S. Wood, *The Radicalism of the American Revolution* (New York, 1992). For a more specific discussion of economic motivation, see Daniel Vickers, "Competency and Competition: Economic Culture in Early America," *William and Mary Quarterly*, 3d ser., 47(1990):3–29. On the connection between masculinity and independence, see Cindy Sondik Aron, *Ladies and Gentlemen of the Civil Service: Middle Class Workers in Victorian America* (New York, 1987); Mary H. Blewett, *Men, Women, and Work: Class, Gender, and Protest in the New England Shoe Industry, 1780–1910* (Urbana, 1988); and Wayne A. Lewchuk, "Men and Monotony: Fraternalism as a Managerial Strategy at the Ford Motor Company," *Journal of Economic History* 53(1993):824–856.

54. Quoted in Aron, *Ladies and Gentlemen of the Civil Service*, 26.

55. Aron, *Ladies and Gentlemen of the Civil Service*, 34.

56. Quoted in Aron, *Ladies and Gentlemen of the Civil Service*, 36. A handful of high-status occupations serve as exceptions that prove the rule. For example, retiring masters of whaling ships had effectively to be bribed by owners (who feared harm to their vessels) before they were willing to accept the risks associated with partnership. See Lee A. Craig and Charles R. Knoeber, "Manager Shareholding, the Market for Managers, and the End-Period Problem: Evidence from the U.S. Whaling Industry," *Journal of Law, Economics and Organization* 8(1992):607–627. To give another instance, my own research in bank records indicates that young men eagerly sought positions as cashiers. Apparently, the status in the community that derived from control of access to credit offset the disadvantages of employee status.

Upward mobility out of clerkships seems to have been less common in England, but whether this difference was a result of a lack of concern for independence or of the relative abundance of labor is not clear. See, for example, David Lockwood, *The Blackcoated Worker: A Study in Class Consciousness,* 2d ed. (Oxford, Eng., 1989), 19–35.

Table 6. Tax Assessments of Partnerships in 1845, by Partners' Experience

	Avg. Assessment of All Firms (in $)	Avg. Assessment of Firms Paying $25 or More (in $)	% of Firms Paying Less than $25
All Partners Experienced	12,737	22,103	42%
Some Partners Experienced	12,463	24,925	51%
All Partners Inexperienced	2,743	11,808	72%

Notes: The average assessment of all firms is based on the assumption that firms not paying at least $25 in tax had no assessed property. The purpose of the calculation is purely heuristic. A partner was considered experienced if he was listed as engaged in some type of business in 1840.

Sources: Boston City Directory, 1840 and 1845; Boston, Tax Assessors, "List of Persons."

their demands for labor over the long run solely with salaried clerks; after some period of time, they had to offer valued employees a share in the business or else risk losing them to other concerns or to independent proprietorship. If the knowledge and experience these men had accumulated in their jobs made losing them a costly proposition, then firms would have to acquiesce in their desire for promotion to partnership. Nonetheless, as Table 3 shows, firms formed in this manner (that is, firms formed of what I am calling experienced and inexperienced partners) had lower survival rates than partnerships made up entirely of experienced businessmen, even though the average wealth holdings of the two groups of firms were comparable (see Table 6). Judging from the fate of partnerships in the R. G. Dun sample, it is unlikely that all or even most of the non-surviving firms failed. The high rate of dissolution is, however, a good indication that these partnerships did not work well in important ways. Promoting employees to partnerships, in other words, was not always sufficient to keep their expertise within the firm.

What about the 35 percent of the firms in which none of the partners was listed with an occupation in the 1840 directory—that is, in which none of the partners was experienced? It is unlikely that the members of these firms valued each other for their business know-how. Nor does it seem probable that they joined together because they expected to have too much work to handle on their own; new firms are not usually overwhelmed by customers. It is much more likely that a common need for capital brought these partners together. A comparison of Tables 5 and 6 suggests that few of them had the financial resources to go into business on their own, but by pooling their resources they could lay in a minimal stock of goods or purchase essential tools and machinery. Regardless of the risk involved, young men apparently preferred this option to working for someone else as a clerk and hoping to be taken into the business at some point. Although the directories may have missed some instances where men in this group served previously as clerks, it is doubtful that any of them worked for the equally inexperienced men with whom they formed partnerships. Rather, it is more likely that they quit other jobs in order to go into business for themselves.

Firms in this category had the lowest rate of survival. Only 17 percent of the partnerships whose members all lacked experience (that is, who were not listed, or not listed with an occupation, in the 1840 directory) survived until 1850, as opposed to 33 percent of the firms with at least one experienced member and 53 percent of those in which both members had some kind of experience (see Table 3). Again, though it is impossible to tell how many of the firms in these various categories actually failed, we do know that 37 percent of the partners in completely inexperienced firms were not listed in the Boston directory in 1850, compared with 18 percent of the rest of the sample. Disappearance from the city is probably a good proxy if not for failure then for a lack of success. In any event, the dramatically lower survival rates for firms with inexperienced members suggest at the very least that the partnership arrangement did not work satisfactorily for the parties involved.

The popularity of the small partnerships that so many Bostonians formed during the early nineteenth century seems not to have resulted from any real economic advantage that such firms had over single proprietorships, but rather from what the young men involved in them sought to avoid—relations of dependence. If the analysis offered here is correct—and it is important to emphasize that at this point it should be accepted only provisionally—the popularity of partnerships in early-nineteenth-century Boston provides a provocative example of the way in which values can affect business structures.[57] The implications of this conclusion for the operation of the economy, however, are less certain. On the one hand, it is possible to argue that young men's reluctance to accept positions of dependence promoted the formation of firms and hence the competitiveness and dynamism of the economy. Moreover, businessmen working for the success of their own firms may have been more innovative than those working for others. In a period when the skills necessary for invention were widely available, the preference for independent proprietorship may thus have operated as a stimulus to technical change.[58] On the other hand, it is possible to argue that young men's reluctance to serve as clerks beyond a probationary period increased the instability of firms and thus inhibited the accumulation over time of the firm-specific capabilities that recent research has suggested are so important for success.[59] The same reluctance also may have kept the size of individual businesses small. In effect, the only way that firms could grow was by taking on new partners, but the difficulties and risks associated with the partnership form of organization worked to limit this avenue of expansion. Not only were partnerships generally small, but relatively few of them survived even five years. The main exceptions, as we have seen, were those firms that joined together partners with the same last name. Presumably the familiarity and discipline that

57. One point to bear in mind is the small number of manufacturing firms in the sample. Kenneth L. Sokoloff found a statistically significant relationship between the size of manufacturing firms and multiple ownership for the early 19th century, suggesting that increasing the number of partners added to the capital of the firm. He also found that New England firms were more likely to have multiple owners than firms elsewhere in the Northeast, suggesting the existence of a strong regional effect. Both findings indicate that caution is in order in generalizing beyond Boston from the results of this article. See "Industrialization and the Growth of the Manufacturing Sector in the Northeast, 1820–1850" (Ph.D. diss., Harvard Univ., 1982), 270–277.

58. On the widespread availability of technological knowledge and the patterns of invention that resulted, see Kenneth L. Sokoloff, "Inventive Activity in Early Industrial America: Evidence from Patent Records, 1790–1846," *Journal of Economic History* 48(1988):813–850; and Sokoloff and B. Zorina Khan, "The Democratization of Invention During Early Industrialization: Evidence from the United States, 1790–1846," *Journal of Economic History* 50(1990):363–378.

59. See, for example, Richard R. Nelson and Sidney G. Winter, *An Evolutionary Theory of Economic Change* (Cambridge, Mass., 1982).

family ties embodied helped to overcome the limitations of the partnership form. Before the size of firms could increase significantly, therefore, ways had to be found to acculturate men to positions of dependence. In the second half of the century changing conditions would require firms to face this challenge.[60]

60. See Angel Kwolek-Folland, *Engendering Business: Men and Women in the Corporate Office, 1870–1950* (Baltimore, 1994); Landry, "Corporate Incentives for Managers," 39–41; and Aron, *Ladies and Gentlemen of the Civil Service*, 139–161.

John Quincy Adams (1767–1848), 1826. Engraved by Asher B. Durand after Thomas Sully. Collection of the Massachusetts Historical Society.

The Politics of Honor: The Massachusetts Conservative Elite and the Trials of Amalgamation, 1824–1829

Harlow W. Sheidley

WHEN WORD REACHED Boston that the House of Representatives had elected John Quincy Adams sixth president of the United States, cannons "announced the welcome news," and " 'Night was turned into day' "[1] as citizens congratulated one another for having given "a second President to the Union."[2] On inauguration day, the wealthy conservative business and professional elite of Massachusetts led Boston, the state, and all New England in celebration, hosting an elaborate dinner at Faneuil Hall. Adorned with a triumphal arch, the room was festooned with flags, eagles, flowers, shrubs, trees, birds, banners, portraits, and statues marking Adams's ascendancy and the great men and events of the state's and nation's history. Official odes and toasts suggested that Adams's election provided "new proof of the moral weight of New England."[3]

That the Massachusetts conservatives hosted this banquet is surely ironic. They had never forgiven Adams for his apostasy in supporting Jeffersonian policies, including the embargo, which had directly threatened their economic interests. However, the sectional pride evinced at this celebration had been a principal factor in their support of his candidacy. Chafing under the sway of the Virginia Dynasty and still suffering from national opprobrium for their sponsorship of the ill-timed Hartford Convention,

1. Edward Cruft[?] to [James?] Lloyd, Feb. 16, 1825, Adams Papers, Massachusetts Historical Society, microfilm ed., reel 467.

2. Joseph E. Sprague to John Quincy Adams, Feb. 15, 1824 [i.e., 1825], Adams Papers, reel 467.

3. [Boston] *Columbian Centinel*, Mar. 5, 1825; *Independent Chronicle & Boston Patriot*, Mar. 5, 1825; *National Aegis* (Worcester, Mass.), Mar. 9, 1825; and "Odes for the Fourth of March," Adams Papers, reel 468.

the elite had come to believe that for sectional reasons it was "a matter of necessity to support" Adams.[4]

More than sectional pride was at stake, however. Political power was a necessary adjunct to the Massachusetts conservatives' status and economic well-being. Centering around approximately forty interlocking families, such as the Lowells, the Perkinses, the Otises, and the Lawrences, based in Boston and Essex County, this privileged group was still in the process of consolidating in the 1820s. Its fortunes had largely originated in commerce, but in this decade it was laying the foundations of American industrial capitalism by establishing textile factories throughout New England. Through business, kinship, political, and communications networks, this same elite also dominated Massachusetts's banking, legal system, professions, and cultural and charitable organizations. Through the Federalist party, this group had long controlled state politics.[5]

Political power, in turn, had buttressed the elite's economic power. At the national level, spokesmen had tirelessly promoted policies that favored their commercial enterprises, such as establishing favorable tonnage duties, tariffs, and a national banking system. Political power at the state and local levels was no less crucial to their economic success. The state legislature, for example, granted bank charters and thereby had the ability not only to facilitate elite banking enterprises but also to block the aspirations of rivals. Control of Boston's newly created municipal government helped them in their real estate ventures and in numerous other ways.[6]

Despite such obvious power, the conservatives' continued rule was not assured in the 1820s. The transfer of their capital from commerce to industry occurred during these years and created a temporary division in elite ranks over protective tariffs. Initially the conservatives had united in favor of free trade. Thus, not surprisingly, when Congress debated the tariff of

4. Ezekiel Webster to Daniel Webster, Jan. 28, 1822, Charles M. Wiltse et al., eds., *The Papers of Daniel Webster: Correspondence* (Hanover, N.H., 1974–1986), 1:304 (hereafter cited as *DWPC*).

5. For general discussions of the Boston elite in the early national period, see Robert F. Dalzell, *Enterprising Elite: The Boston Associates and the World They Made* (Cambridge, Mass., 1987), passim; Frederic C. Jaher, *The Urban Establishment: Upper Strata in Boston, New York, Charleston, Chicago, and Los Angeles* (Urbana, Ill., 1982), 15–156; and Harlow W. Sheidley, "Sectional Nationalism: The Culture and Politics of the Massachusetts Conservative Elite, 1815–1836" (Ph.D. diss., Univ. of Connecticut, 1990), vii–viii, 27–44, and passim.

6. Jaher, *Urban Establishment*, 26–29.

1824, Daniel Webster, in consultation with Thomas Handasyd Perkins, Israel Thorndike, Nathan Appleton, Amos Lawrence, and others, vigorously opposed it in Congress.[7] But by 1827, the elite had split over this issue. In anticipation of more tariff legislation in 1828, Henry Lee communicated with such influential southern free-traders as Robert Y. Hayne and George McDuffie[8] and wrote a pamphlet against protection in behalf of Bostonians opposed to the tariff.[9] Meanwhile, however, Abbott Lawrence attended the Harrisburg convention composed of delegates from thirteen states whose purpose was to devise a high-tariff strategy.[10] In a political shift that reflected the movement of capital into industry, Webster actively supported the tariff of 1828 in the Senate, but in so doing, he did not please all of his constituents. His supporters held a public dinner in his honor in Boston on June 5, designed "to keep him up against the outcry of the mercantile interest," who nonetheless "very generally declined any participation in the affair."[11] As late as 1830, conservatives remained divided over the tariff. Lee and Appleton ran against each other for Congress, with Appleton and protection finally defeating Lee and free trade.[12]

The elite's overriding unity of economic interests based on the interlocking nature of their enterprises and the continued flow of capital into industry, however, predicated their eventual political cohesion on matters of policy. As National Republicans and, later, Whigs, they would support the "American System"—a sound national bank that sustained a uniform currency, a protective tariff to promote domestic industries, and state and federal support for internal improvements—designed to foster the expansion of the market economy. Jacksonian attacks on an activist federal government only solidified elite agreement on policy issues. By 1832, then, the

7. Maurice G. Baxter, *One and Inseparable: Daniel Webster and the Union* (Cambridge, Mass., 1984), 105–106.

8. See Nathaniel Silsbee to Thomas W. Ward, Dec. 22, 1827, box 2, Thomas Wren Ward Papers, Massachusetts Historical Society; Nathaniel Goddard et al. to Robert Hayne, Dec. 5, 1827, copy, Ward Papers bound vol.; and George McDuffie to [Henry Lee?], Jan. 20, 1828, box 3, Lee Family Papers, Massachusetts Historical Society.

9. Henry Lee, *Report of a Committee of the Citizens of Boston and Vicinity, Opposed to a Further Increase of Duties on Importations* (Boston, 1827).

10. Edward Stanwood, *American Tariff Controversies in the Nineteenth Century* (1903; reprint, New York, 1967), 1:263–265.

11. Charles F. Adams to J. Q. Adams, June 10, 1828, Adams Papers, reel 486.

12. Thomas H. O'Connor, *Lords of the Loom: The Cotton Whigs and the Coming of the Civil War* (New York, 1968), 35.

Boston conservatives knew what they were against as well as what they were for.[13]

Such temporary internal division over specific policies did not constitute the greatest challenge to the elite's continued rule. As a group, they were deeply suspicious of competitive popular politics and remained wed to a hierarchical, organic, and deferential social and political ethos that held that those at the social apex were to resolve conflicts, proclaim truth, and rule in the best interests of those below. Yet, as these conservative business and professional leaders well understood, their values were increasingly suspect in a democratizing political culture. Not only had they been proscribed nationally, they faced popular insurrection at home. The market revolution, of which they were at the forefront, was generating cultural, political, and economic conflict among classes as the cash nexus penetrated traditional relationships, disrupting forever the household economy of yeoman and artisan alike.[14] Thus in 1820, the nascent "Middling Interest," a coalition of disaffected Federalist tradesmen and mechanics with whom the Republicans allied, realizing that their economic interests were antithetical to those of the conservative elite, had campaigned against and defeated Boston's incumbent Federalist board of selectmen and had gone on to mount a serious if unsuccessful challenge to the Federalist congressional candidate for the Suffolk County seat in the fall.[15] The conservatives successfully beat back the forces of reform in the state constitutional convention of 1820–1821[16] and authored Boston's municipal charter in

13. See, for example, Baxter, *One and Inseparable*, chaps. 12 and 14. For a general discussion of conservative values and programs, see Daniel Walker Howe, *The Political Culture of the American Whigs* (Chicago, 1979), esp. chaps. 1–3, 5, and 9.

14. See, for example, John L. Brooke, *The Heart of the Commonwealth: Society and Political Culture in Worcester County, Massachusetts, 1713–1861* (Cambridge, 1989), esp. chaps. 9 and 10; Christopher Clark, *The Roots of Rural Capitalism: Western Massachusetts, 1780–1860* (Ithaca, N.Y., 1990), esp. part 4; Paul G. Faler, *Mechanics and Manufacturers in the Early Industrial Revolution: Lynn, Massachusetts, 1780–1860* (Albany, N.Y., 1981), chaps. 9 and 10; Allan Kulikoff, *The Agrarian Origins of American Capitalism* (Charlottesville, Va., 1992), chap. 1; Jonathan Prude, *The Coming of Industrial Order: Town and Factory Life in Rural Massachusetts, 1810–1860* (Cambridge, 1983), parts 2 and 3; and Charles Sellers, *The Market Revolution: Jacksonian America, 1815–1846* (Oxford, 1991), chap. 1, and passim.

15. Andrew R. L. Cayton, "The Fragmentation of 'A Great Family': The Panic of 1819 and the Rise of the Middling Interest in Boston, 1818–1822," *Journal of the Early Republic* 2(1982):150–152.

16. Harlow W. Sheidley, "Preserving 'The Old Fabrick': The Massachusetts Conserva-

1822. But they failed to install Harrison Gray Otis as the city's first mayor, and they lost control of state government in the gubernatorial election of 1823, when the Republican William Eustis defeated Otis. Eustis's reelection the following year confirmed the Republicans' hold on the state and signaled the demise of Bay State Federalism.[17]

The elite's support of Adams thus represented in part a pragmatic response to these political defeats and the disintegration of the Federalist party. If the conservatives' values and economic policies were to be upheld nationally, they needed to fashion a new vehicle to power and a stable base at home from which to operate. Further, the need for unity among the elite would be rendered even more urgent in the coming decade. During the 1830s, the Democratic and Workingmen's parties, among others, gave voice to social, political, and economic discontent spawned by the expanding market economy and emerging industrial order. Those who upheld the traditional culture and economy and who desired a more egalitarian society as well as those who embraced the market revolution but wished to broaden opportunity to gain access to power themselves mounted serious campaigns against the conservatives' continued hegemony.[18] Amalgamation, or fusion, with moderate Republicans was the elite's chosen strategy to maintain their political power. Nor was their support of Adams entirely hypocritical. Adams partook deeply of the conservative ethos. As president, he promulgated a program of national development compatible with elite economic interests, while advocating social hierarchy, reciprocity, and moral stewardship.[19] Adams's "manly & honourable" course fully vindicated New England conservatism.[20]

Yet in four short years Adams was driven from office, his New England precepts and program rejected by the nation. Even more foreboding for

---

tive Elite and the Constitutional Convention of 1820–1821," *Proceedings of the Massachusetts Historical Society* 103(1991):114–137.

17. Ronald P. Formisano, *The Transformation of Political Culture: Massachusetts Parties, 1790s–1840s* (New York, 1983), 120–123.

18. Formisano, *Transformation of Political Culture*, chaps. 10 and 12; Sellers, *Market Revolution*, passim; and Arthur B. Darling, *Political Changes in Massachusetts, 1824–1848: A Study of Liberal Movements in Politics* (New Haven, Conn., 1925), passim.

19. See, for example, John Quincy Adams, "Inaugural Address" and "First Annual Message," James D. Richardson, ed., *A Compilation of the Messages and Papers of the Presidents, 1789–1897* (Washington, D.C., 1896–1899), 2:294–317.

20. Jeremiah Mason to Joseph Story, Dec. 17, 1825, Joseph Story Papers, William Clements Library, University of Michigan, Ann Arbor, microfilm ed., reel 2 (hereafter cited as Story Papers, UM).

the strategy of amalgamation, his presidency closed in a bitter public dispute with the Massachusetts elite that was symptomatic of the limitations of their political culture. Although the conservatives did indeed regain control of state government through the fusion National Republican party following the election of Levi Lincoln, Jr., as governor in 1825, their political standing was always more insecure than is sometimes assumed.[21]

Despite the strong economic interests shared by the conservative elite, the process of party realignment in Massachusetts was very uneven in its progress, as former partisan foes competed with one another for place and advancement within the new party structure, visiting political instability on the Bay State during Adams's four years in office and threatening the conservatives' rule. Finally, however, the difficulties of amalgamation and party realignment derived less from such obvious structural problems than they did from the elite's loyalty to a traditional concept of politics in which personal honor and rectitude of character, not simply effective advocacy of class interests, were equivalent to political merit.

Adams's concept of public office epitomized the elite's perception of the political process. He maintained that the federal government was a matter of "personal consideration and influence," in which public officials were elected on the basis of "Reputation." The government was then organized as in a "pyramid, at the point of which was the chief, under whom men of high consideration, though not equal to his, naturally found their places." Officials were sorted by such attributes as age, experience, and merit into their appropriate ranks in this ruling hierarchy.[22] Holding such a view of the government, Adams and fellow members of the elite inevitably conceived politics not so much as dispassionate competition between two parties and two contending programs but as a highly personal process that reflected one's own status, character, and principles. Significantly, Adams believed that the presidential election entailed nothing less than a national referendum on all his personal and public attributes, arguing that "failure of success" would constitute "a vote of censure by the nation."[23] If elections were judgments of personal merit and probity, it followed that the elite perceived the opposition to be motivated by envy and bent on destroying one's

21. See, for example, Formisano, *Transformation of Political Culture*, 81–82, 123–127; and Richard P. McCormick, *The Second American Party System: Party Formation in the Jacksonian Era* (Chapel Hill, 1966), 41–49.

22. Charles F. Adams, ed., *Memoirs of John Quincy Adams, Comprising Portions of His Diary from 1795 to 1848* (Philadelphia, 1874–1877), 6:245–246 (Feb. 4, 1824).

23. Adams, *Memoirs*, 6:323–324 (May 8, 1824).

reputation. Thus Adams maintained that the "secret history" of Monroe's administration amounted to "one continued series of intrigues" to deprive him of the presidency. To this end, politicians had engaged "in crying me down and disgracing me in the estimation of the people."[24]

This association of politics with character was inherent in the political culture of the elite, and such backward-looking attitudes and values ultimately proved the major barrier to their unity, hindering their political success. Ironically, they had attained their high status partly because their fathers had thrived in an older political culture where such values had obtained. But for amalgamation to proceed smoothly and successfully in the 1820s, conservatives needed to abandon their conception of politics as moral justification and character approbation and recognize that only a harmonious party could effectively expand their power and promote their business interests. This they were unable to do. Instead, their highly developed sense of political honor embroiled them in verbal duels over familiar issues that had formerly divided them, forcing them to rush to the bar of public opinion in an unceasing quest for vindication. Entangled in the imperatives of their political style, the elite finally turned on Adams, attacking his character, motives, and politics even as he was rejected by the nation at large.

Even without the elite's highly moralistic and traditional perception of politics, party realignment in Massachusetts would have been a difficult process. The conservatives had not needed to forge a new party vehicle so long as the Federalists retained control of state politics, yet they lacked discretion in failing to prepare for the day when their hold on state government would be challenged, and cooperation and conciliation would be required. Their insistence that Otis be the gubernatorial nominee in 1823 created a reservoir of ill-will among Republicans, further impeding amalgamation. For many he personified high Federalism and the "treason" of the Hartford Convention, the religious tyranny of the Unitarians, and the arrogance and oppression of the Boston aristocracy.[25]

24. J. Q. Adams to L. C. Adams, Oct. 7, 1822, Worthington C. Ford, ed., *Writings of John Quincy Adams*, (New York, 1913–1917), 7:315–318.

25. For analyses of the election, see Formisano, *Transformation of Political Culture*, 120–123; Samuel E. Morison, *The Life and Letters of Harrison Gray Otis, Federalist: 1765–1848* (Boston, 1913), 2:240–244; and William G. McLoughlin, *New England Dissent, 1630–1833: The Baptists and the Separation of Church and State* (Cambridge, Mass., 1971), 2:1197–1205.

Adams's own candidacy created other hurdles to amalgamation. His problematic political identity as a Republican who had once been a Federalist made him a particularly vulnerable national candidate and fueled local partisan squabbles. Recognizing that "the presence of the Federalists . . . [would] do much more hurt than good," Adams insisted that he be nominated for president in Massachusetts only by Republicans.[26] Accordingly, exclusively Republican caucuses first endorsed Adams, then nominated him, and finally put forth a ticket of strictly Republican electors "pledged" to him, leaving state Federalists with no public role in the presidential campaign.[27] In response, Daniel Webster and others advised Federalists to withhold support from Adams until it was actually needed, hoping that such leverage would eventually earn them influence within a new party structure based on amalgamation. Accordingly, when the contested election went before the House, Webster, in return for interceding on Adams's behalf, extracted a "pledge" from Adams that he would not proscribe Federalists from his administration. Webster thus signaled Massachusetts and New England Federalists to unite with moderate Republicans and tie their own political futures to the success of amalgamation.[28]

Understanding Webster perfectly, Bay State Federalists took the lead in joining with Adams Republicans to form a conservative party of "all good men."[29] Several weeks after Adams's victory in the House, a Federalist caucus endorsed the Republican nominees for governor and lieutenant governor.[30] The Federalists' goal in so doing was to sustain those "things which as public men, we most value." Federalist leaders could support Levi Lincoln, Jr., precisely because he was now "ready to maintain sound princi-

26. William Plumer, Jr., to William Plumer, Jan. 3, 1822, Everett S. Brown, ed., *The Missouri Compromises and Presidential Politics, 1820–1825: From the Letters of William Plumer, Junior, Representative from New Hampshire* (1926; reprint, New York, 1970), 70–75, 74. See also Adams, *Memoirs*, 5:478 (Jan. 3, 1822).

27. See *Independent Chronicle & Boston Patriot*, Jan. 25, 1823, and June 16, 1824; P. P. F. Degrand to J. Q. Adams, Jan. 17, 1824; P. P. F. Degrand to J. Q. Adams, Jan. 22, 1824; William C. Jarvis to John Adams, Jan. 24, 1824; and William C. Jarvis to J. Q. Adams, Jan. 24, 1824, all in Adams Papers, reel 464.

28. For Webster's role in this election, see Shaw Livermore, Jr., *The Twilight of Federalism: The Disintegration of the Federalist Party, 1815–1830* (Princeton, N.J., 1962), 172–196; Baxter, *One and Inseparable*, 109–118; and Irving H. Bartlett, *Daniel Webster* (New York, 1978), 103–107.

29. James T. Austin to H. G. Otis, Apr. 7, 1820, Harrison Gray Otis Papers, Massachusetts Historical Society, microfilm ed., reel 7.

30. Darling, *Political Changes*, 46; *Independent Chronicle and Boston Patriot*, Feb. 19, 1825; and *Salem* [Mass.] *Gazette*, Feb. 18, 1825.

ples," having cured his "democratic itching" by serving on the state's supreme court for a year.[31] Past differences, conservatives assured one another, were merely of historical interest; the "principles" of the two parties "are identical in relation to future measures and policy."[32] And in this election, the amalgamation movement prevailed.[33]

Despite this achievement, and Lincoln's subsequent victories, the process of party realignment did not proceed easily and smoothly. Rather, it was agonizing and complex. Not only did Federalists and Republicans have to sort themselves out into National Republicans and Democrats, but splinter and single-issue groups like the Free Bridge party, the Lottery party, and the Mill Dam party constantly disrupted political equilibrium. Nor were party personnel firmly fixed within these various factions. At any given election the same individual might appear on two or three otherwise mutually exclusive tickets. William Sullivan was surely not alone in lamenting, "I do not know of what side I am—nor of what side anybody is—nor who is up—nor who is down," or in his amazement that "Washington federalists are spreading their garments for Jeffersonian Democrats to walk upon—while the Demos say we want no such auxiliaries."[34]

Adding to the difficulties of party formation, former Federalists and Republicans within the amalgamation movement frequently disagreed over issues of patronage and office—ultimately over which faction would benefit from and retain control of the new party as it was coming into existence. Intense competition for office and patronage among supposed allies had potentially disastrous implications for elite aspirations. For example, in the state elections of April 1825, not only were three senatorial tickets— Federalist, Union, and Democratic—generally offered with overlapping personnel, which was confusing enough,[35] but protest was strident and vocal over the composition of the amalgamation, or Union, tickets, with both Federalists and Republicans seeking the advantage. One paper praised the decision to include candidates from both old parties, observing that "the

31. Isaac Parker to Daniel Webster, Feb. 19, [1825], in Wiltse, *DWPC*, 2:26–28, 26.

32. *Salem* [Mass.] *Gazette*, Apr. 1, 1825.

33. Formisano, *Transformation of Political Culture*, 81–83; and Darling, *Political Changes*, 46.

34. William Sullivan to William Tudor, Sept. 10, 1826, "Manuscripts—Large," Massachusetts Historical Society.

35. *Boston Courier*, Apr. 6, 1825. Compare the Republican ticket for Essex District given in the *Essex Register* (Salem, Mass.), Mar. 21, 1824, to the Union ticket given in the *Salem* [Mass.] *Gazette*, Mar. 25, 1825.

only subject in controversy is the preference which is given to particular individuals."³⁶ Precisely the point.

The ramifications of such political strife stood fully revealed in the elections for the state legislature in April and May of 1827, when the popular vote failed to decide some races. For example, in the conservative bastion of Suffolk County, four of Boston's six senate seats had to be filled by legislative vote because a plethora of competing tickets practically assured that no candidate could win a majority of ballots cast.³⁷ In response, amalgamation leaders in Boston reorganized their party, purging county and ward committees of any Jacksonians in anticipation of the May elections for the lower house,³⁸ but to no avail. Once again voters faced a confusing array of tickets,³⁹ and only eight candidates received the majority of votes required to claim victory, leaving Boston severely underrepresented in the legislature the ensuing year.⁴⁰ Conservatism had not yet found a satisfactory vehicle for its expression in the political arena.

Webster's election to the United States Senate by the state legislature that same year was a welcome and notable victory for the elite's strategy.⁴¹ Nonetheless, the circumstances of that election, coupled with the recent spring election difficulties, suggest that the conservative coalition remained highly unstable. The amalgamationists' choice for senator ultimately came down to Lincoln, the governor under whom fusion had originally succeeded and whom Adams backed,⁴² and the Federalist war-horse Webster, amalgamation's symbol and spokesman in the United States House of Representatives. The legislature could be counted on to support a fusion nomi-

36. *Massachusetts Spy and Worcester Advertiser*, Mar. 30, 1825.

37. I calculated that at least five tickets were offered, including two Republican tickets, one Federal Republican ticket, one Amalgamation ticket, and one Free Bridge ticket. See *Boston Courier*, Apr. 2, 1827; *Independent Chronicle & Boston Patriot*, Mar. 31, 1827; [Boston] *American Statesman and City Register*, Mar. 24 and Apr. 3, 1827; and *Boston Daily Advertiser*, Mar. 16 and 30 and Apr. 2, 1827.

38. Edward Everett to Henry Clay, Apr. 22, 1827, letterbook copy, Edward Everett Papers, Massachusetts Historical Society, microfilm ed., reel 25. See also Edward Everett to John Binnes [i.e., Binns], Apr. 22, 1827, letterbook copy, Everett Papers, reel 25; and *Boston Daily Advertiser*, Apr. 19, 21, 23, and May 8, and 10, 1827.

39. See *Boston Courier*, May 10, 1827.

40. Boston was entitled to 30 representatives. For victors, see *Boston Daily Advertiser*, May 12, 1827. In the run-off election no candidate from any party received the required majority; *Boston Daily Advertiser*, May 18, 1827.

41. Webster was elected by both houses overwhelmingly on June 7, 1827, receiving nearly 2/3 of the votes of each. See George T. Curtis, *Life of Daniel Webster* (New York, 1870), 1:296, n. 1; and Baxter, *One and Inseparable*, 139.

42. Adams, *Memoirs*, 7:141–142 (Aug. 11, 1826).

nee.[43] Through his services on behalf of Adams, Webster had, in a sense, earned the seat.[44] Yet amalgamation leaders remained uneasy. Some Republicans, they reasoned, would support Webster as a former Federalist who could keep his "Federal friends" in line.[45] But others were sure to oppose his selection precisely because of his Federalist affiliations, thereby putting the existence of the coalition at risk.[46] Furthermore, Webster had deeply offended some Federalists by his zealous promotion of fusion, and his election could well alienate those very extremists that the more pragmatic conservatives sought to rein in.[47]

The amalgamation party ultimately selected Webster as its candidate, having reached the conclusion that to lose Lincoln as governor would be to risk the party's disintegration over the choice of his successor. Party leaders realized that electing Webster's successor in Congress also appeared "quite too hazardous to be attempted,"[48] and indeed, despite the fusion leaders' understanding that a former Republican would fill Webster's vacant House seat, the legislature elected the Federalist Benjamin Gorham over both the fusion and Jacksonian candidates, creating further disarray in amalgamation ranks.[49]

Nonetheless, sectional and economic interests together provided a greater degree of cohesion among fusionists in 1828 than at any previous time. When they denounced the Jacksonian "cry against New England" and rallied behind Adams out of a "just regard to our own rights and duties,"[50] amalgamationists could claim a party victory in the state elections as never before. In Essex County, for example, only two senate tickets were

43. Daniel Webster to Henry Clay, May 18, 1827, Wiltse, *DWPC*, 2:202–204; and Darling, *Political Changes*, 53.

44. For Webster's role as administration spokesman, see Baxter, *One and Inseparable*, chaps. 8 and 9.

45. J. E. Sprague to Edward Everett, May 9, 1827, Everett Papers, reel 2. See also Edward Everett, Diary, May 7, 1827, Everett Papers, reel 36.

46. Amalgamation Republicans faced the charge that they had sold out to Federalism in the local elections of 1827. See [Boston] *Massachusetts Journal*, Mar. 10, 1827; and Edward Everett to Joseph E. Sprague, May 8, 1827, letterbook copy, Everett Papers, reel 25.

47. Edward Everett to [J. Q. Adams], May 21, 1827, Adams Papers, reel 480.

48. Nathaniel Silsbee to Henry Clay, May 23, 1827, in Curtis, *Webster*, 1:298–299. Lincoln's unpopular veto of the Warren Bridge doubtless contributed to the choice of Webster. See Formisano, *Transformation of Political Culture*, 193–195.

49. See *Boston Courier*, July 16 and 23, 1827; [Boston] *Massachusetts Journal*, July 21, 1827; and *Independent Chronicle & Boston Patriot*, July 28, 1827.

50. Daniel Webster, "Dinner at Faneuil Hall [June 5, 1828]," *The Writings and Speeches of Daniel Webster*, National ed. (Boston, 1903), 2:11–24, 22–24.

offered,[51] and the entire Union ticket won with no seats left contested.[52] In the county's races for state representative, the victory was not as complete, but the Union ticket again predominated.[53] Suffolk County voters faced a confusing array of tickets, as they had in previous years,[54] but in notable contrast to the events of 1827, the entire Administration Amalgamation senatorial ticket won,[55] and the party was triumphant in the representative election as well.[56] Adams's own campaign reflected the party realignment in his home state. Unlike that of 1824, the legislative caucus of June 1828 supported him without distinction of party. Republican Thomas L. Winthrop and Federalist Samuel Lathrop headed the list as electors at large. Republican leaders such as H. A. S. Dearborn and Joseph E. Sprague and Federalist stalwarts such as Leverett Saltonstall and Abbott Lawrence served on the central committee.[57] Adams entered this election backed by a solid local coalition.

Despite this apparent triumph of amalgamation, which resulted in the control of Massachusetts politics by the newly-christened National Republicans, and Adams's victory within the state, amalgamation had not yet provided the elite with a political vehicle that could reliably sustain their power at home and effectively promote their values nationally. Adams's local victory belied the chaos that had engulfed state politics during his entire presidential term. Such political instability was perhaps an inevitable accompaniment to amalgamation and party realignment. Disputes over patronage and party tickets reflected the inherent competition among ambitious rivals for preferment within a new party structure. But such disputes were also symptomatic of a much more serious impediment to elite cohesion. An impassioned and debilitating debate about the past motives, actions, and principles of the Federalist and Republican parties stalled fusion in Massachusetts at crucial moments. And this debate, in turn, was emblematic of the liabilities of the elite's political ethos in a democratizing political culture.

Participants in this debate over the recent past were trying to define and defend prior political divisions, divisions which they were convinced rested on principles and individual character. Controversies from the recent past

51. *Salem* [Mass.] *Gazette*, Mar. 28 and Apr. 1, 1828.
52. *Salem* [Mass.] *Gazette*, Apr. 8, 1828.
53. *Salem* [Mass.] *Gazette*, May 13 and 16, 1828.
54. *Boston Statesman*, Apr. 3, 1828; and *Boston Courier*, Apr. 7, 1828.
55. *Boston Courier*, Apr. 10, 1828.
56. *Boston Statesman*, May 10, 1828.
57. [Boston] *Massachusetts Journal*, June 14, 1828.

were particularly disruptive to the quest for cohesion because of the significance these conservatives attached to history. To them, the historical record represented much more than a simple catalog of disputes over policies
and issues. They viewed history in the traditional manner as a compendium
of moral lessons, or as *"Philosophy teaching by Example."*[58] Individuals
read history to discover wise principles of behavior for men and nations
that could be applied to the present. In this process, the reader could not
remain neutral but had to make judgments about past actions and especially the historical actors themselves. On these judgments the present and
future well-being of the nation depended. History, then, was not only a
laboratory wherein to dissect the past, but also an indispensable guide to
the future. The highest of moral dramas, its lessons could not be ignored,
but compelled action.[59] This moral view of history colored the conservatives' perception of present politics as well. Because history demonstrated
that even a malefactor remained "true to his character" though "false to
everything else,"[60] one's political behavior, past and present, was indicative
of one's intrinsic merit and probity. Campaigns therefore became moral
combats in which one defended his own record and attacked that of his
opponent, with history providing the materials to guarantee one's own fame
while blasting the opposition to lasting infamy.[61] The elite's conception of
history's uniquely moral purposes and their highly personal perception of
political transactions combined to lock them into an endless debate over
the recent past that undermined the unity they needed in order to attain
their larger political goals.

The record of past inter- and intra-party conflict, which the elite ran-
sacked in their quest for personal vindication, would have proved sufficiently divisive without the moral imperatives they attached to it. It included the bitter rivalry between the fledgling Federalist and Republican
parties of the 1790s. It also embraced the feud between John Adams and
the "high Federalists" that had led to his defeat in 1800, the flirtation with

58. J. Q. Adams to C. F. Adams, Feb. 18, 1822, letterbook copy, Adams Papers, reel 147.

59. For a good statement of this historical purpose see [William Sullivan], "Preface to
the Second Edition," *Familiar Letters on Public Characters, and Public Events, from the
Peace of 1783, to the Peace of 1815,* 2d ed. (Boston, 1834), [v]–xv.

60. J. Q. Adams to C. F. Adams, Jan. 13, 1829, letterbook copy, Adams Papers, reel 148.

61. See J. Q. Adams to G. W. Adams, Nov. 19, 1826, letterbook copy, Adams Papers, reel
148; Timothy Pickering, *Review of the Correspondence Between the Honourable John
Adams, Late President of the United States, and the Late William Cunningham, Esquire
Beginning in 1803, and Ending in 1812* (Salem, Mass., 1824), 4–5; William Plumer to J. Q.
Adams, Sept. 1, 1830; and William Plumer, Jr., to J. Q. Adams, Sept. 16, 1830, both in
Adams Papers, reel 492.

secession carried on by some Federalists during Jefferson's presidency, Massachusetts's resistance to the embargo, and the Hartford Convention. This record of bitter divisions and sectional excesses was in itself damaging to elite cohesion.

However delighted the Massachusetts conservatives were at the prospect of a native son in the White House, John Quincy Adams's candidacy and presidency were destined to broaden the controversy over the past. As a living symbol of former divisions both within Federalist ranks and between Federalists and Republicans, Adams could only have created hardships for all his followers. Because he was the son of the second president, he and his Federalist supporters had to meet the charge that his father had willfully destroyed the Federalist party to satisfy his own ambition. And because he himself had left the Federalist party to support the dreaded Jefferson, Adams and his followers in both parties had to counter the accusation that he was a political sycophant lacking any principles whatsoever. As Rufus King, a former leader of Massachusetts Federalism, predicted, if Adams were elected, "all of N. England that is virtuous or enlightened, will be persecuted & degraded; manners, laws, principles will be changed and deteriorated."[62]

Adams's first presidential campaign in Massachusetts took place within the context of an historical debate between Federalists and Republicans over Federalist intentions in calling the Hartford Convention. This strident argument was not precipitated by Adams's candidacy but was generated by Otis's bid for the office of governor in 1823. Eventually, Otis was defeated, pulled down by the Hartford Convention, which hung "like a Mill stone round . . . [his] neck."[63] In his inaugural address, Governor Eustis continued the Republican offensive, attacking the Federalists' insidious sectional politics and treasonous motives, while maintaining that the Republican victory had "redeemed" the state's reputation.[64]

The Republicans thus guaranteed that the Hartford Convention would again be a central issue in the gubernatorial campaign of 1824, keeping alive the destructive flames of historical controversy. In response, the Federalist party appealed to voters' "regard for their individual honour and rep-

---

62. Rufus King to Christopher Gore, Nov. 22, 1816, Charles R. King, ed., *The Life and Correspondence of Rufus King: Comprising His Letters, Private and Official, His Public Documents, and His Speeches* (1894–1900; reprint, New York, 1971), 6:35–36, 36.

63. P. P. F. Degrand to J. Q. Adams, Apr. 22, 1823, Adams Papers, reel 459.

64. "Speech of His Excellency William Eustis, To Both Branches of The Legislature of Massachusetts; Delivered June 4, 1823," Broadside Collection, 1823, American Antiquarian Society, Worcester, Mass.

utation," charging that Eustis had done "all in his power to defame his predecessors in office, to dishonour the memory" of deceased patriots, and "to traduce and degrade the character of his native state."[65] Federalist newspapers then impugned the practices of the Jefferson and Madison administrations to justify their party's resistance.[66] Republican papers responded by recounting the history of Federalist treason from 1790 to 1815.[67] Otis then entered the fray with his second public defense of the Hartford Convention and blamed Massachusetts's waning national influence on local Republicans, who continued to attack the past policies of the state government.[68] Republicans again returned fire.[69] Recognizing that the continuance of this bitter historical feud made it impossible for the state's Federalists and Republicans to defend and advocate him in unity, Adams wisely remained silent even after adherents wishing to establish his Republican credentials reissued his *Review of the Works of Fisher Ames*, a scathing attack on high Federalism originally published in 1808.[70] For Adams, to have intervened would have been to risk alienating one of the two wings of his supporters.

Into this multi-layered historical debate burst the publication, in the late summer of 1823, of John Adams's confidential correspondence with his friend and kinsman William Cunningham, written between 1803 and 1812,

65. Federal Party, Massachusetts, *To the Electors of Massachusetts* ([Boston ?], 1824), [1], 3.

66. See *Boston Gazette*, as quoted in *Columbian Reporter, and Old Colony Journal* (Taunton, Mass.), Mar. 24, 1824; *Hampden Journal* (Springfield, Mass.), Mar. 17, 1824; [Boston] *Columbian Centinel*, Jan. 3 and 10 and Feb. 28, 1824; *Franklin Herald and Public Advertiser* (Greenfield, Mass.), Mar. 2, 1824; and *Boston Daily Advertiser*, Mar. 19 and 29, 1824.

67. See, for example, the series entitled "The American," signed "George Washington," in the *Independent Chronicle & Boston Patriot*, which ran through February and March 1824.

68. Harrison G. Otis, *Otis's Letters in Defence of the Hartford Convention and the People of Massachusetts* (Boston, 1824), first published as a series of signed letters in the [Boston] *Columbian Centinel*, February–Apr. 21, 1824. For his first defense, see [Otis], *Letters Developing the Character and Views of the Hartford Convention: By "One of the Convention,"* (Washington, D.C., 1820).

69. See, for example, *National Aegis* (Worcester, Mass.), Mar. 24 and 31 and Apr. 7, 1824; and the series, "Remarks on a Series of Letters Published in the Columbian Centinel, by the Hon. H. G. Otis," signed "Gerry," [Boston] *American Statesman & City Register*, which began Mar. 11, 1824.

70. *Independent Chronicle & Boston Patriot*, Nov. 9, 1822. For the ensuing difficulties, see, for example, *Independent Chronicle & Boston Patriot*, Nov. 16, Dec. 28, 1822, and Jan. 11, Feb. 12, and Apr. 23, 1823; [Boston] *Columbian Centinel*, Nov. 16, 1822; and *Massachusetts Spy and Worcester Advertiser*, Jan. 14, 1824.

which would ultimately draw the younger Adams out.[71] In these letters the senior Adams had vented his distrust of the populace, his antipathy to political parties, and his disapproval of Thomas Jefferson—all standard Federalist fare certain to antagonize his son's Republican supporters. But he also dwelt with particular bitterness and in graphic detail on the incompetence of his fellow Massachusetts Federalist Timothy Pickering as secretary of state. Adams justified his dismissal of Pickering from his cabinet by calling into question the actions, motives, and characters of the leading high Federalists who had opposed his own reelection. He also defended his son's support of Jefferson's embargo.[72]

The exhumation of these invectives reopened old divisions among former Federalist partisans. Republican papers supporting John Quincy Adams could not resist publishing a spate of articles castigating the high Federalists of 1798–1801[73] and praising the younger Adams's support of Jefferson,[74] activity that contributed to the disarray in the ranks of his Federalist backers. Ultimately the Adams Federalist press, unable to disassociate the candidate from his father, was forced to side with John Adams against the Hamiltonian wing of the party.[75] This of course drew forth the full ire of the anti-Adams Federalist press, which condemned father and son and gleefully republished, in support of its position, Hamilton's vicious assault on John Adams's politics and character, written during the presidential campaign of 1800.[76]

By 1824, then, the public had been treated to a full-dress review of ancient political animosities rather than to a discussion of immediate issues. Left to the ordinary channels of press commentary, the stir created by the publication of this old correspondence might have subsided. But, ap-

71. For the political motives behind the publication on the part of Cunningham's son, a Jacksonian, see Page Smith, *John Adams* (New York, 1962), 2:1133; and Adams, *Memoirs*, 6:176–177 (Sept. 9, 1823).

72. John Adams, *Correspondence between the Hon. John Adams, Late President of the United States, and the Late Wm. Cunningham, Esq., Beginning in 1803, and Ending in 1812* (Boston, 1823).

73. *Independent Chronicle & Boston Patriot*, Sept. 17, 1823.

74. See the series "John Quincy Adams," signed "Fenella," in the *Essex Register* (Salem, Mass.), October–December 1823.

75. See the series "Correspondence Reviewed" in the [Boston] *Columbian Centinel*, Sept. 17–27, 1823.

76. See "Mr. Coleman's Remarks on Pres. Adams' Correspondence," *Salem* [Mass.] *Gazette*, Oct. 21, 1823, which began a series from the *New York Evening Post* attacking the Adamses. See also *Salem* [Mass.] *Gazette*, Nov. 14, 1823. The *Gazette* ran Hamilton's letter throughout November 1823.

palled by the possibility that John Adams and his "friends" might "escape just censure & reproach," Timothy Pickering decided at this point that he was obliged to "step forth in vindication" of the "characters" of his high-Federalist colleagues.[77] Accordingly, he published a book-length review of the correspondence the following May,[78] anticipating with pleasure that "the whole 'noble family of' Adams," "alike impudent & malevolent," would come to regret the pamphlet.[79] Pickering maintained that the high Federalists had not supported Adams in 1800 because they refused to be responsible for the reelection of a man of such "boundless vanity, disgusting egotism, repulsive self-sufficiency, and an ambition so inordinate as to be capable of sacrificing principles, system, and consistency, to personal gratification."[80] He then blasted the son for supporting the embargo, charging that in return for blind allegiance to Jefferson, John Quincy Adams had been amply rewarded with offices.[81]

While the press debated the significance of Pickering's *Review*,[82] the younger Adams at first decided to let "the personalities of the last century . . . pass the river of Lethe."[83] But Pickering's assertion that his support of the embargo demonstrated a "blind & unlimited confidence in the Executive, incompatible with the independence of a member of the Legislature,"[84] rankled. Adams finally went to the bar of public opinion himself. In search of "vindication of my own character,"[85] he reissued his public letter to Harrison Gray Otis of March 31, 1808, originally written in response to Pickering's public letter calling for state interposition.[86] In a new appendix

77. Timothy Pickering to John Lowell, Oct. 20, 1823, draft, Timothy Pickering Papers, Massachusetts Historical Society, microfilm ed., reel 15.

78. Pickering, *Review*, passim.

79. Timothy Pickering to Richard Peters, Oct. 21, 1823, signed draft, Pickering Papers, reel 15.

80. Pickering, *Review*, 110.

81. Pickering, *Review*, 41–63.

82. See, for example, *Columbian Reporter, and Old Colony Journal* (Taunton, Mass.), May 26, 1824; *Salem* [Mass.] *Gazette*, May 21, 1824; and *Franklin Herald and Public Advertiser* (Greenfield, Mass.), June 29, 1824.

83. J. Q. Adams to John B. Davis, May 20, 1824, letterbook copy, Adams Papers, reel 147.

84. J. Q. Adams to Joseph E. Sprague, May 16, 1824, letterbook copy, Adams Papers, reel 147.

85. J. Q. Adams to John Rutherford, Aug. 16, 1824, letterbook copy, Adams Papers, reel 147.

86. John Quincy Adams, *A Letter to Mr. Harrison Gray Otis, a Member of the Senate of Massachusetts, on the Present State of Our National Affairs, with Remarks upon Mr. T. Pickering's Letter, to the Governor of the Commonwealth, with an Appendix, Written July, 1824* (Baltimore, 1824).

he gave his reasons for voting for the embargo, defended the measure itself, and referred disparagingly to the subsequent Hartford Convention. Pickering, of course, replied.[87]

Thus a quarrel which had originally focused on John Adams's presidency broadened to include New England's obstructionism under the Jefferson and Madison administrations. It thereby flowed into the current controversy raging over the Hartford Convention engendered by local politics. During the waning months of the presidential campaign, local papers continued to feature Adams's quarrel with Pickering and defended the past policies of their own parties to the severe detriment of amalgamation behind Adams.[88] Adams supporters accused one another, and by implication the state, of everything from venality to treason in a debilitating historical battle ill-suited to promote unity in support of New England's not-so-favorite son. The highly developed sense of political honor shared by the elite, and their eternal quest for vindication, ran counter to their larger political goals and economic interests. Adams succeeded to the presidency with his Massachusetts supporters in hostile disarray.

Governor Eustis's death in February 1825, however, removed a major obstacle to party realignment in Massachusetts. In supporting the new Republican gubernatorial candidate, Levi Lincoln, Jr., Federalists were not endorsing the man who had used the state's highest office to attack their party's integrity and patriotism. Thus amalgamation formed a new context for Adams's reelection campaign in Massachusetts. Nonetheless, even the progress made by fusionists could not prevent another raging historical debate from subsuming Adams's second presidential campaign.

Although the opposition continued to exploit the historical record for partisan ends during Adams's reelection campaign,[89] those within the fusion movement made a conscious effort to facilitate cooperation between former opponents. Papers endorsing amalgamation sent up a nearly universal chorus that previous political differences were no longer relevant, being mere matters of speculation that did not "affect the question of the

87. [Boston] *American Statesman & City Register*, Aug. 28, 1824.

88. [Boston] *Columbian Centinel*, May 15, 22, and 29, 1824; *Independent Chronicle & Boston Patriot*, Sept. 1 and Oct. 30, 1824; *National Aegis* (Worcester, Mass.), July 14, 1824; [Boston] *American Statesman*, Sept. 4 and "*Extra*," July 30, 1824; [Boston] *Repertory*, Sept. 4, Oct. 2, 23, 26, 28, and Nov. 2, 1824; and *Salem* [Mass.] *Gazette*, Aug. 6, 24, and Sept. 7, 1824.

89. See Samuel F. Bemis, *John Quincy Adams and the Union* (New York, 1956), 132–134; and Livermore, *Twilight of Federalism*, chap. 10.

fitness of men for office."[90] That this lesson was repeated so often, however, suggests that amalgamation leaders still feared the disruptive power of past political differences and the moral imperatives attached to those differences. Nonetheless, in marked contrast to the election of 1824, Adams supporters in Massachusetts entered the final months of his reelection campaign comparatively unified. It is therefore particularly ironic that Adams himself, in the waning days of that campaign, publicly asserted that New England Federalists had plotted treason in 1808. His accusation was understandably received with "perfect wrath & fury" by Boston Federalists[91] and left a shambles in fusion ranks. The ensuing public debate lasted well into the spring of 1829, threatening to eviscerate the fledgling National Republican party in Massachusetts. The controversy, which involved questions of sectional loyalty, national allegiance, and individual character, moved through several distinct phases but never really progressed, as both former Federalists and Adams sought to vindicate themselves by employing the historical record to discredit the past and present character and motives of the other.

Events led Adams to drop his bombshell. In September 1827, William B. Giles, desiring to establish Jefferson's opposition to Adams's administration, published a confidential letter from Jefferson, dated December 26, 1825. The letter mainly criticized Adams's program for national development, but it also implied that Adams had accused the New England Federalists of treasonable intent in 1808.[92] Adams wisely maintained silence. Then in October 1828, keen to establish that Adams, in informing Jefferson of a Federalist plot, had acted out of a profound national commitment and not personal ambition, a supporter from Virginia, Archibald Stuart, published a copy of a letter from Jefferson to Giles dated the day before the one Giles had published.[93] Indeed, in this letter Jefferson attested to Adams's integrity in telling him of a plot by certain eastern citizens, from "Massachusetts particularly," to separate peaceably from the Union.[94] Because factual er-

90. *Boston Daily Advertiser*, Mar. 24, 1827. See also [Boston] *Massachusetts Journal*, Oct. 18, 1827, and July 5, 1828; *Massachusetts Spy* (Worcester, Mass.), Mar. 21, 1827; *Salem* [Mass.] *Gazette*, Apr. 27 and May 11, 1827, and Mar. 18, 1828; and *Independent Chronicle & Boston Patriot*, Dec. 15, 1827.

91. Edward Everett to Alexander H. Everett, Nov. 1, 1828, Everett Papers, reel 3.

92. Thomas Jefferson to William B. Giles, Dec. 16, 1825, extract, in Henry Adams, ed., *Documents Relating to New-England Federalism, 1800–1815* (Boston, 1905), 6–9.

93. See Archibald Stuart to Thomas J. Randolph, Oct. 11, 1828; Thomas J. Randolph to Archibald Stuart, Oct. 11, 1820; and enclosure, Thomas Jefferson to William B. Giles, Dec. 25, 1825, all in H. Adams, *Documents*, 10–13.

94. Thomas Jefferson to William B. Giles, Dec. 25, 1825, in H. Adams, *Documents*, 12.

rors in the letter made it appear that Adams had accused New England Federalists of planning separation with the aid of the enemy during the War of 1812, Adams authorized a reply, which was published in the *National Intelligencer* in his name on October 21. This corrected errors and summarized both his March 1808 interview with Jefferson and the contents of various letters he had written to congressmen in the fall and winter of 1808–1809, in which he urged them to repeal the embargo to prevent open resistance by New England Federalists, civil war, and British intervention. Adams specifically recollected informing correspondents that the object of these Federalists for several years had been the "dissolution of the Union, and the establishment of a separate confederation," which he knew from "unequivocal evidence, although not provable in a court of law."[95]

This statement could not have failed to elicit the furious controversy that ensued. From Boston, Charles Francis Adams believed his father's action to have been impolitic at the very least. He had ascertained that the Federalists, having acted "zealously" in his father's cause, had been "disinclined to revive old recollections" and were "willing to confess that both sides had committed errors." Nor had they deemed Jefferson's letter worthy of correction. But Adams's own "renewed denunciation" of New England Federalism had "startled their pride," and they felt themselves "in honour bound to reply with spirit."[96] The president's son was surely correct. Given the efforts to heal old party wounds, prudence dictated silence. Why indeed had Adams "after enduring the pelting of the storm with such exemplary patience for four years . . . exploded at the last moment"?[97]

It was precisely because Adams shared so deeply the political culture of the conservative elite that he could not remain silent. If the Federalists were "honour bound" to reply to his statement, he was equally compelled to set the historical record straight. Because history was a repository of moral lessons and a mirror reflecting one's character, the events must be correctly recorded. The errors in Jefferson's letter offered Adams the opportunity to clear his name from the perennial accusations of demagoguery, apostasy, and ambition. Clear in his mind were the three lessons he wished the nation to imbibe from this historical exercise: that he had been the first to warn Jefferson of a danger to the integrity of the Union; that he

95. "From the 'National Intelligencer' of Oct. 21, 1828," in H. Adams, *Documents*, 23–26.
96. C. F. Adams to J. Q. Adams, Dec. 17, 1828, letterbook copy, Adams Papers, reel 157.
97. A. H. Everett to [E. Everett], Jan. 14, 1829, Hale Family Papers, Manuscript Division, Library of Congress, Washington, D.C.

had been "the efficient cause" of the embargo's repeal and had thus saved the nation from "civil War"; and that Jefferson, even though he disagreed with Adams's present politics, "to the last moment of his life . . . bore witness . . . to the integrity and disinterestedness of my conduct at that trying time."[98] The New England Federalists maintained that Jefferson's "palpable errors" rendered his entire letter "doubtful" and thus made Adams's reply unnecessary.[99] For Adams, publishing the correction was imperative precisely because he wanted Jefferson's letter to be believed.

Amalgamation ground to a halt as the combatants enmeshed the entire elite community in a battle over the past. To rescue "*Character* . . . the dearest possession of an honourable, elevated mind,"[100] New Englanders reviewed past politics and replied to Adams in kind, even though it was understood that rending the "community" into "two furious parties" risked sectional and personal political impotence.[101] Both sides sought self-vindication through historical narrative, and in defending their own probity, all were obeying the imperatives of a traditional political culture in which character and reputation, not specific policies advocated, constituted one's political capital. The elite's political culture thus hindered their effective leadership, placing in jeopardy a tenuous unity made even more necessary now that Jacksonian Democracy was at the helm of state.

On November 27, 1828, thirteen of Boston's most powerful Federalist leaders, including Otis, Perkins, William Sullivan, William Prescott, and John Lowell, addressed a private letter to Adams asking for the names of those whose object had been the dissolution of the Union and for the evidence on which his charge was based.[102] Adams refused to comply, taunting that to accuse men who believed in state interposition with dis-

98. J. Q. Adams to C. F. Adams, Dec. 8, 1828, Adams Papers, reel 489.

99. C. F. Adams to J. Q. Adams, Dec. 17, 1828, letterbook copy, Adams Papers, reel 157.

100. *Boston Daily Advertiser*, Nov. 18, 1828.

101. [Boston] *Massachusetts Journal*, Dec. 2, 1828.

102. The original letter is H. G. Otis et al. to John Quincy Adams, Nov. 26, 1828, Adams Papers, reel 488. I have used the version published in H. Adams, *Documents*, 43–45. It was signed by H. G. Otis, Israel Thorndike, T. H. Perkins, William Prescott, Daniel Sargent, John Lowell, William Sullivan, Charles Jackson, Warren Dutton, Benjamin Pickman, Henry Cabot for the deceased George Cabot, C. C. Parsons for the deceased Theophilus Parsons, and Franklin Dexter for the deceased Samuel Dexter. Otis, Sargent, Perkins, Sullivan, Jackson, and Thorndike had all been central committee members, as had the deceased Dexter and Parsons. See James Banner, *To the Hartford Convention: The Federalists and the Origins of Party Politics in Massachusetts, 1789–1815* (New York, 1970), 240, n. 6.

unionism was to charge "them with nothing more than with acting up to their principles."[103] Twelve of the thirteen Federalists then issued a pamphlet defending Massachusetts Federalism, reprinting all the documents in the controversy including their private letter to Adams and his reply.[104] They explained the necessity of upholding "the public reputation of high-minded men," which was the "common property" of all those who had "embarked in the same cause" and the defense of which was a duty of "Honorable men" that must take precedence over any "fear of awakening long-extinguished controversies."[105] Having clarified their own high motives, they attacked those of Adams, whom they portrayed as seeking only political advancement in the past and revenge in the present. They then gave a patriotic gloss to the history of New England Federalism and concluded that the delegates to the Hartford Convention had preserved "the civil and political liberty which had been . . . . bequeathed to them."[106] It was Adams's craven and duplicitous behavior, not New England's past course, that was responsible for the section's fall from national grace. His secret betrayal had caused Massachusetts "lasting dishonor."[107]

Adams immediately reissued this pamphlet from Washington, appending documents of his own.[108] He also commenced a long and tortured book-length reply, which he withheld from publication but which was finally published by Henry Adams in 1877.[109] As newspapers and private correspondents debated the merits of each side in the "civil war" that was sapping New England's strength,[110] Adams poured his wounded sense of

103. J. Q. Adams to H. G. Otis et al., Dec. 30, 1828, in H. Adams, *Documents*, 46–62, 58.

104. H. G. Otis et al., "Appeal to the Citizens of the United States," in H. Adams, *Documents*, 63–92. Franklin Dexter did not join in the appeal. This appeal was prepared by a committee of five, which included Jackson, Otis, Sullivan, Lowell, and Prescott. The final draft was prepared by Lowell and Otis. See Bemis, *Adams and the Union*, 175, n. 46.

105. Otis et al., "Appeal," 69, 64.

106. Otis et al., "Appeal," 80–81.

107. Otis et al., "Appeal," 90.

108. John Quincy Adams, *Correspondence between John Quincy Adams, Esquire, President of the United States, and Several Citizens of Massachusetts Concerning the Charge of a Design to Dissolve the Union Alleged to Have Existed in that State. To Which Are Now Added Additional Papers, Illustrative of the Subject* (Washington, D.C., 1829).

109. John Quincy Adams, "To the Citizens of the United States," in H. Adams, *Documents*, 107–329.

110. C. F. Adams to J. Q. Adams, Feb. 26, 1829, letterbook copy, Adams Papers, reel 157. For the varied public and private reactions, see, for example, *National Aegis* (Worcester, Mass.), Feb. 11 and Apr. 1, 1829; *Independent Chronicle & Boston Patriot*, Feb. 14, 1829; *Springfield* [Mass.] *Republican*, Mar. 4, 1829; *Pittsfield* [Mass.] *Sun*, Feb. 19, 1829; *Boston Statesman*, Feb. 10, 1829; [Boston] *Evening Bulletin and United States Republican*,

political honor into this latest undertaking. Convinced that he had "a great moral lesson" to teach the country through his exposition,[111] he denied that the Hartford Convention was the product of "patriotic pilgrims,"[112] and insisted that it stood as "a perpetual *memento mori* to every deliberate projector of disunion throughout this confederate republic."[113] Eventually, Adams lost control of his voice as a disinterested narrator impartially pronouncing the lessons of history to his audience, and the manuscript degenerated into a personal vendetta against Otis. Accusing Otis of trying to rob his children of their "best inheritance . . . —the good name of their father,"[114] Adams, on page after page, attacked his opponent's character and motives, accusing him of dissembling, stupidity, jealousy, and cowardice. "Stand forth, Harrison Gray Otis, before the people of this Union, our common country," Adams called out from the depths of his anger, humiliation, and despair. "The question is between you and me. The question is between the Hartford Convention and the Union."[115]

This historical controversy, inadvertently initiated by a supporter of Adams who wished to defend the president's reputation, was publicly debated in the Massachusetts press well into May 1829 and beyond. Edward Everett, in an attempt to put out the fire before it consumed the section's political prospects,[116] convinced Adams to delay his reply to the Federalists seeking names and evidence.[117] During this reprieve Everett wrote to Per-

---

Feb. 12, 1829; *Salem* [Mass.] *Gazette*, Feb. 13 and 17, 1829; *Boston Advertiser*, Feb. 19, 1829; *Boston Courier*, Feb. 9, 1829; [Boston] *Massachusetts Journal*, Feb. 12 and Mar. 7 and 10, 1829; [Boston] *Columbian Centinel*, Feb. 11, 1829; C. F. Adams to J. Q. Adams, Feb. 26, 1829, letterbook copy, Adams Papers, reel 157; George Harrison to H. G. Otis, [Feb. 10, 1829?]; Col. Ro[bert] Troup to H. G. Otis, Feb. 12, 1829; John W. Ames to H. G. H. G. Otis, Feb. 14, 1829; Joseph Hopkinson to H. G. Otis, Feb. 15, 1829; W. H. Dillingham to H. G. Otis, Feb. 19, 1829; Col. Robert Troup to H. G. Otis, Feb. 26, 1829; *"Political Penitent,"* to Otis et al., Mar. 4, 1829, all in Otis Papers, reel 9; Edward Everett to A. H. Everett, Feb. 15, 1829, letterbook copy, Everett Papers, reel 25; Benjamin Waterhouse to [J. Q. Adams], Feb. 16, 1829, Adams Papers, reel 490; and Daniel Webster to Achsah Pollard Webster, Feb. 19, 1829, in Webster, *DWPC*, 2:399–400.

111. Adams, *Memoirs*, 8:115 (Mar. 18, 1829).

112. J. Q. Adams, "To the Citizens," 214.

113. J. Q. Adams, "To the Citizens," 328.

114. J. Q. Adams, "To the Citizens," 217.

115. This passage was not published by Henry Adams. See [J. Q. Adams], "An Answer to the Appeal of certain Federalists 1829," 226–227, Adams Papers, reel 246.

116. Edward Everett to [A. H. Everett], Dec. 15, 1828, Everett Papers, reel 3.

117. See Adams, *Memoirs*, 7:79 (Dec. 4, 1828); Edward Everett, Diary, Dec. 4, 6, and 7, 1828, Everett Papers, reel 36; and [Boston] *Evening Bulletin and United States Republican*, Feb. 12, 1829.

kins in an attempt to convince him that neither personal nor political honor required more than a public denial of the Federalists' involvement in a disunionist plot. New England's national influence depended on the success of amalgamation, and amalgamation, he warned, would be destroyed by a *"public controversy,"* plunging "us again into the frightful discord from w'h we have just emerged."[118] Similarly, Charles Francis Adams counseled his father to exercise the utmost "delicacy and discrimination" in this instance in order to avoid dividing "our society" irretrievably.[119] Unity was necessary to counter the Democracy in the Bay State.[120]

Such pragmatic counsel went unheeded, and the long "public controversy" rendered amalgamation ever more elusive. Exercising great diplomacy and tact, Joseph Story, himself a former Republican whose conservative credentials had not been fully ratified until 1820, finally succeeded in bringing it to a halt. He agreed to read Adams's book manuscript but insisted to the president that Adams's "integrity" had never been questioned, a blatant falsehood. Furthermore, he informed Adams of a "disposition" "in the public mind" to let the matter rest.[121] Recognizing that his attack on Otis, who deserved only "calm contempt," had been too passionate,[122] fearing he would lose the ensuing controversy in a combined attack from Federalists and Jacksonians,[123] and worrying that publication would strengthen the alliance between Jackson and former Federalists, which he believed threatened the integrity of the Union,[124] Adams accepted the honorable exit Story provided, agreeing "immediate publication" was unnecessary.[125]

The suppression of Adams's reply was fortunate; its publication would

118. Edward Everett to T. H. Perkins, Dec. [7], 1828, letterbook copy, Everett Papers, reel 25. See also Edward Everett to T. H. Perkins, Dec. 20, 1828, letterbook copy; and Edward Everett to T. H. Perkins, Jan. 3, 1829, Everett Papers, reel 25.

119. C. F. Adams to J. Q. Adams, Dec. 3, 1828, Adams Papers, reel 489. See also C. F. Adams to L. C. Adams, Nov. 15, 1828, Adams Papers, reel 488; and C. F. Adams to J. Q. Adams, Nov. 20, 1828, letterbook copy, Adams Papers, reel 157.

120. C. F. Adams to J. Q. Adams, Dec. 17, 1828, letterbook copy, Adams Papers, reel 157.

121. Joseph Story to J. Q. Adams, Oct. 2, 1829, in William W. Story, *Life and Letters of Joseph Story* (Boston, 1851), 2:13–17.

122. J. Q. Adams to William Plumer, Sept. 24, 1830, letterbook copy, Adams Papers, reel 150. See also J. Q. Adams to Joseph Story, Nov. 4, 1829, letterbook copy, Adams Papers, reel 149.

123. J. Q. Adams to William Plumer, Sept. 24, 1830, letterbook copy; and J. Q. Adams to William Plumer, Jr., Sept. 30, 1830, letterbook copy, both in Adams Papers, reel 150.

124. J. Q. Adams to C. F. Adams, Dec. 22, 1830, letterbook copy, Adams Papers, reel 144.

125. J. Q. Adams to Joseph Story, Nov. 4, 1829, letterbook copy, Adams Papers, reel 149.

only have further strained the cohesion the conservatives needed to be effective politically in opposition to Jacksonian Democracy and an aggressive southern sectionalism. Adams's manuscript nonetheless evinces the durability of the conservatives' archaic political culture and illuminates its limitations in the face of the new politics. As long as prior political divisions elicited such moral and personal judgments, the past would remain a major arena for debate, however harmful that debate proved to be to elite political unity and however damaging such a historical review was to the section's avowed patriotism.

One of the most remarkable complications stemming from Adams's public controversy with the Federalists was the criminal libel suit Daniel Webster instigated against Theodore Lyman, Jr., in December 1828, for even Webster was not immune to the imperatives of the traditional political culture. Ambitious but also politically shrewd, he had been the major initiator of amalgamation within New England and had worked ceaselessly on the political aspects of party building, promoting partisan presses, building coalitions with fusion parties in other states, and defending Adams's program throughout his presidency. He had deplored Otis's gubernatorial race in 1823 precisely because the past issues it raised had caused political disarray in Massachusetts.[126] He equally regretted Adams's initial statement of October 21, believing it "impolitic" because it "put in extreme jeopardy . . . amalgamation."[127] Nonetheless, when Lyman, a former Federalist and member of the Boston elite, published an editorial in the *Jackson Republican* declaring that Adams "distinctly asserts" that Webster was among those engaged "in a plot to dissolve the Union,"[128] Webster did not hesitate to rush to the defense of his own character by charging Lyman with libel. The indictment was appropriately framed "under the law of *scandalum magnatum*, or slander of great men," which was never adopted as part of American common law,[129] and during the trial the prosecution maintained that Lyman's charge had created a "stain . . . on the escutcheon

126. Daniel Webster to Joseph Story, May 12, 1823, Wiltse, *DWPC*, 1:327–328.

127. C. F. Adams to J. Q. Adams, Dec. 3, 1828, Adams Papers, reel 489.

128. [Boston] *Jackson Republican*, Oct. 29, 1828.

129. Josiah H. Benton, Jr., *A Notable Libel Case: The Criminal Prosecution of Theodore Lyman, Jr. by Daniel Webster in the Supreme Judicial Court of Massachusetts, November Term, 1828* (Boston, 1904), 35. For the trial record, see John W. Whitman, *Report of a Trial in the Supreme Judicial Court, Holden at Boston, Dec. 16th and 17th, 1828, of Theodore Lyman, Jr., for an Alleged Libel on Daniel Webster, a Senator of the United States, Published in the Jackson Republican, Comprising All the Documents and Testimony Given in the Cause, and Full Notes of the Arguments of Counsel, and the Charge of the Court. Taken in Short Hand* (Boston, 1828).

of . . . [Webster's] reputation."[130] Although Webster was clearly concerned with his character and standing, his motives in bringing suit were political. In order to pursue high national office successfully, he needed to distance himself from Hartford Convention Federalism.[131] Unfortunately, however, in pressing charges, Webster only perpetuated and publicized the conservatives' crippling controversies.

Once again the nation was treated to the spectacle of the Massachusetts elite savaging the reputation of their native-born president, as the court proceedings called into question neither Lyman's nor Webster's character. Instead, Adams's own character was on trial, in an action entirely argued, witnessed, and presided over by members of the conservative elite who had formerly adhered to the Federalist party. Adams would receive no chance at justice, being presumed guilty at the outset.[132] Chief Justice Isaac Parker, in charging the jury, argued that if Lyman had supplied the names of the alleged traitors not to "prejudice" those persons but to illustrate "the extreme injustice of Mr. Adams' accusation against the leaders of the federal party," then he was not guilty of libel.[133] Under this charge, the jury was unable to agree on a verdict, and the case was ultimately dropped,[134] but not until Adams, Webster, and the conservative leaders had all incurred further stains on the reputations they had sought to wash clean. In pressing charges, Webster once again exposed the disarray of Massachusetts conservatives to national scrutiny, discrediting their claim to national leadership, so recently in their grasp.

The spectacular bloodletting among Massachusetts's business and professional leaders following upon the publication of Jefferson's correspondence with Giles brought Adams's presidency to an ironically fitting conclusion. His entire term had been haunted by the political instability in his native state. The elite's strategy of forging a new political party, consisting of all

130. Whitman, *Report of a Trial*, 7.

131. That this was Webster's aim was clearly understood in Boston. See Edward Everett to A. H. Everett, Nov. 15, 1828, letterbook copy, Everett Papers, reel 25; Samuel A. Eliot to Jared Sparks, Nov. 25, 1828, Jared Sparks Papers, Houghton Library, Harvard University, Cambridge, Mass.; H. G. Otis to George Harrison, [Feb. 26, 1829], Otis Papers, reel 9; and C. F. Adams to J. Q. Adams, Jan. 21, 1829, letterbook copy, Adams Papers, reel 157.

132. For those involved in the case see Benton, *Notable Libel Case*, 31, 35, 46, 51, 52, 63–64, 67, 74–76, 77, and 79. See also J. Q. Adams to C. F. Adams, Dec. 31, 1828, letterbook copy, Adams Papers, reel 148.

133. Whitman, *Report of a Trial*, 71–72.

134. Benton, *Notable Libel Case*, 102–103.

the "good men" in both old parties, in order to sustain their local and national power, uphold their conservative values, and advance their economic interests, had been undermined by their equation of political actions with individual character and probity. In an atmosphere rent by recriminations Massachusetts's newly named National Republican party, the political vehicle for conservative aspirations, issued its first official address in February 1829. The late election, it asserted bravely, had left fewer "seeds of . . . animosity" in "this ancient Commonwealth . . . than in almost any other of our sister republics." The Bay State possessed a "unity of sentiment" regarding current issues, and "political feuds of former times" had been "renounced" with "magnanimity."[135]

Clearly, the Boston-based elite saw the need for unity to achieve their political goals and to sustain their economic interests, but wishing simply would not make it so. They stood on the verge of a new decade and a new political era under Jackson, exhausted by intestine debates that political pragmatists like Edward Everett recognized could only squander their political capital. Ultimately, the conservatives' ability to lead their state and nation was limited not so much by temporary conflicts over tariff policy or the structural difficulties involving issues of place and patronage inherent in party realignment as it was by their conception of what leadership was and how it was attained. Because political contests involved self-vindication and validated important moral lessons, they were fought to the death at the bar of public opinion. Unable successfully to apply the practical lessons garnered from the election of 1828, the elite would again find themselves crippled by their moralistic and intensely personal view of politics in state elections of the 1830s. Ultimately, such local quarrels plagued Webster's first bid for the presidency in the election of 1836.[136] The concept that elections represented referenda on one's character was suitable, perhaps, to the deferential political culture of the eighteenth century; it was ill-adapted to the party competition of a newer era and ill-suited to sustain the unity needed to promote nationally the values and program of the Massachusetts elite. Their very perception of politics, then, which had served them and their fathers so well in an earlier era, countered the political aspirations of the Massachusetts elite, threatening to undermine their local rule while depriving them of national power.

135. [Boston] *Columbian Centinel*, Feb. 21, 1829.
136. Sheidley, "Sectional Nationalism," chap. 8.

Joshua B. Smith (1813–1879). Photograph. Collection of the
Massachusetts Historical Society.

Power and Social Responsibility:
Entrepreneurs and the Black Community
in Antebellum Boston

Lois E. Horton and James Oliver Horton

A TRADITIONAL HISTORY of American business is most likely to focus on issues leading directly to the bottom line. These include the organizational strategy for market expansion, for distribution, for controlling raw materials, and for stabilizing or reducing labor costs.

> Business is business the Little Man said,
> A battle where anything goes.
> Where the only gospel is "get ahead",
> and never spare friends or foes.[1]

Business was business for the black entrepreneurs of Boston no less than for their Yankee counterparts. They, too, worried about the bottom line, but this was not their whole story. Their responsibilities extended to the line of community concerns. Black entrepreneurs were expected to provide leadership to the community, offer apprenticeships for the young, serve as role models for those struggling with oppression and limited opportunities, and be an argument against theories of racial inferiority. In short, their business ventures were expected not only to benefit themselves individually, but to benefit the black community as a whole.

This close association between black entrepreneurs and their communities was not unique. Businessmen in immigrant communities likewise were expected to contribute to community projects and social services. Boston's Irish entrepreneurs supported the Catholic Church and its efforts to bring needed services to poor Irish immigrants, and many helped finance the activities of such groups as the Charitable Irish Society. Two

---

1. Berton Braley, "Business is Business," in Joseph Morris and St. Clair Adams, eds., *Silver Linings: Poems of Hope and Cheer* (New York, 1927).

generations ago Oscar Handlin described immigrant shopkeepers who provided credit and whose businesses became neighborhood meeting places. All nineteenth-century entrepreneurs had to be mindful of community relations and of the good name on which their credit was based, but it was in poor communities, immigrant and African-American, that the tension between communal values stressing social responsibility and the individualistic values of capitalism was most apparent. Handlin argued that those in the immigrant community most likely to be successful were those who could keep this tension in balance. "To create capital in America," he observed, "meant also a slighting of traditional obligations, the exploitation rather than the succor of neighbors."[2]

For people in communities suffering the disadvantages of discrimination, the tensions between accepted business practice and community responsibility were significant. Although this was true for immigrants, because severe racial restrictions targeted black people of all classes, and because the black community in Boston was small, blacks in business there in the antebellum period were bound to the community with extraordinarily strong ties. African Americans were expected to contribute what they could to the community's mutual effort, and since cash was often in short supply even in the top ranks of black society, goods, services, personal efforts, and space were often the most common forms of philanthropic participation. In antebellum Boston, as elsewhere, every black man, woman, and child was expected to act not only as an individual but also as a contributing member of the community and the race. From the pulpits, the newspapers, and every public podium, the word was broadcast that loyalty to the race was highly valued and that the disloyal risked strong community sanctions. African Americans depended on their professionals and on businesspeople to bring respectability to the race. From the platform of Boston's Faneuil Hall, doctor, dentist, lawyer, teacher, and black activist John Rock, then a young man of thirty-five years, addressed a large crowd with this well-worn message, repeated over generations:

> The colored man who by dint of perseverance and
> industry, educates and elevates himself, prepares
> the way for others, gives character to the race
> and hastens the day of general emancipation.[3]

2. Oscar Handlin, *The Uprooted* (New York, 1951), 92.

3. *Liberator*, Mar. 12, 1858, reprinted in Thomas R. Frazier, ed., *Afro-American History: Primary Sources*, shorter ed. (New York, 1971), 75.

African-American success was a collective victory, not merely an individual achievement. Those who established an enterprise, secured influence, and acquired wealth were valued community resources. It was not wealth itself that Rock encouraged, but the power that accrued to wealth, power that could be used for the benefit of the race. "We do not expect to occupy a much better position [as a race] than we now do," he concluded, "until we shall have our educated and wealthy men, who can wield a power that cannot be misunderstood."[4]

Rock's statements reflected community expectations, expectations that have a long and constant history among African Americans. Much of the traditional scholarship focusing on class within African-American society and often emphasizing class division and separation would suggest that entrepreneurs seldom met those expectations. Yet, unlike the aristocrats of color described by Willard Gatewood in his study of black elites of the late nineteenth and early twentieth centuries, most of antebellum Boston's black entrepreneurs were not socially distanced from the masses of blacks in the city.[5] The presence of a black business class in antebellum Boston did reflect such differentiation as W. E. B. DuBois found in Philadelphia at the end of the nineteenth century. But, unlike DuBois's Philadelphians, Boston black entrepreneurs did not constitute a class so distinct from other blacks that little held them to the rest of the African-American community. Nor did their uncertain economic status make "it difficult for them to spare much time and energy in social reform."[6] On the contrary, their status and access to resources made them critical to African-American political protest and community support. This study seeks to modify the notion that class generally separated blacks from one another without suggesting that African-American society was monolithic and undifferentiated, as black entrepreneurs often lived more comfortably than most in their community. Yet, like all black people they faced frequent humiliation and threats of violence, found the protection of authorities unreliable, and were susceptible to being kidnaped into slavery. As a small group in a relatively small and concentrated black community, and perhaps because they were even more vulnerable than their immigrant counterparts, Boston's antebellum black entrepreneurs were more connected to and dependent upon others in their community than most studies of class in black society would suggest.

4. Frazier, *Afro-American History*, 75.
5. Willard B. Gatewood, *Aristocrats of Color: The Black Elite, 1880–1920* (Bloomington, 1990).
6. W. E. B. DuBois, *The Philadelphia Negro* (1899; reprint, New York, 1970), 317.

The 1850s, when Rock spoke, were especially trying times for black people all over the country. Federal law had strengthened the ability of slavery to reach out from the South, recapture fugitives, and even kidnap those who had never been enslaved. The highest court in the nation judged African Americans a stateless people with "no rights the white man was bound to respect."[7] Many white reformers suggested that blacks leave America, and some did resettle in Liberia, Haiti, Canada, or other countries. Yet most blacks refused to accede to the power of slavery, vowing not to be slaves, not to leave, and trying not to despair. Instead they resisted by asserting their rights as Americans, and the entrepreneurs especially supported this resistance.

The calls at mid century for black business achievement for the good of the race were not new. Blacks had long equated individual black success with racial pride. A generation earlier Maria W. Stewart had urged Boston's black men to take up trades and open businesses, to establish themselves as prosperous community members. She called on them to demonstrate their manhood and the manhood of the race, by which she meant pride, autonomy, and citizenship.[8] Throughout the antebellum years many of the hopes of black America rested on the actions of black entrepreneurs. Their numbers were small and their opportunities severely limited, but black businessmen and businesswomen were vitally important to the sustenance and progress of the antebellum free black community in the North. Although slavery had been abolished in Massachusetts a few years after the Revolution, many of the African Americans who lived there were not far removed from that degraded status. Unlike the gradual emancipation in New York, Pennsylvania, and New Jersey, freedom in the Bay State came quickly as a result of a state supreme court ruling. Yet slavery remained a familiar institution among Massachusetts blacks throughout the antebellum period in the personal memories of those who had known bondage in the state during the eighteenth century, in stories told to later generations, and in the more recent experiences of those who continued to emigrate or escape from southern states where slavery still existed.[9]

7. This was the opinion of Chief Justice of the Supreme Court Roger B. Taney in the Dred Scott case of 1857. Don E. Fehrenbacher, *The Dred Scott Case: Its Significance in American Law and Politics*, (New York, 1978).

8. Marilyn Richardson, ed., *Maria W. Stewart: American's First Black Woman Political Writer: Essays and Speeches* (Bloomington, 1987).

9. Arthur Zilversmit, *The First Emancipation: The Abolition of Slavery in the North* (Chicago, 1967). For an excellent comparative treatment of African-American rights in the

Most of the former slaves and their descendants had neither the time nor the opportunity to accumulate the capital necessary for business enterprises. Prejudice and discrimination further hampered black initiatives, making those who did manage to succeed in business all the more remarkable. From two-thirds to three-quarters of those African Americans who were employed in antebellum cities worked at low-level jobs requiring little skill or education. Typically they were day laborers, seamen, or domestic servants whose employment was often insecure or sporadic.[10] Everyone, no matter what his or her occupational rank, was expected to play a role in racial progress. Robert Roberts, a household servant, provided written instructions for other domestics so that they might conduct themselves with dignity, performing their tasks with pride and reflecting positively on the race, but there was little doubt that establishing a business was the preferred role for an enterprising African American.[11]

Among skilled workers and entrepreneurs, some had occupations, like carpentry, shoemaking, or blacksmithing, that could have been learned in slavery or in freedom. Ironically, free black people sometimes had greater opportunities to utilize their skills and form businesses in southern cities, under the paternalistic support of influential whites, than they had in northern cities. Few of Boston's skilled black workers were able to establish businesses equivalent to that of Charleston's Ralph Burnet, master blacksmith. Although not wealthy, he made a comfortable living providing goods and services for the surrounding plantations. Typically, black craftsmen in the South set up "primitive shanties" on the outskirts of town at a convenient crossroads near a country store. In the 1848 industrial census of Charleston almost half of the eighty-nine blacksmiths in the area were African American. The vast majority were slaves, reflecting the fact that in the antebellum South manual labor of any kind was disparaged as fit only for blacks and lowly whites.[12] This often gave African-American craftsmen a clear opportunity for enterprise. "The Negro blacksmith," W. E. B. DuBois later wrote, "held almost absolute sway in this line, which included the

---

North, see Paul Finkleman, "Prelude to the Fourteenth Amendment: Black Legal Rights in the Antebellum North," *Rutgers Law Journal* 17(1986):415–482.

10. James Oliver Horton and Lois E. Horton, *Black Bostonians: Family Life and Community Struggle in the Antebellum North* (New York, 1979).

11. Robert Roberts, *The House Servant's Directory*, (Boston, 1827).

12. John Michael Vlach, *By the Work of Their Hands: Studies in Afro-American Folklife* (Ann Arbor, 1991).

Table 1. Black Workers in Selected Occupations Listed in the Boston City Directory

	1841	*1845*	*1848–1849*
barbers & hairdressers	37	37	50
clothing dealers	25	20	23
boardinghouse keepers	5	5	10
laborers	41	47	82
seamen	33	55	31

many branches of forgery and other trades which are now classified under different heads from that of the regular blacksmith."[13]

In Boston there were few such opportunities. In the city directories and the census records of the antebellum period, listings of African-American blacksmiths, carpenters, and brick masons are extremely rare. Just over one-fourth of all black workers in the city were craftsmen or entrepreneurs in 1850 as well as in 1860, while more than seven of every ten were low-skilled or unskilled. Those Boston blacks who established businesses were disproportionately mulatto and likely to have been born in the Northeast, especially New England, although a sizable number of migrants employed craft and business skills brought with them from the South.[14] Most opened service-oriented operations. Many of these entrepreneurs, such as hair-dressers and some barbers and musicians, likely served a mainly white clientele. However, a substantial number of black businesses were sustained by black sponsorship or patronage, and if these were not always the most financially stable, from the standpoint of black community needs they were often the most significant. The most common black business enterprises were dealerships selling new and used clothing to a largely seafaring clientele, boardinghouse keeping, an endeavor that also served many seamen, and barber and hairdressing shops (see Table 1).

Although only a small number of black business operators were listed, they were almost surely overrepresented among all African Americans in the historical record because they were more likely to be residentially-stable property owners than blacks who were unemployed, partially or irregularly employed, or working in unskilled or service jobs. City directo-

13. W. E. Burghardt DuBois and Augustus Granville Dill, eds., *The Negro American Artisan*, (Atlanta, 1912), 35.
14. Horton and Horton, *Black Bostonians*.

Table 2. Selected Occupations of Black Workers

	1850	*1860*
barber & hairdresser	48	97
clothing dealers	9	21
boardinghouse keepers	5	5
laborers	117	106
seaman	141	132
domestics	56	205

ries were especially skewed, since they were primarily business directories and so were most likely to list middle-class workers and entrepreneurs. A somewhat more reliable listing of occupations, though still with a middle-class bias, may be found in the federal census taken every ten years. In both the 1850 and 1860 U.S. censuses for Boston the occupational categories of laborer and seaman comprised the vast majority of black male workers, with domestics accounting for the largest number of black female employees (see Table 2).

Obviously it was not easy for a black person to enter the business world even at the lowest levels. Yet, against all odds, a few exceptional men were highly successful during this period. In Boston, clothing dealer John P. Coburn, barber Peter Howard, and caterer Joshua B. Smith counted among the most prominent and successful black businessmen. James W. Stewart, who had served in the U.S. Navy during the War of 1812, established himself as a shipping agent and engaged in fitting out whaling and fishing vessels from his shop on Broad Street, the only one of its kind run by a black man.[15] Sailors could go to David Walker's clothing shop, first on Dock Square and then at 24 Brattle Street, to supply themselves with clothing and other gear. Walker was a free black migrant from North Carolina who moved to Boston in 1824. His business was probably of a kind often referred to as a "slop shop," where sailors sold clothing and equipment to bartenders to raise money for shoreside entertainment. Such shops recycled these goods, making a profit by reconditioning them, then reselling them to sailors about to leave port. Although these were small businesses they were significant, for they allowed the black proprietors and their families a measure of economic and social independence.[16]

Boston's black business community was notable, but its leaders did not

15. Richardson, *Maria W. Stewart*.
16. Charles Wiltse, ed., *David Walker's Appeal* (New York, 1965).

compare to the giants in other northern cities who were nationally known and internationally influential. Among the wealthiest and best known in the early nineteenth century were James Forten, the sailmaker in Philadelphia; Thomas Downing, the restauranteur in New York; and the shipowner and sea captain Paul Cuffe in New Bedford. Yet Boston's black business community was connected to these and other well-known and well-positioned business leaders through both commercial channels and networks of political and social activism. Paul Cuffe's shipping enterprise brought goods for Boston's black entrepreneurs to buy and sell, goods often including trade items from the West Indies with special appeal to African-American tastes. When he decided to organize a trading operation with the African colony of Sierra Leone, Cuffe turned to African-American institutions in various east coast cities for aid. Members of the African Society of Boston, many of whom were businessmen, endorsed Cuffe's efforts and recruited and screened settlers for the colony.[17]

Although black Bostonians respected successful entrepreneurs for their business accomplishments, they valued them even more for their contributions to the well-being and progress of the community. Black entrepreneurs found concrete ways to express their sense of responsibility to the community, sometimes by engaging in philanthropy.

Their membership and contributions helped sustain benevolent and mutual aid societies, religious and fraternal organizations, and literary societies, but because their livelihoods were often economically precarious, their subsidy was most likely to take the form of service. They gave financial support to significant community causes like antislavery and education, but they also provided their time and their places of business to meet community needs.

Successful members of the black community were especially likely to be involved in activities related to education and to the abolition of slavery. The career of William P. Powell exemplifies the range of their endeavors. Powell was born free in New York State in 1807. His mother was free, but his father, Edward Powell, was a slave who received his freedom under New York's gradual emancipation in 1827. Powell served as a sailor, married a woman from Plymouth, Massachusetts, and opened a boardinghouse for sailors in New Bedford. He was one of a small group of black men who addressed the Massachusetts legislature in 1837 protesting racial discrimination. Concerned about the limitations of segregated education for black

17. Lamont Thomas, *Rise to be a People* (Urbana, 1986); Rosalind Wiggins, ed., *Captain Paul Cuffe's Logs and Letters, 1808–1817* (Washington, D.C., 1996).

children, he worked for the integration of the public schools. To promote abolition and the education of young people, he chaired the Young Men's Wilberforce Debating Society in New Bedford.[18]

With a keen sense of commitment, black entrepreneurs made arrangements that enabled the community to benefit from their endeavors even after their deaths. The will of Thomas Cole, an antislavery activist and businessman in Boston during the 1830s and 1840s, illustrates the values of a man of relatively modest means. Cole was a hairdresser with a shop on Congress Street, later removed to Atkinson, and a home on Southac Court off of Southac (later Phillips) Street. He was a charter member of the Massachusetts General Colored Association, a local black antislavery group, and was active in church and fraternal organizations. Upon his death in 1847 his estate totaled just under $3,000. After providing for the settlement of his debts and his funeral expenses, Cole left separate bequests to his minister, the minister's wife, and two friends, one the woman who cared for him before he died. He also left money to his nephew, to fellow hairdressers and friends John T. Hilton and Alfred G. Howard, and to Hilton's young son Thomas. Cole carefully distributed the remainder of his estate in accordance with his sense of community responsibility. He left $400 to the Odd Fellows lodge with specific instructions that it be used for the funeral expenses of members and to aid their widows and orphans. He charged the deacons of the African Baptist Church, also called the First Independent Baptist Church, on Belknap (later Joy) Street with using his $300 bequest for "the relief of the sick, poor, and destitute members." Any remaining property was to be distributed to charities chosen by his friends and executors, Hilton and Howard. Two other provisions of his will provide an interesting glimpse of Cole's perception of his community's needs. He left his books to the Adelphic Union Library Association, a literary, discussion, and self-improvement group organized by black men a few years before. Should his nephew not reach the age of majority, his $300 bequest and its proceeds were to be used to build a meeting hall for blacks.[19]

African-American entrepreneurs made up a disproportionate number of those who led Boston's black protest organizations and who represented the community at local, regional, and national protest meetings, as even a cursory look at the records of the state meetings of Massachusetts blacks illustrates. At the statewide gatherings of 1854, held in Boston, clothing

18. C. Peter Ripley, et al., eds., *Black Abolitionist Papers* (Chapel Hill, 1985–1992), 3:303n.

19. Horton and Horton, *Black Bostonians*; Carol Buchalter Stapp, *Afro-Americans in Antebellum Boston: An Analysis of Probate Records* (New York, 1993), 164.

dealer Lewis Hayden sat on the committee appointed to investigate the possibility of founding a manual labor school for the training and education of black youth. Blacksmith Joel W. Lewis and clothing dealer Jonas Clark served on the convention's executive committee. Clothier E. F. B. Mundrucu was a vice president of the state convention in 1858, and barber John J. Smith along with caterer Joshua B. Smith served on that convention's business committee. At the national conventions Boston's black entrepreneurs were similarly active. Robert Roberts, a printer, and James G. Barbadoes, a hairdresser and later a clothing dealer, represented Boston at the 1831 convention in Philadelphia, and Barbadoes was appointed vice president. The men returned the next year. Barbadoes went on to serve at several conventions throughout the decade, joined at various times by hairdresser John Hilton and tailor Henry Weeden.[20]

The list of founders and early officers of the Massachusetts General Colored Association shows the importance of independent entrepreneurs to community organizations. The most famous of the founders was David Walker. The Boston agent for New York's *Freedom's Journal*, the first African-American newspaper in the country, founded in 1827, Walker authored a fiery antislavery tract, his *Appeal*, in 1829. His exhortation to the slaves to recover their manhood and rise up against their masters infuriated southern slaveholders, who put a price on his head, and suspicions were aroused when he was found dead on Bridge Street in Boston in 1830. Another founder of the association was barber Walker Lewis, a member of an established Boston family. His father, Thomas, was an original officer of the African Society, a mutual aid organization, a founding member of the African Baptist Church, and active in the African Masonic Lodge and in the early campaign for a black school in the city. Walker Lewis moved to Lowell and opened a barbershop there in 1830, but he and his family remained active in Boston's antislavery work for generations.[21]

In 1833 the Massachusetts General Colored Association became an auxiliary of the newly created, integrated New England Anti-Slavery Society. At that time the officers were Thomas Dalton, president, William G. Nell, vice president, and James G. Barbadoes, secretary. Formerly a bootblack, Dalton operated a clothing store on Brattle Street and was so successful

20. This pattern of black entrepreneurs overrepresented among the community leadership was not unique to antebellum Boston. See James Oliver Horton and Stacy Flaherty, "Black Leadership in Antebellum Cincinnati," in Henry Louis Taylor, Jr., ed., *Race and the City: Work, Community, and Protest in Cincinnati, 1820–1970* (Urbana, 1993), 70–95.

21. Ripley, *Black Abolitionist Papers*, 3:387n.; James Oliver Horton, *Free People of Color: Inside the African American Community* (Washington, D.C., 1993).

that at his death he left an estate of $50,000. Barbadoes was a stalwart of the abolition movement in Boston beginning in the mid 1820s. He represented the community at the black national conventions from 1831 to 1834 and served on the board of managers of the American Anti-Slavery Society from 1833 to 1836. Combining entrepreneurial interests and his commitment to racial progress, Barbadoes moved his family to Jamaica in 1840 with the intention of starting a silkworm industry there and died of malaria the following year.[22]

The delegate whom the Massachusetts General Colored Association appointed to the New England Anti-Slavery Society was businessman Joshua Easton. He was the son of prominent turn-of-the-century manufacturer James Easton, a blacksmith who served under George Washington during the Revolutionary War, helping to build Boston's fortifications on Dorchester Heights. James Easton educated himself, and he and some other black men combined their resources and opened a forge and nail factory in Bridgewater, Massachusetts. He operated the factory for twenty years, making nails, edge tools, and anchors, and doing ironwork for the construction of the Tremont Theatre in Boston and for the Boston Marine Railway. For the advice he gave black entrepreneurs in Boston, Easton became known as the "Black Lawyer." He involved his sons Caleb, Joshua, Sylvanus, and Hosea in the business, and the factory became a family enterprise. Joshua Easton and Hosea Easton, who eventually became a minister, were charter members of the Massachusetts General Colored Association.[23]

Black businessmen provided funds and facilities to support the antislavery and civil rights work of white abolitionists as well as the activities of their own community. When William Lloyd Garrison and Isaac Knapp started publishing *The Liberator* in Boston in 1831, they did so with borrowed type, a sparsely furnished rented office, and a small amount of credit. The contributions of a few friends and the moral and financial support of Philadelphia's James Forten made publication of the radical abolitionist paper possible. It was Forten who forwarded the $54 in advance proceeds from the paper's first twenty-seven subscribers, all of them black. Garrison and his paper, attacked and denounced from both the South and the North, were sustained by the black community. Boston's African Americans were especially important, providing Garrison with ap-

22. Horton and Horton, *Black Bostonians*; Nell, *Colored Patriots of the American Revolution* (1855; reprint, New York, 1968); Ripley, *Black Abolitionist Papers*.
   23. Nell, *Colored Patriots*, 33.

prentices Thomas Paul, Jr., and William C. Nell, agents for his paper and other publications, subscribers, and financial support.[24]

Not only did local businessmen work to effect change through community organizations; many involved their own businesses in the causes of education, abolition, and aid to fugitive slaves. Capt. Paul Cuffe, one of the most successful businessmen in New England, the son of an African-born slave and an Indian mother, operated a school at his home in Westport, where he taught navigation to local youths. He was committed to the freedom of his people, and in 1810 he sailed for the British colony in Africa called Sierra Leone. Cuffe hoped to gain permission from the abolitionists and merchants of England who controlled the colony to establish a trade between Sierra Leone and the United States that would show such a venture could be profitable even if it did not include trading in slaves. He also became convinced that the colony was a suitable and desirable place for colonization by American free blacks. The War of 1812 interrupted Cuffe's plans, but late in 1815 he embarked for Africa carrying thirty-four settlers on his ship, including five families from Boston. Cuffe financed the journey of many of these with his own money.[25]

Black businesses manifested the entrepreneurs' sense of community responsibility in many different ways. The Eastons operated a school for the young people associated with their factory in Bridgewater, bringing the benefits of education to children sent to work at an early age and, undoubtedly, attempting to counter the education offered by a society that, Hosea Easton contended, taught "that a Negro is part monkey." The factory and the school emphasized strict rules of morality and economic probity, and the factory operated on temperance principles, refusing to make the customary provisions of alcoholic beverages to workers.[26]

Boardinghouse keepers frequently acted in service to community members, especially because many boardinghouses rented lodging to sailors who faced special dangers each time their ships put into port in a slave state. Often, free black sailors were jailed while they were in port, with incarceration costs charged to the ship and sometimes passed on to the sailor. One person to whom sailors in trouble could turn was the operator of the boardinghouse where they generally stayed in their home port. When a sailor

24. Wendell Phillips Garrison and Francis Jackson Garrison, *William Lloyd Garrison, 1805–1879: The Story of His Life Told by His Children* (Boston, 1885–1889).

25. Thomas, *Rise to be a People*; Wiggins, *Captain Paul Cuffe's Logs and Letters*.

26. Nell, *Colored Patriots*; Hosea Easton, "Founded in Avarice" from *A Treatise on Intellectual Character . . .* (Boston, 1837) in Herbert Aptheker, *A Documentary History of the Negro People in the United States* (New York, 1951), 1:168.

named John Tidd was jailed in New Orleans in 1834, his papers attesting to his free status and his clothing were confiscated. In this condition he was in danger of being sold into slavery, so he wrote to boardinghouse keeper Arthur Jones to ask for aid. Jones organized residents of the boardinghouse and together with other businessmen convinced the Massachusetts governor to aid Tidd and support a campaign to protest such imprisonment.[27]

Fugitive slaves who came to Boston with the intent either to settle there or to make their way to Canada depended on aid from many people in the antebellum community, but they were especially indebted to direct aid from black businessmen. Lawyer Robert Morris defended captured fugitives; Dr. John Rock cared for them when they were sick or injured; and clothing dealers such as John R. Manley, Jonas W. Clark, and James Scott replaced fugitives' slave garb with clothing suitable for freedom. The account book of the Vigilance Committee of Boston lists the names of clothing dealer Lewis Hayden, who also sheltered fugitives, and John Taylor, who boarded them at his "temperance house" in the city.[28]

Black barbershops were particularly important in the community's network of informal organizations aiding fugitive slaves. Barbers played many roles in the community and their shops were places where people gathered to discuss political issues, find out about available jobs, buy concert tickets, and even rehearse their parts in plays and musical performances. Massachusetts Sen. Charles Sumner often visited John J. Smith's barbershop at Staniford and Green streets to gather news and check the political and social pulse of the black community. Smith, who had migrated to Boston from Richmond, Virginia, was himself active in the politics of the community, representing Boston at national black conventions during the 1850s. Other barbershops, including Thomas Cole's on Atkinson Street and Peter Howard's on Cambridge Street, doubled as stations on the underground railroad.[29]

Antebellum black entrepreneurs acted on their sense of responsibility to the community by providing many types of material aid to individuals and by contributing their time and resources to organizations working to benefit the race. Yet their social responsibility also extended as well to more

27. Horton and Horton, *Black Bostonians*.

28. Horton and Horton, *Black Bostonians*; Boston City Directory, 1848–1849; Francis Jackson, "Account Book of the Vigilance Committee of Boston," manuscript, Massachusetts Historical Society.

29. John Daniels, *In Freedom's Birthplace* (Cambridge, Mass., 1914); for information on Boston's barbershops as political and social gathering places, see Horton and Horton, *Black Bostonians*.

symbolic functions. They saw themselves as representing African Americans for the rest of society, charged with proving the moral worth and humanity of blacks. Like middle-class white businessmen of the time, black businessmen preached that those who aspired to success must of necessity be sober and trustworthy in their business dealings. This was important advice for all entrepreneurs who depended on credit and on the promises of their associates, but it was especially important for those belonging to a group many presumed to be morally inferior and less intelligent. By all reports, it was the unimpeachable conduct of Capt. Paul Cuffe and his all-black crew that allowed them to sail up the river to the eastern shore of Maryland in the heart of slaveholding territory in the late eighteenth century and to trade unmolested. The Yankee trader with respectable credentials made sure his crew acted with "conciliating propriety" and left Maryland with a valuable cargo of Indian corn.[30]

When the First Annual Convention of the People of Color met in Philadelphia in 1831, black leaders made their values clear. They emphasized their belief that the progress of the race and the attainment of black rights depended on "education, temperance and economy," the values of the growing nineteenth-century middle-class business culture. Among its first orders of business, the convention established committees charged with putting these principles into action by raising funds for a college. The institution, to be located in New Haven, was to provide a "scientific" education but also, through a manual training program, opportunities for students to earn their education and "obtain a useful Mechanical or Agricultural profession." Businessmen were well represented on the committee, which included James Forten of Philadelphia, Thomas Downing of New York, and James Barbadoes and Hosea Easton of Boston, the latter formerly a businessman but then a minister.[31]

For three days in early August 1853 crowds of Boston's black people gathered first at the Twelfth Baptist Church, then later at the Belknap Street Baptist Church to listen to a series of lectures by prominent African Americans on the broad theme, "Prejudice and Opportunity." Local leaders, including Lewis Hayden, spoke at length, encouraging debate and "urging the necessity of individual as well as united action." At the invitation of the Boston meeting Frederick Douglass had come up from New

30. Thomas, *Rise to be a People*, 17.

31. Howard Holman Bell, ed., *Minutes of the Proceedings of the National Negro Conventions, 1830–1864* (New York, 1969), 5–6. This June 1831 meeting in Philadelphia was officially called the First Annual Convention, although there had been an earlier organizational meeting in September 1830, also in Philadelphia.

Bedford where he was lecturing. As one in attendance recalled, "the colored citizens . . . [were] anxious once more to gaze upon the manly form and listen to the thrilling eloquence" of one who had lived among them but had recently moved away to western New York. Douglass was an inspiration to Boston blacks and, indeed, to blacks everywhere. He had sprung from slavery to stand as a living refutation of the charges of inferiority and incapacity leveled at the race. He was what a century later African Americans would term a "role model" pointing the way to racial progress. Douglass was certainly not the only living testimony to black achievement, and he urged black people to insure that future generations would not want for examples of African-American success.[32]

Douglass encouraged blacks to learn trades and establish businesses. Whites, even abolitionist friends, could not be depended on, he said, for too many did "not reduce their theory to practice" by employing blacks in honorable trades or providing apprenticeships for black youth. If African Americans were to improve themselves and the prospects for their race, Douglass argued, "we must . . . do something for ourselves," and those who had already achieved must pass along their knowledge and skill to the young. "Some of us have trades. We must teach them to our children. They must be taught to make boots, as well as black them; to construct bridges, as well as walk over them."[33]

There was controversy and a difference of opinion at the Boston meetings over the wisdom of establishing an exclusively black manual labor school, which Douglass favored. Black lawyer Robert Morris opposed the plan, saying that excluding whites "depreciated" the school. Others agreed, stating that there was no advantage to blacks in excluding whites from the school and that Douglass had "somehow missed the mark." Douglass defended his point, but the matter had not been resolved by the end of the lecture series, nor would it be for some time to come. The above exchange illustrates both the diversity of opinion and the shared viewpoints among free blacks. There was disagreement on whether an integrationist or separatist approach to racial progress would prove most effective, but there was

32. *Frederick Douglass' Paper*, Aug. 12, 1853, quoted in John W. Blassingame, ed., *The Frederick Douglass Papers* (New Haven, 1979–1992), 2:441.

33. Blassingame, *Frederick Douglass Papers*, 2:443. There is a body of evidence to substantiate this charge, made by a number of black abolitionists, that white abolitionists discriminated against black workers. James McCune Smith publicly indicted many white abolitionists at the annual meeting of the American and Foreign Anti-Slavery Society in 1852. See Horton and Horton, *Black Bostonians*, and Bertram Wyatt-Brown, *Lewis Tappan and the Evangelical War Against Slavery* (New York, 1971).

complete agreement that those who had achieved had a special responsibility to "uplift the race." Racial progress demanded "pursuing an honorable employment, reflecting credit upon themselves, and those with whom they are by complexion and position identified."[34]

Throughout the antebellum period, from David Walker's writing in the 1820s to the public statements and printed words of activists in the 1850s, community leaders continued to preach the values of industry and economy and to see their own efforts as contributions to the elevation of the race. Their successes constituted an argument for black equality, and they took on their shoulders the responsibility of proving to their doubting countrymen that they and their fellow African Americans were human beings worthy of full citizenship. When George T. Downing, a successful second-generation restauranteur and hotel operator from Providence, was elected president of the August 1859 national convention in Boston, he delivered an opening address that clearly stated his belief that the advancement of the race depended on the power to be obtained through the success of at least some African Americans.

In the fight against racial injustice Downing urged blacks to exercise their right to vote where they could, but he argued that commanding respect for black rights would also require the attainment of wealth and learning. Downing asserted that blacks had already demonstrated that they possessed one of the requisites for power in American society—"moral character." Learning and wealth, the other two sources of power and progress, were most clearly the province of black entrepreneurs.[35] Membership in Boston's antebellum black business community did not insure social activism. There were entrepreneurs apparently unassociated with protest or community service, but clearly such involvement was valued and even expected. However, community needs were so great that they could not carry this burden alone. Black professionals, especially ministers and teachers, were deeply involved in community service, as were sailors, dock workers, domestic workers, and many others on the lower rungs of the black community's economic ladder. Yet, entrepreneurs often brought more resources to the effort. Their participation in antebellum Boston reflected, in part, the size of the black community, too small perhaps to encourage the social stratification that scholars have noted for much larger post-Civil War or late-nineteenth-century black communities in major

34. W. H. Logan, speaking before the Boston meeting, *Frederick Douglass' Paper*, Aug. 12, 1853, quoted in Blassingame, *Frederick Douglass Papers*, 2:444.

35. William Wells Brown, *The Black Man, His Antecedents, His Genius, and His Achievements*, 4th ed. (1865; reprint, Salem, N.H., 1992), 251.

northern cities. Antebellum Boston also reflected a distinctly northern type of social structure among African Americans, much less stratified than was true in large southern port cities like Charleston or New Orleans. Elsewhere we have argued that these regional social patterns became less distinct after the Civil War, during the last decades of the century and especially in the early twentieth century, when large numbers of southern blacks migrated to northern cities.[36] In the pre-Civil War years, when Boston's blacks of all economic levels and occupational groups shared neighborhoods and associated with one another daily, it is not surprising that black professionals and entrepreneurs understood the responsibilities of privilege and met the community's expectations that they would act cooperatively in the solidarity of race.

36. Michael P. Johnson and James L. Roark, *Black Masters: A Free Family of Color in the Old South* (New York, 1984). Horton, *Free People of Color*, 139–144.

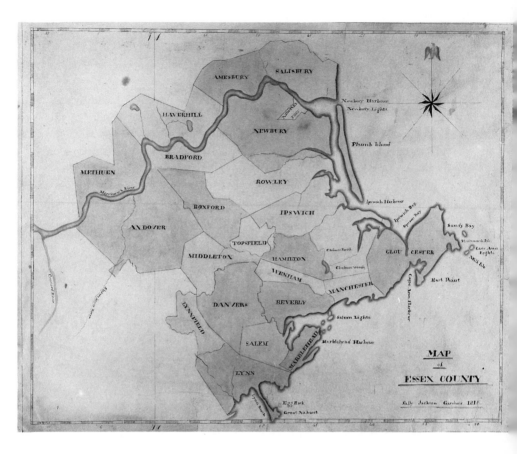

Map of Essex County, 1816. Ink and Watercolor by Sally Jackson
Gardner. Collection of the Massachusetts Historical Society.

The Making of an Empire:
Boston and Essex County, 1790–1850

Benjamin W. Labaree

IN HIS INAUGURAL address to the Boston City Council in January 1849 Mayor John Prescott Bigelow declared that

> The long winter of New England isolation is broken:—she now warms and flourishes in friendly and thrifty intercourse with the luxuriant West; and it is not too much to anticipate that the day will come when there will be no greater nor more prosperous city upon the American continent than the City of the Pilgrims.[1]

The completion a few years before of a rail connection between Boston and the Hudson River via the Western Rail Road from Worcester seemed reason enough for the mayor's optimism. Even more promising was the soon-to-be completed link with Canada and the St. Lawrence River valley at Ogdensburg, New York, over the rails of a half-dozen cooperating companies in northern New England. To commemorate the latter achievement Boston treated itself to a three-day Railroad Jubilee in September 1851, culminating in a dinner for 3,600 on the Common attended by President Millard Fillmore and the governor-general of Canada, the Earl of Elgin and Kincardine.[2] The long quest for a route of its own to "the luxuriant West" was over. Boston's re-emergence as a metropolis of the first rank seemed near at hand.[3]

Bostonians' quest for reliable links to the interior began in the last decade of the eighteenth century. As the lingering postrevolutionary depression

1. "Inaugural Address to the City Council. By John Bigelow. Jan. 1, 1849," reprinted in *The Railroad Jubilee: An Account of the Celebration Commemorative of the Opening of Railroad Communication between Boston and Canada, September 17th, 18th, and 19th, 1851* (Boston, 1852).

2. Howard Mumford Jones, "The Unity of New England Culture," *Proceedings of the Massachusetts Historical Society* 79(1967):75–76.

3. The humorously patronizing letter of congratulation from New York's Gov. Wash-

gradually receded and the new Federal government assumed power in 1789, Boston's merchants anticipated a return to the level of maritime activity that had put their port well ahead of New York and close to Philadelphia in the years just before the war.[4] Boston's maritime fleet had suffered severe wartime losses, but so too had most of its New England rivals. New Bedford had already begun to specialize in whaling. The growth of Providence was still largely a gleam in the eye of the Brown brothers, and to the north, both Portsmouth and Portland were too distant to challenge Boston's effort to expand its hinterland.

Boston's most serious competition for hegemony came from the ports of Essex County. Taken collectively, the populations of Salem, Marblehead, Gloucester, and Newburyport exceeded Boston's 18,000 by 30 percent in 1790, and in 1794 (the first year for which discrete figures are available) they owned about the same amount of shipping (66,369 tons) as did Boston (66,962).[5] Between them, Salem and Newburyport served as market towns for almost all of Essex County's nearly 60,000 people. In addition to a fairly good network of roads through most of the county these two towns relied on river and coastal transportation to serve their hinterlands. Highways and

ington Hunt offers a delightful antidote to the pontificating addresses and stuffy letters of regret that fill the pages of the official account of the celebration:

> We the people of New York . . . have seen you invading our soil, filling our valleys, boring our mountains at some points, levelling them at others, and turning your steam engines loose upon us to run up and down, roaming at large throughout our borders. Indeed, it has long been evident that you intended to ride over us in your efforts to entice away our western brethren. . . . [But] I am somewhat curious to know at what point your next encroachments will begin. There are limits to human endurance, and I must warn you to pause and take breath before making fresh tracks upon our territory. We have never desired to monopolize the Western trade. After yielding to you a share sufficient to satisfy any but an inordinate and grasping ambition, enough will remain for us.—*Railroad Jubilee*, 207–208.

4. Ports were assessed in terms of their average annual tonnage entered and cleared for the five-year period 1768–1772, calculated from Customs 16/1 (Public Record Office, London). Philadelphia ranked first, with 84,338 tons, Boston second with 76,597, Charleston third at 61,575 tons, and New York fourth with 51,825 tons of shipping entered and cleared. Maritime enterprise during the first decade after the Revolution is difficult to document, but on the strength of its coastal trade Boston would appear to have been more active than either Philadelphia or New York in the early 1790s. U.S. Congress, *American State Papers: Commerce and Navigation*, various years.

5. Calculated from *American State Papers: Commerce and Navigation*. The year 1794 is the first for which tonnage figures are available for separate customs districts. For the same year New York owned 94,062 tons of shipping and Philadelphia, 74,169.

water routes linked Essex County with Boston as well, but in no sense was the "province" a dependent of Boston. Its seaports maintained their own trading routes to the Canadian maritimes, Great Britain, the European continent, and Asia, and they dominated trade with such of the West Indies as were open to American vessels. In 1791 Essex County exported slightly over $1,000,000 worth of American produce from its fisheries, farms, and forests, just $75,000 less than the exports of Boston itself.[6]

In the eighteenth and early nineteenth centuries seacoast communities could increase their wealth through a variety of maritime activities. First Marblehead and then Gloucester supported large fleets of fishing vessels, for example, while Bath and Waldoboro, Maine, on the other hand, prospered as shipbuilding centers. Some ports grew wealthy by specializing in commercial relations with particular regions of the world. Salem's early pepper trade with the East Indies and its later domination of commerce with East Africa are examples. A town might even succeed in combining a number of these activities, as did Newburyport for a time, with shipbuilding, fishing, and trade with the West Indies. But every merchant knew that only those coastal communities that became entrepôts for a prosperous hinterland could themselves expect to develop into flourishing seaports. New England presented a particular challenge because of the convex arc of its coastline from Portland, Maine, to Fairfield, Connecticut. The region's numerous coastal towns had therefore to compete with each other in the struggle to control overlapping segments of territory in the interior. In contrast, the gently concave coastline from New York to Cape Hatteras gave ports in those regions more room to develop their own hinterlands.

Unlike its major east coast rivals, New York, Philadelphia, and later Baltimore, Boston had no natural routes to the interior. Neither the Mystic River nor the Charles offered access further than a few miles inland. To the south, the Blackstone River valley led southeast out of Massachusetts toward the developing port of Providence, and in New England's central valley the Connecticut River ran south to Long Island Sound, where New York took over its trade.[7] Although the Merrimack penetrated northern New England for a distance of about 150 miles, it met the sea 40 miles north of Boston, at Newburyport. Boston's extensive coastal trade, the most active of any American port in the colonial period, was at best only partial compensa-

6. Figures compiled from United States Census, 1790, and *American State Papers: Commerce and Navigation*.

7. George Adams, *The Massachusetts Register for the Year 1853* . . . (Boston, 1853) makes much of the natural disadvantages that Boston had to overcome.

tion for the absence of a natural route to an interior hinterland. Boston's leaders would have to take more aggressive measures if they intended to contend for prominence in the competitive postwar world of commerce.

At Newburyport, for instance, forward-looking local merchants had already begun to improve their port's inland access. In 1791 a group of investors financed construction of the Essex-Merrimack toll bridge, which crossed the river three miles upstream and opened an overland route into New Hampshire. A canal dug the same year from the Merrimack through the salt marshes to Hampton provided a second route to New Hampshire's coastal communities. Another passage led south through Plum Island Sound to a short canal that gave access to the Ipswich River and, later, all the way to Essex. In 1792 several Newburyporters, including some of the bridge investors, were incorporated as The Proprietors of the Locks and Canals on Merrimack River. This group undertook to facilitate the passage of timber and other commodities along the river by constructing a canal around the thirty-two-foot drop at Pawtucket Falls in Chelmsford. Four years and $50,000 later the Pawtucket Canal opened to traffic, marred only by a prophetic accident at the opening ceremonies that dumped company officials into the waterway. Merchants of Newburyport had high hopes that these improvements would insure the port a steady supply of ship timber and extend its hinterland well into the interior of Massachusetts and New Hampshire by the river that flowed past their waterfront to the sea.[8]

Even before the first flatboats had reached Newburyport, however, several Boston investors had begun to investigate the possibility of building a canal of their own into the interior. At first they considered the suggestion of General Henry Knox for a waterway connecting the Connecticut River at Millers Falls to Boston but ultimately discarded the idea as impracticable, as indeed it was, given the limited engineering skills of the time.[9] Then in 1793 the General Court granted a charter to The Proprietors of the

8. Essex–Merrimack Bridge Papers, Historical Society of Old Newbury; John J. Currier, *History of Newburyport, Mass. 1764–1905* (Newburyport, 1906), 1:147, 368–372. On the canal: actually the first raft of boards went through the uncompleted waterway in mid April 1795; [Newburyport] *Impartial Herald,* Apr. 14, 1795; Benjamin W. Labaree, *Patriots and Partisans: The Merchants of Newburyport, 1764–1815* (Cambridge, Mass., 1962), 98–99; Harry C. Dinmore, "Proprietors of Locks and Canals: The Founding of Lowell," in Arthur L. Eno, Jr., ed., *Cotton was King: A History of Lowell, Massachusetts* (Lowell, 1976), 70–71; Robert Weible, ed., *The Continuing Revolution: A History of Lowell, Massachusetts* (Lowell, 1991), 11–12.

9. Christopher Roberts, *The Middlesex Canal, 1793–1860* (Cambridge, Mass., 1938), 19–25.

Middlesex Canal, headed by James Sullivan, attorney general of Massachusetts. This group planned to capture the hinterland of New Hampshire for the port of Boston by building a canal to the Charles River from the Merrimack River at Middlesex Village, close to the southernmost point in its course. The directors chose to defer extending the system further north and west by a waterway that would join the Merrimack and Connecticut rivers in New Hampshire.

Several businessmen of Medford, through whose town the canal would pass, comprised a significant segment of the original investors, but within a few years they had sold most of their shares to Bostonians of more considerable means. Joseph Barrell, Christopher Gore, Andrew Craigie, Oliver Wendell, and William Tudor were among the first wealthy Bostonians to support the project, but several of them, like Craigie, bailed out early, and Barrell needed help carrying his eighty shares. Over a thirteen-year period each share was assessed a total of $610, a considerable burden for some of the investors. Construction took place under the guidance of the self-educated engineer Loammi Baldwin. When finished on the last day of December 1803, the waterway required thirteen locks to carry traffic up and over a rise of 107 feet along its twenty-seven mile route. In the next decade the canal's directors invested heavily in building additional locks that extended the navigation of the Merrimack River all the way to Concord, New Hampshire, some fifty miles upstream from the canal entrance at Middlesex Village.[10]

The Middlesex Canal succeeded in its immediate objective of diverting the flow of at least some of interior New Hampshire's resources to Boston. It brought down lumber, cordwood for fuel, and other wood products like shingles and clapboards. Cargoes of ship timber made possible the establishment of Thacher Magoun's famous shipyard on the Mystic River at Medford. Shippers could move their bulk commodities by the canal at about half the cost of transportation by land and were therefore in a better position to compete with coasting vessels that brought similar goods from Maine. Shippers could also patronize teamsters as a competitive alternative because of their ability to deliver door-to-door.[11] Upstream cargoes, on the other hand, remained difficult to obtain until after the establishment of mills at Lowell, Massachusetts, and Nashua and Concord, New Hampshire, which provided larger markets. Overall, the Middlesex Canal did not

10. Roberts, *Middlesex Canal*, 41–43, 114, 124–135.

11. See the nine reasons offered by the canal agent to explain why some shippers might have preferred transporting their goods overland, in Roberts, *Middlesex Canal*, 149–151.

prove to be a financial success. The Proprietors delayed issuing their first dividend until 1819, and total payments before operations ended in 1854 never matched the capital outlays assessed against the stockholders.[12]

In a larger sense, however, the Middlesex Canal had a significance that reached beyond its modest economic role. It was America's first complex waterway. Builders of other canals, most notably those who constructed the Erie Canal, learned many lessons from Boston's pioneering effort. And if the Middlesex Canal did not exactly open up the interior of New England to the merchants of Boston, it surely helped to rekindle interest in the project to connect western Massachusetts with the coast at Boston. In 1826 a special commission studied the possibility of a canal all the way to the Hudson, via Fitchburg, Millers Falls, and a tunnel through Hoosic Mountain, but the General Court found the estimated cost, $6,000,000, out of the question.[13] Nor were private investors willing or able to step forward. There was nothing inherently wrong with the route itself, which railroad builders would adopt a half-century later, but it was not meant for a canal. New England's topography made the construction of any east-west waterway prohibitively expensive. In the 1830s Massachusetts investors of both public and private funds would be glad they had not squandered their capital on building a western canal.

For the citizens of Newburyport the completion of the Middlesex Canal was a mortal blow, killing whatever chance their town might have had to become the entrepôt for the entire Merrimack Valley. When Newburyport's Proprietors of Locks and Canals learned about the rival project, they complained that its objective was nothing less than "to ruin the trade of our river from its old and natural channel to the waters of Boston Harbour."[14]

12. Roberts, *Middlesex Canal*, 159–187; Charles F. Adams, Jr., "Canal and Railroad Enterprise," in Justin Winsor, ed., *The Memorial History of Boston, including Suffolk County, Massachusetts, 1630–1880* (Boston, 1881), 4:111–113. A description of the Merrimack River's canal system as of 1815 is reprinted in Timothy Dwight, *Travels in New England and New York*, ed. Barbara Miller Solomon with Patricia M. King (Cambridge, Mass., 1969), 1:294–296.

13. Adams, "Canal and Railroad Enterprise," 113–116.

14. Proprietors of Locks and Canals, *Directors' Records*, 1:77, as quoted in Weible, *Continuing Revolution*, 12. Weible downplays the competition between the Pawtucket and Middlesex canals, pointing out that at least two men owned stock in both companies. Writing in 1881 Boston's Charles Francis Adams, Jr., expressed a different point of view in his chapter on canals and railroads for the *Memorial History of Boston*: "The Merrimac once threatened to drain off the interior of New Hampshire to Portsmouth [*sic*], unless

Salem's irascible Jeffersonian diarist, the Reverend William Bentley, predicted with just a hint of sympathy for Federalist Newburyport that the town was unlikely to rise to its former prosperity were the Middlesex Canal to prove successful.[15] To be sure, those who hoped to navigate the Merrimack faced other problems, including obstructions in the river below Pawtucket Falls and a shifting bar at its mouth. But the opportunity to extend the port's influence upstream would have been more than sufficient incentive to invest in the engineering necessary to overcome these obstacles and improve the river channel, as indeed was done in later decades.[16]

Long before the Middlesex Canal had begun to syphon off the natural resources of the Merrimack Valley for Boston, Essex County suffered the continuing loss of an even more valuable resource, some of its most enterprising men of business. In the 1790s, after graduating from Harvard, Newburyport natives Patrick Tracy Jackson and his brother-in-law, Francis Cabot Lowell, decided to settle in Boston, where the latter's father, John, (another Newburyport native) served as judge of the Massachusetts Superior Court. Patrick's father, Jonathan, remained in Newburyport for a few more years, but he too moved to Boston in 1796. Among other merchants who moved to Boston after doing business along the Merrimack in this era was John Coffin Jones. From Beverly came several members of the Cabot and Lee families, and later the prominent merchant Israel Thorndike. In 1808, Salem lost William Gray, its wealthiest shipowner, who followed Stephen Higginson and several other merchants from the area; Marblehead's Hoopers, also merchants, came after Gray.

---

something were done to control events." Adams's imperial perspective, if not his ignorance of northern New England geography, might in part be explained by the fact that his father had been a director of the canal company for over 20 years (1830–1852), and both John Adams and John Quincy Adams had been among the early stockholders. It is clear from newspaper references to "the very considerable benefit which will result from the navigation both up and down" the river that Newburyporters saw the Merrimack Valley as a market for their imports as well as a source of ship timber and other wood products. *Impartial Herald*, Feb. 13. 1795. It should be noted that in colonial years, Boston, Salem, and Newburyport shared overland traffic along the Merrimack Valley. Percy W. Bidwell and John I. Falconer, *History of Agriculture in the Northern United States, 1620–1860* (reprint, New York, 1941), 141.

15. William Bentley, *The Diary of William Bentley, D.D.* (Salem, 1905–1914), 4:335, 344.

16. "Lieut. Col. Anderson's Report of the Survey of Newburyport Harbor, transmitted with the letter from the Secretary of War to the Nineteenth Congress, Feb. 1827." A copy is at the Historical Society of Old Newbury. New York, Philadelphia, and ports situated near the mouths of rivers regularly employed dredges to keep channels clear for shipping.

For those who remained in the county Boston drew steadily closer in the first decades of the nineteenth century with the construction of three major turnpikes that linked the farthest corners of Essex County with the metropolis. The Salem Turnpike, the Newburyport Turnpike, and the Essex Turnpike, which connected Andover with Salem, made travel to and trading with Boston both cheaper and easier than ever before, especially after Newburyport's Benjamin Hale introduced major improvements to the safety and comfort of the stagecoaches then in use. Four-horse wagons carried freight in both directions on a regular basis, and the Eastern Stage Company, founded in 1818, served the population residing north and east of Boston with a well organized system of transportation that survived until after the coming of the railroads. The fact that much of the capital for these turnpikes came from county merchants suggests that the initiative for improved transportation came from the outlanders rather than from Bostonians. Essex investors who hoped that these turnpikes would be money-earners, however, were sorely disappointed. Newburyport's turnpike cost almost as much as the Middlesex Canal to build (nearly $500,000) and paid only meager dividends.[17]

Throughout the good years of neutral trade from 1793 to the Embargo of 1807 the four Essex County ports managed to stay fairly close to Boston in both maritime activity and population. The shipping they owned totaled 114,156 tons in 1810, not too far behind Boston's 149,169, and their aggregate population stood at 32,090, just twelve hundred fewer people than Boston's 33,250. In fact, Essex County as a whole still had over twice the population of Boston's Suffolk County. But the War of 1812 took a far heavier toll on the smaller ports of Essex County than on Boston. At war's end their tonnage was down nearly 25 percent from its prewar high to just over 86,675, while Boston's dropped only 8 percent to 137,009. Although both regions would subsequently experience further decline, Boston's was less severe. The census of 1820 showed that the population of the Essex ports suffered a net loss of 500 from their 1810 totals, while Boston gained more than 10,000. Marblehead and Newburyport were worst hit; the former lost 60 percent of its shipping, along with a measure of its population,

17. D. Hamilton Hurd, comp., *History of Essex County, Massachusetts* . . . (Philadelphia, 1888), 1:lxvi–lxxvi; James D. Phillips, "Transportation in Essex County," *Essex Institute Historical Collections* 85(1949):245–258; Currier, *History of Newburyport*, 1:377, 394–398.

while the latter's tonnage dropped by more than a third and its population decreased by 800.[18]

"Nothing will restore this town to its former state of prosperity so effectively," wrote the editor of the *Impartial Herald* in September 1817, "as making the Merrimack navigable." He and others proposed the construction of a canal around Hunt's Falls below the Pawtucket, and two years later the town's leading merchants were incorporated as the Proprietors of the Merrimack Canal to tackle the project.[19] But before work began these efforts were overtaken by the momentous events that transformed the Pawtucket Falls into a major industrial site, and most Newburyporters gradually abandoned the hope that their town might still become the entrepôt for the entire Merrimack Valley. By no means did the community retreat from the sea altogether, however. The banks of the Merrimack continued as a major shipbuilding region until the Civil War, and Newburyporters maintained a lively fishing fleet as well. But the town no longer sent its own vessels to Europe or Asia, its West Indies trade dwindled, and its commerce with the Maritime provinces increasingly was carried in Canadian bottoms. Newburyport's shipowners shifted their business to the carrying trade, freighting cargoes from New Orleans, the Chesapeake, or New York to Great Britain and the Continent, their vessels rarely if ever returning to their nominal homeport. "Newburyport has withered under the influence of Boston," Caleb Cushing concluded in 1825, noting a process that would accelerate thereafter. At the same time, Salem was also losing its function as a market town. "The direction of all the turnpikes to Boston," Bentley observed as early as 1816, "has much injured the inland trade of Salem." The citizens "go almost by instinct to Fanueil [*sic*] Hall Market," he remarked on another occasion.[20]

Although Boston suffered far less than its Essex County neighbors from the vicissitudes of the War of 1812, its own maritime commerce was also slow to recover. The port's total tonnage further declined by 1820, with particularly heavy losses in vessels registered for foreign commerce, down

18. *American State Papers: Commerce and Navigation*; Census of 1820.

19. *Impartial Herald*, Sept. 19, 26, 1817; Currier, *History of Newburyport*, 1:149.

20. Benjamin W. Labaree, "The Search for Recovery. New England Outports after the War of 1812: Newburyport as a Case Study," in Conrad E. Wright, ed., *Massachusetts and the New Nation* (Boston, 1992), 54–63; Cushing quoted in Samuel Eliot Morison, *The Maritime History of Massachusetts, 1783–1860* (Boston, 1921), 216; for Bentley, *Diary*, 4:348, 392.

more than 30 percent since 1810.[21] At an average construction cost of forty dollars per ton, Boston's investment in deepwater shipping had therefore dropped by almost $1,500,000 in ten years. Not until the mid 1830s did Boston once again own as much shipping in foreign trade as it had in 1810. The decline in its deepwater fleet was, however, partially offset by a sharp increase in coastal vessels, largely at the expense of the Essex County ports.[22]

Meanwhile, two sons of Newburyport, Francis Cabot Lowell and his brother-in-law Patrick Tracy Jackson, along with Nathan Appleton and several other Boston capitalists, were laying the groundwork for the future. The cotton textile mill they founded in 1813 at Waltham, with the engineering help of Newbury native Paul Moody, became the mold for the factory system that would revolutionize the Massachusetts economy.[23] In 1821, their search for a greater source of waterpower than the Charles could provide took them to the Merrimack River's Pawtucket Falls. There they marveled at the thirty-two-foot drop and the waterway built by Newburyport's Proprietors of Locks and Canals a quarter-century before. Jackson's father, Jonathan, a prominent Newburyport merchant in the Revolutionary era, had been the first president of the Proprietors, and when he died in 1810 his son Patrick Tracy and his brothers inherited their father's shares. Through the agency of Thomas March Clark, yet another Newburyport merchant, who had overseen construction of the Pawtucket Canal, the Boston Manufacturing Company quickly and quietly bought up over 300 acres of land at the falls and then took over the canal company's facilities with a straight stock swap. The mill town that resulted from the harnessing of the Merrimack at Pawtucket Falls was appropriately named for Francis Cabot Lowell, who had died in 1817.[24]

It is not within the scope of this essay to trace the development of Lowell by the Boston Associates, for technically speaking, Lowell is in Middlesex

21. *American State Papers: Commerce and Navigation.*

22. See Benjamin W. Labaree, "Essex County Outports, 1810–1815," *Essex Institute Historical Collections* 119(1983):63–69.

23. See Robert F. Dalzell, Jr., *Enterprising Elite: The Boston Associates and the World They Made* (Cambridge, Mass., 1987), 5–44, for the beginnings of the Boston Manufacturing Co. and the roles of Lowell and Jackson. See also, Robert F. Dalzell, Jr., "The Boston Associates and the Rise of the Waltham-Lowell System: A Study in Entrepreneurial Motivation," in Weible, *Continuing Revolution*, 39ff.

24. Dalzell, *Enterprising Elite*, 47–49; Weible, "East Chelmsford, 1775–1821," 11–13; and Patrick M. Malone, "Canals and Industry: Engineering in Lowell, 1821–1880" in Weible, *Continuing Revolution*, 138–139.

County, not Essex. But the rise of Lowell was important to Essex for several reasons. First, it changed the primary use of the Merrimack River from a navigational waterway to a source of industrial power.[25] Cargoes could still reach Boston via the Middlesex Canal because it left the Merrimack about one mile upstream of the dam at Lowell, but Newburyport's link with the upper river was compromised when the Pawtucket Canal was transferred to the Boston Manufacturing Company. Second, the building of the Merrimack's first factory town at Lowell, the river's southernmost point, confirmed Boston as the entrepôt for the Merrimack Valley. In the 1820s the Middlesex Canal was available to carry building materials and raw cotton to Lowell and the finished cloth downstream.[26]

But the canal was slow-going, expensive to maintain, and worst of all, closed by ice and snow for several months each winter. Following the lead of Patrick Tracy Jackson, a number of the Boston Associates concluded that the twenty-seven-mile route between Lowell and Boston was a natural candidate for a railroad. Their Boston & Lowell line was the first public railroad to receive a charter from the General Court, on June 5, 1830, although the lines to Worcester and to Providence managed to go into service before the B & L did. Jackson took the initiative in ordering two locomotives from their English builder, Robert Stevenson, determining the route, and (perhaps more important than he could have known) accepting Stevenson's rail gauge of four feet, eight and one-half inches, which thereafter became the standard for American railroads. The Boston & Lowell opened for service in June 1835 and within a few years established connections with other lines up the Merrimack Valley through Nashua and Manchester to Concord, New Hampshire.[27]

Although the Boston & Lowell itself did not enter Essex County, it

25. See Theodore Steinberg, *Nature Incorporated: Industrialization and the Waters of New England* (Cambridge, 1991), 56–60.

26. Had Jackson and Appleton chosen instead the 26-foot drop at Deer Jump Falls, where they in fact would establish Lawrence as a milltown in 1845, the Salem-Beverly harbor might have won a larger share of valley business because of its proximity to that site.

27. R. Richard Conard, "The First Locomotive on the Boston & Lowell Railroad," *B & M Bulletin* (September 1985), 7–9; Balthasar H. Meyer, *History of Transportation in the United States before 1860* (Washington, 1913), 322–323; Tom Nelligan and Scott Hartley, *The Route of the Minuteman* (New York, 1980), 43–44; and on the railroad gauge: Albro Martin, *Railroads Triumphant: The Growth, Rejection and Rebirth of a Vital American Force* (New York, 1992), 43–44. George P. Baker, *The Formation of the New England Railroad Systems: A Study of Railroad Combination in the Nineteenth Century* (Cambridge, Mass., 1937), 100–105; Malone, "Canals and Industry," 149–150.

allowed the Andover & Wilmington Railroad, built in 1836 with capital funds from Phillips Academy and the Andover Theological Seminary,[28] to reach Boston over its tracks. This local line was extended eastward to Haverhill in 1837 and became the nucleus of what would be consolidated as the Boston & Maine Railroad in 1842. From Haverhill it then ran north-east through Exeter and Dover, New Hampshire, to Portland, Maine. Three years later the B & M built its own line into Boston, ending its dependence on Boston & Lowell rails and connecting the Merrimack Valley towns of Haverhill, Bradford, Andover, and Lawrence directly with the city. By this time Boston interests had swallowed up the little Andover & Wilmington Railroad, just as the Boston Associates had taken over Newburyport's Locks and Canals Company in 1821.[29]

Meanwhile the coastal towns of Essex County gained their own access to Boston with the opening in 1838 of the Eastern Railroad, whose early investors and managers were predominantly county residents. Upon its completion two years later the main line ran from a depot in East Boston (requiring a harbor crossing by ferry from downtown Boston) north through Lynn, Salem, Ipswich, and Newburyport, and on to Portsmouth, New Hampshire. In 1842 it connected into Portland over the same railroad that the Boston & Maine leased for that purpose, the two roads signing a joint agreement. At Portland they later worked together to engage the Penobscot Steam Navigation Company, by which they would offer service to the rest of eastern Maine. In 1847 the Eastern completed its Cape Ann branch through Beverly and Manchester to the thriving fishing port of Gloucester. Yet another branch of the Eastern (at first a subsidiary called the Essex Railroad) ran northwest to the mills at Lawrence.[30]

The introduction of railroads could not have come at a more critical time for Boston. As we have seen, the city's commercial activity had relied heavily on coastal shipping, leaving the interior communities of eastern and central New England difficult to access. Yet by the end of 1847, a little more than twelve years after the opening of the Boston & Lowell Railroad, Boston had become the hub of a transportation system that ran 76 miles up

28. Most of the original endowment for the seminary came from the largess of two Newburyport merchants, William Bartlett and Moses Brown.

29. Baker, *New England Railroad Systems*, 145–148.

30. Baker, *New England Railroad Systems*, 147; Francis B. C. Bradlee, *The Eastern Railroad: A Historical Account of Early Railroading in Eastern New England* (Salem, 1917), 4–32; Charles J. Kennedy, "Railroads in Essex County a Century Ago" *Essex Institute Historical Collections* 95(1959):137–148; for Lawrence, see Donald B. Cole, *Immigrant City: Lawrence, Massachusetts, 1845–1921* (Chapel Hill, 1963).

the Merrimack Valley to Concord, New Hampshire, 109 miles northward to Portland, Maine, and by steamer, another 60 miles or so along the coast into Penobscot Bay. This network tied every significant seaport and manufacturing center north of Boston to the metropolis. At the same time other railroads linked Boston to neighboring areas that lay to the west and to the south, where trains connected at Fall River and other ports with steamboat service to New York. Looking eastward, Bostonians were delighted when in 1840 Samuel Cunard chose Boston as the U.S. terminal for his steamship line. (They were equally dismayed when he switched to New York eight years later!)

As important as it was that they strengthen their grip on nearby communities, however, some of Boston's leaders had more ambitious goals. They had been troubled by their city's lack of access to the west, by which they clearly meant not only western Massachusetts but the greater west that lay beyond the Hudson River. With its foreign-commerce fleet frozen at 1805 levels Boston's hope of competing with New York as a major American entrepôt may have seemed more than ever an unattainable dream. But like other American ports New York was experiencing its own problems in regaining the levels of foreign commerce it had attained in the years before the War of 1812. Although by 1830 its total fleet was twice Boston's, the ports were about even in the important category of tonnage registered for foreign trade. The difference between them, and it was significant, lay in the fact that more than twice as much tonnage entered and cleared at New York as at Boston. Almost the only advantage Boston had was that it lay nearly a day closer to Europe than did New York.[31]

The completion of the Erie Canal in 1825 seemed to some observers the

31. This difference between tonnage "owned" and tonnage "entered and cleared" tells us that New York attracted far more vessels owned elsewhere, including in foreign countries, than did Boston. *American State Papers: Commerce and Navigation.*

The question of Boston's relative prosperity in 1830, which Dalzell usefully discusses in *Enterprising Elite*, 86–87, n. 14, can never be definitively answered because the necessary statistics are incomplete. As far as foreign commerce is concerned, however, it is clear that Boston was in a mild recession in 1830. If one looks at *tonnage*, in 1826, the first year for which figures are available, 233,891 tons of shipping entered and cleared Boston on foreign voyages. This total declined to 206,736 tons by 1830 and would not reach the 1826 level again until 1832. The *value* of exports and imports carried by these vessels declined from a pre-recession high of $21,310,475 in 1825 to 1830's low of $13,528,801 before recovering in 1832. It is difficult to see how the merchants cited by Dalzell could have ignored a 36.5 percent decline in the value of their city's foreign trade! For other evidence of Boston's economic conditions, see William H. Pease and Jane H. Pease, *The Web of Progress: Private Values and Public Styles in Boston and Charleston, 1828–1843* (New York, 1985), 23–24.

final nail in Boston's coffin. But to the promoters of a railroad from Boston to the Hudson River New York's new waterway offered an opportunity to reach not only upstate New York but the whole of the northwest.[32] The normal handling of cargoes shipped via the Erie Canal involved their transfer at Albany into Hudson River vessels whose progress depended on wind and tide. As the Board of Directors of Internal Improvements reported in 1829:

> The western parts of the state, and the northern and western parts of New York, and even the western states, if a rail road were established from Boston to the Hudson river, might regularly receive supplies, to a large amount from Boston, which without this improvement will be necessarily sought from some other market [i.e., New York City].[33]

In fact, the board noted, Boston already imported over 20,000 tons of cargo directly from Albany by coasting schooners that sailed down the Hudson River right past New York City. And Boston sent out nearly 6,000 tons of goods to Albany by the same route. The promoters strongly believed that their railroad would encourage a significant increase in this two-way traffic in just a few years of operation.[34]

The advocates of the western railroad were keenly aware that New York had taken over the trade of much of the Massachusetts interior. They noted how Worcester County business went down the Blackstone to Providence and thence through Long Island Sound to New York. Similarly, Connecticut Valley trade ran downriver to Hartford or Middletown or via the Farmington Canal to New Haven and thence by steamer on to New York. Including Berkshire County's commerce via the Hudson River, the commissioners reckoned that Boston was losing at least 50,000 tons of internal

32. Massachusetts Board of Internal Improvements, *Report of the Board of Directors of Internal Improvements of the State of Massachusetts on the Practicality and Expediency of a Rail-road from Boston to the Hudson River* . . . (Boston, 1829), 50–51.

33. *Report of the Board of Directors*, 50–51.

34. *Report of the Board of Directors*, 28–30. Stephen Salisbury, *The State, the Investor, and the Railroad: The Boston & Albany, 1825–1867* (Cambridge, Mass., 1967), 36, argues that reaching new manufacturing sites was the primary goal of the early western railroad movement in Massachusetts, rather than, as suggested by Edward C. Kirkland, in his *Men, Cities, and Transportation: A Study in New England History, 1820–1900* (Cambridge, Mass., 1948), 1:92–124, that the movement was a response to the Erie Canal. The evidence, however, seems to suggest both motives. One might wonder why, if providing Boston with a direct link to upstate New York and the west were not important, the promoters proposed to incur the additional expense of crossing the Taconic mountains into the Hudson Valley at all. See Dalzell, *Enterprising Elite*, 86, n. 12, for a fuller discussion of this issue.

trade in this way each year. Not only would their railroad plug these "leaks" but it would also enhance the value of the farmland in those regions served by the line. In addition it would undoubtedly lead to the identification of sites along rivers and streams of the interior suitable for industrial development. Boston could then become the "central mart" where the products of new western factories would be sold, thus attracting both domestic and foreign purchasers. At present, the commissioners warned, New York was very close to gaining an insurmountable lead in that role.[35]

Completed in 1841 at a cost of over $7,000,000, the Western Rail Road extended Boston's service from Worcester through Pittsfield to Albany, a total distance of over 200 miles, and connected it with the Erie Canal. Before the end of the decade, once further rail links were completed in the west, Boston, Massachusetts, and St. Louis, Missouri, would be linked by a continuous line of railroads. The Western proved to be an immensely successful road during its first decade of operation. By 1848 it was carrying almost 200,000 tons of freight east and another 80,000 tons west each year, earning its stockholders the maximum allowable dividend of 8 percent in the process. The Western brought to Boston a significant share of the foodstuffs consumed by its rapidly expanding population and provided access to an important market for the Commonwealth's manufactures. But flour could still go all the way from Albany to Liverpool, England, via the Hudson and New York City for the same cost at which it traveled from Albany to Boston by rail. To make matters worse, in response to the Massachusetts line New York rushed to completion its own "western railroad," the Erie. In the end, then, the Western Railroad did little to strengthen Boston's challenge to New York's supremacy as the major exporter of western produce. And when Great Britain repealed the Corn Laws in 1846 New York was in a better position than ever before to take advantage of the expanding market for grain products. Nevertheless Boston's maritime spokesmen remained doggedly optimistic throughout the 1840s. Introducing the merchants of Boston to the first issue of his *Boston Shipping List and Commercial and Underwriters' Gazette*, the publisher insisted that

> Boston, with its steamship communication with Europe, and its railroad traveling and carrying facilities to all parts of the interior, and more particularly with *the West*, must necessarily be a great commercial depot.[36]

35. *Report of the Board of Directors*, 40, 44, 49.
36. *Boston Shipping List, Prices Current, Commercial and Underwriters' Gazette*, Sept. 2, 1843, 2. The journal itself was a remarkable testimony to the publishers' faith in

In the end Boston failed to make a serious dent in New York's domination over the major routes of commerce—internally to the western states, along the coast to the southern and gulf ports, and across the Atlantic by both sailing packet and steamship to Great Britain'and the European continent. By mid century New York even threatened Boston's trade with China and the East Indies. Boston had to settle for becoming the unchallenged *entrept* for that region of New England that lay north of Cape Cod. But first it had to overcome local competition from Portland, Portsmouth, and the four ports of Essex County, Salem-Beverly, Newburyport, Gloucester, and Marblehead, for to a considerable extent Boston's rise came at their expense.

Several kinds of evidence show the price Essex County paid for Boston's growth. For several decades after the War of 1812 Salem had remained a significant seaport, with extensive trading contacts in South America, the Mediterranean, along the coast of India, and throughout the Dutch East Indies, particularly in Sumatra. Its shipowners kept a hand in the China trade until mid century, a commerce that took their vessels all over the Pacific in search of commodities suitable for sale at Canton. But during the 1840s Boston began to take over Salem's trade with the East Indies. In 1850 Salem had only six clearances for the East Indies while Boston had eighty. Not only was Boston Harbor better suited for the larger vessels being used by mid century, but its railroad network made it a far better distributor of imports.[37] Partly in response to this loss Salem merchants expanded their trade with West African ports and then added Madagascar, Zanzibar, and other places along the east coast of Africa to their list of destinations. This trade remained a Salem specialty until the 1850s, when Boston took most of it over as well.[38]

In the period from 1830 to 1850 the aggregate tonnage of shipping owned in the four Essex County ports rose by 30 percent. At the same time, however, Boston's fleet grew by 137 percent, widening its marginal advan-

---

Boston's maritime future. In addition to the usual marine list with arrivals and departures, it included the names and locations of every vessel in port and reviewed prices, supplies on hand, and demand for each of 40-odd commodities on the Boston market.

37. *Hunt's Merchants' Magazine* 24(1851):477. A number of those vessels clearing Boston for the East however, were Salem-owned, and even many of those of Boston registry were commanded by Salem captains.

38. Morison, *Maritime History*, 217–224; Joseph B. Hoyt, "Salem's West Africa Trade, 1835–1863 and Captain Victor Francis Debaker," *Essex Institute Historical Collections* 102(1966):56, 70–71; Edward H. Berman, "Salem and Zanzibar:1825–1850" *Essex Institute Historical Collections* 105(1969):339–340.

tage from twice to four times that of its northern neighbors. Furthermore, an increasing number of Essex-owned vessels left their home ports to enter the carrying trade out of Boston or New York and never returned. This was one reason why entrances and clearances of American-flag vessels at Essex County ports declined by more than 20 percent between 1830 and 1850. In contrast, Boston's American-flag traffic increased by 142 percent, 11.5 times that of its neighbors to the north. Both areas showed an increase in foreign-flag shipping activity, but Boston's rose far more rapidly.[39] One would expect that as Boston commerce grew the city would come to dominate the import market of Massachusetts at the expense of the smaller ports. But somewhat surprisingly it also began during these decades to export much of Essex County's domestic produce as well. By 1860 Boston was shipping out $400,000 worth of boards and other lumber products annually in contrast to Newburyport's $3,000. The manufacture of boots and shoes was a major industry in Essex County; yet when it came to the export of these items, Boston's trade exceeded the northern ports' $3,700 total by nearly $200,000. The export of dried and pickled fish provides another example. Although it controlled the fishery itself with a fleet thirty times greater than that of Boston, Essex County exported only $67,300 of its own catch, while the larger port sent out $375,600. Only Salem among the county's textile manufacturing towns managed to export any of its own cloth.[40]

To a great extent Boston's hegemony came about through the remarkable growth of its coastal fleet. At the beginning of the nineteenth century Essex County had a greater tonnage enrolled as coasters than did Boston, but after the War of 1812 the larger port overtook its neighbors. By 1830 Boston's coastal fleet was twice that of the Essex ports and at mid century three times its size. In the same twenty-year period the number of coasting vessels arriving annually at Boston doubled from 3,000 to an astounding 6,000, or very nearly twenty a day throughout the year. The records for just one week in mid September 1850 illuminate the wide range of Boston's coastal commerce. Nearly half of the 154 arrivals brought in lumber, lime, and perhaps granite from a dozen or more ports along the Maine coast. From Philadelphia came thirty-one barks, brigs, and schooners loaded with

39. These figures are compiled from several sources: *American State Papers: Commerce and Navigation*; Boston Board of Trade, *Sixth Annual Report . . . 1860* (Boston, 1860), and *Seventh Annual Report . . . 1861* (Boston, 1861).

40. *American State Papers: Commerce and Navigation*. See also, Labaree, "Essex County Outports," 69.

coal and flour, while twenty-three vessels of British registry hailed from the Canadian Maritimes, probably carrying coal, plaster of paris, and some lumber. Sixteen vessels entered from New York, eleven from other New England ports, and one from New Orleans—a large bark that brought in a cargo of raw cotton for shipment by rail to the Merrimack Valley mills.[41]

As important as coastal commerce was to the growth of Boston as New England's entrepôt, the railroad seemed to have a more immediate and devastating effect on the ports of Essex County.[42] In less than two years after the Eastern Railroad reached Salem in 1838 the number of Boston firms regularly advertising in the *Salem Gazette* considerably increased. Notices of unique services like packet lines running from Boston to Baltimore, Savannah, or New Orleans were to be expected, but ads that touted such wares as sugar, coffee, wine, and carpeting leveled a direct challenge at local shopkeepers. Most issues of the *Gazette* ran fifteen or twenty such advertisements. One Boston firm inadvertently revealed the pecking order current in the commercial world. "Just returned from NEW YORK with a large and valuable stock of NEW SPRING GOODS," proclaimed E. F. Newhall in a double-column display advertisement.[43] Newburyport lay far enough north to escape for awhile the long arm of the Boston retailer. But only for a decade. By 1850, ten years after the Eastern Railroad reached town, "Pettingill's Boston Business Directory" began to appear as a regular feature on the back page of the daily *Impartial Herald*, occupying three of four columns and advertising the goods and services of no fewer than sixty Boston businesses.[44]

One should not imagine that Boston's expansion touched only the seaports of Essex County and not its inland areas. A comparison of property valuations shows the effect on the county as a whole. From its standing as the state's wealthiest county at the beginning of the century (with an almost

41. *American State Papers: Commerce and Navigation*; *Boston Shipping List and Price-Current*, Jan. 1, 1851; *Hunt's Merchants' Magazine* 6(1841):184. Because coasting vessels did not always enter at the customhouse these arrival figures are conservative; Labaree, "Essex County Outports," 67–68.

42. In respect to the relative effects of these two modes of carrying goods I have modified the views I expressed in "Essex County Outports."

43. *Salem Gazette*, various issues; Apr. 3, 1840 for "NEW SPRING GOODS."

44. *Impartial Herald*, Oct. 29, 1850, and later issues. From reading several hundred issues of each newspaper I have the impression that the *Herald* carried more general news, including items from or about Boston, than did the *Salem Gazette* in these years. Perhaps Salem readers had begun to subscribe to Boston journals as a primary source of information. (Unfortunately, William Bentley is no longer alive to illuminate the point!)

$1,000,000 margin over Boston's Suffolk County) by 1850 Essex had sunk to third place after both Suffolk and Middlesex. While Suffolk's share of the state's wealth nearly doubled in that period, from 18.9 percent to 36.4, Essex County's fell by half, from 20 percent to less than 10 percent. Boston's growth affected other counties as well. Aside from the whaling county of Bristol, Middlesex was the only other county besides Suffolk to increase its share of the state's wealth over the first half of the nineteenth century, mostly on the strength of its textile mills. Comparing the changing valuations of Boston and Salem reveals a pattern almost identical to that of their respective counties. Salem's share of the combined wealth of Massachusetts cities and towns dropped almost 50 percent while Boston's nearly doubled.[45]

The railroads by which Boston expanded its influence changed the surrounding countryside in irreversible ways. From the first talk of a western railroad the seaboard farmers feared the effect of western produce on their markets. One railroad advocate, when confronted at the State House by farmers who asked what they should do with their farms, told them, "Turn them into strawberry fields; that will make them pay!"[46] To be sure, some local farmers did take up the cultivation of fruits, but in the production of their former staples—rye, wheat, corn, beef, pork, mutton, wool, and butter—the farmers of Essex County simply could not compete. Instead of providing pork to Boston, for instance, farm families now obtained western pork from the city. The region's sheep population declined by 50 percent in the single decade 1840–1850.[47]

Farmers received plenty of advice at their county agricultural society's annual meetings. Allen W. Dodge urged his listeners at the 1842 Essex gathering to resurrect their apple orchards; three years later Mr. Stone drew his audience's attention to manure—from cattle, ashes, fish, seaweed, and the newest idea: guano from the Pacific islands. In seeking a cure for the ills that beset the eastern farmer, the speakers uniformly refused to criticize the railroad itself, for to do so would be to oppose progress. "It were idle, if not unwise," said Mr. Dodge, "to complain of that which promotes the general

45. Boston Board of Trade, *Sixth Annual Report . . . 1860; Seventh Annual Report . . . 1861; Hunt's Merchants' Magazine* 16(1847):436, 440; 24(1851):252.

46. "Influence of Railroads on Agriculture," *Hunt's Merchants' Magazine* 27(1852):759–760.

47. Ben: Perley Poore, "Early Farming in Essex County," *Transactions of the Agricultural Society of Massachusetts for the Year 1856* (Boston, 1856), 12–13; Percy W. Bidwell, "The Agricultural Revolution in New England," *American Historical Review* 26(1921): 689–692.

good. . . . I ask any candid and enlightened farmer," he continued, "if he would have Massachusetts, if he could, stripped of those iron avenues which connect her . . . with the far West and far East. . . . No," Dodge concluded, "I am persuaded that your good sense revolts from such a wish." E. H. Derby, Esq., scion of Salem's once great merchant family, joined in the praise of railroads as a benefit to the farmers of neighboring Middlesex County whom he addressed in 1847, asking his audience "have not the suburban dairy farms been required for building-lots at treble prices?" Mr. Derby did not explain what the landless farmers were supposed to do with the rest of their lives after selling out. As late as 1856, however, Newbury's gentleman farmer, Ben: Perley Poore, exhorted his listeners "to deepen their furrows, to increase their supplies of home-made fertilizers . . . and above all, to raise a generation of working boys and girls."[48]

In the end of course both Mr. Derby and Mr. Poore were right. Many Essex County farmers did sell their lands for housing construction. And those who remained on the land did raise a generation of working boys and girls, but many of those children left the farm and found work in the mills and workshops of Lowell, Lawrence, and Boston itself. These losses of farmland and labor both contributed to falling agricultural production and the reversion of once-arable fields and meadows to woodlands.[49] As Derby predicted, the more accessible fields were sold as building lots to a new type of resident who lived in the countryside but worked in Boston—the commuter. When the Boston & Maine completed its own tracks into the city in 1845 it promoted the suburbs along its route as ideal places to live.[50]

In the summer of 1851 the people of Boston celebrated what they considered to be the completion of the effort to reach out and connect their city

48. Allen W. Dodge, "Address . . . 1842," *Essex Agricultural Society Transactions January 1842* (Salem, 1842), 10–13; "Mr. Stone's Address," *Essex Agricultural Society Transactions January 1845* (Salem, 1846), 10–11; Poore, "Early Farming in Essex County," 14; "E. H. Derby's Address to the Middlesex Agricultural Society," *Transactions of the Agricultural Societies of Massachusetts for the Year 1847* (Boston, 1848), 216.

49. For the impact of railroads on the landscape and related issues, see Leo Marx, *The Machine in the Garden* (New York, 1964); John Stilgoe, *Metropolitan Corridor: Railroads and the American Scene,* (New Haven, 1983); Stilgoe, *Common Landscape of America, 1580 to 1845* (New Haven, 1982); Stilgoe, *Borderland: Origins of the American Suburb, 1820–1939* (New Haven, 1988); John Brinckerhoff Jackson, *Discovering the Vernacular Landscape* (New Haven, 1984). The writings of Henry David Thoreau and Ralph Waldo Emerson remain valuable sources for studying the changes that took place.

50. The term "commuter" seems to have appeared when, in 1838, a group of thrifty

with the rest of America. Now, a century and a half later, the physical evidence of their world is disappearing before our eyes. The farms and orchards around Boston went first, as Derby predicted. But could he and his generation have imagined that so much of the railroad system, with its stations and roundhouses and locomotives, would go as well? And the wharves and warehouses from which Boston's merchants hoped to send the produce of the west have all but vanished, and the sailing packets and steamships as well.

Perhaps in the summer of 2001 the City of Boston will treat itself to another Jubilee, this one to commemorate the completion of the Central Artery Project. In a sense the purpose of this enormous undertaking is similar to that of its predecessor. Just as Boston's nineteenth-century railroad network made it possible for white-collar workers to take up residence outside the city on the farmlands of Essex County and elsewhere and become the first commuters, so too the Central Artery is designed to allow their white-collar descendants to remain commuters by driving into the city each day in their single-occupant vehicles. Will any of the 10,000 guests who dine in the Fleet Center in September 2001 in celebration pause to wonder how long their highways and bridges, tunnels, interchanges, and off-ramps will last?

Salem residents who worked in Boston asked the new Eastern Railroad to issue them "season" tickets at reduced or commuted prices. The Eastern agreed, other railroads followed suit, and the "commuter" was born. Charles J. Kennedy, "Commuter Services in the Boston Area, 1835–1860," *Business History Review* 36(1962):155–159.

Massachusetts General Hospital, [1846]. Engraving. Collection of the Massachusetts Historical Society.

What the Merchants Did with Their Money:

Charitable and Testamentary Trusts

in Massachusetts,

1780–1880

Peter Dobkin Hall

NO GROUP OF AMERICANS better knew the difficulties of accumulating and preserving wealth than did a select group of New England merchants, those who founded prominent Boston families in the late eighteenth and early nineteenth centuries. At the same time, few knew better the capacity of wealth to corrupt and weaken its inheritors. In looking to secure the future of their families and their city, the merchants faced the dual problem of consolidating and maintaining their wealth, while also ensuring it remained a source of continuing vitality and strength from generation to generation.

Few of these merchants had started as wealthy men, so they knew all too well the hazards to which new fortunes were subject. Not many could claim deep roots in the city where they had made good—they could not depend on circles of well-established kinsmen to help them out. None could look to the state or to the law as a bulwark to defend their interests—government was passing into the hands of an electorate less than friendly to the proper-tied, and the law, especially as it affected the inheritance of property, was inimical to the transmission of large fortunes between generations. To maintain their wealth in the face of incredible economic risk and political turbulence, and to pass it on more or less intact to their progeny, whose competence was ever threatened by inevitable tendencies to extravagance and folly, would require remarkable knowledge and skill.

The research on which this study is based was made possible through the generous support of the AAFRC Trust for Philanthropy, the Aspen Institute's Nonprofit Sector Research Fund, and the Lilly Endowment, Inc. An earlier version of this paper appeared as Working Paper #214 of the Program on Non-Profit Organizations, Yale University.

Reflecting in 1859 on Boston's prosperity during the previous century, Dr. Oliver Wendell Holmes tersely summarized the fundamental problem of the city's emergent upper class. "It is in the nature of large fortunes to diminish rapidly, when subdivided and distributed," wrote Doctor Holmes in 1859,

> A million is the unit of wealth, now and here in America. It splits into four handsome properties; each of these into four good inheritances; these, again, into scanty competences for four ancient maidens,—with whom it is best the family should die out, unless it can begin again as its great-grand-father did. Now a million is kind of golden cheese, which represents in a compendious form the summer's growth of a fat meadow of craft or commerce; and as this kind of meadow rarely bears more than one crop, it is pretty certain that sons and grandsons will not get another golden cheese out of it, whether they milk the same cows or turn in new ones. In other words, the millionocracy, considered in a large way, is not at all an affair of persons and families, but a perpetual fact of money with a variable human element . . . Of course, this trivial and fugitive fact of personal wealth does not create a permanent class, unless some special means are taken to arrest the process of disintegration in the third generation. This is so rarely done, at least successfully, that one need not live a very long life to see most of the rich families he knew in childhood more or less reduced, and the millions shifted into the hands of the country-boys who were sweeping stores and carrying parcels when the now decayed gentry were driving their chariots, eating their venison over silver chafing-dishes, drinking Madeira chilled in embossed coolers, wearing their hair in powder, and casing their legs in boots with silken tassels.[1]

Holmes echoed a set of concerns all too familiar to wealthy Brahmins of his time, who were keen students of history and morbidly prone to draw lessons from it. Their Prescott had sharply etched the rise and fall of the Spanish empire; their Motley had traced the trajectory of the Dutch republic; their essayists and travelers keenly observed the struggles of the British aristocracy to maintain its place, as well as the determination of Great Britain's manufacturing and commercial classes to ennoble themselves.

The Law of Inheritance

Alexis de Tocqueville, so many of whose observations had been shaped and informed by his conversations with eminent Bostonians of the previous

---

1. Oliver Wendell Holmes, *Elsie Venner, A Romance of Destiny* (1859; reprint, New York, 1961), 19.

generation, had posited partible inheritance as the central, driving dynamic of American society.

"The law of inheritance was the last step to equality," Tocqueville wrote. It ought, he believed, "to be placed at the head of all political institutions" because it exercised such an "incredible influence upon the social state of a people":

> When the legislator has once regulated the law of inheritance, he may rest from his labor. The machine once put in motion will go on for ages, and advance, as if self-guided, towards a point indicated beforehand. When framed in a particular manner, this law unites, draws together, and vests property and power in a few hands; it causes an aristocracy, so to speak, to spring out of the ground. If formed on opposite principles, its action is still more rapid; it divides, distributes, and disperses both property and power. Alarmed by the rapidity of its progress, those who despair of arresting its motion endeavor at least to obstruct it by difficulties and impediments. They vainly seek to counteract its effect by contrary efforts; but it shatters and reduces to powder every obstacle, until we can no longer see anything but a moving and impalpable cloud of dust, which signals the coming of the Democracy.[2]

Neither Tocqueville nor Holmes doubted the extraordinary power of partible inheritance. It created the social conditions of equality that made necessary republican government. And, outside the South, it had prevented the long-term accumulation of wealth and the emergence of aristocracy. But while the Frenchman, writing in the early 1830s, believed that efforts to "arrest its motion" were doomed to failure, the canny Holmes, writing a generation later, was willing to concede that "special means" could be taken to arrest "this process of disintegration."

Moderating the force of partible inheritance posed special difficulties for Bostonians of the late eighteenth century. The division of estates between surviving children had been a cornerstone of the colony's social order, providing the religiously-mandated patriarchal household with the land, labor, and skills to fulfill the multitude of tasks imposed upon it by state and church.[3] After nearly two hundred years, the legitimacy of childrens' claims

---

2. Alexis de Tocqueville, *Democracy in America* (1840; reprint, New York, 1945), 1:49–51.

3. Studies of partible inheritance and its impact on New England society include: George L. Haskins, "The Beginnings of Partible Inheritance in the American Colonies," *Yale Law Journal* 51(1942):129ff.; Philip J. Greven, Jr., *Four Generations: Population, Land, and Family in Colonial Andover, Massachusetts* (Ithaca, 1970); Bernard Farber,

to paternal estates was the bedrock of the population's conception of testamentary justice. These attitudes had been reinforced by the Revolution, which both promoted concepts of legal equality and explicitly identified entail and primogeniture with the Old World traditions that Americans had repudiated.

While primogeniture, entail, and trusts, mechanisms capable of ensuring the intact transmission of estates within families over extended periods of time, had long existed as a part of English law, the New England colonists had generally refused to permit their use or even to allow the creation of the legal jurisdictions necessary for their enforcement. Thus, in 1804, we find the Supreme Judicial Court of Massachusetts declining to enforce a testamentary trust on the grounds that "if the conveyance was in *trust*, this court could not have compelled the execution of it; and, until the legislature shall think it proper to give us further powers, we can do nothing upon subjects of *that* nature."[4]

Unlike other legal instruments, trusts require a special form of legal authority called equity jurisdiction. Unlike the common law, which is concerned with *past* acts, equity is concerned with enforcing *future* acts. In addition, trusts involve coextensive property rights which are divided between the trustee, who is the *legal* owner (and who has the right to buy, sell, or rent the property, as if it were his own), and the beneficiary, who is the *equitable* owner (and who has enforceable claims on the use of the trust property).[5] Historically, neither future acts nor the coextensive legal rights and equitable rights associated with trusts were enforceable by the courts of most states after the Revolution.[6]

Guardians of Virtue: Salem Families in 1800 (New York, 1972); John J. Waters, "Patrimony, Succession, and Social Stability: Guilford, Connecticut, in the Eighteenth Century," *Perspectives in American History* 10(1976):131–160; and Peter Dobkin Hall, *The Organization of American Culture, 1700–1900: Private Institutions, Elites, and the Origins of American Nationality* (New York, 1982).

4. Prescott v. Tarbell, 1 Mass. (1 Williams) 208 (1804).

5. Austin Wakeman Scott, *The Law of Trusts* (Boston, 1939), 1:3–8.

6. General works covering postrevolutionary legal developments and giving attention to interstate differences include: Roscoe Pound, *The Formative Era of American Law* (Boston, 1938); William E. Nelson, *Americanization of the Common Law: The Impact of Legal Change on Massachusetts Society, 1760–1830* (Cambridge, Mass., 1975); and Morton J. Horowitz, *The Transformation of American Law, 1780–1860* (Cambridge, Mass., 1977). Works giving particular attention to the development of equity jurisdiction include: Edwin H. Woodruff, "Chancery in Massachusetts," *Law Quarterly Review* 5(1889):370–386; Spencer Liverant and Walter H. Hitchler, "A History of Equity in Pennsylvania," *Dickin-*

Despite this, the founders of wealthy merchant families appear to have viewed trusts as a promising solution to the challenge of passing wealth intact between generations while also ensuring that the capital it represented remained undivided and available for investment. A trust estate could be left in the care of a trustee who would manage and invest it for the benefit of a testators' descendants. The property itself would remain undivided, but the descendants would receive, in more or less equal proportion, the shares in parental estates that they had reason to expect.

The merchant family founders had a further reason to explore the possibilities offered by trusts. At the end of the eighteenth century, they had begun encouraging shifts in their sons' occupational choices.[7] Before the Revolution, all the sons of merchants tended to follow their fathers into trade, in many cases regardless of their aptitudes or inclinations. In the postrevolutionary years, perhaps in deference to individual desires but more likely with an eye to managing risk, consolidating capital, and ensuring that the sons with the greatest entrepreneurial skills succeeded to the business, a pattern of occupational diversification began to appear.[8] Usually only one son went into trade; the rest became physicians, attorneys, clergymen, scholars, and gentlemen of leisure. Income from trusts could help maintain the life-styles of non-merchant sons, as well as add to their professional capabilities the financial resources to ensure them leadership in their fields.

son Law Review 37(1933):156–183; William L. Curran, "The Struggle for Equity Jurisdiction in Massachusetts," *Boston University Law Review* 31(1951):269–296; Stanley N. Katz, "The Politics of Law in Colonial America: Controversies over Chancery Courts and Equity Law in the Eighteenth Century," Donald Fleming and Bernard Bailyn, eds., *Law in American History* (Cambridge, Mass., 1971), 257–288; John H. Langbein, "Chancellor Kent and the History of Legal Literature," *Columbia Law Review* 93(1993):547ff.; A. W. Scott, "Charitable Trusts in New York," *New York University Law Review* 26(1951): 2, 251ff.

7. My study of occupational choices by sons of the Amory, Cabot, Codman, Higginson, Jackson, Lawrence, Lowell, and Peabody families in the period 1680–1900 reveals a steady trend away from business careers: between 73 and 92 percent of the sons of fathers born between 1680 and 1739 entered business; fewer than half of the sons of fathers born between 1760 and 1839 did so. For the 1829–1839 birth cohort, the proportion of sons entering business dropped to less than 30 percent. On changing patterns of career choice in merchant, artisan, and professional families, see Hall, *Organization of American Culture*, 35–54, and "Family Structure and Class Consolidation among the Boston Brahmins," (Ph.D. diss., State Univ. of New York–Stony Brook, 1973).

8. For evidence that Boston merchant fathers were encouraging sons to make their own occupational choices by the early years of the 19th century, see James Jackson Putnam, *A Memoir of Dr. James Jackson* (Boston, 1905).

These occupational patterns facilitated the shift from partnership to corporations as the basic form of business enterprise.[9] Because partnerships made each member of a firm liable for the actions of every other member, and because there was no way of limiting the partners' personal liability for debts incurred by the firm, such organizations were unsuited to the high-risk activities of postrevolutionary commerce. More to the point, partnerships required a degree of personal trust and confidence among firm members that was likely to exist within a family, yet was often absent as investors who were not related by blood or marriage endeavored to pool their capital.

The lists of incorporators and stockholders in Boston's earliest bank, insurance, and bridge ventures clearly suggest that they were efforts to combine the economic resources of unrelated families and to serve the greater interests of the merchant community while avoiding the pitfalls of the partnership form of organization. The board members of the Massachusetts Bank, for example, included representatives of the city's major family groups engaged in commerce.[10] This collectivist character became even more evident in 1818, with the establishment of the "Suffolk System," a consortium of Boston banks whose purpose was to protect the city's

9. While many Boston merchants conducted business "on their own account" in sole partnerships, the core families of the Brahmin group overwhelmingly favored partnership firms. The composition of partnership firms in the Cabot, Higginson, Jackson, Lee, and Lowell families changed significantly between the early 18th and the mid 19th centuries: through the first half of the 18th century, more than half their partnerships were between close relatives—fathers, sons, or brothers. After the mid 18th century, they were more likely to establish firms with more distant relatives-in-laws, uncles, or cousins—or with non-kin. After 1820, sons, if they went into business at all, most frequently chose to work in corporate settings—in banks, insurance companies, or textile mills—rather than in partnership firms. See Hall, "Family Structure," 6–111.

10. The first board of directors of the Massachusetts Bank also included representatives of the two principal mercantile factions in the city: native Bostonians, including Thomas Russell (a cousin of the Amorys, Carys, and Codmans), Edward Payne (an Amory in-law), William Phillips (a business associate of Payne's), Jonathan Mason (a partner and in-law of Phillips), Samuel A. Otis (connected with the Grays, Carys, Blakes, and Warrens), Samuel Breck, and James Bowdoin (a political appointee); and Essexmen, including Stephen Higginson (a Cabot cousin), John Lowell (an in-law, through successive marriages, to the Higginson, Cabot, and Russell families), Oliver Wendell (a cousin of Isaac Smith and Jonathan Jackson), Isaac Smith (a cousin of Wendell and Jackson), and George Cabot (who was related to the Higginsons, Jacksons, Lees, and Lowells). On this, see Hall, *Organization of American Culture*, 345–346.

specie deposits from raids by country banks and non-Boston financial interests.[11] The early decades of the nineteenth century were marked by the emergence of a civic mentality whose purpose was to advance and tie together the interests of Boston and its leading families or, as one historian of trusteeship put it, to "preserve a continuing and dominating position for these families in the affairs of Boston and its surrounding territories."[12]

The family founders were aware that the legal issues framing private trusts were closely related to those involving the establishment and enforcement of charitable and educational trusts. In fact, they took as their example English organizations that had the eleemosynary trust as their foundation and hoped to shape comparable institutions in Massachusetts. Yet the history of trusts in the state was inauspicious. Although Massachusetts could boast trusts dating back to the early seventeenth century, many of these had suffered extraordinary mismanagement, due to the inexperience of colonial jurists and the absence of equity jurisprudence.[13] Therefore, resolving the legal status of these instruments was central to the founders' private and public purposes. This task took on particular urgency after 1800, as the merchants' political influence began to diminish and the opposition initiated legislative attacks on their control of Harvard and other New England colleges.

Building an American Equity Jurisdiction

The first two decades of the nineteenth century witnessed extraordinary economic and political turbulence. The Napoleonic Wars and Jefferson's Embargo shattered Boston's commerce. Religious dissenters, artisans, and farmers formed a Democratic-Republican coalition which successfully challenged the long-standing political dominance of the "wealthy, learned, and respectable." The merchant group itself was split deeply over religious

11. On capital pooling, see Gerald T. White, *History of the Massachusetts Hospital Life Insurance Company* (Cambridge, Mass., 1957). On the Suffolk Bank and the "Suffolk System," see David Rice Whitney, *The Suffolk Bank* (Cambridge, Mass., 1878). Justin Winsor's *Memorial History of Boston, including Suffolk County, Massachusetts, 1630–1880* (Boston, 1880–1881), also gives a good account of the integrated nature of Boston finance.

12. Donald Holbrook, *The Boston Trustee* (Boston, 1937), 7.

13. See, for example, Charles P. Bowditch, *An Account of the Trust Administered by the Trustees of the Charity of Edward Hopkins* (Boston, 1889).

questions, as Unitarian and Trinitarian Congregationalists struggled to control the state's churches and emerging cultural and charitable institutions.[14]

Legal issues were at the center of the struggle. The nature of the law itself, as well as questions of judicial authority and architecture, preoccupied the legislatures of the revolutionary and postrevolutionary era. Many Americans viewed the common law, the collective body of judicial precedents stretching back into English history, as a "tatter'd Gothic garment," tainted with feudal solicitude for aristocracy and church. Under Jefferson's leadership, Virginia in the 1770s undertook a "revisal of the laws" intended to reject entirely the English legal heritage, repealing the common law, and building from the ground up a legal system suitable to republican government.[15] Other states followed suit to a greater or lesser extent.

While Massachusetts followed a generally less radical course than did Virginia, the attitude of its legislators towards equity was unyieldingly hostile and stemmed from a number of sources.[16] Equity powers were regarded as unsuitable for a democratic state because of the broad discretionary powers they granted the judiciary. Looking to the English experience with chancery courts, which exercised equity powers, Americans were keenly aware of the protracted, inaccessible, expensive, and often incomprehensible nature of equity proceedings. Even lawyers distrusted equity because of its seeming irrationality, sympathizing with the remark of seventeenth-century jurist Lord Selden that "equity is a roguish thing. 'Tis all one as if they should make the standard for measur[ing] the chancellor's foot."[17] As a result of this hostility, the Massachusetts Constitution of 1780, though generally a very conservative document, explicitly denied the Common-

14. On the emergence of these institutions in the late 18th and early 19th centuries, see Conrad Edick Wright's important study, *The Transformation of Charity in Postrevolutionary New England* (Boston, 1992), and Peter Dobkin Hall, *Inventing the Nonprofit Sector: Essays on Philanthropy, Voluntarism, and Nonprofit Organizations* (Baltimore, 1992).

15. On Jefferson's attitude toward the common law, see his "Revisal of the Laws of Virginia," in Adrienne Koch, ed., *The American Enlightenment* (New York, 1965), 296–298. On the impact of Jeffersonian attitudes toward charitable trusts, see E. S. Hirshler, "A Survey of Charitable Trusts in Virginia," *Virginia Law Review* 25(1939):109–116. A good account of the struggle between legal ideologies can be found in Howard S. Miller, *Legal Foundations of American Philanthropy* (Madison, 1961).

16. The best summary of the reasons for Massachusetts's hostility toward equity can be found in Curran, "Struggle for Equity Jurisdiction," 269–273.

17. Quoted in "Equity," in *Encyclopedia Britannica, Eleventh Edition* (New York, 1911), 9:727.

wealth's courts equity powers. These were reserved, as in the old province charter, to the legislature, to which petitioners must continue to appeal for equitable remedies.

Despite these discouraging events, a handful of determined lawyers promoted efforts to grant equity powers to the courts. Chief among them was Joseph Story, a young Republican representative from Salem.[18] In 1808, Story was named chairman of a committee to investigate and report on the matter. The members drafted a bill proposing the establishment of a separate court of equity and offering a view of the subject that was strikingly different from the traditional understanding.[19] First of all, Story pointed out the extent to which equity was more than a collection of irrationalities. Properly interpreted, equity not only could broadly pertain to a wide variety of issues, including commercial disputes, land titles, and wills, but also had a capacity to assume a "steady and well-defined shape" and to be "limited by . . . fixed rules" of interpretation and application.[20]

Story particularly emphasized the extent to which American conditions precluded the evils that had beset equity courts in England. In America, Story wrote, the nearly universal practice of partible inheritance and the rejection of feudal mechanisms like entail had simplified the process of wealth transmission and reduced the family conflicts so often seen in the settlement of estates in the Old World.[21] Although America's unique circumstances and republican ideals had liberated property relations from monarchical and medieval institutions, Story argued that the failure to establish equity jurisdiction gave individuals too much freedom in disposing of their property. Unless the courts were empowered to regulate certain kinds of property relations, the country stood in danger "of having our most valuable estates locked up in mortmain, and our surplus wealth pass away in specious or mistaken charities, founded upon visionary or useless

18. On Story's championship of equity, see Curran, "Struggle for Equity Jurisdiction"; R. Kent Newmyer, *Supreme Court Justice Joseph Story: Statesman of the Old Republic* (Chapel Hill, 1985); and William W. Story, ed., *Life and Letters of Joseph Story* (Boston, 1851). Langbein's masterful article "Chancellor Kent and the History of Legal Literature" helps put Story's contributions into context.

19. Curran refers to Story's unpublished 1808 report to the legislature, which I have been unable to locate. Evidently Story's 1820 article, "Chancery Jurisdiction," published as an unsigned piece in the *North American Review* 9(1820):161ff., is an expanded version of that report. The essay appears under Story's by-line in William W. Story, ed., *The Miscellaneous Writings of Joseph Story* (Boston, 1852), 148–179.

20. Story, "Chancery Jurisdiction," 151.

21. Story, "Chancery Jurisdiction," 153.

schemes, to the impoverishment of friends, and the injury of the poor and deserving of our own countrymen."[22] Without equity, neither the interests of "idiots and lunatics, as to the guardianship of their persons, and the management of their estates, and the protéction of their rights"—nor those of orphans—could be adequately safeguarded.[23]

No less important, in Story's view, was the ability to deal with "bills for specific performance of contracts," a matter of growing importance in America's burgeoning economy. Story condemned the exercise of equity powers by the legislatures, which, often under political influence or popular pressures, had tended to "dispense with a strict compliance" of the terms of contracts "when no accident, mistake, or fraud" had prevented their fulfillment.[24] Under these circumstances, equity had been misused, with officials "acting upon a thousand fancies of imaginary hardship" to grant relief from obligations even in cases where the petitioner had "utterly failed to comply with the conditions of sale, within the period stipulated by the express letter of his contract."[25] "We have known," Story wrote, of "specific performance sought, and reluctantly denied, after the lapse of more than thirty years, when all the original parties were dead, and the land, which was a wilderness, was become a settled and cultivated country."[26] This kind of uncertainty, delay, and dissatisfaction was intolerable in a rational economic setting.

Story's arguments in favor of equity resonated with the Boston merchants' emerging awareness of the need to strike a balance between the desire to secure property and the need to ensure that their wealth remained a source of continuing vitality and strength for their families and their class. On the one hand, equity, by protecting contracts from meddling legislatures and vexatious suits over estates and land titles, would ensure legal transformation that could have far-reaching impacts on commerce, real estate, charities, and testation. On the other, it promised to ensure the free circulation of property essential to a growing entrepreneurial economy.

Despite Story's learned and eloquent report and the backing of influential politicians from both parties, the legislature defeated "An Act Providing for Relief in Equity." The measure was again introduced in 1810, but was once more defeated, a loss "due in no small measure to Representative

22. Story, "Chancery Jurisdiction," 156.
23. Story, "Chancery Jurisdiction," 157.
24. Story, "Chancery Jurisdiction," 158.
25. Story, "Chancery Jurisdiction," 159.
26. Story, "Chancery Jurisdiction," 159.

Story's own party, which won its first statewide victory in that year."[27] The growing strength of the Republicans benefited Story's career, even as his beliefs moved in a more conservative direction. In 1811, President Madison appointed Story to the United States Supreme Court. Once on the court, Story began handing down decisions that had much more in common with the tenets of the Federalists, who promoted the growth of federal over state power, the strength and stability of institutions to counter popular influence, and a legal infrastructure favorable to economic development.

As his reputation grew, Story began gathering influential allies in the legal profession and, perhaps more importantly, building his ties to powerful Boston mercantile interests.[28] As one biographer described Story's political transformation, he "not only joined Massachusetts conservatives but wished to lead them."[29] Though neither wealthy nor well-connected, his Harvard degree, his evident brilliance, and his outstanding service as a director of two Salem banks drew him into the most powerful circle of Boston leaders. He became an intimate of John Lowell, the city's preeminent conservative, and this brought him into contact with the "Merrimac Men"—the Cabots, Jacksons, Lees, and other relatives of Lowell who were pioneering industrial development in the state. His aesthetic interests brought him friendship with the city's well-connected intellectuals, including publisher George Ticknor (who had married into a textile fortune), Edward Everett (who married a daughter of insurance magnate Peter Chardon Brooks), and Josiah Quincy, Jr. (possessor of a private fortune based in Boston real estate).

Story's reward for his "apostasy" was closer involvement with Harvard, which had become the core institution of the emerging Brahmin class and the "intellectual nerve center of conservative ideas."[30] In 1818, he was elected to the Board of Overseers; in 1827, he became a Fellow of the Corporation; and in 1829, he became Dane Professor of Law and, in effect, head of the law school. His Harvard affiliation strategically positioned him as a scholar, teacher, and jurist to exert an extraordinary influence on the thinking of the legal profession in Massachusetts and beyond. He expanded his ideas about equity, originally set forth in reports to the state legislature,

27. Curran, "Struggle for Equity Jurisdiction," 274.
28. On Justice Story's place among the Boston elite, see Ronald Story, *The Forging of an Aristocracy: Harvard and the Boston Upper Class, 1800–1870* (Middletown, Conn., 1980).
29. Newmyer, *Joseph Story*, 163.
30. Newmyer, *Joseph Story*, 165.

into influential articles for popular audiences [including an important article in the *North American Review* (1820)] and into legal treatises [for example, *Commentaries on Equity Jurisprudence as Administered in England and America* (1836)].[31] A constellation of merchant-funded eleemosynary organizations elected him to their boards; as the nineteenth century wore on, these groups came to define the institutional boundaries of the emerging Brahmin class.

Though he had become a national figure, Story remained intensely engaged in Massachusetts politics. He continued to push for a grant of equity powers to the Supreme Judicial Court, despite the opposition of its Chief Justice, Isaac Parker, who decried judicial discretion.[32] (Strong support from Judge Charles Jackson, a kinsman of the Cabots, Higginsons, Jacksons, Lees, and Lowells, helped to counter Parker's influence). In February of 1817, with surprisingly little public comment or debate, the legislature was persuaded to pass an act granting the Supreme Judicial Court full equity powers in matters affecting trusts. Three years later, when Massachusetts held a constitutional convention, Story attended as a delegate from Salem and was made chairman of the committee on the judiciary. Its members recommended the creation of a separate chancery court, on the model established in New York, but the proposal was defeated by the full convention, of which Isaac Parker, Story's old adversary, was president. Still Story and his allies pushed ahead and, through the 1820s, succeeded in persuading the legislature to increase incrementally the state courts' equity powers.

Law and Institutions

The new legal environment favorable to the creation and enforcement of trusts was in every sense an achievement of the emerging Brahminate. Against deeply rooted traditions and well-organized popular hostility, this influential minority had brought into being an arena of activity that provided the basis for passing on its wealth, relatively intact, to future generations, for pooling its collective economic resources, and for building up its identity and influence as a class. At the same time, both the process and the product by which these goals were achieved suggests the complexity of the merchant group's intentions. They did not want to create an aristocracy

31. Joseph Story, *Commentaries on Equity Jurisprudence as Administered in England and America* (Boston, 1836).

32. Again, Curran gives the definitive account of Story's activities with regard to equity in the period 1817–1820.

along the European model; despite their growing wealth, they continued to see themselves as a capitalist class. And, largely self-made men themselves, they recognized that their continuing vitality depended on their ability to, in Holmes' words, "drain off" the "promising young author and rising lawyer and large capitalist" from wherever they could be found.[33] This was evidenced in their willingness to recruit talented outsiders like Joseph Story.

Striking this balance between the desire for exclusivity (witness their imperative to define themselves as a group and to pool their resources) and the need for inclusivity (which compelled them to recruit talented outsiders and to ensure that only the most competent of their own progeny assumed positions of responsibility) was no easy task. Boston merchants, in fact, were unique among America's emergent urban elites in meeting the challenge. Although Philadelphia and New York were both larger and richer, enjoying incalculably greater access to the natural resources and interior markets essential to economic growth, their sharp religious divisions and imperfect legal architecture hampered the capacity of their elites to pool their resources for either economic or institutional purposes. While Boston would never give rise to great fortunes on the scale of Stephen Girard's or John Jacob Astor's, neither Philadelphians nor New Yorkers (until the end of the nineteenth century) would create cultural and educational institutions as influential as Harvard, the Massachusetts General Hospital, or the Boston Museum of Fine Arts. Nor would either group present to society a class of leaders who, despite its relative lack of political power, would so firmly and successfully dominate the civic life of their respective regions over the course of more than a century.[34]

The legal environment and the institutions to which it gave rise made

33. Oliver Wendell Holmes, *Autocrat of the Breakfast Table* (1858; reprint, New York, 1957), 119–120.

34. Perhaps the best study of the differences between the elites and the institutional cultures of Boston, New York, Philadelphia, and other cities is E. Digby Baltzell's *Puritan Boston and Quaker Philadelphia: Two Protestant Ethics and the Spirit of Class Authority and Leadership* (New York, 1979). See also, Peter Dobkin Hall, "Cultures of Trusteeship in the United States," in Hall, *Inventing the Nonprofit Sector*, 135–206. While they do not seek to make explicit comparisons between New York and other cities, the following studies shed important light on this issue: Thomas Bender, *New York Intellect: A History of Intellectual Life in New York City, from 1750 to the Beginnings of Our Own Time* (New York, 1987); Bender, *Intellect and Public Life: Essays on the Social History of Academic Intellectuals in the United States* (Baltimore, 1993); David C. Hammack, *Power and Society: Greater New York at the Turn of the Century* (New York, 1982); Sam Bass Warner, *The Private City: Philadelphia in Three Periods of Growth* (Philadelphia, 1968).

the crucial difference. While Chancellor James Kent of New York was unquestionably the chief figure in Americanizing equity and in successfully promoting equity jurisprudence in the Empire State, his efforts were hampered by Jacksonian opponents who limited the proportion of estates decedents could leave to charity, limited the size of institutional endowments, and placed all the state's eleemosynary institutions—including churches— under state regulation. While Kent's efforts assured wealthy New Yorkers an extraordinary freedom in their private testamentary arrangements, legal and political barriers as well as ethnic and religious conflicts within the elite prevented the establishment and funding of institutions with the potential for broad public influence.[35]

Philadelphians labored under similar disabilities. Dominated by back-country Democrats, its legislature annulled the *Statute of Charitable Uses* after the Revolution, removing the legal basis for the enforcement of charitable trusts, and steadfastly refused for decades thereafter to grant state courts equity powers. While Pennsylvania's "common law courts proved exceedingly imaginative in compensating by incorporating parts of equity law and procedure into their own proceedings," neither these expedients nor the informal arrangements wealthy Philadelphians used to create and enforce testamentary trusts were any substitute for the "steady and well-defined shape" of a body of jurisprudence "limited by fixed rules" of interpretation and application.[36] Despite the city's impressive financial and in-

35. The best account of Kent's influence is in Langbein, "Chancellor Kent," 547ff. On Jacksonian strictures on charitable giving and trust making, see James Barr Ames, "The Failure of the 'Tilden Trust'" in Ames, *Lectures on Legal History and Miscellaneous Legal Essays* (Cambridge, 1913), 285–297, and Scott, "Charitable Trusts in New York," 152–175. See also, John S. Whitehead, *The Separation of College and State: Columbia, Dartmouth, Harvard, and Yale, 1776–1876* (New Haven, 1973).

A more recent study by Stanley N. Katz, Barry Sullivan, and C. Paul Beach, "Legal Change and Legal Autonomy: Charitable Trusts in New York, 1777–1893," in *Law and Society Review* 3(1985):51–89, argues that New York's hostility to charities was an artifact of the state's legal system and that strictures on them were not as severe as earlier scholars had assumed.

36. Katz, "The Politics of Law," 271. Erwin N. Griswold provides a fine description of the impact that the unofficial status of equity in Pennsylvania had on the development of testamentary trusts in the Keystone state in *Spendthrift Trusts under the New York Statutes and Elsewhere* (Albany, 1947), 21–22:

In the early part of the [19th] century there were no equity courts in Pennsylvania, and the law courts did not have equity powers. The result was that if a man had what elsewhere would have been regarded as an equitable right, there was little or no means of dealing with it in Pennsylvania. Creditors were therefore unable to reach the

tellectual resources, the development of great institutions of education and culture under elite patronage would not occur until the end of the nineteenth century. And, while the city's elite could produce a handful of outstanding individuals, it would never produce, in a quantity comparable to Boston, a steady stream of national leaders.[37]

Trusts in Massachusetts: The First Wave, 1820–1833

The Massachusetts legislature established the judicial framework for equitable remedies, but the substance of equity was built up by precedents established on a case by case basis. Suits brought by Boston merchants not surprisingly loomed large in this process, since they, more than any other group, possessed estates large and complex enough to require the "special means" needed to counteract the erosive force of partible inheritance.

Cases defining the fundamentals of trust law came in three major waves, each roughly correlated with generational removes from the founders of the early family trusts. The first wave, which came before the courts in the 1820s, concerned the most basic features of trusts: their immunity from the claims of creditors and other third parties; the fiduciary responsibilities of

---

interest of the beneficiary, since there was no procedure at law for that purpose. In this state of the law, the courts became accustomed to interests owned by beneficiaries which could not be reached by creditors. When, in later years, the Pennsylvania courts gradually acquired equity powers, spendthrift trusts had become firmly established, and an accepted part of the law.

37. Baltzell concisely, if crudely, posits the differences between Boston's and other cities' capacities to produce leaders in the first chapter of *Puritan Boston and Quaker Philadelphia*:

[a] clue to the relationship between hierarchy and leadership is suggested by [John] Gardner's list of Founding Fathers. *All* these men were reared in Massachusetts or Virginia; *none* was reared in the colony of Pennsylvania, though Philadelphia was the largest city in the new nation and contained perhaps the wealthiest, most successful, gayest, and most brilliant elite in the land. Not only had Pennsylvanians little to do with taking the lead in our nation's founding, but the state has produced very few distinguished Americans throughout our history. . . . Thus, [the] list of 400 notable Americans in the *Encyclopedia of American History* (1965) shows that Massachusetts produced twice as many prominent individuals as did Virginia and more than three times as many as Pennsylvania. As might be expected, moreover, Virginia led in the proportion of men of power and authority (including presidents of the United States); Massachusetts, providing a more balanced group of leaders, excelled in arts and letters; Pennsylvanians were more likely to be men of innovation and change, a large proportion of whom made their careers outside the state. Indeed, the sole president from Pennsylvania, James Buchanan, was one of the weakest in American history. [4–5]

trustees; and the length of time a private trust could be permitted to last before its *corpus* was distributed. The second wave came in the 1850s, focusing on the rights of beneficiaries under trust estates, and resulted largely from challenges to restrictive trust provisions by beneficiaries. The third wave, decided in the 1870s, was concerned with the immunity of estates from the claims of third parties, in particular, the validity of spend-thrift trusts.

The first major trust case decided by the Supreme Judicial Court tested a provision that many early nineteenth-century merchants had routinely at-tached to their trust instruments, one that protected principal and income from claims made by the beneficiaries' creditors. For example, Boston merchant Jonathan Jackson in his will established a trust to guarantee that his daughters' share of his estate would be protected from their husbands and from claims by their husbands' creditors:

> if either of my daughters who are now married. viz. Hannah Lowell and Sarah Gardner, or either of . . . my other two Daughters after being married, should at any time stand in need of assistance for their comfortable support, and maintenance, I authorize and direct the said trustees to pay over the said interest or produce to such of my daughters as have most need. . . . But in every case of such payment to any married daughter, the same shall go and be paid to and for the sole, separate, and peculiar use of the said Daughter, and the same or any part thereof shall not be paid to her husband. Nor shall the principal sum, nor the interest, nor the produce thereof be in any manner subject to be charged or liable to the claims, controul, debts, or encumbrances of any husband of either of my daughters.[38]

The landmark case testing such provisions that came before the court in 1824 involved neither a large estate nor a Boston merchant family. But the decision rendered did much to reassure the elites that their estates would be secure from the claims of creditors. *Braman* v. *Stiles* concerned a tes-tator from rural Worcester County who, after providing for his wife and three of his sons by straightforward distributions of money and property, ordered that

> whatever shall fall to the part or share of my son Jonas Stiles, shall be deposited by my executor in the hands of my sons, Luther Stiles and Barney Stiles, and be retained by them, and dealt out to the said Jonas for his comfort and advantage, according to their best judgment and discretion.[39]

38. Quoted in Kenneth Wiggins Porter, *The Jacksons and the Lees: Two Generations of Massachusetts Merchants, 1765–1844* (Cambridge, Mass., 1937), 383–384.

39. Braman v. Stiles, 19 Mass. (2 Pickering) 461 (1824).

Farmer Stiles had, in effect, created a trust, named one of his sons as a beneficiary, and designated the others as trustees with the power to distribute principal and interest at their discretion. In 1823, one of the creditors of the improvident Jonas, in an effort to recover monies owed him, brought attachment proceedings against "all the interest of Jonas Stiles in the real estate of which his father died seised." Because satisfying this claim would require liquidating the estate, the Stiles brothers resisted and the case came before the Supreme Judicial Court.

Chief Justice Parker wrote an opinion strongly safeguarding the intentions of testators and endorsing the integrity of the trust. "Nothing can be more clear," he declared,

> than that the testator . . . intended that his sons, Luther and Barney, should be the trustees of Jonas, as to every thing which was the subject matter of this provision; and such intention was lawful, for he having the power of disposing of his property as he pleased, had a right to prevent it from going to the creditors of his son, or from being wasted by the son himself, if, as was probable, he had become incapable of taking care of property. Creditors have no right to complain; for unless such disposition can be made, without doubt testators, in like situations would give their property to their other children.[40]

Of particular interest here is Parker's willingness to extend the protection of the courts, which had traditionally defended the interests of women, children, and lunatics, to include property dedicated to the support of a person who was legally competent. This was a clear shift in judicial thinking away from the protection of incompetent *persons* towards a concern for the integrity of *estates*. Of further interest is the court's sanction of the broad discretion given to trustees, thus empowering them to act as they saw fit, without written instructions. Taken together, these features of the decision were important steps towards enabling testators to preserve their wealth intact, regardless of the capabilities and desires of their heirs.

Few cases have had greater impact on the character of American trusts testamentary and charitable than *Harvard College and Massachusetts General Hospital* v. *Amory*, which set the "prudent man" standard for fiduciaries.[41] Brought before the court in 1829, the case involved the will of Boston merchant John McLean, the husband of Ann (Amory) McLean, who died in 1823 leaving the sum of $50,000 in trust and appointing his

40. Braman v. Stiles, 464.

41. Harvard College and Massachusetts General Hospital v. Amory, 26 Mass. (9 Pickering) 446–465 (1830).

brothers-in-law, Jonathan and Francis Amory, as trustees. Income from the trust was to be paid to McLean's widow during her lifetime. On her death, the principal was to be divided between Harvard and MGH.

The trustees invested the principal in the stock of manufacturing corporations, particularly the Boston and Merrimack companies, in which the Amorys and their kinsmen owned substantial interests. The college and the hospital took exception to this, claiming that although the large dividends yielded by such investments benefited the widow McLean, they "disregarded the interests of the respondents" because of their fluctuating value and (since manufacturing companies did not enjoy limited liability) exposed the estate to "total loss." In effect, the plaintiffs asked the court to rule on two questions: 1) how much discretion could trustees be permitted in making investment decisions; 2) whether beneficiaries had the right to question the discretionary powers of trustees in these matters.

In this case, the court ruled against the college and the hospital. Justice Samuel Putnam's opinion considered the allegation that the Amorys had invested imprudently and to the detriment of the remaindermen by exploring the safety of all possible kinds of investment. He found that all had a significant potential to fail: the security of government bonds depended on the vagaries of politics; the security of real estate investments depended on the validity of titles; the value of stocks was subject to the uncertainties of the marketplace. One factor, in Putnam's view, made "the promises and conduct of private corporations which are managed by substantial and prudent directors" a more secure investment than any other: unlike government, he wrote, private corporations "are amenable to the law. The holder may pursue his legal remedy and compel them or their officers to do justice. But the government can only be supplicated." Justice Putnam gave this litany of insecurity a ringing conclusion:

> All that can be required of a trustee to invest, is, that he shall conduct himself faithfully and exercise a sound discretion. He is to observe how men of prudence, discretion and intelligence manage their own affairs, not in regard to speculation, but in regard to the permanent disposition of their funds, considering the probable income, as well as the probable safety of the capital to be invested.[42]

Putnam went on to point out that the testator himself, "a man of extraordinary forecast and discretion, in regard to the management of his property," whose "vast accumulation could not be ascribed to accidental causes, but to

42. Harvard College and Massachusetts General Hospital v. Amory, 459–461.

calculation and reflection," had obviously considered the securities questioned by the remaindermen prudent investments, since he had "invested nearly half his property in manufacturing stock." His inclinations, Putnam suggested, were "entitled to great consideration" in assessing the decisions of his trustees and seemed to justify their actions.[43]

Having vigorously defended the power of trustees to invest at their discretion, Putnam concluded by further protecting them from accountability to beneficiaries by declaring that they were not liable for losses resulting from their investment decisions:

> Trustees are justly and uniformly considered favourably, and it is of great importance to bereaved families and orphans, that they should not be held to make good, losses in the depreciation of stocks or the failure of the capital itself, which they held in trust, provided they conduct themselves honestly and discreetly and carefully, according to the existing circumstances, in the discharge of their trusts. If this were held otherwise, no prudent man would run the hazard of losses which might happen without any neglect or breach of good faith.[44]

This decision tremendously expanded the power and independence of trustees by giving them almost complete discretion to invest funds as they saw fit, free from the restraints of interested parties. At the same time, the standard of prudence set for trustees by the court was, it appeared, the same that their peers in Boston's financial community had come to expect. In the end, this decision introduced a degree of rationality into the investment process: a common standard of prudence made the investment process less idiosyncratic and less subject to the interests of particular families, in effect establishing a legal basis for pooling economic resources to serve the collective interests of the merchant families as a group.

Most importantly, by sanctioning trustees' ability to invest in manufacturing, railroad, insurance, and other stocks and by protecting them from the threat of endlessly vexatious suits by disgruntled beneficiaries, the court both released family money into a common pool, making it available for rational investment in the broader economy, and transformed trustees into key intermediaries in this process.

From this point on, particular individuals who specialized in managing trust estates, the trustees of charitable endowments, and firms like the Massachusetts Hospital Life Insurance Company (MHLI) began to assume greater and greater centrality in Boston's financial community. By

43. Harvard College and Massachusetts General Hospital v. Amory, 462, 463.
44. Harvard College and Massachusetts General Hospital v. Amory, 465.

1850, the MHLI had become the largest commercial lender in New England and a key player in underwriting the region's textile and railroad industries.[45] Specialized trust managers—Boston Trustees, as they came to be known—could, by mid century, be found on the boards of directors of virtually every major enterprise in and (as Boston's role as a center of investment banking began to grow) beyond Massachusetts.[46]

Putnam's decision, in freeing capital from family control, further signaled the separation of management and ownership that was, as Berle and Means would point out nearly a century later, the distinguishing characteristic of the modern economic order.[47] As it turned out, it was also the distinguishing characteristic of modern class structure: by placing capital under the best possible management, but also by consolidating and rationalizing its use, this arrangement constituted one of the "special means" to assure that the millionocracy would not be merely a "perpetual fact of money with a variable human element."

Finally, the separation of ownership and management, with its emphasis on competence, ensured that the financial core of the emerging Brahmi-

45. White's *History of the Massachusetts Hospital Life Insurance Company* gives the best overall account of the merchants' use of trusts for pooling capital and the role of this process in the rise of Boston as a center of investment banking in the antebellum period.

46. A scholarly study of the "Boston Trustee" has yet to be written. Holbrook's *The Boston Trustee* sheds valuable light on the subject, as do John P. Marquand's article "Boston," *Fortune* 7(1933):27–29, 32–36, 98–106; William J. Sheehan's "Unique to Boston Are the Famous 'Boston Trustees,'" *Boston Transcript*, July 21, 1934; and the biographies of such notable trustees as Philip Dexter and William Minot in their respective Harvard classbooks.

A stockholder protest by J. C. Ayer, *Some of the Uses and Abuses in the Management of Our Manufacturing Corporations* (Lowell, 1863), provides striking insight into the growing power of trustees. While Ayer directed most of his barbs at the MHLI, they are equally applicable to private trustees, since the leading ones also served as officers and directors of the companies in which they invested. Describing the power of trustees, Ayer wrote: "by their position, with the affairs of the Corporation closed to all but themselves, they can buy stock when it has been prosperous, and sell out to the innocent public when it has been unfortunate. . . . Manufacturing stocks are holden in large proportion by women, widows, orphan children, charitable institutions, and retired old men, who are dependent on them for their support. The proxy vote of nearly all of these can always be gathered by the officers because they alone know who they are" (16).

47. Adolph A. Berle, Jr., and Gardiner C. Means, *The Modern Corporation and Private Property* (New York, 1933). For an account of the separation of ownership and management in the administration of the financial affairs of wealthy families, see George M. Marcus and Peter Dobkin Hall, *Lives in Trust: The Fortunes of Dynastic Families in Late Twentieth Century America* (Boulder, 1992), and George M. Marcus, ed., *Elites: Ethnographic Issues* (Albuquerque, 1983).

nate would embody a capacity to recruit talented outsiders, thereby helping to maintain the group's vitality. While Brahmin lore is replete with
stories about wealthy Bostonians' genealogical obsessions, the ranks of the
city's economic and cultural leadership were, in fact, constantly replenished by talented individuals who were not descendants of elite postrevolutionary family founders. At the same time, scions of Boston merchant families did not hesitate to move out into the economic mainstream—banking
in New York, managing railroads in Illinois, setting up mining ventures in
Michigan—and, in so doing, they assured Boston's elite a central role in the
development of a national economy, not only as a supplier of capital, but as
the *avant garde* of managerial and, later, technological expertise.[48]

But these achievements still lay in the future. Despite the important first
steps taken by the courts, in the 1830s the law of trusts remained largely
undefined. And perhaps the most significant unresolved issue concerned
the *duration* of trusts. This was no small matter. Debate on the subject
was politically charged: even Story himself criticized the ways in which
English law had hampered the growth of a free economy and empowered
oppressive aristocratic and ecclesiastical institutions through entails, restrictive trust provisions, and the uncontrolled growth of endowed charities. In their efforts to Americanize equity, Boston merchants sought to
strike a balance between its conservative and liberalizing possibilities: limiting the duration of trusts to prevent the partition of estates, while avoiding
the hazards of great wealth passed on, generation after generation, to un-
worthy descendants.

The last key case in the first wave of trust decisions made by the Supreme Judicial Court focused on this issue. As in *Braman* v. *Stiles*, it did not
involve a famous family or a great estate. But the learned judges used this
simple matter concerning a rural will as a pretext for drawing the broadest
possible conclusions. The case, *Nightingale* v. *Burrell*, came before the
Court in 1833.[49] It involved the 1793 will of a testator who provided that his
farm would be divided between his two daughters, that they should hold
their portions for their lifetimes, and, if one of them should die without
issue, her share should go to the surviving daughter and her children. This
provision was clearly an effort to ensure that the farm remained in the
testator's family and to prevent its division and sale to strangers on the
death of one or another of his daughters. Though not a trust estate, since no

48. The best discussion of this is Gabriel Kolko's essay "Brahmins and Businessmen," in
Barrington Moore and Kurt Wolfe, eds., *The Critical Spirit: Essays in Honor of Herbert
Marcuse* (Boston, 1967).
49. Nightingale v. Burrell, 32 Mass. (15 Pickering) 104ff. (1833).

trustee was named and the heirs held title to the property, the case bore on trusts because the will's provisions limited the heirs' ability to dispose of the property.

Following the will's probate, the two daughters divided the land by deeds. In 1806, one of the daughters sold her portion to William Walter, a Boston merchant, who permitted both women to remain on the property as tenants, with the provision that, at their decease, he would take possession. At the time no one objected to this arrangement. In 1829, one of the daughters died, survived by her husband, but leaving no children. The surviving sister sued for possession of her late sibling's share of the farm, arguing that her father's will had provided that, on the death of one of his daughters without issue, the survivor should take the whole estate.

Lawyers for the estate of the deceased sister argued that the testator had created an illegal entail and that, even if his instructions were interpreted as an executory devise, the contingency of surviving children was too remote for the provision to be valid. Lawyers for the surviving sister asserted that the provision was not an entail because the land vested in one of the daughters and thus was not too remote. The testator, they argued, had not provided that the land should go to his heirs in perpetuity (which would be an illegal entail); the limitation on selling the property applied merely within the lifetimes of his daughters. Thus, they argued, the testator's provision was valid, and the sale of the land to a third part was void, because it attempted to dispose of property that was not the heirs' to dispose of.

Chief Justice Lemuel Shaw delivered the opinion in the case. The lengths to which he went in expanding its implications make it clear that he viewed it as a signal opportunity to explore the frontiers of legal doctrine. The core of the decision hinged on Shaw's precedent-setting application of the Rule Against Perpetuities. This rule was a guideline, developed over time in English law, to prevent testators from creating perpetual trusts, which were defined as estates "inalienable, though all mankind join in the conveyance . . . a thing odious in the law, and destructive to the commonwealth; it would stop commerce and prevent the circulation of property."[50] Though first enunciated in the seventeenth century, British courts did not define its final form until 1833, the same year in which Justice Shaw handed down his decision in *Nightingale* v. *Burrell*.[51]

While the Rule Against Perpetuities required that property vest at some

50. Jarius Ware Perry, *A Treatise on the Law of Trusts and Trustees* (Boston, 1872), 345.
51. Guy Newhall, *Future Interests and the Rule Against Perpetuities in Massachusetts* (Boston, 1942), 55.

point, there was endless litigation concerning *when* this should occur. The guideline adopted by Shaw was to require

> that [the property] vest within the compass of a life or lives in being, at the time the devise takes effect, that is, at the death of the testator, and twenty-one years and the fraction of a year after, otherwise such executory devise is wholly void.[52]

Thus, in simplest terms, the rule as enunciated by Shaw set three generations from the testator as the maximum duration of a trust. In theory, however, the rule could be broadly interpreted, since "life or lives in being" at the time the trust or devise was made did not refer to any specific persons. In England, for example, it became common to make the "lives in being" all the lineal descendants of Queen Victoria, which made trusts, if not perpetual, able to endure for a considerable period of time.

Again, the adoption of the Rule Against Perpetuities by Massachusetts courts, where men who increasingly favored or who were, like Justices Jackson and Putnam, related by blood or marriage to the Brahminate presided, underscores the complexity of the merchant group's social goals. Anglophiles though they were, they were not seeking to become an aristocracy through the creation of "special means" that would entirely insulate them from the democratizing forces of partible inheritance or the rigors of the marketplace. They knew, rather, that their strength as a group depended on their continuing commitment to commerce and manufacturing.

There was a more immediately practical reason for the Brahminate to favor adoption of the rule. If perpetuities were permitted, each succeeding generation would increase the number of beneficiaries to be supported by such trusts, and the amount of income available to each individual would decrease over time. Perpetuities would, in other words, subject estates to the same problems of partition and diminished resources that the merchants were trying to avoid in the first place. In addition, perpetuities would tend to reinforce the interests of individual families over those of the group as a whole. For if property could not vest, the primary reason for intermarriage within the group would disappear, since it would not be possible to consolidate estates in any meaningful sense. Without widespread endogamy, the children of merchant families would marry non-Bostonians and would scatter their talents and their shares in family fortunes. Even as the first generation of merchant family founders was dying off and their fortunes were passing to a generation of heirs who enjoyed unprecedented privileges and wealth, the group remained keenly aware of

52. Nightingale v. Burrell, 111.

the dilemmas presented by inherited wealth and the tensions between "an audacious will to power and the cautious reckoning of gain."[53]

Trusts in Massachusetts: The Second Wave, 1850–1869

While the activism of the Supreme Judicial Court did much to set guidelines for the administration and enforcement of trusts, these applied only in cases brought before the court and to trusts established once doctrine had been set forth. The guidelines did not apply to older trusts that had previously been established and remained unchallenged. Appropriately, given the maturation of the first "inheritor" cohort of merchant family descendants, the second wave of legal decisions involved efforts to define the rights of beneficiaries under trusts and to clarify further the powers and duties of trustees.

Not surprisingly, given the tendencies of earlier decisions and the growing amount and economic significance of property held in trust, the direction of court decisions during this period further increased the power of trustees and diminished the rights of beneficiaries. Trustees' discretionary power was enhanced by two decisions, one set forth in 1855, the other in 1868. Two other major decisions, although they voided the trusts in question, further increased the power of trustees by clarifying the rules by which funds could be legally restricted.

The case of *Perkins* v. *Hays* involved the widow of a prominent Boston merchant who was the beneficiary of a life trust established under her husband's will. After his death, she remarried.[54] When her second husband found himself unable to pay his debts, she agreed to assign a portion of her trust income to satisfy his obligations. On learning of this arrangement, the trustees refused to release the funds, and the woman brought suit.

The court's decision favored the trustees' action, establishing the doctrine that testators could specify the uses to which their bounty could be put and granting trustees the discretion to decide whether certain uses were appropriate. This meant that beneficiaries could not, as in this case, pledge away income in anticipation of receiving it, since that would deprive trustees of their power to ensure that trust income would be applied to the uses set forth by the testator or dictated by their judgment.

The second case, *Minot* v. *Paine*, concerned the definition of trust income specifically, whether dividends paid in stock rather than money

53. Ronald Story, "Class Development and Cultural Institutions in Boston, 1800–1870" (Ph.D. diss., State Univ. of New York—Stony Brook, 1972), 421.

54. Perkins v. Hayes, 69 Mass. (3 Gray) 405ff. (1855).

should be treated as income payable to beneficiaries or as additions to principal, subject to the control of the trustee.[55] The court's controversial decision, known as the Rule in Minot's Case, held that stock dividends, however made, should be treated as capital, and cash dividends, however credited, should be treated as income payable to beneficiaries. Needless to say, the rule worked very much to the advantage of trust estates, which could, when corporations paid dividends in stock, substantially increase their capital. And, given the leading positions many of them had assumed on corporate boards by the 1860s, it enabled trustees to use their influence to see to it that dividends were paid in stock rather than cash.

The decision sparked outrage in elite legal circles. Brahmin lawyer John Osborne Sargent, a Harvard overseer and member of the Porcellian Club, lampooned its reasoning in a series of angry articles and pamphlets. "Walking over Cambridge Bridge the other afternoon," he wrote in one,

I was accosted by a gentleman who touched his hat politely, and begged to direct my attention to an Egyptian pyramid in the distance.

I looked with both eyes, and could see nothing but the Bunker Hill Monument.

"But, sir," said he, observing that I did not entirely agree with him, "you must admit that it is in the nature of an Egyptian pyramid."

"Certainly, sir," I replied, "they are both built of stone."

"Then, sir, I am not far out of the way in saying that it represents, and that we must regard it as an Egyptian pyramid?"

. . . I was getting a little uneasy under this, for though my accostant, in his white tie and black frock, was a perfect gentleman, there was something clearly wrong about him. So I replied, "By all means," and was continuing on my way.

"Please understand, sir," said he, gently obstructing my passage, "that I hold that structure to be an Egyptian pyramid on the banks of the Nile. Yes, sir, that must be regarded as settled. I said so yesterday. Good afternoon, sir."

Poor fellow, I observed to myself, as he took his leave,—poor fellow! escaped, probably, from Somerville [the mental hospital]. But he has a very judicial air. Can it be possible that he is one of the ——! I should not otherwise have suspected it, perhaps—but then his mode of reasoning is so similar to that of the bench![56]

55. Minot v. Paine, 99 Mass. 101ff. (1868).
56. John Osborne Sargent, *The Rule in Minot's Case, Again* (New York, 1872), 5–6. Sar-

Sargent had clearly missed the point of the decision. While it may have been true that to identify principal with stock dividends did not make any more sense than to identify the Bunker Hill Monument with the pyramids of Egypt, the court's concerns were not guided by common sense but by the exigencies of economic reality. Thus Sargent's protracted protest (he wrote three lengthy pamphlets on the case), like earlier protests against the power of trustees, was in vain. And, while his views were apparently widely shared in the Boston legal community, his colleagues kept their opinions to themselves, no doubt wary of the awesome power of the professional and institutional trustees who benefited so greatly from the decision.

Other important cases coming before the court in this period involved efforts to break trusts set up by merchant family founders Robert Gould Shaw (d. 1854) and Israel Thorndike (d. 1832). Both trusts contained straightforward devises designed to maximize accumulation and minimize partition before the distribution of their principal. Shaw left property to one of his daughters in a trust that, on her death, was to pay $20,000 to her widower and bar him from any future share in the estate, with the remainder to be divided into separate trust funds for her children, granting to them the power to bequeath their funds as they saw fit.[57] The Thorndike trust, made twenty years earlier, was simpler: it provided that a sum should be placed in trust in the Massachusetts Hospital Life Insurance Company for a period of fifty years. At the end of this period, the funds were to be distributed among those persons who were his legal heirs. To this, Thorndike added the provision that, should any of his heirs find themselves in need before the final distribution of the estate, they could petition his trustees for relief—which the trustees could grant at their discretion.[58]

In both of these cases, the court applied the Rule Against Perpetuities, but in a more refined form. As set forth by Justice Shaw in *Nightingale* v.

---

gent's other writings on the case include *The Rule in Minot's Case* (New York, 1870) and *A Third Chapter in Minot's Case* (New York, 1874).

Sargent's arguments anticipated by nearly a century the "total return" concept that became popular among many endowment portfolio managers during the 1960s. Events served to substantiate the wisdom of the Rule in Minot's Case. As institutions which treated capital gains as income discovered to their grief, this practice increased revenues in boom times, but had catastrophic consequences when securities prices fell, as they did in the early 1970s. On this, see William L. Cary and Craig B. Bright, *The Law and Lure of Endowment Funds* (New York, 1969) and *The Developing Law of Endowment Funds* (New York, 1974).

57. Sears v. Russell, 74 Mass. (8 Gray) 86ff. (1857).

58. Thorndike v. Loring, 81 Mass. (15 Gray) 391 (1860).

Burrell, the rule stated that an estate must vest within the term of a life or lives in being, twenty-one years and nine months. But Shaw did not deal with the question of whether, in setting up a trust, contingencies must be specified to ensure that the estate would vest by the expiration of that period. In *Sears* v. *Russell*, the court had gone to some lengths to state that, even though events took place within the term allowed by the rule, a trust would be void if these events were incidental to the terms of the will. The court ruled the Shaw trust void and ordered the estate to be distributed immediately to the heirs. Reasoning along similar lines, it also broke the Thorndike trust.

The "laughing heirs" won these battles, but the war was won by the testators and trustees, whose capacity to control estates and deploy Brahmin family resources for collective purposes was greatly strengthened. Over time, testators became less concerned with perpetuities, resorting to other, more effective methods. According to a 1933 *Fortune* magazine article on Boston, by the early twentieth century, it had become

> the accepted practice for the young Forbes or Lowell whom the Rule Against Perpetuities would make outright owner of several millions of gilt-edged bonds to reestablish voluntarily his family trust. And failing the voluntary act, there [were] always enough uncles and aunts to see that the deed in any case was done.[59]

Again, this affirms the effort, evident from the early nineteenth century, to guard against rendering wealth and the descendants who inherited it economically useless. The capacity to make and remake trusts offered the merchant class the flexibility essential for maintaining its vitality and for effectively deploying its collective resources.

Trusts in Massachusetts: The Third Wave, 1865–1882

The final stage in trust law development is significant both for its part in Massachusetts's own legal history and for its bearing on legal developments in other states and at the federal level. While Massachusetts had gone further than any other state in upholding the wishes of testators with regard to the disposition of their property, analogous developments had taken place in other states where commerce and industry had produced wealthy urban elites. As noted earlier, in both New York and Pennsylvania, urban upper classes had nurtured methods—albeit somewhat different ones—of

59. Marquand, "Boston," 36.

keeping their estates intact and favoring the desires of testators over the claims of beneficiaries and creditors.

Through the years in which these developments had occurred, no occasion had arisen to test these arrangements in the federal courts (in striking contrast to the situation of charitable trusts, which had been extensively reviewed). In 1875, a creditor of the beneficiary of a "spendthrift" trust brought suit to challenge the validity of the device. The case, *Nichols* v. *Eaton*, an appeal from the U.S. District Court of Rhode Island, involved clauses in the will of a testator who had created a trust estate for her four children. To this trust she attached a stipulation providing that,

> if her sons . . . should alienate or dispose of the income to which they were entitled under the trusts of the will, or if, by reason of bankruptcy or insolvency, or any other means whatsoever, said income shall no longer be personally enjoyed by them respectively, but the same would become payable to some other person, then the trust expressed in said will . . . should immediately cease. . . . In that case, during the life of such son, that part of the income of the trust fund was to be paid to the wife and children, or wife and child, as the case may be, of such son; and, in default of any objects of the last mentioned trust, the income was to accumulate in augmentation of the principal fund.[60]

An additional stipulation instructed the trustees, in the case of bankruptcy or insolvency, to pay at their discretion "such part of the income to which my . . . sons would have been entitled under the preceding trusts in case the forfeiture hereinabove had not happened."[61] Such methods of protecting trust income from seizure by or assignment to creditors was nothing new to Massachusetts law, whose courts had confirmed their legality as early as the 1820s.

In 1867, one of the sons failed in business and assigned all of his property to satisfy his creditors. Following the testator's instructions, the trustees stopped his income, an event that prompted one assignee to bring suit in federal circuit court. When the trustees' action was upheld, the assignee appealed to the United States Supreme Court. Attorneys for the assignee argued that a trust that secured the enjoyment of wealth free from liability for debts was "void on grounds of public policy as being in fraud of the rights of creditors."[62] The court, however, took a very different stance, even as it acknowledged English cases that had sustained this viewpoint. The

60. Nichols v. Eaton, 91 U.S. 716, 718 (1875).
61. Nichols v. Eaton, 719.
62. Nichols v. Eaton, 721–722.

majority took particular pains to draw distinctions between the law of trusts as it had developed in England and the United States and, in a manner that followed Story's conception of an equity jurisprudence framed by the unique nature of American institutions, upheld the trust. After pointing out the extent to which American bankruptcy statutes protected part of a debtor's property from seizure, the court underscored the importance of the peculiarly public nature of testamentary and property records:

> in this country, all wills or other instruments creating such trust estates are recorded in public offices, where they may be inspected by every one; and the law in such cases imputes notice to all persons concerned of all of the facts which they might know by inspection. When, therefore, it appears by the record of a will that the devisee holds this life estate or income, dividends, or rents or real property payable to him alone, to the exclusion of the alienee or creditor, the latter knows, that, in creating a debt with such a person, he has no right to look to that income as means of discharging it. He is neither misled nor defrauded when the object of the testator is carried out by excluding him from any benefit in such a devise.[63]

This ruling went far beyond even Massachusetts's historic solicitude for protecting trust estates. Certainly, *Braman* v. *Stiles* had protected the trust estate itself from the claims of a beneficiary's creditors; *Perkins* v. *Hays* had taken the doctrine a bit further in ruling that a beneficiary could not alienate or assign income in anticipation of receiving it. It seems likely, moreover, that Boston lawyers were already creating such trusts before *Nichols* v. *Eaton*. The 1874 edition of Jarius Ware Perry's *Treatise on the Law of Trusts and Trustees* suggests that

> a trust may be so created that no interest vests in the *cestui que trust* [the beneficiary]; consequently, such interest cannot be alienated, as where property is given to trustees to be applied in their discretion for the use of a third person, no interest goes to the third person until the trustees have exercised their discretion.[64]

However, Perry's dictum did not appear in his 1872 edition, nor had it yet been challenged in the Massachusetts courts. So it can be assumed that sanction for the practice came from the federal case.

Of course, the federal ruling did not obligate the states to accept its principles, so it was only a matter of time before they were challenged. This occurred in Massachusetts in 1882, when a small Boston bank, the Broad-

63. Nichols v. Eaton, 726.
64. Perry, *Treatise on the Law of Trusts*, chap. 386a.

way National, sued a beneficiary and his trustee, asking the court to apply income from a trust created by the defendant's brother to satisfy a debt.[65] In this case, the court, capping nearly a century of decisions, affirmed the ability of testators to use trusts to protect both the income and principal of their estates from the claims of third parties. The language of the decision echoed, though with somewhat more candor, the decision in *Nichols* v. *Eaton*:

> it is argued that investing a man with apparent wealth tends to mislead creditors, and to induce them to give him credit. The answer is, that creditors have no right to rely upon property thus held, and to give him credit upon the basis of his estate which, by the instrument of creating it, is declared to be inalienable by him, and not liable for his debts. By the exercise of proper diligence they can ascertain the nature and extent of his estate, especially in this Commonwealth, where all wills and most deeds are spread upon the public records.[66]

These decisions outraged portions of the legal community. One of the more notable protests came from the heart of the Brahminate itself in the form of a book, *Restraints on the Alienation of Property* (1882), written by John Chipman Gray, an eminent Boston lawyer and Royall Professor of Law at Harvard.[67] The book, which went through successive editions, denounced the court decisions upholding spendthrift trusts as contrary to the public interest, to legal precedents, and, ultimately, to national survival. "One of the worst results of spendthrift trusts," Gray declared

> is the encouragement it gives to a plutocracy, and to the accumulation of a great fortune in a single hand, through the power it affords to rich men to assure undisturbed possession of wealth to their children, however weak or wicked they may be.[68]

While assuring his readers that the courts had acted out of ignorance rather than a desire to "perpetuate a privileged class whose power and wealth should not be endangered by the weakness or folly of particular members,"

65. Broadway National Bank v. Adams, 133 Mass. 170ff. (1882).
66. Broadway National Bank v. Adams, 173–174.
67. John Chipman Gray, *Restraints on the Alienation of Property* (Boston, 1895).
68. Gray, *Restraints on the Alienation of Property*, v. Gray's sentiment was echoed by Harvard law professor Erwin N. Griswold, who described spendthrift trusts as devices "designed to protect the fortunes of Pennsylvania manufacturers and Massachusetts shipping and textile overlords from the depredations of their extravagant, and none too competent progeny." *Spendthrift Trusts under the New York Statutes and Elsewhere–Including Insurance Proceeds* (Albany, 1947), 31.

Gray took pains to point out the dangerous consequences that were likely to flow from these decisions. Linking them to the radical agitations of newly unionized workers and restive farmers, Gray declared,

> to a frame of mind and a state of public sentiment like this, spendthrift trusts are most congenial. If we are all to be cared for, and have our wants supplied, without regard to our mental and moral failings, in the socialistic Utopia, there is little reason why in the meantime, a father should not do for his son what the State is then asked to do for us all. . . . My modest task has been to show that spendthrift trusts have no place in the system of the Common Law. But I am no prophet, and certainly do not mean to deny that they may be in entire harmony with the Social Code of the next century. Dirt is only matter out of place; and what is a blot on the escutcheon of the Common Law may be a jewel in the crown of the Social Republic.[69]

Gray's influential protest not only reiterated the tension between "an audacious drive for power" and the "cautious reckoning of gain" that had characterized Brahmin testation from its beginnings; it also reflected the extent to which social Darwinism had heightened and sharpened these concerns in the post-Civil War period.

Even before the war, pundits like Dr. Holmes had fretted over the debilitating tendencies of wealth. "The weak point in our chryso-aristocracy," he wrote in *The Autocrat of the Breakfast Table*,

> is the same I have alluded to in connection with cheap dandyism. Its thorough manhood, its high-caste gallantry, are not so manifest as the plate glass of its windows and the more or less legitimate heraldry of its coach panels. It is very curious to observe of how small account military folks are held among our Northern people. Our young men must gild their spurs, but they need not win them. The equal division of property keeps the younger sons above the necessity of military service. Thus the army loses an element of refinement, and the moneyed upper class forgets what it is to count heroism among its virtues. Still I don't believe in any aristocracy without pluck as its backbone. Ours may show it when the time comes, if ever it does come.[70]

Holmes wrote these words during the spring of 1858. The young Brahmins, his own son included, would very soon have a chance to "win their spurs."

But even the wartime heroism of the best and brightest of the young Brahmins, celebrated by Thomas Wentworth Higginson in the *Harvard Memorial Biographies* as a vindication of "those classes, favored in worldly

69. Gray, *Restraints on the Alienation of Property*, ix–x.
70. Holmes, *Autocrat*, 244–245.

fortune, which would elsewhere form an aristocracy," was insufficient to allay the anxieties that men like John Chipman Gray had evinced by the 1880s.[71] The immense growth of new commercial and industrial fortunes, combined with rising economic turbulence and social disorder, intensified their concern that the Brahmin class would unfit itself for the ever harsher "struggle for existence." And he feared that spendthrift trusts would tip the balance between "audacious will" and "cautious reckoning" dangerously far in the direction of the latter—and that the spiraling accumulation of wealth would give rise to the economic and social senility characteristic of decadent European aristocracies. Gray had no objection to the existence of classes. But, as a social Darwinist, he insisted that such groups must be founded in strength, competence, and force of will. As he wrote in comparing *laissez-faire* with newer social ideas, "the old doctrine was a wholesome one, fit to produce a manly race, based on sound morality and wise philosophy; and that new doctrine is contrary thereto."[72]

Wealth and Charity: The Public Dimensions of Private Wealth

The accumulation, consolidation, and transmission of wealth are private acts. But they inevitably have public dimensions. When one portion of a community proves to be more economically adept, it not only alters relationships between all groups but also each group's perception of itself. This is especially true in societies like New England's, where egalitarian traditions, rooted in Puritanism and nurtured by the Revolution, remained strong.

At mid century, the Boston families who Dr. Holmes would label "the Brahmin class of New England" were still very much engaged in making money and had not yet found a distinct identity which set them apart from the rest of the community. They did not live in residential enclaves, generally avoided conspicuous displays of their wealth, and sent their children to play on the Common and to be educated in public schools like Boston Latin. As citizens of means, they naturally maintained an intense interest in public affairs, running for elective office and serving on local boards and committees. To the extent that they conceived of themselves as a group at all, they appear to have framed their common purposes in public rather than private terms.

71. Thomas Wentworth Higginson, ed., *The Harvard Memorial Biographies* (Cambridge, Mass., 1866), v.
72. Gray, *Restraints on the Alienation of Property*, x.

A variety of circumstances forced Boston's wealthy to change their understanding of themselves and their relationship to their community. As Holmes would note by the 1850s, wealth, especially inherited wealth, led them to develop increasingly distinctive lifestyles. "We are forming an aristocracy . . . in this country," he wrote in 1854,

> not a *gratia-Dei*, nor a *jure-divino* one,—but a *de-facto* upper stratum of being, which floats over the turbid waves of common life like the iridescent film you may have seen spreading over the water about our wharves,—very splendid, though its origin may have been tar, tallow, train-oil, or other such unctuous commodities. . . . Of course, money is its corner-stone. . . . Money kept for two or three generations transforms a race,—I don't mean merely in manners and hereditary culture, but in blood and bone. Money buys air and sunshine, in which children grow up more kindly, of course, than in close, back streets; it buys country places to give them happy and healthy summers, good nursing, good doctoring, and the best cuts of beef and mutton. . . . As the young females of each successive season come on, the finest specimens among them, other things being equal, are apt to attract those who can afford the expensive luxury of beauty. The physical character of the next generation rises in consequence. It is plain that certain families have in this way acquired an elevated type of face and figure.[73]

As their lifestyles and ambitions began to be more distinguished by their money and their urban situation, the merchants' religious inclinations began to diverge from those of other citizens. As country people fell under the sway of evangelicals, the urban wealthy tended increasingly towards more rational forms of religious expression. Although the roots of this divergence lay deep, originating in theological conflicts dating back to the Great Awakening, over time it became an increasingly political struggle that centered on issues of institutional control.

Deep-seated social tensions underlay these political and religious differences.[74] The conflict between rural and urban interests intensified after the 1780s, manifesting itself as a struggle between the merchants and lawyers of the coastal cities and backcountry farmers and artisans. Rural resistance to the efforts to discharge the state's revolutionary war debt (much of it owed to the merchants) through taxation was widespread and in some places took the form of armed rebellion. This animosity was fueled by a

73. Holmes, *Autocrat*, 244–245.

74. On social and economic change in New England society in this period, see James A. Henretta, *The Evolution of American Society* (Lexington, Mass., 1973). See also, Hall, *Organization*, 35–78.

deeper crisis in rural society, as diminishing resources and an increasing population forced the children of farmers to leave the land. Those without resources sought to earn their living as unskilled day laborers and factory operatives in the towns and cities; those with the means to do so went west.

Urban artisans suffered a similar crisis of diminishing expectations, which contrasted starkly with the merchants' burgeoning fortunes. The days when an apprentice could confidently expect to become a journeyman and, eventually, a master craftsman and proprietor of his own workshop were past. The migration of rural youth seeking entry into the trades, together with the efforts of artisans to provide for their own sons, overwhelmed the occupational structure. In addition, promises of opportunity in the New World and the political and economic crises in the Old drew to America increasing numbers of foreign artisans (and, by the 1840s, unskilled laborers), who vied for work with the native-born. As competition intensified, success depended increasingly on one's entrepreneurial skills and technological innovation. In this race, only a few men emerged as leaders, as employers, or as brokers of the skills and products of others.

In town and in the country, circumstances compelled increasing numbers of people to define their political, economic, and religious interests quite differently than did the "wealthy, learned, and respectable," the merchants, ministers, lawyers, and magistrates who had traditionally taken the lead in public affairs. Many joined the ranks of the Jeffersonians, yet even those who remained in the Federalist fold harbored deep resentment at the growing scale and power of urban wealth.

By the beginning of the nineteenth century, the merchants found themselves increasingly isolated from Boston's masses, as strangers filled the community and old patterns of deference broke down. While they continued to maintain a firm hold on state and local political life, their place was endangered by the Jeffersonians' ascendancy on the national level. Although a handful of merchants enthusiastically backed Jefferson, the vast majority remained loyal Federalists. As the victors distributed the spoils— judgeships, postmasterships, customs posts, and other appointive offices— among themselves, the merchants' influence necessarily diminished.[75]

The merchants found themselves increasingly disenfranchised. As their political power waned, they sought to devise alternative means of advanc-

75. On changes in political life during the early years of the 19th century, see Noble E. Cunningham, *The Jeffersonian Republicans in Power: Party Operations, 1801–1809* (Chapel Hill, 1963); Paul Goodman, *The Democratic-Republicans in Power* (Cambridge, 1964); and W. A. Robinson, *Jeffersonian Democracy in New England* (Boston, 1916).

ing their interests. Their efforts focused increasingly on eleemosynary institutions, entities which could influence public life, but which did not require—at least to the degree necessary for government service—electoral sanction. Money, strategically deployed in the form of gifts and bequests to educational and charitable institutions, could maintain the merchants' public influence if their political efforts failed to do so.[76]

But carrying these plans forward was no simple matter. Just as the legislature had the power to design the state's judicial architecture, and so profoundly shape how private individuals could or could not transmit their wealth, so it retained extraordinary power over charitable and educational institutions which, as chartered corporations, were considered public not private entities. While individuals had supported Harvard since the seventeenth century and enabled the school to accumulate a considerable endowment, the state had been the college's greatest financial supporter and, through the Board of Overseers, retained a major voice in its governance.[77] Given this, it was hardly surprising that the merchants' efforts to construct an alternative to political power focused to such a degree on issues of institutional control.

Tensions between the merchants and their opponents broke out in the open in 1803, over the future of two key positions at Harvard: the Hollis Professorship of Divinity and the college presidency. The rural clergy and their urban allies insisted that the incumbent of the Hollis chair should be, as the deed of gift to the college had stated, a "man of solid learning in Divinity, of sound and orthodox principles."[78] To them, this meant a conservative Trinitarian Calvinist. When the question of succession to the Hollis professorship was initially raised, the conservative clergy still wielded considerable influence over the college, and their champion, President Joseph

76. On the use of nonpolitical voluntary associations by the declining "aristocratic party" in the early 19th century, see Tocqueville, *Democracy in America*, 186–187.

77. On the relative contributions of public and private supporters to Harvard, see Seymour E. Harris, *The Economics of Harvard* (New York, 1970). Story, *Forging*, and Whitehead, *Separation*, give the best accounts of the financial and administrative dimensions of the process of privatization that began in 1780 and was completed in 1865, when elected alumni representatives replaced *ex officio* elected officials on the board of overseers.

78. Samuel Eliot Morison, *Three Centuries of Harvard* (Cambridge, 1936), 188. On the background and outcome of the Unitarian/Trinitarian struggle at Harvard, see Conrad Wright, *The Beginnings of Unitarianism in America* (Boston, 1955); Conrad Wright, "The Election of Henry Ware: Two Contemporary Accounts Edited with Commentary," *Harvard Library Bulletin* 17(1969):245–278; and Daniel Walker Howe, *The Unitarian Conscience: Harvard Moral Philosophy, 1805–1861* (Cambridge, Mass., 1970).

Willard, declared that he "would sooner cut off his hand than lift it up for an Arminian Professor."[79] Willard's death in 1804 broadened the dimensions of the struggle.

The conflict was inherently political, since, under the charter of 1780, Harvard's Board of Overseers included the entire membership of the upper house of the state legislature. And the upper house, because of its property qualification, was dominated by Federalist laymen who were sympathetic to the religious liberals. In February of 1805, the board voted to confirm Henry Ware, a Unitarian, as the Hollis professor. The battle over the presidency was no less heated and, after a protracted struggle, another Unitarian, Samuel Webber, became president of Harvard. The orthodox Calvinists broke with Harvard, establishing their own theological seminary at Andover. Orthodox families also abandoned the college, preferring to send their sons to Yale or to new institutions like Williams and Bowdoin, where Trinitarians still held sway.

The struggle for control of Harvard commenced a series of acrimonious conflicts that would shake every congregation in eastern Massachusetts, as Trinitarians and Unitarians fought over the doctrinal soundness of their ministers and, when congregations split, over the ownership of church properties. These disagreements frequently ended up in the courts, where overwhelmingly Federalist and Unitarian jurists decided against the Trinitarians in case after case. Slowly but inexorably, the urban elite extended its control over the tax-supported churches of the countryside, forcing the Trinitarians to establish their own congregations, which were supported by voluntary contributions.[80]

As the merchants consolidated their control of Harvard and the established churches, the legislature, whose lower house remained predominantly Trinitarian in its sympathies, declined to provide Harvard, hitherto regarded as a public institution, with further financial support. Boston's Federalist and largely Unitarian merchant community did not hesitate to make up for this deficiency with private contributions, a willingness that was fueled by the election in 1810 of John Thornton Kirkland, who had married into the Cabot family, as president of the college. Unlike Yale, which faced the challenge of diminished state support by turning for financial sustenance to its broadly dispersed alumni, Harvard and the constellation of institutions that grew up around it would be built on the

79. Morison, *Three Centuries*, 188.
80. On the legal dimensions of the controversy, see Leonard W. Levy, *The Law of the Commonwealth and Chief Justice Shaw, 1830–1860* (New York, 1967), 29–42.

donations and bequests of a small circle of wealthy Boston merchants and manufacturers.

In 1810, even as the college was engaged in a bruising struggle with the Jeffersonian legislature over the composition of its governing boards, the city's wealthy continued to come forward with philanthropic proposals, like the initiative for establishing the Massachusetts General Hospital, in which they quite clearly still sought to represent a public that was less and less inclined to extend them electoral legitimacy. Physicians James Jackson and John Collins Warren, who drafted the proposal, were very much a part of Boston's emerging mercantile elite. Jackson was the son of Jonathan Jackson, president of the Boston Bank and treasurer of Harvard; one brother, Patrick Tracy Jackson, was already a successful merchant and, within two years, would become partners with his cousin Francis Cabot Lowell to establish the textile mill at Waltham that would bring the industrial revolution to Massachusetts; another brother, Charles, sat on the Supreme Judicial Court. While the hospital proposal nominally addressed the health-care needs of a growing urban population, it was also part and parcel of the elite's effort to extend its control over the medical profession by tying clinical training, which had been a very profitable sideline for physicians, to Harvard and its medical college.[81]

In February of 1811, the legislature granted a charter to the Massachusetts General Hospital. It provided for a Board of Visitors consisting of public officials—the governor, lieutenant governor, the speaker of the House, and the chaplains of both houses—and a Board of twelve self-perpetuating trustees. The state also provided modest financial support: it granted the corporation a piece of Boston real estate, "with authority to sell the same and use the proceeds at pleasure, provided that within five years an additional sum of one hundred thousand dollars should be obtained by private subscriptions and donations."[82] It also donated the labor of state convicts for preparing the stone that would be used to erect the hospital's first building. In exchange, the corporation was expected to support "thirty of the sick and lunatic persons chargeable to the Commonwealth" (this provision was subsequently modified, for fear that it would make the institution "merely a pauper establishment").

81. For a text of the proposal, see James Jackson and John Collins Warren, "Circular Letter Addressed to Several of Our Wealthiest and Most Influential Citizens, for the Purpose of Awakening in Their Minds an Interest in the Subject of a Hospital (1810)" in Nathaniel I. Bowditch, *History of the Massachusetts General Hospital* (Boston, 1872), 3–9.
82. Bowditch, *History of the Massachusetts General Hospital*, 8–9.

One of the first acts of the trustees was an attempt to meet the $100,000 challenge grant from the state. "Not ambitious of being the guardians of a charity *merely nominal*," they declared, we

> are satisfied that the sum affixed by the Legislature as the condition of its grant, is so small, when compared with the wealth of individuals and the greatness of the State, that no plea arising from "the hardship of the times," and "the general embarrassment of affairs," or "the claims of other charities," can or ought to avail the community. If such a proposal as this fail, it will be, in the judgement of the undersigned, decisive of the fate of the establishment. It will then be apparent that *the will is wanting* in the public to patronize such an undertaking; and that the honor of laying the foundation of a fabric of charity so noble and majestic must be left for times when a higher cast of character predominates, and to a more enlightened and sympathetic race of men.[83]

The trustees proceeded to produce a thousand copies of a pamphlet urging support for the hospital and to divide themselves into committees responsible for soliciting particular individuals. In addition, they organized ward committees for door-to-door fundraising within the city of Boston, as well as committees to reach residents in Salem, Beverly, New Bedford, Plymouth, Charlestown, Medford, Cambridge, Roxbury, and Newburyport. Within three days, the committees had collected pledges totaling $78,802—within another two weeks, the sum has risen to $93,969. Eventually, the hospital succeeded in collecting more than $140,000 from 1,047 subscribers. Of these, 245 gave $100 or more.

Although the institution was intended to benefit the whole state, almost all of the contributions came from Boston and surrounding towns. More significantly, the ten largest donors contributed nearly 40 percent of the total raised. This tendency for giving to be concentrated among a handful of wealthy patrons would become the characteristic pattern of Boston philanthropy (unlike Trinitarian philanthropy, which sought to cast a broader net and to emphasize broad participation). Despite the importance its founders had already ascribed to leadership by a benevolent elite, the rhetoric with which the hospital was inaugurated still celebrated the initiative in communitarian terms of "all classes of . . . citizens combining and concentrating their efforts."[84] Gradually, however, the merchants would begin to come to grips with their isolation. In the hospital's second fund drive in

83. Bowditch, *History of the Massachusetts General Hospital*, 19–20.
84. Robert F. Dalzell, Jr., *Enterprising Elite: The Boston Associates and the World They Made* (Cambridge, Mass., 1987), 127.

1844, donations were even more concentrated among the wealthy—with only 200 gifts, almost all in amounts of $500 or more. More importantly, the elite would begin to ascribe its generosity to its worthiness to lead and to point to its philanthropy as a justification for its wealth.

Despite growing political tensions, affluent Bostonians of 1810 had only begun to conceive of themselves as a class apart. This is evident in the circular for the hospital, whose language suggests that they had not yet clearly distinguished between *charity* (palliative, religiously justified activities to help the poor and dependent) and *philanthropy* (systematic, politically-justified benevolence in support of elite educational and cultural institutions which often served to extend their social influence). Over time, these two strands of benevolence would begin to diverge, with purely charitable activities such as poor relief falling more often into the sphere of churches and public agencies, and philanthropic activities becoming almost exclusively the domain of private institutions controlled and funded by the elite.

Five years after the issuance of its charter, the legislature authorized the hospital to increase its revenues by granting annuities on lives. To take advantage of this potentially lucrative privilege, the trustees in 1819 established the Massachusetts Hospital Life Insurance Company, a for-profit corporation that was to share its earnings with the hospital. The company, which was also granted the power to manage personal, testamentary, and institutional endowment trusts, within a few years became the largest financial enterprise in New England and a major source of capital for the textile and railroad industries. Naturally, the boards of the hospital and the insurance company were tightly interconnected, and the key players on both boards were chief figures in the city's financial, commercial, and manufacturing communities. The establishment of the MHLI marked the union of the Brahmins' public and private purposes as well as the convergence of the laws of charitable and testamentary trusts under the protective umbrella of equity jurisprudence.

Families and Philanthropy

The 1830s marked the take-off point for the fortunes of the families who would eventually constitute the core of Boston's "Brahmin" elite. The textile industry, still experimental in the 1820s, grew rapidly in the '30s, thanks to tariff protection, a steady supply of inexpensive southern cotton, a rapidly growing domestic market for manufactured goods, improved transportation, and abundant capital. The leading textile firms, still closely held by a handful of interrelated extended families including, most notably, the Appletons, Cabots, Jacksons, Lawrences, and Lowells, produced a flood of wealth, which accumulated faster than it could be spent. Boston industrialists poured these funds into new ventures: railroads, banks, insurance, real estate, iron, shipping, and lumber, which yielded more profits.

Boston's wealthiest families, despite their growing resources, lived austerely. They did not build great estates or entertain lavishly. Nor did they emulate other would-be aristocrats by withdrawing from active civic and economic participation. But the scope and scale of their fortunes, which grew unremittingly, made it increasingly difficult to sustain the fiction that they were merely the better off portion of a still-integrated urban community. Not only were they rich, but their wealth—thanks to trusts, to its emerging corporate character, and to the growing tendency to distinguish its enjoyment from its competent management—became noticeably more permanent with each succeeding generation. As this occurred, spokesmen for the group became increasingly preoccupied with the problem of selecting and training competent leaders and managers from among their number and with justifying the possession in terms of the dominant egalitarian and democratic values of American society.

In part, the merchants responded to these challenges by further expanding their commitment to the city's charitable and educational institutions, an obligation that flowed from their need to maintain and extend their public influence. (This was not mere vanity; their continuing economic success depended on a capacity to shape public opinion and maintain public order.) At the same time, as more of their sons decided against careers in business, supporting educational and other institutions that helped to enhance the status of the professions became in itself a form of wealth transmission. To be sure, Harvard, Massachusetts General Hospital, the Athenaeum, and the host of other privately-supported eleemosynary institutions founded and funded by the merchants provided public benefit. But the private advantages that accrued to the extended families of those who sat on their boards and contributed generously, by gift and bequest, to their fundraising efforts cannot be underestimated.[85]

85. On Harvard's shift towards recruiting members of the elite as faculty, see Story, *Forging*, 57–88. MGH was no less closely tied to the merchants who governed and funded it: the hospital's first two staff physicians, both of whom served for more than twenty years, were James Jackson, son of merchant Jonathan Jackson and husband of Elizabeth Cabot, and John Collins Warren, whose father-in-law, merchant Jonathan Mason, was a co-founder and director of the Massachusetts Bank. Later appointments also drew from the

By the 1830s, Harvard had become the central institution for socializing the sons of elite families, as well as for recruiting talented and ambitious young men into commercial and eleemosynary enterprises.[86] As young businessmen and professionals built their careers after graduation, service on corporate and charitable boards began to be regarded as an important indicator of leadership ability, as well as a testing ground for advancement to greater responsibilities in both the worlds of commerce and charity. By the 1850s, the emerging Brahminate would recognize its leaders not merely by the amount of wealth they possessed, but by their service on an elaborate hierarchy of boards that directed the city's increasingly well-endowed charitable, educational, and eleemosynary institutions. Individuals who linked the worlds of finance and benevolence, through their control of their own enterprises and their power to invest the assets of testamentary trusts and institutional endowments, were able to shape collectively the city's economic direction, while at the same time assuring the continuing influence of its elite families. This move from the mere transmission of wealth towards systematic *inter vivos* investment in the human capital necessary for sustaining the Brahmins and their influence was of immense significance and, more than anything else, denoted their transformation into a coherent and cohesive *class*.

Through the 1820s and '30s, the merchants' sense of themselves as a group apart continued to be reinforced by political conflict. Following the earlier pattern of Jeffersonianism, Jacksonian politics in Massachusetts involved not only electoral and economic challenges from newly enfranchised "common men," but a continuation of the struggle between Trinitarians and Unitarians. These involved not only ongoing attacks on elite influence over Harvard, but also the establishment of rival institutions that sought to shape public opinion.

---

pool of merchant sons, including Henry Ingersoll Bowditch, Samuel Cabot, Henry J. Bigelow, Algernon Coolidge, J. B. S. Jackson, Francis Minot, George W. Otis, George and Samuel Parkman, George C. Shattuck, Benjamin S. Shaw, D. H. Storer, and J. Mason Warren.

86. In the cohort of sons born to the Amory, Cabot, Codman, Higginson, Jackson, Lawrence, Lee, Lowell, and Peabody families between 1760 and 1779 (who came to maturity in the years 1780–1799), fewer than 30 percent attended Harvard. For sons born after 1760, the proportion climbed steeply: 55 percent of the 1780–1799 cohort attended; 80 percent of the 1800–1819 and 1820–1839 cohorts attended. Initially, merchants might choose college education as a way of steering their sons into non-business occupations. But by the second quarter of the 19th century, they were making higher education available to all of their sons. One reason for this, it appears, is that Harvard came to be viewed as an arena for testing the competence of future business and professional leaders.

If, on the one hand, the Brahmins' wealth made it difficult for them to claim to be "of the people," on the other hand it expanded their capacities to influence the masses. Nowhere is this more evident than in the founding of the Lowell Institute, a prototype of the modern foundation, established under the will of John Lowell, Jr. (1799–1836), the son of textile industry pioneer Francis Cabot Lowell.[87] A politically active lawyer and a leader of the Unitarian forces, Lowell was keenly aware of the struggle between the two for public influence, as well as the extent to which Trinitarian leaders like Lyman Beecher were using public lecture series—the lyceums—as recruiting grounds for their cause.

But Lowell's concerns went well beyond religion and politics. He was no less concerned with the problem of articulating the relationship of wealth to the new lifestyles that were transforming his city. With thousands of young men and women flocking to public lectures and other forms of entertainment, it was quite clear that private libraries like the Boston Athenaeum and increasingly exclusive educational institutions like Harvard could never hope to influence the broader public. To do this, the wealthy would have to be willing "to raise the character of the community" by proactively influencing the form and content of popular culture.

Naturally, in an open market for public edification, the elite could not force audiences to attend lectures of a more "elevated" sort, such as those the institute offered. Nevertheless, by making attendance at the programs free of charge and by providing the resources to attract "star quality" lecturers, the institute enjoyed a considerable competitive advantage over its rivals, which had to depend on admission fees to remunerate speakers. In effect, it represented an assertion of elite control over popular culture (the lecturers, after all, were chosen by the institute's single trustee, who was required to be a lineal descendant of the Lowell family) justified in a language of "public improvement."

87. One of the most complete accounts of the Lowell Institute can be found in Ronald Story's chapter on the subject in "Class Development and Cultural Institutions," 42. See also Edward Weeks, *The Lowells and Their Institute* (Boston, 1966); Ferris Greenslet, *The Lowells and Their Seven Worlds* (Boston, 1946); and Harriette Knight Smith, *The History of the Lowell Institute* (Boston, 1898). For the background of John Lowell, Jr., the founder, especially his thinking on religious and political issues, see Edward Everett, *A Memoir of Mr. John Lowell, Jun., Delivered as the Introduction to the Lectures on His Foundation, in the Odeon, 31st December, 1839* (Boston, 1840). For a sense of the audience for popular lectures and the significance of political and denominational competition, see Lyman Beecher, *The Autobiography of Lyman Beecher*, Barbara M. Cross, ed. (Cambridge, Mass., 1961), 2:107–111.

For all the rivalry that existed among religious and political factions, the Unitarian elite benefited significantly from the "moral reform" agitations of the Trinitarians and other evangelicals. In the 1820s, the latter launched a crusade against the city's theaters. These were "all constructed after the manner of the English theatres of that period—with 'refreshment rooms' so called, which were in reality common grog-shops, contiguous to them or within easy access, with an entrance directly from the pit and first row of boxes. Free admission was granted to women to the 'third row' "—with predictable moral consequences.[88] The evangelicals shut down the theaters in short order. Elite organizations like the Boston Academy of Music took up occupancy in some of them, like the Federal Street Theatre. The evangelicals purchased others, such as the Tremont Theatre, dedicating them to religious purposes and public lectures.

Under its first trustee, the founder's nephew John Amory Lowell, the institute flourished. Lowell was a man of both extraordinary financial acumen and high intellect. The list of Lowell lecturers during his tenure represents a veritable pantheon of the most eminent figures in American science, literature, political economy, philosophy, and theology. The lectures were so immensely popular that crowds crushed the windows of the Old Corner Bookstore where the tickets were distributed and certain series had to be repeated by popular demand. By 1860, the institute had virtually put all other lecture series out of business.

The Lowell Institute was paradigmatic, both drawing together the earlier tendencies of Brahmin benevolence and setting for it new directions. First and foremost, it underscored the relationships between the private domain of testation and the public domain of philanthropy, suggesting by its example that charitable bequests, rather than being idiosyncratic gestures, should boldly serve the collective interests of the class. Secondly, in requiring that the sole trustee be a lineal descendant of the Lowell family, it unabashedly tied together private and public stewardship. At the same time, the institute set a pattern for elite cultural intervention that would recur later in the century, when investment banker Henry Lee Higginson established the Boston Symphony Orchestra.[89] This nonprofit entity entered a rich and complex setting of voluntary and proprietary musical organizations that served a broad public. But its substantial financial resources,

88. Smith, *History of the Lowell Institute*, 8–9.

89. On the BSO as a cultural paradigm, see Paul J. DiMaggio, "Cultural Entrepreneurship in Nineteenth Century Boston," in DiMaggio, ed., *Nonprofit Enterprise in the Arts: Studies in Mission and Constraint* (New York, 1986), 41–62.

combined with the prestige of its patrons, enabled it within a few years virtually to monopolize the top musical talent in the city, as well as bring to Boston audiences an array of international stars that fee-dependent organizations could not rival. Nonprofit museums would impact proprietary exhibitions of art and natural wonders in a similar manner.

The Crystallization of Brahmin Philanthropy

In an 1845 article for the *North American Review*, Harvard Treasurer Samuel Atkins Eliot attempted to summarize the remarkable commitment of Boston wealth to eleemosynary purposes, a benefaction that he regarded, and correctly so, as being unrivaled by any other American city.[90] Eliot's purposes were twofold: first, he was attempting to show the role of private giving in the development of the city's charitable, cultural, educational, and religious life; second, he was trying to articulate and justify the public role of private wealth.

Eliot began by referring to an earlier effort, President Quincy's 1830 address at the bicentennial celebration of Boston's settlement, which, in its published form, included a list of charitable, educational, religious, and moral societies and institutions that Bostonians had supported during the first three decades of the nineteenth century. These, taken together with the amount of money each received, suggested that Boston's benevolent inclinations distinguished it from other cities.[91] Because Boston's population had nearly doubled and its wealth vastly increased in the fifteen years since Quincy's estimates, Eliot believed that it had "become a question of deep interest" to "enumerate the principal objects of Boston liberality" to see "how far, and it what particular ways, the character of Boston has been or is to be affected by such a sudden development of its resources, and such an immense accession to its physical and commercial strength."

Choosing to ignore the intense political and religious conflicts that still raged in Massachusetts (as he wrote, the Trinitarians were mounting yet another effort to regain control of Harvard), Eliot proceeded to delineate a model of civil society in New England that downplayed the importance of government and stressed the importance of private initiative. "Our institutions," he wrote,

90. [Samuel Atkins Eliot,] "Public and Private Charities of Boston," *North American Review* 61(1845):135–159.

91. [Eliot,] "Public and Private Charities," 135–136.

are not of the nature of those paternal governments which assume all their subjects to be in a state of pupilage, and will not suffer them to act for fear of their acting amiss,—the object of whose parental care seems to be rather to check than to promote the development of the infant energies of their people. Our civil polity partakes more of the character of another family relation, equally delightful to the imagination and the heart, and may be called fraternal government. The true idea of a government of the people is that of an association, the members of which are ready to aid each other not merely in the attainment of those objects in which they have a common interest, but also to reach such as may be particularly desirable to only one or two of the number.[92]

Eliot praised the extraordinary liberality of Bostonians, listing the "great variety of purposes" for which money was voluntarily bestowed, including "thirty-one societies or institutions having religious objects, twenty-six for purposes of literary education, and twenty-five for the relief of physical and moral wants," as well as thirty-one "other objects of more or less general interest" and "no less than thirteen subscriptions for monuments to the memory of as many honored individuals."[93] He worried, however, about the "obvious effects arising from this multiplicity and subdivision of institutions of benevolence."[94] While conceding that interorganizational rivalries stimulated "the activity and industry of all," leading not only to higher levels of giving, but also to "an unseen under-current of kindness and active benevolence, which may be some compensation for the harshness, suspicion, and injustice which they are apt to indulge," Eliot feared that "the multiplicity of objects" would diminish the resources of each.[95] His was, in effect, a plea for Bostonians to give to established institutions—to consolidate and target their donations, much as they had their investment capital. (And, it should be remembered, Eliot's audience, the readers of the *North American Review*, primarily comprised members of the elite.) Here, Eliot applied to the domain of charity themes traditionally voiced with reference to the partition of estates.

Eliot similarly appropriated the reasoning behind the Prudent Man Rule in criticizing the tendency of some givers to limit and restrict "the uses to which funds may be applied, to such a degree, that, when the circumstances of society change even but slightly, the means provided for a pre-

92. [Eliot,] "Public and Private Charities," 139–140.
93. [Eliot,] "Public and Private Charities," 148–149.
94. [Eliot,] "Public and Private Charities," 149.
95. [Eliot,] "Public and Private Charities," 149.

vious state of things are no longer applicable to the corresponding wants of the present and succeeding times." Pointing to the example of the trusts "for the benefit of young married mechanics in the cities of Boston and Philadelphia" established under the will of Benjamin Franklin, Eliot asked,

> What would he have felt, had he known that in thirty years after his death it would have become difficult, and in fifty years almost impossible, to find persons of such a description, and in such situations, as he required; and that his money, instead of circulating among young mechanics, was quietly accumulating by adding to it the yearly interest accruing on the stock in which it was invested?

He continued, "if Franklin's sagacity could not foresee for a score of years what was to occur in a class with whose interests, habits, and character he was entirely familiar, who shall presume to direct future generations?"[96] "The only way in which a man can do permanent good with the money which he must leave behind him," Eliot asserted, echoing Justice Putnam's dictum in *Harvard College* v. *Amory,* "is to trust something to the discretion of those who will follow him."

Eliot concluded his essay with a *paean* to the class that produced such individuals and a set of reflections on how it related to the community. Americans, Eliot declared, had avoided the "artificial arrangements [that] have separated the apparent interests of one class from those of another, and have led the one to look down, and the other to look up, through so many generations, that at length men have really, practically, forgotten that they belong to the same race of animals.[97] In contrast to Europe, he wrote,

> our situation, our institutions, and our habits set us perfectly free. The oppression of the mass by the few is rendered impossible by the public institutions, and is driven, by the habits of thinking and feeling generated by those institutions, from the wish and thought of any one as much as it is from his power.[98]

An essential element in producing this happy situation is, Eliot argued, the absence of forms of government that leave "to the political powers to do every thing, whether for weal or woe, which can be done by society." "Here," he declared,

> the subject takes much of the matter into his own hands, and does many things far better than any government could possibly do them; and at the

96. [Eliot,] "Public and Private Charities," 150–153.
97. [Eliot,] "Public and Private Charities," 152–154.
98. [Eliot,] "Public and Private Charities," 154–155.

same time he requires his government to do well all that it can do; and it is a fact, that a much larger amount has been distributed by the individual inhabitants of Boston than by the City government, in the same term of time, for the same, or similar, purposes. This is done freely, voluntarily, by no compulsion of any sort, from the motive that springs up in the breast of one, and is communicated to many, be it benevolence, vanity, love of influence, ambition, or whatever else may be imagined.[99]

Philanthropy and voluntarism, in other words, not only prevented the formation of permanent class divisions, but also assured that society would be "knit together by feelings and by interests intertwining in every direction, and scarcely can one bond be broken without its being widely felt and speedily repaired."[100]

Eliot used these arguments to deny the charges of critics that the wealthy exercised undue influence in public life: "Riches alone," he continued,

do not enable a man to be much of an oppressor anywhere, and in this country the rich man can make no figure at all in that line. There must be position and privilege superadded to wealth to make it possible to oppress, and in New England neither that position nor that privilege can be attained by any body. So far is the rich man from having attained them, that he is, in truth, farther from them than other persons. He is jealously watched, constantly suspected.[101]

The ultimate proof of the powerlessness of the wealthy, Eliot somewhat disingenuously concluded, lay in his account of Boston philanthropies. The large sums gathered from the "mites of the generous poor" suggested that philanthropy presented an even playing field in which all could support the causes and institutions in which they believed. And the sums given by the "generous rich" for an equally wide variety of purposes suggested that the influence of the wealthy had "been exerted, in this country, only for beneficent purposes."[102]

Eliot's essay is striking, in light of his evident ambitions, for its failure to articulate a fully satisfactory rationale for the existence of his class. While the beginning of the piece exudes pride in the Brahmins' generosity, the second half, which decries the ingratitude of the masses, points to the elite's failure to persuade anyone but themselves of their indispensability. Part of the problem lay, no doubt, with Eliot's conception of his peers as a

99. [Eliot,] "Public and Private Charities," 155–156.
100. [Eliot,] "Public and Private Charities," 156.
101. [Eliot,] "Public and Private Charities," 157.
102. [Eliot,] "Public and Private Charities," 158.

coherent group—as he portrays them they are merely affluent and meritorious, representing, as Dr. Holmes would remark a few years later, "a permanent fact of wealth with a variable human element." Only their riches distinguish them from the broader community with which Eliot still repeatedly expresses strong identification. Not until the Brahmins (as Holmes would dub them in 1859) fully came to terms with the reality of their wealth and the way in which it really did make them different from everybody else, would Boston's elite be able effectively to assert its claims to leadership.

In 1860, on the eve of the Civil War, Eliot again surveyed the growth of Boston's charities for the popular press.[103] The tone of this essay is considerably different from his earlier one: as spokesman for the city's patricians, he had a far clearer sense of who they were as a group and of the distinctive nature of their role as community leaders. The defensiveness of the 1845 essay was notably absent, perhaps because the influx of mostly Catholic immigrants and the rising political challenge they represented had led the battling Protestant factions finally to find common cause and to settle their long-standing differences in the intervening years. "It is with great satisfaction," he wrote,

> that we observe in our present list so many associations, whose names and objects are new; which have, indeed, begun to exist since 1845, and which show, or tend at least to show, that the resources upon which public spirit may draw are neither hoarded nor exhausted. The old institutions are kept up, and new ones are formed, very generally by voluntary contribution; in a few instances only, by permanent funds; and thus successive generations meet new occasions, without forgetting the perpetual wants of society.[104]

He concluded, "it is to intellectual culture in all departments of the mind," therefore,

> that we desire to call the attention of the philanthropic among us, most particularly in the present state of our institutions and our charities. It would seem that all other departments to which liberality may be called to extend its benefactions are now more or less faithfully provided for. Elementary education, physical suffering, poverty, old age, and mental infirmity, are all furnished with the means of supply or relief.[105]

103. [Samuel Atkins Eliot,] "Charities of Boston," *North American Review* 91(1860): 149–165.
104. [Eliot,] "Charities of Boston," 151.
105. [Eliot,] "Charities of Boston," 165.

The major remaining challenge was "the proper and sufficient collegiate education of our own young men." Furthermore,

> We shall deem no labor lost which shall tend in any degree to arouse the community of our age and nation to a sense of the importance of affording to all who seek it the means of the most thorough and accurate instruction in every branch of human knowledge. By this process we shall not only raise the standard and increase the product of intellectual studies and pursuits, but we shall secure for all future time the great charities, and the religious and literary institutions, which are the protection, the ornament, and the glory of nations.[106]

Eliot's analysis of Boston charity denotes some fundamental shifts both in the Boston elite's view of itself and in its understanding of philanthropy. Most importantly, he considered the city's model of charitable activity to have *national* implications: he evoked Bostonians as an example for the elites of other cities to follow. Secondly, while in his earlier essay he had been unwilling to prioritize philanthropic objectives, advocating instead a synergy among all benevolent activities, by 1860 Eliot would unambiguously assert that certain institutions were more important—and hence more worthy of support—than others.

By the 1850s, Harvard had grown to serve the elite whose wealth had transformed the provincial public college into the nation's leading private university: the college had become, as Henry Adams wrote, the Brahmins' "ideal of social self-respect"—a basic credential for class membership. But it also served a broader public, helping Boston, as Holmes would write, to "drain a large watershed of intellect" and leading it to attract to it the "promising young author and rising lawyer and large capitalist" and "the prettiest girl."[107] Eliot's reforms further extended Boston's "suction range," broadening Harvard's cultural influence in a way that both paralleled and to a significant extent undergirded the growing scale and scope of the city's economic interests, which would include the financing of major western railroads and such pioneer "high tech" firms as General Electric and the American Telephone and Telegraph Company.

But in being transformed into institutions of national significance, Harvard and the constellation of cultural and scientific enterprises to which it was tied (the Athenaeum, the American Academy of Arts and Sciences, the Museum of Natural History, the Boston Symphony Orchestra, the Museum of Fine Arts, the Lowell Institute, the Massachusetts General Hospi-

106. [Eliot,] "Charities of Boston," 165.
107. Holmes, *Elsie Venner*, 119–120.

tal, the Perkins Institution for the Blind) ultimately transcended the city of their origins. Although Boston would be eclipsed by New York as the nation's financial center, the pattern it set for elite philanthropy would not only profoundly affect the wealthy in other metropolitan areas, but would lead to the creation of a new national elite based on educational and professional credentials. This "new middle class" of experts, serving in corporations; in government; and in institutions of culture, health care, and social welfare would lead the nation into the twentieth century.

More importantly, just as Greece conquered Rome, Boston would have a far greater impact on New York and other metropolitan centers than they would have on Boston. As New York's economic importance grew after the Civil War—and with it, private fortunes—that state's legal obstacles to devoting private wealth to public purposes became more evident. The watershed event, which occurred in 1887, involved the New York courts' ruling against the Tilden Trust, an attempt by corporate lawyer and presidential candidate Samuel Tilden to leave a substantial portion of his multi-million dollar estate in trust for charitable purposes.[108] Because New York's laws forbade bequests to charitable corporations not yet in being and because the courts regarded Tilden's charitable purposes, which he left to his trustees to define, as too vague, the trust was declared void.[109]

The failure of the Tilden Trust set off a storm of protest and concern, sparking an orchestrated campaign supported by financier-philanthropists like J. P. Morgan (who was, not coincidently, a major benefactor of Harvard) and led by such men as Harvard Law School Dean James Barr Ames. "Melancholy the spectacle must always be," Ames intoned in a widely-circulated article published on the eve of the New York legislature's debate on revising the state's charities laws,

> when covetous relatives seek to convert to their own use the fortune which a testator has plainly devoted to a great public benefaction. But society is powerless in a given case, so long as the forms of law are observed. When, however, charitable bequests have been repeatedly defeated, under cover of law, and that, too, although the beneficent purpose of the testator was

108. Tilden v. Green, *Reports of Cases Decided in the Court of Appeals of the State of New York* (Albany, 1892), 29ff. See also, Alexander Clarence Flick, *Samuel Jones Tilden: A Study in Political Sagacity* (New York, 1939), 508–519.

109. On New York's hostility to charitable trusts, see Scott, "Charitable Trusts," and Ames, "Failure of the Tilden Trust." Major New York court decisions overturning charitable bequests included Williams v. Williams, 8 New York 525 (1866), Bascom v. Albertson, 24 New York 584 (1866), and Cornell University v. Fiske, 136 U.S. 152 (1890).

unmistakably expressed in a will executed with all due formalities, and although the designated trustees were ready and anxious to perform the trust reposed in them, one cannot help wondering if there is not something wrong in a system of law which permits this deplorable disappointment of the testator's will and the consequent loss to the community. The prominence of the testator, and the magnitude of the "Tilden Trust," which has recently miscarried, have aroused so general an interest that this seems a peculiarly fit time to consider the legal reasons for the failure of that and similar charitable bequests in New York.[110]

Ames's concern, shared by civic-minded New Yorkers and their Boston allies, was that without legal capacity to devote private wealth to public purposes, the vast new fortunes of the era would become the basis for a plutocracy, bringing with it not only the weakness and degeneracy associated with inherited wealth, but open class warfare. Against a background of increasingly bitter farmer and labor protest, in 1893, the legislature passed a sweeping revision of the state's charities laws which, in effect, "Bostonized" New York charities.[111] Within twenty years, New York's economic centrality was matched by its philanthropic eminence.

Ironically—and certainly in ways he could not have anticipated—Oliver Wendell Holmes's characterization of Boston as the "hub of the solar system" proved correct at least insofar as the architecture of American institutional culture was concerned. The dominance of private institutions and their unique dependence on individual wealth was in every sense a product of Boston and its merchant family founders. While voluntary associations were, as Tocqueville observed, nearly ubiquitous in America, only in Massachusetts—and only due to the exertions of the Boston merchants—were they allowed to benefit to such an extent from the harvest of the "fat meadow of craft or commerce" as the American economy took off. This represented more than an institutional achievement: the establishment and enrichment of colleges, hospitals, libraries, museums, and other eleemosynary entities was part and parcel of a broader effort to balance the problems of accumulating and preserving wealth against the capacity of wealth to corrupt and weaken its inheritors.

Significantly, not everyone regarded Boston's model of benevolence as

110. Ames, "Failure of the Tilden Trust," 285.
111. For an excellent case study of the "Bostonization" of New York's nonprofit institutions in the 1890s, see James Wooten, "The Emergence of Nonprofit Legal Education in New York," Working Paper #154, Program on Non-Profit Organizations, Yale University, 1990.

genuinely charitable. An 1893 survey, "American Millionaires and Their Public Gifts," published in the influential reform periodical *Review of Reviews*, titled its section on the city, "has not Boston one great public benefactor?" "Our Boston millionaires," the anonymous correspondent declared,

> give money when it is solicited (properly), and they all include in their wills some bequests to Harvard and to the Massachusetts General Hospital. That is all. Of great public benefactions, we have none in Boston. . . . He commends Mr. H. L. Higginson for having instituted the Boston Symphony Orchestra, but adds that the orchestra is now a very lucrative investment rather than a public benefaction. There was once a generous man named Lowell in Boston who endowed the Lowell Institute with a great scheme of free courses and lectures. His good work still lives on. Mrs. Quincy A. Shaw has founded and maintains a number of free kindergartens, and Mr. Daniel S. Forbes, who publishes the *Youth's Companion*, is very generous to Baptist churches and causes. Our correspondent mentions as a typical case a Bostonian who "occasionally gives his distinguished ancestor's autograph to the Massachusetts Historical Society."[112]

To critics, giving that primarily served the interests of the donor's own class was not genuine philanthropy. Nor did they deem the Brahmins' penchant for supporting established institutions rather than creating new ones a particularly creative response to the great challenges of the violent and turbulent nineteenth-century *fin de siècle*. Further, Boston's preference for giving to private, nonprofit corporations stood in sharp contrast to philanthropic practices outside New England, where donations to public institutions were, by far, more common.[113]

Conclusion: The Revolution in Family Wealth Transmission

In an important 1988 article, legal historian John Langbein identifies what he regards as fundamental shifts in the contemporary ethos and practice of wealth transmission in America. "Whereas of old," Langbein writes,

112. "American Millionaires and Their Public Gifts," *Review of Reviews* 7(1893):40–68.
113. The *Review of Reviews* critique integrates numerous examples of such public philanthropy in states outside of New England. In California, for example, the favored object of elite benevolence was the fledgling University of California at Berkeley. For more recent studies of these persistent patterns of philanthropy, see William G. Bowen, Thomas I. Nygren, Sarah E. Turner, and Elizabeth Duffy, *The Charitable Nonprofits: An Analysis of Institutional Dynamics and Characteristics* (San Francisco, 1994), 25–31. See also, Julian Wolpert, "The Geography of Generosity: Policy Remedies for Stingy Places" (unpublished paper, Woodrow Wilson School of Public Affairs, Princeton Univ., 1993) and Hall, "Cultures of Trusteeship."

wealth transmission from parents to children tended to center upon major items of patrimony such as the family farm or the family firm, today for the broad middle classes, wealth transmission centers on a radically different kind of asset: the investment in skills. In consequence, intergenerational wealth transmission no longer occurs primarily upon the death of the parents, but rather, when the children are growing up, hence, during the parents' lifetimes.[114]

This shift from testamentary to *inter vivos* transfers was due not only to changes in the nature of wealth itself, from land assets or shares in a family firm to financial assets (stocks, bonds, bank deposits, mutual fund shares, insurance contracts, and the like), but also, and more significantly, to the growth of human capital—the skills and knowledge that lie at the root of advanced technological life.

Langbein details the immense cost to families of providing for the educational demands of modern economic life, an expense that in 1988 approximated 31 percent of an average family income, arguing that

> for most families, . . . these education expenses represent capital transfers in a quite literal sense: The money comes from savings, that is, from the family's capital; or debt is assumed, meaning that the money is borrowed from the family's future capital.[115]

Langbein heightens the impact of his observations by underscoring the increasing importance of education to Americans:

> in 1870, only 2% of the population was graduating from high school; by 1970 the figure was 75.6%. In 1870 institutions of higher learning in the United States conferred a total of 9,371 degrees, of which 9,370 were bachelor's degrees and exactly one was a doctorate. In 1970 the total number of degrees conferred showed an increase of more than a hundredfold over 1870. The figure stood at 1,065,000, of which almost 30,000 were Ph.D. or equivalent degrees.[116]

Yet Americans' expenditures for formal education ballooned throughout the nineteenth century, growing from $9.2 million in 1840 to $289.6 million in 1900. By 1959 the figure had reached $23.9 billion (4.8 percent of gross national product), and by 1987 the figure stood at $282.1 billion (7 percent of gross national product).

Langbein does not break down the differences between the costs of

114. John H. Langbein, "The Twentieth Century Revolution in Wealth Transmission," *Michigan Law Review* 86(1988):723.
115. Langbein, "Wealth Transmission," 733.
116. Langbein, "Wealth Transmission," 731.

public and private education, nor does he consider philanthropic giving in support of education.[117] Doing so would doubtless further strengthen his hypothesis, since his study is concerned with wealth transmission among the upper and upper-middle classes, the propertied groups mostly likely to patronize private institutions and who, traditionally, have been their most significant source of donations and bequests.

The rising cost of education, combined with the increasing extent to which educational investment had become the essential "provision in life" that could rescue children from the harsh fate of becoming unskilled laborers, led Langbein to conclude that "in today's economic order, it is education more than property, the new human capital rather than the old physical capital, that similarly advantages a child."[118]

This shift from passing on wealth by will to *inter vivos* transfers in the form of investments in human capital is paralleled by a striking change in what Langbein calls the "Ethos of Inheritance," in ways which have affected even the holders of great wealth. "The new pattern," he argues, "has become a social norm, a norm so powerful that it has begun to chip away at the ethos of older notions of inheritance." Citing a *Fortune* magazine story on inheritance, Langbein points to the views of a number of "extremely wealthy people who planned to leave their children only token inheritances":

> Warren Buffett, the billionaire chairman of the Berkshire Hathaway holding company, said he planned to leave each of his three children only a few hundred thousand dollars: having put the children through college, Buffett said he expected them "to carve out their own place in this world." It would be "harmful" and "antisocial" to set up his children with "a lifetime supply of food stamps just because they came out of the right womb." Buffett's $1.5 billion will go to charity. So will the $50 million fortune of a New York entrepreneur named Eugene Lang, who sent his three children to college, gave each "a nominal sum" after college, and plans to disinherit them. He explained to the *Fortune* reporter: "To me inheritance dilutes the motivation that most young people have to fulfill the best that is in them. I want to give my kids the tremendous satisfaction of making it on their own."[119]

Langbein regards Buffett and Lang as exceptional not only in their hostility toward conventional modes of inheritance, but also in the novelty of

117. In 1990, these amounted to more than $12 billion, according to Virginia A. Hodgkinson et. al., *Nonprofit Almanac, 1992–1993* (San Francisco, 1992), 112.

118. Langbein, "Wealth Transmission," 733.

119. Langbein, "Wealth Transmission," 736–737.

their views, which, he argues, "would have been inconceivable a century or more ago." "Can we imagine," Langbein asks, "the twelfth Earl of Carlisle arranging for the dissipation of the family seat, in order to stimulate the thirteenth Earl to the challenge of reacquiring it?" Exceptional and novel though they might be, Langbein believes that these attitudes toward conventional wealth transmission are "not only quite exceptional," but also "historically very recent and also very American." Behind them, in his opinion, are two novel ideas:

> the assumption that wealth is largely fungible, that there is no great sentimental attachment nor any particular social significance to the family's existing patrimony. That is why Mr. Buffett could liken his fortune to a pile of food stamps, and why Mr. Lang could hope that his children would experience the satisfaction of "making it on their own." By it, he means, something like it, but not the identical property. This notion that wealth is fungible is an idea that fits the new forms of wealth better than the old, an idea that fits American circumstances better than English or European. You're much more likely to be sentimental about your ancestors' manor house than about the family's portfolio of marketable securities.
>
> More and more, Americans expect personal wealth to take the form of earned income, that is, we expect it to be a return on human capital. Messrs. Buffett and Lang have taken that expectation to its limit; in their eyes, conventional wealth transfer has lost its legitimacy. The esteem associated with holding property really now applies only to earned income, to property that embodies the fruits of human capital. In this sense, the revolution in family wealth transmission, which is overwhelmingly an event of the broad middle classes, touches even the holders of great wealth.[120]

Langbein's overall assessment of changing patterns in American wealth transmission is brilliantly insightful and substantially correct. But he is quite wrong in arguing that either the shift from transfer of assets to investment in human capital or the "new ethos of inheritance" is particularly new. The fundamental elements of the revolution in wealth transmission first emerged among Boston's merchant families more than a century ago. An ethos of inheritance that emphasized anxiety about the corrupting potential of inherited wealth led the merchants to limit their descendants' access to capital and to devise institutional means of ensuring that individuals in each generation would have to prove themselves before assuming positions of responsibility. The Bostonians pioneered changes in the nature of wealth itself, shifting their financial assets from family firms to diversified holdings

120. Langbein, "Wealth Transmission," 737–738.

of stocks, bonds, and real estate, often held in testamentary and charitable trusts. This shift facilitated the diversification of childrens' occupational choices, which not only reduced family demands on capital, but sustained the status of children in non-business occupations. Massive investment in human capital, both in the form of direct expenditure and in the form of philanthropic giving, served a variety of purposes, including underwriting occupational strategies, capital pooling, and extending the influence of the merchant group as its political power diminished. In other words, Lang-bein's revolution comprises the essential conditions for the transformation of Boston's merchant families of the early nineteenth century into the cohesive and coherent class that, by the twentieth century, had emerged as the preeminent economic, political, and cultural force.

It seems only fair to add that the ethos of inheritance that contemporary entrepreneurs like Buffet and Lang have expressed strikingly parallels not only the thinking of Brahmins like Oliver Wendell Holmes and John Chipman Gray, but also that of non-Brahmins like Andrew Carnegie, whose 1889 essay, "Wealth," is probably the single most influential piece ever written on the subject. "Why should men leave great fortunes to their children?" Carnegie asked, when

> Observation teaches us that, generally speaking, it is not well for the children that they should be so burdened. Neither is it well for the State. . . . It is not the exception, however, but the rule, that men must regard; and, looking at the usual result of enormous sums conferred upon legatees, the thoughtful man must shortly say, "I would as soon leave to my son a curse as the almighty dollar."[121]

"The growing disposition to tax more and more heavily large estates left at death," Carnegie continued,

> is a cheering indication of the growth of a salutary change in public opinion. . . . Men who continue hoarding great sums all their lives, the proper use of which for public ends would work good to the community from which it chiefly came, should be made to feel that the community, in the form of the State, cannot thus be deprived of its proper share. By taxing estates heavily at death the State marks its condemnation of the selfish millionaire's unworthy life.[122]

Carnegie was not content to give advice to his fellow tycoons. Acting on his belief that "he who dies rich dies disgraced," the Great Ironmaster spent

121. Andrew Carnegie, "Wealth" [1886], in Carnegie, *The Gospel of Wealth and Other Timely Essays* (1886; reprint, New York, 1900), 10.
122. Carnegie, "Wealth," 11.

the last twenty years of his life giving his money to charitable institutions. Although few of his contemporaries went to these lengths, the elaborate efforts of the Rockefellers and other dynastic families to institutionalize their fortunes and to train their children to regard their wealth as a stewardship responsibility suggest that Carnegie's views were not idiosyncratic.

Though Langbein discounts important aspects of the earlier history of wealth transmission in America, his article nevertheless directs our attention toward a largely unexplored research frontier: the ways in which the elites and their institutions influenced the behavior and attitudes of the American people as a whole. The historiography of elites—and the heated debates it has engendered—has for too long been preoccupied with whether these groups really existed and, if so, whether their presence really mattered. Over the past thirty years, a substantial body of disinterested scholarship has conclusively demonstrated their existence. But the question of their influence—and how this was brought to bear—remains largely unaddressed.

Earlier efforts to deal with the question of influence were flawed by their use of rationalistic power models, which treated elites as monolithic and focused on their collective motives and intentions (which were all too often inferred, *post hoc*, from their actions). Recent work in the fields of organization theory and the social history of technology offer alternative models— models which treat such things as organizational structures (and, potentially, legal practices) as forms of *technology* whose evolution can be traced and analyzed using social construction paradigms.[123] Because these paradigms are designed to explain complex and contradictory motives and behavior, multiple constituencies, and unintended outcomes, they are infinitely more suitable for interpreting historical data and for addressing vexing questions about the influence of elites and the interrelationships of family, community, locality, region, and nation.

123. I refer specifically to the concepts in two major collections of essays, Walter W. Powell and Paul J. DiMaggio's *The New Institutionalism in Organizational Analysis* (Chicago, 1991), and Wiebe E. Bijker, Thomas P. Hughes, and Trevor Pinch, *The Social Construction of Technological Systems* (Cambridge, 1987). Powell and DiMaggio's theoretical insights are especially valuable because of the authors' close attention in their previous work to institutions in their historical settings. In the Bijker collection, I especially recommend Trevor Pinch and Wiebe Bijker's essay, "The Social Construction of Facts and Artifacts: Or How the Sociology of Science and the Sociology of Technology Might Benefit Each Other." For an effort to deal with elites and artifacts as a process of social construction, see Peter Dobkin Hall, "Organization as Artifact: A Study of Technological Innovation and Management Reform, 1893–1906," in James Gilbert, ed., *The Mythmaking Frame of Mind: Social Imagination and American Culture* (Belmont, 1993), 178–208.

Contributors

Jonathan M. Chu is Associate Professor of History
at the University of Massachusetts-Boston.

Patricia Cleary is Associate Professor of History
at California State University-Long Beach.

William M. Fowler, Jr., is Chairman of the Department of History
at Northeastern University
and Co-Editor of *The New England Quarterly*.

Peter Dobkin Hall is a research scientist in the Program
on Non-Profit Organizations at Yale University.

David Hancock is Associate Professor of History
at the University of Michigan-Ann Arbor.

James Oliver Horton is Benjamin Banneker Professor
of History and American Studies
at The George Washington University.

Lois E. Horton is Professor of American Studies
at George Mason University.

Benjamin W. Labaree is Professor of History and Environmental Studies,
Emeritus, Williams College.

Naomi R. Lamoreaux is Professor of History and Economics
at the University of California-Los Angeles.

Lisa B. Lubow teaches history at the University of Hartford.

Contributors

Margaret E. Newell is Assistant Professor of History
at The Ohio State University.

Harlow W. Sheidley is Assistant Professor of History
at the University of Colorado at Colorado Springs.

John W. Tyler is Editor of Publications
of the Colonial Society of Massachusetts.

Katheryn P. Viens is Director of the Old Colony Historical Scoiety,
Taunton, Massachusetts

Barbara McLean Ward is Associate Editor, *Encyclopedia of New England
Culture*, University of New Hampshire, and Lecturer, Museum Studies
Program, Tufts University.

Conrad Edick Wright is Worthington C. Ford Editor of Publications
and Director of the Center for the Study of New England History
at the Massachusetts Historical Society.

Mary Saracino Zboray is an independent scholar in Atlanta, Georgia.

Ronald J. Zboray is Associate Professor of History
at Georgia State University.

Index

～

Abbot, William, 126

Abbott, Horace, 270n

Account books, 23, 32, 33, 54. *See also* Education

Act for the Encouragement of Trade, 66

Act Providing for Relief in Equity, 374–375

Adams, Abigail, 124, 131n, 146; on economy, 129, 133, 139, 142

Adams, Charles Francis, 316, 320

Adams, Charles Francis, Jr., 348n–349n

Adams, George, 265n

Adams, Henry, 318, 413

Adams, John, 1, 133, 309, 310–313

Adams, John Quincy, 308; as president, 301, 302–303, 310, 322–323; Daniel Webster and, 304, 307, 321; Democratic party and, 320–321; Edward Everett and, 319; Embargo and, 312; engraving (illustration), 296; Federalist party and, 301, 311, 317–319, 322; Harrison Gray Otis and, 313, 319, 320; Hartford Convention and, 319; John Adams and, 311–312; Joseph Story and, 320; Levi Lincoln, Jr., and, 306; Massachusetts elite and, 301, 303, 304, 307, 308, 314; presidential campaign of, 310, 314–315; Republican party (Jeffersonian) and, 301, 312; *Review of the Works of Fisher Ames* and, 311; Thomas Jefferson and, 313, 315–317; Timothy Pickering and, 313–314

Adams, Samuel, Sr., 16n, 119

Adelphic Union Library Association, 333

Advertising, 17, 39, 261; handbill (illustration), 38; in newspapers, 43, 45, 52, 81, 360

Africa, 345, 358

African Americans: among Boston town poor, 183; and antislavery movement, 333; and boardinghouses, 336–337; and colonization movement, 328, 336; and education, 334; and philanthropy, 332;
and social responsibility, 325–341; artisans, 329–330; as servants, 183; barbershops and fugitive slaves, 337; blacksmiths, 329–330; Boston, 330, 331; business community, 337; businessmen and antislavery movement, 333–336; businessmen as community representatives, 337–338; businessmen as role models, 337–338; churches, 333, 338; community leadership, 325–341; community organizations, 332–334; conventions, 333–334, 335, 338; education, 334, 338–339; in colonial Boston, 32; New Bedford, 332–333; New York business community, 332; occupations in Boston, 330–331; Philadelphia business community, 327. *See also* individual names

African Baptist Church, Boston, 334

African Society, 332; and Thomas Lewis, 334

Agricultural goods, 89; Essex Co., 361; in revolutionary era, 127, 132, 134–136, 145; shortages, 131. *See also* individual products

Albany, N.Y., 356

Alleyne, Thomas, 142

Almy, William, 285

Almy and Brown, 285

American Academy of Arts and Sciences, 413

American Anti–Slavery Society, 335

"American System," 299

American Telephone and Telegraph Co., 413

Ames, James Barr, 414–415

Amory, Francis, 369n, 381-383

Amory, John, 77

Amory, Jonathan, Sr., 77, 113, 171, 382–383

Amory, Thomas, 37n, 86, 113

Amory family, 405n

Anderson, John, 35

Andover & Wilmington Railroad, 354

Index

Index

Belknap Street Baptist Church, 338
Bell, Jonathan, 191–192
Benjamin, Mr., 146
Benjamin, Asher, 187, 202
Benson, George, 285
Bentley, William, 349, 351
Bequests: among women entrepreneurs,
  51–53. *See also* Estates, Inheritance,
  Trusts
Bernard, Francis, 159
Bethune, George, 81n, 86, 89, 90
Bethune, Nathaniel, 89, 90
Bigelow, Henry J., 405n
Bigelow, John Prescott, 343
Billerica, Mass., 15
Birdcalls, 32
Bissett, Robert, 75n
Blank books, 256
Blinn, Daniel, 35
Blount, Thomas, 152
Boardinghouses: and African Americans,
  336–337; and book trades, 225–228,
  252n
Board of Trade, 16, 18
Boat builders, 88
Boilers, 136
Bonds, 117
Bonnets, 46
Book trades, 213–215; and Boston econ-
  omy, 214–215, 220–221; and industrial-
  ization, 215n, 218–219, 224–231, 261;
  and political views, 258–259, 262; bookbinders, 222, 225, 240, 247; booksellers,
  212, 222, 225, 228–230, 240–243, 247–
  249, 261, 264; Boston as center of, 213–
  214, 239, 255; class divisions in, 225,
  230, 257–262; expansion and fluctua-
  tion, 219–225, 230–234, 259–262; geography of workplaces and residences,
  218–219, 225, 230, 243–250; longevity
  of businesses, 239, 260; occupational
  definitions, 215n, 224, 241, 264; occupational mobility, 241–242; proletarianization, 218, 225–228, 243; stability of
  businesses, 230–240, 259–262
Boston., Mass., 1851 Railroad Jubilee,
  343, 362–363; African-Americans artisans, 330; African–American business
  community and fugitive slaves, 337;
  African-American business community
  and social responsibility, 325–341;

African–American churches, 334;
African–American community leadership, 325–341; African–American elite,
325–341; African–American manual
training school, 334; American terminus
for Cunard Line, 355; and environs,
343–363; banks, 371; and Erie Canal,
355–356; and hinterlands, 343–344; as
center of American trade, 10; as center
of economic policy, 3; as center of internal development, 14; as information
center, 239; as transportation hub, 354–
355; black occupations, 330; book
trades, 211–267; Boston & Maine Railroad promotes suburban living, 362;
Brahmins described, 396–397; building
trades, 181–209; business partnerships
in, 269–295; businesses, 330, 331; Central Artery Project, 363; changes in
street names, 245n; city directory of,
279n; class structure, 121, 257–262,
365–421; colonial merchant community,
98–119; colonial standard of living, 7;
colonial trade, 36, 67–68, 157–158;
commerce disrupted, 371; commercial
decline, 351–352; competition among
colonial retailers, 46; competition with
Charleston, S.C., 63, 65, 70, 78, 80, 82,
95; competition with Essex Co., Mass.,
344–345, 352, 358–359, 360–362; competition with Gloucester, 358; competition with Marblehead, 358; competition
with Newburyport, 82, 358; competition
with Newport, R.I., 14; competition with
New York, N.Y., 10, 14, 63, 65, 70, 78, 80,
82, 83, 93, 95, 356-358; competition with
other cities, 3, 6, 10, 14–15, 81–85; competition with Philadelphia, Penn., 10, 63,
65, 70, 78, 80, 82, 83, 93–95; competition
with Portland, Me., 358; competition
with Portsmouth, N.H., 14, 358; competition with Salem, 14, 63, 84–85, 93–95,
358; cultural influence on New York,
N.Y., 414; development of book–trades
districts, 243–250, 252–259, 261; East
India trade, 358; economic and political
turbulence, 371; economic impact of
Revolutionary War, 101–103, 116–119,
146; economy compared with Essex Co.,
350; economy in nineteenth century,
220–221; elite control of, 298; elite

Index

Boston., Mass. (*cont.*)
recruitment of talent, 377, 385; elites of, 297–323; entrepot for New England Atlantic ports, 358; ethnic community leadership, 325–326; Federalist party in, 300, 315, 317; Franklin mechanic trust, 410; goldsmiths, 23–37; Harvard College, 413–414; hinterlands, 345–346; influence of railroads, 361; literary culture of, 214; marine insurance industry, 156–166; municipal charter and, 300–301; neighborhood development, 198; partnerships in, 278, 280–291, 293–295; philanthropic boards, 405; philanthropy: S. A. Eliot on, 408–413; political representation of, 306n; poor, 183-184; population growth, 83; rail network and foreign trade, 358; real estate development, 195–203; real estate speculation, 196–197; standardization of carpenter prices, 187; syphons off Essex Co. business leaders, 349; taxable wealth, 182; tax lists, 182n; town meeting, 16; trade in nineteenth century, 177; trade in revolutionary era, 101, 116–119, 160, 163–165; trade with Albany, N.Y., 356; trade with southern colonies, 10, 37; wine trade in, 63, 65, 67-70, 73, 74, 77–85, 93–95; women in, 39–61, 279n. *See also* Trade, individual neighborhoods, individual trades

Boston, Siege of, 99, 113, 119
Boston Academy of Music, 407
Boston & Lowell Railroad, 353
Boston & Maine Railroad, 354, 362
Boston and Roxbury Mill Corporation, 198
Boston Associates, 197, 352
Boston Athenaeum, 404, 406, 413
Boston Bank, 178–179
Boston Custom House, 195n
Boston Manufacturing Co., 352, 353
Boston Marine Insurance Company, 166–179
Boston Marine Railway, 335
Boston Museum of Natural History, 413
Boston Neck, 15
Boston Port Act, 100
Boston Society for Encouraging Industry and Employing the Poor, 19
Boston Symphony Orchestra, 407–408, 413, 416

Boston Theatre, 190, 200, 201, 203, 205
Bourn, Benjamin, 31
Bowditch, Henry Ingersoll, 405n
Bowdoin, James, 111, 119, 370n; 1786 proclamation by (illustration), 120
Bowdoin College, 400
Boyer, James, 34n
Boylston, Thomas, 115n
Bradford, John, 117
Brads, 32
Braid, 32; Haarlam, 136
Braman v. Stiles, 380–381, 385, 393
Brandon, Benjamin, 89
Brandon, John, 90
Brandy, 81, 88
Braziers, 88
Breck, Samuel, 111, 117, 370n
Bricklayers, 88
Bridgen, Edward, 46–47, 49, 53–54, 56
Bridges, 251, 255, 346, 370
Bridgewater, Mass.: African–American nail factory, 335
Brigantines, 35
Broad Street Association, 198–199
Broadway National Bank, 393–394
Broadway National Bank v. Adams, 393–394
Brokers, 88
Bromfield, John, 271
Brookfield, Mass., 140–141
Brooks, Edward, 162
Brooks, Peter Chardon, 162–165, 177–178
Brown, Charles, 260
Brown, Enoch, 88
Brown, James, 260
Brown, Moses, 285, 354n
Brown, Nicholas, 285
Brown, Samuel, 163
Brown, Smith, 285
Brown and Benson, 285
Brown and Ives, 285
Brown family, 167
Bruce, Stephen, 116
Brushes, 32
Buckingham, Joseph T., 259
Buckles, 34
Buffett, Warren: estate, 418, 419, 420
Building costs, 190, 192–193, 200
Building manuals, 186
Building materials, 191, 193, 199, 201, 202, 208n

Index

Index

Chandler, Hannah Gardiner, 33–34
Chandler, John, 33
Chandler, Mary, 33
Chandlers: and book trades, 242; as wine merchants, 88
Chardon, Peter, 16n
Charitable Irish Society, 325
Charity, 148; among the poor, 183; and J. Story, 376
Charles II, 66n
Charles River Bridge, 14, 27, 82
Charleston, S.C.: and domestic trade, 82; and international trade, 63, 65, 67–68, 70; and wine trade, 78–79, 80; black businesses, 329; shipping industry, 82; trade competition with Boston, 63, 65, 70, 78, 80, 82, 95
Charlestown, Mass.: book trades in, 251
Chauncy, Charles, 124–125, 131–132
Cheap, Thomas, 75n
Cheese, 36
China: as personal asset, 92
Choate, Joseph, 95n
Choate family, 16n
Chocolate, 8
Cider, 66n, 80n, 86n
Cinnamon water, 81
Civil Service, 291
Clapp, David, Jr., 251n
Clark, Jonas W., 334; and fugitive slaves, 337
Clark, Thomas March: and Boston Manufacturing Co., 352
Class, 397–398; and African Americans, 325–341; and credit access, 6, 7; and debt, 148; and Harvard College, 405, 413; and inheritance, 367; and Loyalism, 98–100, 111–115; and philanthropy, 410–413; and wine consumption, 77; austerity of wealthy, 404; Boston, 90–91, 105, 109, 365–421; conflict, 121, 257–262; divisions in book trades, 225, 230; elite recruitment, 413; O. W. Holmes on, 366; recruitment of talent, 377, 385; separation of ownership and management of companies, 384; socio–economic mobility, 98–100, 103–117, 119; status among goldsmiths, 26–27, 29–30, 37; status among merchants, 90, 105, 109; wealthy as class apart, 403
Cleland, William, 162

Clerks, 68n, 289, 291n, 292, 293, 294
Clocks, 92
Cloth: as import good, 89, 136; as retail item, 43, 46, 54, 60n, 126; manufacture, 42
Clothing, 54, 89
Clouston, William, 197n
Coates, Mary, 53n
Coburn, John P., 331
Cod, 64n, 79, 85, 89
Codman, John, Jr., 111, 116; real estate holdings, 182–183
Codman, John, Sr., 111
Codman family, 119, 369n, 405n
Coffee houses: and marine insurance, 153–154
Coffin, Francis, 271
Cole, Thomas, 337; antislavery activities, 333; estate, 333
Colman, John: and Atlantic merchants, 8; and Land Bank (1739–1741), 16–17; and wine trade, 81n, 86; as paper money advocate, 10, 11, 15, 17, 20
Colonization: and Paul Cuffe, 336; of free blacks, 328
Columbia (ship), 118, 163
Columbian Insurance Company, 172
Combs, 13, 32, 35
Commodities, 130, 132–133, 139, 144; money as, 123; prices in revolutionary era, 124, 127, 160
Common Law, 272
Commonwealth: as common good, 3, 4, 11, 12, 28; Bay colonists' notions of, 2n
Coney, John, 30
Congregationalists: and Harvard College, 399–400; division from Unitarians, 371–372
Constables, 105, 141, 148
Consumption, 2; alcohol, 66n; and class division, 7; and female community, 61; and local trade, 45; and Loyalism, 57; and women in business, 39–40, 43; cider, 80n; colonial habits of, 46; consumer production, 215; impact on economy in revolutionary era, 135–136, 148; in paper money debates, 5, 7–9, 11; in revolutionary era, 105; regulation, 86; rum, 80; versus English habits of, 49; wine, 65, 68, 76–77, 80, 81, 86
Contracting services, 191–192

Index

Index

Dartmouth College Case, 273

Davidson, George, 170

Davis, Caleb: and economy in revolutionary era, 126, 145–147; and use of credit in revolutionary era, 126, 131, 144; and wine trade, 89n; as military supplier, 117

Davis, Joshua, 183

Davis, Solomon, 87n

Davis, Thomas, 166–169, 176–179

Day, Jackie, 50, 54

Dearborn, H. A. S., 308

Dearden, Ann, 51

Deblois, Gilbert, 46, 54

Debt: and socio–economic status, 148; debt instruments, 123, 136, 143; debtor's prison, 142; discounts on, 126, 131; economic function, 125, 133, 136; experience of debtors, 125, 130–131, 136, 141, 143–145; in paper money debates, 2, 6–7, 12, 13n; in revolutionary era, 121, 135, 142; insolvency, 141, 143–148; Revolutionary War and, 117; value of, 124, 130, 143–144, 148; women and, 45. *See also* Bankruptcy

Dedham, Mass., 15

Deflation: *See* Inflation

De la Lande and Fynje: Dutch firm, 133

Democratic party, 301, 305, 306, 307; in Massachusetts, 317, 320; John Quincy Adams and, 320–321

Denyer, James, 75n

Derby, E. H., 363; praises railroads, 362

Derby, Elias Hasket, 99, 125, 126, 131

Derby, Richard, 74, 77, 94, 95

Development: and credit, 126; and opportunities for women, 39–40, 41; and population growth, 83; internal and colonial Boston, 14; internal and Land Bank (1739–1741), 16–17; in paper money debates, 3–5, 9, 10, 12, 13–17, 20; public, 15

Dexter, Aaron, 171

Dexter, Franklin, 317n

Dighton, Mass., 15

Distilling, 81, 88, 109, 136, 215

Distribution, 261; in book trades, 218

Diversification, 3, 146, 261; among colonial artisans, 23–25, 28; among colonial goldsmiths, 31, 37; view of paper money advocates, 13, 20

Dodge, Allen W.: on Essex Co. agriculture, 361–362

Dodge, B.W., 277, 289

Dodge, James, 183

Doggett, Noah, 87n

Dolphin (ship), 173

Douglass, Frederick, 338–339

Douglass, William, 5, 18

Downing, George T., 340

Downing, Thomas, 332, 338–339

Dowse, Joseph, 158

Dowse, Samuel, 34

Dram–shops, 86

Dress: in paper money debates, 8, 12

Drew, Sylvester, 87n

Driscoll, J. Francis, 264

Dry goods, 50, 89, 214–215

DuBois, W. E. B., 327, 329–330, 341

Duck, 81

Dudley, Paul, 7, 13n

Dudley family, 8

Duer group: real estate speculators, 196

Dummer, Jeremiah, 26

Dunbar, Melzar, 192

Dutton, Warren, 317n

Dyer, Ebenezer, 206

Earrings, 39

East, Henrietta Maria, 44n

East Boston Manufacturing Company, 277

Eastern Railroad, 354, 360

Eastern Stage Company, 350

East India Company, 78

East India trade: and Salem, 345

Easton, Caleb, 335

Easton, Hosea, 335, 336, 338–339

Easton, James, 335

Easton, Joshua, 335

Easton, Sylvanus, 335

Eaton, Joseph, 201, 208

Eayers, Moses, Jr., 188

Eayers, Moses, Sr., 188

Economic behavior: individual, 122–126, 129, 132, 139, 142–147

Economic depressions: of 1839, 279. *See also* Inflation

Economic discourse, 1–4, 10–11; liberalism, 10, 15, 20

Editors, 222–225, 230, 241. *See also* Book trades

Education: accounting, 49; among merchants, 90; and African Americans, 334, 336, 338–339; and religion, 399–400;

Index

and social class, 404–405; available to women, 42, 47–48, 49, 50–51, 53n, 55; literacy, 48–49

Edwards, Abigail Fowle Smith, 27, 32

Edwards, John, 30

Edwards, Samuel, 27, 30, 32–33

Edwards, Thomas, 30, 32

Eldredge, Charles: versus Joseph Jenkins, 204–205

Electrotype plates, 215

Elgin and Kincardine, Earl of, 343

Eliot, Samuel Atkins: on Boston philanthropy, 408–413

Elliot, Samuel, 109

Ellison, William, Jr., 188

Ellison, William, Sr., 188

Employment: opportunities for women in colonies, 42, 52. *See also* Craftsmen, Occupational mobility, specific trades

England: and colonial trade, 36, 66–67; and hard–money policy, 18–19; and insurance industry, 155; and paper money debates, 18, 20; and wine trade, 78, 80; clerks in, 291n; Court of Vice Admirality, 171; economic impact of military presence, 134; economy of British Empire, 122, 136, 153; marine insurance in, 152; opposition to Land Bank (1739–1741), 17; Parliament, 17-20, 155; trade with in revolutionary era, 118, 134–136; trade with Portugal, 66n, 67

Engravers, 222, 225, 247. *See also* Book trades

Entail: and equity courts, 373

Entrepreneurship: and artisans in colonial Boston, 23–37; and Boston real estate development, 198; and paper money debates, 3, 8–9, 13, 14; in book trades, 225, 231n, 261; weakness among Boston merchants, 65, 93–95, 117–118; women and, 39–61

Equity Law, 368, 371–376; and J. Kent, 378; and New York, 377–378; and Pennsylvania, 377–378; and politics, 373–376, 378; court proposed, 373; J. Selden on, 372; J. Story favors court jurisdiction, 373–376; Massachusetts Constitution of 1780 on, 372–373; politicization of, 374; Republican party opposes, 375

Erie Canal, 348; and Boston, 355–356

Erving, John, Jr., 113–115

Erving, John, Sr., 90, 113

Essex Co., Mass., 297–323; and Boston, 343–363; and railroads, 360; business leaders move to Boston, 349; commercial connections, 345; competition with Boston, 344–345, 350, 352, 358–359, 360–362; map (illustration), 342; political parties in, 307–308; railroads and agriculture, 361–362

Essex–Merrimack Toll Bridge, 346

Essex Railroad, 354

Essex Turnpike, 350

Estates: Boston merchants, 30–34, 90–91, 365–421. *See also* Bequests, Inheritance, Trusts

"Eumenes" (pseud.), 125

Eustis, Jane, 44n, 52, 59–60

Eustis, William, 301, 310, 311, 314

Everett, Edward, 319, 323, 375

Exchange. *See* Trade

Exchange Coffee House, 202

Exportation, 9, 10, 35. *See also* Importation Trade

Faneuil, Peter, 17

Faneuil Hall, 297

Fans, 54

Farming, 82–83; and colonial exports, 83; and economy, 131–132, 144–145, 149, 184; and paper money debates, 3, 6, 7, 9, 11, 13n; and pricing in revolutionary era, 125; and use of credit, 6, 126, 128; local exchange with goldsmiths, 29; prices of farms, 142, 144–145; support for Land Bank (1739–1741), 17; support for paper money, 2, 9, 13, 20–21

Fashion: and English imports, 39, 45, 54, 61; and women shopkeepers, 46, 50, 61

Federalist party, 303; Alexander Hamilton and, 312; Daniel Webster and, 306, 307, 321; decline of, 300–301; divisions in, 311–313, 314; Hartford Convention and, 310, 318; in Boston, 315, 317; John Adams and, 309; John Quincy Adams and, 301, 304, 310, 311, 317–319, 322; Levi Lincoln, Jr., and, 314; mechanics and, 300; Republican (Jeffersonian) party and, 304, 310, 311; secession and, 316, 320; social composition of, 298; tradesmen and, 300; War of 1812 and, 316. *See also* Hartford Convention

Federal Street Theatre, 407

Index

Fetridge & Co. Periodical Arcade (illustration), 210
Fiction: and book trades, 259
Fillebrown, James, 190
Fillmore, President Millard, 343
Firewood, 36
First Independent Baptist Church, Boston: receives bequest, 333
Fishing, 82, 85; fish as currency, 85; fisheries, 14, 85; fishhooks, 32, 35; Gloucestor, 345; impact of Revolutionary War, 101; trade, 66n, 67, 79, 169; in paper money debates, 13; Marblehead, 345; Massachusetts, 82, 85, 345; Newburyport, 345, 351; Salem, 85
Fitch, Timothy, 87n
Flax, 16n, 173
Fleischer, Charles, 146
Fletcher, Samuel, 81n
Flour, 64n, 80, 117n
Forbes, Daniel S., 416
Forten, James, 332, 335, 338–339
Fort Hill, Boston: development of, 198
Fowler, Jacob, 79
Fox, Gilbert, 263
France: economic impact of military presence, 131, 134–135; economy in revolutionary era, 137; in Revolutionary War, 100, 102, 117; partnerships and, 271; subsidies for revolutionary government, 133–134, 137; trade with in revolutionary era, 118, 122, 132–133, 134–136
Franklin, Benjamin: mechanic trusts, 410
Franklin Place, Boston, 193
Free Bridge party, 305, 306n
Freeholders, 128, 132
Free trade, 28; in paper money debates, 3, 9, 10, 11, 20. *See also* Trade
French, Hannah, 265
French and Indian Wars, 71–73, 85. *See also* War
Fruit, 64n
Furniture: as personal assets, 92

Gardiner, Elizabeth, 34
Gardner, Mass., 139
Garrison, William Lloyd, 335–336
Gatewood, Willard: on African–American elite, 327
Gay, Calvin, 95n
Gender: and goods carried by male and female shopkeepers, 50; consciousness of among women shopkeepers, 40–41, 55, 58, 61. *See also* Women
General Court, 111; and Land Bank (1739–1741), 17–18; and marine insurance, 164; and paper emissions, 4, 138; and paper money debates, 14, 15, 18; and tax policy, 141, 143, 144, 147–148; charters granted, 165; incorporation of Massachusetts Bank, 162
General Electric Co., 413
George III, 122n
Gerry, Elbridge, 97
Gerry, Thomas, Jr., 79
Gerry, Thomas, Sr., 79
Giles, William B., 315–316, 322
Gill, Moses, 111
Gillam, Elizabeth, 51
Gillam, Jane, 51
Gilman, John S., 270n
Gin, 136n. *See also* Liquor
Girard, Stephen, 377
Glass, 13, 136
Glass bottles, 277–278
Gleason, Frederick, 258–259
Gloucester, Mass.: and commercial rivalry with Boston, 344–345, 358; fishing fleet, 345
Gloves, 45, 54, 60n
Goldsmiths, 26–37; and local exchange, 29, 34; and merchant ventures, 26; and private lending, 26; class status, 26–27, 29–30; English, 26n. *See also* Artisans, Silversmiths
Gold wares, 36, 92; cup by Jacob Hurd (illustration), 22
Goods in trade, 29. *See also* Trade
Gordon, Alexander, 79n
Gordon, James, 75n
Gore, Christopher: and Middlesex Canal, 347
Gorham, Benjamin, 307
Gould, Robert, 87n
Granaries, 14
Grant, Samuel, 92
Gray, Harrison, 260
Gray, John, 113
Gray, John Chipman, 420; and "spendthrift" trusts, 396; *Restraints on the Alienation of Property*, 394–395
Gray, William, 349

Index

Green, Joseph, 89, 90
Green, Joseph, Jr., 90
Greene, Anne Gould, 33–34
Greene, Benjamin, 26n, 33–36
Greene, Nathaniel, 33, 34
Greene, Rufus, 33–35
Greene, Thomas, 33–35
Greene, William, 34
Greenleaf, William, 145
Gresham's Law, 130n
Griffin, James, 81, 87n
Grosse, Thomas, 81n, 86
Groton, Conn., 36
Guilds. *See* Craft guilds
Gunpowder, 123
Gunsmiths, 42

Haddock, William, 75n
Hadley, Mass., 15
Hadley & Stanwick, 202
Hale, Benjamin: improves stagecoaches, 350
Hall, Lott, 79, 95
Hamilton, Alexander, 117, 147n, 312
Hamilton, John, 174
Hammers, 29
Hancock, John: and Madeira consumption, 77; and wine trade, 84, 94; as merchant, 111; on socio–economic mobility among merchants, 101
Hancock, Thomas, 77
Handkerchiefs, 32, 132
Handlin, Oscar, 326
Hardware, 50
Harrisburg, Penn., 299
Hartford, Conn., 36
Hartford Convention, 297, 303, 310; Daniel Webster and, 322; Federalist party and, 318; Harrison Gray Otis and, 311; John Quincy Adams and, 319; Timothy Pickering and, 314. *See also* Federalist party
Hartshorne, Rolun, 200
Harvard College, 90, 404, 406, 416; and Boston cultural institutions, 413–414; and class conflict, 257–258; and class structure, 375, 377, 413; and estate of John McLean, 381–383; and merchant support, 400–401; and paper money debates, 4, 11; and recruitment of elite, 405; Unitarian Controversy, 399–400

Harvard College and Massachusetts General Hospital v. *Amory*, 410; and "prudent man" standard, 381–383
Harvard Memorial Biographies: by T. W. Higginson, 395–396
Haskins, E. Lac, 291
Haskins, Ralph, 187, 191
Hatch, Crowell, 163
Hats, 60n
Hatton, E., 153
Hawes, Edward, 184
Hawes, William T., 277
Hayden, Lewis, 334, 338; and fugitive slaves, 337
Hayne, Robert Y., 299
Hays, Moses Michael, 162
Hazard, Samuel, 105
Hearsey, Thomas, 200, 201, 205
Hebron, Conn., 36
Hemp, 13, 16n, 122n
Hiccox, Matthew, 75n
Higginson, Henry Lee, 416; and Boston Symphony Orchestra, 407–408
Higginson, John, 126
Higginson, Stephen, 99, 111, 116, 125, 349, 370n
Higginson family, 369n, 370n, 405n
Hill, Richard, 74, 80
Higginson family, Richard, 405n
Hill, Richard, 369n, 370n
Hilton, John T., 333
Hilton, Thomas, 333
Holbrook, Darius, 206–207
Holland, Park, 135
Holmes, Oliver Wendell, 367, 411, 415, 420; debilitating tendencies of wealth, 395; on Boston Brahmins, 396–397; on class structure, 377; on elite recruitment, 413; on inheritance, 366
Homer, John, 87n
Homes: and standard of living, 33, 91–92; boarding and boardinghouses, 225–228, 252n; residential locations in book trades, 219, 225, 230, 243–247, 250–257, 261–262
Hoosic Tunnel, 348
Hose, 54, 88
Howard, Alfred G., 333
Howard, Peter, 331, 337
Hucksters, 105
Hughes, Samuel, 81n

435

Index

Hull, John, 26
Hume, David, 11, 12
Hunt, Washington, 343n–344n
Hunt, William, 81n
Hurd, Jacob, 26n, 30–31, 32; cup by (illustration), 22
Hurd, John, 161–164
Hurd, William L., 263
Hutchinson, Shrimpton, 90n, 92
Hutchinson, Thomas, 4, 5, 15, 17–18
Hutchinson family, 8, 99

Importation: and women shopkeepers, 42–43, 57–60; British manufactures, 8, 19, 45, 118, 135–137; by artisan entrepreneurs, 27; by colonial goldsmiths, 29, 31–37; demand for imported goods, 127, 131, 135, 142, 148; economic role in revolutionary era, 132, 139; expansion in mid eighteenth century, 20, 45; illegal activities, 84, 92, 94, 123; in paper money debates, 4, 5, 13; manufactured goods, 36; non–importation agreement, 20, 57–60, 101–102, 113; re-exportation, 67–68, 70, 74; regulation, 8, 11–12. *See also* Exportation, Merchants, Trade
Income: among Boston merchants, 99n, 103–117; among Boston population, 104–105, 145–146. *See also* Property, Wealth
India, 78, 80
India Wharf, Boston, 190, 198–200, 208. *See also* Proprietors of India Wharf
Individualism, 1, 11–12
Industrialization: corporations and, 273; goldsmiths and, 24; investment capital and, 274–275; of book trades, 215n, 218–219, 224–231, 247n, 261
Industry, 14; decline in eighteenth century, 81–82; view of paper money advocates, 9, 12
Inflation, 23, 29; and colonial goldsmiths, 30; impact on merchant community, 103–104, 105; in revolutionary era, 123–132, 136, 143–144, 147. *See also* Currency, Economic depressions
Ingraham, Joseph Holt, 257–258
Inheritance: A. de Tocqueville on, 366–367; and Boston merchants, 365–421; and social structure, 367; entail, 368; O. W. Holmes on, 366; partible, 367–371;

and equity courts, 373; primogeniture, 368. *See also* Bequests, Estates, Trusts
Inman, Elizabeth Murray: *See* Murray, Elizabeth
Inman, Ralph, 39n, 81n
Inns, 33, 80, 88
Insurance, 83n, 158, 165, 197, 370. *See also* Marine insurance
Insurance Company of North America, 176–177
Investment: capital, 276–277; early industrialization and, 274–275; in book trades, 229; in government notes, 142; in Massachusetts Bank, 162; in national governments, 133; in postrevolutionary era, 195; in revolutionary era, 123, 127, 131, 135–136, 138–139, 142, 144, 149, 160; international, 133, 148; strategies, 196; view of paper money advocates, 12. *See also* Capital
Ipswich, Mass., 15
Ireland: and wine trade, 78
Iron, 13, 16n, 35, 81
Ives, Thomas P., 285

Jackson, Andrew, 323
Jackson, Charles, 317n, 387; favors judicial equity jurisdiction, 376
Jackson, Henry: and Boston Marine Insurance Company, 174; as trustee of Boston Theatre, 201; Boston merchant, 190; real estate speculation, 196
Jackson, James: and establishment of Massachusetts General Hospital, 401, 404n
Jackson, Jonathan, 271, 276, 349, 352, 401, 404n
Jackson, J.S.B., 405n
Jackson, Mary, 51n
Jackson, Patrick Tracy, 349, 352, 353, 401
Jackson and Bromfield, 276
Jackson family, 369n, 370n, 404, 405n
Jacksonians: *See* Democratic party
Jackson Republican (periodical), 321
Jailhouse, 200
Jaquith, Moses, 263
Jefferson, Thomas, 310, 311; Embargo of, 312; John Adams and, 312; John Quincy Adams and, 313, 315–317; Virginia legal revisions, 372; William Giles and, 322
Jeffries, James, 160
Jenkins, Joseph, 185–186, 203–205

Index

Index

Index

Merchants (*cont.*)

bers, 101–102, 108; opposition to Land Bank (1739–1741), 17; political views, 98–100, 103, 111–115; shifts in revolutionary era, 97–103, 105–116, 119; support for Land Bank (1739–1741), 17; support for Harvard College, 400–401; support for Massachusetts General Hospital, 401–403. *See also* Business Community, Importation, Traders, Wine merchants

Mergers: in book trades, 260

Merrimack River, 82, 345, 346, 351, 353

Metalwares, 27, 29, 32

Metalworking, 214–215

Methuen Treaty, 66n

Middle colonies: and international trade, 83

Middlemen: and paper money debates, 4–5, 8, 18n; women entrepreneurs as, 47

Middlesex Canal, 346–349, 353

Middlesex Co., Mass.: railroads and agriculture, 362

Midwives, 42

Military contractors, 8, 116–117

Military forces: impact on economy in revolutionary era, 131–132, 134–135. *See also* Revolutionary War, War

Mill Dam party, 305

Millinery wares, 43, 52, 54

Milton, Mass., 36

Ministers, 88

Minot, Francis, 405n

Minot, Jonas Clarke, 95n

Minot, T.M. and J., trade bill (illustration), 268

Minot v. *Paine*, 388–391; Rule in Minot's Case, 389–390

Mittens, 32

Mixer & Pitman, 277

Monroe, James, 303

Montesquieu, Michel de Montaigne, 12

Moodey, Paul, 352

Moore, John, 81n

Morgan, J. P., 414

Morris, Robert (financier), 117

Morris, Robert (lawyer), 337, 339; and fugitive slaves, 337

Motley, John Lothrop, 366

Mowat, James, 75n

Mt. Vernon Proprietors: real estate speculators, 198

Mun, Thomas, 10

Mundrucu, E. F. B., 334

Murdock, William, 75n

Murray, Anne, 54, 56

Murray, Charlotte, 55

Murray, Elizabeth, 61; as middleman for other shopkeepers, 47; association with English merchants, 45–47; correspondence with Christian Barnes, 59; decision to remain in Boston, 39, 41; difficulties with debt, 45; early years in Boston, 44–45; growing success and independence, 46; handbill (illustration), 38; knowledge of colonial fashion, 46; life with brother James, 41; marriage to James Smith, 47; marriage to Thomas Campbell, 47; mentors Anne and Elizabeth Cuming, 47; mentors Jeany McNeal, 48; mentors Polly Murray, 48–51, 54, 56; political views in revolutionary era, 60; travel to London, 46–47; use of newspaper advertising, 45–46

Murray, James, 41, 46–47, 60

Murray, John, 44, 48, 55

Murray, Polly, 48–51, 53–56, 58

Museum of Fine Arts, Boston, 413; and class structure, 377

Music dealers, 225

Mutton, 361

Mystic River, 82

Nails, 13, 29, 32

Naish, William, 75n

Nason, Seth, 201, 208

National Intelligencer, 316

National Republican party, 299, 302, 305, 308, 315, 323

Naval stores, 14, 214

Necklaces, 39

Needles, 32

Nell, William C.: *Liberator* apprentice, 336

Nell, William G.: and New England Anti–Slavery Society, 334

Netherlands: loans to revolutionary government, 133–134, 137; trade with in revolutionary era, 122–123, 135–136

Neufville, Jean De & Sons, 131n

New Bedford, Mass.: African Americans, 332–333; specializes in whaling, 344

Newburyport, Mass., 82; and internal im-

Index

Paper money (*cont.*)
incentive to productivity, 3, 7, 9; as stimulus to independence, 20; as transatlantic concern, 16; Bank of England notes, 4; colonial bills, 5, 6, 18, 36; debates, 1–4, 9, 10–11, 13–15, 16, 20; depreciation, 4, 5, 17n, 18; emissions, 15; in revolutionary era, 126–127, 129, 133–134, 137–139; Land Bank (1739–1741) notes, 17; Massachusetts bills, 4, 18, 30; regulation, 18; use for local trade, 6, 8; use in Massachusetts Bay Colony, 3–4, 20; paper money advocates: appeal to voters, 3, 15, 20; as critics of English policy, 1, 16; assumptions shared with opponents, 4; attitude toward balance–of–trade theory, 3, 9; attitude toward local regulations, 3; economic discourse used, 12, 20; political economy envisioned, 1, 2, 3, 9, 11, 13–14, 16–17, 20; use of Puritan values, 3; paper money opponents: and Massachusetts Bay Colony development, 15–16; appeal to British authority, 16; appeal to voters, 3; assumptions shared with advocates, 4; attitude toward credit access, 6, 7; attitude toward internal trade, 8; attitude toward international trade, 5; attitude toward regulation, 4; attitude toward specie, 4; political economy envisioned, 4, 8. *See also* Currency, Specie
Parker, Isaac, 322; opinion in *Braman v. Stiles*, 381; opposes judicial equity jurisdiction, 376
Parkman, Ebenezer, 16n
Parkman, George, 405n
Parkman, Samuel, 118, 405n
Parliament: *See* England
Parsons, C. C., 317n
Parsons, Ebenezer, 111, 116
Parsons, Theophilus, 317n
Partnerships, 370n.; and corporations, 370; and liability, 370; capital and, 276; clerks and, 289, 292-294; composition of, 284–293; corporations and, 274–276; craftsmen and, 278, 281, 283, 286; dissolution of, 270n, 283–284, 292; family relationships and, 284–286, 370; formation of, 276, 278-280, 286–287; growth of, 278-280; in Boston, 280–283, 293–295; in France, 271; in Providence, R.I., 285; labor agreements and, 277; limitations

of, 270–271; manufacturing and, 294n; masculinity and, 293–295; merchants and, 278n–279n, 286; silent partners and, 281n; wealth of, 288; whaling masters and, 291n; women and, 276n
Paskoff, Paul, 274
Pattern books, 186
Paul, Thomas, Jr., 336
Pawtucket Canal, 346, 352, 353
Payne, Edward, 87n, 160–162, 370n
Payne, William, 161–162, 171
Peabody family, 405n
Pell, Hester, 396n
Pell, Samuel, 53n
Penknife cases, 32
Pennsylvania: agricultural production, 131; and equity, 377–378; annuls Statute of Charitable Uses, 378; corporations in, 274; trust law, 391–392
Penobscot Steamship Navigation Co., 354
Perfume, 171
Periodical offices, 224, 249; Fetridge & Co. Periodical Arcade (illustration), 210
Periodicals, 249, 258–259. *See also* specific titles
Perkins, Thomas Handasyd, 118, 299, 317, 320
Perkins Institution for the Blind, 414
Perkins v. Hays, 388–391, 393
Perry, Jarius Ware: *Treatise on the Law of Trusts and Trustees*, 393
Petticoats, 39, 45
Philadelphia, Penn.: African-American business community, 327; and book trades, 213; and colonial trade, 10; and cultural institutions, 378–379; and domestic trade, 80, 82; and international trade, 63, 65, 68, 70, 92, 94; and marine insurance, 156, 158, 164, 172–173; and wine trade, 74, 78–80, 95; artisanal entrepreneurship in, 25; class structure, 377; economy in revolutionary era, 101n, 102–103, 131, 134; Franklin mechanic trust, 410; merchant community, 106n; population growth, 83; shipping industry, 82; trade competition with Boston, 10, 63, 65, 70, 78, 80, 82, 83, 93–95; women shopkeepers in, 43
Philanthropy: and African Americans, 332; and class strucure, 410–413; and wealth, 396–416; S. A. Eliot on, 408–413

Index

Phillips, John, 89
Phillips, S., Jr., 126
Phillips, William, Jr., 117
Phillips, William, Sr., 111, 117, 370n
Phillips Academy, 354
Pickering, Thomas, 312
Pickering, Timothy, 312–313, 314
Pickman, Benjamin, 317n
Pictures, 32
Pigs, 145
Pins, 29, 32, 35
Piracy, 118–119, 169–170
Pitch, 35, 36
Pitson, James, 86n
Poe, Edgar Allan, 259
Pollard, Benjamin, 157–158
Pollard, Sidney, 274
Polley, John, 183
Poore, Ben: Perley, 362
Popular Party, 2n, 9, 11, 16
Population growth, 83, 213, 219–220
Pork, 35, 361
Porter, Elisha, 141
Portland, Me.: commerce, 344; competition with Boston, 358
Portsmouth, N.H.: and colonial trade, 14–15; and wine trade, 74, 95; commerce, 344; trade competition with Boston, 14, 358
Portugal: and marine insurance, 174; and wine trade, 75; trade with colonies, 83; trade with England, 66n, 67
Postlethwayt, Malachy, 68n
Poverty, 42, 148, 183–184
Powell, Edward, 332
Powell, William, 87n
Powell, William P., 332–333
Pownall, Thomas, 159
Prescott, William, 317
Prescott, William Hickling, 366
Presses, 256
Price, Ezekiel, 159, 161
Pricing: carpenters, 187; fluctuations in revolutionary era, 123–135, 141, 143–145; of farms, 137, 142
Prince (farm hand to Abigail Adams), 124
Pringle, John, 75n
Printers, 212, 222–229, 240–243, 246–257, 262, 264; women as, 42. *See also* Book trades
Prints: as personal assets, 92

Privateering, 136; and Boston economy, 119; and Boston merchant community, 106, 111, 116; and international trade, 73; and marine insurance, 160, 171–172; and wine trade, 92
Privy: constructed, 191, 192
Processions: tradesmen, 185
Production, 124; and concepts of wealth, 28; in paper money debates, 13n
Productivity, 101; in paper money debates, 3, 7, 9, 11, 13; of goldsmiths, 29–30
Professions: and family diversification strategy, 369–370
Proletarianization: of book trades, 218, 225–228, 243, 257, 261; of building trades, 203–209; of goldsmithing, 24
Property: and economy in revolutionary era, 142, 145; and tax collection in revolutionary era, 140; assets of merchant community in revolutionary era, 101. *See also* Income, Land
Proprietors of India Wharf, 198–199, 208
Proprietors of the Locks and Canals on Merrimack River, 348, 352; incorporated, 346
Proprietors of the Merrimack Canal: incorporated, 351
Protest: food riots, 115n; popular support for Land Bank (1739–1741), 17–18
Providence, R.I., 167, 285, 344
Provincetown, Mass., 174
"Prudent Man" rule, 382–383
Publishers, 212, 215n, 224, 229, 240–243, 264. *See also* Book trades
Publishers' Row, 245, 247n, 255
Purcell, Mary, 52
Puritans, 3, 11, 65
Putnam, Samuel, 387, 410; and international trade, 70n, 89; opinion in *Harvard College and Massachusetts General Hospital* v. *Amory*, "prudent man" rule, 382–383

Quebec, 70n, 89
Quincy, Edmund, 17, 81n
Quincy, Josiah: on Boston philanthropy, 408
Quincy, Josiah, Jr., 375

Railroad Jubilee, 1851, 343, 362–363
Railroads, 352–358; and Boston, 252, 255, 258, 361; and Essex Co., Mass., 360; and

Index

Index

Salvage, marine, 174

Sargent, Daniel, 116, 170, 317n

Sargent, John Osborne: on Rule in Minot's Case, 389–390

Satin, 39

Satinets, 277

Sawmills, 14, 126

School construction, 15

Schoolmasters, 88

Schooners, 35

Scissors, 29, 32

Scotland, 146

Scott, James: and fugitive slaves, 337

Scott, John, 75n

Scott, Long Bill, 144

Sea otter, 171

Searle, John, 74n

Sears, David, 117

Sears, Isaac, 106, 116

Sears v. *Russell*, 391

Sedgwick, Theodore, 134

Selby, Thomas, 86

Selden, John: on equity law, 372

Seven Years' War, 19–20

Sewall, Samuel, Jr., 17

Sewall family, 8, 167

Shannon, James Noble, 126, 144

Shattuck, George C., 405n

Shattuck, William, 116

Shaw, Mrs. A. Quincy, 416

Shaw, Benjamin S., 405n

Shaw, Jesse, 194

Shaw, Lemuel: opinion in *Nightingale* v. *Burrell*, 386–388, 390–391

Shaw, Robert Gould: estate, 390–391

Shaw family, 390–391

Shays's Rebellion, 121, 135

Shepard, Allan, 259n

Shepherd, Benjamin, 131

Shipbuilding, 163; artisan entrepreneurs and, 26; Boston, 81; in colonial shipping ventures, 35; in Massachusetts Bay Colony, 14; in paper money debates, 14; Maine, 345; Newburyport, 345, 351; Salem, 85

Shipowners, 125; and marine insurance, 152–154, 156, 158, 170

Shipping, 145–146, 154, 156; Boston industry, 82; Lloyd's Coffee House and, 154; marine insurance and, 151–152, 157, 173; pursued by artisan entrepre-

neurs, 27, 32–37; record–keeping, 68n; regulation, 84; Salem, 84–85; tariffs, 163–164

Ships: as personal assets, 92; in colonial shipping ventures, 35; sale of, 154; salvage of, 174. *See* Marine insurance

Shipwrights, 35, 42

Shirley, William, 18, 19, 90, 159

Shoemakers: women as, 42

Shoes, 45

Shopkeeping, 40, 106n, 107–108, 145; among colonial artisans, 24, 29, 31–32; and Loyalism, 57; and newspaper advertising, 45, 52; and paper money debates, 8; and use of credit, 8, 126; and wine trade, 88; business with English merchants, 45, 46–47, 54; competition among shopkeepers, 46, 54; importance of location and, 52, 55; occupational definition, 109; primary goods carried, 45, 50; skills required, 47–49; socio–economic role criticized, 28; support for Land Bank (1739–1741), 17; women and, 39–61. *See also* Retailers

Shrimpton, Samuel, 66n

Shute, Samuel, 9

Sierra Leone: and colonization movement, 336

Sigourney, Daniel, 187, 192–193

Sigourney, Elisha, 202–203

Silk, 39, 88, 92

Silver, Rollo, 264–265

Silversmiths, 30. *See also* Artisans, Goldsmiths

Silver wares, 36, 92

Simpson, Charles, 35, 36

Slaters, 192

Slavery, 32, 175–176, 328, 337. *See also* Trade

Sleght, Elizabeth Pell, 53n

Slitting mills, 13

Sloane, Robert, 79n

Sloops, 35

Smalley, Thomas, 174

Smethurst, Gamaliel, 95n

Smith, Adam, 11

Smith, Elizabeth Murray: *See* Murray, Elizabeth

Smith, Isaac, 27, 32, 370n

Smith, James, 39n, 47

Index

Index

Index

Tradespeople: Federalist party and, 300; goldsmiths and, 29, 36; pricing and, 125; procession, 185. *See also* Book trades

Transport (periodical), 259

Transportation: and book trades, 213, 246, 252, 255, 258, 261. *See also* Railroads

Traveller (ship), 170, 175

Treatise on the Law of Trusts and Trustees, by J. W. Perry, 393

Treaty of Utrecht, 4

Tremont Theatre, 257, 335, 407

Trimmings, 39, 54

Trowbridge, John Townsend, 228n

Truck–pay system, 9, 17n

Trumbull, John, 143

Trumpets, 32

Trusts: and Boston merchants, 369–396; and legal environment, 376–379; and liability of trustees, 383; duration, 385–388; fiduciary responsibilities of trustees, 381–385; immunity from creditors, 379–381; immunity from third–party claims, 391–396; in Massachusetts law, 379–396; Massachusetts Supreme Judicial Court on, 379–396; merchants establish, 365–396; powers of trustees, 381; "prudent man" standard, 381–383; rights of beneficiaries, 388–391; Rule Against Perpetuities, 386–388; Rule in Minot's Case, 389–390; varieties, 371. *See also* Bequests, Estates, Inheritance

Tucker, Josiah, 122n

Tudor, William, 347

Tufts, Cotton, 129, 138–139, 146

Turnpikes, 350

Tweezers, 32

Twelfth Baptist Church, Boston: African American, 338

Twine, 81

Type, 215, 229, 260. *See also* Book trades

Ulysses (ship): Gouache attributed to Corné (illustration), 150

Unemployment, 86

Union Bank, 27, 166–167

Union party, 305, 308

Unitarians, 303; and Harvard College, 399–400; and moral reform, 407; division with Trinitarians, 371–372, 399–400

United States Congress: and economic policy in revolutionary era, 122, 129, 138, 163–164; and international debt in revolutionary era, 142; creation of navy, 169; tariffs and, 298–299

United States Constitution: tradesmen's procession honoring, 185

United States Navy, 277; and international trade, 168–169

United States Supreme Court, 173

Upton, Mass., 140

Uring, Nathaniel: as wine merchant, 67

Value, 123–129, 130–134, 138, 141–145, 147–148; concept, 12, 123, 128n, 133

Vance, Hugh, 11

Van Schaack, Henry, 134

Vigilance Committee of Boston: and fugitive slaves, 337

Vincent, Ambrose, 81n, 86

Virginia: legal revisions, 372

Wages, 17n, 27n, 84, 124–125. *See also* Labor

Waistcoats, 88

Waldoboro, Me., 345

Waldron, Samuel, 190

Walker, Benjamin, 27n

Walker, David, 331, 340; and Massachusetts General Colored Association, 334

Waller, James, 47, 53–54

Walley, Abiel, 81n, 86

Walley, Thomas, 111

Walter, William: and *Nightingale* v. *Burrell*, 386

Waltham, Mass.: textile mill established, 352

War: and marine insurance, 158–160, 168–169, 176–179; impact on international trade, 71–72, 82–83, 118–119. *See also* French and Indian War, Military forces, Revolutionary War, War of 1812, War of Austrian Succession, War of Jenkins' Ear

Ward, Benjamin C., 271–272, 276

Ward, William, 271–272

Ware, Henry: named Hollis Professor, 400

Warehouses, 84, 92

Warner, Sam Bass, 200

War of 1812, 239, 247, 316

War of Austrian Succession, 71, 83

War of Jenkins' Ear, 71

Warren, James, 98

Index

Index

Winniett, John, 87n
Winslow, Edward, 26–27
Winslow, Isaac, 27n
Winslow, Joshua, 17, 27n
Winter, Stephen, 34n
Winthrop, Thomas L., 308
Wise, John, 11, 12, 13, 20
Wiswall, Oliver, 200, 201; and Boston Theatre, 205
Women: and banking, 26n; and business opportunities in colonial Boston, 40–43, 47; and colonial fashion, 61; and family connections, 44, 58; as consumers, 61; as entrepreneurs, 33–34, 39–61; as merchants, 42; as shopkeepers, 39–61; gender consciousness among, 40–41, 55, 58, 61; in 1860 Boston City directory, 279n; political views, 57–60; longevity of businesses, 43; partnerships and, 276n; primary goods carried, 42–43, 50. *See also* Gender
Woodman, Charles, 183
Woodstock, Conn.: and colonial trade, 36
Wool, 361
Woolens, 89
Worcester, Mass., 15, 36, 141, 142, 147
Worcester Co., Mass., 2n, 17n, 140
Workingmen's parties, 301

Yale University, 90, 400
Young Men's Wilberforce Debating Society, 333